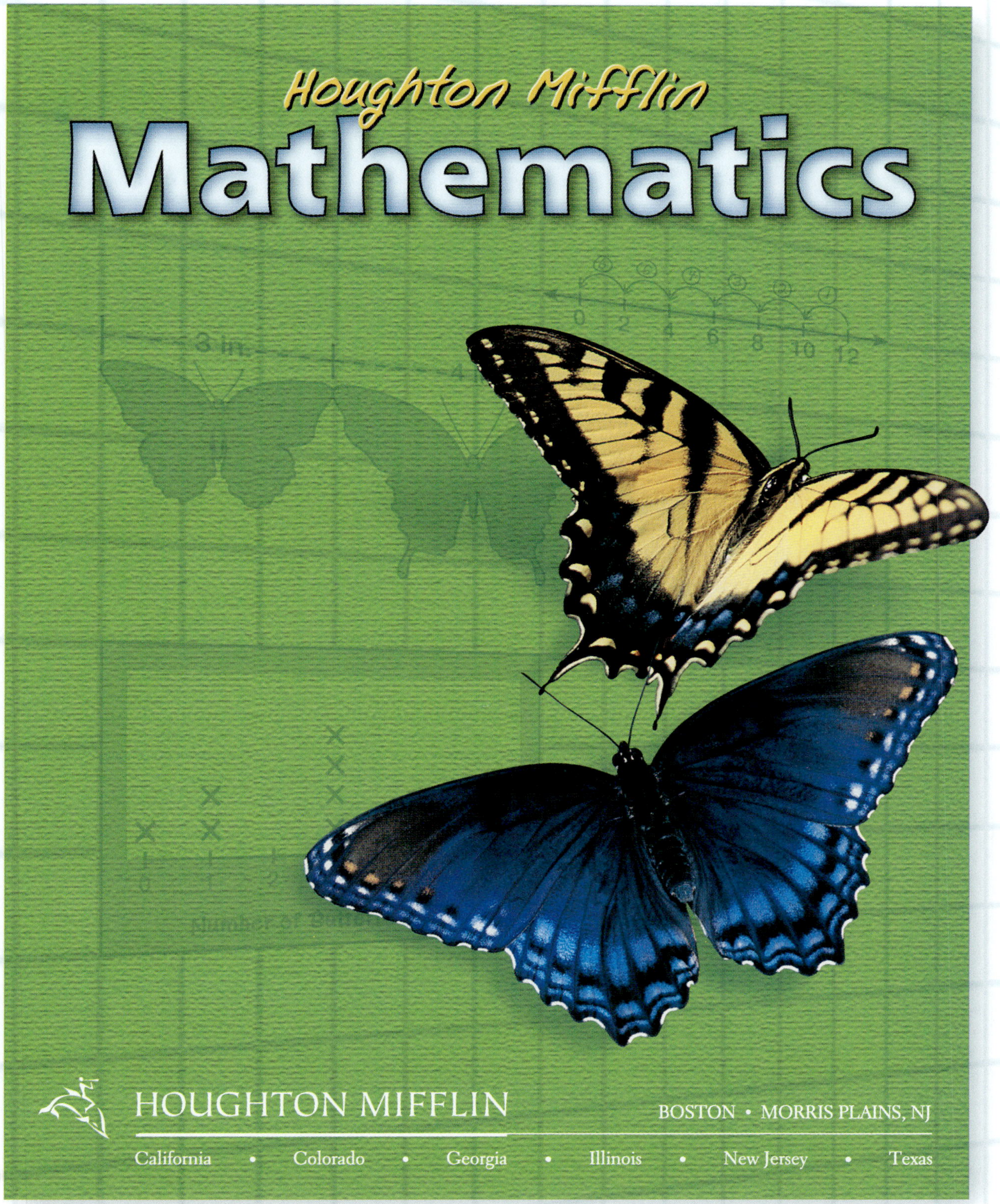

ISBN 0-618-09977-8

2 3 4 5 6 7 8 9 VH 06 05 04 03 02 01

Authors

Senior Authors

Dr. Carole Greenes
Professor of Mathematics Education
Boston University
Boston, MA

Dr. Miriam A. Leiva
Distinguished Professor of Mathematics Emerita
University of North Carolina
Charlotte, NC

Dr. Bruce R. Vogeli
Clifford Brewster Upton Professor of Mathematics
Teacher's College, Columbia University
New York, NY

Program Authors

Dr. Matt Larson
Curriculum Specialist for Mathematics
Lincoln Public Schools
Lincoln, NE

Timothy D. Kanold
Director of Mathematics
Adlai E. Stevenson High School
Lincolnshire, IL

Dr. Jean M. Shaw
Professor of Elementary Education
University of Mississippi
Oxford, MS

Dr. Lee Stiff
Professor of Mathematics Education
North Carolina State University
Raleigh, NC

Content Reviewers

Lawrence Braden (Grades 5–6)
Mathematics Teacher
St. Paul's School
Concord, NH

Dr. Don Chakerian (Grades 3–4)
Emeritus Professor of Mathematics
University of California
Davis, CA

Dr. Kurt Kreith (Grades 3–4)
Emeritus Professor of Mathematics
University of California
Davis, CA

Dr. Liping Ma (Grades K–2)
Independent Scholar
Palo Alto, CA

Dr. David Wright (Grades 5–6)
Professor of Mathematics
Brigham Young University
Provo, UT

Teacher Reviewers

Grade K

Mary Benedetto
John Barry Elementary School
Chicago, IL

Marcia Neuski
Marconi Community Academy
Chicago, IL

Mary Yoveff
St. James School
Belvidere, IL

Grade 1

Cris Lee
Little Woods School
St. Charles, IL

Karen Illyin
Washington Elementary School
Waukegan, IL

Donna Kelly
Emerson School
Maywood, IL

Pat Pulido
Stevenson School
Melrose Park, IL

Len Mitnaul
Woodrow Wilson Elementary School
Trenton, NJ

Grade 2

Pat Burns
Maplebrook Elementary School
Naperville, IL

Joan Janopoulos
Garfield School
Maywood, IL

Linda Mallek
Clearview Elementary School
Waukegan, IL

Michelle Kuhn
Melrose Park School
Melrose Park, IL

Diane Maksay
Refkin Elementary School
Glendale Heights, IL

Janet Rhodes
Nichols Elementary School
Nichols, NY

Grade 3

Nancy Fister
Reba O. Steck Elementary School
Aurora, IL

Karen Holly
Robert Healy Elementary School
Chicago, IL

Margie Henricksen
Andrew Cooke Magnet School
Waukegan, IL

Kathy Ruggerio
Mark Sheridan Academy
Chicago, IL

Joanne Stevens
Nichols Elementary School
Nichols, NY

Grade 4

Lorraine Bujan
Mark Sheridan Magnet School
Chicago, IL

Robin Gillette
Nichols Elementary School
Nichols, NY

Mary Mitchell
McKinley School
New Brunswick, NJ

Ron Metcalf
Barbara B. Rose Elementary School
South Barrington, IL

Mary Peterson
Long Beach Elementary School
Montgomery, IL

Grade 5

Chuck Freundt
Meadow Glens Elementary School
Naperville, IL

Patricia Heintz
PS 92 Queens
Corona, NY

Kristen Mellish
Whittier Elementary School
Downers Grove, IL

Grade 6

Linda Hunt
O. A. Thorp Scholastic Academy
Chicago, IL

Judy O'Neill
Gwynedd Mercy Academy
Spring House, PA

Mary Ryan
Barrington Middle School
Barrington, IL

Janet Schild
Madison Jr. High School
Naperville, IL

Getting Started

Welcome to Houghton Mifflin Mathematics! Before you begin to use this book, take a quick look and check out some of its special features. That way, you'll be able to get the most out of every lesson!

Using the Lessons

There is something new to learn in each lesson. Here are some things to watch for as you take a quick look at some of the lessons in the book.

- ***Different Ways*** boxes show that sometimes there is more than one way to solve a problem.
- ***Explain Your Thinking*** questions help you check to see if you understand important ideas in the lesson.
- ***Ask Yourself*** questions guide your thinking about how to do the math.

Learning Math Vocabulary

Math is about more than just numbers! To read, write, and talk about math, it helps to know the correct vocabulary words to use.

- ***Reading Mathematics*** pages will help remind you of math vocabulary words you already know and prepare you for the new chapter.
- ***Vocabulary*** boxes will list important math words that will be used in the lesson. These words are usually highlighted in the lesson—so you can't miss them!
- ***Using Vocabulary*** feature boxes will remind you of the important math words in the chapter.

Using Special Features

Show What You Know

Are you ready for a riddle or to learn about a whole different number system? These pages give you different ways to use the math you have just learned.

Number Sense

These pages show you that there is more than one way to solve a problem or think about a math idea. Then you can use the way that makes the most sense to you!

These feature boxes are full of fun facts about things in the world around you that relate to math.

Have you ever heard the expression "Use your head"? This is the place to do it!

Algebra is a special kind of math that you will use more and more as you get older. But why wait? You can get ready for algebra now!

Look for Internet references. You can use the Web to find brainteasers and other fun and challenging math activities to do!

Getting Started

Becoming a Better Problem Solver

Problem solving is one of the most important reasons to learn to do mathematics. Here are the four parts of a problem-solving plan that can help you become a better problem solver.

Understand

Be sure you really understand the problem.

- Reread the problem carefully.
- Retell the problem in your own words.
- List the information given in the problem.
- Decide what you need to find.

Plan

Make a plan to solve the problem.

- Think about the problem and decide how you will try to solve it.
- Choose a strategy to use—see the list on page ix for some choices.
- Choose a method to use, such as estimation, mental math, or paper and pencil.

Solve

Find the answer.

- Carry out the plan.
- Adjust your plan or try a different strategy if needed.
- Check your computations to be sure they are correct.

Look Back

Check that your answer makes sense.

- Did you answer the question that was asked?
- Is your answer labeled correctly?
- Is your answer reasonable?

Problem-Solving Strategies

Many different strategie scan be used to solve problems. As you learn and practice different strategies, you will soon know which one to use for different kinds of problems.

Remember, when it comes to problem solving:

- Sometimes you can use several different strategies.
- Sometimes you can use a combination of strategies.
- Sometimes you can use your own strategy.

Here are the strategies you will learn about and use this year.

Problem-Solving Strategies

These strategies can be used for many different kinds of problems.	These strategies are usually used for specific types of problems.
Use Models to Act It Out	Find a Pattern
Draw a Picture	Use Logical Thinking
Write a Number Sentence	Work Backward
Make a Table	Guess and Check
Solve a Simpler Problem	

Now that you know something about the math book you'll be using this year, let's get started! Turn the page to find out what you will be learning in the months to come.

Contents

Remembering Basic Facts

Chapter 1 Place Value

Money and Time

Addition and Subtraction

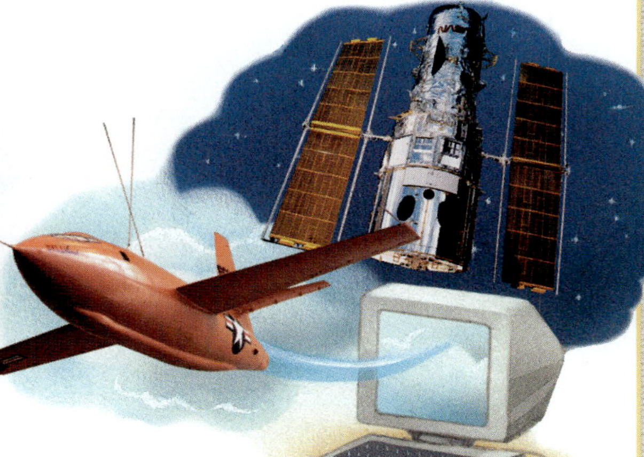

Measurement

Multiplication Concepts

Multiplication Facts

Geometry and Measurement

Division Concepts

Division Facts

Chapter 10 Data and Probability

Fractions and Decimals

Multiplying and Dividing

Book Resources

Remembering Addition Facts to 10

Add.

0 + 4	1 + 8	2 + 1	3 + 1	0 + 2	6 + 2
9 + 0	2 + 0	5 + 0	10 + 0	1 + 2	0 + 7
2 + 7	1 + 3	0 + 8	3 + 7	6 + 0	5 + 3
0 + 10	9 + 1	5 + 2	8 + 1	3 + 0	6 + 3
1 + 0	2 + 5	4 + 4	1 + 5	1 + 4	3 + 6
7 + 3	0 + 0	0 + 1	4 + 2	6 + 4	6 + 1
2 + 6	5 + 1	3 + 5	5 + 4	2 + 4	2 + 8
1 + 9	7 + 1	0 + 6	2 + 3	3 + 4	4 + 0
0 + 5	8 + 0	4 + 3	1 + 6	0 + 3	1 + 7
2 + 2	8 + 2	5 + 5	3 + 3	4 + 6	4 + 1
7 + 2	1 + 1	0 + 9	3 + 2	7 + 0	4 + 5

Remembering Addition Facts to 20

Add.

3 + 10	6 + 7	6 + 6	7 + 6	9 + 6	3 + 8
8 + 9	9 + 10	0 + 10	4 + 8	4 + 6	6 + 10
9 + 5	8 + 4	2 + 8	6 + 8	3 + 7	7 + 7
1 + 10	6 + 4	5 + 7	10 + 5	10 + 4	10 + 10
8 + 8	5 + 6	9 + 4	8 + 7	9 + 3	10 + 7
5 + 5	9 + 9	1 + 9	5 + 10	10 + 3	7 + 8
6 + 5	7 + 5	10 + 2	9 + 2	10 + 8	9 + 7
7 + 3	10 + 9	8 + 3	8 + 5	5 + 9	8 + 6
2 + 10	4 + 9	7 + 10	9 + 1	10 + 1	9 + 8
7 + 4	8 + 10	10 + 0	4 + 7	5 + 8	6 + 9
3 + 9	8 + 2	2 + 9	7 + 9	10 + 6	4 + 10

Remembering Subtraction Facts to 10

Subtract.

6 − 1	5 − 0	8 − 4	10 − 9	5 − 2	2 − 2
4 − 1	7 − 6	8 − 8	5 − 5	10 − 4	9 − 6
5 − 1	10 − 3	7 − 5	9 − 9	3 − 2	7 − 0
9 − 1	0 − 0	7 − 2	1 − 1	9 − 3	4 − 3
4 − 0	3 − 3	8 − 6	10 − 8	9 − 5	1 − 0
10 − 1	9 − 8	7 − 1	9 − 2	8 − 2	5 − 3
2 − 1	9 − 7	10 − 10	6 − 4	7 − 7	8 − 7
9 − 4	6 − 0	6 − 5	8 − 0	5 − 4	3 − 0
10 − 8	8 − 5	10 − 2	4 − 4	10 − 0	6 − 3
7 − 4	9 − 0	8 − 1	6 − 2	7 − 3	8 − 3
10 − 5	6 − 6	3 − 1	2 − 0	4 − 2	10 − 6

Remembering Subtraction Facts to 20

Subtract.

11 − 10	19 − 0	15 − 0	12 − 9	15 − 10	16 − 7
14 − 6	11 − 1	20 − 10	18 − 8	13 − 4	18 − 0
14 − 7	16 − 0	12 − 0	17 − 7	19 − 10	13 − 3
11 − 8	12 − 6	14 − 9	12 − 5	13 − 10	17 − 0
16 − 8	12 − 2	18 − 10	13 − 7	17 − 9	13 − 6
15 − 9	14 − 5	16 − 6	12 − 10	18 − 9	11 − 7
15 − 6	14 − 4	11 − 3	17 − 10	12 − 7	13 − 0
14 − 8	12 − 3	11 − 4	19 − 9	16 − 10	15 − 8
11 − 0	14 − 9	12 − 8	15 − 5	13 − 9	11 − 6
10 − 0	16 − 9	13 − 5	11 − 9	14 − 10	12 − 4
15 − 7	17 − 8	14 − 0	20 − 0	11 − 5	13 − 8

Skip Counting

Copy and complete. Count by 2s to 100.

2	4	___	___	10
___	___	16	18	20
22	___	26	28	___
32	34	___	___	40
___	44	46	48	___
___	54	___	58	60
62	64	___	___	70
72	___	76	___	80
82	84	___	88	___
___	94	96	98	___

Copy and complete. Count by 5s to 100.

5	___	15	___	___
30	___	40	___	50
55	60	___	___	75
___	85	___	95	___

Skip Counting

Copy and complete. Count by 10s to 200.

10	____	____	40	____
60	____	____	90	____
____	120	____	____	150
160	____	180	____	____

Copy and complete. Count by 3s to 60.

3	6	____	12	____
18	____	24	____	30
____	____	____	42	____
48	51	____	57	____

Copy and complete. Count by 4s to 100.

4	____	12	____	20
____	28	____	36	40
44	____	52	56	____
64	68	____	____	80
____	88	____	96	100

CHAPTER 1

Place Value

Why Learn About Place Value?

Place value can help you understand the meaning of numbers. It can also help you compare and order them.

If you like to collect things, such as rocks, coins, or books, you can use place value to keep track of the number of items in your collection.

Look at the children playing in the ball crawl. It's easy to count the number of children. Place value can help you count the number of balls.

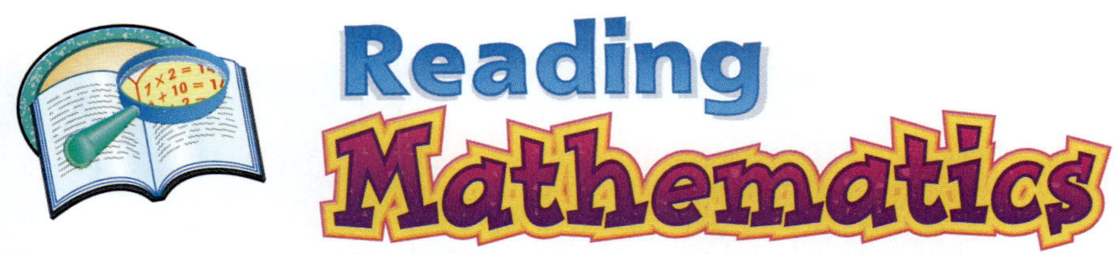

Reviewing Vocabulary

Understanding math language helps you become a successful problem solver. Here are some math vocabulary words you should know.

digit	the symbol used to write a number
place value	the value of a digit determined by its place in a number
is greater than ($>$)	the symbol used to compare two numbers when the greater number is written first
is less than ($<$)	the symbol used to compare two numbers when the lesser number is written first
equal to ($=$)	the symbol used to compare two numbers when the value of each number is the same

Reading Words and Symbols

When you read mathematics, sometimes you read only words, sometimes you read words and symbols, and sometimes you read only symbols.

Look at the different ways you can describe 385.

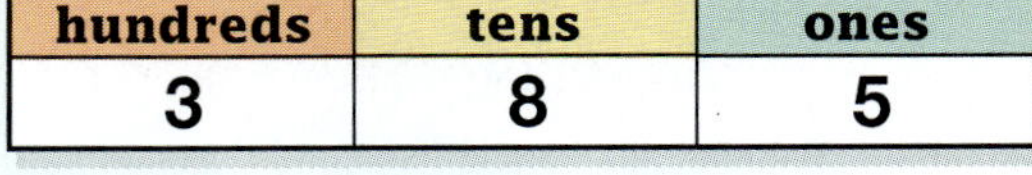

hundreds	tens	ones
3	8	5

- 385 has three digits.
- 385 has 3 hundreds, 8 tens, and 5 ones.
- 385 is read as three hundred eighty-five.
- 385 is between 300 and 400.
- $385 > 384$
- $385 < 386$

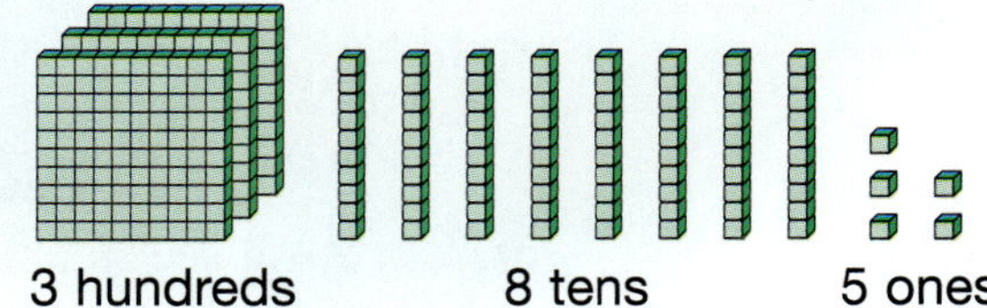

Try These

1. Write each sentence using numbers and symbols.
   - **a.** Eighty-six is greater than eighty-five.
   - **b.** Two hundred sixty is equal to two hundred sixty.
   - **c.** Four hundred is less than five hundred.
   - **d.** Seventy-five is greater than fifty-seven.

2. Tell whether the 3 is in the *ones, tens,* or *hundreds* place.

a. 138	**b.** 370	**c.** 31	**d.** 563
e. 938	**f.** 83	**g.** 377	**h.** 34

3. Write the numbers in order from least to greatest.

   a. 65 73 45 **b.** 175 204 192 **c.** 1,973 1,745 1,945

4. Write *true* or *false* for each sentence.
   - **a.** Ten ones is equal to one ten.
   - **b.** A two-digit number is greater than a three-digit number.
   - **c.** Ten tens is equal to 1,010.
   - **d.** Four hundred thirty-two is greater than four hundred twenty-three.

Upcoming Vocabulary

Write About It **Here are some other vocabulary words** you will learn in this chapter. Watch for these words. Write their definitions in your journal.

round	**one thousand**
expanded form	**ten thousands**
standard form	**hundred thousands**
word form	

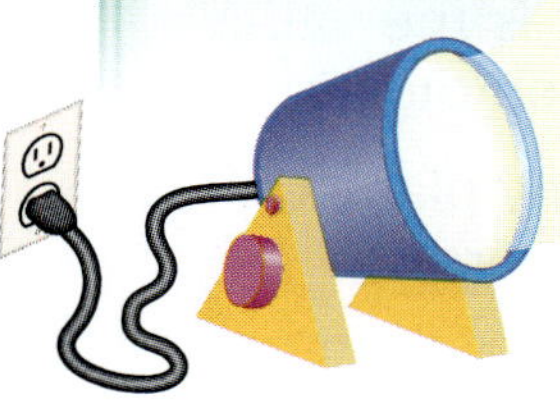

Numbers Through 999

You will learn about place value of numbers to 999.

New Vocabulary
expanded form
standard form
word form

Learn About It

Numbers are made up of digits. The value of each digit depends on its place in a number.

This shoe is 118 inches long. It is the longest shoe in the world! A place-value chart can help you understand the value of each digit in the number 118.

hundreds	tens	ones
1	1	8

The value of the 1 is 100. The value of the 1 is 10. The value of the 8 is 8.

Different Ways to Write a Number

You can use **expanded form.**	You can use **standard form.**	You can use **word form.**
100 + 10 + 8	118	one hundred eighteen

Explain Your Thinking

► In the number 304, what is the meaning of the zero in the tens place?

Guided Practice

Write each number in two other ways. Use standard form, expanded form, and word form.

1. 200 + 40 + 7 **2.** 300 + 9 **3.** 465

4. two hundred thirty-eight **5.** 4 hundreds 9 tens 4 ones

Ask Yourself
- What is the value of each digit?
- Do any places have zeros?

Independent Practice

Write each number in standard form.

6. 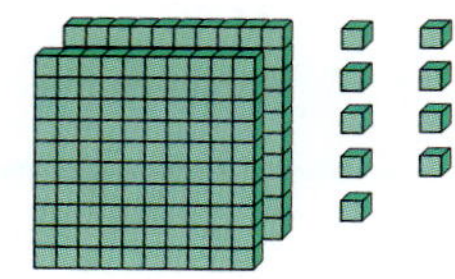

7. 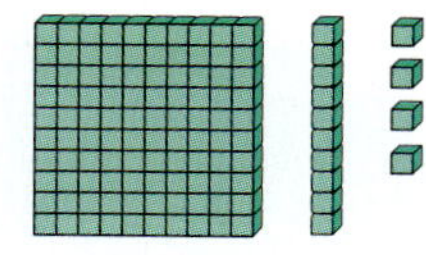

8. 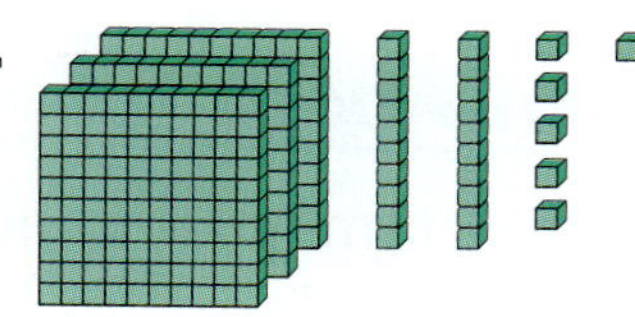

9. 900 + 80 + 6

10. 400 + 20 + 3

11. 100 + 50

12. 200 + 60 + 5

13. 700 + 3

14. 400 + 80 + 1

15. 6 hundreds 8 ones

16. 5 hundreds 9 tens

17. 3 hundreds 5 tens 2 ones

18. 2 hundreds 3 tens 9 ones

Write the place of the underlined digit. Then write its value.

19. $\underline{1}76$ **20.** $8\underline{9}3$ **21.** $3\underline{1}0$ **22.** $42\underline{7}$ **23.** $\underline{5}51$ **24.** $7\underline{4}9$

25. $\underline{2}67$ **26.** $35\underline{7}$ **27.** $\underline{9}28$ **28.** $64\underline{8}$ **29.** $47\underline{0}$ **30.** $5\underline{6}6$

Problem Solving • Reasoning

Use Data **Use the table for Problems 31–33.**

31. Cal says that the longest bicycle is eight hundred seventy-six inches long. Is he correct? Explain why or why not.

32. How would you write the length of the smallest biplane in expanded form? in word form?

33. **Analyze** Look at the numbers in the table. Which number has the greatest tens digit?

Item	Length
Smallest biplane	106 in.
Longest bicycle	876 in.
Smallest car	100 in.

Mixed Review • Test Prep

Add or subtract. *(pages xxii, xxiv)*

34. $6 + 2$

35. $3 - 1$

36. $7 - 4$

37. $5 + 3$

38. $8 + 2$

39. $9 - 6$

40 Which shows counting by 5s? *(page xxvi)*

A 10, 15, 20, 25

B 4, 6, 8, 10

C 3, 6, 9, 12

D 15, 20, 30, 40

Extra Practice See Set A on page 40.

Round Two-Digit Numbers

You will learn how to round numbers to the nearest ten.

New Vocabulary
round

Learn About It

The King family is riding in a bike-a-thon. The sign shows the distance children, teenagers, and adults will ride. Rounded to the nearest 10 miles, how far will each group ride?

Bike-a-thon

Children	12 miles
Teenagers	15 miles
Adults	17 miles

One way to **round** a number is to round it to the nearest ten.

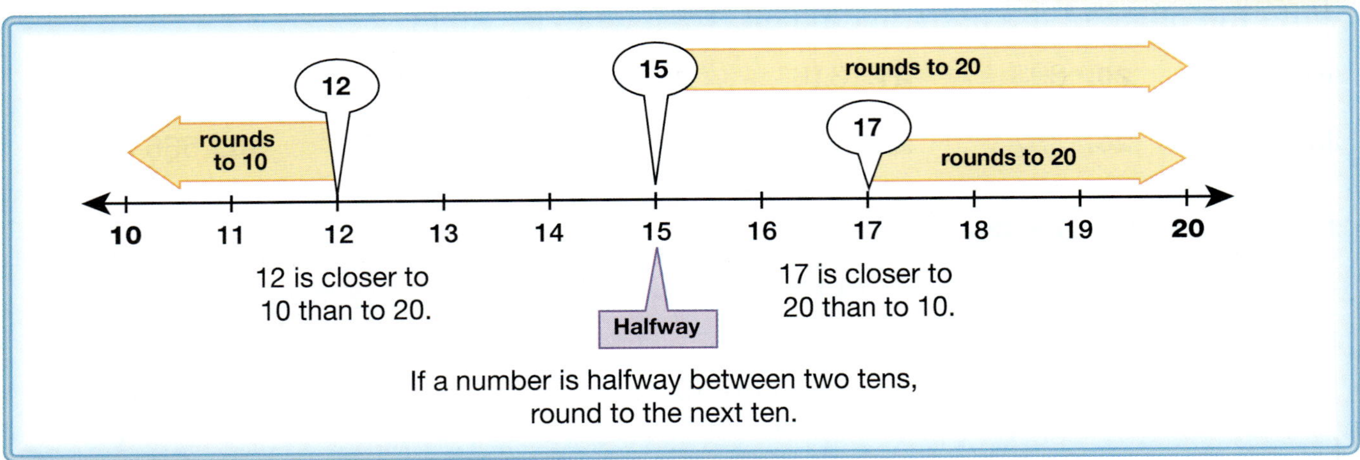

Solution: When rounded to the nearest 10 miles, children will ride 10 miles and teenagers and adults will ride 20 miles.

Another Example

Money

What is 23¢ rounded to the nearest ten cents?

What is 26¢ rounded to the nearest ten cents?

23
rounds to 20¢
26
rounds to 30¢
20 21 22 23 24 25 26 27 28 29 30

Explain Your Thinking

► What is the least number that rounds to 20?

► Are rounding rules different when you round money? Explain.

Guided Practice

Round each amount to the nearest ten or ten cents.

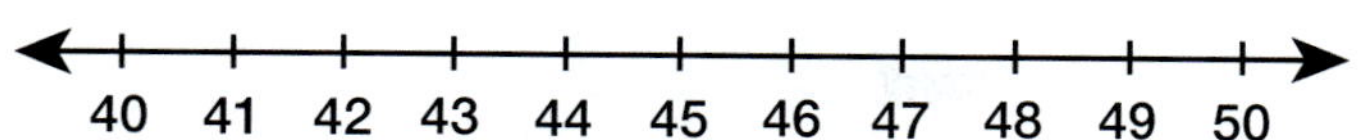

1. 41 **2.** 48¢ **3.** 43 **4.** 45¢ **5.** 44

6. 49 **7.** 45¢ **8.** 46 **9.** 42¢ **10.** 47¢

Ask Yourself

- Which ten is the number closest to?
- What do I do if the number is halfway between two tens?

Independent Practice

Round each amount to the nearest ten or ten cents.

11. 81 **12.** 53 **13.** 67 **14.** 47 **15.** 15 **16.** 73

17. 42¢ **18.** 68 **19.** 34¢ **20.** 75 **21.** 13¢ **22.** 86

23. 79¢ **24.** 51 **25.** 82¢ **26.** 57¢ **27.** 15¢ **28.** 93

Problem Solving • Reasoning

29. A park has 38 miles of bike trails. Rounded to the nearest ten miles, how many miles is that?

30. **Analyze** If Katie rounds the number of hours she biked last month to the nearest ten hours, she would say that she biked for 60 hours. What is the least number of hours she might have biked? How do you know?

31. **Patterns** One week Min rode her bike 2 miles. The next week she rode it 6 miles. The week after that she rode it 10 miles. If the pattern continued, how many miles did Min likely ride her bike in the fifth week?

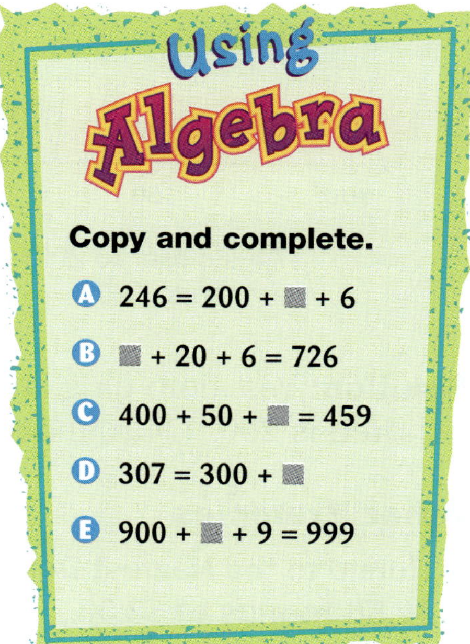

Mixed Review • Test Prep

Add or Subtract. *(pages xxii–xxv)*

32. 6 + 3 **33.** 17 − 4 **34.** 12 + 7 **35.** 8 − 2 **36.** 5 + 9

37 Which is another way to write 400 + 30 + 3? *(pages 4–5)*

A 43 **B** 403 **C** 430 **D** 433

Extra Practice See Set B on page 40.

Round Three-Digit Numbers

You will learn how to round numbers to the nearest hundred or to the nearest ten.

Review Vocabulary
round

Learn About It

Marta and Ali have collected 174 pieces of sea glass. Marta says that there are about 200 pieces. Ali says that there are about 170 pieces. Can they both be right?

When you round a three-digit number, you can **round** to the nearest hundred or to the nearest ten.

Different Ways to Round

Round 174 to the nearest hundred.

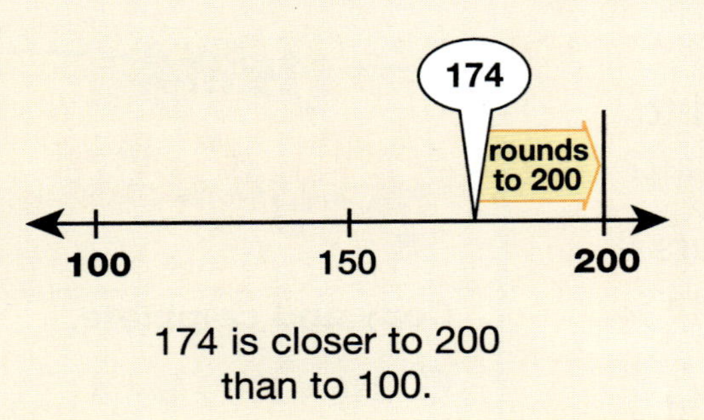

174 is closer to 200 than to 100.

Round 174 to the nearest ten.

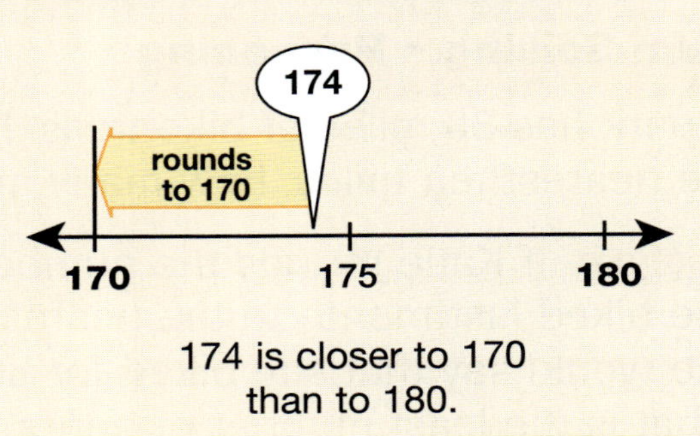

174 is closer to 170 than to 180.

Solution: Yes, both girls are right. 174 rounded to the nearest hundred is 200. 174 rounded to the nearest ten is 170.

Other Examples

A. Round to the Nearest Dollar
$2.56 rounds to $3.00.

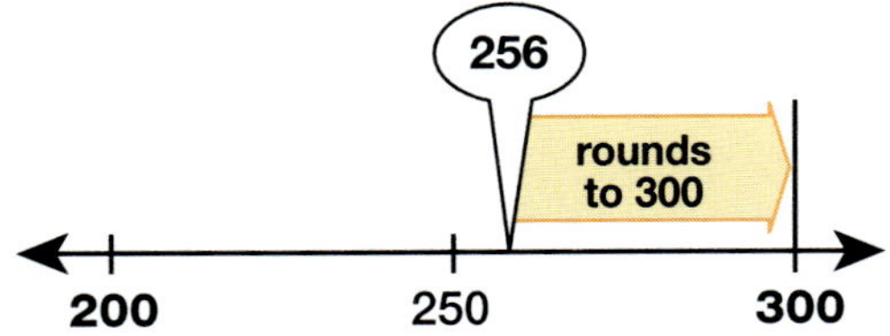

B. Round to the Nearest Ten Cents
$2.56 rounds to $2.60.

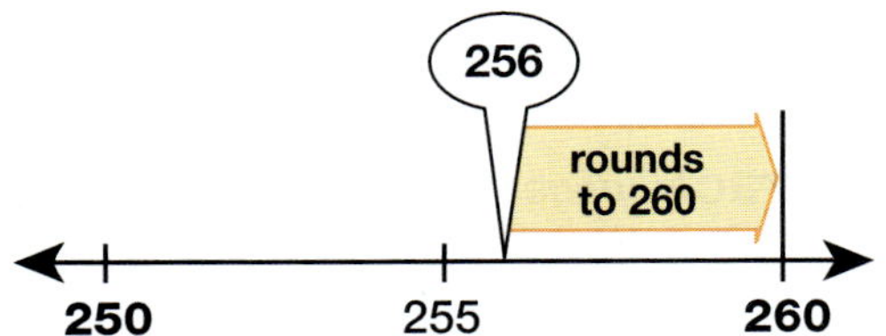

Explain Your Thinking

► If you round a number to the nearest ten and the nearest hundred, which gives a better estimate? Will they ever be the same? Explain your answer.

Guided Practice

Round to the nearest hundred or dollar.

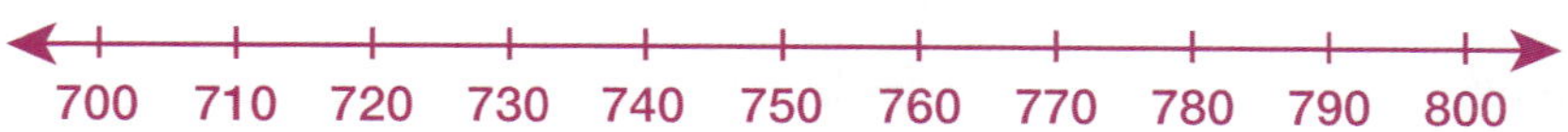

1. 743 **2.** $7.68 **3.** 791 **4.** 729

5. 774 **6.** 736 **7.** 705 **8.** $7.50

Ask Yourself

- Which hundred is the number closer to?
- What should I do if the number is halfway between two hundreds?

Independent Practice

Write the two hundreds each number is between.

9. 466 **10.** 735 **11.** 243 **12.** 588

13. 370 **14.** 654 **15.** 195 **16.** 349

Write the two tens each number is between.

17. 334 **18.** 575 **19.** 601 **20.** 827

21. 853 **22.** 704 **23.** 496 **24.** 182

Round to the nearest hundred or dollar.

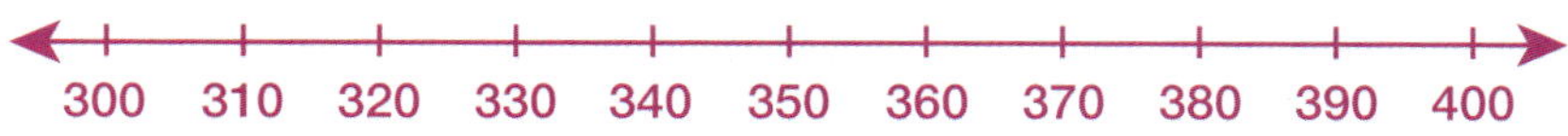

25. 400 **26.** 322 **27.** $3.59 **28.** 361

29. 306 **30.** $3.84 **31.** 338 **32.** $3.50

Round to the nearest ten or ten cents.

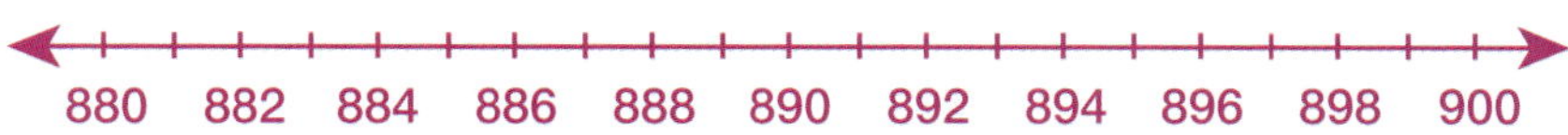

33. 889 **34.** $8.94 **35.** 883 **36.** 885

37. $8.81 **38.** 897 **39.** $8.92 **40.** 886

Round to the place of the underlined digit.

41. $\underline{6}55$ **42.** $1\underline{8}9$ **43.** $\$\underline{9}.27$

44. $\underline{4}72$ **45.** $\$7.\underline{3}3$ **46.** $3\underline{5}7$

Problem Solving • Reasoning

Solve. Choose a method.

Computation Methods

• Mental Math • Estimation • Paper and Pencil

47. Lisa has 15 rocks in her rock collection. She gives 1 rock to each of 6 friends. How many rocks does she have left?

48. William has 207 sports cards, 119 erasers, and 275 shells. Which of William's collections has about 200 items in it?

49. **Explain** Tyrell has 185 glass marbles and 212 plastic marbles. He says that he has about 200 of each kind of marble. Why does he use the same number to tell how many of each kind of marble he has?

50. **Compare** Ada has a comic-book collection. She has 18 adventure comic books and 23 mystery comic books. Does she have more than 30 comic books?

Mixed Review • Test Prep

Add or subtract. *(pages xxiii–xxv)*

51. 5 − 3 **52.** 7 + 4 **53.** 9 + 8 **54.** 16 − 8 **55.** 9 − 4

56. 17 − 9 **57.** 10 + 9 **58.** 14 − 9 **59.** 6 + 9 **60.** 7 + 6

Which numbers are likely to come next in each pattern? *(page xxvi)*

61 2, 4, 6, ___, ___, ___

A 10, 12, 14 **C** 8, 9, 10
B 8, 10, 12 **D** 7, 8, 9

62 1, 3, 5, ___, ___, ___

F 7, 9, 11 **H** 7, 8, 9
G 6, 7, 8 **J** 6, 8, 10

Logical Thinking

Analogies

Look at the way the first set of numbers is related. Choose the letter that shows a similar relationship for the second pair.

63. **14** is to **8 + 6** as **18** is to ___.

A 8 + 8 **C** 6 + 8
B 9 + 9 **D** 8 + 14

64. **7** is to **12 − 5** as **6** is to ___.

F 11 − 6 **H** 13 − 9
G 14 − 5 **J** 15 − 9

Extra Practice See Set C on page 40.

Practice Game

What's My Number?

Use what you know about place value to play this game with a partner. Try to guess your opponent's number before he or she guesses your number.

What You'll Need

For each player

- *place-value chart*

Players 2

Here's What to Do

1. Each player thinks of a 3-digit number and secretly writes it down.
2. Players take turns asking questions that can be answered yes or no to figure out the other number.

   Sample questions
   - Is the number an even number?
   - Is the digit in the hundreds place greater than 5?
3. Players continue asking questions. The first player to figure out the other player's number scores 1 point.
4. Repeat Steps 1 to 3. The first player to score 3 points wins the game.

Hmmm . . . I wonder what number he chose!

Share Your Thinking How can the place-value chart help you keep track of the answers to the questions you asked?

Problem-Solving Skill: Estimated or Exact Amounts

You will learn how to decide if numbers are being used to show an exact amount or an estimated amount.

Sometimes you need to decide if numbers are being used to show an exact amount or an estimated amount.

Ostriches cannot fly, but they can run! Ostriches can run more than 30 miles an hour. They can be up to 8 feet tall. They have 2 toes on each foot. An ostrich egg weighs more than 3 pounds. An empty ostrich egg costs $6.25.

Sometimes numbers are used to show estimates.

Words such as *more than, almost, over, up to,* and *about* tell you that amounts are estimated, not exact.

Do you know exactly how fast an ostrich can run?
No, you know that an ostrich can run *more* than 30 miles an hour.

Do you know exactly how tall an ostrich is?
No, you know that an ostrich can be *up to* 8 feet tall.

Sometimes numbers are used to show exact amounts.

Exact amounts are amounts that have been counted.

Do you know exactly how much an empty ostrich egg costs?
Yes, an empty ostrich egg costs $6.25.

Do you know exactly how many toes an ostrich has on each foot?
Yes, an ostrich has 2 toes on each foot.

Look Back What other estimated amount can you find in the paragraph above on ostriches?

Right: The bald eagle has been the national symbol of the United States since 1782. *Left*: The great blue heron uses its long neck and bill to catch food.

Guided Practice

Solve.

1. Joshua counted 15 blue herons in a salt marsh. Is "15 blue herons" an exact amount or an estimated amount?

Did Joshua count the herons?

2. Almost 75,000 bald eagles once nested in the United States. Is "almost 75,000" an exact amount or an estimated amount?

Is there a word clue before the number?

Choose a Strategy

Solve. Use these or other strategies.

Problem-Solving Strategies

- **Draw a Picture**
- **Write a Number Sentence**
- **Guess and Check**

3. On a nature hike, Stephanie took 18 pictures of birds. Then she took 10 pictures of other animals. How many pictures of animals did Stephanie take in all?

4. A small and a large eagle poster cost $12 together. A large poster costs $4 more than a small poster. How much does each poster cost?

5. Eric checks out two library books. The book about eagles has 42 pages. The book about ducks has almost 50 pages. Eric says that the books have about 90 pages in all. Is he correct? Explain why or why not.

6. There are three birds' eggs on display. The eggs are lined up in a row. The robin's egg is not next to the ostrich's egg. The blue jay's egg is to the left of the ostrich's egg. In what order are the birds' eggs on display?

7. Penguins can be very heavy. One penguin weighs 53 pounds. Another penguin weighs 71 pounds. What is each penguin's weight to the nearest ten pounds?

8. **Write About It** One day, almost 40 birds came to a bird feeder. The next day, more than 40 birds came to the feeder. On which day did more birds come to the feeder? Explain.

Extra Practice See 1–4 on page 43.

Quick Check

Check Your Understanding of Lessons 1–4

Write the place of the underlined digit.
Then write its value.

1. $\underline{7}6$ **2.** $9\underline{3}$ **3.** $24\underline{8}$ **4.** $\underline{5}62$ **5.** $7\underline{8}4$

Round to the nearest ten or ten cents.

6. 51 **7.** 83¢ **8.** 29 **9.** 45 **10.** 78¢

Round to the underlined digit.

11. $\underline{6}80$ **12.** $\$9.\underline{7}5$ **13.** $\underline{1}34$ **14.** $\underline{7}55$ **15.** $\$\,5.\underline{4}1$

Solve.

16. On Tuesday, Jenny's baseball team won their game by a score of 5 to 3. More than 60 fans came to watch. Is the number of fans an exact amount or an estimate? Explain.

17. There are 14 players on Jenny's baseball team. In Tuesday's game, 2 players got hits. Is the number of players on Jenny's team an exact amount or an estimate?

How did you do?

If you had difficulty with any items in the Quick Check, you can use the following pages for review and extra practice.

Items	Review These Pages	Do These Extra Practice Items
1–5	pages 4–5	Set A, page 40
6–10	pages 6–7	Set B, page 40
11–15	pages 8–10	Set C, page 40
16–17	pages 12–13	1–4, page 43

Test Prep • Cumulative Review

Maintaining the Standards

Choose the letter of the correct answer.

Use the table for Questions 1–2.

Grade	Number of Toys
1	159
2	230
3	179

1. If the number of toys collected by the third grade is rounded to the nearest ten, what is the rounded number?
   A 18
   B 100
   C 180
   D 200

2. If the number of toys collected by the first grade is rounded to the nearest hundred, what is the rounded number?
   F 100
   G 150
   H 160
   J 200

3. Which number is equal to 700 + 60?
   A 7,600 **C** 761
   B 760 **D** 76

4. How is four hundred fifty written in standard form?
   F 4,500 **H** 450
   G 4,050 **J** 405

5. Kathy says that her mystery number has a nine in the tens place. Which number could be her mystery number?
   A 91
   B 329
   C 952
   D 1,923

6. Jeffers School has 572 students. What is the value of the underlined digit in <u>5</u>72?
   F 5
   G 50
   H 500
   J 5,000

7. Michael has 206 trading cards. Which words mean 206?
   A twenty-six
   B two hundred sixty
   C two thousand sixty
   D two hundred six

8. Megan and her family visited a zoo that has 560 different kinds of animals. Write the number in expanded form.

   Explain How did you find your answer?

Safe Site

Internet Test Prep
Visit **www.eduplace.com/kids/mhm** for more *Test Prep Practice.*

Modeling One Thousand

You will learn how one thousand is related to hundreds and tens.

New Vocabulary
one thousand

Learn About It

Use grid paper to explore one thousand.

Look at the paper square on the right. Suppose you made a line of 1,000 squares this size. How long would the line be? How is 1,000 related to 1, 10, and 100? Divide your class into 10 teams to find out.

Paper Square

Materials
grid paper
10 crayons
scissors
tape

Step 1 Choose a team color. Use a crayon in your team's color to fill in a strip of 10 squares on grid paper. Cut out the strip. Then color and cut out 9 more strips of 10 squares.

Step 2 Look at your strips.

- How many strips do you have?
- How many squares do you have?

Make a table like the one on the right. Fill in the first row of the table.

Number of Teams	Number of Strips	Number of Squares
1		
2		
3		
4		
5		
6		
7		
8		
9		
10		

Step 3 Tape your team's 10 strips in a line. Be sure not to overlap any squares. Now join another team. Tape both teams' strips together in a line. Then fill in the second row of your table.

Step 4 Work as a class to tape all of the strips together. Then complete your table.

Try It Out

Use your completed table to help you answer each question.

1. How many squares were in each strip?
2. How many strips did each team have?
3. How many squares did each team have?
4. Together how many strips did all of the teams make?
5. How many squares in all were there?
6. How many groups of 100 squares were there?

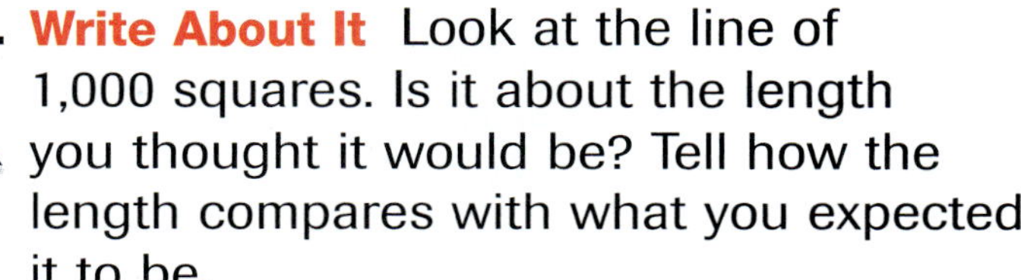

7. **Write About It** Look at the line of 1,000 squares. Is it about the length you thought it would be? Tell how the length compares with what you expected it to be.

Tell whether each is greater than, less than, or equal to 1,000.

8. 8 boxes of 100 pencils
9. 9 boxes of 1,000 craft sticks
10. 10 bags of 10 muffins
11. 10 bags of 100 letters

Write about it! Talk about it!

Use what you have learned to answer these questions.

12. Look at the table you completed. What pattern do you notice in each row? in each column?
13. If you know how many tens there are in 100, how can you find the number of tens in 700?
14. For which would you need a larger container: 1,000 grains of sand or 1,000 marbles? Explain.

Place Value to Thousands

You will learn about place value of numbers to thousands.

Learn About It

Dancing dragons are a fun part of Chinese parades. The longest dancing dragon ever made had 3,760 people in it. That means the dragon had 7,520 legs!

A place-value chart can help you understand the value of each digit in 7,520.

thousands	hundreds	tens	ones
7	5	2	0

The value of the 7 is 7,000. The value of the 5 is 500. The value of the 2 is 20. The value of the 0 is 0.

Different Ways to Write a Number

You can use expanded form.
7,000 + 500 + 20

You can use standard form.
7,520
A comma is used to separate thousands and hundreds.

You can use word form.
seven thousand, five hundred twenty

Explain Your Thinking

► In what ways are 7,520 and 5,720 similar? different?

Guided Practice

Write each number in two other ways. Use standard form, expanded form, and word form.

1. 4,900

2. eight thousand, seventy-three

3. 9,000 + 80 + 7

4. 3,000 + 200 + 30 + 5

Ask Yourself

- What is the value of each digit in the number?
- Are there any places that have zeros?

Independent Practice

Write each number in standard form.

5. 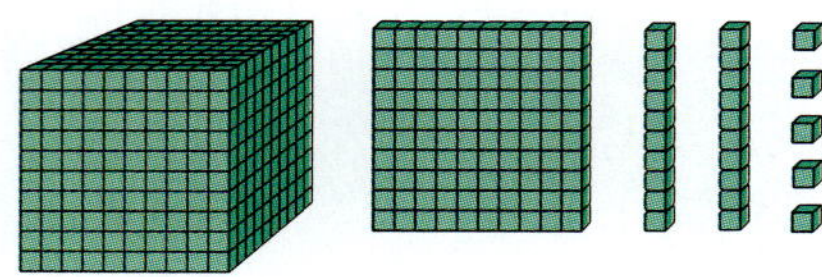

6. 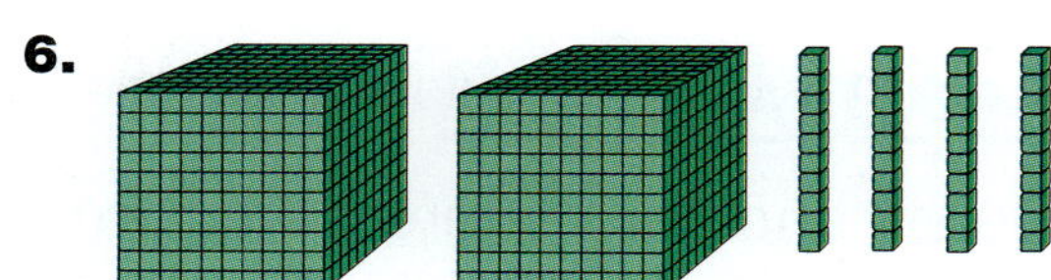

7. 3,000 + 500 + 6 **8.** 2,000 + 7 **9.** 9,000 + 30

10. 7,000 + 400 + 80+ 2 **11.** 4,000 + 90 **12.** 3,000 + 80 + 6

13. 6 thousands 2 hundreds

14. 5 thousands 4 hundreds 7 tens 9 ones

15. 9 thousands 1 hundred 7 tens

16. 8 thousands 9 tens 2 ones

17. three thousand, twenty-five

18. one thousand, three hundred twelve

19. seven thousand, eight hundred fifty-nine

Write the place of the underlined digit. Then write its value.

20. <u>3</u>,780 **21.** 4,<u>0</u>59 **22.** 1,8<u>3</u>9 **23.** 9,2<u>3</u>5 **24.** 2,50<u>9</u>

25. 6,<u>1</u>85 **26.** <u>9</u>,142 **27.** 3,54<u>7</u> **28.** <u>4</u>,108 **29.** 3,<u>6</u>70

Problem Solving • Reasoning

Use Data **Use the table for Problems 30–32.**

City Parades	
Event	**Number of Marchers**
Chinese New Year	4,521
Memorial Day	3,697
Fourth of July	5,279
Thanksgiving	4,027

30. Write the number of marchers in the Fourth of July parade in expanded form.

31. **Analyze** In which parade does the number of marchers have a 7 in the ones place and a 9 in the tens place?

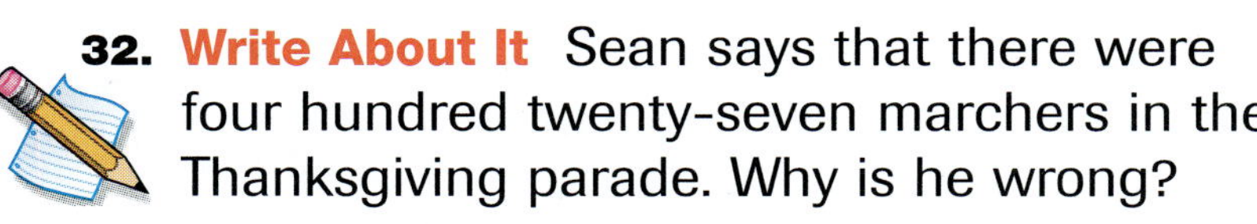

32. **Write About It** Sean says that there were four hundred twenty-seven marchers in the Thanksgiving parade. Why is he wrong?

Mixed Review • Test Prep

Round each number to the nearest ten and hundred. *(pages 8–10)*

33. 372 **34.** 505 **35.** 143 **36.** 894 **37.** 267

38 Which is equal to five? *(pages xxii–xxv)*

A 10 − 3 **B** 3 + 2 **C** 19 − 9 **D** 13 + 2

Extra Practice See Set D on page 41.

Compare Numbers

You will learn how to compare numbers.

Learn About It

Derek and Jan entered their frogs in a frog derby. Derek's frog jumped 124 inches and Jan's frog jumped 128 inches. Whose frog jumped the greater distance?

Which is greater, 124 or 128?

Different Ways to Compare Numbers

You can use a number line.

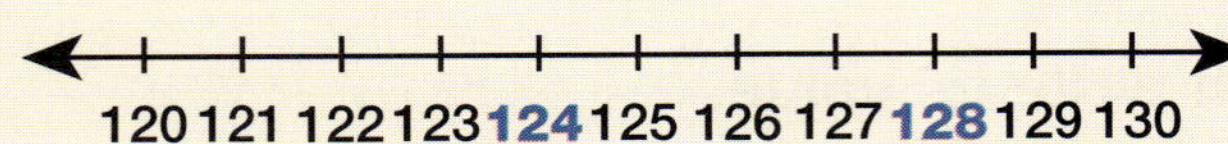

124 is to the left of 128.

So $124 < 128$
and $128 > 124$.

You can use a place-value chart.

hundreds	tens	ones
1	2	4
1	2	8

↑ same ↑ same ↑ 4 ones $<$ 8 ones

So $124 < 128$
and $128 > 124$.

Solution: Jan's frog jumped the greater distance.

Remember:
$>$ means "is greater than"
$<$ means "is less than"

Explain Your Thinking

► Suppose you are comparing 468 and 493. Do you need to compare the numbers in the ones place? Why or why not?

Another Example

Comparing Four-Digit Numbers

Which is less, 2,758 or 2,798?

thousands	hundreds	tens	ones
2	7	5	8
2	7	9	8

↑ same ↑ same ↑ 5 tens $<$ 9 tens

So $2{,}758 < 2{,}798$.

Guided Practice

Compare. Write >, <, or = for each ●.

1. 35 ● 37 **2.** 77 ● 97 **3.** 239 ● 156

4. 190 ● 109 **5.** 1,157 ● 1,157 **6.** 2,347 ● 2,357

Ask Yourself

- Which digits should I compare first?
- Which sign should I write?

Independent Practice

Compare. Write >, <, or = for each ●.

7. 50 ● 98 **8.** 70 ● 70 **9.** 99 ● 43 **10.** 100 ● 98

11. 99 ● 44 **12.** 790 ● 970 **13.** 98 ● 89 **14.** 164 ● 164

15. 105 ● 150 **16.** 199 ● 201 **17.** 3,497 ● 4,271 **18.** 2,809 ● 2,804

Problem Solving • Reasoning

19. Last year 8,341 people came to the frog derby. This year 8,304 people came. Did more people come this year or last year?

20. **Compare** Serena brought 2 frogs named Leaper and Ribbit to the derby. One frog jumped 142 inches and the other jumped 148 inches. If Leaper jumped farther than Ribbit, how far did each frog jump?

21. **Analyze** Jeff used the digits 2, 5, 7, and 9 to make as many four-digit numbers as he could that are less than 5,000. What numbers did Jeff make? He used each digit in each number.

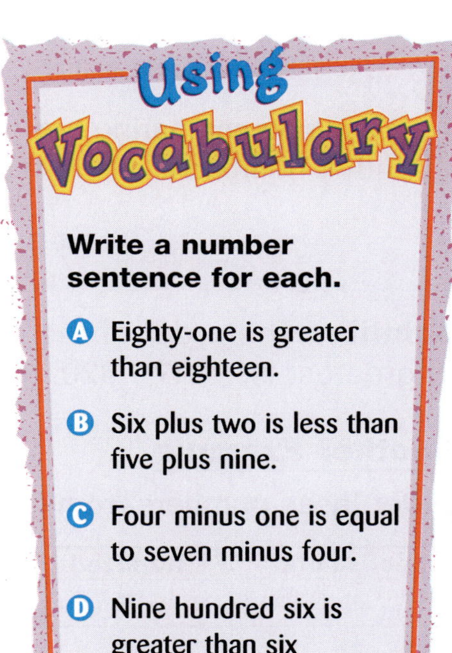

Mixed Review • Test Prep

Write the value of the underlined digit. *(pages 18–19)*

22. 1,4$\underline{7}$6 **23.** $\underline{5}$,723 **24.** 8,$\underline{1}$04 **25.** 9,35$\underline{8}$ **26.** $\underline{2}$,419

Choose the letter of the correct number. *(pages 18–19)*

27 4,031 = 4,000 + ■ + 1

A 0 **C** 30
B 10 **D** 300

28 6,805 = 6,000 + ■ + 5

E 8,000 **G** 80
F 800 **H** 0

Extra Practice See Set E on page 41.

Ordering Numbers

You will learn how to put numbers in order.

Learn About It

Look at the waterfalls at the right. Write the heights of the waterfalls in order from least to greatest.

Use a place-value chart to order 317; 640; and 620 from least to greatest.

Vernal Falls
317 feet

Feather Falls
640 feet

Bridalveil Falls
620 feet

- Start at the left to compare digits in the greatest place first.
- Continue comparing the other numbers.

hundreds	tens	ones
3	1	7
6	4	0
6	2	0

3 hundreds < 6 hundreds, so 317 is the least number.

2 tens < 4 tens, so 620 < 640.

Solution: The order of the numbers from least to greatest is: 317 620 640.

Another Example

Order these numbers from greatest to least: 564 1,752 554.

thousands	hundreds	tens	ones
	5	6	4
1	7	5	2
	5	5	4

1,752 is the greatest number.

5 = 5, so compare tens.

6 > 5, so 564 > 554

The order from greatest to least is: 1,752 564 554.

Explain Your Thinking

► Why is 1,752 greater than 564 even though the first digit of 564 is greater than the first digit of 1,752?

Guided Practice

Write the numbers in order from greatest to least.

1. 99 89 92

2. 777 771 780

3. 1,400 1,539 1,578

4. 165 1,257 309

> **Ask Yourself**
> - Which place should I look at first?
> - Which number is greatest?

Independent Practice

Write the numbers in order from least to greatest.

5. 71 89 30

6. 561 34 87

7. 459 121 834

8. 100 329 562

9. 1,449 1,756 3,863

10. 1,348 5,790 1,484

Write the numbers in order from greatest to least.

11. 53 74 60

12. 129 347 12

13. 7,893 7,080 7890

14. 1,976 1,960 1,944

15. 670 671 675

16. 19 16 61

Problem Solving • Reasoning

Use Data **Use the table for Problems 17–20.**

17. Write the height of Comet Falls in expanded form.

18. **Compare** Order the heights of the waterfalls from greatest to least.

19. **Estimate** Are Comet Falls and Virginia Falls about the same height? Explain.

20. **Write Your Own** Use the table to write a problem about the falls. Then give it to a classmate to solve.

Waterfall Heights

Waterfall	Height
Victoria	355 feet
Nevada	594 feet
Comet	320 feet
Virginia	315 feet

Mixed Review • Test Prep

Compare. Write >, <, or = for each ●. *(pages 20–21)*

21. 458 ● 485

22. 540 ● 541

23. 6,117 ● 6,107

24. 8,878 ● 8,788

What is the missing number? *(page xxii)*

25 ■ + 8 = 10

A 18 **B** 10 **C** 8 **D** 2

Extra Practice See Set F on page 41.

Round Four-Digit Numbers

You will learn how to round four-digit numbers to the nearest thousand, hundred, or ten.

Learn About It

Kevin displays his art on his own Web site. To the nearest thousand, how many people have visited Kevin's Web site so far?

You can round the number to find an estimate.

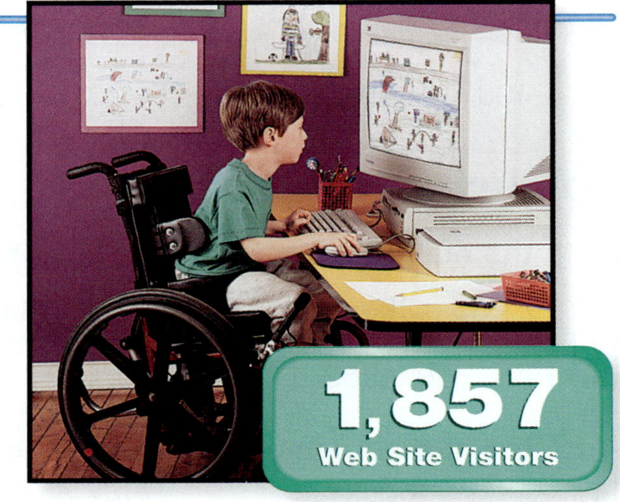

1,857
Web Site Visitors

Different Ways to Round

You can use a number line.

Find 1,857 on the number line. Then decide whether it is closer to 1,000 or to 2,000.

1,857 is closer to 2,000 than to 1,000. So round to 2,000.

1,857 — rounds to → 2,000

1,000 1,100 1,200 1,300 1,400 1,500 1,600 1,700 1,800 1,900 2,000

Another way is to follow these steps.

Step 1 Circle the digit in the place you want to round to.

(1), 8 5 7
↑
thousands place

Step 2 Underline the digit to the right of the circled digit.

(1), 8 5 7
↑
underlined digit

Step 3
- If the underlined digit is 5 or greater, increase the circled digit by 1.
- If the underlined digit is less than 5, do not change the circled digit.
- Then change all digits to the right of the circled digit to zeros.

(1), 8 5 7
↓
2 , 0 0 0

$8 > 5$
Change 1 to 2.

Write zeros to the right.

1,857 rounds to 2,000.

Solution: To the nearest thousand, 2,000 people have visited Kevin's Web site.

Other Examples

A. Round to the Nearest Hundred

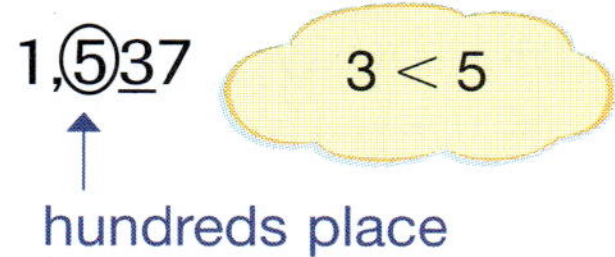

1,537 **rounds to** 1,500

B. Round to the Nearest Ten

1,537 **rounds to** 1,540

Explain Your Thinking

► Can a three-digit number round to 1,000? Explain why or why not.

Guided Practice

Round to the nearest thousand.

1. 2,857 **2.** 1,915 **3.** 5,064

Round to the nearest hundred.

4. 6,588 **5.** 1,445 **6.** 4,109

Round to the nearest ten.

7. 8,913 **8.** 4,532 **9.** 1,915

Ask Yourself

- To what place am I rounding?
- What digit is in the place to the right of the rounding place?
- Is that digit greater than, less than, or equal to 5?

Independent Practice

Round to the nearest thousand.

10. 2,885 **11.** 8,250 **12.** 3,491 **13.** 5,658 **14.** 7,199

15. 5,291 **16.** 4,763 **17.** 1,539 **18.** 6,714 **19.** 9,483

Round to the nearest hundred.

20. 4,399 **21.** 3,511 **22.** 136 **23.** 6,015 **24.** 7,780

25. 157 **26.** 903 **27.** 8,075 **28.** 923 **29.** 3,485

Round to the nearest ten.

30. 9,809 **31.** 611 **32.** 1,036 **33.** 428 **34.** 7,954

35. 777 **36.** 2,582 **37.** 9,073 **38.** 875 **39.** 333

Problem Solving • Reasoning

Use Data Use the table for Problems 40–44.

40. Look at the number of Web sites shown for each type of festival. Round each number to the nearest thousand.

41. Michael listed the types of festivals from the one with the fewest Web sites to the one with the greatest number of Websites. In what order did he list the festivals?

42. Al, Ben, and Carl each chose a festival to write about. Al's choice has fewer sites than Ben's. Carl's choice has fewer sites than Al's. No one chose dance festivals. Which kind of festival did each boy choose?

43. **Analyze** After the table was made, Ana found one hundred more Web sites about art festivals and 20 more Web sites about dance festivals. Rounded to the nearest thousand, what is the new number of art festival Web sites?

44. **Write About It** Suppose an art Web site was visited by 963 people one day. What is the number of vistors rounded to the nearest hundred? rounded to the nearest thousand? What do you notice about the rounded numbers?

Festival Web Sites

Type	Number of Web Sites
Music	5,293
Food	4,381
Art	5,427
Dance	3,659

Mixed Review • Test Prep

Write the place of the underlined digit. Then write its value. *(pages 18–19)*

45. 4,731 **46.** 8,139 **47.** 1,037 **48.** 7,394

Write the numbers in order from least to greatest. *(pages 22–23)*

49. 94 49 59 **50.** 128 138 183 **51.** 442 4,420 440

Choose the letter of the correct answer. *(pages 4–5)*

52 Which of the numbers below has a 5 in the tens place?

A 4,325 **C** 5,590

B 8,567 **D** 1,959

53 Which of the numbers below has a 7 in the hundreds place?

F 5,278 **H** 2,767

G 7,431 **J** 9,370

Extra Practice See Set G on page 42.

Show What You Know

Even and Odd

Answer each question.

1. What even three-digit numbers can you make using each of the digits 5, 8, and 1?
2. What odd three-digit numbers can you make using the digits 1, 4, and 7?
3. What even two-digit numbers have a 6 in the tens place?

Remember
Even numbers have 0, 2, 4, 6, or 8 in the ones place.
Odd numbers have 1, 3, 5, 7, or 9 in the ones place.

Break the Code

Ancient Egyptians developed a system of numbers using symbols. In this system each symbol is repeated as many times as necessary. The values of the symbols are added.

1. 𓎆𓎆𓏺𓏺𓏺
2. 𓆼𓆼𓍢𓍢𓎆
3. 𓍢𓍢𓏺𓏺𓏺𓏺
4. 𓆼𓎆𓏺

Key:
𓏺 = 1
𓎆 = 10
𓍢 = 100
𓆼 = 1,000

Example: 𓍢𓍢𓎆𓎆𓏺
100 + 100 + 10 + 10 + 1 = 221

What's the Number

Use the clues to solve each problem.

1. I am between 600 and 800. My digits are 5, 6, and 7. What is the least number I can be? What is the greatest number I can be?
2. I am between 500 and 1,000. All of my digits are odd. What is the least number I can be? What is the greatest number I can be?

Problem-Solving Strategy: Find a Pattern

You will learn how to solve problems by finding a pattern.

Sometimes you can use a pattern to help you solve a problem.

Problem The numbers on the first four mailboxes on Jesse's street are 6003, 6007, 6011, and 6015. If the pattern continues, what are the numbers likely to be on the next three mailboxes?

Understand

What is the question?

What are the numbers likely to be on the next three mailboxes?

What do you know?

The first four numbers are 6003, 6007, 6011, and 6015.

Plan

How can you find the answer?

Look for a pattern in the given numbers.

Solve

Find a pattern.

6003 → +4 → 6007 → +4 → 6011 → +4 → 6015

The numbers increase by 4 each time.

To go from one number to the next, add 4 each time.

The next three numbers are 6019, 6023, and 6027.

Look Back

Look back at the problem.

If the pattern continues, which place value will remain unchanged the longest?

Remember:
- Understand
- Plan
- Solve
- Look Back

Guided Practice

Solve these problems, using the Find a Pattern strategy.

1. There are seven houses on Jim's street. The house numbers of the first four houses are 9004, 9008, 9012, and 9016. If the pattern continues, what are the numbers on the next three houses likely to be?

Which part of the number is changing? How is it changing?

2. In May Amanda got 2 new customers on her paper route. In June she got 4 new customers. In July she got 6 new customers. If this pattern continues, how many new customers will she likely get in August?

How does the number of new customers change each month?

Choose a Strategy

Solve. Use these or other strategies.

Problem-Solving Strategies

- **Write a Number Sentence**
- **Make a Table**
- **Use Logical Thinking**

3. There are 2,563 trees in Paula's town. There are 60 oak trees, 2,000 maple trees, and 500 spruce trees. The rest are birch trees. How many birch trees are there? Explain how you know.

4. Tickets to a neighborhood block party cost $3 each. The Paulson family needs 4 tickets, the Loma family needs 6 tickets, and the Smith family needs 8 tickets. How much will each family spend?

5. Look at the numbers below. What is the next number likely to be?

   1, 2, 4, 7, ____

6. What are the next two numbers in the pattern below likely to be?

   120, 117, 114, 111, ____, ____

7. What is the greatest 4-digit number that can be made with the digits 3, 1, 6, and 4?

8. If the pattern below continues, how many trees are likely to be planted next to the house on the far right?

Extra Practice See 5–8 on page 43.

Quick Check

Check Your Understanding of Lessons 5–10

Write the place of the underlined digit.
Then write its value.

1. 4,<u>5</u>78 **2.** 1,8<u>9</u>3 **3.** <u>8</u>,792 **4.** 6,34<u>2</u>

Compare, Write $>$, $<$, or $=$ for each ●.

5. 48 ● 84 **6.** 910 ● 901 **7.** 3,275 ● 3,271

Order the numbers from greatest to least.

8. 716 3,562 87 6,731 175

9. 1,437 2,763 876 1,932 2,458

Round to the place of the underlined digit.

10. <u>3</u>,687 **11.** 1,<u>7</u>32 **12.** <u>8</u>,168 **13.** 3,<u>2</u>51

Solve.

14. Jason played 4 computer games. These where his scores.

2,496 2,596 2,696 2,796

If the pattern in the scores continues, what will Jason's next score likely be? Explain.

How did you do?

If you had difficulty with any items in the Quick Check, you can use the following pages for review and extra practice.

Items	Review These Pages	Do These Extra Practice Items
1–4	pages 16–19	Set D, page 41
5–7	pages 20–21	Set E, page 41
8–9	pages 22–23	Set F, page 41
10–13	pages 24–26	Set G, page 42
14	pages 28–29	5–8, page 43

Test Prep • Cumulative Review

Maintaining the Standards

Choose the letter of the correct answer.

1. A music store sold 3,060 CDs in the last month. Which of the following is equal to 3,060?

   A 300 + 60
   B 3,000 + 6
   C 3,000 + 600
   D 3,000 + 60

2. A music auditorium holds 4,579 people. What is this number rounded to the nearest hundred?

   F 4,000
   G 4,500
   H 4,600
   J 5,000

3. Look at the pattern below.

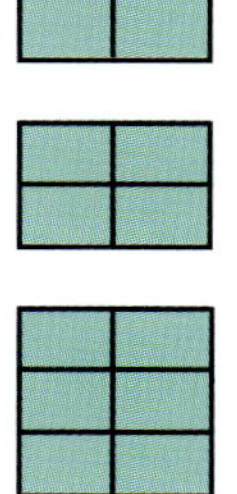

   If the pattern continues, how many tiles will likely be in the next figure?

   A 6
   B 7
   C 8
   D 10

4. What is the least whole number you can make using the digits 5, 3, 9, and 1?

   F 3,159 **H** 3,591
   G 1,395 **J** 1,359

5. Which of the following is a true statement?

   A 8,541 $<$ 8,451
   B 7,032 $>$ 7,310
   C 2,099 $<$ 2,960
   D 4,501 $>$ 4,510

6. Peter rounded the number of students in his school to 2,000. If he rounded to the nearest hundred, which of the following could be the number of students in his school?

   F 1,981 **H** 2,096
   G 2,085 **J** 2,562

7. Look at the numbers below.

   2, 5, 8, 11, _____

   What is the next number in the pattern likely to be?

   A 12 **C** 14
   B 13 **D** 15

8. Write the value of the underlined digit in <u>3</u>,902.

   Explain How did you find your answer?

Safe Site

Internet Test Prep
Visit **www.eduplace.com/kids/mhm** for more *Test Prep Practice.*

LESSON 11

Place Value to Ten Thousands

You will learn about the place value of numbers to ten thousands.

New Vocabulary
ten thousands

Learn About It

Mount McKinley is in Denali National Park in Alaska. It is the highest mountain in North America.

A place-value chart can help you understand the value of 20,320.

ten thousands	thousands	hundreds	tens	ones
2	0	3	2	0

Mount McKinley
(elevation: 20,320 feet)

Different Ways to Write 20,320

You can write it in expanded form.
20,000 + 300 + 20

You can write it in standard form.
20,320

You can write it in word form.
twenty thousand, three hundred twenty

Explain Your Thinking

► If a five-digit number has no hundreds, is there a digit in the hundreds place? Use a place-value chart to explain.

Guided Practice

Write each number in two different ways. Use standard form, expanded form, or word form.

1. 50,644

2. 90,000 + 8,000 + 300 + 80 + 5

3. 1 ten thousand 6 hundreds 9 ones

4. twenty-five thousand, two hundred sixty-one

Write the value of the digit 4 in each number.

5. 54,602 **6.** 47,005 **7.** 10,345

Ask Yourself

- What is the value of each digit in the number?
- Are there any places that have zeros?

Independent Practice

Write each number in standard form.

8. 90,000 + 90 + 9

9. 20,000 + 1,000 + 400 + 50 + 9

10. 9 ten thousands 9 tens

11. 1 ten thousand, 8 hundreds 9 tens 7 ones

12. eighty thousand, eight

13. sixty thousand, one hundred fifty-nine

14. five hundred sixty-one

15. three thousand, eight hundred thirteen

16. eighty-three thousand, four

17. twenty-nine thousand, thirty-three

Write the place of the underlined digit. Then write its value.

18. $\underline{1}0{,}700$ **19.** $\underline{4}59$ **20.** $1{,}28\underline{7}$ **21.** $\underline{8}5{,}097$

22. $5\underline{2}{,}681$ **23.** $\underline{5}9{,}104$ **24.** $\underline{8}0$ **25.** $44{,}\underline{4}44$

Problem Solving • Reasoning

Use Data **Use the table for Problems 26–29.**

26. Write the height of Mount Everest in word form.

27. **Compare** Which is higher, Mount Fuji or Mount Cook?

28. Round the height of Mount Fuji to the nearest thousand.

29. **Compare** If you round the heights of Mount Fuji and Mount Cook to the nearest hundred, are the rounded heights the same? Why or why not?

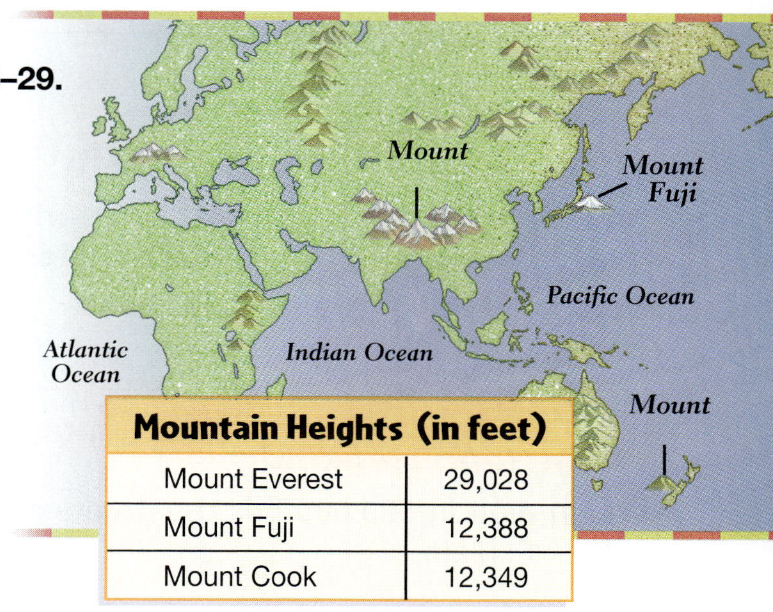

Mountain Heights (in feet)	
Mount Everest	29,028
Mount Fuji	12,388
Mount Cook	12,349

Mixed Review • Test Prep

Round each number to the underlined place. *(pages 24–26)*

30. $3{,}9\underline{1}7$ **31.** $7{,}\underline{6}34$ **32.** $\underline{4}{,}810$ **33.** $\underline{2}{,}500$ **34.** $9{,}6\underline{3}3$

35 Which makes the number sentence true? *(pages xxii–xxiv)*

4 + 6 = ____

A 10 − 4 **B** 6 − 4 **C** 4 + 10 **D** 6 + 4

Extra Practice See Set H on page 42.

Place Value to Hundred Thousands

You will learn about the place value of greater numbers.

New Vocabulary
hundred thousands

Learn About It

Time can really add up! There are 525,600 minutes in a 365-day year.

A place-value chart can help you understand the value of 525,600.

hundred thousands	ten thousands	thousands	hundreds	tens	ones
5	2	5	6	0	0

Different Ways to Write a Number

You can write it in expanded form.
500,000 + 20,000 + 5,000 + 600

You can write it in standard form.
525,600

You can write it in word form.
five hundred twenty-five thousand, six hundred

Explain Your Thinking

► Which digit in 525,600 has the greatest value? Explain.

► Why is it important to write zeros in the ones and the tens places in 525,600?

Guided Practice

Write each number in standard form.

1. 800,000 + 400 + 80 + 2

2. 100,000 + 9,000 + 900 + 10

3. one hundred fourteen thousand, four

Ask Yourself
- What is the value of each digit?
- Are there any places that have zeros?

Write the value of the underlined digit.

4. <u>6</u>54,703 **5.** 10<u>4</u>,592 **6.** 987,<u>3</u>24 **7.** 1<u>2</u>0,846

Independent Practice

Write each number in standard form.

8. 200,000 + 3,000 + 800 + 20 + 8

9. 900,000 + 900 + 90 + 9

10. two hundred thousand, six hundred thirteen

11. 600,000 + 10,000 + 1,000 + 300 + 90 + 8

12. four hundred sixty-nine thousand, eight hundred seventy-seven

13. one hundred four thousand, seven hundred twenty-one

Write the place of the underlined digit. Then write its value.

14. <u>3</u>12,700 **15.** 961,<u>4</u>78 **16.** 28<u>3</u>,506 **17.** 2<u>3</u>4,087

18. 4<u>9</u>0,625 **19.** <u>2</u>05,617 **20.** 951,<u>2</u>74 **21.** 61<u>7</u>,510

Problem Solving • Reasoning

22. There are 604,800 seconds in a week. What place value does the digit 6 have in 604,800?

23. **Analyze** Kelley wrote a six-digit number. One digit was zero. The other digits were odd. No two digits were the same. The number was the greatest number Kelley could make using these digits. What number did Kelley write?

24. Sam is counting by 5s starting with 43,965. How many numbers will he say before he has to start saying "forty-four thousand"?

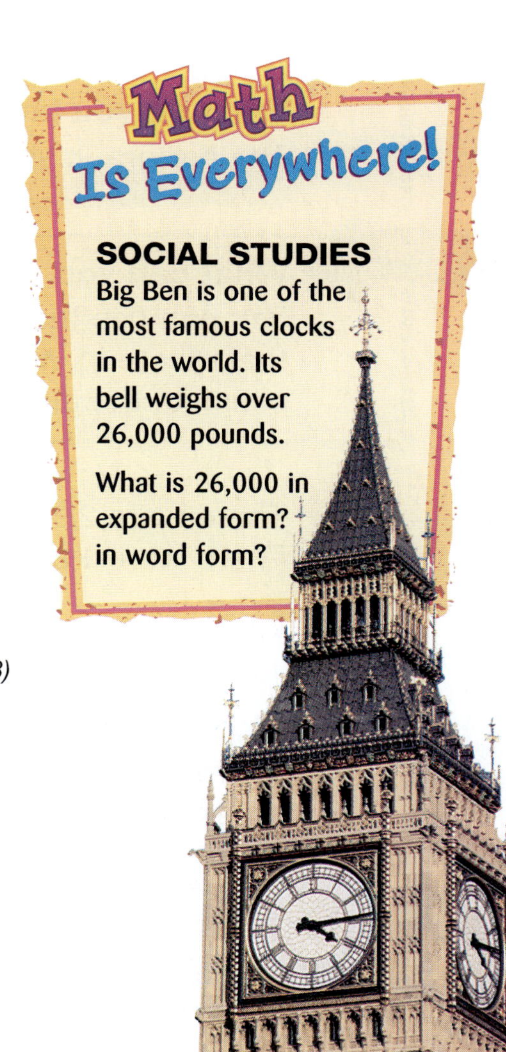

Mixed Review • Test Prep

Order the numbers from greatest to least. *(pages 22–23)*

25. 761 816 787

26. 1,564 1,530 1,548

27. 492 498 625

28. 1,259 1,349 1,243

29 If the pattern below continues, which number is likely to be next? *(page xxvii)*

64, 68, 72, 76, ____

A 78 **B** 80 **C** 82 **D** 84

Extra Practice See Set I on page 42.

Problem-Solving Application: Read a Graph

You will learn how to use a graph to help you solve problems.

You can get information from a graph to help you solve problems.

Problem An aquarium put on special shows each week for a month. Look at the bar graph. About how many more people visited the dolphin show the first week than the second week?

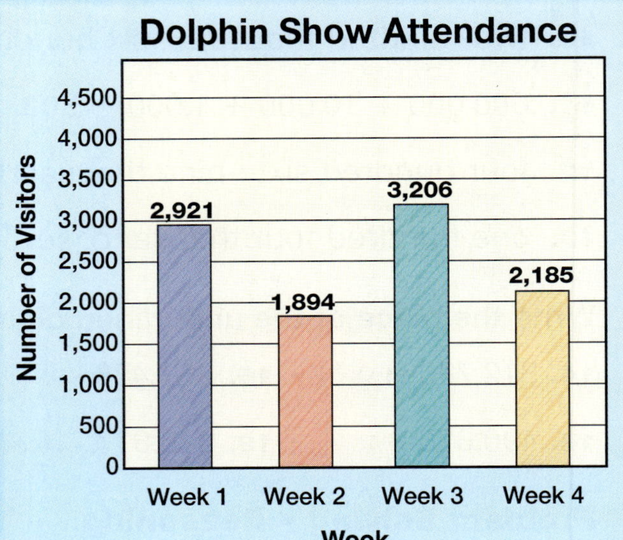

What is the question?

About how many more people visited the dolphin show in Week 1 than in Week 2?

What do you know?

The bar graph shows how many visitors there were each week.

Plan

What can you do to find the answer?

You can use the bar graph to find how many visitors there were in Week 1 and Week 2. Then you can estimate the difference.

Solve

There were 2,921 visitors in Week 1.
There were 1,894 visitors in Week 2.

2,921	rounds to	3,000
1,894	rounds to	− 2,000
		1,000

There were about 1,000 more visitors in Week 1 than in Week 2.

Look back at the answer.

Is the answer an exact number or an estimated amount?

Remember:
- Understand
- Plan
- Solve
- Look Back

Guided Practice

Use the graph on page 36 for Problems 1 and 2.

1. About how many more visitors were there in Week 3 than in Week 4?

   Think: What was the attendance in each week?

2. List the attendance for each week from greatest to least.

   Think: Which bar is tallest? Which bar is shortest?

Choose a Strategy

Solve. Use these or other strategies.

Problem-Solving Strategies

- **Guess and Check**
- **Write a Number Sentence**
- **Use Logical Thinking**

The graph on the right shows the number of videos sold in the aquarium gift shop in June. Use the graph to answer Problems 3–7.

3. Which two videos had about the same number of sales?
4. About how many turtle videos and fish videos were sold?
5. Order the number of each kind of video sold from greatest to least.
6. About how many more whale videos were sold than seal videos?
7. In July, 100 more seal videos were sold than in June. How many seal videos were sold in July?

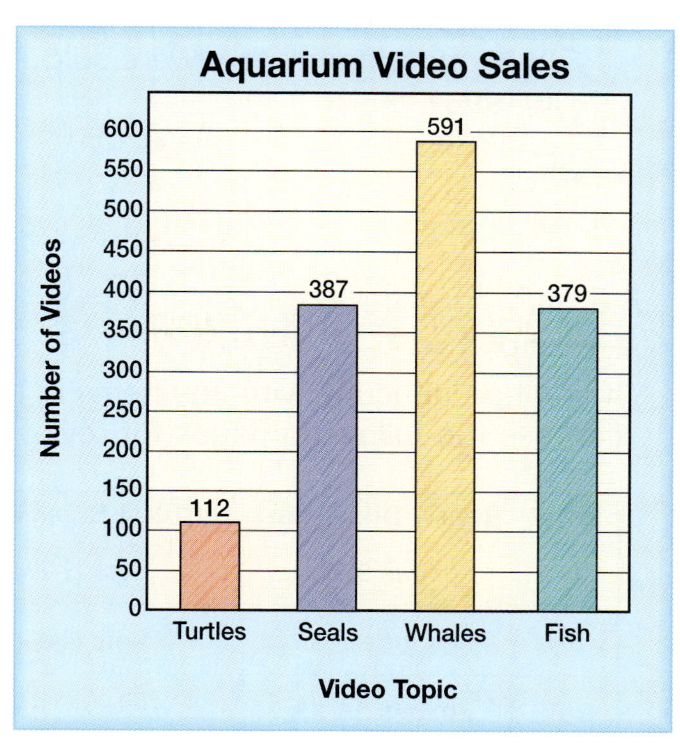

Extra Practice See 9–11 on page 43.

Quick Check

Check Your Understanding of Lessons 11–13

Write each in standard form.

1. 60,000 + 3,000 + 500 + 40 + 3

2. 400,000 + 6,000 + 200 + 70 + 5

3. forty-five thousand, six hundred forty-six

4. three hundred thousand, two hundred twenty-five

Write the place of the underlined digit.
Then write its value.

5. $4\underline{6},712$ **6.** $\underline{2}7,592$ **7.** $472,3\underline{7}4$ **8.** $\underline{1}43,617$

Solve.

9. In which year were computer sales highest? How many computers were sold that year?

10. How would the graph change if 1,000 more computers were sold in 1996?

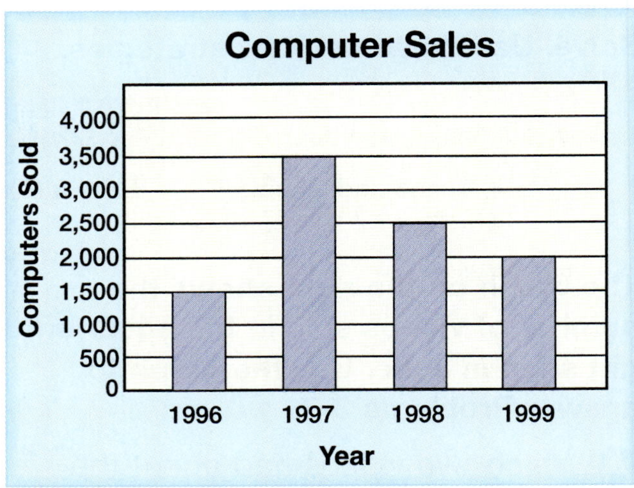

How did you do?

If you had difficulty with any items in the Quick Check, you can use the following pages for review and extra practice.

Items	Review These Pages	Do These Extra Practice Items
1–4	pages 32–35	Sets H–I, page 42
5–8	pages 32–35	Sets H–I, page 42
9–10	pages 36-37	9–11, page 43

Test Prep • Cumulative Review

Maintaining the Standards

Choose the letter of the correct answer.

1. A stadium seats nine thousand, forty-seven people. How is this number written in standard form?

   A 947 **C** 9,407
   B 9,047 **D** 9,470

2. Which of the following shows numbers in order from least to greatest?

   F 4,060 4,120 5,016 3,270
   G 5,016 4,120 4,060 3,270
   H 3,270 4,120 4,060 5,016
   J 3,270 4,060 4,120 5,016

3. Which of the following is equal to 705?

   A 70 + 5
   B 700 + 50
   C 70 + 50
   D 700 + 5

4. Mr. Anderson received 2,476 votes in the last election. What is this number rounded to the nearest thousand?

   F 1,000 **H** 2,500
   G 2,000 **J** 3,000

5. What is the value of the underlined digit in 6,1<u>5</u>2?

   A 5 **C** 50
   B 5,000 **D** 500

Use the table to answer Questions 6–7.

Major Zoos	
Location	**Number of Different Kinds of Animals**
Bronx	607
Cincinnati	712
Denver	672
San Diego	800

6. Which lists the zoos in order from the one that has the greatest number of different kinds of animals, to the one that has the least number?

   F San Diego, Cincinnati, Denver, Bronx
   G Bronx, Denver, Cincinnati, San Diego
   H San Diego, Denver, Cincinnati, Bronx
   J Cincinnati, San Diego, Denver, Bronx

7. If the Bronx Zoo rounded its figure to the nearest ten, what would the rounded number be?

   Explain How did you find your answer?

Safe Site

Internet Test Prep
Visit **www.eduplace.com/kids/mhm** for more *Test Prep Practice.*

Extra Practice

Set A (Lesson 1, pages 4–5)

Write each number in standard form.

1. 6 hundreds 7 tens 5 ones
2. 2 hundreds 4 tens 3 ones
3. 4 hundred ten
4. 7 hundred ninety-three
5. 300 + 20 + 7
6. 100 + 6
7. 500 + 90 + 3
8. 400 + 10 + 9
9. 100 + 80 + 2
10. 600 + 70
11. 200 + 5
12. 300 + 8

Write the value of the underlined digit.

13. $\underline{2}54$
14. $78\underline{3}$
15. $4\underline{2}0$
16. $6\underline{6}1$
17. $32\underline{8}$
18. $\underline{5}16$
19. $\underline{1}67$
20. $47\underline{5}$
21. $\underline{9}84$
22. $5\underline{3}9$
23. $28\underline{0}$
24. $6\underline{7}0$

Set B (Lesson 2, pages 6–7)

Write the two tens each number is between.

1. 21
2. 55
3. 82
4. 69
5. 71
6. 37

Round each number to the nearest ten or ten cents.

7. 34
8. 57¢
9. 23
10. 65¢
11. 91¢
12. 42

Set C (Lesson 3, pages 8–10)

Write the two hundreds each number is between. Then write the two tens each number is between.

1. 908
2. 127
3. 651
4. 768
5. 345
6. 408
7. 847
8. 379
9. 566
10. 239
11. 468
12. 371

Round to the nearest hundred or dollar. Then round to the nearest ten or ten cents.

13. 688
14. $2.58
15. 977
16. 708
17. $4.29
18. $9.06
19. 135
20. 350
21. $5.90
22. 234
23. $7.52
24. 295

Extra Practice

Set D *(Lesson 6, pages 18–19)*

Write each number two other ways. Use standard form, expanded form, and word form.

1. 3,472 **2.** 2,000 + 20 + 6 **3.** 8,701 **4.** 7,000 + 900 + 20

5. four thousand, nine hundred eleven **6.** eight thousand, thirty-two

7. two thousand, sixty-seven **8.** nine thousand, three hundred

Write the value of the underlined digit.

9. 1,71$\underline{2}$ **10.** $\underline{6}$,341 **11.** $\underline{3}$,498 **12.** 8,$\underline{2}$56

13. 8,1$\underline{3}$4 **14.** 4,47$\underline{8}$ **15.** 7,$\underline{9}$21 **16.** $\underline{2}$,576

Set E *(Lesson 7, pages 20–21)*

Write >, <, or = for each ●.

1. 70 ● 78 **2.** 77 ● 72 **3.** 80 ● 70 **4.** 73 ● 75

5. 40 ● 60 **6.** 35 ● 10 **7.** 55 ● 45 **8.** 25 ● 25

Compare. Write >, <, or = for each ●.

9. 52 ● 520 **10.** 212 ● 112 **11.** 289 ● 298

12. 7,001 ● 5,999 **13.** 6,792 ● 6,792 **14.** 3,981 ● 3,993

Set F *(Lesson 8, pages 22–23)*

Order the numbers from greatest to least.

1. 46 78 24 **2.** 342 324 365 **3.** 242 442 244

4. 997 797 967 **5.** 1,001 1,101 1,010 **6.** 7,914 7,409 7,810

Order the numbers from least to greatest.

7. 47 76 64 **8.** 684 865 575 **9.** 727 712 721

10. 7,543 7,453 7,354 **11.** 8,080 8,800 8,088 **12.** 1,148 1,140 1,180

Extra Practice

Set G (Lesson 9, pages 24–26)

Round to the nearest thousand.

1. 5,890 **2.** 8,519 **3.** 3,777 **4.** 6,042 **5.** 4,807

Round to the nearest hundred.

6. 645 **7.** 210 **8.** 1,543 **9.** 5,365 **10.** 7,456

Round to the nearest ten.

11. 65 **12.** 558 **13.** 727 **14.** 9,227 **15.** 2,405

Set H (Lesson 11, pages 32–33)

Write each number two other ways. Use standard form, expanded form, and word form.

1. 50,000 + 700 + 40 + 3

2. seventy thousand, forty-seven

3. 7 hundreds 5 tens 2 ones

4. 9 ten thousands 5 hundreds 6 ones

Write the value of the underlined digit.

5. 4$\underline{1}$ **6.** 1,$\underline{5}$07 **7.** 6$\underline{3}$0 **8.** $\underline{7}$,834 **9.** $\underline{3}$2,994

Set I (Lesson 12, pages 34–35)

Write each number in standard form.

1. 700,000 + 20,000 + 5,000 + 30 + 5

2. six hundred ninety-three thousand

3. 300,000 + 40,000 + 2,000 + 700 + 60 + 1

4. one hundred twenty-seven thousand, seventy

Write the value of the underlined digit.

5. $\underline{8}$,549 **6.** $\underline{1}$4,137 **7.** 600,0$\underline{9}$3 **8.** 5,$\underline{5}$04 **9.** $\underline{3}$12,562

Extra Practice • Problem Solving

Solve. *(Lesson 4, pages 12–13)*

1. Greyhounds can run at speeds of about 40 miles per hour. Is "about" 40 an exact amount or an estimate?

2. Heather's town received almost 3 inches of rain in June. Is this an estimate or an exact number?

3. Jo bought a bag of 85 dog biscuits. Do you know exactly how many biscuits there are in the bag?

4. More than 550,000 people live in the city where Ms. Jefferson was born. Is "more than 550,000" an exact amount or an estimate?

Find a pattern to solve each problem. *(Lesson 10, pages 28–29)*

5. The XZ Bicycle Company makes dirt bikes. The model numbers of the bikes are X110Z, X220Z, X330Z, and X440Z. If the pattern continues, what will the next model number likely be?

6. A running team lines up to get their running shirts. The first five shirts are numbered 710, 712, 714, and 716. If the pattern continues, what numbers will likely be on the next 3 shirts?

7. Robert is planting tulips. He plants 3 tulips in Row 1, 6 tulips in Row 2, and 9 tulips in Row 3. If he continues this pattern, how many tulips will Robert likely plant in Row 6?

8. There are 4 third-grade classrooms. The first 3 classrooms are numbered 3304, 3504, and 3704. If the pattern continues, what is the number likley to be on the fourth classroom?

Use the graph to solve. *(Lesson 13, pages 36–37)*

9. Which grade has twice as many players as Grade 2?

10. How many more third-grade players are there than fourth-grade players?

11. Order the grades from the one with the least number of players to the one with the greatest number of players.

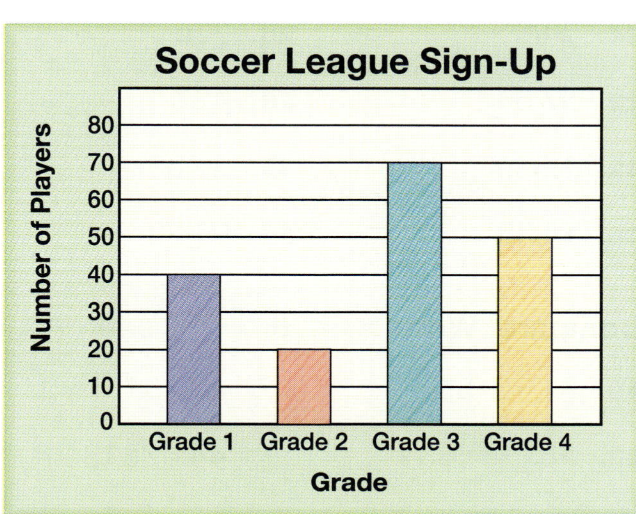

Chapter Review

Reviewing Vocabulary

Match each vocabulary word with an example.

1. expanded form	**a.** three thousand, two hundred fifty
2. standard form	**b.** 3000 + 200 + 50
3. word form	**c.** 3,250

Reviewing Concepts and Skills

Write each number in standard form. *(pages 4–5, 18–19, 32–33)*

4. 300 + 40 + 7 **5.** 7,000 + 500 + 10 + 9 **6.** 800 + 70 + 2

7. 600 + 3 **8.** 1,000 + 200 + 30 + 6 **9.** 3,000 + 900 +60+2

10. 3 hundreds 9 tens 5 ones **11.** 9 hundreds 2 tens 4 ones

12. 6 thousands 8 tens 3 ones **13.** 2 thousands 7 tens 2 ones

14. five hundred sixty-nine **15.** seven thousand, four hundred fifty

Write the value of the underlined digit. *(pages 4–5, 18–19, 32–33)*

16. 714 **17.** 3,329 **18.** 25 **19.** 6,800

20. 1,597 **21.** 4,637 **22.** 951 **23.** 8773

Round to the place of the underlined digit. *(pages 6–7, 8–10, 24–26)*

24. 74¢ **25.** 22¢ **26.** $4.32 **27.** 950

28. $7.54 **29.** 421 **30.** 744 **31.** 936

32. 1,349 **33.** 2,385 **34.** 1,856 **35.** 7,840

36. $4.35 **37.** 9,823 **38.** 6,045 **39.** 4,317

Compare. Write $>$, $<$, or $=$ for each ●. *(pages 20–21)*

40. 81 ● 55 **41.** 91 ● 91 **42.** 348 ● 346

43. 483 ● 834 **44.** 7,813 ● 3,813 **45.** 6,491 ● 6,489

Write the numbers in order from least to greatest. *(pages 22–23)*

46. 83 76 91

47. 77 71 79

48. 327 312 302

49. 776 687 677

50. 1,127 1,112 1,211

51. 3,822 3,288 3,832

Write the numbers in order from greatest to least.

52. 45 54 42

53. 748 478 847

54. 381 318 338

55. 3,122 3,202 3,149

56. 2,481 2,488 2,478

57. 9,669 9,996 9,696

Solve. Use the graph for Question 58. *(pages 12–13, 24–25, and 36–37)*

58. In which months were there more than 1,000 customers? Which month came closest to having 2,000 customers?

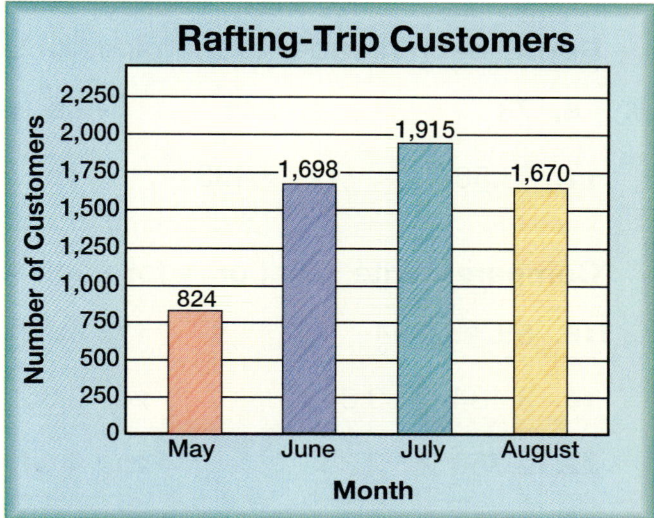

59. In September, there were about 1,200 customers. Is 1,200 an exact amount or an estimate?

60. One week, Lee biked 20 miles. The next week he biked 25 miles, and the week after that he biked 30 miles. If the pattern continues, how many miles will he likely bike the fourth week?

Brain Teaser Math Reasoning

Round and Round

Ken is thinking of a number.

- Rounded to the nearest ten, it is 250.
- Rounded to the nearest hundred, it is 300.

What could Ken's number be? List all of the possible answers.

Internet Brain Teasers
Visit **www.eduplace.com/kids/mhm** for more *Brain Teasers.*

Chapter Test

Write each number in standard form.

1. 4 hundred thousands 3 ten thousands 6 thousands 7 tens 5 ones
2. six hundred twenty-seven thousand, two hundred eight
3. 500,000 + 30,000 + 7,000 + 800 + 40 + 2
4. five ten thousands three thousands six hundreds four tens five ones
5. 400,000 + 6,000 + 200

Round each number to the place of the underlined digit.

6. $\underline{7}8$ **7.** $\underline{5}4$¢ **8.** $\underline{8}85$ **9.** $\underline{2}5$¢ **10.** $\underline{9}43$

11. \$3.$\underline{5}6$ **12.** $\underline{7}$,493 **13.** $\underline{1}$,802 **14.** $\underline{5}$,802 **15.** $\underline{7}50$

Compare. Write >, <, or = for each ●.

16. 59 ● 594 **17.** 391 ● 391 **18.** 6,384 ● 6,382

19. 3,484 ● 3,844 **20.** 2,850 ● 2,870 **21.** 5,480 ● 5,485

22. 2,750 ● 2,865 **23.** 4,442 ● 4,452 **24.** 7,983 ● 983

Write the numbers in order from least to greatest.

25. 73 77 71 **26.** 452 388 512

27. 732 772 734 **28.** 3,852 3,528 3,582

29. 1,856 1,854 1,850 **30.** 2,712 2,721 712

Solve.

31. Some friends are planning a 24-mile bike trip. After they bike 4 miles, they will stop to rest. They will stop again after they have biked a total of 8 miles. They'll make another rest stop after they have gone 12 miles. How many more rest stops will the friends likely make before they finish their bike trip?

Use the graph below to answer Problems 32–33.

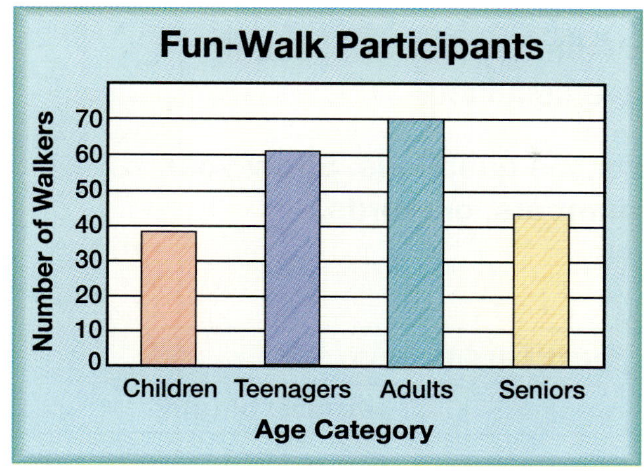

32. Order the number of walkers by age category from greatest to least.

33. There are about 220 walkers in the Fun Walk. Is that an exact amount or an estimate? Explain.

Write About It

Solve each problem. Use correct math vocabulary to explain your thinking.

1. Jamal rounded the number 2,584 to 2,600. Leah rounded the same number to 2,590.

- **a.** Explain and show how Jamal rounded the number.
- **b.** Explain and show how Leah rounded the number.
- **c.** Explain and show a different way to round the number.

2. Lois wrote 90,150 in word form. She wrote "nine thousand, fifteen." Her answer was not correct.

- **a.** Write the correct word form of the number 90,150.
- **b.** Explain what Lois did wrong.

Another Look

The table below shows the number of baseball cards five students have collected.

Use the table to answer the questions. Show your work using pictures, numbers, or words.

Sport Card Collections	
Name	**Number of Cards**
Tim	1,213
Laura	860
David	678
Tina	772
Joe	673

1. List the numbers in the table in order from greatest to least. Which student has the greatest number of cards? the least number?

2. Why do you have to look at the ones place to decide if David or Joe has the most cards?

3. Round the numbers in the table to the nearest hundred. Can you use the rounded numbers to list the card collections in order from greatest to least? Explain why or why not. What would be the advantage of rounding the numbers to the nearest ten?

4. **Look Back** Compare the numbers in the table to the the rounded numbers you found for Question 3. Which rounded numbers are greater than the actual numbers? Which are less? Explain your answer.

5. **Analyze** Suppose Tim gave away 200 cards. Would he still have the greatest number of cards? Explain how you know.

Enrichment

Different Ways to Write a Number

You can use what you know about regrouping to write numbers in different ways.

Here are 4 ways to write the number 35.

- 3 tens 5 ones
- 2 tens 15 ones
- 1 ten 25 ones
- 35 ones

Here are 4 ways to write the number 350.

- 3 hundreds 5 tens
- 2 hundreds 15 tens
- 1 hundred 25 tens
- 35 tens

Write each of these numbers in four different ways.

1. 65

a. 6 tens ____ ones

b. ____ tens 15 ones

c. ____ tens ____ ones

d. ____ ones

2. 104

a. ____ hundred ____ ones

b. ____ tens ____ ones

c. ____ tens ____ ones

d. ____ ones

Write each of these numbers in two other ways.

3. 251 **4.** 4,300 **5.** 626

6. 368 **7.** 9,452 **8.** 7,582

Explain Your Thinking

Using only tens, can you write the number 703? Explain.

Money and Time

Why Learn About Money and Time?

It's important to learn about money and time since you use them both almost every day.

Whenever you buy a snack or a game, you're using money. If you know you have to be at soccer practice at 4 o'clock or that you can play outside until 5 o'clock, you're using time.

All these people are in a race. Someone is measuring the time it takes the winner to finish the race. The measurement of time is not only important in sports but in many areas of life.

Reviewing Vocabulary

Understanding math language helps you become a successful problem solver. Here are some math vocabulary words you should know.

cent sign (¢)	the symbol used to show cents
decimal point (.)	the symbol used to separate dollars and cents
dollar sign ($)	the symbol used to show dollars
minutes	the unit of time that is equal to 60 seconds
hour	the unit of time that is equal to 60 minutes
month	the unit of time that is one of the twelve parts that a year is divided into
year	the unit of time that is equal to twelve months
calendar	a table that shows the days of the week and the months of the year in order

Reading Words and Symbols

When you read mathematics, sometimes you read only words, sometimes you read words and symbols, and sometimes you read only symbols.

Look at the ways you can show money.

- 46¢
- $0.46
- forty-six cents

Look at the ways you can show time.

- 4:00
- 4 o'clock
- four o'clock

- 4:30
- four-thirty
- half past four

Try These

1. Replace each ■ with a dollar sign, a cent sign, or a decimal point.

   a. ■3.50 **b.** 78■ **c.** $1■25 **d.** ■42

   e. 19■ **f.** $4■08 **g.** ■1.99 **h.** 2■

2. Write each amount by using a dollar sign. Then write each amount by using a cent sign.

   a. twenty-three cents **b.** seven cents

   c. thirty-three cents **d.** seventy-nine cents

3. Use the words on the right to complete the story.

   Jason was at kick-ball practice for two ____ in the afternoon. The next ____, he played in a kick-ball game. There is another game one ____ from now. His team hopes to win 12 games this ____.

   Vocabulary
   month
   day
   year
   hours

4. Write *true* or *false* for each sentence.

   a. The time on the clock is three o'clock.

   b. There are sixty minutes in one hour.

   c. The short hand is the minute hand.

Upcoming Vocabulary

Write About It **Here are some other vocabulary words** you will learn in this chapter. Watch for these words. Write their definitions in your journal.

half-dollar	**ordinal numbers**
quarter	**leap year**
nickel	**decade**
equivalent	**century**

Value of Money

You will learn the value of dollars, dimes, and pennies.

Review Vocabulary
dollar sign ($)
decimal point (.)

Learn About It

Susan's dad gave her a piggy bank for her birthday. She put 1 dollar, 1 dime, and 1 penny in the bank. What's the total value of the money in the bank?

1 dollar
100 cents
100¢

1 dime
10 cents
10¢

1 penny
1 cent
1¢

Dollars	Dimes	Pennies
1	1	1

one dollar and eleven cents
$1.11
dollar sign **decimal point**

There is $1.11 in the bank.

Other Examples

A. Zero Dollars

Dollars	Dimes	Pennies
0	4	2

forty-two cents
$0.42 or 42¢

B. Zero Dimes

Dollars	Dimes	Pennies
2	0	4

two dollars and four cents
$2.04

C. Zero Pennies

Dollars	Dimes	Pennies
7	4	0

seven dollars and forty cents
$7.40

Explain Your Thinking

▶ Look at the examples above. What do the numbers after the decimal point stand for? What do the numbers before the decimal point stand for?

Guided Practice

Write each amount, using a dollar sign and a decimal point.

1. 

2. 

Ask Yourself

- Did I place the decimal point between the dollars and cents?
- Did I remember to write the dollar sign?

Independent Practice

Write each amount, using a dollar sign and a decimal point.

3. 

4. 

5. eight dollars and forty-four cents

6. five dollars and eighteen cents

7. three dollars and ninety cents

8. eleven dollars and six cents

Problem Solving • Reasoning

9. Clare has 3 jars of pennies. They are shown at the right. Use a dollar sign and a decimal point to write the value of the money in each of the jars.

10. **Analyze** Toby had 8 dimes and 30 pennies in his bank. He took out half of the dimes. What is the value of the money left in the bank?

11. Maribel has \$6.15 in her bank. How much will she have if she adds 1 dollar, 2 dimes, and 1 penny to her bank?

Mixed Review • Test Prep

Compare. Write >, or <, or = for each ●. *(pages xxii–xxv)*

12. 4 + 6 ● 11 − 4

13. 6 − 2 ● 2 + 2

14. 3 + 7 ● 4 + 8

15 What is 2,466 rounded to the nearest ten? *(pages 24–26)*

A 2,500 **B** 2,470 **C** 2,460 **D** 2,400

Extra Practice See Set A on page 88.

Count Coins and Bills

You will learn how to name and count coins and bills.

New Vocabulary
half-dollar
quarter
nickel

Learn About It

Each coin below is worth a different amount. You can find the total value of the coins by counting.

dollar	**half-dollar**	**quarter**	**dime**	**nickel**	**penny**
one dollar 100¢ $1.00	fifty cents 50¢ $0.50	twenty-five cents 25¢ $0.25	ten cents 10¢ $0.10	five cents 5¢ $0.05	one cent 1¢ $0.01
$1.00 →	$1.50 →	$1.75 →	$1.85 →	$1.90 →	$1.91

The total value of the coins is $1.91.

Another Example

Count Bills and Coins

$10.00 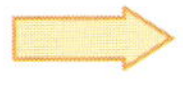 $15.00 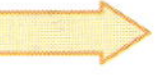 $15.50  $15.75 → $16.00 → $16.10

The total value of the bills and coins is $16.10.

Explain Your Thinking

► Why do people often start with the bill or coin of greatest value when they count money? If you start with a different bill or coin will the answer be different?

Guided Practice

Write each amount, using a dollar sign and a decimal point.

1. 

2. 

Ask Yourself

- What is the value of each bill and coin?
- Did I count the money in order from greatest to least value?

Independent Practice

Write each amount, using a dollar sign and a decimal point.

3. 

4. 

5. 

6. 

7. 1 dollar, 1 half-dollar, and 7 nickels

8. 1 five-dollar bill, 3 dollar coins, 2 quarters, and 4 nickels.

9. 3 half-dollars, 1 quarter, and 3 pennies

10. 6 quarters, 2 dimes, 1 nickel, and 3 pennies

Problem Solving • Reasoning

11. **Patterns** Sakima saved 1 quarter a day for 5 days. Complete the pattern to find how much money she had saved by the fifth day.

$0.25, $0.50, $0.75, ____, ____

12. **Logical Thinking** Mike has 5 coins that total 96¢. What are the five coins?

13. **Write About It** Dan has 2 quarters, 3 dimes, and 4 nickels. Lu has 1 half-dollar, 1 quarter, 1 dime, and 10 pennies. Who has more money? Explain.

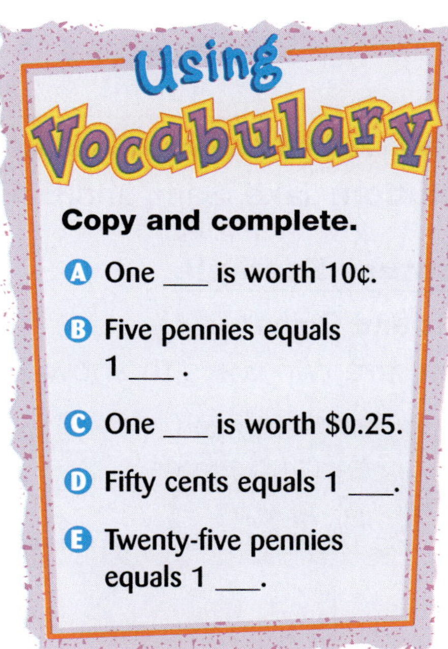

Copy and complete.

A One ___ is worth 10¢.

B Five pennies equals 1 ___ .

C One ___ is worth $0.25.

D Fifty cents equals 1 ___.

E Twenty-five pennies equals 1 ___.

Mixed Review • Test Prep

Round each number to the nearest ten. *(pages 6–7, 8–10)*

14. 48 **15.** 52 **16.** 133 **17.** 286 **18.** 399

19 What is the value of the digit 7 in 473,946? *(pages 34–35)*

A 700,000 **B** 70,000 **C** 7,000 **D** 700

Extra Practice See Set B on page 88.

Equivalent Amounts

You will learn how to show the same amount of money in different ways.

New Vocabulary
equivalent

Learn About It

Jake, Sam, and Emma are at a yard sale. Look at the coins below. How much money does each person have to spend?

Find the value of each group of coins.

Solution: Jake, Sam, and Emma each have 50¢.

Amounts of money that are equal in value are said to be **equivalent**.

Another Example

Bills and Coins

Here are two ways to show $11.25.

Explain Your Thinking

- Look back at the example. Draw another way to show $11.25, by using the fewest number of bills and coins.
- Describe as many ways as you can to show 75¢. What way uses the fewest coins? the most coins?

Guided Practice

Find the value of the amount for each exercise on the left. Then write the letter of the equivalent amount on the right.

1. 1 half-dollar, 3 dimes
2. 2 half-dollars, 1 quarter, 1 nickel
3. 5 quarters, 1 nickel
4. 8 dimes

A.

B.

Ask Yourself

- What is the value of each bill or coin?
- What is the total amount?
- Did I remember to use a decimal point and dollar sign?

Independent Practice

Find the value of the amount for each exercise on the left. Then write the letter of the equivalent amount on the right.

5. 1 half-dollar, 2 dimes, 2 nickels
6. 15 one-dollar bills, 2 quarters
7. 8 dimes
8. 1 dollar, 5 quarters
9. 9 quarters
10. 3 five-dollar bills, 5 dimes
11. 3 quarters, 5 pennies
12. 4 half-dollars, 5 nickels

A.

B.

C.

Use a dollar sign and a decimal point to write each value.

13. 15 pennies and 2 dimes
14. 3 dollars, 8 dimes, and 4 pennies
15. 4 quarters, 6 dimes, and 4 nickels
16. 10 dollars, 4 quarters, and 3 dimes
17. Look at the objects on the right. Write the money amounts in order from least to greatest.

Write two different ways to show each amount using coins and bills.

18. 5¢ **19.** 75¢ **20.** $15.00 **21.** $5.50 **22.** $10.10

Use the fewest number of coins and bills to show each amount.

23. 13¢ **24.** 60¢ **25.** 95¢ **26.** $14.00 **27.** $6.40

Problem Solving • Reasoning

Solve. Choose a method. Use the sign for Problems 28–31.

Computation Methods

- Estimation
- Mental Math
- Paper and Pencil

28. Steve wants to buy 1 video game and 1 puzzle. He has $3.00. Does Steve have enough money to buy both the video game and the puzzle? Explain.

29. **Analyze** Suppose you have quarters, dimes, and nickels. What coins would you use to buy a card game if you wanted to use the fewest coins possible?

30. Matt bought 5 board games at the yard sale. How much did they cost?

31. **Logical Thinking** Tony used 5 coins to buy a puzzle. What coins could Tony have used?

32. **Compare** Sally has 2 quarters, 3 dimes, and 4 nickels. Vicky has 3 quarters, 1 dime, 2 nickels, and 5 pennies. Does the person with more coins also have more money? Explain why or why not.

Mixed Review • Test Prep

Round each number to the nearest hundred. *(pages 8–9, 24–25)*

33. 9,737 **34.** 862 **35.** 4,155 **36.** 8,682 **37.** 997

38 Find the sum of 9 and 8. *(pages xxii–xxiii)*

A 98 **B** 18 **C** 17 **D** 1

Extra Practice See Set C on page 88.

Practice Game

Count It Up!

Practice counting money amounts by playing this game with a partner. Try to be the first person to reach the "target amount"!

What You'll Need

Players 2

For each pair

- *a number cube labeled 1 to 6*
- *play money (1¢, 5¢, 10¢, 25¢, and 50¢ coins; 6 of each)*

Here's What to Do

1. Players decide on a target amount between $2 and $5.
2. The first player rolls the number cube. The number rolled is the number of coins the player has to pick. The player can pick any combination of coins.
3. The first player counts his or her money and records the total value of the coins.
4. Players take turns repeating Steps 2 and 3. After each turn, players add the new amount to the amount he or she has already recorded. The first player to reach the target amount exactly wins!

Share Your Thinking At the start of the game, is it better to pick coins of higher value or of lower value? Explain.

Count Change

You will learn how to count change.

Learn About It

Jason is in the toy store with his grandfather. They buy a puzzle that costs $3.44 and pay with a ten-dollar bill. How much change should they receive?

One way to find the change is to count up from the cost of the toy.

- Start with the cost of the toy.
- Count coins and bills until you have reached the amount paid.

Amount Paid

$6.56 is the change.

- Then, count the bills and coins used to make the change.

Solution: They should receive $6.56 in change.

Explain Your Thinking

► When people count change, they often start with the coin of least value. Why is that so?

Guided Practice

Find the correct change. List the coins and bills used.

1. You paid with $1.00.

2. You paid with $5.00.

Ask Yourself

- What amount do I start with?
- What coins do I need?
- What bills do I need?

Independent Practice

Find the correct change. List the coins and bills used.

3. You paid with 50¢.

4. You paid with $2.00.

5. You paid with $10.00.

6. You paid with $1.00.
You bought stickers for $0.78.

7. You paid with $5.00.
You bought a magazine for $2.85.

8. You paid with $10.00.
You bought an action toy for $7.64.

9. You paid with $10.00.
You bought a puzzle for $8.99.

Copy and complete the table below. List the coins and bills you might receive as change.

	Amount Paid	Cost of Item	Change
10.	$1.00	$0.73	?
11.	$5.00	$3.95	?
12.	$10.00	$7.80	?
13.	$15.00	$11.49	?

Problem Solving • Reasoning

Jani, Meg, and Alan each bought one of the items shown at the right. Each child gave the clerk $3.00. What did each child buy?

Puzzle Book $2.70; Crayons $2.85; $2.25; $2.95

14. Jani's change was 1 nickel and 1 dime.

15. Meg's change was 3 quarters.

16. Alan's change was 5 pennies.

Mixed Review • Test Prep

Round each number to the underlined place.
(pages 6–7, 8–9, and 24–26)

17. $\underline{7}8$ **18.** $3\underline{2}3$ **19.** $\underline{4}19$ **20.** $2{,}\underline{8}44$ **21.** $7{,}\underline{8}75$

22 What is 6,140 rounded to the nearest hundred? *(pages 24–26)*

A 6,000 **B** 6,100 **C** 6,140 **D** 6,200

Extra Practice See Set D on page 89.

Problem-Solving Skill: Choose the Operation

You will learn when to use addition or subtraction to solve a problem that involves money.

Sometimes you need to decide whether you should add or subtract to solve a problem that involves money.

At the school's used-book sale, Leta had 90¢ to spend. She spent 50¢ on a book about birds and 30¢ on a book about fish.

You should add to find the total amount.

How much did Leta spend on the two books?

```
  50¢ ←cost of bird book
+ 30¢ ←cost of fish book
  80¢ ←total cost of the two books
```

You should subtract to find the part that is left.

How much money did Leta have left after buying the 2 books?

```
  90¢ ←amount Leta started with
− 80¢ ←amount Leta spent on the two books
  10¢ ←amount left over after buying the books
```

You should subtract to compare two amounts.

How much more did Leta spend on the bird book than the fish book?

```
  50¢ ←cost of bird book
− 30¢ ←cost of fish book
  20¢ ←how much more spent on bird book
```

Look Back Suppose the two books cost 40¢ each. Would Leta have enough money to buy both? Explain your answer.

A bookmobile brings books to neighborhoods where there are no libraries.

Guided Practice

Tell whether you would add or subtract. Then solve.

1. Lilia is a day late in returning her 4 books to the library. The fine is 10¢ per book. How much money does Lilia have to pay in fines?

Do you need to find the total amount or part of the amount?

2. Ted is buying books at the school book sale. He has \$6. He spends \$4 on mystery books. How much money does Ted have left?

Do you need to find the total amount or part of the amount?

Choose a Strategy

Solve. Use these or other strategies.

Problem-Solving Strategies

- **Use Logical Thinking**
- **Find a Pattern**
- **Write a Number Sentence**

3. Keith bought two books for 20¢ each and one book for 10¢. After paying for the books, he had 10¢ left. How much money did Keith have at the start?

4. Josephine wants to buy three paperback books. The books cost 10¢, 20¢, and 30¢. How much money does Josephine need to buy all three books?

5. Noah has 1 dollar bill, 2 quarters, 4 dimes, 1 nickel, and 3 pennies in his pocket. How much money does Noah have in coins?

6. Phil wants to buy a book that costs a quarter. He needs a dime more than he has now. How much money does Phil have now?

7. Jim, Kay, Ann, and Leo each bought books at the book sale. Jim spent more than Ann. Kay spent the most. Ann spent more than Leo. Write the names of the students in order from the one who spent the most to the one who spent the least.

8. Here is the beginning of a pattern. If the pattern continues, how many stars will be in the sixth group?

Extra Practice See 1–4 on page 91.

Check Your Understanding of Lessons 1–5

Write each amount, using a $ sign and a decimal point.

1.

2.

3. six dollars and forty-eight cents

4. twelve dollars and five cents

Copy and complete each sentence.

5. One quarter equals ___ nickels.

6. One dollar equals ___ quarters.

Compare the amounts. Write >, <, or = for each ●.

7. 3 dimes ● 1 quarter

8. 3 quarters ● 1 dollar

9. 1 half-dollar ● 5 dimes

10. 2 dimes ● 3 nickels

Solve.

11. Fred buys a poster that costs $2.65. He gives the clerk $5.00. What is the correct change? List the bills and coins that Fred might receive.

12. Laura is in a gift shop. She has $10 to spend. She spends $4 on a key ring and $3 on a bookmark. How much money does Laura have left?

How did you do?

If you had difficulty with any items in the Quick Check, you can use the following pages for review and extra practice.

Items	Review These Pages	Do These Extra Practice Items
1–4	pages 54–57	Sets A–B, page 88
5–10	pages 58-60	Set C, page 88
11	pages 62-63	Set D, page 89
12	pages 64-65	1–4, page 91

Test Prep • Cumulative Review

Maintaining the Standards

Write the letter of the correct answer. If the correct answer is not here, choose NH.

1. Cindy bought a book and paid for it with these bills and coins. How much did the book cost?

A $6.19
B $6.34
C $6.59
D $6.79

2. Mallory's mystery number is equal to 300 + 20. What is Mallory's mystery number?

F 32
G 302
H 320
J 3,020

3. What is the value of these coins?

A 46¢
B 51¢
C 56¢
D 65¢

4. Robert used these bills to buy this toy.

How much change should he receive?

F 12¢ **H** 32¢
G 22¢ **J** 40¢

5. There were 12 problems on a math test. Paula got 3 problems wrong. How many problems did she get right?

A 15 **C** 9
B 11 **D** NH

6. Which of the following shows the numbers in order from least to greatest?

F	64	642	604	6,400
G	6,400	642	604	64
H	64	604	642	6,400
J	604	64	642	6,400

7. Sandy made 9 bracelets and Carrie made 8 bracelets. How many bracelets did they make altogether?

Explain How did you find your answer?

Internet Test Prep
Visit **www.eduplace.com/kids/mhm** for more *Test Prep Practice.*

Hour, Half-Hour, Quarter-Hour

You will learn how to tell time to the hour, half-hour, and quarter-hour.

Learn About It

Tyler has a busy schedule. You can see his morning activities below. Look at the clocks. The short hand shows hours. The long hand shows minutes.

Units of Time		
1 day	=	24 hours
1 hour	=	60 minutes
1 half-hour	=	30 minutes
1 quarter-hour	=	15 minutes

Getting Up

Write as

- six-fifteen
- fifteen minutes after six
- quarter after six
- 6:15

Getting Dressed

Write as

- six-thirty
- thirty minutes after six
- half past six
- 6:30

Eating Breakfast

Write as

- six forty-five
- forty-five minutes after six
- fifteen minutes before seven
- quarter to seven
- 6:45

On Bus to School

Write as

- seven o'clock
- 7:00

A.M. is used for the hours from 12 midnight to 12 noon.

11:00 A.M.

P.M. is used for the hours from 12 noon to 12 midnight.

11:00 P.M.

Explain Your Thinking

► How many complete turns around the clock does the hour hand make in one day?

Guided Practice

Write each time in at least two ways.

1. 

2. 

3. 

Ask Yourself

- How many hours does the clock show?
- How many minutes does the clock show?

Independent Practice

Write each time in at least two ways.

4. 

5. 

6. 

7. 

Write each time by using numbers.

8. quarter after five **9.** half past seven **10.** two o'clock

Choose the most reasonable time for each activity.

11. eating breakfast

a. 7:00 A.M. **b.** 1:00 A.M.
c. 7:00 P.M. **d.** 4:00 P.M.

12. going home from school

a. 4:30 A.M. **b.** 3:30 P.M.
c. 9:30 A.M. **d.** 11:30 P.M.

Problem Solving • Reasoning

13. **Patterns** Trains leave a station at 4:45 P.M., 5:00 P.M., 5:15 P.M., and 5:30 P.M. If the pattern continues, what time is the next train likely to leave?

14. **Analyze** Which time is closer to 5:00, half past five or 4:45?

Mixed Review • Test Prep

Add or subtract. *(pages xxii–xxv)*

15. 11 + 5 **16.** 17 − 4 **17.** 9 + 3 **18.** 14 − 6

19 What is another way to write 5,000 + 70 + 2 ? *(pages 18–19)*

A 5,720 **B** 5,702 **C** 5,072 **D** 572

Extra Practice See Set E on page 89.

Time to Five Minutes

You will learn how to tell time to five minutes.

Learn About It

Carla is on a school trip with her class to Washington, D.C. They are waiting to take a tour of the Capitol Building. How can you read the time shown on the clock?

Different Ways to Tell Time

One way to read the time is to tell the number of minutes **after the hour**.

- The **hour hand** is between 9 and 10, so the time is after 9 o'clock.
- The **minute hand** is on the 7. Start at the 12 and count ahead by 5-minute steps.

Write: 9:35

Read: nine thirty-five, or 35 minutes after 9

Remember: It takes 5 minutes for the minute hand to move from one number to the next.

Another way to read the time is to tell the number of minutes **before the hour**.

- The **hour hand** is between 9 and 10, so the time is before 10 o'clock.
- The **minute hand** is on the 7. Start at the 12 and count back to the 7 by 5-minute steps.

Write: 9:35

Read: 25 minutes before 10

Solution: The time 9:35 can be read as:

- nine thirty-five
- 35 minutes after 9
- 25 minutes before 10

Another Example

A. Minutes After the Hour

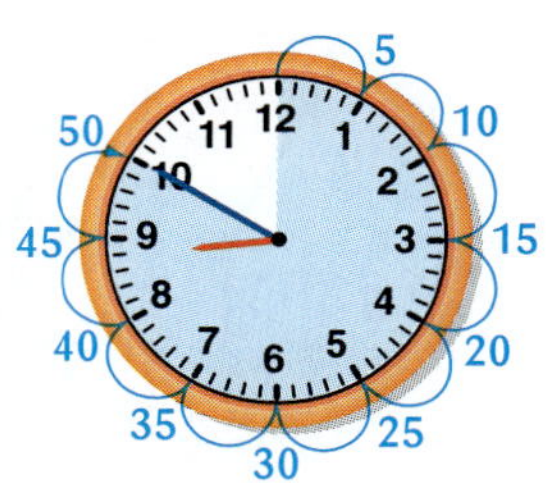

50 minutes after 8
8:50

B. Minutes Before the Hour

10 minutes before 9
8:50

▲ Capitol Building, Washington D.C.

Explain Your Thinking

► If a clock shows 40 minutes after 9, how can you tell how many minutes before 10?

Guided Practice

Write each time as minutes after and before an hour.

1. 

2. 

3. 

Ask Yourself

- Where is the hour hand pointing?
- Where do I start counting by 5-minute steps? Where do I stop counting?

Independent Practice

Write each time as minutes after and before an hour.

4. 

5. 

6. 

7. 

8. 

9. 

10. 

11. 

For Exercises 12–17, write the letter of the clock that shows each time.

12. five fifty-five

13. 25 minutes after 11

14. 11:25

15. 5 minutes before 6

16. 5:55

17. eleven twenty-five

Clock A

Clock B

Algebra • Equations **Copy and complete.**

18. 1 hour = _____ minutes

19. 2 hours = _____ minutes

20. 60 minutes = _____ hour

21. 180 minutes = _____ hours

22. 120 minutes = _____ hours

23. 30 minutes = _____ hour

Copy and complete. Use *minutes*, *hours*, or *days*.

24. Watching a movie takes about 2 ____ .

25. Eating breakfast takes about 15 ____ .

26. A cross-country drive takes about 10 ____ .

27. Brushing your teeth takes about 2 ____ .

Problem Solving • Reasoning

Use the information at the right for Problems 28 and 29.

28. There are 8 boys, 6 girls, and 2 teachers in Carla's tour group. Is the group large enough to make reservations for a group tour?

29. A tour bus arrives at the Capitol at 2:20 P.M. What is the earliest time the tourists can tour the Capitol?

30. **Write About It** The hour hand on Carla's watch points between the 10 and the 11. The minute hand points at 8. Carla says the time is 10:40. Theo says it is almost ten minutes to 8. Who is right? Explain.

Mixed Review • Test Prep

Add or subtract. *(pages xxii–xxv)*

31. $7 + 4$ **32.** $8 - 8$ **33.** $9 + 5$ **34.** $10 - 3$ **35.** $17 + 3$ **36.** $20 - 10$

Choose the letter of the correct answer.

37 $9 + 8 = ■$

A 1 **B** 7 **C** 17 **D** 18

38 $15 - ■ = 6$

F 9 **G** 10 **H** 11 **J** 20

Visual Thinking

Using a Time Line

A time line can be used to show when things happen.
The time line below shows the 24 hours in a day.
The hours from midnight to noon are A.M. hours.
The hours from noon to midnight are P.M. hours.

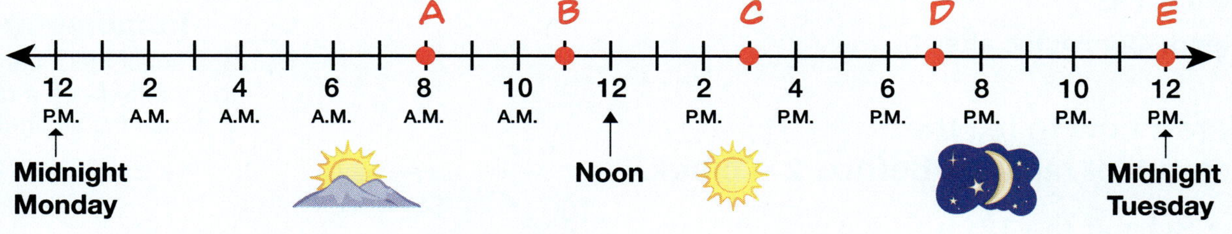

Write the time for each of the letters on the time line above. Use A.M. and P.M.

39. A **40.** B **41.** C **42.** D **43.** E

Match each time with the most likely activity.

44. 10 P.M. **a.** eating lunch

45. 8 A.M. **b.** sleeping in bed

46. 1 P.M. **c.** eating breakfast

47. 10 A.M. **d.** working in school

48. **Write Your Own** Make your own time line for a day.

Extra Practice See Set F on page 89.

Time to the Minute

You will learn how to tell the number of minutes after the hour and before the hour.

Learn About It

Bill is getting ready to record a children's story on tape. The time that Bill started recording his story is shown on the clock at the right. How can you read the time shown on the clock?

Different Ways to Tell Time

Here's how to tell the number of minutes **after 1 o'clock.**

- Start at the 12.
- Count ahead by 5-minute steps.
- Then count the remaining minutes.

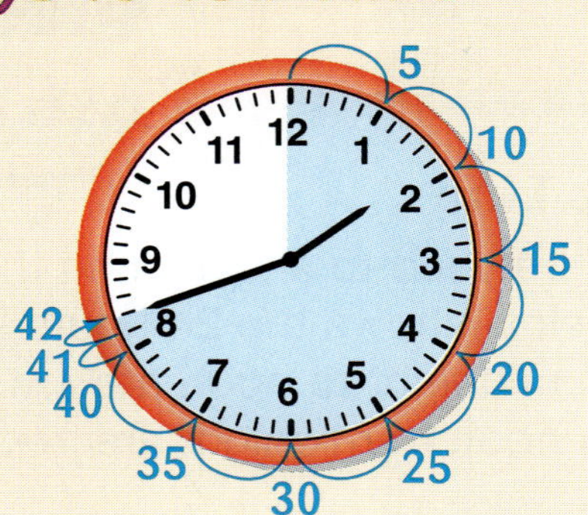

Write: 1:42
Read: 42 minutes after 1

Remember:
Each small mark between the numbers on a clock stands for 1 minute.

Here's how to tell the number of minutes **before 2 o'clock.**

- Start at the 12.
- Count back by 5-minute steps.
- Then count the remaining minutes.

Write: 1:42
Read: 18 minutes before 2

Solution: The time 1:42 can be read as,
- one forty–two
- 42 minutes after 1
- 18 minutes before 2

Explain Your Thinking

► Why does 42 minutes after 1 tell the same time as 18 minutes before 2?

Guided Practice

Write each time as minutes after and before the hour.

1. 
2. 
3. 

Ask Yourself

- Where do I start counting by 5-minute steps? Where do I stop counting?
- What do I count by next?

Independent Practice

Write each time, in words.

4. 7:31 5. 9:59 6. 11:17 7. 5:43 8. 8:46

Write each time as minutes after and before an hour.

9. 
10. 
11. 
12. 

Problem Solving • Reasoning

Use Data The table shows the times each student started to record his or her story. Use the table for Problems 13–15

Reading Times	
Name	**Starting Time**
Anita	2:05 P.M.
Bill	1:42 P.M.
Fran	2:54 P.M.
Karyn	1:18 P.M.
Miguel	2:28 P.M.
Pedro	3:30 P.M.

13. Using words, write the starting time for the student who recorded their story first.

14. Which students started to record their stories between 1:30 and 2:00? between 2:00 and 2:30?

15. **Compare** List the students in order from the one who recorded first to the one who recorded last.

Mixed Review • Test Prep

Compare. Write >, <, or = for each ●. *(pages 20–21)*

16. 864 ● 874 17. 5,740 ● 740 18. 2,261 ● 2,162 19. 1,909 ● 1,099

20. What is another way to write 6 ten thousands? *(pages 32–35)*

A 60 **B** 6,000 **C** 60,000 **D** 600,000

Extra Practice See Set G on page 90.

Problem-Solving Strategy: Use Logical Thinking

You will learn how you can use logical thinking to solve a problem.

Sometimes you need to use logical thinking to solve a problem.

Problem Aaron, Beth, Celia, and David have music lessons today. Each lesson is 30 minutes long. Aaron's lesson is at 1:30 P.M. Beth's lesson is the last lesson of the day. David's lesson is 1 hour after Celia's lesson. What time is David's lesson? What time is Celia's lesson?

Understand

What do you need to find?

You need to find the times of David's lesson and Celia's lesson.

What do you know?

- Aaron's lesson is at 1:30 P.M.
- Beth has the last lesson.
- David's lesson is 1 hour after Celia's.

Plan

How can you solve the problem?

You can use logical thinking to organize what you know.

Solve

Start with what you know.

- Aaron's lesson is at 1:30 P.M.
- Beth has the last lesson.
- There are 2 lessons left 1:00 P.M. and 2:00 P.M.
- David's lesson is 1 hour after Celia's.

Time	Student
1:00 P.M.	
1:30 P.M.	Aaron
2:00 P.M.	
2:30 P.M.	Beth

So David's lesson is at 2:00 P.M. and Celia's lesson is at 1:00 P.M.

Look Back

Look back at the problem.

Does the answer match the facts in the problem?

Remember:
- Understand
- Plan
- Solve
- Look Back

Guided Practice

Solve these problems, using the Logical Thinking strategy.

1. Adam, Rita, Mike, and Sharon each bought a music book. The books cost \$4, \$6, \$7, and \$8. Mike spent \$6. Rita spent less than Adam did. Sharon spent the most. How much did each student spend?

How much did Sharon spend?

2. Tom, Josie, Pat, Mick, and Nancy are in a music recital. Tom plays first. Pat plays before Nancy and after Mick. Josie plays last. In what order will the students play in the recital?

How can you use a table to organize the facts?

Choose a Strategy

Solve. Use these or other strategies.

Problem-Solving Strategies

- Find a Pattern
- Use Logical Thinking
- Act It Out

3. Juanita has 4 coins in her pocket. She will use the coins to buy a new folder for her sheet music. The total value of the coins is 50¢. Two of the coins are alike. What are the four coins Juanita has in her pocket?

4. Mary's piano lesson costs \$10. She paid for her lesson with a \$5 bill, some \$1 bills, and quarters. She used the same number of quarters as \$1 bills. How many of each bill and coin did Mary use?

5. Cindy, Zack, Joe, and Pam take singing lessons. Their lessons cost \$15, \$18, \$20, and \$25 each. Joe's lesson costs the least. Cindy pays the most. Zack pays less than Pam. How much does each person pay for a singing lesson?

6. On Monday, Jan practiced the piano for 20 minutes. On Tuesday, she practiced for 30 minutes. On Wednesday, she practiced for 40 minutes. If this pattern continues until Friday, how many minutes will Jan likely practice on Friday?

Extra Practice See 5–8 on page 91.

Elapsed Time

You will learn how a clock can help you tell when an activity will end or how long an activity will be.

Learn About It

The Mexican Folk Dancers practice every Saturday. Suppose the practice starts at 12:00 noon and ends at 1:30 P.M. How long is the practice?

If you know the starting time and the ending time, you can find how long the practice lasts.

Start at 12:00.

Count the hours.
12:00 to 1:00 is 1 hour.

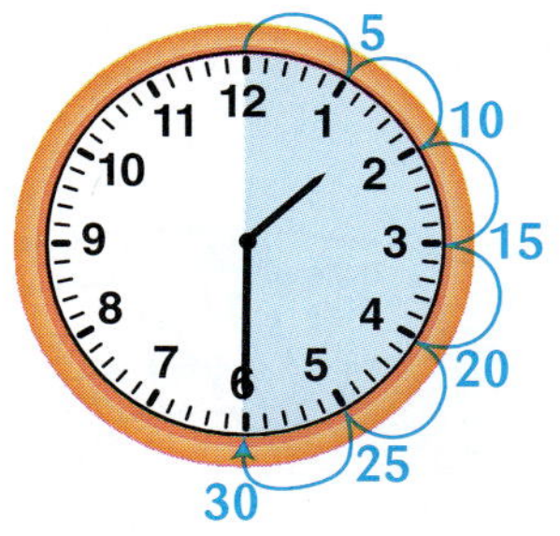

Then count the minutes.
1:00 to 1:30 is 30 minutes.

Solution: The practice is 1 hour and 30 minutes long.

If practice starts at 10:00 A.M. and lasts 50 minutes, what time does the practice end?

If you know when the practice starts and how long it lasts, you can find when the practice ends.

Start at 10:00.

Count ahead 50 minutes to 10:50.

Solution: The practice ends at 10:50 A.M.

Explain Your Thinking

► Without using a clock, can you tell how long a practice from 7:00 P.M. TO 9:30 P.M. lasts?

Guided Practice

Tell what time it will be

1. in 3 hours

2. in 20 minutes

3. in 45 minutes

Ask Yourself

- At what time do I start counting?
- Do I need to count hours?
- Do I need to count minutes?

Independent Practice

Tell what time it will be

4. in 5 minutes

5. in 35 minutes

6. in 1 hour

7. in 3 hours

Look at each pair of times. Write how much time has passed.

8. Start: 7:30 A.M.
End: 7:40 A.M.

9. Start: 10:10 P.M.
End: 10:55 P.M.

10. Start: 9:30 A.M.
End: 11:30 A.M.

Problem Solving • Reasoning

11. One Sunday the Mexican Folk Dancers practiced from noon until 2:00 P.M. and from 5:00 P.M. until 6:30 P.M. How long did they practice in all?

12. **Analyze** Three dance groups are performing between 12:00 noon and 1:30 P.M. Suppose each group's performance lasts 30 minutes. Write the time each performance starts.

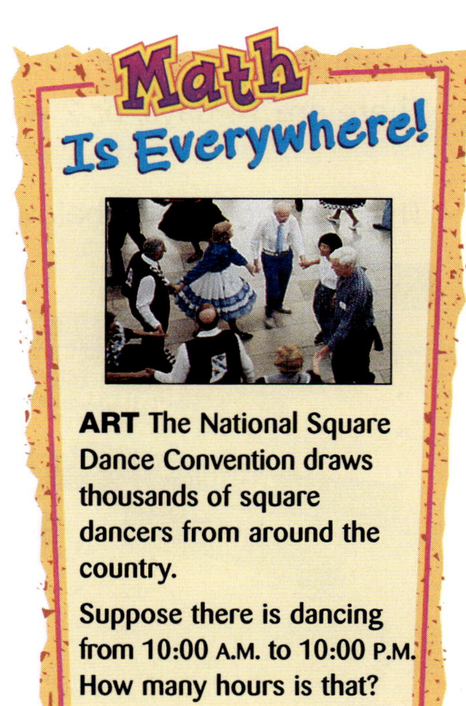

ART The National Square Dance Convention draws thousands of square dancers from around the country.

Suppose there is dancing from 10:00 A.M. to 10:00 P.M. How many hours is that?

Mixed Review • Test Prep

Write each number in expanded form. *(pages 32–35)*

13. 25,401 **14.** 14,306 **15.** 22,041 **16.** 101,101

17 What is the value of 3 quarters, 2 dimes, and 3 nickels? *(pages 56–57)*

A \$0.98 **B** \$1.10 **C** \$1.23 **D** \$1.35

Extra Practice See Set H on page 90.

Use a Calendar

You will learn how to read and use a calendar.

New Vocabulary
ordinal numbers

Learn About It

A calendar shows the days of the week and the months of the year. Alana and her dad are going to the football game on Saturday, November 9.

Find Saturday, November 9, on the calendar below.

November

Sunday	Monday	Tuesday	Wednesday	Thursday	Friday	Saturday
					1	2
3	4	5	6	7	8	9 Football Game
10	11 Veterans Day	12	13	14	15	16
17	18	19	20	21	22	23
24	25	26	27	28 Thanksgiving	29	30

Calendar Units
1 week = 7 days
1 year = 12 months
1 year = 52 weeks

Write: November 9 **Read:** November ninth

Now find November 23.

Count the number of days from November 9 to November 23.

There are 14 days, or 2 weeks.

The yearly calendar below shows the months in order.

There are 12 months in a year.

Ordinal numbers are used to show order or position.

Here are some ordinal numbers that are often used when talking about the days shown on a calendar.

1st first	2nd second	3rd third	4th fourth	5th fifth	6th sixth	7th seventh
8th eighth	9th ninth	10th tenth	11th eleventh	12th twelfth	13th thirteenth	14th fourteenth
15th fifteenth	16th sixteenth	17th seventeenth	18th eighteenth	19th nineteenth	20th twentieth	21st twenty-first
22nd twenty-second	23rd twenty-third	24th twenty-fourth	25th twenty-fifth	26th twenty-sixth	27th twenty-seventh	28th twenty-eighth
29th twenty-ninth	30th thirtieth	31st thirty-first				

Look at the monthly calendar pages on the previous page. January is the first month of the year. November is the eleventh month of the year. Which is the fifth month?

Explain Your Thinking

- ► Look back at the November calendar. How many days in November are Thursdays? How many days are Fridays? Why is the number of Thursdays different from the number of Fridays?
- ► Why doesn't each month of a calendar start on a Sunday?

Guided Practice

Use the calendars on page 80 for Exercises 1–10. Write the name of each month.

1. 4th month **2.** 1st month **3.** 7th month

4. 3rd month **5.** 9th month **6.** 2nd month

Write the day of the week.

7. November 3 **8.** November 11 **9.** November 20

10. What is the date of the second Tuesday in November?

Ask Yourself

- How do I find the day of the week when I know the date?
- How do I find the date when I know the day of the week?

Independent Practice

Use the May calendar for Exercises 11–15.

11. What date is the Flower Show?

12. What day of the week is May 16?

13. What is the date of the third Monday?

14. What date comes after May 31?

15. What day of the week is Mother's Day?

May

Sunday	Monday	Tuesday	Wednesday	Thursday	Friday	Saturday
			1	2	3	4
5	6	7	8	9	10	11
12 Mother's Day	13	14 Flower Show	15	16	17	18
19	20	21	22	23	24	25
26	27 Memorial Day	28	29	30	31	

Name the month that is 3 months after each month.

16. May **17.** August **18.** March **19.** December

Name the month that is 2 months before each month.

20. June **21.** November **22.** April **23.** February

Problem Solving • Reasoning

Use the calendar above for Problems 24 and 25.

24. **Estimate** About how many weeks are there between Mother's Day and Memorial Day?

25. What day of the week is the last day of April? Explain how you know.

26. **Compare** Suppose you were at camp from July 1 to July 20. Your friend was at camp from July 6 to July 20. How much longer were you at camp than your friend?

27. **Write Your Own** Write two or three questions using the calendars in the lesson. Use ordinal numbers in your questions. Then give your questions to a classmate to answer.

Mixed Review • Test Prep

Find each missing number. *(pages 4–5, 18–19)*

28. 40 + ■ = 46

29. 200 + 90 = ■

30. 300 + ■ + 8 = 378

31. ■ + 900 + 70 + 6 = 1,976

32 What is another way to write five thousand, nine hundred eight? *(pages 18–19)*

A 5,980 **B** 5,098 **C** 5,908 **D** 598

Extra Practice See Set I on page 90.

Show What You Know

Estimating Time

15 minutes
1 hour
6 hours
10 days

Use the sign at the right to complete the story.

1. Today the family vacation began. Jody got up early. It took her ____ to eat breakfast. **2.** Then the family got in the car. The airport was 50 miles away, so it took ____to get there.

3. The flight from New York to San Diego takes about ____.

4. The family is going to be on vacation for ____.

Before and After

It's important to label times after midnight and before noon as A.M. and times after noon as P.M. Write each time shown below. Label each A.M. or P.M.

1. Five minutes before noon

3. One hour after 11:30 A.M.

5. 8 minutes after noon

2. 3 hours before 1 P.M.

4. 45 minutes after midnight

6. 2 hours before 12:15 P.M.

What Time Is It?

Use the clues to find each time.

1. The time is between 5 A.M. and 7 A.M. The hour digit is even.

The sum of the minute digits is 6.

You say the number of minutes when you count by 5s.

2. The time is between 6 P.M. and 8 P.M. The hour digit is odd.

The minute hand is between 2 and 3.

The sum of the minute digits is 3.

Problem-Solving Application: Use a Schedule

You will learn how to read and use a schedule.

A schedule is a table that lists the times for events or activities.

Problem Jill and Linda are at day camp. They want to choose an activity that starts at 9:00 A.M. and lasts more than one hour. Which activity should they choose?

DAILY ACTIVITIES

Activity	Starting Time	Ending Time
Hiking	9:00 A.M.	10:00 A.M.
Tennis	9:00 A.M.	10:15 A.M.
Arts and crafts	10:30 A.M.	12:00 noon
In-line skating	9:00 A.M.	10:00 A.M.
Horseback riding	10:00 A.M.	12:00 noon
Swimming	1:00 P.M.	2:30 P.M.

Understand

What do you need to find?
You need to find the activities that start at 9:00 A.M. and are more than 1 hour long.

What do you know?
The starting and ending times for all the activities are listed in the schedule.

Plan

How can you solve the problem?
Find the activities that start at 9:00 A.M. and continue past 10:00 A.M.

Solve

Look at the column labeled *Starting Time*.
Three activities start at 9 A.M.
- Hiking
- Tennis
- In-line skating

Now look at the column labeled *Ending Time*.
The activities end at different times.
- Hiking ends at 10:00 A.M.
- Tennis ends at 10:15 A.M.
- In-line skating ends at 10:00 A.M.

Tennis lasts for more than 1 hour. So the girls should choose tennis.

Look Back

Look back at the schedule. Is there another activity that starts at 9:00 A.M. and lasts more than 1 hour?

Remember:
- Understand
- Plan
- Solve
- Look Back

Guided Practice

Use the schedule on page 84 for Problems 1 and 2.

1. Which activities could Jill and Linda choose to do between 10:00 A.M. and 12:00 noon?

Does the activity have to start exactly at 10:00 A.M.?

2. Is it possible for a camper to do more than three activities on the same day? Explain your thinking.

How many of the activities happen at the same time?

Choose a Strategy

Solve. Use these or other strategies. Use the schedule on page 84 for Problems 3–6.

Problem-Solving Strategies

- **Find a Pattern**
- **Use Logical Thinking**
- **Make a Table**

3. Mario wants to do an activity that lasts exactly 2 hours. Which activity should he choose?

4. Brad just finished tennis lessons. How many minutes does he have to wait to do arts and crafts?

5. Would it be possible for Mary Beth to do both the arts and crafts activity and swimming? Why or why not?

6. Liz wants to do an activity that comes after hiking but before lunch. Lunch is at 12:00 noon Which activities could she choose?

7. Campers who pass a swimming test can take diving lessons. The diving lessons start on July 17 and last for 5 days. What is the date of the last diving lesson?

8. Brian signed up for 12 days of camp. He attends every Monday, Tuesday, and Thursday. His first day is a Monday. What weekday is Brian's tenth day of camp?

9. There were 4 teams in a relay race, Team A, Team B, Team C, and Team D. Team B finished in second place. Team D won the race. Team C beat Team A. List the teams in the order in which they finished the race.

Extra Practice See 9–10 on page 91.

Quick Check

Check Your Understanding of Lessons 6–12

Write each time as minutes after and before the hour.

1. 

2. 

3. 

Write how much time has elapsed.

4. Start: 5:25 A.M.
End: 5:45 A.M.

5. Start: 6:30 P.M.
End: 8:30 P.M.

6. Start: 1:10 P.M.
End: 1:45 P.M.

Use the calendar at the right to answer the questions.

7. What day of the week is June 7?

8. What is the date 3 weeks after June 5?

9. Write the ordinal number for the first Tuesday in June.

June						
Sun.	Mon.	Tues.	Wed.	Thurs.	Fri.	Sat.
				1	2	3
4	5	6	7	8	9	10
11	12	13	14	15	16	17
18	19	20	21	22	23	24
25	26	27	28	29	30	

Solve.

10. Mark has 5 coins in his pocket. The value of the coins is 60¢. Three of the coins are alike. What are Mark's coins?

How did you do?

If you had difficulty with any items in the Quick Check, you can use the following pages for review and extra practice.

Items	Review These Pages	Do These Extra Practice Items
1–3	pages 68–75	Sets E–G, page 89–90
4–6	pages 78–79	Set H, page 90
7–9	pages 80–82	Set I, page 90
10	pages 76–77	5–8, page 91

Test Prep • Cumulative Review

Maintaining the Standards

Write the letter of the correct answer.

1 Harold worked for one half-hour. How many minutes did he work?

A 15 **C** 45
B 30 **D** 60

2 Barbara gave the clerk \$4.00 for a game that cost \$3.19. How much change should she receive?

F 71¢ **H** 81¢
G 79¢ **J** 99¢

3 Which of the following shows numbers in order from least to greatest?

A 3,475 3,582 3,487 3,579
B 3,582 3,579 3,487 3,475
C 3,475 3,487 3,579 3,582
D 3,487 3,475 3,579 3,582

4 Maria's birthday is one week and two days after February 10th. When is Maria's birthday?

February						
Sun.	Mon.	Tues.	Wed.	Thurs.	Fri.	Sat.
1	2	3	4	5	6	7
8	9	10	11	12	13	14
15	16	17	18	19	20	21
22	23	24	25	26	27	28

F February 17
G February 19
H February 20
J February 28

5 Melanie left her house at 8:00 A.M. She arrived at school at 8:20 A.M. How long did it take Melanie to get to school?

A 5 minutes
B 15 minutes
C 20 minutes
D 60 minutes

6 Kathy practices 15 minutes every day for a spelling bee. What part of an hour is 15 minutes?

F one quarter
G one half
H three quarters
J one whole

7 Which symbol makes this a true statement?

785 ⬬ 748

A $>$
B $<$
C $=$
D $+$

8 What number should go in the box to make this number sentence true?

$7 + ■ = 13$

Explain How did you find your answer?

Safe Site

Internet Test Prep
Visit **www.eduplace.com/kids/mhm** for more *Test Prep Practice.*

Extra Practice

Set A (Lesson 1, pages 54–55)

Write each amount, using a $ sign and a decimal point.

1. 

2.  

3. four dollars and eighteen cents

4. seven dollars and forty-three cents

Set B (Lesson 2, pages 56–57)

Write each amount, using a $ sign and a decimal point.

1. 

2.  

3. 1 five-dollar bill, 3 one-dollar bills, 1 half-dollar, 6 nickels

4. 1 ten-dollar bill, 1 five-dollar bill, 9 quarters, 8 dimes, 14 pennies

Set C (Lesson 3, pages 58–60)

Find the value of the amount for each exercise on the left. Then write the letter of the equivalent amount on the right.

1. 3 quarters, 5 dimes, 4 nickels
2. 2 dollar bills, 1 half-dollar, 4 nickels
3. 5 half-dollars, 1 dime, 2 nickels
4. 1 dollar bill, 1 quarter, 2 dimes

A.  

B. 

Write two different ways to show each amount using coins and bills.

5. 17¢ 6. 89¢ 7. $1.25 8. $4.20 9. $12.00 10. $15.05

Extra Practice

Set D (Lesson 4, pages 62–63)

Find the correct change. List the coins and bills used.

1. You paid with 50¢.
   You bought a pencil for 27¢.
2. You paid with $1.00.
   You bought six apples for $0.91.
3. You paid with $5.00.
   You bought barrettes for $3.19.
4. You paid with $5.00.
   You bought a toy car for $4.29.

Set E (Lesson 6, pages 68–69)

Write each time in at least two ways.

1. 
2. 

3. 
4. 

Write each time by using numbers.

5. three o'clock
6. half past nine
7. quarter after two
8. one-fifteen
9. quarter to five
10. twelve forty-five

Set F (Lesson 7, pages 70–72)

Write each time as minutes after and before an hour.

1. 
2. 

3. 
4. 

Write each time by using numbers.

5. twenty minutes after three
6. ten minutes before nine
7. five minutes before six
8. five minutes after eleven
9. ten minutes after two
10. thirty minutes before four

Extra Practice

Set G (Lesson 8, pages 74–75)

Write each time as minutes after and before an hour.

1. 
2. 
3. 
4. 

Write each time, in words.

5. 7:17 6. 11:23 7. 2:31 8. 5:11 9. 12:47 10. 4:41

Set H (Lesson 10, pages 78–79)

Tell what time it will be

1. in 30 minutes

2. in 2 hours

3. in 10 minutes

Look at each pair of times. Write how much time has elapsed.

4. Start: 8:10 A.M.
End: 8:40 A.M.

5. Start: 6:15 A.M.
End: 6:35 A.M.

6. Start: 10:15 P.M.
End: 11:00 P.M.

7. Start: 3:10 P.M.
End: 7:10 P.M.

Set I (Lesson 11, pages 80–82)

Write the name of each month.

1. 3rd month 2. 8th month 3. 1st month 4. 11th month

5. What month is 2 months after April?
6. What month is 3 months before March?
7. What date is 3 days before July 4th?

Extra Practice • Problem Solving

Tell whether you would add or subtract. Then solve. *(Lesson 5, pages 64–65)*

1. Jacob bought three books that cost $2 each. How much did Jacob pay for the three books?
2. Meg needs $7 to buy stickers. She has $4 now. How much more money does she need?
3. Kyle buys 4 toy cars at a fair. The cars cost 10¢, 30¢, 20¢, and 30¢. How much does Kyle spend on the 4 cars?
4. Heather has 70¢ to spend at a used-toy sale. She buys a yo-yo for 20¢. How much money does she have left?

Solve these problems, using the Logical Thinking strategy. *(Lesson 9, pages 76–77)*

5. Joanna, Rita, Lou, and Kimberly each bought an animal key chain. The key chains cost $3, $3, $2, and $4. Rita spent the least. Lou's and Joanna's key chains cost the same amount. How much did Kimberly spend on her key chain?
6. Steve, Luke, Sam, and Al all take half-hour gymnastics lessons. The last lesson starts at 3:00. Steve's lesson is at 1:30. Al's lesson is at 3:00. Luke's lesson is before Al's lesson, but 1 hour after Steve's lesson. What time does Sam's lesson start?
7. Kerry has 7 coins in her pocket. The total value of the coins is $1.50. Three of the coins are alike. She has one nickel. What coins does Kerry have?
8. Marie spent $7 on animal toys. The cow cost $2. The duck was $1 more than the cow. Marie also bought a bear. How much did the bear cost?

Solve. Use the schedule. *(Lesson 12, pages 84–85)*

9. Alan and Luis want to enter the sack race. What other events can they enter?
10. Betsy wants to see who wins the long jump. Her friend Mai wants to see who wins the high jump. How long will Betsy have to wait for Mai to meet her for lunch?

Field Day Schedule

Activity	Starting Time	Ending Time
Sack Race	9:00 A.M.	10:00 A.M.
Relay Race	9:00 A.M.	10:15 A.M.
Long Jump	10:00 A.M.	11:15 A.M.
High Jump	10:30 A.M.	11:30 A.M.

Chapter Review

Reviewing Vocabulary

Write *true or false* for each sentence.
Give examples to support your answers.

1. A decimal point separates dollars and cents.
2. Equivalent amounts of money have the same value.
3. A year is 51 weeks.
4. Every month on a calendar begins on a Monday.
5. There are 120 minutes in 2 hours.

Reviewing Concepts and Skills

Write each amount using a $ sign and a decimal point. *(pages 54–57)*

6. 

7. 

8. four dollars and ninety cents

9. seven dollars and fifty-five cents

10. 1 five-dollar bill, 1 quarter, and 7 nickels

11. 4 quarters, 3 dimes, 1 nickel, and 4 pennies

Find the correct change. List the coins and bills used. *(pages 62–63)*

12. You paid with $5.00. You bought a book for $3.25.

13. You paid with $10.00. You bought a hat for $5.69.

Write the time as minutes after and before an hour. *(pages 68–73)*

14. 

15. 

16. 

Write each time by using numbers. *(pages 68–75)*

17. nine-fifteen **18.** half past noon **19.** quarter after two

20. four fifty-three **21.** eight past seven **22.** eleven forty-nine

Write what time it will be. *(pages 78–79)*

23. in 15 minutes

24. in 2 hours

25. in 40 minutes

Write the month that is 5 months after each month. *(pages 80–82)*

26. June **27.** November **28.** February **29.** April

Solve. Use the schedule for Problem 30.
(pages 64-65; pages 76–77, pages 84–85)

30. Mary and Ed are touring a TV studio to watch shows being made. They are going to see the *TRex* show. Can they watch another show as well? Explain.

Show	Starting Time	Ending Time
Guessing Game	12:00 P.M.	12:30 P.M.
TRex	12:00 P.M.	1:15 P.M.
Starshine	1:30 P.M.	3:00 P.M.

31. Ginette has 85¢ in her pocket. After giving a quarter and a dime to a friend, she has 2 coins left. What are the coins?

32. Julia has 30¢ in her bank, 20¢ in her wallet, and a dime in her coat pocket. How much money does Julia have?

Brain Teasers Math Reasoning

THIRTEEN COINS

Jane has 13 coins that are worth 82¢ altogether. What are the coins?

CLOSE HANDS

For which of these times are the hands of a clock closest together: 1:05, 9:45, or 6:30?

Internet Brain Teasers
Visit **www.eduplace.com/kids/mhm** for more *Brain Teasers.*

Chapter Test

Write each amount, using a $ sign and a decimal point.

1. 

2. 

3. five dollars and eighty-two cents

4. four dollars and three cents

5. 1 ten-dollar bill, 1 quarter, 4 nickels, and 1 penny

6. 1 five-dollar bill, 3 quarters, 7 dimes, and 6 pennies

Write two different ways to show each amount, using coins and bills.

7. 85¢

8. $1.30

9. $6.55

10. $17.00

Write the time as minutes after and before the hour.

11. 

12. 

13. 

14. 

15. 

16. 

Look at each pair of times. Write how much time has elapsed.

17. Start: 9:20 A.M.
End: 9:30 A.M.

18. Start: 3:10 A.M.
End: 3:35 A.M.

19. Start: 10:15 P.M.
End: 11:45 P.M.

Write the name of each month.

20. 2nd month

21. 10th month

22. 4th month

23. 7th month

Solve.

24. Eric, June, Margo, and Jeff have $9 between them. Margo has $2 more than Jeff. Eric has $1 more than Margo. Jeff has $1. How much money does June have?

25. Alena wants to buy a frog eraser that costs 80¢. She has 30¢. How much more money does she need to buy the eraser?

Write About It

Solve each problem. Use correct math vocabulary to explain your thinking.

1. Sue and her father are going on a fishing trip. They are leaving on April 2 and returning home on the second Tuesday in April.

a. On what day are Sue and her father leaving?

b. On what date will they return?

c. How many days will they be gone?

APRIL						
Sunday	Monday	Tuesday	Wednesday	Thursday	Friday	Saturday
1	2	3	4	5	6	7
8	9	10	11	12	13	14
15	16	17	18	19	20	21
22	23	24	25	26	27	28
29	30					

2. Mike has two dimes, a quarter, and three nickels. Paco has a half-dollar and two dimes. Mike says to Paco, "I have six coins, and you only have three, so I have more money than you do."

a. Is Mike right or wrong? Explain your answer.

b. Mike doesn't have enough money to buy a pack of trading cards that costs $1. Paco offers to lend him the money. What coins should Paco give Mike?

Another Look

Use the information below to find the answer to each question.

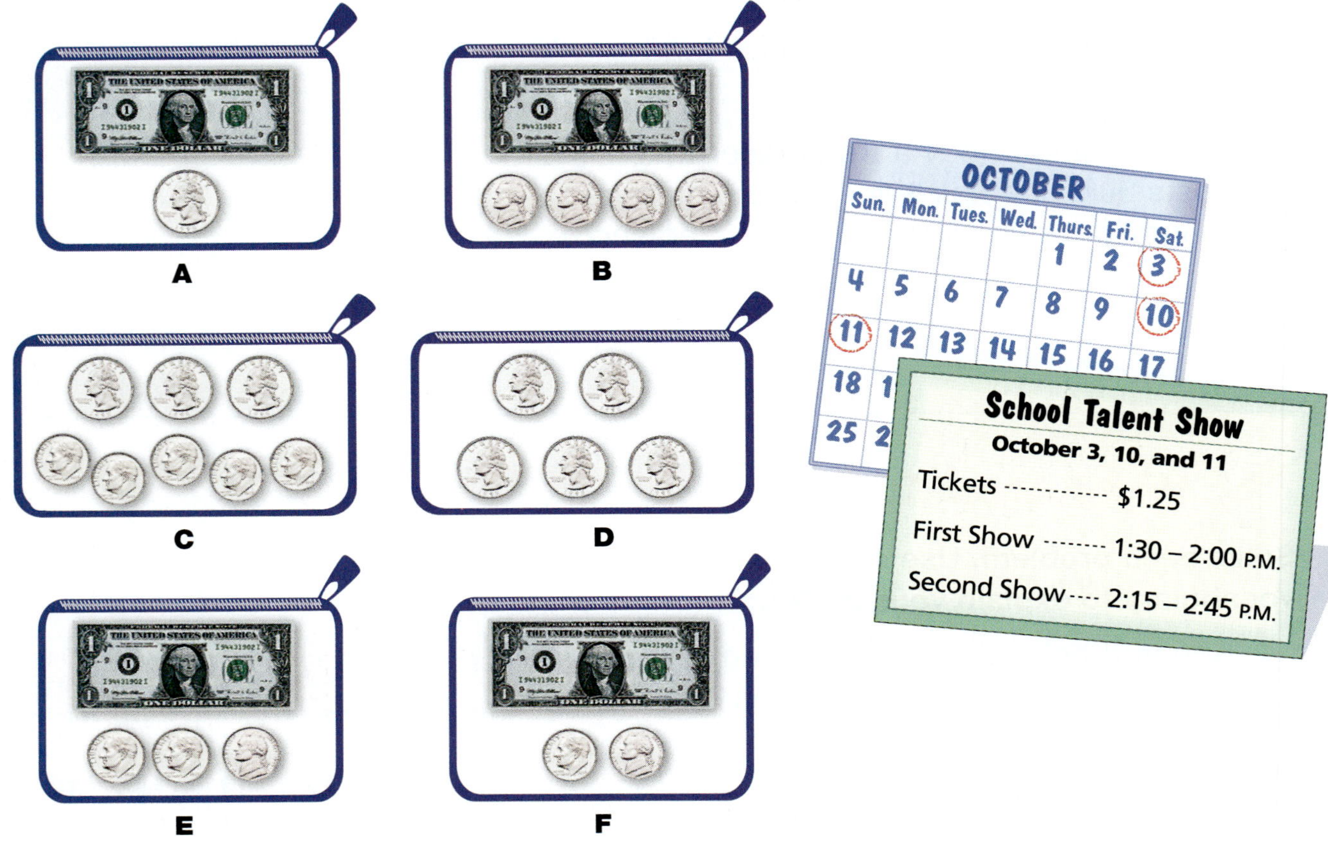

1. Write the letter of each purse that shows the exact amount of money needed for one ticket.

2. The sign shows the starting and ending times for the shows.

- **a.** How long does each show last?
- **b.** How many minutes are there between the end of the first show and the beginning of the second show?
- **c.** Tina missed the shows on October 3. How many days does she have to wait from October 3 until the next show?

3. **Look Back** Look at the sets of coins above that do not show the amount of money needed for a ticket. What coins could you add to each set to show the price of one ticket?

4. **Analyze** Suppose you pay for a ticket with a $5 bill. What is the fewest number of bills and coins you could get as change?

Enrichment

Using Calendar Skills

A year usually has 365 days. However, every fourth year we add an extra day to the month of February. Such a year is called a **leap year**, and it is 366 days long.

This modern version of the classic poem, shown below, will help you remember how many days are in each of the months of a year.

New Vocabulary
leap year
decade
century

Thirty days are in September,
April, June, and November;
All of the rest have thirty-one
Except for February,
Which has twenty-eight,
Until leap year when it has twenty-nine.

Calendar Units		
1 year	=	12 months
1 year	=	52 weeks
1 year	=	365 days
1 **leap year**	=	366 days
1 **decade**	=	10 years
1 **century**	=	100 years

Use the poem and the table to answer Questions 1–6.

1. How many months have 30 days? 31 days?
2. How many days does April have? does October have?
3. How many days does February have in a leap year?
4. If your dog is 10 years old, how many decades old is that?
5. How old is your cousin if he has lived exactly 2 decades and 2 years?
6. If your great-grandmother has lived exactly 1 century and 5 years, how old is she?

Explain Your Thinking

Suppose you are 9 years old and you were born on February 29. How many times would you have celebrated your birthday on February 29? Explain.

Addition and Subtraction

Why Learn About Addition and Subtraction?

There are many activities in which you use addition and subtraction.

When you keep score in a game, you're using addition. When you use part of your allowance to buy something, you can use subtraction to figure how much money you have left.

The people in this picture are riding on a bicycle path. At the end of the ride, they can add the number of miles in each section of the bike path to find the total distance that they've ridden.

Reviewing Vocabulary

Understanding math language helps you become a successful problem solver. Here are some math vocabulary words you should know.

number sentence	a sentence that uses symbols to show how numbers are related
addend	a number that is added
addition	an operation on two or more numbers to find the sum
sum	the answer in an addition problem
subtraction	an operation on two numbers to find the difference
difference	the answer in a subtraction problem

Reading Words and Symbols

When you read mathematics, sometimes you read only words, sometimes you read words and symbols, and sometimes you read only symbols.

There are different ways to write and read addition sentences.

$$\begin{array}{r} 45 \\ +\ 31 \\ \hline 76 \end{array}$$

45 ← addend
+ 31 ← addend
76 ← sum

$45 + 31 = 76$

45 and 31: addends; 76: sum

- ▶ 45 plus 31 equals 76.
- ▶ The sum of 45 and 31 is 76.
- ▶ 31 added to 45 equals 76.

There are different ways to write and read subtraction sentences.

$$\begin{array}{r} 86 \\ -\ 52 \\ \hline 34 \end{array}$$

34 ← difference

$86 - 52 = 34$

34: difference

- ▶ 86 minus 52 equals 34.
- ▶ The difference between 86 and 52 is 34.
- ▶ 52 subtracted from 86 equals 34.

Try These

1. Write *addend, sum,* or *difference* to describe each blue number.

a. 6 + 9 = 15

b.
$$\begin{array}{r} 12 \\ +\ 7 \\ \hline 19 \end{array}$$

c. 18 − 9 = 9

d.
$$\begin{array}{r} 24 \\ +\ 45 \\ \hline 69 \end{array}$$

2. Write *true* or *false* for each sentence.

a. The sum in an addition problem is always less than one of the addends.

b. Changing the order of the addends does not change the sum.

c. When you subtract zero from a number, the difference is zero.

d. Subtraction is the opposite of addition.

3. Write each as a number sentence.

a. 9 subtracted from 17 equals 8.

b. 58 minus 23 equals 35.

c. 54 added to 45 equals 99.

d. The difference between 66 and 5 is 61.

e. 72 plus 56 equals 128.

Upcoming Vocabulary

Write About It **Here are some other vocabulary words** you will learn in this chapter. Watch for these words. Write their definitions in your journal.

Commutative Property of Addition

Associative Property of Addition

Zero Property of Addition

regroup

estimate

LESSON 1

Addition Properties

You will learn about three special rules that are used in addition.

New Vocabulary
Commutative Property
Zero Property
Associative Property

Learn About It

The three addition properties listed below are special rules that can help you when you add.

Commutative Property Changing the order in which numbers are added does not change the sum.

5 + 3 = 8
(5: addend, 3: addend, 8: sum)

You can add down.

$$\begin{array}{r} 5 \\ +\ 3 \\ \hline 8 \end{array} \downarrow$$

3 + 5 = 8
(3: addend, 5: addend, 8: sum)

You can add up.

$$\begin{array}{r} 5 \\ +\ 3 \\ \hline 8 \end{array} \uparrow$$

Zero Property The sum of any number and zero is that number.

4 + 0 = 4

Associative Property Changing the way in which addends are grouped does not change the sum.

(6 + 4) + 3
10 + 3 = 13

6 + (4 + 3)
6 + 7 = 13

You can use parentheses to show which numbers to add first.

Explain Your Thinking

► Describe three ways to find 8 + 2 + 6. Is one way easier than the others? Explain your thinking.

Guided Practice

Find each sum.

1. $6 + 3$ $3 + 6$	**2.** $0 + 4$ $4 + 0$	**3.** $9 + 8$ $8 + 9$
4. $(7 + 3) + 5$ $7 + (3 + 5)$	**5.** $(8 + 4) + 6$ $8 + (4 + 6)$	**6.** $(8 + 2) + 0$ $8 + (2 + 0)$

Ask Yourself

- Which addition property can I use?
- How can I group the addends so that they are easier to add?

Independent Practice

Find each sum.

7.	**8.**	**9.**	**10.**	**11.**	**12.**
$\begin{array}{r} 2 \\ 7 \\ +\ 8 \\ \hline \end{array}$	$\begin{array}{r} 5 \\ 8 \\ +\ 3 \\ \hline \end{array}$	$\begin{array}{r} 2 \\ 7 \\ +\ 4 \\ \hline \end{array}$	$\begin{array}{r} 2 \\ 0 \\ +\ 9 \\ \hline \end{array}$	$\begin{array}{r} 1 \\ 5 \\ +\ 4 \\ \hline \end{array}$	$\begin{array}{r} 3 \\ 2 \\ +\ 1 \\ \hline \end{array}$

13. $5 + 3 + (2 + 8)$ **14.** $5 + 4 + (7 + 2 + 1)$ **15.** $(3 + 7) + 6 + 2 + 3$

n **Algebra • Properties** **Find the missing addends.**

16. $4 + 6 = 6 + \blacksquare$	**17.** $9 + \blacksquare = 9$	**18.** $5 + (6 + 3) = (5 + \blacksquare) + 3$
19. $5 + 3 = \blacksquare + 5$	**20.** $0 + \blacksquare = 7$	**21.** $(7 + 4) + \blacksquare = 7 + (\blacksquare + 2)$

Problem Solving • Reasoning

22. **Patterns** Nina is planting flowers in her garden on the right. If she continues the pattern, what color flowers is she likely to plant in the eleventh row? Explain.

23. **Analyze** There were 6 lilies, 5 tulips, 4 daisies, and 1 rose in Meg's basket. After she gave away 2 lilies, 2 daisies, and 1 tulip, how many flowers were left?

Mixed Review • Test Prep

Write the numbers in order from least to greatest. *(pages 22–23)*

24. 15 67 76 **25.** 44 19 21 **26.** 405 550 505 **27.** 1,101 1,000 100

28 Which number has a 4 in the thousands place? *(pages 32–33)*

A 56,442 **B** 18,474 **C** 24,749 **D** 42,341

Extra Practice See Set A on page 146.

Regroup Ones

You will learn how to regroup ones when you add.

New Vocabulary
regroup

Learn About It

Imala and her mother sold clay pots at a Native American craft fair. They sold 159 large pots and 118 small pots. How many clay pots did they sell?

Add. **159 + 118 = ■**

Find 159 + 118.

Step 1 Show 159 and 118.

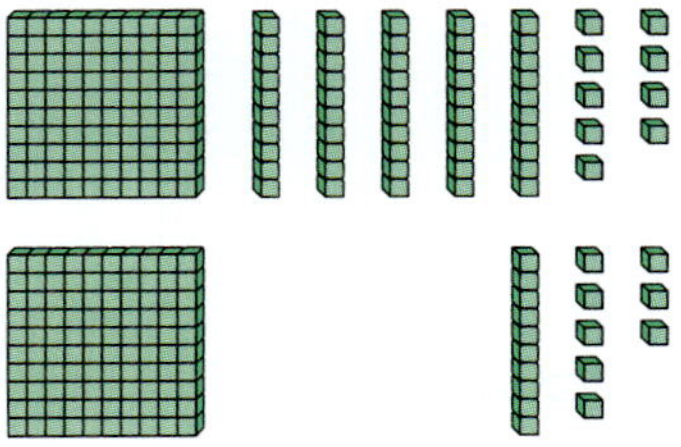

$$\begin{array}{r} 159 \\ +118 \\ \hline \end{array}$$

Step 2 Add the ones.
9 ones + 8 ones = 17 ones

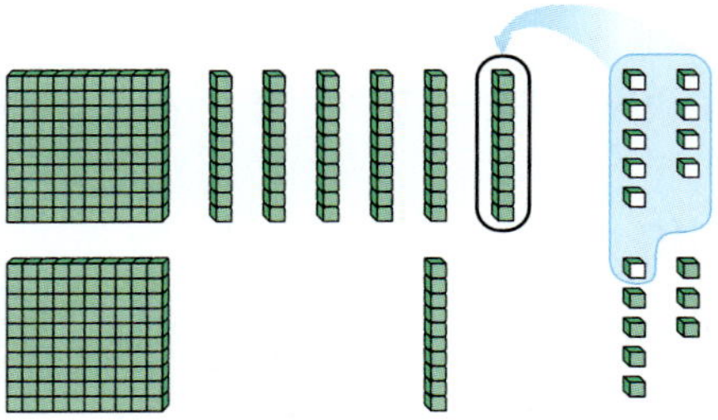

$$\begin{array}{r} ^{1}\\ 159 \\ +118 \\ \hline 7 \end{array}$$

Regroup 17 ones as 1 ten 7 ones.

Step 3 Add the tens.
1 ten + 5 tens + 1 ten = 7 tens

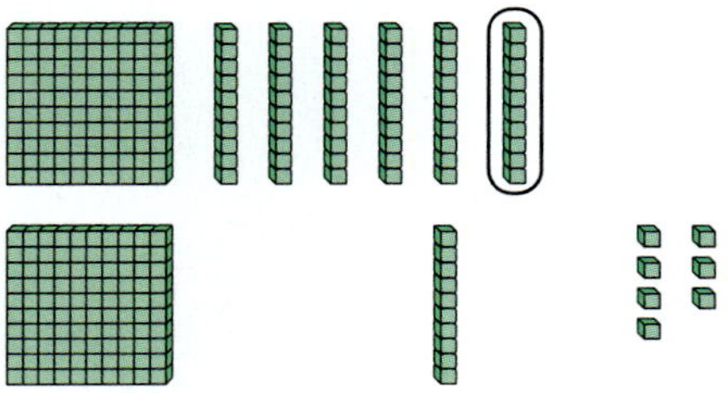

$$\begin{array}{r} ^{1}\\ 159 \\ +118 \\ \hline 77 \end{array}$$

Step 4 Add the hundreds.
1 hundred + 1 hundred = 2 hundreds

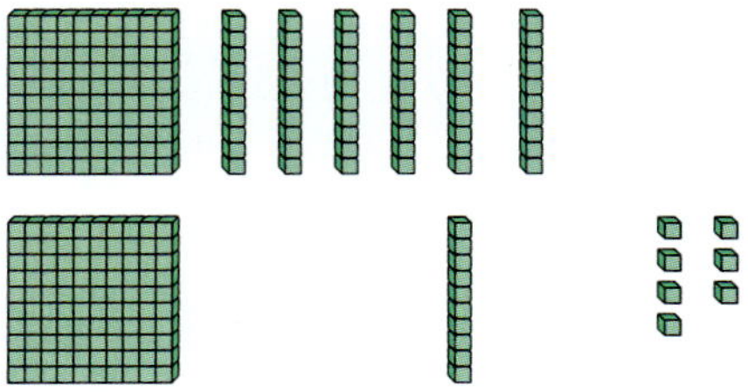

$$\begin{array}{r} ^{1}\\ 159 \\ +118 \\ \hline 277 \end{array}$$

Solution: They sold 277 clay pots.

Other Examples

A. Two-Digit Numbers

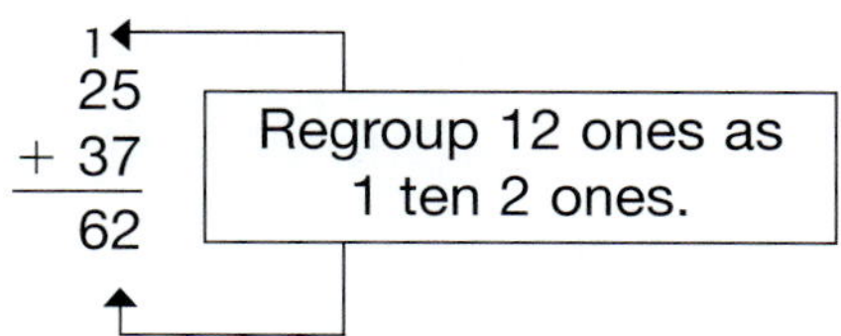

B. Money

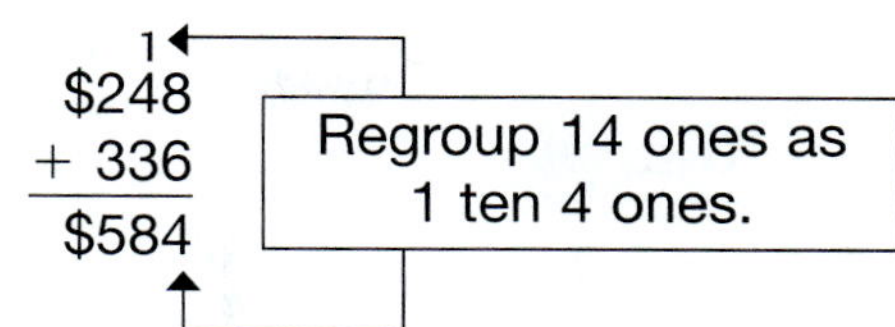

Explain Your Thinking

► When you add, why is it important to line up the ones digits and the tens digits correctly?

► How can you tell when you need to regroup?

Guided Practice

Add.

1. $35 + 27 **2.** 658 + 234 **3.** 263 + 129

4. 52 + 27 **5.** 643 + 228 **6.** $337 + $318

Ask Yourself

- What is the sum of the ones?
- Do I need to regroup ones?

Add. Then write *yes* for each exercise where you regrouped ones to make a ten.

7. 34 + 62 **8.** 23 + 68 **9.** 354 + 127 **10.** 438 + 224 **11.** 859 + 140

Independent Practice

Find each sum.

12. $37 + 19 **13.** 58 + 26 **14.** 17 + 39 **15.** $19 + 75 **16.** 72 + 18

17. 105 + 729 **18.** 205 + 107 **19.** $837 + 148 **20.** 243 + 548 **21.** 156 + 627

22. 72 + 26 **23.** 354 + 213 **24.** 572 + 419 **25.** $121 + $732

26. $541 + $317 **27.** 548 + 129 **28.** 634 + 126 **29.** 362 + 29

Algebra • Functions

Complete each table by following the rule.

Rule: Add 28

	Input	Output
30.	54	■
31.	47	■
32.	65	■
33.	31	■

Rule: Add 126

	Input	Output
34.	337	■
35.	112	■
36.	568	■
37.	324	■

Rule: Add $135

	Input	Output
38.	$437	■
39.	$229	■
40.	$564	■
41.	$820	■

Problem Solving • Reasoning

42. Jake bought a package of beads. There were 175 large beads and 115 small beads in the package. How many beads did Jake buy?

43. **Logical Thinking** Anna spent $18 on dolls and clay pots. The dolls cost $4 each, and the pots cost $3 each. How many of each did Anna buy?

44. **Measurement** The fair was open from 9 A.M. to 6 P.M. each day. How many hours was the fair open during two days?

45. On Saturday, 312 people visited the fair. On Sunday, 468 people visited the fair. How many people visited the fair during the two days?

46. There were 46 dancers in the morning show and 44 different dancers in the afternoon show. How many dancers were in the two shows?

47. **Money** At the fair, Sharma spent $4 on a gift for her sister and $3 on a snack for herself. If Sharma brought $10 to the fair, how much money does she have left?

Mixed Review • Test Prep

Round each number to the nearest ten. *(pages 6–10, 24–26)*

48. 56 **49.** 32 **50.** 568 **51.** 794 **52.** 2,508 **53.** 3,497

Choose the letter for the correct answer. *(pages 18–19, 32–33)*

54 Which number shows forty thousand, five hundred sixty?

A 4,560 **C** 40,560
B 40,506 **D** 40,000,560

55 Which number shows three thousand, sixteen?

F 3,016 **H** 3,160
G 3,106 **J** 30,016

Extra Practice See Set B on page 146.

Adding in Different Ways

Here are two different ways to add.

This is how Doug does addition.

$$\begin{array}{r} 57 = 50 + 7 \\ +\ 22 = 20 + 2 \\ \hline 70 + 9 = 79 \end{array}$$

So 57 + 22 = 79.

How does writing 57 as 50 + 7 and 22 as 20 + 2 help Doug add?

$$\begin{array}{r} 46 = 40 + 6 \\ +\ 35 = 30 + 5 \\ \hline 70 + 11 = 81 \end{array}$$

So 46 + 35 = 81.

How does writing 46 as 40 + 6 and 35 as 30 + 5 help Doug add?

This is how Jan does addition.

$$\begin{array}{r} 57 \\ +\ 22 \\ \hline \end{array} \qquad \begin{array}{r} 57 \\ +\ 20 \\ \hline 77 \\ +\ 2 \\ \hline 79 \end{array}$$

Think: 22 = 20 + 2

So 57 + 22 = 79.

How does thinking of 22 as 20 + 2 help Jan add?

$$\begin{array}{r} 46 \\ +\ 35 \\ \hline \end{array} \qquad \begin{array}{r} 46 \\ +\ 30 \\ \hline 76 \\ +\ 5 \\ \hline 81 \end{array}$$

Think: 35 = 30 + 5

So 46 + 35 = 81.

How does thinking of 35 as 30 + 5 help Jan add?

Try These

Find each sum. Use Doug's, Jan's, and the standard method.

1. $\begin{array}{r} 27 \\ +\ 54 \\ \hline \end{array}$ **2.** $\begin{array}{r} 81 \\ +\ 16 \\ \hline \end{array}$ **3.** $\begin{array}{r} 66 \\ +\ 28 \\ \hline \end{array}$ **4.** $\begin{array}{r} 32 \\ +\ 44 \\ \hline \end{array}$ **5.** $\begin{array}{r} 63 \\ +\ 29 \\ \hline \end{array}$

Explain Your Thinking

► How are the three methods alike? How are they different?

Regroup Ones and Tens

You will learn that when you add, sometimes you have to regroup both ones and tens.

Review Vocabulary
regroup

Learn About It

Larry built a model village, using 3-D puzzles. The train station puzzle has 272 pieces and the library puzzle has 378 pieces. How many puzzle pieces did Larry use to build the train station and the library?

Add. **272 + 378 = ■**

Find 272 + 378.

Step 1 Add the ones.
2 + 8 = 10

$$\begin{array}{r} {}^{1} \\ 272 \\ +\ 378 \\ \hline 0 \end{array}$$

Regroup 10 ones as 1 ten 0 ones.

Step 2 Add the tens.
1 + 7 + 7 = 15

$$\begin{array}{r} {}^{1\,1} \\ 272 \\ +\ 378 \\ \hline 50 \end{array}$$

Regroup 15 tens as 1 hundred 5 tens.

Step 3 Add the hundreds.
1 + 2 + 3 = 6

$$\begin{array}{r} {}^{1\,1} \\ 272 \\ +\ 378 \\ \hline 650 \end{array}$$

Step 4 Check by adding upward.

$$\begin{array}{r} {}^{1\,1} \\ 272 \\ +\ 378 \\ \hline 650 \end{array} \uparrow$$

Solution: Larry used 650 puzzle pieces.

Another Example

Money

$$\begin{array}{r} {}^{1\ \ 1} \\ \$3.45 \\ +\ 2.98 \\ \hline \$6.43 \end{array}$$

Bring down the decimal point and the dollar sign.

Explain Your Thinking

- ▶ Why do you sometimes need to regroup when you add?
- ▶ How are adding whole numbers and adding money alike? How are they different?

Guided Practice

Find each sum.

1. 67 + 75

2. 374 + 148

3. $2.94 + 6.76

4. $4.28 + 1.79

Ask Yourself

- What is the sum of the ones? Do I have to regroup?
- What is the sum of the tens? Do I have to regroup?

Independent Practice

Add. Check by adding upward.

5. 354 + 549

6. 278 + 134

7. $4.45 + 3.75

8. 689 + 239

9. 243 + 498

10. $5.75 + 3.28

11. 149 + 778

12. $6.24 + 2.89

13. 636 + 192

14. $1.51 + 3.28

15. 135 + 648

16. 477 + 239

17. 234 + 498

18. 313 + 485

19. $3.82 + $5.35

20. 134 + 183

21. 435 + 208

22. $4.23 + $1.72

Problem Solving • Reasoning

23. A hobby store sold 175 more puzzles than board games. If the hobby store sold 256 board games, how many puzzles did it sell?

24. Taylor has twice as many model cars as Brian has. If Brian has 8 model cars, how many model cars does Taylor have?

25. **Analyze** A rocket display was visited by 57 people. An airplane display was visited by 26 more people than visited the rocket display. How many people visited the two displays?

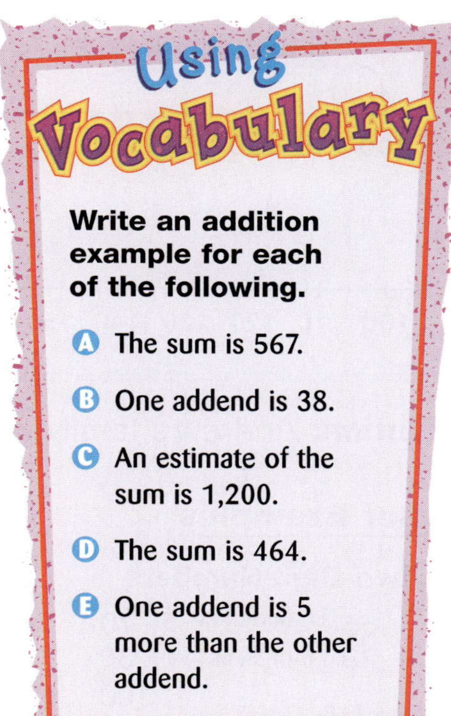

Write an addition example for each of the following.

A The sum is 567.

B One addend is 38.

C An estimate of the sum is 1,200.

D The sum is 464.

E One addend is 5 more than the other addend.

Mixed Review • Test Prep

Write each number. *(pages 4–5, 18–19)*

26. 600 + 70 + 9

27. 800 + 60 + 7

28. 4,000 + 500 + 30 + 2

29. 3,000 + 200 + 10 + 1

30 Which of these is equal to 3 quarters and 3 dimes? *(pages 58–60)*

A $0.90 **B** $0.95 **C** $1.05 **D** $1.30

Extra Practice See Set C on page 146.

Estimate Sums

You will learn how to round numbers to estimate sums.

New Vocabulary
estimate

Learn About It

Andrew's family is driving 208 miles from Salt Lake City to Idaho Falls. Then they are driving 182 miles farther to Yellowstone National Park. About how far will they drive?

If you do not need an exact answer, you can estimate. When you **estimate**, you find an answer that is close to the exact answer.

Estimate the distance Andrew's family will drive.

Estimate 208 + 182.
Round each number to the greatest place.
Then add.

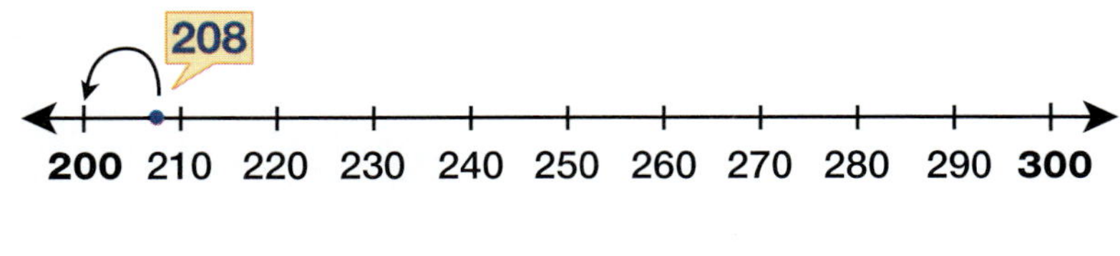

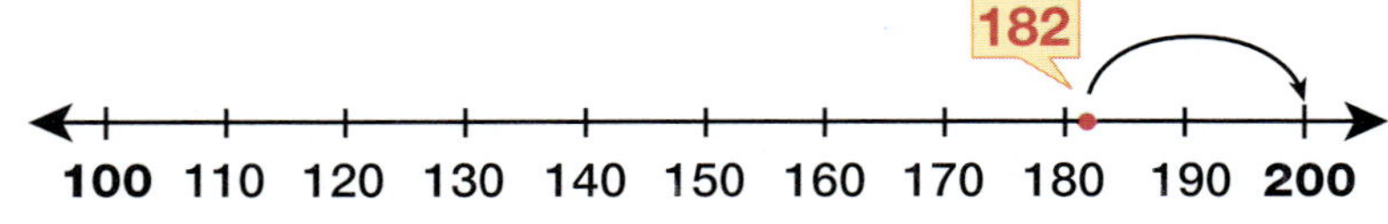

208	rounds to	200
+ 182	rounds to	+ 200
		400

Solution: Andrew's family will drive *about* 400 miles.

Other Examples

A. Two-Digit Numbers

65	rounds to	70
+ 29	rounds to	+ 30
		100

65 + 29 is *about* 100.

Remember
Since the ones digit in 65 is 5, 65 rounded to the nearest 10 is 70.

B. Money

$1.86	rounds to	$2.00
+ 4.15	rounds to	+ 4.00
		$6.00

$1.86 + $4.15 is *about* $6.00.

Explain Your Thinking

► Explain how you can tell if the estimated sum is greater or less than the exact answer?

Guided Practice

Round each number to the greatest place. Then add.

1. 54 + 65 **2.** 68 + 43 **3.** 53 + 87

4. 225 + 572 **5.** 376 + 533 **6.** $3.32 + $1.42

Ask Yourself

- To what place should I round each number?
- How many zeros should the estimate have?

Independent Practice

Round each number to the greatest place. Then add.

7. 47 + 64 **8.** 29 + 37 **9.** 53 + 49 **10.** 71 + 17 **11.** 36 + 42

12. 346 + 389 **13.** $2.84 + 1.72 **14.** 384 + 525 **15.** $6.55 + 1.07 **16.** 164 + 837

17. $8.34 + 1.26 **18.** 314 + 726 **19.** $6.72 + 3.61 **20.** 521 + 228 **21.** $1.29 + 4.21

22. $8.52 + $2.84 **23.** 311 + 918 **24.** 224 + 572 **25.** $6.84 + $2.75

Problem Solving • Reasoning

Use the sign for Problems 26 and 27.

26. **Estimate** About how many campsites are nearby for Andrew's family to choose from?

27. **Money** How much would it cost Andrew and his family to enter the park and spend 3 nights at the Indian Creek campsite?

28. Andrew's family spent $185 for food and $120 for gasoline on their camping trip. About how much did they spend for food and gasoline?

Mixed Review • Test Prep

Name each month. *(pages 80–82)*

29. The tenth month of the year **30.** The fifth month of the year

31 What is 7,860 rounded to the nearest hundred? *(pages 24–26)*

A 7,000 **B** 7,800 **C** 7,900 **D** 8,000

Extra Practice See Set D on page 146.

Problem-Solving Skill: Exact Answer or Estimate

You will learn when you need an estimate and when you need an exact answer.

Before you start to solve a problem, you must decide whether you need an estimate or an exact answer.

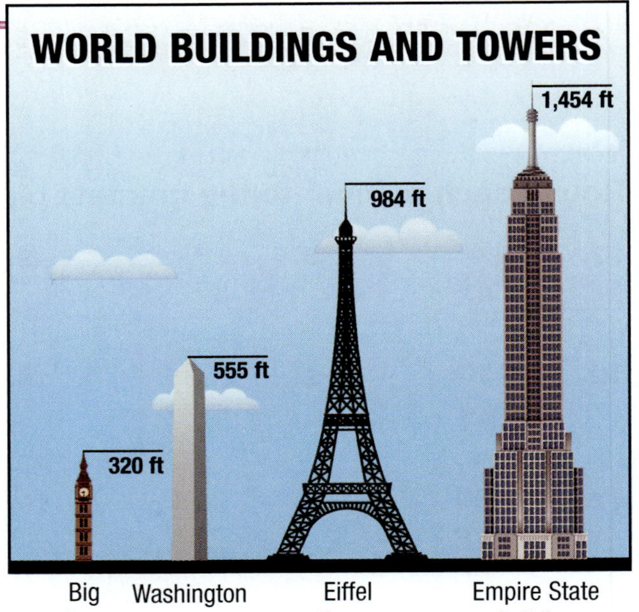

Think about this situation.

Landmark Tower in Japan is 416 feet taller than the Washington Monument.

What do you know?

- Landmark Tower is 416 feet taller than the Washington Monument.
- The height of the Washington Monument is 555 feet.

Sometimes you need an exact answer.

Suppose someone asks you, "How tall is Landmark Tower?"

Since the question asks for the exact height, you need to find 555 feet + 416 feet.

$$\begin{array}{r} \overset{1}{5}55 \text{ feet} \\ +\ 416 \text{ feet} \\ \hline 971 \text{ feet} \end{array}$$

Landmark Tower is 971 feet tall.

Sometimes you need an estimate.

Suppose someone asks you, "About how tall is Landmark Tower?"

Since the question asks "about how tall," your answer can be an estimate.

555 rounds to 600 feet
\+ 416 rounds to + 400 feet
1,000 feet

Landmark Tower is about 1,000 feet tall.

Look Back Suppose someone asked you about the number of windows in the Empire State Building. When might an exact number be needed? When might an estimate be enough?

The Petronas Twin Towers, in Kuala Lumpur, Malaysia, are among the world's tallest buildings.

Guided Practice

Use the information on page 112. Write whether you need an estimate or an exact answer. Then solve.

1. A city is planning to build a tower that is 475 feet taller than Big Ben in London, England. How tall will the new building be?

   Think: How tall is Big Ben?

2. The Petronas Towers are 499 feet taller than the Eiffel Tower in Paris, France. Are the Towers greater than 1,500 feet tall?

   Think: Can you estimate to solve?

Choose a Strategy

For problems 3-6 write whether you need an estimate or an exact answer. Then solve. Use these or other strategies.

Problem-Solving Strategies

- **Draw a Picture**
- **Use Logical Thinking**
- **Write a Number Sentence**

3. During a tour of New York, 32 more people visited the Empire State Building than the World Trade Center. If 29 people visited the World Trade Center, how many people visited the Empire State Building?

4. Central Plaza is 672 feet taller than the Washington Monument. The Petronas Towers are 256 feet taller than Central Plaza. About how much taller are the Petronas Towers than the Washington Monument?

5. Suppose you get on an elevator on the 40th floor of a building. The elevator goes up 2 floors, then down 6 floors, then up 3 floors. What floor are you on now?

6. Library Tower in California has 18 more floors than Society Tower in Ohio. If Society Tower has 57 floors, how many floors does Library Tower have?

7. **Write About It** Two tour groups want to go to the Eiffel Tower. One group has 33 people. The other has 28 people. In what situation might it be an advantage to know the exact number of people?

8. The World Trade Center is taller than the Empire State Building but shorter than the Petronas Towers. The Empire State Building is taller than the Landmark Tower. List the buildings in order from shortest to tallest.

Extra Practice See 1–4 on page 149.

Quick Check

Check Your Understanding of Lessons 1–5

Find the missing numbers.

1. $3 + 6 = 6 + \blacksquare$

2. $5 + \blacksquare = 5$

3. $2 + 5 + 4 = 5 + \blacksquare + 4$

Add.

4. $\begin{array}{r} 37 \\ +\ 28 \\ \hline \end{array}$

5. $\begin{array}{r} 567 \\ +\ 226 \\ \hline \end{array}$

6. $\begin{array}{r} \$3.64 \\ +\ 2.18 \\ \hline \end{array}$

7. $\begin{array}{r} 46 \\ +\ 57 \\ \hline \end{array}$

8. $\begin{array}{r} 394 \\ +\ 226 \\ \hline \end{array}$

9. $\begin{array}{r} \$1.98 \\ +\ 2.29 \\ \hline \end{array}$

Round each number to the greatest place. Then add the rounded numbers.

10. $\begin{array}{r} 23 \\ +\ 36 \\ \hline \end{array}$

11. $\begin{array}{r} 593 \\ +\ 241 \\ \hline \end{array}$

12. $\begin{array}{r} 112 \\ +\ 382 \\ \hline \end{array}$

13. The driving distance from Albany, New York, to New York City is 160 miles. The distance from New York City to Baltimore, Maryland, is 197 miles. How many miles is it from Albany to Baltimore?

14. The driving distance from San Diego, California, to Los Angeles is 118 miles. The distance from Los Angeles to San Francisco is 384 miles. About how many miles is it from San Diego to San Francisco?

How did you do?

If you had difficulty with any items in the Quick Check, you can use the following pages for review and extra practice.

Items	Review These Pages	Do These Extra Practice Items
1–3	pages 102–103	Set A, page 146
4–6	pages 104–106	Set B, page 146
7–9	pages 108–109	Set C, page 146
10–12	pages 110–111	Set D, page 146
13–14	pages 112–113	1–4, page 149

Test Prep • Cumulative Review

Maintaining the Standards

Choose the letter of the correct answer. If a correct answer is not here, choose NH.

1. Kennedy School students collected labels from cans. The third grade collected 247 labels, and the fourth grade collected 236 labels. How many labels did they collect in all?

   A 13 **C** 483
   B 411 **D** NH

2. What time does the clock show?

   F 1:45 **H** 2:45
   G 2:15 **J** 3:00

3. Tara played soccer for one and a half hours. Which number sentence could be used to find the number of minutes Tara played soccer?

   A $60 + 30 = \blacksquare$
   B $60 + 60 = \blacksquare$
   C $60 - 30 = \blacksquare$
   D $60 - 15 = \blacksquare$

4. Which of the following is equal to 305?

   F $30 + 5$
   G $300 + 50$
   H $30 + 50$
   J $300 + 5$

Use the table for Questions 5–6.

Cookie Sale	
Cookie	**Boxes Sold**
Chocolate chip	495
Mint	493
Peanut butter	572

5. About how many boxes of chocolate chip cookies were sold?

   A 300
   B 500
   C 600
   D 700

6. How many boxes of chocolate chip cookies and mint cookies were sold?

   F 818
   G 878
   H 918
   J NH

7. The Hart family traveled 169 miles on Monday and 183 miles on Tuesday. How many miles did they travel in all?

   Explain How did you find your answer?

Safe Site

Internet Test Prep
Visit **www.eduplace.com/kids/mhm** for more *Test Prep Practice.*

LESSON 6

Column Addition

You will learn how to add 3 or more addends.

Learn About It

Jana's class collected items for a recycling project. They collected 124 cans, 78 plastic bottles, and 52 glass bottles. How many items did the class collect?

Add. **124 + 78 + 52 = ■**

Find 124 + 78 + 52.

Step 1 Add the ones.
4 + 8 + 2 = 14 ones

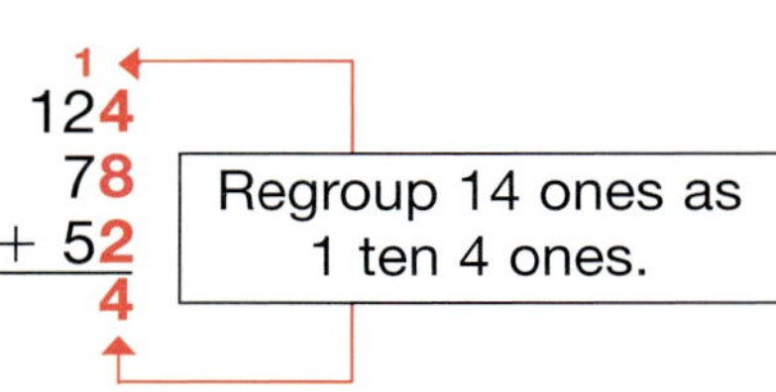

Be sure to line up the numbers correctly.

Step 2 Add the tens.
1 + 2 + 7 + 5 = 15

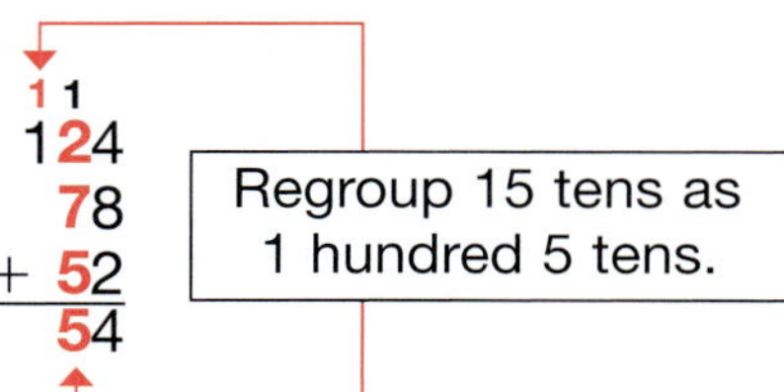

Step 3 Add the hundreds.
1 + 1 = 2

```
  1 1
  124
   78
+  52
  254
```

Solution: The class collected 254 items.

Check your work.
You can check by adding upward.

```
  1 1
  124 ↑
   78 |
+  52 |
  254
```

Other Examples

A. Money

```
   2 1
  $1.62
   2.99
+  4.76
  $9.37
```

B. Regroup Hundreds

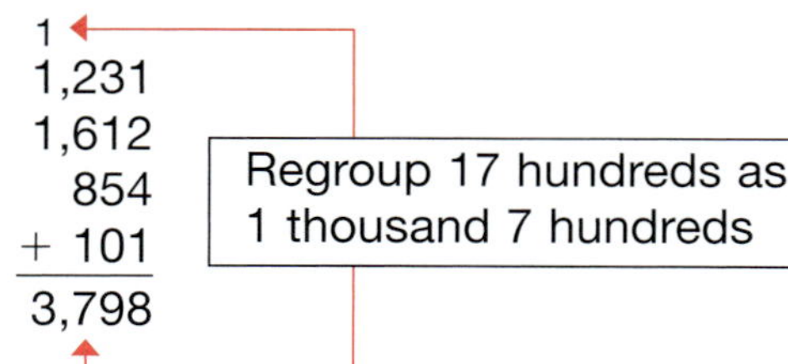

Explain Your Thinking

► What is the greatest number of ones you would ever regroup as tens when you add three numbers?

Guided Practice

Find each sum.

1. $\begin{array}{r} 62 \\ 15 \\ +\ 17 \\ \hline \end{array}$ **2.** $\begin{array}{r} \$1.54 \\ 2.18 \\ +\ 4.63 \\ \hline \end{array}$ **3.** $\begin{array}{r} 18 \\ 243 \\ +\ 71 \\ \hline \end{array}$ **4.** $\begin{array}{r} 601 \\ 319 \\ +172 \\ \hline \end{array}$

5. 32 + 28 + 41 + 36 **6.** 370 + 320 + 345

Ask Yourself

- What is the sum of the ones? Do I have to regroup?
- What is the sum of the tens? Do I have to regroup?

Independent Practice

Add. Check by adding in a different order.

7. $\begin{array}{r} 12 \\ 14 \\ +\ 42 \\ \hline \end{array}$ **8.** $\begin{array}{r} 25 \\ 25 \\ +\ 45 \\ \hline \end{array}$ **9.** $\begin{array}{r} 51 \\ 24 \\ +\ 63 \\ \hline \end{array}$ **10.** $\begin{array}{r} 67 \\ 33 \\ +\ 21 \\ \hline \end{array}$ **11.** $\begin{array}{r} \$42 \\ 33 \\ +\ 13 \\ \hline \end{array}$

12. $\begin{array}{r} 381 \\ 252 \\ +\ 211 \\ \hline \end{array}$ **13.** $\begin{array}{r} \$5.25 \\ 1.46 \\ +\ 1.24 \\ \hline \end{array}$ **14.** $\begin{array}{r} 704 \\ 372 \\ +\ 118 \\ \hline \end{array}$ **15.** $\begin{array}{r} \$3.06 \\ 1.09 \\ +\ 2.50 \\ \hline \end{array}$ **16.** $\begin{array}{r} 588 \\ 236 \\ +\ 118 \\ \hline \end{array}$

17. $\begin{array}{r} 128 \\ 34 \\ +\ 19 \\ \hline \end{array}$ **18.** $\begin{array}{r} 45 \\ 438 \\ +\ 226 \\ \hline \end{array}$ **19.** $\begin{array}{r} 549 \\ 735 \\ +\ 76 \\ \hline \end{array}$ **20.** $\begin{array}{r} 23 \\ 238 \\ 340 \\ +\ 152 \\ \hline \end{array}$ **21.** $\begin{array}{r} 1,121 \\ 225 \\ 321 \\ +\ 425 \\ \hline \end{array}$

22. 23 + 24 + 41 **23.** 134 + 16 + 32 + 40 **24.** \$5.65 + \$1.20 + \$2.25

25. 142 + 68 + 13 **26.** 184 + 15 + 79 + 12 **27.** \$1.28 + \$2.82 + \$1.63

Algebra • Expressions **Compare. Use $>$, $<$, or $=$ for each $\bigcirc$.**

28. 36 + 0 $\bigcirc$ 36 − 0 **29.** 18 + 6 $\bigcirc$ 18 − 6

30. 24 + 5 $\bigcirc$ 24 + 6 **31.** 54 − 3 $\bigcirc$ 54 − 4

32. 29 + 34 $\bigcirc$ 34 + 29 **33.** 23 + 38 $\bigcirc$ 19 + 42

Write *true* or *false*. Give an example to support your answer.

34. Changing the order of the addends changes the sum.

35. The sum of two numbers is never equal to one of the addends.

Problem Solving • Reasoning

Solve. Choose a method. Use the graph for Problems 36–39.

Computation Methods

- Mental Math
- Estimation
- Paper and Pencil

36. How many bottles has Mr. Campo's class collected in all?

37. About how many cans have been collected?

38. The students used some of the glass bottles for art projects. They used 45 bottles for flower vases, 10 bottles for sculptures, and 35 bottles for sand art. How many glass bottles were used in all?

39. **Analyze** Mrs. Lee's class collected 13 more plastic bottles and 11 more glass bottles than Mr. Campo's class. How many bottles did the two classes collect altogether?

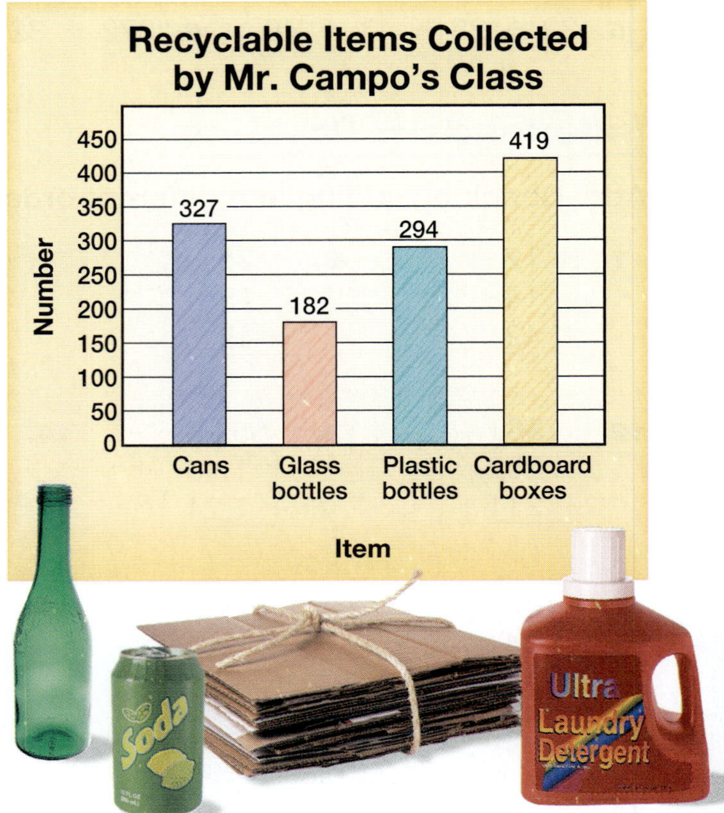

Mixed Review • Test Prep

How many days are there in each month? *(pages 80–82)*

40. April **41.** August **42.** November **43.** January

44 Where should the minute hand point if it is 1:45? *(pages 68–69)*

A 1 **C** 9
B 3 **D** 12

45 What time does the clock show? *(pages 70–72)*

F 3:25 **H** 2:25
G 4:25 **J** 5:15

Extra Practice See Set E on page 147.

Practice Game

Add It Up!

Practice addition by playing this game with a partner.
Try to be the first person to earn 50 points!

What You'll Need

- *a number cube labeled 1 to 6*
- *a number cube labeled 4 to 9*

Players
2

Here's What to Do

1. The first player rolls both number cubes and writes a two-digit number using the rolled numbers. Then he or she rolls both cubes again and writes another two-digit number.
2. The first player then finds the sum of the two numbers. The other player checks that the addition is correct. The ones digit of the sum is the number of points that the first player earns for this turn.
3. Players take turns repeating Steps 1 and 2. Each player keeps a record of his or her total number of points. The first player to reach a total of 50 points wins.

Share Your Thinking Suppose you always write the greatest ones digit possible in each addend. Will that always give you the greatest possible ones digit in the sum? Give an example to support your thinking.

LESSON 7

Add Greater Numbers

You will learn how to add 2 four-digit numbers.

Learn About It

The bowl sculpture at the right was built with 1,135 cans. The taxi was made from 1,566 cans. How many cans were used to build both sculptures?

Add. **1,135 + 1,566 = ■**

Find 1,135 + 1,566.

Step 1 Add the ones.
5 + 6 = 11

```
     1
  1,135
+ 1,566
      1
```

Regroup 11 ones as 1 ten 1 one.

Step 2 Add the tens.
1 + 3 + 6 = 10

```
    1 1
  1,135
+ 1,566
     01
```

Regroup 10 tens as 1 hundred 0 tens.

Step 3 Add the hundreds.
1 + 1 + 5 = 7

```
    1 1
  1,135
+ 1,566
    701
```

Step 4 Add the thousands.
1 + 1 = 2

```
    1 1
  1,135
+ 1,566
  2,701
```

Check your work. Estimate to the nearest hundred.

```
  1,135  rounds to    1,100
+ 1,566  rounds to  + 1,600
                      2,700
```

2,701 is a reasonable answer.

Solution: There were 2,701 cans used to build both sculptures.

Other Examples

A. Money

```
   1 1 1
  $23.45
+  19.79
  $43.24
```

B. Zeros in the Addends

```
   1   1
   1,603
 + 3,509
   5,112
```

Explain Your Thinking

► Why can you add numbers in a different order to check that your sum is correct?

Guided Practice

Find each sum. Estimate to check.

1. 3,838 + 2,165 **2.** $79.25 + 11.54 **3.** 4,025 + 3,082

Ask Yourself

- What is the sum of each column of digits? Do I need to regroup?

Independent Practice

Find each sum. Estimate to check.

4. 4,128 + 2,354 **5.** $15.99 + 23.25 **6.** 3,192 + 5,466 **7.** 3,834 + 2,788 **8.** 1,709 + 3,402

9. $35.29 + 17.64 **10.** 5,617 + 1,828 **11.** 4,829 + 2,354 **12.** 2,198 + 1,362 **13.** 3,872 + 4,129

14. 1,345 + 3,224 **15.** 3,103 + 1,903 **16.** 5,380 + 1,046 **17.** $24.68 + $12.99

18. 4,872 + 1,958 **19.** 6,134 + 3,453 **20.** 4,198 + 4,726 **21.** $40.36 + $38.25

Problem Solving • Reasoning

22. During Game Week, the third grade used 1,678 more dominoes to build a path than the second grade. If the second grade used 1,543 dominoes, how many dominoes did the third grade use?

23. **Analyze** Will has 12 more dominoes than Eric. Eric has 72 dominoes. How many dominoes do the boys have together?

24. **Write About It** Laura used 1,516 cards to build a house. Justin has 948 cards, and Carlos has 580 cards. Can Justin and Carlos build a house that uses as many cards as Laura's? Explain.

Mixed Review • Test Prep

Round each number to the nearest hundred. *(pages 24–26)*

25. 3,638 **26.** 8,495 **27.** 5,312 **28.** 2,883

29 Which sum is closest to 800? *(pages 110–111)*

A 564 + 186 **B** 516 + 180 **C** 437 + 163 **D** 696 + 185

Extra Practice See Set F on page 147.

Problem-Solving Strategy: Guess and Check

You will learn how to use the Guess and Check strategy to solve a problem.

The wingspan of the butterfly in the picture is 2 centimeters more than that of the moth. Together the two lengths total 62 centimeters. What is the wingspan of the butterfly? What is the wingspan of the moth?

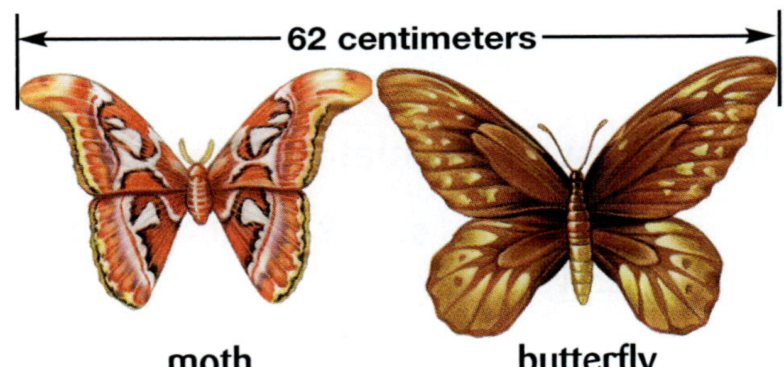

Understand

What are the questions?

- What is the wingspan of the butterfly?
- What is the wingspan of the moth?

What do you know?

- The two lengths total 62 centimeters.
- The wingspan of a butterfly is 2 centimeters more than that of a moth.

Plan

How can you solve the problem?

Guess two numbers whose difference is 2. Then add to check to see if their sum is 62. Then continue guessing and checking until you find numbers that work.

Solve

First Guess: 31 and 29

Check: $31 + 29 = 60$

$60 < 62$

60 is too small. Guess again.

Second Guess: 32 and 30

Check: $32 + 30 = 62$

$32 - 30 = 2$

30 and 32 are correct.

The wingspan of the butterfly is 32 centimeters.
The wingspan of the moth is 30 centimeters.

Look Back

Look back at the solution.

How can you use the results of one guess to decide what your next guess should be?

The Tooth Cave ground beetle is an endangered species in the United States.

Guided Practice

Solve these problems, using the Guess and Check strategy.

1. In the United States, there are 9 more endangered species of butterflies than endangered species of beetles. Together, the total is 25. How many endangered species of butterflies are there in the United States? How many beetles?

What should the sum of the two numbers be?

2. Emily and Jacob each found different sites on the Internet about grasshoppers. Emily found 4 more sites than Jacob found. The total number of sites they found was 18. How many sites did each of them find?

How much greater is one number than the other?

Choose a Strategy

Solve. Use these or other strategies.

Problem-Solving Strategies

- **Guess and Check**
- **Use Logical Thinking**
- **Write a Number Sentence**

3. Lin has 6 more butterfly pictures than Bea. Together they have 22 butterfly pictures. How many butterfly pictures does each girl have?

4. Billie Joe saw 28 birds in the park. He saw 23 more birds as he walked home from the park. About how many birds did Billie Joe see?

5. A class had 21 caterpillars. They all turned into either butterflies or moths. There were 3 more moths than butterflies. How many of each insect were there?

6. **Write About It** John has 15 more pictures of butterflies than of moths. If he has 18 pictures of moths, does he have more than 50 pictures in all? Explain.

7. Shani drew 4 pictures of insects. She drew a grasshopper first. She drew a ladybug before she drew a butterfly but after she drew a cricket. In what order did she draw the pictures?

Extra Practice See 5–7 on page 149.

Quick Check

Check Your Understanding of Lessons 6–8

Find each sum.

1.
```
  12
  23
 +41
```

2.
```
  28
  63
 +50
```

3.
```
 $263
  341
+  25
```

4.
```
  435
  207
 +684
```

Add.

5.
```
  3,254
 +2,138
```

6.
```
  $12.68
 + 35.47
```

7.
```
  5,726
 +1,537
```

8.
```
  4,765
 +3,258
```

9. Kyle cut two boards for his art project. One board is 6 centimeters longer than the other. The two lengths added together are 76 centimeters. What are the lengths of the two boards?

10. Allison has 30 more coins in her collection than Shelby has. The total number of coins in both collections is 340. How many coins does each person have?

How did you do?

If you had difficulty with any items in the Quick Check, you can use the following pages for review and extra practice.

Items	Review These Pages	Do These Extra Practice Items
1–4	pages 116–118	Set E, page 147
5–8	pages 120–121	Set F, page 147
9–10	pages 122–123	5–7, page 149

Test Prep • Cumulative Review

Maintaining the Standards

Choose the letter of the correct answer. If a correct answer is not here, choose NH.

1. Paul took 15 minutes to clean his room. He finished at 2:00 P.M. Which clock shows the time he began?

   A 1:45 **C** 1:35
   B 1:50 **D** 2:15

2. What is the total cost for both items?

   F $7.48
   G $8.48
   H $8.75
   J NH

3. Kim used 98 beads for one necklace and 75 beads for another necklace. Which number sentence could be used to find the total number of beads used?

   A 98 − 75 = ■
   B 98 + 75 = ■
   C ■ + 75 = 98
   D ■ − 98 = 75

Use the table for Questions 4–5.

Ticket Sales	
Movie	**Tickets Sold**
100 Hounds	315
Flying South	298
Sleepy Kitten	512

4. How many tickets were sold for 100 Hounds and Flying South?

   F 183 **H** 613
   G 603 **J** 750

5. How many tickets were sold all together?

   A 800 **C** 1,025
   B 925 **D** 1,125

6. Sal's lunch costs $4.75 and Jill's lunch costs $3.50. What is the total cost of the lunches?

   F $7.25 **H** $8.50
   G $8.25 **J** NH

7. What number should go in the box to make this number sentence true?

   5 + ■ = 11

   Explain How did you find your answer?

Safe Site

Internet Test Prep
Visit **www.eduplace.com/kids/mhm** for more *Test Prep Practice.*

LESSON 9 Subtraction Strategies and Properties

You will learn ways to find differences in subtraction.

Learn About It

Here are some subtraction strategies and properties.

Subtraction Strategies

Count Back

When you subtract 1, 2, or 3, you can count back.

Find 11 − 2.

5 6 7 8 9 10 11 12 13 14 15

Start at 11. Count back 2 numbers.
You end up at 9.

11 − 2 = 9

Count Up

When you subtract numbers that are close, you can count up.

Find 13 − 10.

5 6 7 8 9 10 11 12 13 14 15

Start at 10. Count up to 13.
You counted 3 spaces.

13 − 10 = 3

Subtraction Properties

Subtract Zero

When you subtract 0 from a number, the difference is that number.

Find 3 − 0.

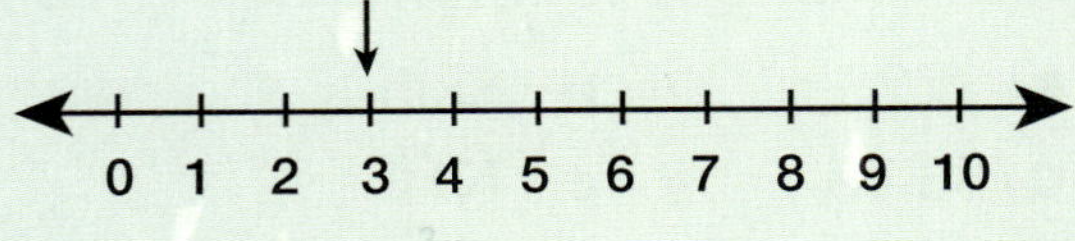

3 − 0 = 3

Subtract a Number From Itself

When you subtract a number from itself, the difference is zero.

Find 6 − 6.

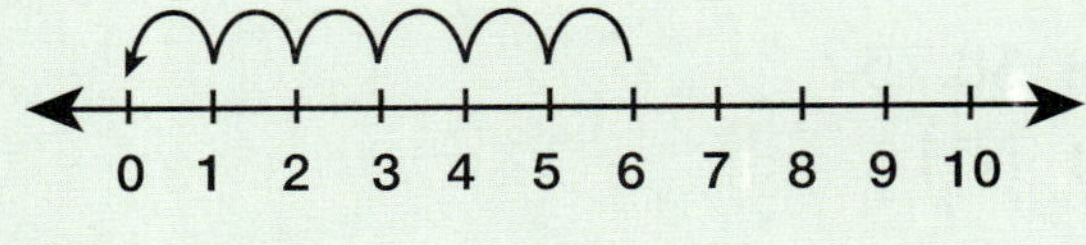

6 − 6 = 0

Explain Your Thinking

► Use a number line to show whether it is easier to count up or count back to find 8 − 1.

Guided Practice

Find each difference.

1. 12 − 3 **2.** 11 − 9 **3.** 10 − 3 **4.** 10 − 10

5. 18 − 0 **6.** 14 − 5 **7.** 16 − 16 **8.** 13 − 3

Ask Yourself

- Are the numbers the same?
- Is one of the numbers zero?

Independent Practice

Subtract.

9. 11 − 1 **10.** 15 − 0 **11.** 13 − 10 **12.** 18 − 18 **13.** 17 − 9 **14.** 12 − 2

15. 16 − 8 **16.** 10 − 7 **17.** 14 − 0 **18.** 12 − 4 **19.** 17 − 17 **20.** 16 − 10

21. 13 − 13 **22.** 16 − 0 **23.** 12 − 3 **24.** 13 − 11 **25.** 19 − 19

26. 12 − 8 **27.** 14 − 14 **28.** 15 − 8 **29.** 19 − 0 **30.** 14 − 9

Algebra • Properties **Find each missing number.**

31. 13 − ■ = 13 **32.** ■ − 15 = 0 **33.** 0 = 16 − ■ **34.** 11 − 11 = ■

35. ■ − 0 = 18 **36.** ■ − 14 = 0 **37.** ■ − 20 = 0 **38.** 0 = 17 − ■

Problem Solving • Reasoning

39. I am the difference when 0 is subtracted from 24. What number am I?

40. The difference is 0 when I am subtracted from 16. What number am I?

41. Think about 15 − 5. Will you get the same answer when you count back from 15 as when you count up from 5? Explain.

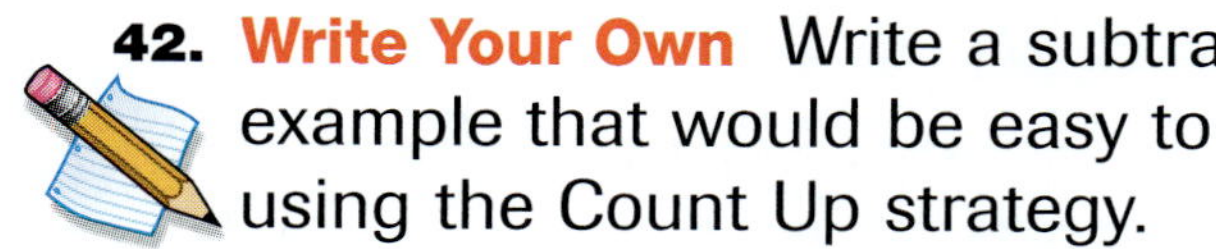

42. **Write Your Own** Write a subtraction example that would be easy to solve by using the Count Up strategy.

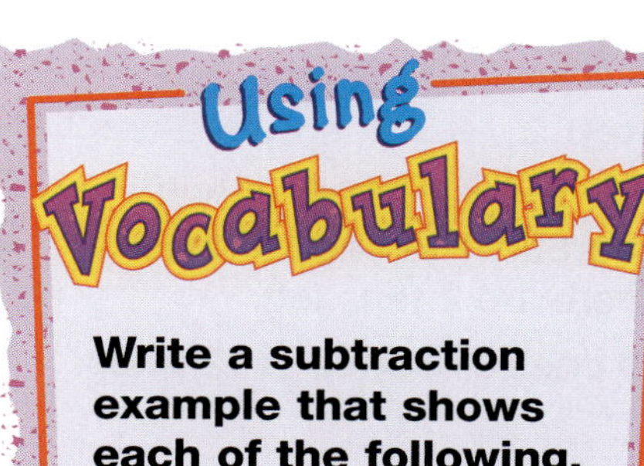

Write a subtraction example that shows each of the following.

- **A** The difference is 4.
- **B** The number subtracted is 8.
- **C** A number is subtracted from 9.
- **D** The difference is 0.
- **E** The difference is 1.

Mixed Review • Test Prep

Write each amount in a way that uses the fewest coins. *(pages 58–60)*

43. 55¢ **44.** 81¢ **45.** 37¢ **46.** 46¢ **47.** 24¢ **48.** 12¢

49 Which number equals 7,000 + 40 + 3? *(pages 18–19)*

A 743 **C** 7,403

B 7,043 **D** 7,000,403

Extra Practice See Set G on page 147.

LESSON 10

Regroup Tens

You will learn how to regroup tens as ones when you subtract.

Learn About It

Tanisha rode on two roller coasters at Funland Amusement Park. The Tornado is 332 feet high and the Comet is 119 feet high. How much higher is the Tornado than the Comet?

Subtract. **332 − 119 = ■**

Find 332 − 119.

Step 1 Show 332.

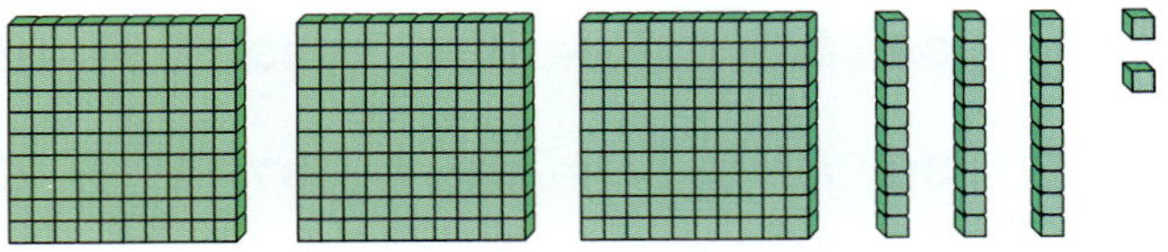

$$\begin{array}{r} 332 \\ -119 \\ \hline \end{array}$$

Step 2 9 > 2, so there are not enough ones to subtract. Regroup 1 ten as 10 ones. There are 2 tens left.

10 ones + 2 ones = 12 ones

$$\begin{array}{r} {}^{2\,12} \\ 3\not{3}\not{2} \\ -119 \\ \hline \end{array}$$

Step 3 Now you can subtract the ones.

12 ones − 9 ones = 3 ones

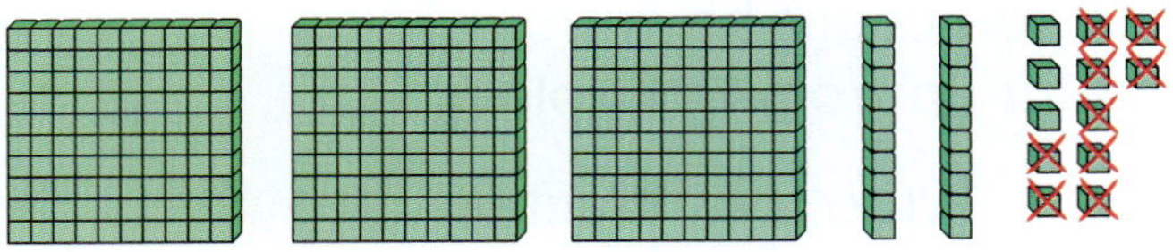

$$\begin{array}{r} {}^{2\,12} \\ 3\not{3}\not{2} \\ -119 \\ \hline 3 \end{array}$$

Step 4 Subtract the tens.

2 tens − 1 ten = 1 ten

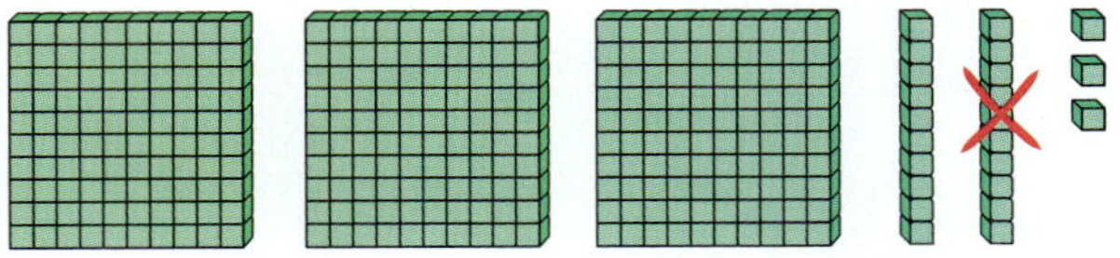

$$\begin{array}{r} {}^{2\,12} \\ 3\not{3}\not{2} \\ -119 \\ \hline 13 \end{array}$$

Step 5 Subtract the hundreds.

3 hundreds − 1 hundred = 2 hundreds

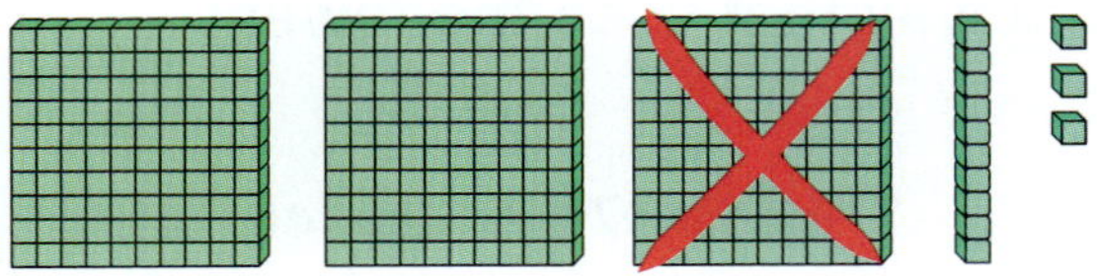

$$\begin{array}{r} {}^{2\,12} \\ 3\not{3}\not{2} \\ -119 \\ \hline 213 \end{array}$$

Solution: The Tornado is 213 feet higher than the Comet.

Other Examples

A. Two-Digit Numbers

$$\begin{array}{r} \scriptstyle 3\,18 \\ \not{4}\not{8} \\ -\,2\,9 \\ \hline 1\,9 \end{array}$$

B. Money

$$\begin{array}{r} \scriptstyle 6\,12 \\ \$7\not{7}\not{2} \\ -\,2\,1\,4 \\ \hline \$5\,5\,8 \end{array}$$

C. Zero in the Tens Place

$$\begin{array}{r} \scriptstyle 3\,16 \\ 8\not{4}\not{6} \\ -\,3\,0\,9 \\ \hline 5\,3\,7 \end{array}$$

Explain Your Thinking

- ▶ Why is it helpful to show that you regrouped 1 ten?
- ▶ How can you tell by looking at an exercise if you need to regroup a ten as ten ones?

Guided Practice

Subtract.

1. $96 − 27 **2.** 45 − 18 **3.** $964 − 381 **4.** 878 − 162

5. 67 − 38 **6.** 438 − 119 **7.** $875 − $432

Ask Yourself

- Are there enough ones to subtract?
- If there are not enough ones, what should I do?

Subtract. Then write yes for each exercise where you regrouped a ten to make 10 ones.

8. 535 − 126 **9.** 829 − 423 **10.** 837 − 345 **11.** 436 − 218 **12.** 943 − 117

Independent Practice

Find each difference.

13. $78 − 39 **14.** 81 − 56 **15.** 55 − 17 **16.** $63 − 44 **17.** 36 − 28

18. 432 − 116 **19.** 265 − 128 **20.** $693 − 266 **21.** 731 − 708 **22.** 963 − 457

23. $91 − $15 **24.** 53 − 29 **25.** $52 − $41 **26.** 87 − 49

27. 765 − 432 **28.** 873 − 225 **29.** 541 − 316 **30.** 45 − 28

Algebra • Functions Complete each table by following the rule.

Rule: Subtract 36

	Input	Output
31.	58	
32.	62	
33.	75	
34.	89	

Rule: Subtract $154

	Input	Output
35.	$286	
36.	$572	
37.	$785	
38.	$991	

Rule: Subtract 328

	Input	Output
39.	769	
40.	544	
41.	496	
42.	651	

Problem Solving • Reasoning

Use Data Use the table for Problems 43–45.

43. **Compare** How much higher is the Tiger roller coaster than the Runner?

44. If the Comet's height is increased by 24 feet, how much shorter than the Tiger will the Comet be?

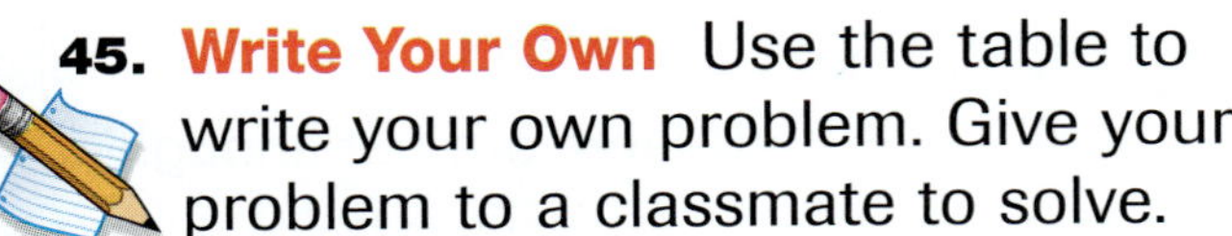

45. **Write Your Own** Use the table to write your own problem. Give your problem to a classmate to solve.

Roller Coaster Heights

Roller Coaster	Height
Comet	119 feet
Runner	228 feet
Tiger	274 feet
Tornado	332 feet

46. **Analyze** A car on the Tiger holds twice as many riders as a car on the Comet. A car on the Comet holds 4 fewer riders than a car on the Tornado. If a car on the Tornado holds 12 riders, how many riders does a car on the Tiger hold?

47. **Logical Thinking** Sue, Julissa, and Kira were in line to ride the Runner. Julissa was not first. Sue was behind Kira. Kira was right in front of Julissa. Who was first in line?

Mixed Review • Test Prep

Write the value of the underlined digit. *(pages 4–5, 18–19, 32–33, 34–35)*

48. $42\underline{2}$ 49. $7{,}\underline{7}89$ 50. $2\underline{6}{,}354$ 51. $41{,}6\underline{8}3$ 52. $2\underline{5}8{,}072$

53. What time is it 3 hours after 6:00 P.M.? *(pages 78–79)*

A 9:00 A.M. **C** 9:00 P.M.

B 3:00 P.M. **D** 3:00 A.M.

Extra Practice See Set H on page 147.

Number Sense

Subtracting in Different Ways

Here are two different ways to subtract.

This is how Carla does subtraction.

$$\begin{array}{r} 67 \\ -\ 9 \\ \hline \end{array} \quad \begin{array}{r} 67 \\ -\ 7 \\ \hline 60 \\ -\ 2 \\ \hline 58 \end{array}$$

Think: $9 = 7 + 2$

So $67 - 9 = 58$.

How does thinking of 9 as 7 + 2 help Carla subtract?

$$\begin{array}{r} 52 \\ -\ 37 \\ \hline \end{array} \quad \begin{array}{r} 52 \\ -\ 2 \\ \hline 50 \\ -\ 30 \\ \hline 20 \\ -\ 5 \\ \hline 15 \end{array}$$

Think: $37 = 2 + 30 + 5$

So $52 - 37 = 15$.

How does thinking of 37 as 2 + 30 + 5 help Carla subtract?

This is how Jeb does subtraction.

$$\begin{array}{r} 67 \\ -\ 9 \\ \hline \end{array} \quad \begin{array}{c} +1 \\ +1 \end{array} \quad \begin{array}{r} 68 \\ -\ 10 \\ \hline 58 \end{array}$$

So $67 - 9 = 58$.

How does adding 1 to each number help Jeb to subtract?

$$\begin{array}{r} 52 \\ -\ 37 \\ \hline \end{array} \quad \begin{array}{c} +3 \\ +3 \end{array} \quad \begin{array}{r} 55 \\ -\ 40 \\ \hline 15 \end{array}$$

So $52 - 37 = 15$.

How does adding 3 to each number help Jeb to subtract?

Try These

Find each difference. Use Carla's, Jeb's, and the standard method.

1. $\begin{array}{r} 43 \\ -\ 7 \\ \hline \end{array}$ **2.** $\begin{array}{r} 22 \\ -\ 9 \\ \hline \end{array}$ **3.** $\begin{array}{r} 54 \\ -\ 6 \\ \hline \end{array}$ **4.** $\begin{array}{r} 87 \\ -\ 28 \\ \hline \end{array}$ **5.** $\begin{array}{r} 52 \\ -\ 36 \\ \hline \end{array}$

Explain Your Thinking

► How are the three methods alike? How are they different?

Regroup Tens and Hundreds

You will learn that when you subtract, sometimes you have to regroup both tens and hundreds.

Learn About It

A male lion weighed 430 pounds. A female lion weighed 285 pounds. How much more did the male weigh than the female?

Subtract. **430 − 285 = ■**

Find 430 − 285.

Step 1 5 > 0, so you need to regroup 1 ten as 10 ones.

```
   2 10
  4 3̸ 0̸
− 2 8 5
```

Step 2 Subtract the ones.
10 − 5 = 5

```
   2 10
  4 3̸ 0̸
− 2 8 5
      5
```

Step 3 8 > 2, so you need to regroup 1 hundred as 10 tens.

```
    12
  3 2̸ 10
  4̸ 3̸ 0̸
− 2 8 5
      5
```

Step 4 Subtract the tens.
12 − 8 = 4

```
    12
  3 2̸ 10
  4̸ 3̸ 0̸
− 2 8 5
    4 5
```

Step 5 Subtract the hundreds.
3 − 2 = 1

```
    12
  3 2̸ 10
  4̸ 3̸ 0̸
− 2 8 5
  1 4 5
```

Step 6 Check by using addition.

Problem	**Check**
430	145
− 285	+ 285
145	430

The numbers are the same, so the difference is correct.

Solution: The male weighed 145 pounds more than the female.

Another Example

Money

```
    12
  8 2̸ 14
 $9̸ .3̸ 4̸
− 3 .4 5
 $5 .8 9
```

Bring down the decimal point and the dollar sign.

Explain Your Thinking

- How is subtracting money like subtracting whole numbers?
- Why do you sometimes need to regroup in more than one place?

Guided Practice

Find each difference.

1. 624 − 378

2. \$8.52 − 1.74

3. 962 − 141

4. \$7.28 − 3.49

> **Ask Yourself**
> - Are there enough ones to subtract?
> - Are there enough tens to subtract?

Independent Practice

Subtract. Check by adding.

5. 436 − 158

6. 658 − 379

7. \$7.23 − 2.35

8. 542 − 167

9. 824 − 537

10. \$9.53 − 4.78

11. 318 − 139

12. \$4.52 − 1.74

13. 764 − 291

14. 687 − 353

15. 458 − 121

16. \$8.42 − \$1.79

17. 574 − 268

18. 438 − 175

19. 536 − 289

20. 764 − 132

21. \$8.35 − \$4.71

22. 412 − 263

Problem Solving • Reasoning

23. A male Siberian tiger weighs 650 pounds. A female tiger weighs 365 pounds. How much lighter is the female than the male?

24. **Measurement** At a zoo, animals are fed every 4 hours 4 times a day. If the last feeding is at 6 P.M., at what times are the animals fed each day?

25. **Write About It** Kathy took 162 pictures of a giant panda on Monday. Then on Tuesday she took 128 more pictures. Can she make two collages that each use 150 pictures? Explain.

SCIENCE River hippos usually stay underwater for 3 to 5 minutes at a time. However, they can stay underwater for up to 30 minutes!

Suppose a hippo stays underwater for a quarter of an hour. How many minutes is that?

Mixed Review • Test Prep

Compare. Use >, <, or = for each ⬭. *(pages 58–60)*

26. 7 dimes ⬭ 7 nickels

27. 1 quarter, 3 nickels ⬭ 4 dimes

28 What is the value of the 4 in 78,402? *(pages 4–5, 18–19, 32–33)*

A 40,000 **B** 4,000 **C** 400 **D** 40

Extra Practice See Set I on page 148.

Estimate Differences

You will learn how to round numbers to estimate differences.

Learn About It

The Mustangs scored 292 points during the basketball playoffs this year! That is 112 more points than they earned last year. About how many points did the Mustangs earn last year?

The word *about* tells you that you do not need an exact answer.

Estimate the number of points the team earned last year.

Estimate 292 − 112.

Round each number to the greatest place.
Then subtract.

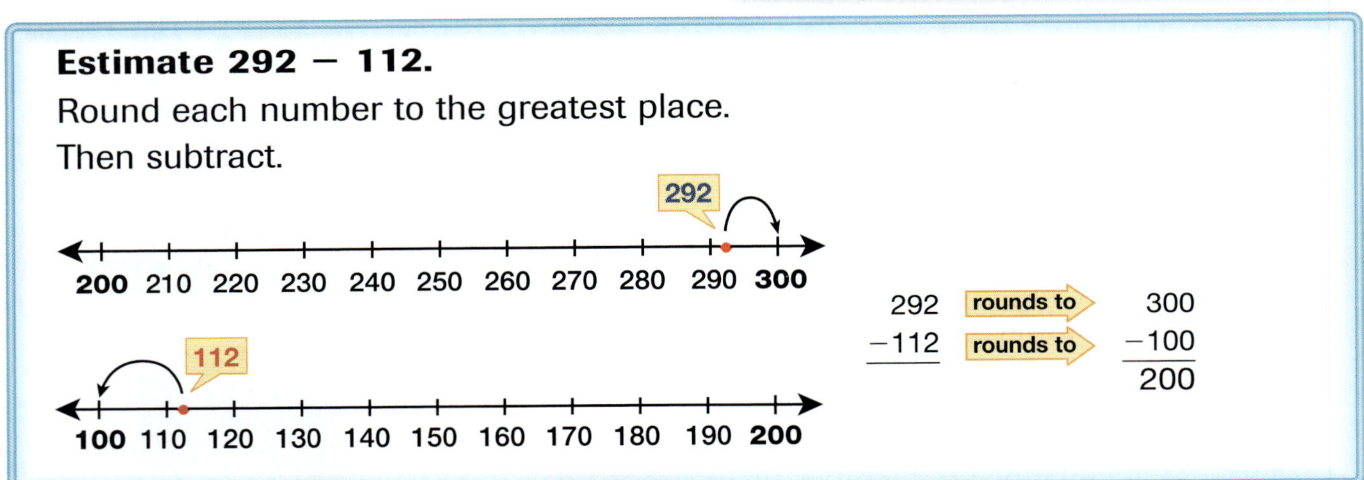

292	rounds to	300
−112	rounds to	−100
		200

Solution: The Mustangs earned *about* 200 points last year.

Other Examples

A. Two-Digit Numbers

85	rounds to	90
− 57	rounds to	− 60
		30

85 − 57 is about 30.

Remember
Since the ones digit in 85 is 5, 85 rounded to the nearest ten is 90.

B. Money

\$4.35	rounds to	\$4.00
− 2.27	rounds to	− 2.00
		\$2.00

\$4.35 − \$2.27 is about \$2.00.

Explain Your Thinking

► How can you use estimation to decide if a difference is reasonable?

Guided Practice

Round each number to the greatest place. Then subtract.

1. 528 − 364 **2.** 78 − 61 **3.** 234 − 132

4. $6.25 − $2.87 **5.** 736 − 187 **6.** $7.62 − $3.48

Ask Yourself

- What place should I round each number to?
- How many zeros should the estimate have?

Independent Practice

Round each number to the greatest place. Then subtract.

7. 84 − 61 **8.** 91 − 44 **9.** 42 − 26 **10.** 39 − 18 **11.** 48 − 22

12. $8.83 − 5.49 **13.** 777 − 192 **14.** $709 − 612 **15.** 941 − 811 **16.** $7.85 − 4.70

Problem Solving • Reasoning

Use Data **Use the table for Problems 17–19.**

17. About how many more points did the Mustangs score than the Hawks?

18. Last year the Bulldogs scored 384 points during the playoffs. How many more points did they score last year than this year?

19. **Write About It** In what situation might it be an advantage to know the exact number of points scored by all of the teams? In what situation might an estimate be enough?

Total Points Scored During Playoffs This Year

Team	Points
Mustangs	292 points
Cougars	218 points
Bulldogs	178 points
Hawks	109 points

Mixed Review • Test Prep

Add. *(pages 104–106)*

20. 43 + 28 **21.** 27 + 65 **22.** 12 + 79 **23.** 45 + 38

24 Which of the following numbers is greater than 1,732 and less than 2,867? *(pages 22–23)*

A 1,723 **B** 2,872 **C** 2,859 **D** 1,730

Extra Practice See Set J on page 148.

Quick Check

Check Your Understanding of Lessons 9–12

Subtract.

1. $\begin{array}{r} 11 \\ -\ 11 \\ \hline \end{array}$

2. $\begin{array}{r} 14 \\ -\ 9 \\ \hline \end{array}$

3. $\begin{array}{r} 16 \\ -\ 0 \\ \hline \end{array}$

4. $\begin{array}{r} 13 \\ -\ 2 \\ \hline \end{array}$

5. $\begin{array}{r} 15 \\ -\ 3 \\ \hline \end{array}$

Find each difference. Check by adding.

6. $\begin{array}{r} 43 \\ -\ 28 \\ \hline \end{array}$

7. $\begin{array}{r} 874 \\ -\ 465 \\ \hline \end{array}$

8. $\begin{array}{r} 635 \\ -\ 128 \\ \hline \end{array}$

9. $\begin{array}{r} 523 \\ -\ 394 \\ \hline \end{array}$

10. $\begin{array}{r} \$8.24 \\ -\ 4.86 \\ \hline \end{array}$

Round each number to the greatest place. Then subtract the rounded numbers.

11. $\begin{array}{r} 64 \\ -\ 32 \\ \hline \end{array}$

12. $\begin{array}{r} 78 \\ -\ 22 \\ \hline \end{array}$

13. $\begin{array}{r} 458 \\ -\ 261 \\ \hline \end{array}$

14. $\begin{array}{r} 614 \\ -\ 263 \\ \hline \end{array}$

15. $\begin{array}{r} 941 \\ -\ 552 \\ \hline \end{array}$

16. Jake's class is selling tickets to their class play. There are 452 seats in the auditorium. The class has sold 275 tickets. How many more tickets do they need to sell to fill the auditorium?

How did you do?

If you had difficulty with any items in the Quick Check, you can use the following pages for review and extra practice.

Items	Review These Pages	Do These Extra Practice Items
1–5	pages 126–127	Set G, page 147
6–8	pages 128–130	Set H, page 147
9–10, 16	pages 132–133	Set I, page 148
11–15	pages 134–135	Set J, page 148

Test Prep • Cumulative Review

Maintaining the Standards

Choose the letter of the correct answer. If a correct answer is not here, choose NH.

1. The school band has 42 boys and 27 girls. How many more boys than girls are in the band?
   - **A** 5
   - **B** 15
   - **C** 25
   - **D** 69

2. Look at the table below.

Input	Output
80	65
70	55
60	45

   What is the rule?
   - **F** Input − 15 = Output
   - **G** Input + 15 = Output
   - **H** Input − 10 = Output
   - **J** Output − 10 = Input

3. Pablo saved $5.59. The cap he wants costs $7.95. How much more money does Pablo need to buy the cap?
   - **A** $2.00
   - **B** $2.36
   - **C** $2.44
   - **D** $3.54

4. What is the value of the underlined digit in 2,3<u>4</u>7?
   - **F** 4,000
   - **G** 40
   - **H** 400
   - **J** 4

5. The Hall family will drive a total of 624 miles to Los Angeles. They have already driven 279 miles. How many more miles do they have to drive?
   - **A** 345
   - **B** 355
   - **C** 903
   - **D** NH

6. Abby uses these bills to buy the stuffed animal.

   How much change should she get?
   - **F** 40¢
   - **G** 50¢
   - **H** 51¢
   - **J** 61¢

7. John, Larry, and Mike collect baseball cards. John has 75 cards. Larry has 92 cards, and Mike has 59 cards. How many more cards does Larry have than Mike?

   Explain How did you find your answer?

Safe Site

Internet Test Prep
Visit **www.eduplace.com/kids/mhm** for more *Test Prep Practice.*

LESSON 13

Subtract Greater Numbers

You will learn how to subtract four-digit numbers.

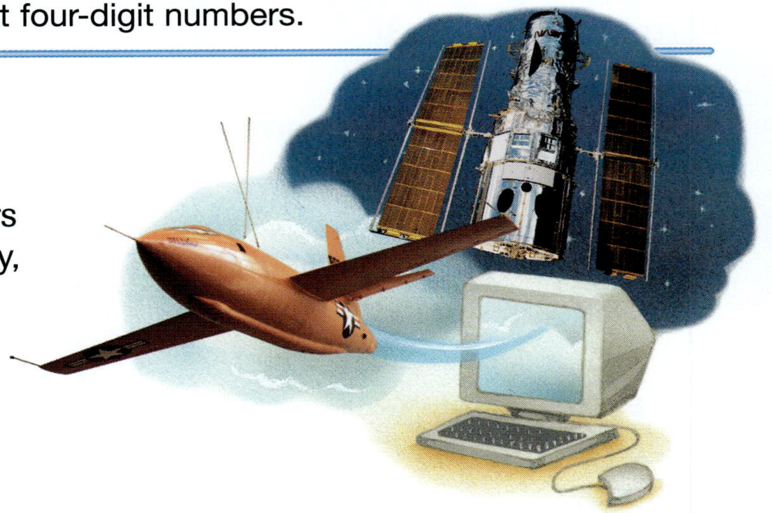

Learn About It

Did you know that the National Air and Space Museum offers virtual tours on the Internet? Suppose one Saturday, 5,632 people took virtual tours while 3,445 people visited the museum. How many more people took virtual tours than visited the museum?

Subtract. **5,632 − 3,445 = ■**

Find 5,632 − 3,445.

Step 1 5 > 2, so you need to regroup 1 ten as 10 ones.

$$\begin{array}{r} \scriptsize{2\,12} \\ 5{,}6\not{3}\not{2} \\ -\ 3{,}445 \\ \hline \end{array}$$

Step 2 Subtract the ones. **12 − 5 = 7**

$$\begin{array}{r} \scriptsize{2\,12} \\ 5{,}6\not{3}\not{2} \\ -\ 3{,}445 \\ \hline 7 \end{array}$$

Step 3 4 > 2, so you need to regroup 1 hundred as 10 tens.

$$\begin{array}{r} \scriptsize{12} \\ \scriptsize{5\,\not{2}\,12} \\ 5{,}\not{6}\not{3}\not{2} \\ -\ 3{,}445 \\ \hline 7 \end{array}$$

Step 4 Subtract the tens. **12 − 4 = 8**

$$\begin{array}{r} \scriptsize{12} \\ \scriptsize{5\,\not{2}\,12} \\ 5{,}\not{6}\not{3}\not{2} \\ -\ 3{,}445 \\ \hline 87 \end{array}$$

Step 5 Subtract the hundreds. **5 − 4 = 1**

$$\begin{array}{r} \scriptsize{12} \\ \scriptsize{5\,\not{2}\,12} \\ 5{,}\not{6}\not{3}\not{2} \\ -\ 3{,}445 \\ \hline 187 \end{array}$$

Step 6 Subtract the thousands. **5 − 3 = 2**

$$\begin{array}{r} \scriptsize{12} \\ \scriptsize{5\,\not{2}\,12} \\ 5{,}\not{6}\not{3}\not{2} \\ -\ 3{,}445 \\ \hline 2{,}187 \end{array}$$

Solution: 2,187 more people took virtual tours than visited the museum on Saturday.

Other Examples

A. Money

$$\begin{array}{r} \scriptsize{12} \\ \scriptsize{3\,\not{2}\,14} \\ \$\not{4}\not{3}.\not{4}6 \\ -\ 28.54 \\ \hline \$14.92 \end{array}$$

B. Zeros

$$\begin{array}{r} \scriptsize{7\,12\,7\,14} \\ \not{8},\not{2}\not{8}\not{4} \\ -\ 3{,}409 \\ \hline 4{,}875 \end{array}$$

Explain Your Thinking

- How would you check to see if your answer was reasonable?
- How would you check your work to see if your answer was correct?

Guided Practice

Subtract.

1. 8,482 − 2,845

2. 6,287 − 1,402

3. $79.18 − 24.26

Ask Yourself

- What is the difference in each column of numbers?
- Do I need to regroup?

Independent Practice

Find each difference. Check by using addition or estimation.

4. 4,828 − 1,476

5. 8,726 − 3,579

6. 3,594 − 1,678

7. $69.25 − 28.39

8. 5,388 − 2,679

9. 9,824 − 6,912

10. $89.72 − 65.95

11. 4,828 − 1,539

12. 7,985 − 4,502

13. $29.25 − 15.12

14. 5,827 − 1,911

15. 7,254 − 3,108

16. 7,629 − 1,815

17. $44.88 − 13.62

18. 8,928 − 6,315

Problem Solving • Reasoning

19. **Estimate** The museum theater has 487 seats, and the planetarium has 230 seats. About how many more seats are in the museum theater?

20. **Analyze** A museum has 5 more displays on the first floor than on the second floor. Together the two floors have 23 displays. How many displays are on each floor?

21. One day, 3,428 people visited a space exhibit, and 1,149 people visited an aircraft exhibit. How many more people visited the space exhibit?

Mixed Review • Test Prep

Add or subtract. *(pages 104–107, 128–129)*

22. 45 + 28

23. 77 − 18

24. 387 + 107

25. 682 − 155

26 What is the sum of $4.18 + $2.31? *(pages 108–109)*

A $1.87 **B** $4.39 **C** $6.49 **D** $6.59

Extra Practice See Set K on page 148.

LESSON 14

Subtract Across Zeros

You will learn how to subtract across zeros.

Learn About It

Kasey collected 300 pennies. She gave 128 of her pennies to her little brother. How many pennies does Kasey have left?

Subtract. **300 − 128 = ■**

Find 300 − 128.

Step 1 There are no ones or tens to subtract from. Regroup 3 hundreds as 2 hundreds 10 tens.	**Step 2** Regroup 10 tens as 9 tens 10 ones.	**Step 3** Subtract ones, tens, and hundreds.
2 10 ~~3~~ ~~0~~ 0 − 1 2 8	9 2 ~~10~~ 10 ~~3~~ ~~0~~ ~~0~~ − 1 2 8	9 2 ~~10~~ 10 ~~3~~ ~~0~~ ~~0~~ − 1 2 8 1 7 2

Solution: Kasey has 172 pennies left.

You can use the same steps when you subtract four-digit numbers.

Find 4,302 − 1,155.

Step 1 $2 < 5$, so you need to regroup. There are no tens to regroup. So regroup 3 hundreds as 2 hundreds 10 tens.	**Step 2** Regroup 10 tens as 9 tens 10 ones.	**Step 3** Subtract ones, tens, hundreds, and thousands.
2 10 4,~~3~~ ~~0~~ 2 − 1,1 5 5	9 2 ~~10~~ 12 4,~~3~~ ~~0~~ ~~2~~ − 1,1 5 5	9 2 ~~10~~ 12 4,~~3~~ ~~0~~ ~~2~~ − 1,1 5 5 3,1 4 7

Explain Your Thinking

► How is regrouping to find 504 − 239 different from regrouping to find 514 − 239?

Guided Practice

Find each difference.

1. 504 − 239   **2.** 900 − 647   **3.** 800 − 726   **4.** 3,405 − 1,267

Ask Yourself

- Are there zeros in the number I am subtracting from?
- If so, what do I do?

Independent Practice

Subtract. Check by using addition or estimation.

5. 707 − 353   **6.** 802 − 577   **7.** 900 − 652   **8.** 700 − 436   **9.** 800 − 725

10. 5,609 − 2,365   **11.** 9,804 − 5,637   **12.** 8,700 − 4,279   **13.** 3,006 − 2,484   **14.** 3,700 − 3,627

15. 808 − 566   **16.** 500 − 288   **17.** 300 − 244

18. 4,702 − 1,391   **19.** 4,400 − 4,211   **20.** 5,008 − 2,125

Problem Solving • Reasoning

21. **Analyze** The library is displaying coins from Asia, Europe, and South America. The number of coins from Asia is twice the number of coins from South America. Use the posters at the right to find the total number of coins on display.

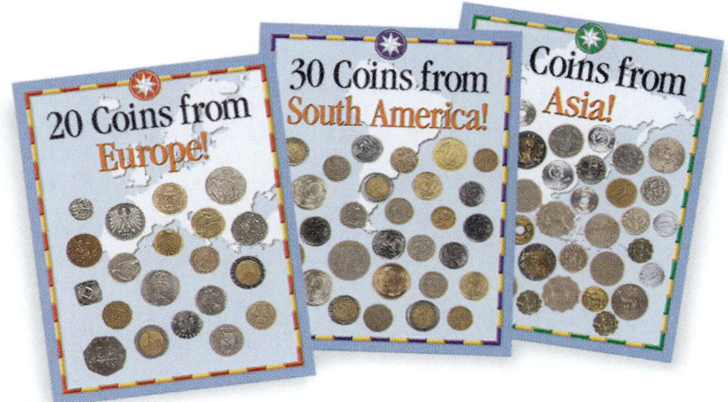

22. The library has 200 coins and 159 bills from Africa. How many more coins than bills from Africa does the library have?

23. **Analyze** Sean has 43 coins in his collection. He has 11 more pennies than nickels. How many nickels are in Sean's collection?

Mixed Review • Test Prep

Round each number to the nearest thousand. *(pages 24–25)*

24. 3,629   **25.** 6,002   **26.** 7,576   **27.** 1,188   **28.** 9,209

29 What is another name for 5 thousands, 7 hundreds 3 tens? *(pages 18–19)*

A 5,730   **B** 573   **C** 5,073   **D** 5,703

Extra Practice See Set L on page 148.

Problem-Solving Application: Use Operations

You will learn how to use addition and subtraction to solve problems.

Sometimes you can use addition and subtraction to solve problems.

Problem A baby is born with 350 bones. As it grows, some of its bones join together. An adult has 206 bones. How many more bones does a baby have?

What is the question?

How many more bones does a baby have?

What do you know?

- An adult has 206 bones.
- A baby is born with 350 bones.

Plan

How can you solve the problem?

Since you want to find how many more bones a baby has than an adult, you need to compare the 2 numbers.

So you should subtract.

Solve

Find 350 − 206.

$$\begin{array}{r} 350 \\ -\ 206 \\ \hline 144 \end{array}$$

A baby has 144 more bones than an adult.

Look back at your answer.

How can you decide if the answer is reasonable by looking back at the problem?

Remember:
- Understand
- Plan
- Solve
- Look Back

Guided Practice

Solve.

1. Human beings grow two sets of teeth: baby teeth and adult teeth. An adult has 32 teeth, and a baby has 20 teeth. How many more teeth does an adult have than a baby?

Do I need to find the total number, or am I comparing numbers?

2. There are many different bones in your body. Your skull has 28 bones. Your spine has 26 bones. How many bones are there altogether in your spine and skull?

Do I need to find the total number, or am I comparing numbers?

Choose a Strategy

Solve. Use these or other strategies.

Problem-Solving Strategies

- **Find a Pattern**
- **Guess and Check**
- **Write a Number Sentence**

3. There are 53 bones altogether in one hand and foot. A hand has one more bone than a foot. How many bones are there in 2 feet?

4. Chiara is 2 inches taller than Paul. Paul is 3 inches shorter than Sam. If Sam is 56 inches tall, how tall is Chiara?

5. A store sells skeleton posters for $12.95 each. Posters of the heart cost one dollar less than skeleton posters. How much would one skeleton poster and one heart poster cost?

6. Exercise is good for bones. One day, Elizabeth did 10 sit-ups. The next day she did 15 sit-ups. The day after that she did 20 sit-ups. How many sit-ups is Elizabeth likely to do on the fifth day? Explain.

7. You use 43 muscles to frown and 15 muscles to smile. How many more muscles do you use to frown than to smile?

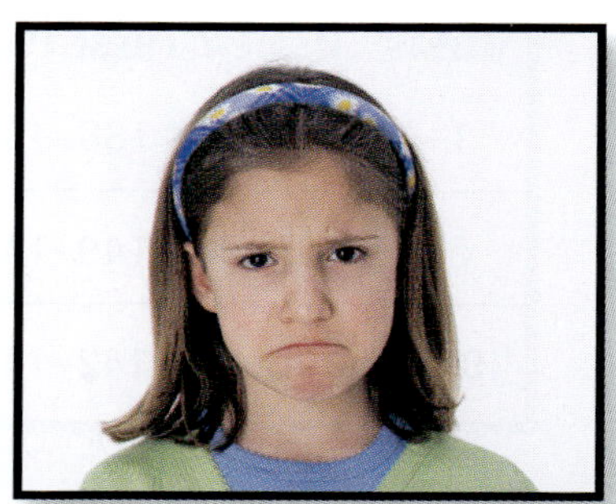

Extra Practice See 8–10 on page 149.

Quick Check

Check Your Understanding of Lessons 13–15

Find each difference. Check by using addition or estimation.

1. $5,676 - 2,464$

2. $\$58.23 - 17.38$

3. $7,162 - 4,539$

4. $9,836 - 3,942$

Find each difference. Check by using addition or estimation.

5. $505 - 274$

6. $903 - 476$

7. $4,307 - 1,452$

8. $6,008 - 2,543$

Solve.

9. Yoshi's family went on vacation. They drove 347 miles the first day and 315 miles the second day. How many miles did they drive altogether? Which operation did you use to find out?

10. Adela is going to visit her grandparents. They live 425 miles away. Adela travels 261 miles the first day. How many miles are left to travel the second day? Which operation did you use to find out?

How did you do?

If you had difficulty with any items in the Quick Check, you can use the following pages for review and extra practice.

Items	Review These Pages	Do These Extra Practice Items
1–4	pages 138–139	Set K, page 148
5–8	pages 140–141	Set L, page 148
9–10	pages 142–143	8–10, page 149

Test Prep • Cumulative Review

Maintaining the Standards

Write the letter of the correct answer. If a correct answer is not here, choose NH.

1 Look at the items below.

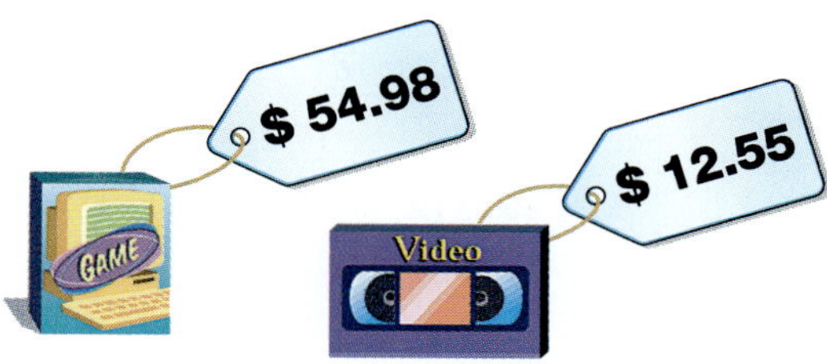

How much more does the game cost than the video?

A $30.00
B $32.48
C $41.43
D $42.43

2 Which of the following is another way to write the time quarter after three?

F 2:45
G 3:30
H 3:45
J NH

3 What number is equal to 6,000 + 400?

A 6,040
B 6,004
C 6,400
D 4,600

4 What is the difference between 3,170 and 2,985?

F 185
G 195
H 1,815
J 6,155

Use the table for Questions 5–7.

River	Length (in miles)
Amazon	4,000
Chang	3,964
Nile	4,160
Huang	3,395

5 Which river is the longest?

A Amazon
B Chang
C Nile
D Huang

6 How many miles longer is the Nile River than the Amazon River?

F 160
G 840
H 8,160
J NH

7 How many miles shorter is the Huang River than the Amazon River?

A 500
B 605
C 1,395
D 7,395

8 Which digit in 3,598 has the greatest value?

Explain How did you find your answer?

Safe Site

Internet Test Prep
Visit **www.eduplace.com/kids/mhm** for more *Test Prep Practice.*

Extra Practice

Set A (Lesson 1, pages 102–103)

Find each sum.

1. 8 4 + 3 **2.** 7 0 + 5 **3.** 8 9 + 4 **4.** 6 5 + 7 **5.** 9 6 + 2 **6.** 8 7 + 4

7. 3 + 2 + (8 + 2) **8.** 9 + (3 + 6 + 1) **9.** (2 + 5 + 3) + 2

Set B (Lesson 2, pages 104–106)

Find each sum.

1. 27 + 69 **2.** \$64 + 28 **3.** 53 + 37 **4.** 47 + 18 **5.** 36 + 35

6. \$307 + 418 **7.** 738 + 216 **8.** 139 + 351 **9.** 546 + 207 **10.** \$127 + 439

11. 37 + 43 **12.** 807 + 125 **13.** \$444 + \$519 **14.** 237 + 148

Set C (Lesson 3, pages 108–109)

Find each sum. Check by adding up.

1. 46 + 87 **2.** 428 + 491 **3.** \$4.86 + 3.29 **4.** 122 + 799 **5.** 319 + 293

6. 246 + 537 **7.** 623 + 148 **8.** 369 + 248 **9.** \$5.74 + \$2.29

Set D (Lesson 4, pages 110–111)

Estimate each sum by rounding to the greatest place.

1. 48 + 55 **2.** 67 + 92 **3.** \$87 + 29 **4.** 23 + 46 **5.** 58 + 33

6. \$5.39 + 3.75 **7.** 540 + 275 **8.** 726 + 109 **9.** \$4.85 + 3.25 **10.** 197 + 732

11. 28 + 53 **12.** 62 + 86 **13.** \$1.83 + \$ 5.27 **14.** 675 + 166

Extra Practice

Set E (Lesson 6, pages 116–118)

Find each sum. Check by adding the numbers in a different order.

1. $\begin{array}{r} 22 \\ 28 \\ +\ 33 \\ \hline \end{array}$ **2.** $\begin{array}{r} 47 \\ 31 \\ +\ 12 \\ \hline \end{array}$ **3.** $\begin{array}{r} 36 \\ 149 \\ +\ 12 \\ \hline \end{array}$ **4.** $\begin{array}{r} 251 \\ 27 \\ +\ 403 \\ \hline \end{array}$ **5.** $\begin{array}{r} 271 \\ 316 \\ +\ 104 \\ \hline \end{array}$

6. 17 + 42 + 34 **7.** 38 + 18 + 192 **8.** 116 + 311 + 12

9. 143 + 212 + 315 **10.** 341 + 213 + 75 **11.** 814 + 25 + 142

Set F (Lesson 7, pages 120–121)

Find each sum.

1. $\begin{array}{r} \$21.79 \\ +\ 33.26 \\ \hline \end{array}$ **2.** $\begin{array}{r} 8{,}873 \\ +\ 1{,}029 \\ \hline \end{array}$ **3.** $\begin{array}{r} \$30.57 \\ +\ 54.61 \\ \hline \end{array}$ **4.** $\begin{array}{r} 1{,}287 \\ +\ 6{,}765 \\ \hline \end{array}$

5. 6,803 + 2,197 **6.** 7,019 + 1,793 **7.** 3,624 + 4,987

8. $36.25 + $43.96 **9.** 5,302 + 3,974 **10.** 2,753 + 5,268

Set G (Lesson 9, pages 126–127)

Subtract.

1. $\begin{array}{r} 16 \\ -\ 2 \\ \hline \end{array}$ **2.** $\begin{array}{r} 9 \\ -\ 7 \\ \hline \end{array}$ **3.** $\begin{array}{r} 17 \\ -\ 0 \\ \hline \end{array}$ **4.** $\begin{array}{r} 18 \\ -\ 18 \\ \hline \end{array}$ **5.** $\begin{array}{r} 19 \\ -\ 1 \\ \hline \end{array}$

6. 15 − 15 **7.** 14 − 2 **8.** 13 − 0 **9.** 11 − 8

Set H (Lesson 10, pages 128–130)

Find each difference.

1. $\begin{array}{r} 71 \\ -\ 57 \\ \hline \end{array}$ **2.** $\begin{array}{r} \$84 \\ -39 \\ \hline \end{array}$ **3.** $\begin{array}{r} 643 \\ -\ 228 \\ \hline \end{array}$ **4.** $\begin{array}{r} 584 \\ -\ 376 \\ \hline \end{array}$ **5.** $\begin{array}{r} 682 \\ -\ 167 \\ \hline \end{array}$

6. 62 − 28 **7.** 76 − 29 **8.** $443 − $225 **9.** 594 − 288

Extra Practice

Set I (Lesson 11, pages 132–133)

Find each difference. Check by adding.

1. $544 - 429$
2. $374 - 126$
3. $833 - 475$
4. $591 - 362$
5. $\$8.74 - 2.68$
6. $4.23 − $2.46
7. 741 − 526
8. 391 − 172
9. 634 − 479

Set J (Lesson 12, pages 134–135)

Estimate each difference by rounding to the greatest place.

1. $67 - 31$
2. $88 - 44$
3. $\$49 - 18$
4. $798 - 312$
5. $\$6.67 - 2.75$
6. 796 − 423
7. $4.91 − $1.86
8. 276 − 158
9. $8.53 − $4.29
10. 435 − 284
11. 619 − 473
12. $7.82 − $6.49
13. 928 − 782

Set K (Lesson 13, pages 138–139)

Find each difference. Check by using addition or estimation.

1. $5{,}739 - 2{,}598$
2. $8{,}916 - 3{,}737$
3. $7{,}565 - 3{,}436$
4. $\$43.11 - 12.87$
5. $4{,}271 - 1{,}355$
6. $4{,}642 - 2{,}158$
7. $6{,}393 - 2{,}295$
8. $9{,}717 - 3{,}925$
9. $3{,}471 - 1{,}968$
10. $7{,}113 - 2{,}197$

Set L (Lesson 14, pages 140–141)

Find each difference. Check by using addition or estimation.

1. $500 - 342$
2. $300 - 111$
3. $705 - 423$
4. $7{,}402 - 3{,}291$
5. $6{,}005 - 4{,}173$
6. 5,302 − 3,291
7. 8,600 − 4,125
8. 7,008 − 5,137

Extra Practice • Problem Solving

Decide whether you need an estimate or an exact answer. Then solve. *(Lesson 5, pages 112–113)*

1. During a tour, 28 more people visited the zoo than the aquarium. If 36 people visited the aquarium, how many people visited the zoo?

2. An elm tree in Randy's yard is 45 feet tall. A sugar maple is 12 feet shorter than the elm tree. How tall is the sugar maple?

3. The Empire State Building in New York is 373 meters tall. A tower on top of the building is 70 meters tall. How tall are the building and the tower?

4. Steve made a model boat that is about 21 inches long. Pam made a model boat that is about 38 inches long. About how much longer is Pam's boat than Steve's boat?

Solve each problem, using the Guess and Check strategy. *(Lesson 8, pages 122–123)*

5. Look at the list below. John spent $4.70. He bought 3 items. What did he buy?

Price List	
Ball	$1.40
Balloon	$1.50
Jacks	$1.30
Toy car	$1.45
Yo-Yo	$1.75

6. A class had 47 tadpoles. The tadpoles became frogs or toads. There were 5 more frogs than toads. How many frogs were there? How many toads were there?

7. Last year, Bess took out 10 more library books than Meg. They took out 106 books in all. How many books did each girl take out?

Use the information in the table to solve. *(Lesson 15, pages 142–143)*

8. How many tickets in all were sold on Saturday for *Game Time* and *Rob's Run*?

9. How many more tickets to *Dinosaur Days* were sold on Saturday than on Sunday?

10. Which movie sold fewer than 1,000 tickets altogether on Saturday and Sunday?

Number of Movie Tickets Sold

Movie	Saturday	Sunday
Dinosaur Days	595	476
Game Time	362	581
Rob's Run	628	745
Top of the World	827	758

Chapter Review

Reviewing Vocabulary

Match the word or words with the definition.

1. **Commutative Property** — **a.** The sum of any number and zero is that number.
2. **Zero Property** — **b.** The way in which addends are grouped does not change the sum.
3. **Associative Property** — **c.** The order in which numbers are added does not change the sum.

Reviewing Concepts and Skills

Find each sum. Check your work. *(pages 102–111, 116–121)*

4. 7 + 6 + 4

5. 8 + 2 + 5

6. 6 + 0 + 4

7. 5 + 4 + 5

8. 9 + 8 + 2

9. 34 + 25

10. 119 + 238

11. 324 + 576

12. 776 + 157

13. \$6.26 + 4.08

14. 53 + 12 + 25

15. 45 + 17 + 28

16. 137 + 20 + 418

17. 6,443 + 1,389

18. \$53.50 + 28.50

19. 4 + (3 + 7) + 2

20. 3 + (8 + 2) + 4

21. 8 + 3 + (6 + 4)

22. 49 + 83

23. 435 + 235 + 12

24. 659 + 423

25. 18 + 310 + 23

26. 5,107 + 8, 911

27. 3,241 + 1,628

Round each number to the greatest place. Then estimate the sum. *(pages 110–111)*

28. 44 + 51

29. 92 + 37

30. 413 + 289

31. 638 + 199

32. 757 + 372

Find each difference. Check by using addition. *(pages126–135, 138–141)*

33. $79 - 34$

34. $92 - 61$

35. $382 - 145$

36. $576 - 189$

37. $\$7.13 - 5.27$

38. $483 - 249$

39. $732 - 521$

40. $\$62.75 - 13.17$

41. $9{,}909 - 7{,}861$

42. $4{,}500 - 2{,}468$

43. 402 − 298

44. $37.64 − $18.85

45. 7,304 − 3,913

Round each number to the greatest place. Then estimate the difference. *(pages 134–135)*

46. $29 - 18$

47. $62 - 38$

48. $517 - 178$

49. $875 - 432$

50. $961 - 504$

51. 69 − 57

52. 311 − 230

53. 918 − 488

Solve. *(pages 112–113, 122–123, 142–143)*

54. A hamburger has 340 calories. A chicken sandwich has 265 calories. How many more calories does the hamburger have than the chicken sandwich?

55. Grace sees a turtle at the zoo that is 115 years old. She sees a marine clam that is 78 years older than the turtle. About how old is the marine clam?

56. Amy and Josh make a total of 65 bookmarks for the school fair. Josh makes 5 more than Amy. How many bookmarks does each child make?

Brain Teasers Math Reasoning

In a Row

Three numbers in a row (such as 3, 4, 5 or 25, 26, 27) add up to 705. What are the numbers?

Oh, Mom

Hillary's mother is two times as old as Hillary will be in 7 years. Hillary is 8. How old is her mother?

Internet Brain Teasers
Visit **www.eduplace.com/kids/mhm** for more *Brain Teasers.*

Chapter Test

Add.

1. $\begin{array}{r} 6 \\ 2 \\ +\ 5 \\ \hline \end{array}$ **2.** $\begin{array}{r} 4 \\ 7 \\ +\ 3 \\ \hline \end{array}$ **3.** $\begin{array}{r} 8 \\ 5 \\ +\ 4 \\ \hline \end{array}$ **4.** $\begin{array}{r} 6 \\ 3 \\ +\ 7 \\ \hline \end{array}$ **5.** $\begin{array}{r} 5 \\ 4 \\ +\ 9 \\ \hline \end{array}$ **6.** $\begin{array}{r} 8 \\ 3 \\ +\ 2 \\ \hline \end{array}$

7. 4 + 3 + 7 + 6 **8.** 8 + (3 + 4 + 3) **9.** 4 + 3 + (4 + 6)

Find each sum or difference.

10. $\begin{array}{r} 47 \\ +\ 21 \\ \hline \end{array}$ **11.** $\begin{array}{r} 84 \\ -\ 23 \\ \hline \end{array}$ **12.** $\begin{array}{r} 648 \\ -\ 529 \\ \hline \end{array}$ **13.** $\begin{array}{r} \$617 \\ +\ 138 \\ \hline \end{array}$ **14.** $\begin{array}{r} 3,021 \\ +\ 2,164 \\ \hline \end{array}$

15. $\begin{array}{r} \$2.05 \\ +\ 7.12 \\ \hline \end{array}$ **16.** $\begin{array}{r} \$43.86 \\ -\ 23.59 \\ \hline \end{array}$ **17.** $\begin{array}{r} 1,279 \\ -\ 915 \\ \hline \end{array}$ **18.** $\begin{array}{r} 5,512 \\ +\ 1,976 \\ \hline \end{array}$ **19.** $\begin{array}{r} 4,005 \\ -\ 1,372 \\ \hline \end{array}$

20. 942 − 794 **21.** 341 + 18 + 407 **22.** 3,405 − 1,639

23. 658 + 275 **24.** \$52.04 − \$3.96 **25.** \$25.97 + \$63.84

Round each number to the greatest place. Then estimate.

26. $\begin{array}{r} 37 \\ +\ 42 \\ \hline \end{array}$ **27.** $\begin{array}{r} 45 \\ -\ 38 \\ \hline \end{array}$ **28.** $\begin{array}{r} 627 \\ -\ 518 \\ \hline \end{array}$ **29.** $\begin{array}{r} 843 \\ +\ 486 \\ \hline \end{array}$ **30.** $\begin{array}{r} 794 \\ -\ 182 \\ \hline \end{array}$

31. 63 + 39 **32.** 82 − 12 **33.** 59 + 42

34. 823 − 219 **35.** 583 − 190 **36.** 741 + 668

Solve.

37. The bicycle was invented in 1791. The motorcycle was invented in 1869. How many years after the invention of the bicycle was the motorcycle invented?

38. There are 318 mystery books in the Grove Street Library. The Fourth Avenue Library has 297 mystery books. About how many mystery books are in both libraries?

39. Juan and Marco collect seashells. Juan has 30 more seashells than Marco. The boys have a total of 106 seashells. How many seashells does each boy have?

40. A gift shop sells T-shirts for $9.50 each and hats for $5.99 each. Brian bought two T-shirts and Laurie bought two hats. How much more money did Brian spend than Laurie?

Write About It

Solve each problem. Use correct math vocabulary to explain your thinking.

1. Ruth says she will add to solve this problem.

   Problem The Ferris wheel at the amusement park can hold 64 people. If 85 people are beginning to get on the Ferris wheel, how many people will have to wait for the next ride?

   a. Do you agree with Ruth? Why or why not?

   b. How would you solve the problem?

   c. How would you check your answer?

2. Look at the way Simon solved this problem, using estimation.

   a. Explain what he did wrong.

   b. Show how to estimate the answer correctly.

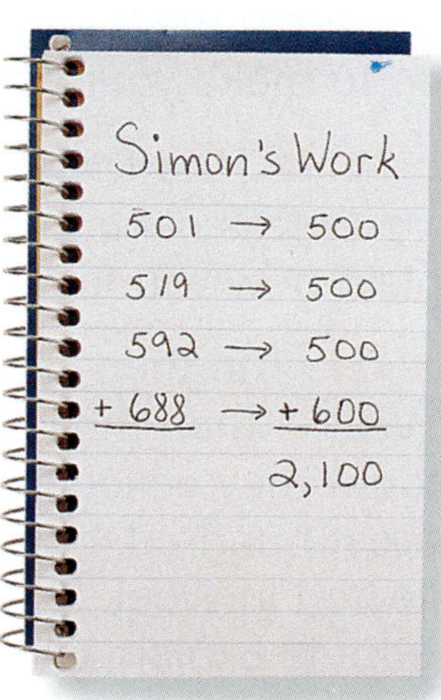

Another Look

Beth's school collected canned food over a period of 3 weeks. The table below shows how many cans of food students from Grade 3 and Grade 4 brought in each week.

Use the table to find the answer to each question.

Can Collection			
Grade	**Week 1**	**Week 2**	**Week 3**
Grade 3	198	199	187
Grade 4	87	98	99

1. How many cans were collected altogether by the third and fourth grades in Week 1? Week 2? Week 3? In which week were the most cans collected by the two grades? In which week were the fewest cans collected? What is the difference between the total number of cans collected in these two weeks?

2. Round to the nearest hundred to estimate the total number of cans the third grade collected in the 3 weeks. Then round to the nearest hundred to estimate the total number of cans the fourth grade collected in the 3 weeks. Show the numbers you used to make your estimates.

3. **Look Back** Did the students in each grade collect more or less cans than the estimated amounts? Explain how you know.

4. **Analyze** The third-graders collected 52 more cans in Week 4 than they did in Week 3. Would the amount they collected in Week 4, rounded to the nearest hundred, be greater than the amount they collected in Week 3, rounded to the nearest hundred? Explain why or why not.

Enrichment

Using a Venn Diagram

The circles of a Venn diagram show how different sets are related. Look at the Venn diagram below. One circle shows all of the red objects. The other circle shows all of the cubes.

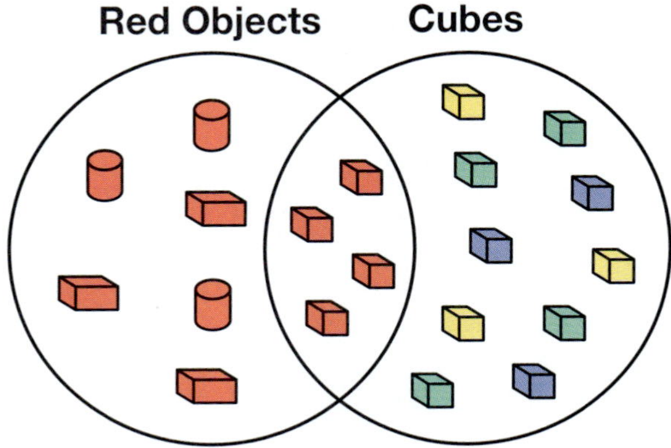

Use the Venn diagram to answer these questions.

1. How many red objects are there?
2. How many cubes are there?
3. How many objects are red and cubes?
4. How many objects are red but not cubes?
5. How many objects are cubes but not red?

Explain Your Thinking

Look at the Venn diagram below. What does the overlapping part of the circles show?

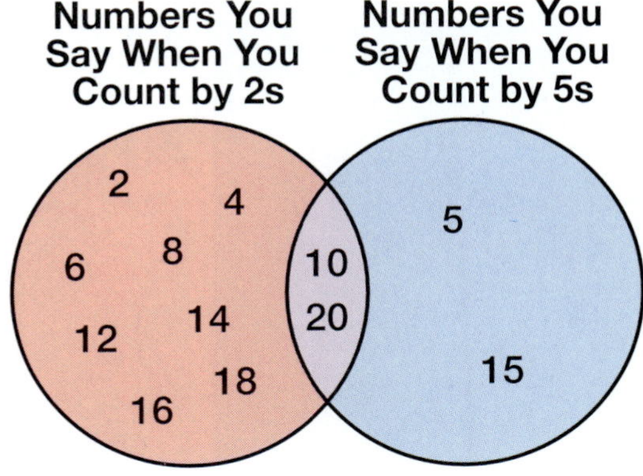

Measurement

Why Learn About Measurement?

Measurement can tell you how long or how heavy something is or how much something can hold.

When you figure out whether a desk will fit along a wall or how much your pet weighs, you are using measurement.

These cooks are making a large pot of *paella* that will feed many people at a festival. The recipe they use tells them how many pounds of peas to add to the pot!

Reading Mathematics

Reviewing Vocabulary

Understanding math language helps you become a successful problem solver. Here are some math vocabulary words you should know.

Customary Units of Measure		
Length	**Capacity**	**Weight**
inch (in.) foot (ft)	cup (c) pint (pt) quart (qt) gallon (gal)	pound (lb)

Metric Units of Measure		
Length	**Capacity**	**Mass**
centimeter (cm) meter (m)	liter (L)	kilogram (kg)

Reading Words and Symbols

When you read mathematics, sometimes you read only words, sometimes you read words and symbols, and sometimes you read only symbols.

You can describe the length, weight, and capacity of an object by using customary units or metric units.

Customary Units

- The fish tank is about 18 inches long.
- It has a weight of about 9 pounds.
- It holds about 10 gallons of water.

Metric Units

- The fish tank is about 45 centimeters long.
- It has a mass of about 4 kilograms.
- It holds about 12 liters of water.

Try These

1. Write the word each abbreviation in the recipe stands for.

Party Punch

3 c cranberry juice	2 pt orange juice
1 qt ginger ale	1 gal apple juice

2. Match the tool with the units it measures. Write *inches, pounds,* or *cups*.

a. 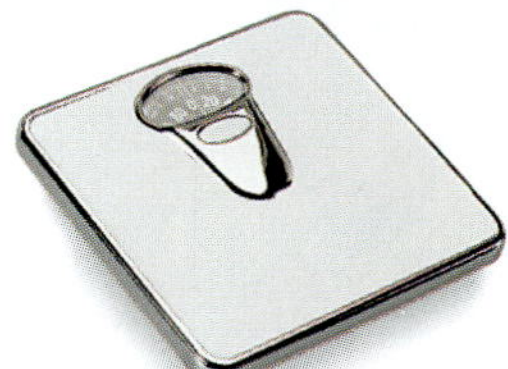

b. 

c. 

3. Write *true* or *false* for each sentence.
   a. A cat can weigh five meters.
   b. You can use kilograms to measure how long a baseball bat is.
   c. Meters can be used to measure how high a ceiling is.
   d. You can measure an amount of juice in liters.

Upcoming Vocabulary

Write About It **Here are some other vocabulary words** you will learn in this chapter. Watch for these words. Write their definitions in your journal.

half inch	**decimeter (dm)**
yard (yd)	**kilometer (km)**
mile (mi)	**milliliter (mL)**
ounce (oz)	**degrees Fahrenheit (°F)**
mass	**degrees Celsius (°C)**
gram (g)	

Measuring Length

You will learn how to tell the length of an object.

Review Vocabulary
inch (in.)

Learn About It

There are many ways to estimate and measure length.

One way is to use a non-standard unit such as a paper clip. Another way is to use an inch ruler.

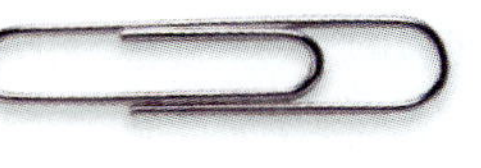

Materials
inch ruler
classroom objects
small paper clips

Use a paper clip. Estimate and then measure the length of the pencil below.

Step 1 Lay paper clips end to end along the picture of the pencil.

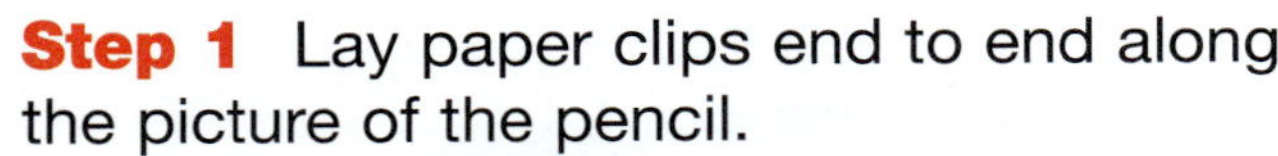

- How many paper clips long is the pencil?
- How close is that to your estimate?

Now use an inch ruler. Estimate and then measure the length of the pencil below to the nearest inch.

Step 2 Line up one end of the pencil with the left end of the ruler.

An **inch (in.)** is a standard unit used to measure length in the customary measurement system.

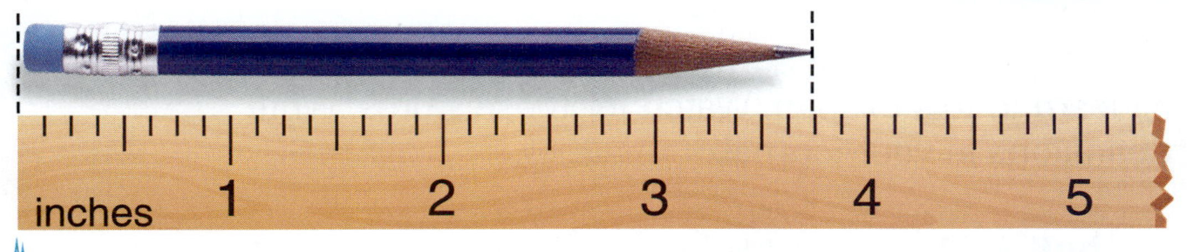

The left end of this ruler is 0 inches.

- Find the inch mark that is closest to the other end of the pencil.
- What is the length of the pencil to the nearest inch? Is this measurement exact? Explain.

Try It Out

1. Find 5 classroom objects to measure. Estimate and measure the length of each object to the nearest inch. Record your work in a table like the one below.

Object	My Estimate	Length to the Nearest Inch

Measure each of the objects below to the nearest inch.

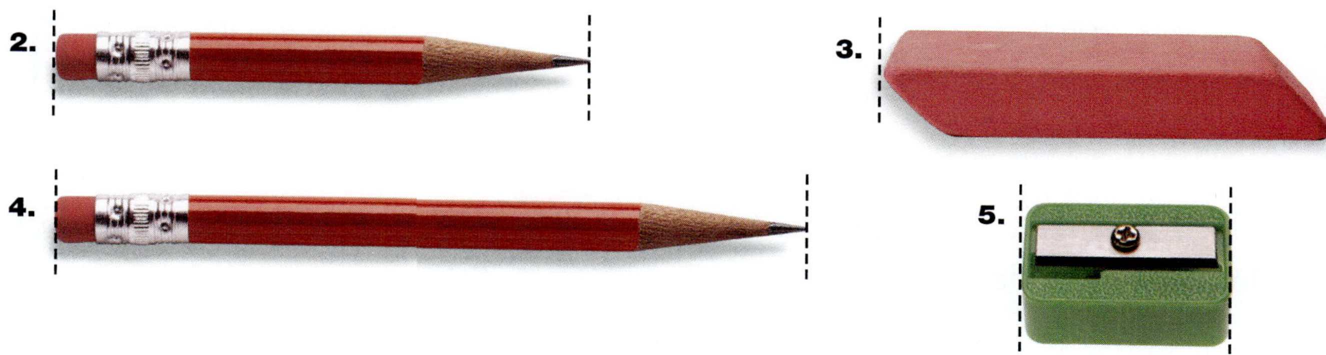

Use a ruler. Draw a line of each length.

6. 3 inches
7. 10 inches
8. 6 inches
9. Name three objects that are about 1 inch long or wide.
10. Find objects in the classroom that are about 6 inches long. Measure the objects to check your estimates.

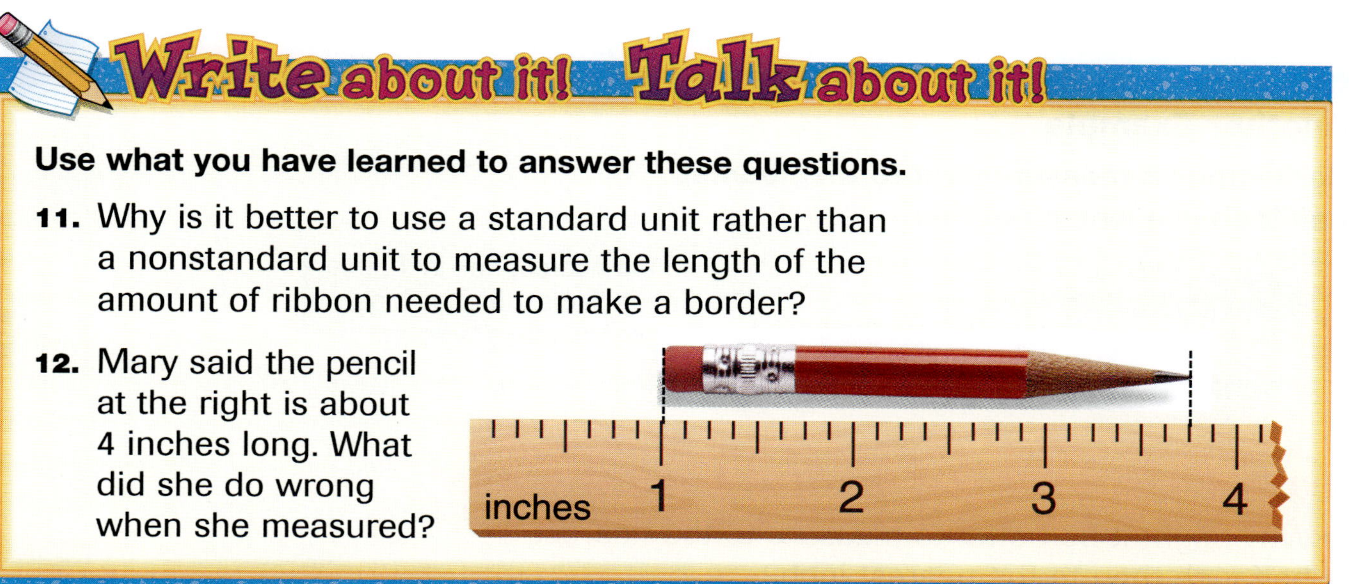

Use what you have learned to answer these questions.

11. Why is it better to use a standard unit rather than a nonstandard unit to measure the length of the amount of ribbon needed to make a border?
12. Mary said the pencil at the right is about 4 inches long. What did she do wrong when she measured?

LESSON 2

Measure to the Nearest Half Inch

You will learn how to measure objects to the nearest half inch.

New Vocabulary
half inch

Learn About It

You can use your ruler to measure the caterpillar to the nearest **half inch**.

How long is this caterpillar to the nearest half inch?

The right end of this caterpillar is closer to the $2\frac{1}{2}$-in. mark than to either 2-in. mark or the 3-in. mark.

To the nearest half inch, this caterpillar is $2\frac{1}{2}$ in. long.

How long is this caterpillar to the nearest half inch?

The right end of this caterpillar is closer to the $2\frac{1}{2}$-in. mark than to the 3-in. mark.

To the nearest half inch, this caterpillar is $2\frac{1}{2}$ in. long.

Another Example

Sometimes a measurement to the nearest half inch is a whole number.

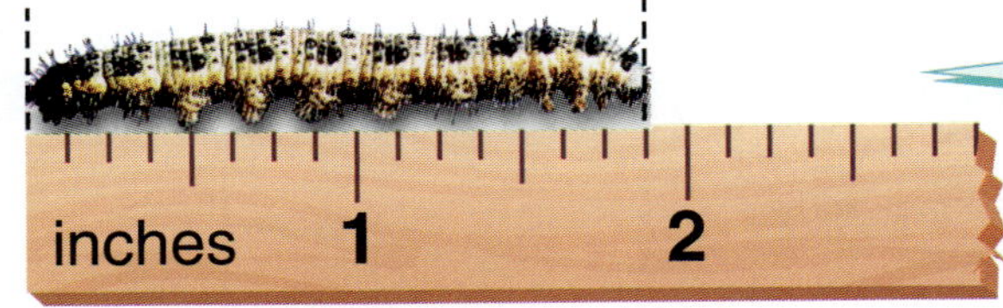

To the nearest half inch, this caterpillar is 2 inches long.

Explain Your Thinking

► Why might it be better to measure to the nearest half inch than to the nearest inch?

Guided Practice

Measure each caterpillar to the nearest half inch.

1. 

2. 

> **Ask Yourself**
> - Which mark on the ruler is closest to the end of the object?

Use an inch ruler. Draw a line of each length.

3. $5\frac{1}{2}$ in. **4.** 7 in. **5.** $2\frac{1}{2}$ in. **6.** 4 in.

Independent Practice

Measure each caterpillar to the nearest half inch.

7. 

8. 

Use an inch ruler. Draw a line of each length.

9. $\frac{1}{2}$ in. **10.** $3\frac{1}{2}$ in. **11.** 5 in.

Problem Solving • Reasoning

12. Matéo and Karen are drawing pictures of butterflies. Matéo drew a butterfly that is $2\frac{1}{2}$ inches wide. Karen drew a butterfly that is 2 inches wider than Matéo's butterfly. How wide is Karen's butterfly?

13. **Analyze** A caterpillar measures $3\frac{1}{2}$ inches long. One end of the caterpillar lies on the 2-inch mark of the ruler. Where on the ruler does the other end of the caterpillar lie?

SCIENCE Butterflies can be large or small. Suppose a blue pansy butterfly is $1\frac{1}{2}$ in. wide. If a monarch butterfly is 3 inches wider than that, how wide is the monarch butterfly?

Mixed Review • Test Prep

Compare. Write >, <, or = for each ⬬. *(pages 4–5, 20–21)*

14. 456 ⬬ 465 **15.** 800 + 90 ⬬ 800 + 9 **16.** 1,008 ⬬ 1,080

17 Which number correctly completes this number sentence? *(pages 4–5)*

$200 + \blacksquare + 9 = 219$

A 10 **B** 19 **C** 21 **D** 100

Extra Practice See Set A on page 198.

Customary Units of Length

You will learn how to use customary units to measure longer lengths.

New Vocabulary
foot (ft)
yard (yd)
mile (mi)

Learn About It

France gave the Statue of Liberty to the United States in 1885. To measure something large you need to use units such as **foot (ft)**, **yard (yd)**, and **mile (mi)**.

Customary Units of Length

1 foot	=	12 inches
1 yard	=	3 feet
1 yard	=	36 inches
1 mile	=	1,760 yards
1 mile	=	5,280 feet

Her nose is almost 5 feet long.

Her hand is more than 5 yards long.

The Statue of Liberty is about 150 feet or 50 yards tall.

Her tablet is about 13 feet wide.

The ship that brought the Statue of Liberty to the United States from France traveled nearly 4,000 miles.

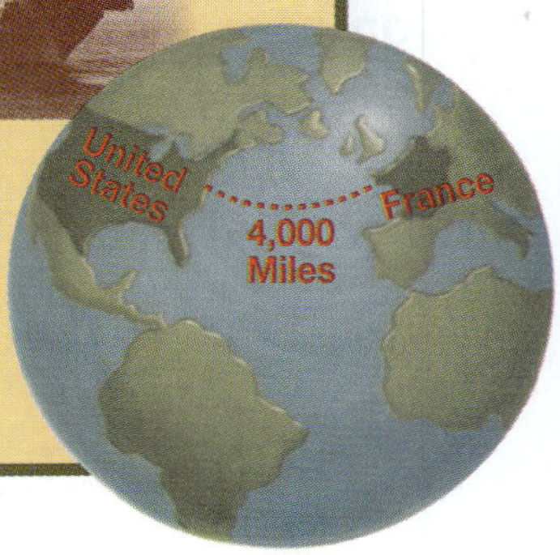

United States
France
4,000 Miles

Explain Your Thinking

- ▶ Why do people use miles instead of feet to measure the distance from France to the United States?
- ▶ Which is greater, 80 inches or 2 yards? Explain.

Guided Practice

Ask Yourself

- Do I need to use a small, medium, or large unit of measure?

Choose the unit you would use to measure each. Write *inch*, *foot*, *yard*, or *mile*.

1. the width of your math book
2. the distance from your home to an airport
3. the length of a football field

Choose the better estimate.

4. The width of your desk
   a. 3 miles **b.** 3 feet
5. The length of a classroom
   a. 10 yards **b.** 10 inches

Independent Practice

Choose the better estimate.

6. the width of a post card
   a. 3 feet **b.** 3 inches
7. the distance across a lake
   a. 4 yards **b.** 4 miles
8. the height of a tall building
   a. 50 miles **b.** 50 yards
9. the length of a dollar bill
   a. 6 inches **b.** 6 yards
10. the length of a boat
    a. 20 feet **b.** 20 miles
11. the distance between two cities
    a. 35 miles **b.** 35 inches
12. the width of your hand
    a. 4 inches **b.** 40 feet
13. the depth of a swimming pool
    a. 80 feet **b.** 8 feet

Algebra • Functions **Find a pattern. Then complete the table. Write the rule you used.**

14.

Feet	1	2	3	4	5
Inches	12	24			

15.

Yards	1	2	3	4	5	6
Feet	3	6	9			

Algebra • Equations Copy and complete.

16. 3 ft = ____ yd **17.** 12 in. = ____ ft **18.** 36 in. = ____ yd

19. 12 ft = ____ yd **20.** 18 ft = ____ yd **21.** 2 ft = ____ in.

22. 36 in. = ____ ft **23.** 4 ft = ____ in. **24.** 6 in. = ____ ft

Compare. Write >, <, or = for each ●.

25. 2 yd ● 2 ft **26.** 5,280 ft ● 1 mi **27.** 1 ft ● 10 in.

28. 1 mi ● 5,250 ft **29.** 12 in. ● 12 ft **30.** 1 yd ● 3 ft

31. 5 ft ● 3 yd **32.** 26 in. ● 2 ft **33.** 6 ft ● 2 yd

Problem Solving • Reasoning

Use Data **Use the table for Problems 34 and 35.**

34. **Compare** Which feature in the table is the greatest?

35. Which is wider, the Statue of Liberty's eye or mouth? Explain your answer.

36. **Logical Thinking** The third-grade and fourth-grade classes made statues in art class. The third grade's statue is taller than the fourth grade's statue. One statue is 2 feet tall. The other is 20 inches tall. How tall is each class's statue? Explain your answer.

37. **Write About It** Would you choose to measure the length of your arm in inches or in yards? Explain your reasoning.

Statue of Liberty Measurements

Feature	Measure
Length of finger	8 ft
Width of eye	3 ft
Length of arm	14 yd
Width of mouth	1 yd
Height of head	17 ft

Mixed Review • Test Prep

Write each number in two other ways. Use standard form, expanded form, or word form. *(pages 18–19)*

38. 203,002 **39.** 6,000 + 300 + 8 **40.** five hundred thirty-one thousand

41. 900,001 **42.** six thousand, three **43.** 8 hundreds 5 tens 5 ones

44 Which expression is closest in value to 50? *(pages 108–109, 140–141)*

A 49 + 5 **B** 60 − 45 **C** 50 + 50 **D** 100 − 75

Extra Practice See Set B on page 198.

Show What You Know

Missing Unit

Pick two different measurement units from the box to complete each number sentence. You can use each unit more than once.

in.
ft
yd

1. 1 ____ $<$ 2 ____

2. 3 ____ $<$ 2 ____

3. 12 ____ = 1 ____

4. 3 ____ = 9 ____

5. 2 ____ $>$ 5 ____

6. 32 ____ $<$ 3 ____

Missing Operations

Complete each number sentence. Use + or −.

1. 1 ft ● 1 ft = 2 ft

2. 3 yd ● 2 yd = 36 in.

3. 15 in. ● 3 in. = 1 ft

4. 10 in. ● 1 in. ● 1 in. = 1 ft

5. 1 yd ● 2 yd ● 1 yd = 12 ft

6. 12 in. ● 12 in. ● 12 in. = 1 yd

Missing Measurements

Pick a measurement from the box to complete each number sentence. You can use each measurement more than once.

1 in.
12 in.
1 ft
1 yd

1. 2 ft + ____ = 1 yd

2. 11 in. + ____ = 1 ft

3. 22 in. + ____ + ____ = 2 ft

4. 2 yd − ____ = 3 ft

5. 4 ft + ____ + ____ = 2 yd

Estimating and Measuring Capacity

You will learn how to estimate and measure the amount a container can hold.

Review Vocabulary
cup (c)
pint (pt)
quart (qt)
gallon (gal)

Learn About It

Capacity is the amount a container can hold. In the customary system, **cup (c)**, **pint (pt)**, **quart (qt)**, and **gallon (gal)** are used to measure capacity.

Use different-size containers and water to estimate and measure capacity.

Materials

water
1-cup container
1-pint container
1-quart container
1-gallon container
different-size containers

Step 1 Use the cup container to fill the pint container. In a table like the one shown, record how many cups are needed to fill the pint.

- How many cups are there in a pint?

Capacity			
	Pint	Quart	Gallon
Cups	2		
Pints			
Quarts			

Step 2 Estimate the number of cups needed to fill the quart and gallon containers. Use the cup container to check your estimates. Record your results in the table.

- How many cups are there in a quart? a gallon?

Step 3 Now estimate the number of pints needed to fill the quart and gallon containers. Use the pint container to check your estimates. Record your results in the table.

- How many pints are there in a quart? in a gallon?

Step 4 Estimate the number of quarts needed to fill the gallon container. Check your estimate and record your results in the table.

- How many quarts are there in a gallon?

Step 5 Now choose a different-size container. Estimate how many cups, pints, quarts, or gallons it holds. Then measure to check your estimate.

- Did the container hold more or less than you estimated?

Step 6 Estimate and then measure the capacity of all the other containers.

Try It Out

Use your table to find the missing measure.

1. 1 gal = ____ qt
2. 1 pt = ____ c
3. 1 qt = ____ pt
4. 2 qt = ____ pt
5. 3 pt = ____ c
6. 2 gal = ____ qt
7. 3 qt = ____ pt
8. 3 gal = ____ qt
9. 1 gal = ____ pt
10. Do you think a kitchen sink holds more or less than 1 gallon of water? Explain.
11. **Write Your Own** Write a rule that helps you find the number of quarts when you know the number of gallons.

Write about it! Talk about it!

Use what you have learned to answer these questions.

12. Do you think these containers could have the same capacity? Explain your thinking. Then describe a way to find out if these containers have the same capacity.

13. Suppose you pour 1 gallon of water into pint containers. Then you pour 1 gallon of water into quart containers. Would you use more pint containers or quart containers? Explain.

Customary Units of Weight

You will learn how to use customary units to measure the amount a container can hold.

Customary Units of Capacity
1 pint = 2 cups
1 quart = 2 pints
1 gallon = 4 quarts

Learn About It

You can use customary units to measure capacity.

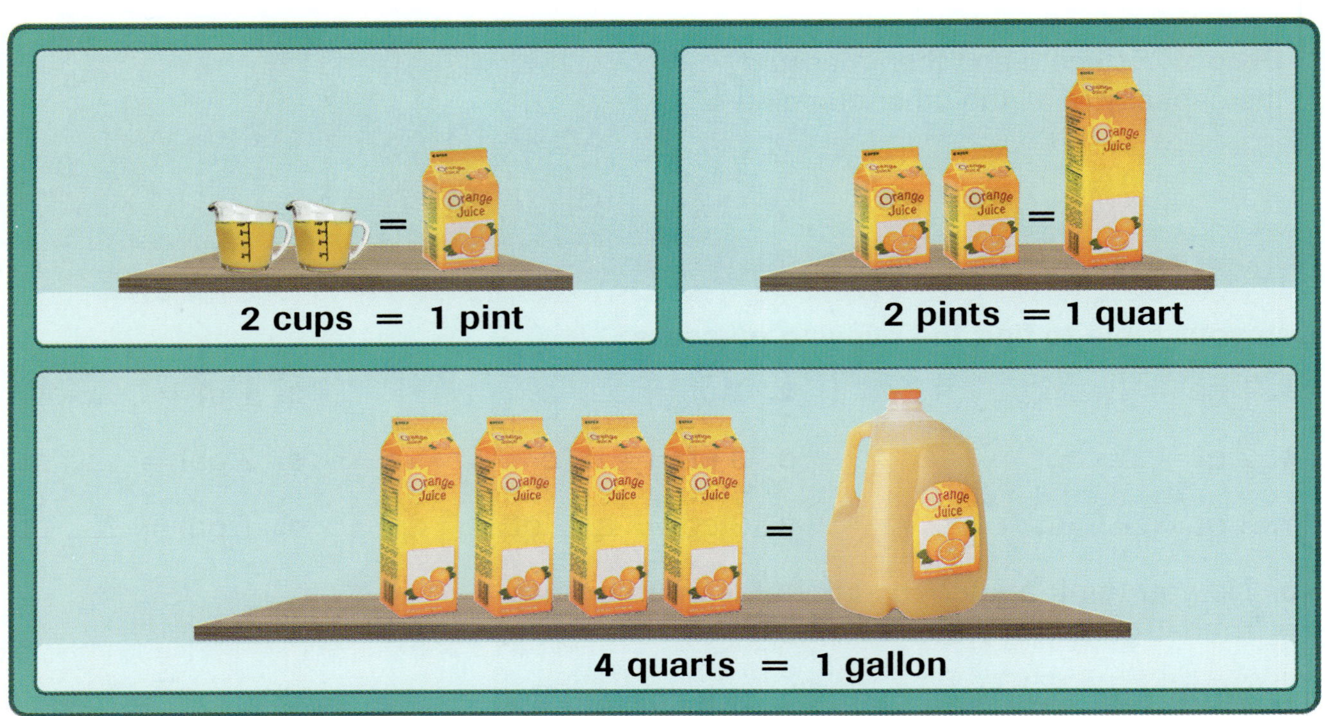

Explain Your Thinking

- ► How many cups equal a half pint?
- ► How many pints equal 4 cups? Explain.

Guided Practice

Ask Yourself

- Do you need to measure a small, medium, or large capacity?
- Which is the smallest unit of measure? the largest unit?

Choose the unit you would use to measure the capacity of each. Write *cup*, *pint*, *quart*, or *gallon*.

1. 

2. 

3. 

Choose the better estimate.

4. puppy's water bowl
1 gallon or 1 pint

5. coffee mug
1 cup or 10 cups

6. car gas tank
20 pints or 20 gallons

Independent Practice

Choose the unit you would use to measure the capacity of each. Write *cup, pint, quart,* or *gallon*.

7. 

8. 

9. 

10. 

Choose the better estimate.

11. baby pool
20 gallons or 20 cups

12. watering can
2 quarts or 200 quarts

13. glass of juice
1 quart or 1 cup

14. bathtub
100 pints or 100 gallons

15. soup bowl
2 cups or 2 quarts

16. aquarium
10 gallons or 10 cups

Algebra • Equations **Copy and complete.**

17. 2 pt = ____ c

18. 4 qt = ____ gal

19. 3 qt = ____ pt

20. 2 pt = ____ qt

21. 8 c = ____ pt

22. 3 gal = ____ pt

Problem Solving • Reasoning

Use the recipe to answer Problems 23–24.

23. **Estimate** About how many pints of punch does this recipe make?

24. If you want to double the recipe, how many cups of lemonade will you need?

25. **Analyze** Aaron has a 12-cup punch bowl. He uses a 1-quart container to fill it. How many times must he pour a quart into the bowl to fill it?

Mixed Review • Test Prep

Write the value of the 4 in each number. *(pages 34–35)*

26. 5,064 **27.** 401,110 **28.** 104,929 **29.** 646 **30.** 2,496 **31.** 49,817

32 Which number completes this number sentence? *(pages 102–103)*

6 + ■ = 11

A 17 **B** 11 **C** 6 **D** 5

Extra Practice See Set C on page 198.

Customary Units of Weight

You will learn how to use customary units to tell the weight of an object.

New Vocabulary
pound (lb)
ounce (oz)

Learn About It

Pound (lb) and **ounce (oz)** are customary units used to measure weight.

You measure a slice of bread or a key in ounces. You measure a loaf of bread or a piano in pounds.

Customary Units of Weight
1 pound = 16 ounces

1 ounce

1 pound

16 one-ounce slices of bread have the same weight as a 1-pound loaf of bread.

Try this activity to estimate and measure weight.

Materials
scale
1-pound weight

Step 1 Find 5 small objects in your classroom. Predict which objects weigh less than, more than, or about a pound.

Step 2 Use the balance scale and the 1-pound weight to check your predictions.

Explain Your Thinking

- ▶ Which is heavier: a pound of pencils or a pound of bricks? Explain.
- ▶ Would you always measure the weight of a small object in ounces? Why or why not?

Guided Practice

Choose the unit that you would use to measure the weight of each. Write *ounce* or *pound*.

1. 

2. 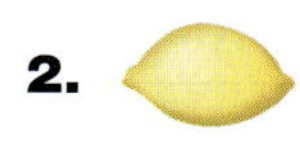

3. 

4. 

5. 

6. 

> **Ask Yourself**
> - Do I need a small or large unit of measure?
> - Which is the smaller unit of measure? the larger unit?

Independent Practice

Choose the unit that you would use to measure the weight of each. Write *ounce* or *pound*.

7. 

8. 

9. 

10. refrigerator

11. cracker

12. paper towel

13. pencil

14. table

15. sponge

Choose the better estimate.

16. a pizza
- **a.** 2 pounds
- **b.** 2 ounces

17. a banana
- **a.** 6 pounds
- **b.** 6 ounces

18. a slice of cheese
- **a.** 1 pound
- **b.** 1 ounce

19. a wooden spoon
- **a.** 10 ounces
- **b.** 100 ounces

20. a turkey
- **a.** 2 pounds
- **b.** 20 pounds

21. a television set
- **a.** 20 ounces
- **b.** 20 pounds

Algebra • Equations **Copy and complete.**

22. 1 lb = ____ oz

23. 3 lb = ____ oz

24. 4 lb = ____ oz

25. 2 lb = ____ oz

26. 8 oz = ____ lb

27. 16 oz = ____ lb

28. 32 oz = ____ lb

29. 48 oz = ____ lb

30. $\frac{1}{2}$ lb = ____ oz

Problem Solving • Reasoning

Use Data **Use the graph for Problems 31–34.**

Fruit Weights	
Fruit	**Weight**
Grapefruit	2 pounds
Pineapple	3 pounds
Watermelon	5 pounds
Apple	$1\frac{1}{2}$ pounds

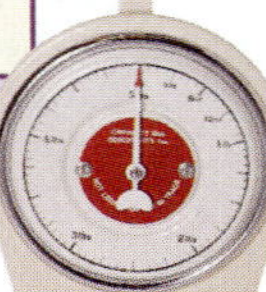

31. Which fruit is the heaviest? How many pounds is it?

32. How many pounds is the pineapple? How many ounces is that?

33. **Compare** Suppose a melon weighs 30 oz. Is it heavier or lighter than the pineapple? How much heavier or lighter is it?

34. **Analyze** How much does the grapefruit weigh? How many ounces is this? Explain.

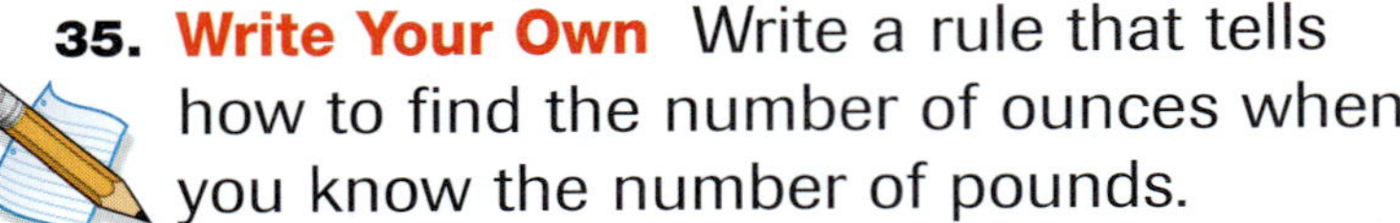

35. **Write Your Own** Write a rule that tells how to find the number of ounces when you know the number of pounds.

Mixed Review • Test Prep

Write each time using numbers. *(pages 68–69)*

36.

37.

38.

Choose the letter of the correct answer. *(pages 56–57)*

39 How much money is shown?

A 23¢ **C** 57¢

B 47¢ **D** $1.07

40 How much money is shown?

F $4.00 **H** 65¢

G 85¢ **J** 55¢

Extra Practice See Set D on page 199.

Practice Game

Match the Measure

Practice what you have learned about measurement by playing this game with a partner.

What You'll Need

- *20 index cards or Teaching Tool 1*

Players
2

Here's What To Do

1. Make 1 set of cards like those in Set A. Make 2 sets of cards like those in Set B.
2. Shuffle all of the cards. Lay them face down in a 4 by 5 array.
3. Take turns turning over 2 cards at a time. You make a match when a unit of measure matches something that would normally be measured in that unit. For example, "feet" and "length of your classroom."

   If you make a match, take the cards. If you do not a make a match, turn the cards back over.
4. Continue taking turns until all the cards have been matched. The player with the most matches wins.

Set A

length of your classroom	distance across the ocean
weight of a cat	water in a sink
height of a third grader	distance to the moon
water in a pool	milk in a small carton
juice in a glass	weight of a desk

Set B

feet	cups
pounds	gallons
miles	

Share Your Thinking Look at the cards in Set B. Could you replace the "cups" card with a "pints" card and play the game again? Explain.

Temperature: Degrees Fahrenheit

You will learn how to tell temperature in degrees Fahrenheit.

New Vocabulary
degrees Fahrenheit (°F)

Fahrenheit

220°
212°F water boils
210°
200°
190°
180°
170°
160°
150°
140°
130°
120°
101°F a hot day
110°
100°
98.6°F normal body temperature
90°
80°
68°F room temperature
70°
60°
50°
40°
32°F water freezes
30°
20°
10°F a cold day
10°
0°
-10°
°F

The thermometer shows 78°F.

Learn About It

On the same day, different places in the United States can have very different temperatures.

Temperatures on January 1

Manawa, Wisconsin
It is 12°F.
That's cold!

San Diego, California
It is 72°F.
That's warm!

A thermometer like the one at the left can be used to measure temperature in **degrees Fahrenheit (°F).**

Explain Your Thinking

► How do the lines between the numbers on the thermometer help you read the temperature?

Guided Practice

Write each temperature. Then write *hot, warm, cool,* or *cold* to describe the temperature.

1. °F 70° 60°

2.

Ask Yourself

- Where is the top of the red line?
- What temperature describes hot? warm? cool? and cold?

Independent Practice

Write each temperature. Then write *hot, warm, cool,* or *cold* to describe the temperature.

3. 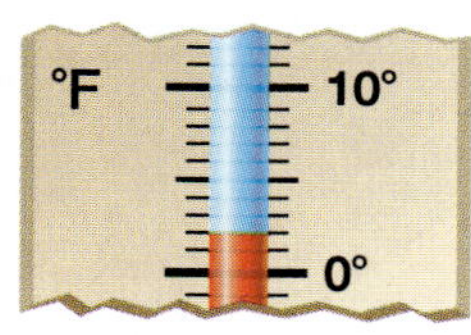

4. 

5. 

6. 

Choose the better estimate of the temperature.

7.  

a. 90°F **b.** 27°F

8.  

a. 50°F **b.** 95°F

9. 

a. 65°F **b.** 18°F

Problem Solving • Reasoning

10. Jeff's temperature is 102°F. Is his temperature above or below normal body temperature?

11. In Hilo, Hawaii, it was 75°F on January 1. On the same day in Hong Kong, China, it was 5 degrees cooler. What was the temperature in Hong Kong?

12. **Analyze** One morning it was 93°F. During the day the temperature rose 6 degrees and then dropped 2 degrees. That evening the temperature fell 3 degrees more. What was the final temperature?

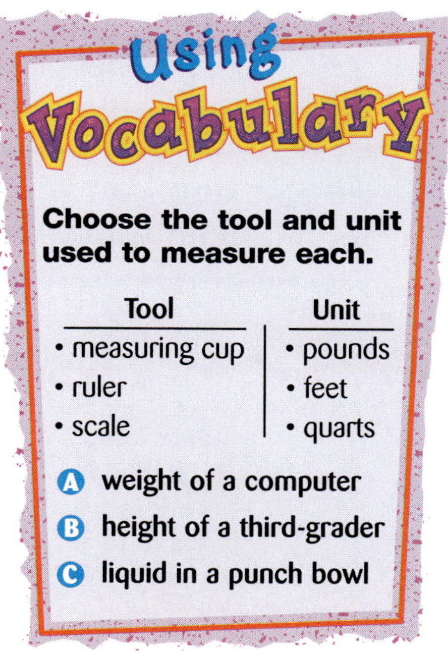

Using Vocabulary

Choose the tool and unit used to measure each.

Tool	Unit
• measuring cup	• pounds
• ruler	• feet
• scale	• quarts

A weight of a computer

B height of a third-grader

C liquid in a punch bowl

Mixed Review • Test Prep

Add. *(pages 102–103)*

13. 5 + 8 + 2 **14.** 4 + 2 + 6 **15.** 3 + 9 + 9 **16.** 9 + 6 + 1

17 Look at the numbers below. What is the fourth number from the left? *(pages 80–82)*

4 6 8 10 12 14

A 14 **B** 10 **C** 8 **D** 4

Extra Practice See Set E on page 199.

Problem-Solving Strategy: Work Backward

You will learn how to solve a problem by working backward.

Sometimes in a problem you can start with what you know and work backward.

Problem Shaun wanted to replace the string on his yo-yo. He cut a piece of string into 2 equal pieces. Then he cut 4 inches off one piece. That gave him a string that was 32 inches long. How long was the original piece of string?

What is the question?

How long was the original piece of string?

What do you know?

- He cut the string into 2 equal pieces.
- He cut 4 inches off one piece.
- The final piece of string was 32 inches long.

How can you find the answer?

Start with what you know. Then work backward.

Solve. Start with the final length of string.

Final Length				Original Length
32 inches	+ **4**	**36 inches**	+ **36**	**72 inches**
4 inches was cut off to get this length.	Work backward. Add 4.	The original string was cut into 2 equal pieces to get this length.	Work backward. Add 36.	

The original piece of string was 72 inches long.

Look back at the problem.

How can you check to see if your answer is reasonable?

Guided Practice

Solve these problems, using the Work Backward strategy.

1. Claire weighed a bag of marbles. Then she added 3 pounds of marbles to the bag. After taking 5 pounds of marbles out, the bag weighed 6 pounds. How much did the bag of marbles weigh in the beginning?

   Think: What information should you start with?

2. Ben is making tails for 4 kites. He cuts a piece of ribbon into 2 equal pieces. Then he cuts each of those pieces into 2 equal pieces. Each piece of ribbon is now 30 inches long. How long was the original piece of ribbon?

   Think: How many pieces of ribbon did Ben have after making all the cuts?

Choose a Strategy

Solve. Use these or other strategies.

Problem-Solving Strategies

- Find a Pattern
- Work Backward
- Guess and Check

3. Sue and her dad went to a toy store. She spent $6 for a bead kit and $4 for a yo-yo. Her dad gave her $5. Sue then had $7. How much money did she have when she arrived at the toy store?

4. Scot put 3 model airplanes on the first shelf of his bookcase, 6 on the second shelf, and 9 on the third shelf. If this pattern continues, how many airplanes is he likely to put on the sixth shelf of the bookcase?

5. Lei put a red ribbon on her toy dog. She put a green ribbon on her toy cat. The red ribbon is 2 inches longer than the green ribbon. Together the ribbons are 30 inches long. How long is each ribbon?

6. Tom collects trading cards. His friend gave him 4 special edition cards. Tom gave 2 of the cards to his brother. Tom bought 24 more cards. If he now has a total of 33 cards, how many cards did Tom start off with?

7. **Analyze** Manuel and Sarah are building a tower. They have a total of 25 blocks. Sarah has 5 more blocks than Manuel. How many blocks does each child have?

8. Lee added 24 inches of track to his train track. Then he removed 8 inches. This made his track 120 inches long. How long was the track before he began changing it?

Extra Practice See 1–2 on page 201.

Quick Check

Check Your Understanding of Lessons 1–8

Measure to the nearest half-inch.

1. 

Find the missing measure.

2. 18 ft = ___ yd

3. 2 yd = ___ ft

4. 1 mi = ___ ft

5. 1 mi = ___ yd

6. 2 ft = ___ in.

7. 3 yd = ___ in.

Choose the better estimate.

8. a cool fall day

58°F 92°F

9. a bowl of soup

2 c 2 qt

10. a bag of potatoes

5 oz 5 lb

Solve.

11. Mr. Jacobs placed a bag of pet food on a scale. Next, he added 2 pounds of food to the bag. After he took out 3 pounds of food, the bag weighed 4 pounds. How much did the bag of pet food weigh to start with?

How did you do?

If you had difficulty with any items in the Quick Check, you can use the following pages for review and extra practice.

Items	Review These Pages	Do These Extra Practice Items
1	pages 160–163	Set A, page 198
2–7	pages 164–166	Set B, page 198
8–10	pages 170–177	Set C, page 198 Set D–E, page 199
11	pages 178–179	1–2, page 201

Test Prep • Cumulative Review

Maintaining the Standards

Choose the letter of the correct answer. If a correct answer is not here, choose NH.

1. Which number sentence could be used to find the number of inches in 3 feet?

   A ■ inches = 12 + 12 + 12
   B ■ inches = 6 + 6 + 6
   C ■ inches = 12 + 12
   D ■ inches = 8 + 8 + 8

2. Which of the following is the best estimate of the amount of water a fish tank can hold?

   F 5 cups
   G 5 pints
   H 5 quarts
   J 5 gallons

3. The population of Sunnydale is 3,944. The population of Oakdale is 3,985. About how many people live in the two cities?

   A 5,000
   B 8,000
   C 10,000
   D 12,000

4. What time does the clock show?

   F 9:30
   G 6:10
   H 5:30
   J 10:30

Use the table to answer Questions 5 and 6.

Input	Output
0	6
3	9
6	12
9	■

5. What is the rule?

   A Input − 6 = Output
   B Input + 6 = Output
   C Output + 6 = Input
   D Output − 10 = Input

6. If the input is 9, what is the output?

   F 16
   G 15
   H 14
   J 10

7. Penny received 600 votes for class president. Jack received 428 votes. How many more votes did Penny receive?

   F 172
   G 228
   H 1,028
   J NH

8. Jamie bought 5 pounds of sugar. How many ounces equal 5 pounds?

   Explain How did you find your answer?

Centimeter and Decimeter

You will learn how to use metric units to measure length.

New Vocabulary
centimeters (cm)
decimeter (dm)

Learn About It

Many countries around the world use the metric system of measurement. **Centimeters (cm)** and **decimeters (dm)** are metric units used to measure length.

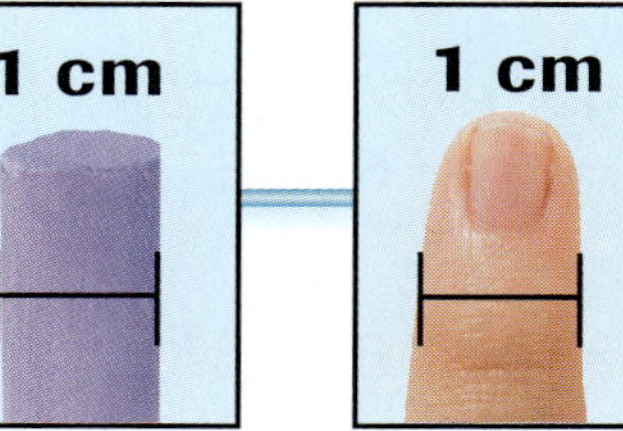

Centimeters are used to measure the lengths and widths of short objects.

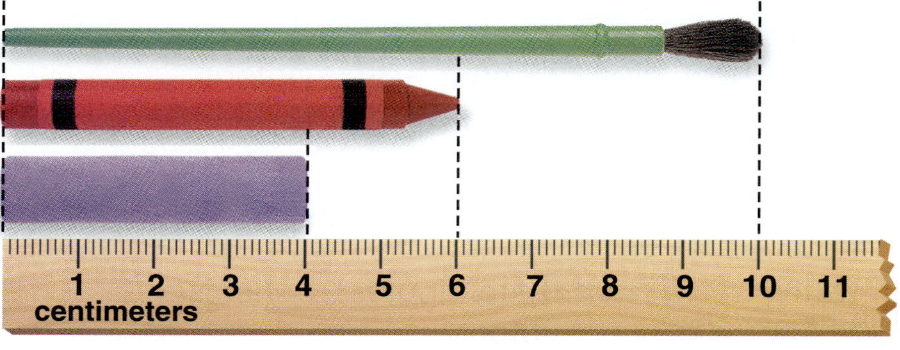

The paintbrush is 10 cm to the nearest cm.

The crayon is 6 cm to the nearest cm.

The chalk is 4 cm to the nearest cm.

Metric Units of Length
1 decimeter = 10 centimeters

Decimeters are used to measure longer objects.

The paintbrush is 1 dm long to the nearest decimeter.

Explain Your Thinking

- ► Suppose you measure a pencil in centimeters and then in decimeters. Is it more centimeters or more decimeters long?
- ► How can you find the number of centimeters if you know the number of decimeters?

Guided Practice

Estimate. Then measure to the nearest centimeter.

1.

2. **3.**

> **Ask Yourself**
> - Which centimeter mark is the closest to the end of the object?
> - Do you need a small or large unit?

Choose the unit you would use to measure each. Write *cm* or *dm*.

4. the width of your finger **5.** the length of your arm **6.** the width of a pencil

Independent Practice

Estimate. Then measure to the nearest centimeter.

7.

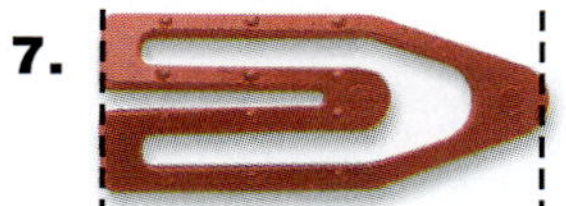

8.

9.

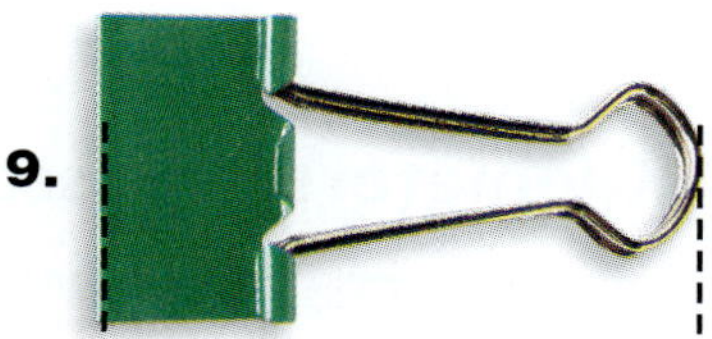

Choose the better estimate.

10. width of a computer
3 dm or 3 cm

11. width of your foot
60 cm or 6 cm

12. length of your shoe
2 cm or 2 dm

Problem Solving • Reasoning

Use Data **Use the picture for Problems 13 and 14.**

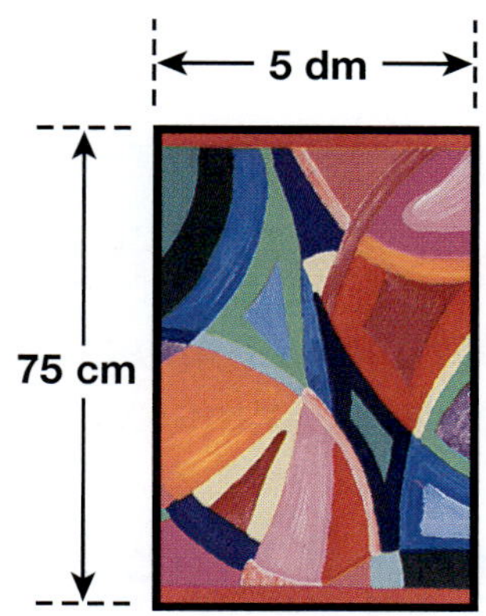

13. Josie painted the picture at the right. Which is greater, the width of the picture or the height of the picture? By how many centimeters is it greater?

14. **Analyze** Tim's picture is 5 cm taller than Josie's picture. How many decimeters tall is Tim's picture?

Mixed Review • Test Prep

For each pattern, write two numbers that are likely to come next. *(pages 28–29)*

15. 12, 14, 16, 18, ____, ____ **16.** 1, 2, 4, 8, ____, ____ **17.** 10, 25, 40, 55, ____, ____

18 Which number is 100 less than 452? *(pages 22–23)*

A 152 **B** 352 **C** 442 **D** 552

Extra Practice See Set F on page 199.

Meter and Kilometer

You will learn how to use metric units to measure greater lengths.

New Vocabulary
meter (m)
kilometer (km)

Learn About It

Meters (m) and **kilometers (km)** are metric units also used to measure length.

Metric Units of Length		
1 meter	=	10 decimeters
1 meter	=	100 centimeters
1,000 meters	=	1 kilometer

Meters are used to measure lengths longer than a centimeter or a decimeter.

1 meter

Kilometers are used to measure long distances.

The George Washington Bridge is about 1 kilometer long.

It takes about 10 minutes to walk 1 kilometer.

Explain Your Thinking

► Would you measure the distance from your home to school in meters or kilometers? Explain your choice.

Guided Practice

Choose the unit you would use to measure each. Write *m* or *km*.

1. width of a classroom
2. length of the Mississippi River
3. distance from New York City to Washington, D.C.
4. depth of a swimming pool

Ask Yourself

- Do you need a small or large unit?
- Which is the smaller unit? the larger unit?

Independent Practice

Choose the unit that you would use to measure each. Write *m* or *km*.

5. distance an airplane flies
6. height of a door
7. length of a ship
8. distance across town
9. length of a table
10. depth of a lake

Choose the better estimate.

11. length of a hockey stick
1 m or 1 km

12. length of a bridge
200 km or 2 km

13. height of a baseball player
2 m or 20 m

14. height of a mountain
4 m or 4 km

15. height of a tree
10 m or 10 km

16. length of a car
5 m or 50 m

Algebra • Equations **Copy and complete.**

17. 1 m = ____ cm
18. 1,000 m = ____ km
19. 10 km = ____ m
20. 10 m = ____ cm
21. 3 km = ____ m
22. 200 cm = ____ m
23. 5 m = ____ cm
24. 40 cm = ____ dm
25. 8 m = ____ cm

Problem Solving • Reasoning

26. **Estimate** A soccer field is about 100 meters long. About how many soccer fields laid end-to-end would cover 1 km? Explain.

27. Which is longer, a 2-kilometer race or a 2,500-meter race? Explain your thinking.

28. **Write Your Own** Write a rule that gives you the number of meters when you know the number of kilometers.

Mixed Review • Test Prep

Solve. *(pages 28–29, 108–109)*

29. 34 + 90
30. 52 − 28
31. 25 + 75
32. 100 − 65

33 What is the value of the 5 in 52,309? *(pages 32–33)*

A 5 ten thousands **B** 5 thousands **C** 5 hundreds **D** 5 ones

Extra Practice See Set G on page 200.

Metric Units of Capacity

You will learn how to use metric units to measure capacity.

New Vocabulary
liter (L)
milliliter (mL)

Learn About It

Liter (L) and **milliliter (mL)** are metric units used to measure capacity.

Metric Units of Capacity
1 liter = 1,000 milliliters

Try this activity to estimate and measure using liters.

Materials
1-liter container
other containers

Step 1 Pick 5 containers. Estimate which of the containers hold less than, more than, or about 1 liter.

Step 2 Use water and the 1-liter container to check your estimates.

Explain Your Thinking

- Why would you use liters instead of milliliters to measure the amount of juice in a pitcher?
- Would you need a larger container to hold 500 mL or to hold 500 L? Explain.

Guided Practice

Choose the better estimate for the capacity of each.

1. 
25 L or 25 mL

2. 
1 L or 10 L

3. 600 L or 6 L

Ask Yourself
- Do you need a small or a large unit?
- Which is the smaller unit? the larger unit?

Choose the unit to measure the capacity of each. Write *mL* or *L*.

4. a bathtub **5.** a spoon **6.** a pitcher

Independent Practice

Choose the better estimate for the capacity of each.

7. 

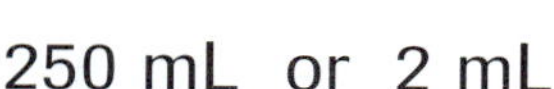

250 mL or 2 mL

8. 

150 L or 150,000 L

9. 1 mL or 100 mL

Choose the unit that you would use to measure the capacity of each. Write *mL* or *L*.

10. a pail **11.** a soup can **12.** a small vase

13. a pond **14.** a drinking glass **15.** a goldfish bowl

Algebra Sense • Equations **Complete.**

16. 1 L = ____ mL **17.** 500 mL = ____ L **18.** 2,000 mL = ____ L

19. 3 L = ____ mL **20.** 5,000 mL = ____ L **21.** 1,000 mL = ____ L

Problem Solving • Reasoning

22. Ed drank 890 milliliters of water. How many milliliters less than a liter did he drink?

23. **Logical Thinking** Judy and Sam each have a bottle. Judy's bottle holds more than Sam's bottle. One bottle has a red label and holds 2 liters. The other bottle has a blue label and holds 1,500 milliliters. What color is the label on Sam's bottle?

24. Toby poured 2,300 mL of water into a bowl. Then Kanisha poured 3 L of water into the same bowl. How much water is in the bowl now?

Mixed Review • Test Prep

Solve. *(pages xxii–xxv)*

25. ■ + 3 = 10 **26.** 9 − 8 = ■ **27.** ■ + 5 = 12

28. 8 = 20 − ■ **29.** 15 = ■ + 7 **30.** 6 + ■ = 16

31 Which of the following is true? *(pages 20–21)*

A $4 + 6 > 12$ **B** $12 < 4 + 6$ **C** $6 + 4 = 12$ **D** $6 + 4 < 12$

Extra Practice See Set H on page 200.

Problem-Solving Skill: Choose a Computation Method

You will learn how to add and subtract by using different methods.

When you solve a problem, you can use mental math, estimation, or paper and pencil.

Use Bob's journal for the problems below.

My Vacation
to the Grand Canyon

Day 1: We traveled 520 kilometers. We saw wheat fields and huge buffalo.

Day 2: We traveled 375 kilometers. We saw a roadrunner.

Day 3: We traveled 342 kilometers. Some of the time we traveled through desert. The Grand Canyon was nearby.

Sometimes you can use mental math.

Bob went on a trip. How many kilometers did he travel during the first two days?

$520 + 375 = ?$

Use mental math to add.

$500 + 375 = 875$

$875 + 20 = 895$

Think: 520 is the same as 500 + 20.

Bob traveled 895 kilometers during the first two days.

Sometimes you can use estimation.

To the nearest hundred kilometers, how many kilometers did Bob travel during the first three days ?

520	rounds to	500
375	rounds to	400
+ 342	rounds to	+ 300
		1,200

Bob traveled about 1,200 km during the first three days of his trip.

Sometimes you can use paper and pencil.

How many more kilometers did Bob travel during the first day than during the second day?

$$\begin{array}{r} \overset{4}{\cancel{5}}\overset{\overset{11}{\cancel{1}}}{\cancel{2}}\overset{10}{\cancel{0}} \\ -\ 375 \\ \hline 145 \end{array}$$

Bob traveled 145 km more the first day.

Look Back Explain why you think each method was chosen for the three problems above.

Remember:
- Understand
- Plan
- Solve
- Look Back

Guided Practice

Solve. Choose mental math, estimation, or paper and pencil. Explain your choice.

1. Bob bought a water bottle for $6.50 and a souvenir magnet for $1.50. He paid with a ten-dollar bill. What was his change?

Can you solve the problem by using mental math?

2. Bob's new water bottle can hold 950 mL of water. If he drinks 2 full bottles of water, about how much water will he drink?

Do you need an exact answer or an estimate?

Choose a Strategy

Solve. Use these or other strategies.

Problem-Solving Strategies
- Find a Pattern
- Write a Number Sentence
- Work Backward

3. The Grand Canyon is 443 kilometers long. It is 16 kilometers wide. How much greater is the length of the Grand Canyon than the width?

4. Bob's family brought 3 bottles of suntan lotion. Each bottle contains 425 mL of lotion. How many mL of lotion did the family bring?

5. The family spent $14.35 for gas on Saturday. On Sunday, they spent $1.25 more than they did on Saturday. How much did they spend for gas altogether?

6. Bob bought some cards and mailed 2 of them. He bought 4 more cards and mailed 3 of them. Then he had 4 cards left. How many cards did Bob buy in at the start?

7. The family saw a sign that said "Camp site–100 km." The next sign said it was 80 km away and the sign after that said it was 60 km away. How far will the family likely be from the campsite when they see the next sign?

8. Bob and his family went on a 3-hour hike. In the first hour, the family hiked 460 meters. In the second hour, they hiked 530 meters and in the third hour they hiked 480 meters About how far did the family hike in all?

Extra Practice See 3–6 on page 201.

Metric Units of Mass

You will learn how to use metric units to measure the mass of an object.

New Vocabulary
gram (g)
kilogram (kg)
mass

Learn About It

Gram (g) and **kilogram (kg)** are metric units used to measure the **mass,** or the amount of matter in an object.

You measure a shoelace or an egg in grams.
You measure a pair of sneakers or a car in kilograms.

Metric Units of Mass
1 kilogram = 1,000 grams

1 gram

1 kilogram

1,000 shoelaces have about the same mass as the sneakers.

Try this activity to estimate and measure mass.

Step 1 Find 5 small objects in your classroom. Estimate which of the objects are less than, more than, or about a kilogram.

Step 2 Use the scale and the kilogram to check your estimates.

Materials
scale
1-kilogram mass

Explain Your Thinking

▶ Do you think a larger item always has a greater mass? Use an example to explain.

Guided Practice

Choose the unit you would use to measure the mass of each. Write *g* or *kg*.

1. 

2. 

3. 

Ask Yourself
- Do I need a small or large unit of measure?

Independent Practice

Choose the unit you would use to measure the mass of each. Write *g* or *kg*.

4. a golf cart
5. a baseball cap
6. a soccer player
7. a horse
8. a tennis ball
9. a pair of goggles

Choose the better estimate.

10. a horse
    6 kg or 600 kg
11. a grapefruit
    500 g or 5 kg
12. a baseball bat
    10 g or 10 kg

Algebra • Equations **Copy and complete.**

13. 1 kg = ___ g
14. $\frac{1}{2}$ kg = ___ g
15. 2,000 g = ___ kg
16. 500 g = ___ kg
17. 3 kg = ___ g
18. 4,000 g = ___ kg

Problem Solving • Reasoning

Use Data **Use the table to solve. Choose a method.**

Computation Methods

- Mental Math
- Estimation
- Paper and Pencil

19. **Compare** Is the mass of a bowling ball less than or greater than 4,000 g? Explain.
20. How many more grams is the mass of a bowling ball than the mass of a basketball?
21. **Analyze** Suppose there is a 900-gram mass on one side of a scale. Which items listed in the table could you use to balance the scale? You can use an item more than once. Is there more than one answer? Explain.

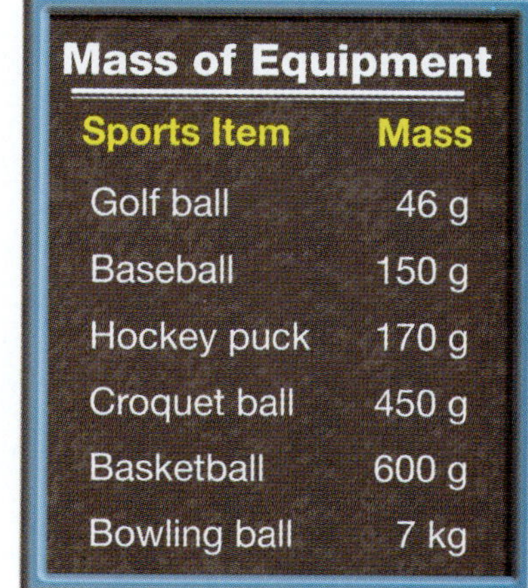

Mass of Equipment

Sports Item	Mass
Golf ball	46 g
Baseball	150 g
Hockey puck	170 g
Croquet ball	450 g
Basketball	600 g
Bowling ball	7 kg

Mixed Review • Test Prep

Compare. Write >, <, or = for each ●. *(pages 20–21, 110–111, 128–131)*

22. 80¢ + 15¢ ● 45¢ + 50¢
23. 67¢ ● 76¢
24. 30 + 21 ● 89 − 45

25. Which number has a 3 in the thousands place? *(pages 34–35)*

A 131,898 **B** 214,359 **C** 143,948 **D** 334,978

Extra Practice See Set I on page 200.

Temperature: Degrees Celsius

You will learn how to tell temperature in degrees Celsius.

New Vocabulary
degrees Celsius (°C)

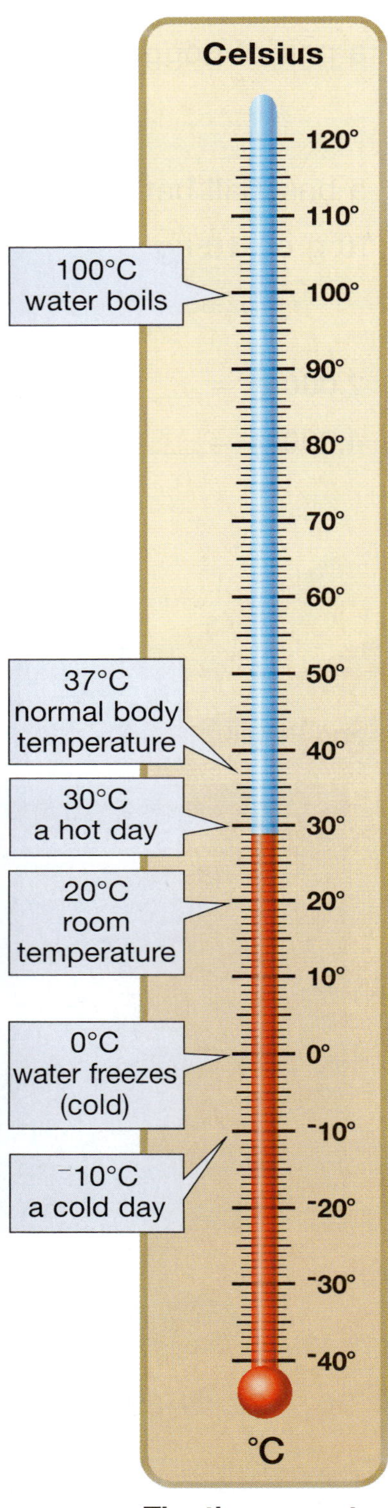

The thermometer shows 29°C.

Learn About It

There are animals that can live in very low temperatures and animals that can live in very high temperatures.

Temperatures on January 1

The desert iguana can live in temperatures as high as 45°C.

The emperor penguin can live in temperatures as low as ⁻30°C.

A thermometer like the one at the left can be used to measure temperature in **degrees Celsius (C)**.

Explain Your Thinking

► The temperature is ⁻5°C. Is this cold or hot? Explain how you know.

Guided Practice

Write each temperature. Then write *hot, warm, cool,* or *cold* to describe the temperature.

1. 

2. 

Ask Yourself

- Where does the red line end?
- What temperature describes hot? warm? cool? cold?

Independent Practice

Write each temperature. Then write *hot, warm, cool,* or *cold* to describe the temperature.

3. 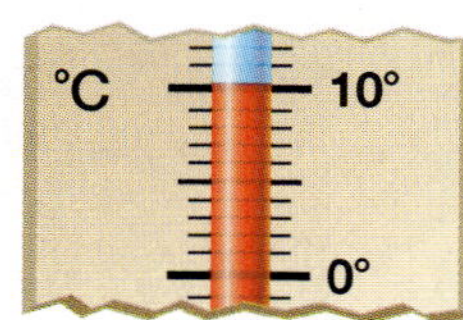

4. 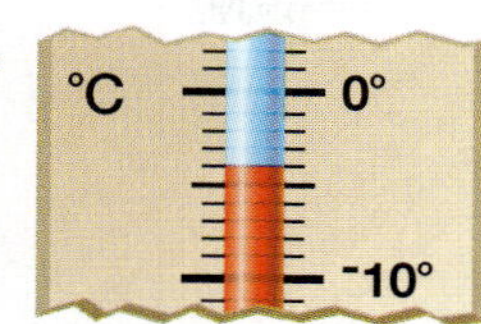

5. 

6. 

Choose the better estimate of the temperature.

7. 

a. ⁻1°C **b.** 27°C

8. 

a. 5°C **b.** 21°C

9. 

a. 10°C **b.** 30°C

Problem Solving • Reasoning

10. Suppose Pat's temperature is 36°C. Is it above or below normal body temperature? By how many degrees is it above or below?

11. **Analyze** Use the thermometer on page 192. What is the difference in temperature between ⁻30°C and 45°C? Explain how you got your answer.

12. **Write About It** Describe an activity you might do outside if the temperature is 28°C.

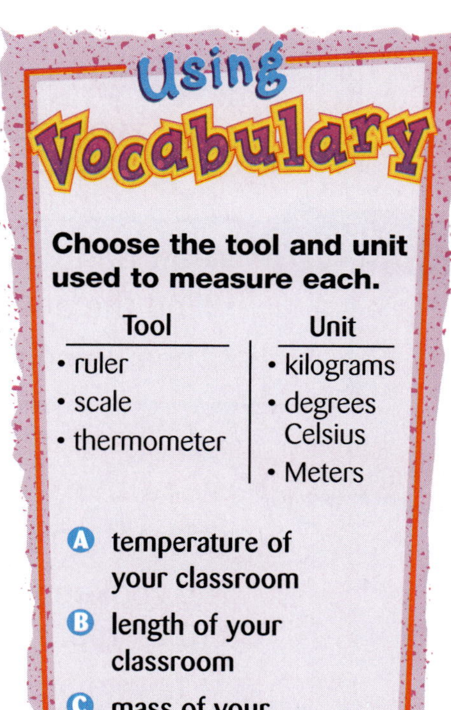

Mixed Review • Test Prep

Round each number to the place value of the underlined digit. *(pages 6–9; 24–25)*

13. 8,901 **14.** 74¢ **15.** 399 **16.** $2.09

17 Which is another name for 95? *(pages 4–5)*

A 7 tens 15 ones **C** 8 tens 15 ones

B 8 tens 5 ones **D** 9 tens 15 ones

Problem-Solving Application: Use Measurement

You will learn how to use what you know about measurement to solve problems.

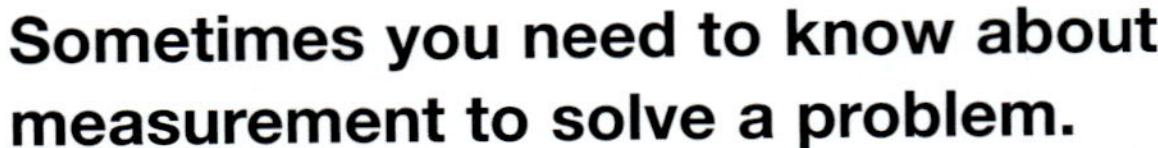

Sometimes you need to know about measurement to solve a problem.

Problem The table at the right shows the amount of food Tara, the elephant, eats in a day. Suppose the zookeeper has 110 pounds of fruit. Does the zookeeper have enough fruit to feed Tara for one week?

Tara's Daily Food

Tara's Daily Food
15 pounds of fruit
3 pounds of bran
38 pounds of carrots
12 pounds of vitamins
80 pounds of yams
$1\frac{1}{2}$ bales of hay

Understand

What is the question?
Does the zookeeper have enough fruit for one week?

What do you know?
- Tara eats 15 lb of fruit each day.
- The zookeeper has 110 lb of fruit.

Plan

What can you do to find the answer?
- Find the amount of fruit needed to feed Tara for one week.
- Then compare that amount with 110 pounds.

Solve

Since there are 7 days in a week, add 15 seven times.

$15 + 15 + 15 + 15 + 15 + 15 + 15 = 105$ pounds

The zookeeper needs 105 pounds of fruit.
$110 > 105$, so the zookeeper has enough fruit.

Look Back

Look back at the problem.
How many more pounds of fruit should the zookeeper buy to have enough fruit for Tara for 2 weeks? Explain your thinking.

This baby elephant is 7 days old. It weighed about 200 lb when it was born. Its mother weighs about 9,000 lb, and its father weighs about 15,000 lb!

Guided Practice

Solve. Use the table on page 194 to help you.

1. Each day Tara is fed 10 pounds of yams during her morning exercises, 10 pounds of yams with breakfast, 20 pounds with lunch, and the rest with dinner. How many pounds of yams is Tara fed with dinner?

Will you need to add or subtract first?

2. When Tara was a newborn, she drank about 7,000 mL of milk each day. At 9 months old, she drank 26 L of milk each day. How much more milk did Tara drink each day when she was 9 months old than when she was a newborn?

How many milliliters are in a liter?

Choose a Strategy

Solve. Use these or other strategies.

Problem-Solving Strategies

- **Find a Pattern**
- **Write a Number Sentence**
- **Use Logical Thinking**

3. Which weighs more, a 25,500-pound truck or three elephants that weigh 8,500 pounds each? Explain.

4. Tara walked 753 meters in a parade. Did she walk more or less than one kilometer? Explain.

5. Gita, Ruby, Billy, and Tara are elephants. Ruby weighs more than Tara. Gita weighs more than Ruby. Billy weighs less than Gita but more than Ruby. Write the names of the elephants in order from heaviest to lightest.

6. Tara, Ruby, Gita, and Billy get extra hay when it is cold outside. The temperature at the zoo was 25°C at 9:00 A.M. By noon the temperature was 3°C higher. Should the zookeeper give them extra hay? Explain your reasoning.

7. Tara's mass was 113 kg at birth. Her mass was 117 kg 3 days later. Six days after birth her mass was 121 kg. If this pattern continues, what will her mass likely be 9 days after birth?

8. On Saturday, 1,234 tickets were sold at the zoo. Additional tickets were sold on Sunday. If 2,302 tickets were sold on the two days, how many tickets were sold on Sunday?

Extra Practice See 7–9 on page 201.

Quick Check

Check Your Understanding of Lessons 9–15

Find the missing measure.

1. 400 cm = ___ m
2. 2 m = ___ cm
3. 2,000 m = ___ km
4. 50 cm = ___ dm

Choose the best estimate.

5. a computer
   15 g   15 kg
6. a paper clip
   1 g   100 g
7. bath water
   10°C   40°C
8. a pitcher of water
   200 mL   2 L

Solve.

9. Anita had 1 kilogram of flour. She used 625 grams in a recipe she was making. About how many grams of flour did she have left? Do you need an exact answer or an estimate?
10. Mike and Tim went jogging. Mike jogged 1,500 meters. Tim jogged 3 kilometers. Who jogged the furthest? How much further? Explain.

How did you do?

If you had difficulty with any items in the Quick Check, you can use the following pages for review and extra practice.

Items	Review These Pages	Do These Extra Practice Items
1–4	pages 182–185	Set F, page 199 Set G, page 200
5–8	pages 186–187, 190–193	Sets H–J, page 200
9–10	pages 188–189, 194–195	3–9, page 201

Test Prep • Cumulative Review

Estimating and Using Metric Units of Measure

Choose the letter of the correct answer. If a correct answer is not here, choose NH.

1. Which of the following is the best estimate of the height of a classroom door?

   A 3 centimeters
   B 3 decimeters
   C 3 meters
   D 3 kilometers

2. If the pattern continues, what is likely to be the next number?

   7, 14, 21, 28, ____

   F 32
   G 35
   H 42
   J 44

3. There are 400 students in a school and 128 students received awards. How many students did not receive awards?

   A 271
   B 300
   C 528
   D NH

4. Which number sentence could be used to find the number of grams in 2 kilograms?

   F ■ grams = 1,000 + 1,000
   G ■ grams = 100 + 100
   H ■ grams = 1,000 − 1,000
   J ■ grams = 1,000 + 1,000 + 100

5. What number should go in the box to make this number sentence true?

   ■ − 19 = 52

   A 33
   B 47
   C 65
   D 71

6. What is the value of the underlined digit in 1,<u>9</u>62?

   F 9
   G 90
   H 900
   J 9,000

7. Which of the following is the best estimate of the amount of water that this drinking glass can hold?

   A 5 liters **C** 2 mL
   B 250 mL **D** 1 liter

8. Manny entered the 5,000-meter run. How many kilometers equal 5,000 meters?

   Explain How did you find your answer?

Safe Site

Internet Test Prep
Visit **www.eduplace.com/kids/mhm** for more *Test Prep Practice.*

Extra Practice

Set A (Lesson 2, pages 162–163)

Measure each object to the nearest half inch.

1. 

2.

3. 

Use an inch ruler. Draw a line of each length.

4. $4\frac{1}{2}$ in.
5. $6\frac{1}{2}$ in.
6. $7\frac{1}{2}$ in.

Set B (Lesson 3, pages 164–166)

Choose the better estimate.

1. The length of your bed
   a. 6 inches b. 6 feet
2. The distance from a home to a school
   a. 3 feet b. 3 miles

Find the missing measure.

3. 3 ft = ____ in.
4. 9 ft = ____ yd
5. 36 in. = ____ yd
6. 4 yd = ____ ft
7. 24 in. = ____ ft
8. 18 in. = ____ ft

Compare. Use >, <, or = for each ●.

9. 2 ft ● 20 in.
10. 39 in. ● 39 ft
11. 12 ft ● 4 yd
12. 5,255 ft ● 1 mi
13. 9 yd ● 30 ft
14. 15 in. ● 1 ft

Set C (Lesson 5, pages 170–171)

Choose the better estimate.

1. large bucket
   a. 2 gallons b. 2 pints
2. glass of milk
   a. 1 cup b. 1 quart

Find the missing measure.

3. 3 pt = ____ c
4. 2 gal = ____ pt
5. 10 c = ____ pt
6. 4 gal = ____ qt
7. 6 qt = ____ pt
8. 6 gal = ____ pt

Extra Practice

Set D (Lesson 6, pages 172–174)

Choose the unit that you would use to measure the weight of each. Write *ounce* or *pound*.

1. 

2. 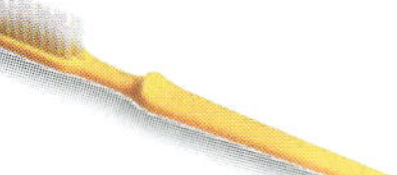

3. 

Choose the better estimate.

4. calculator
   a. 12 lb b. 12 oz

5. cat
   a. 8 lb b. 8 oz

Find the missing measure.

6. 24 oz = ____ lb
7. $2\frac{1}{2}$ lb = ____ oz
8. 64 oz = ____ lb
9. 5 lb = ____ oz
10. 8 oz = ____ lb
11. 7 lb = ____ oz

Set E (Lesson 7, pages 176–177)

Choose the better estimate of the temperature.

1. 
   a. 15°F b. 75°F

2. 
   a. 100°F b. 20°F

3. 
   a. 95°F b. 8°F

Set F (Lesson 9, pages 182–183)

Estimate. Then measure to the nearest centimeter.

1. 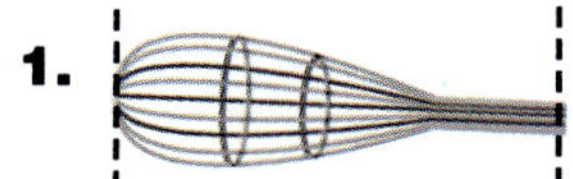

2. 

Choose the better estimate.

3. width of your hand
   a. 50 cm b. 10 cm

4. length of piece of spaghetti
   a. 15 dm b. 15 cm

Extra Practice

Set G (Lesson 10, pages 184–185)

Choose the better estimate.

1. distance a car travels in an hour
   a. 35 m b. 35 km
2. height of a school bus
   a. 8 km b. 8 m

Find the missing measure.

3. 15 m = ____ cm
4. 400 cm = ____ m
5. 2,000 m = ____ km
6. 20 dm = ____ cm
7. 2 km = ____ m
8. 100 cm = ____ m

Set H (Lesson 11, pages 186–187)

Find the missing measure.

1. 4 L = ____ mL
2. 2 L = ____ mL
3. 6,000 mL = ____ L
4. 1,000 mL = ____ L
5. 3,000 mL = ____ L
6. 5 L = ____ mL

Set I (Lesson 13, pages 190–191)

Choose the unit that you would use to measure the mass of each. Write *g* or *kg*.

1. apple
2. lawn mower
3. spoon

Choose the better estimate.

4. egg
   a. 20 g b. 2 g
5. basketball
   a. 500 g b. 50 kg
6. T-shirt
   a. 2 g b. 100 g

Find the missing measure.

7. 4 kg = ____ g
8. 3,000 g = ____ kg
9. 2 kg = ____ g

Set J (Lesson 14, pages 192–193)

Write each temperature. Then write *hot, warm, cool,* or *cold* to describe the temperature.

1. 

2. 

3. 

4. 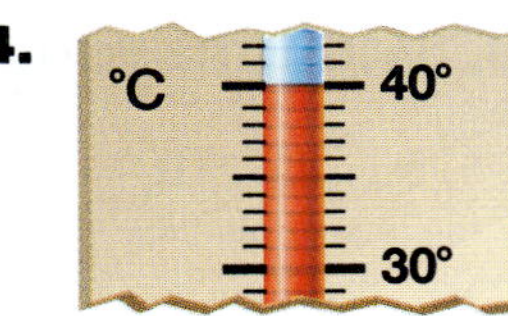

Extra Practice • Problem Solving

Solve these problems, using the Work Backward strategy. *(Lesson 8, pages 178–179)*

1. Yesterday Susan began making a string necklace. Today she braided 4 inches in the morning and 3 inches in the afternoon. Now the necklace is 12 inches long. How long was the necklace at the end of yesterday?

2. Wu made a pitcher of lemonade. He drank 2 cups with lunch and another cup in the afternoon. Then there was 1 pint left in the pitcher. How many cups of lemonade did Wu make?

Solve. Tell if you used mental math, estimation, or paper and pencil. Then explain your choice. *(Lesson 12, pages 188–189)*

3. About 5 liters of water drain out of a bathtub each minute. About how many liters of water drain out in 4 minutes?

4. A school hopes to sell 500 books at a book sale. Today, they sold 382 books. How many more books do they need to sell?

5. John is measuring wood for a birdhouse. He needs two pieces of wood that are 10 inches long and two that are 7 inches long. He has a piece of wood that is one yard long. Will he have enough wood to cut the four pieces? Explain.

6. The temperature on Friday was 40°F. The weather forecaster says that on Saturday it will be 5° lower. By Sunday the temperature will drop 10° more. Water begins to freeze at 32°F. Will the temperature be low enough for water to freeze on Sunday? Explain.

Use the table to solve. *(Lesson 15, pages 194–195)*

7. Was the total weight of all 3 puppies at birth greater than 3 pounds?

8. Which puppy gained the most weight in one month?

9. Puppy 3 gained 2 pounds during the first two weeks. How much weight did it gain the second two weeks?

Puppy Weights

	At Birth (oz)	After 1 Month (oz)
Puppy 1	28	85
Puppy 2	24	64
Puppy 3	19	70

Chapter Review

Reviewing Vocabulary

Decide if each statement is *true* or *false*.

1. The length of a large paper clip is about a foot.
2. Kilogram and gram are metric units of weight.
3. One kilogram is heavier than one gram.
4. These units of length are in order from shortest to longest: foot, inch, mile, yard.
5. These units of length are in order from shortest to longest: centimeter, decimeter, meter, kilometer.

Reviewing Concepts and Skills

Measure each object to the nearest half inch. *(pages 162–163)*

6. 

7. 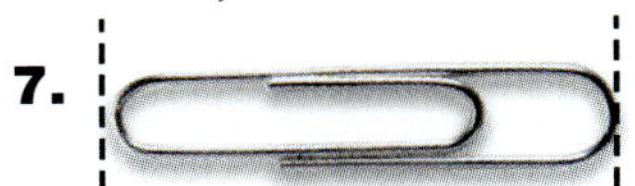

Choose the better estimate.

8. width of a frying pan
   a. 12 ft b. 12 in.
9. pitcher of juice
   a. 1 cup b. 1 quart
10. height of a man
    a. 6 ft b. 6 yd
11. length of a trail
    a. 5 km b. 15 m
12. perfume bottle
    a. 100 mL b. 5 mL
13. bowl of soup
    a. 600 mL b. 6 L

Compare. Use >, <, or = for each ●. *(pages 164–166, 170–174)*

14. 3 yd ● 30 in.
15. 25 in. ● 2 ft
16. 15 ft ● 5 yd
17. 2 gal ● 10 pt
18. 1 qt ● 6 c
19. 2 lb ● 34 oz
20. 30 cm ● 3 m
21. 100 m ● 10 cm
22. 4,000 m ● 4 km
23. 8 kg ● 900 g
24. 2,000 g ● 2 kg
25. 300 mL ● 2 L

Find the missing measure.

26. 24 in. = ____ ft
27. 3 lb = ____ oz
28. 9 pt = ____ c
29. 400 cm = ____ m
30. 4,500 mL = ____ L
31. 8 kg = ____ g

Write each temperature. Then write *hot, warm, cool,* or *cold* to describe each temperature. *(pages 176–177, 192–193)*

32. 

33. 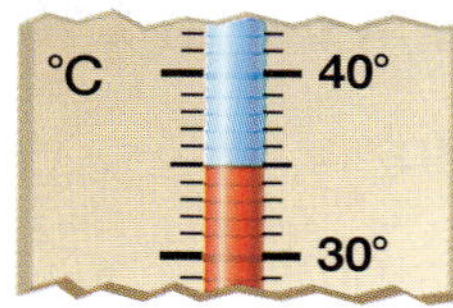

34. 

Solve. *(pages 178–179, 188–189, 194–195)*

35. Ted collects and trades rocks. He traded a 7-lb rock for a 4-lb rock. Now his collection weighs 25 lb. What did his collection weigh before he made the trade?

36. Nan has two jump ropes. One is 10 feet long. The length of the two ropes together is 6 yards. How long is the other jump rope?

37. Patti filled a 5-liter bucket with soapy water to wash her bike. After she finished there was about 1,080 mL of soapy water left in the bucket. About how much soapy water did Patti use?

Brain Teasers Math Reasoning

Unusual Units

Anna made up a new unit of measurement and named it after herself. There are 12 "annas" in 5 yd. How many "annas" would there be in 5 feet?

Pouring Punch

Dan has a 5-cup bottle, a 2-cup bottle, and big bucket. None of the containers are marked. How could Dan use the containers to measure 11 cups of punch?

Internet Brain Teasers
Visit **www.eduplace.com/kids/mhm** for more *Brain Teasers.*

Chapter Test

Use an inch ruler. Draw a line of each length.

1. $9\frac{1}{2}$ in. **2.** 2 in. **3.** $5\frac{1}{2}$ in.

4. 8 cm **5.** $6\frac{1}{2}$ cm **6.** 14 cm

Choose the better estimate.

7. weight of a baseball
a. 30 lb **b.** 13 oz

8. width of a stapler
a. 2 in. **b.** 2 yd

9. glass of juice
a. 2 c **b.** 2 qt

10. bottle of cooking oil
a. 10 L **b.** 1 L

11. height of a door
a. 3 m **b.** 30 m

12. mass of a cow
a. 5 kg **b.** 500 kg

Compare. Use $>$, $<$, or $=$ for each ●.

13. 2 gal ● 10 c **14.** 50 oz ● 4 lb **15.** 6 yd ● 20 ft

16. 4 L ● 500 mL **17.** 1 kg ● 500 g **18.** 3 km ● 4 m

Find the missing measure.

19. 12 c = ____ pt **20.** 5 ft = ____ in. **21.** 5 lb = ____ oz

22. 6,000 g = ____ kg **23.** 50 dm = ____ m **24.** 7 m = ____ cm

25. 9 yd = ____ ft **26.** 8,000 m = ____ km **27.** 9,000 mL = ____ L

Write each temperature. Then write *hot, warm, cool,* or *cold* to describe each temperature.

28.

29.

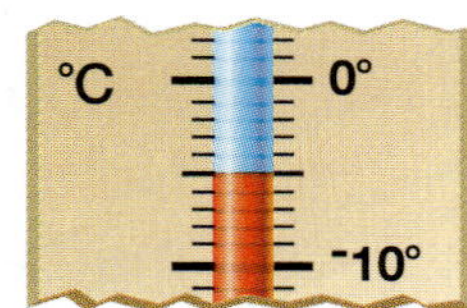

30.

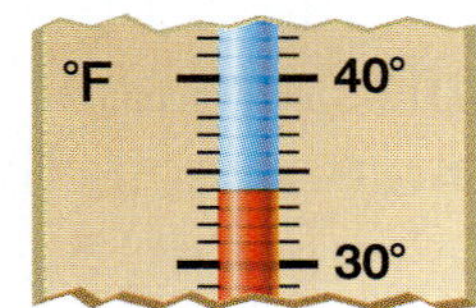

Solve.

31. Jill's gym bag weighs 2 pounds. She forgot to pack her sweatpants, sweatshirt, and sweatsocks. Together they weigh about 18 ounces. How many ounces will her gym bag weigh when she packs these three items?

32. Mario bought orange juice for a party. He also bought 4 gallons of fruit juice. At the party 7 gallons of juice were used and 6 gallons were left over. How many gallons of orange juice did Mario buy?

33. Samantha wants to put a fence around all 3 sides of her herb garden. She needs 7 feet of fencing for each side. Fencing is sold by the yard. How many yards of fencing will Samantha need to buy?

Write About It

Solve each problem. Use correct math vocabulary to explain your thinking.

1. You have 2 gallons of apple cider for a party. There will be 15 people at the party.

   a. You have three 2-quart pitchers. Will these pitchers hold all the cider?

   b. If the cider is served in 1-cup glasses, will there be enough for everyone to have 2 servings?

2. Look at the picture on the right. Joan had to convert decimeters to centimeters. She knows that 1 dm = 10 cm. This is how she converted 3 decimeters into centimeters.

   a. What is wrong with her reasoning?

   b. Show how to find the correct answer.

Another Look

Use the pictures below to find the answer to each question.

1. Look at the pictures of the objects in the top row. Suppose you want to measure how much liquid each object holds. Would you use units of length, capacity, or weight? List the customary units you would use to measure how much liquid each object holds.
2. Look at the pictures of the objects in the bottom row. Suppose you want to measure the height of each object. Would you use units of length, capacity, or weight? List the metric units you would use to measure the height of each object.
3. **Look Back** Which customary units would you use to measure the height of the objects in the bottom row?
4. **Analyze** The measurements of some things can be reported using different units. For example, you could measure the length of a room in feet or in yards. Name four other items that can be measured using different units. List the units you would use to measure each item.

Enrichment

Using a Scale Drawing

A scale drawing is the same shape, but not the same size as the object it pictures.

In this scale drawing, 1 inch stands for 2 feet.

The height of the tiger lily in the scale drawing is 2 inches.

So the height of a real tiger lily is 4 feet.

Use your ruler to measure each flower. Then answer each question.

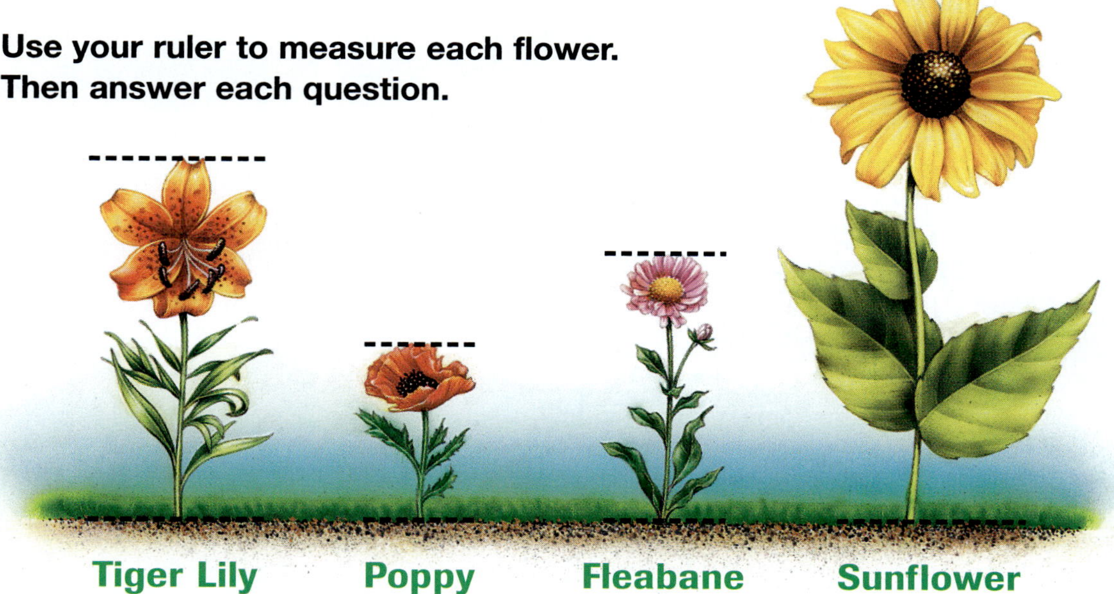

1. What is the height of the poppy in the scale drawing?
2. What is the height of a real poppy?
3. What is the real height of fleabane?
4. How many feet taller is a real sunflower than a real poppy?

Explain Your Thinking

Suppose the height of a real marigold is 2 feet 6 inches. How many inches tall would it be in a scale drawing where 1 inch stands for 2 feet? How did you decide?

Multiplication Concepts

Why Learn About Multiplication Concepts?

Multiplication concepts can help you understand how to find the total number of items when you have equal-sized groups.

If your cat eats 2 cans of food each day, you can use multiplication to find how many cans of food your cat eats each week.

Each of these flowers has 5 petals. You can use multiplication to find the total number of petals on the three flowers.

Reading Mathematics

Reviewing Vocabulary

Understanding math language helps you become a successful problem solver. Here are some math vocabulary words you should know.

equal groups groups that have the same number of objects

multiply to find the total number of objects that are in equal groups

multiplication sentence a sentence that shows how numbers are related when multiplied

product the answer in a multiplication problem

Reading Words and Symbols

When you read mathematics, sometimes you read only words, sometimes you read words and symbols, and sometimes you read only symbols.

All of these describe the same multiplication sentence.

- 2 groups of 10 equals 20.
- 2 times 10 equals 20.
- The product of 2 and 10 is 20.

$$\begin{array}{r} 10 \\ \times\ 2 \\ \hline 20 \end{array} \leftarrow \text{product}$$

$$2 \times 10 = \underset{\substack{\uparrow \\ \text{product}}}{20}$$

Try These

1. Tell if the picture shows equal groups. Write *yes* or *no*.

a.   

b.   

c.  

d.  

2. Tell if 8 is the sum, difference, or product.

a. $\begin{array}{r} 2 \\ \times\ 4 \\ \hline 8 \end{array}$

b. $6 + 2 = 8$

c. $\begin{array}{r} 17 \\ -\ 9 \\ \hline 8 \end{array}$

d. $4 \times 2 = 8$

3. Write each as a multiplication sentence.

a. Two times three equals six.

b. The product of four and ten is forty.

c. Five groups of one equals five.

d. Two multiplied by two equals four.

Upcoming Vocabulary

Write About It **Here are some other vocabulary words** you will learn in this chapter. Watch for these words. Write their definitions in your journal.

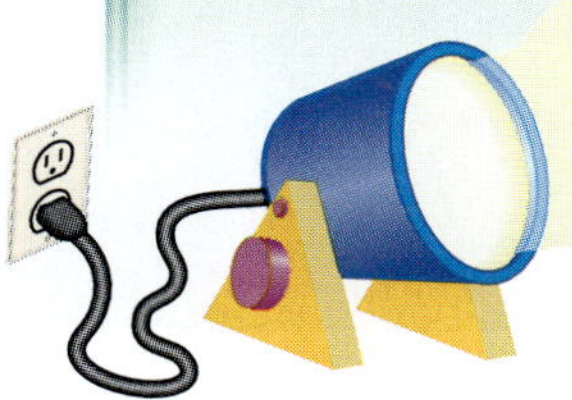

array

factors

Commutative Property of Multiplication

Modeling Multiplication

You will learn that you can think about multiplication as repeated addition.

Review Vocabulary
multiplication

Learn About It

Use counters to model multiplication.

Look at the 3 strips of stickers shown on the right. There are 5 stickers on each strip. How can you find the number of stickers there are in all? Use counters to help you.

Materials

For each pair:
36 counters
6 pieces of paper

Step 1 Use pieces of paper to stand for the strips. Use counters to stand for the stickers. Put 5 counters on each piece of paper.

Step 2 Find the total number of counters.

You can find the total number in different ways.

You can write an addition sentence.

$5 + 5 + 5 = 15$

Think: 3 groups of 5 = 15.

You can write a **multiplication** sentence.

$3 \times 5 = 15$

Read: Three times five equals fifteen.

Think: 3 groups of 5 = 15.

- How many counters are there in all?
- How many stickers are there in all?

Step 3 Now use counters and pieces of paper to make other equal groups. Decide how many counters and pieces of paper to use. Be sure to put the same number of counters on each piece of paper.

Step 4 Find the total number of counters. In a table like the one below, draw a picture of your groups of counters. Then describe your picture by using words, an addition sentence, or a multiplication sentence.

Step 5 Repeat Steps 3 and 4 several times. Record your work in your table.

Draw the Equal Groups	Think	Addition Sentence	Multiplication Sentence
	3 groups of 5	$5 + 5 + 5 = 15$	$3 \times 5 = 15$

Try It Out

Model each set with counters. Then write an addition sentence and a multiplication sentence for each.

1. 4 groups of 3
2. 5 groups of 2
3. 2 groups of 6
4. 5 groups of 4
5. 3 groups of 6
6. 2 groups of 10

Write a multiplication sentence for each.

7. $7 + 7 + 7 + 7 = 28$
8. $3 + 3 + 3 + 3 + 3 + 3 = 18$
9. $4 + 4 + 4 = 12$
10. $5 + 5 + 5 + 5 + 5 + 5 + 5 = 35$

Write about it! Talk about it!

Use what you have learned to answer these questions.

11. Can you write a multiplication sentence to describe this picture? Explain why or why not.

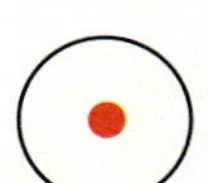
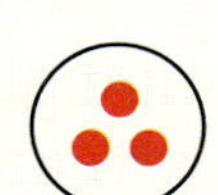

12. Suppose you buy 3 identical packages of stickers. What must you know before you can multiply to find the total number of stickers you bought?

Arrays and Multiplication

You will learn that you can multiply numbers in any order.

New Vocabulary
array
factors
product
Commutative Property

Learn About It

Kevin collects stamps from different countries. He keeps his stamps in an album. How many stamps are on this page of his album?

Look at the array.

The stamps are arranged in an array. An **array** shows objects arranged in rows and columns.

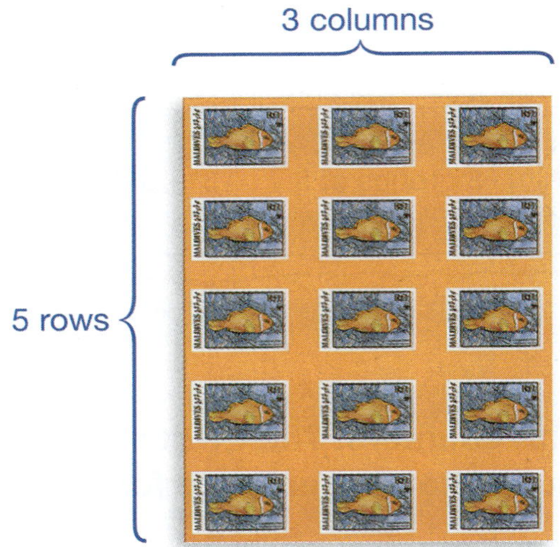

Each row in the array has an equal number of stamps. You can multiply to find the total number of stamps.

$$5 \times 3 = 15$$

5 → rows; 3 → stamps in each row; 15 → total number of stamps

Solution: There are 15 stamps on the page.

Look at the multiplication sentence again. The numbers you multiply are called **factors**. The answer is called the **product**.

$$5 \times 3 = 15$$

5 → factor; 3 → factor; 15 → product

Suppose the page is turned. Does the total number of stamps change?

Compare the two arrays.

3 columns

5 rows

5 columns

3 rows

$5 \times 3 = 15$

5 ↑ rows, 3 ↑ stamps in each row

$3 \times 5 = 15$

3 ↑ rows, 5 ↑ stamps in each row

Remember: The number of rows is the first factor.

The total number of stamps does not change. There are 15 stamps in each array.

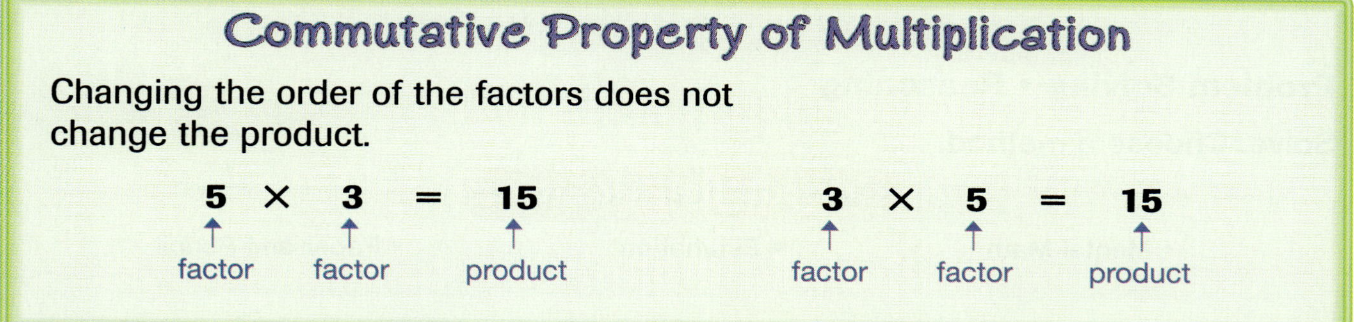

Commutative Property of Multiplication

Changing the order of the factors does not change the product.

$5 \times 3 = 15$

5 ↑ factor, 3 ↑ factor, 15 ↑ product

$3 \times 5 = 15$

3 ↑ factor, 5 ↑ factor, 15 ↑ product

Explain Your Thinking

- Give an example of two different pairs of factors that have the same product.
- How can knowing $4 \times 6 = 24$ help you find 6×4?

Guided Practice

Write a multiplication sentence for each array.

1. 

2.  

> **Ask Yourself**
>
> - How many rows are there?
> - How many are in each row?

Independent Practice

Write a multiplication sentence for each array.

3.

4.

5. 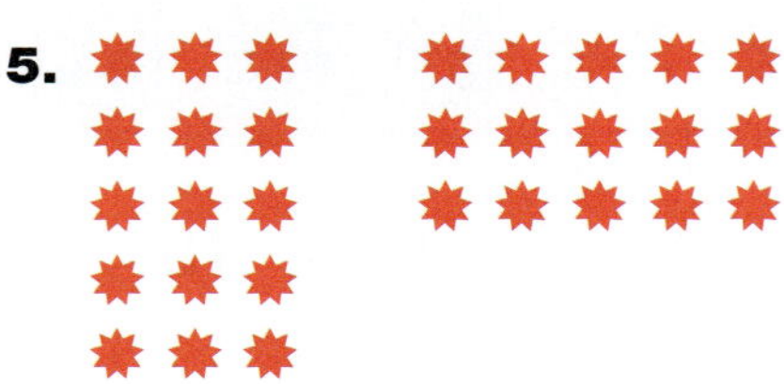

6.

Algebra • Properties **Find each missing number.**

7. $3 \times 5 = 15$
$5 \times 3 = ■$

8. $2 \times 6 = 12$
$6 \times ■ = 12$

9. $8 = 4 \times 2$
$■ = 2 \times 4$

10. $21 = 7 \times 3$
$21 = 3 \times ■$

11. $3 \times 4 = 12$
$4 \times ■ = 12$

12. $30 = 5 \times 6$
$30 = 6 \times ■$

Problem Solving • Reasoning

Solve. Choose a method.

Computation Methods

- Mental Math
- Estimation
- Paper and Pencil

13. Marta has 8 rows of post cards with 3 cards in each row. How many post cards does she have?

14. Mike has 62 stamps. Paul has 38 stamps. About how many more stamps does Mike have?

15. Hallie bought 2 booklets of animal stamps and 3 booklets of flower stamps. Each booklet has 20 stamps. How many stamps did Hallie buy?

16. **Write About It** A stamp machine shows 8 different stamps on display in an array. What are all the different ways the stamps can be arranged?

17. Analyze Hans bought a sheet of stamps that has 4 rows of 5 stamps. Two rows have flowers. Two rows have trees. So far Hans has used 3 flower stamps. How many flower stamps are left?

18. Sarah has 2 rows of 5 stamps left in her booklet of stamps. She wants to mail 12 party invitations. If each invitation needs 1 stamp, will Sarah have enough stamps? Explain why or why not.

Mixed Review • Test Prep

Solve. *(pages 104–106, 108–109, 132–133)*

19. $\begin{array}{r} 25 \\ +\ 64 \\ \hline \end{array}$ **20.** $\begin{array}{r} 78 \\ +\ 95 \\ \hline \end{array}$ **21.** $\begin{array}{r} 308 \\ -\ 47 \\ \hline \end{array}$ **22.** $\begin{array}{r} 519 \\ -\ 328 \\ \hline \end{array}$ **23.** $\begin{array}{r} 493 \\ +\ 728 \\ \hline \end{array}$

Choose the letter for the correct answer. *(pages 128–129, 140–141)*

24 568 − 219 = ■

A 249 **C** 351
B 349 **D** 359

25 704 − 217 = ■

F 487 **H** 587
G 513 **J** 921

Making Arrays

Suppose you have been asked to design a new sheet of stamps. There are 24 stamps, and they need to be arranged in equal rows.

26. One way is shown at the right. What other ways could you design the sheet of stamps?

- Draw a picture to show each way.
- Write a multiplication sentence to describe each picture.

Extra Practice See Set A on page 242.

Multiply With 2

You will learn different ways to multiply when 2 is a factor.

Learn About It

Balloon artists twist and turn balloons into animal shapes. Suppose 2 balloons are needed to make a fish. How many balloons are needed to make 6 fish?

6 (factor) × 2 (factor) = ■ (product) or

$$\begin{array}{r} 2 \leftarrow \text{factor} \\ \times\ 6 \leftarrow \text{factor} \\ \hline ■ \leftarrow \text{product} \end{array}$$

Different Ways to Multiply

You can skip count.

Skip count by 2s until you say 6 numbers.

Say 2, 4, 6, 8, 10, 12.

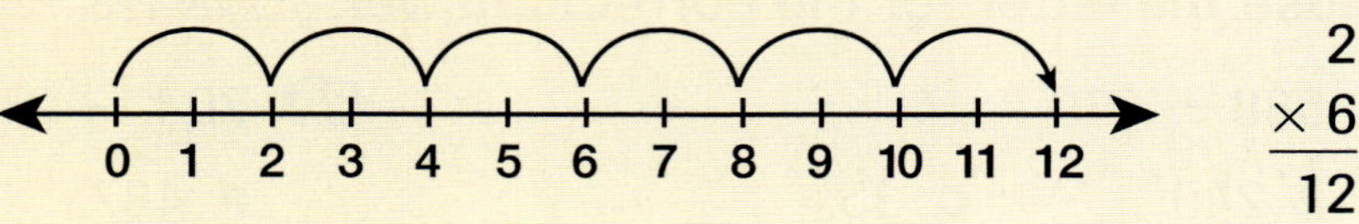

$$\begin{array}{r} 2 \\ \times\ 6 \\ \hline 12 \end{array}$$

You can draw a picture.

Then use repeated addition.

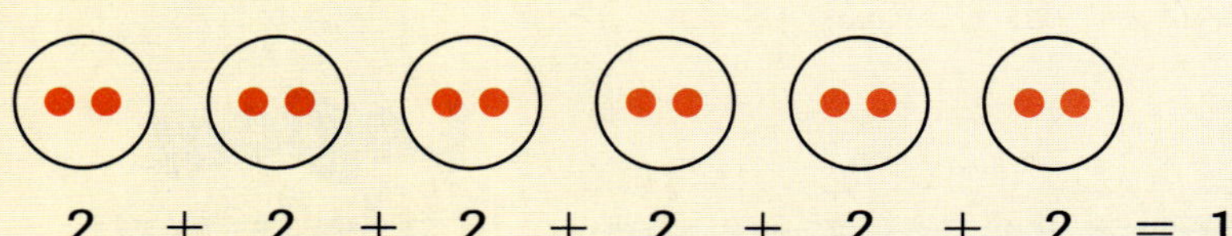

2 + 2 + 2 + 2 + 2 + 2 = 12

You can write a multiplication sentence.

6 × 2 = ■

6 × 2 = 12

Think: 6 groups of 2 = 12.

Solution: 12 balloons are needed to make 6 fish.

Explain Your Thinking

► Why does 6 × 3 equal 3 × 6?

Guided Practice

Multiply.

1. $\begin{array}{r} 2 \\ \times\ 4 \\ \hline \end{array}$

2. $\begin{array}{r} 7 \\ \times\ 2 \\ \hline \end{array}$

3. $\begin{array}{r} 8 \\ \times\ 2 \\ \hline \end{array}$

4. $\begin{array}{r} 2 \\ \times\ 9 \\ \hline \end{array}$

Ask Yourself

- Can the Commutative Property help me?

Independent Practice

Write a multiplication sentence for each picture.

5. 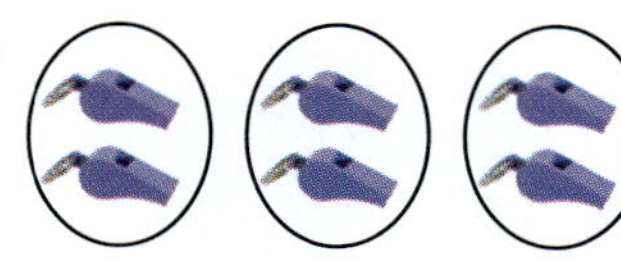

6. 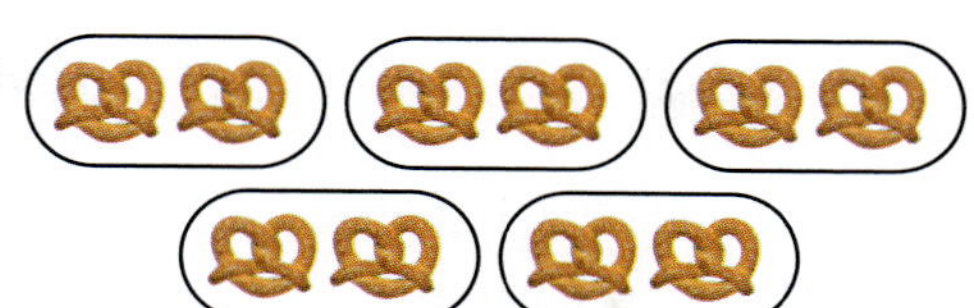

7. 

Multiply.

8. 3×2 **9.** 2×6 **10.** 5×2 **11.** 10×2 **12.** 8×2 **13.** 6×2

14. 2×4 **15.** 2×3 **16.** 7×2 **17.** 9×2 **18.** 1×2 **19.** 2×2

20. 2×9 **21.** 4×2 **22.** 7×2 **23.** 8×2 **24.** 2×10

Problem Solving • Reasoning

Use the information in the sign for Problems 25–27.

25. How much do tickets for 4 children cost?

26. **Money** Rob bought tickets for 3 children and 2 adults. Marie bought tickets for 4 children and 1 adult. How much more money did Rob spend than Marie?

27. **Logical Thinking** George brought money to the fair. After he bought a child's ticket and a turtle balloon, he had $4.00 left. The balloon cost 50¢. How much money did George bring to the fair?

Mixed Review • Test Prep

Write the value of the underlined digit. *(pages 4–5, 18–19, 32–33)*

28. $4\underline{2}8$ **29.** $\underline{8}{,}109$ **30.** $10{,}\underline{7}25$ **31.** $30{,}9\underline{7}6$ **32.** $74{,}\underline{1}84$

33 Which numbers are in order from least to greatest? *(pages 22–23)*

A 248 284 482
B 284 248 824
C 842 428 248
D 284 428 248

Extra Practice See Set B on page 242.

Multiply With 5

You will learn different ways to multiply when 5 is a factor.

Learn About It

Anna has 6 sets of Russian nesting dolls. Each set is made up of 5 dolls. How many dolls does Anna have in all?

Multiply. **6 × 5 = ■** or $\begin{array}{r} 5 \\ \times\ 6 \\ \hline ■ \end{array}$

Different Ways to Multiply

You can skip count.

Skip count by 5s until you say 6 numbers.

Say 5, 10, 15, 20, 25, 30.

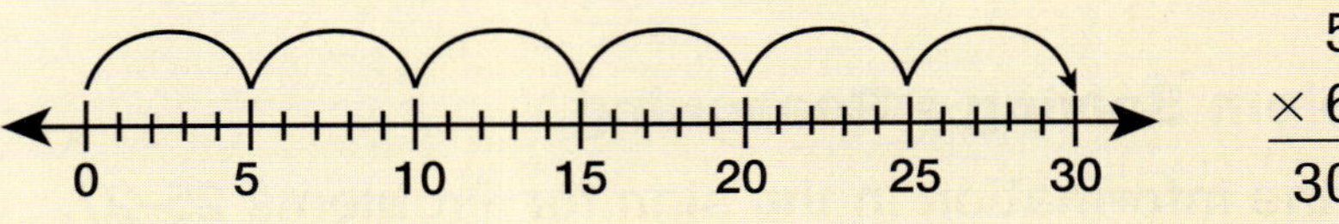

$\begin{array}{r} 5 \\ \times\ 6 \\ \hline 30 \end{array}$

You can draw a picture.

Then use repeated addition.

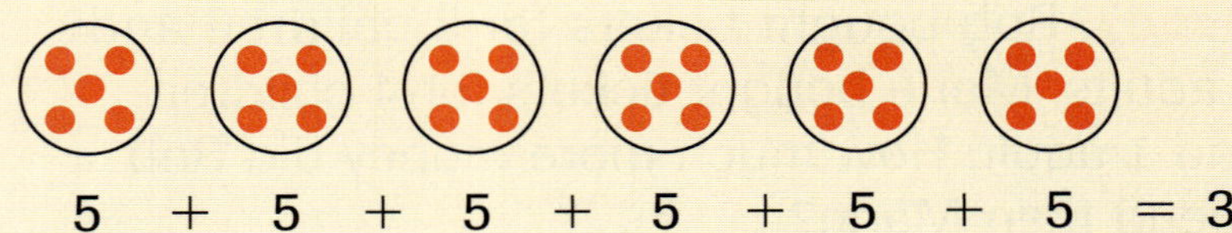

5 + 5 + 5 + 5 + 5 + 5 = 30

You can draw an array.

6 rows of 5 = 30

You can write a multiplication sentence.

6 × 5 = ■

6 × 5 = 30

Think: 6 groups of 5 = 30.

Solution: Anna has 30 Russian nesting dolls in all.

Explain Your Thinking

- When you multiply a number by 5, can the product have a 2 in the ones place? Why or why not?

Guided Practice

Find each product.

1. 5×3
2. 4×5
3. 5×2
4. 7×5
5. 9×5
6. 5×6
7. 8×5
8. 1×5

Ask Yourself

- Are there groups of 5?
- Can the Commutative Property help me?

Independent Practice

Multiply.

9. 5×2
10. 1×5
11. 3×5
12. 5×9
13. 5×6
14. 4×5
15. 5×5
16. 5×7
17. 6×5
18. 5×1
19. 2×5
20. 8×5

Algebra • Equations **Find each missing factor.**

21. $5 \times ■ = 10$
22. $■ \times 5 = 25$
23. $5 \times ■ = 40$
24. $45 = ■ \times 5$
25. $30 = 5 \times ■$
26. $5 \times ■ = 50$
27. $5 = 1 \times ■$
28. $35 = 5 \times ■$

Problem Solving • Reasoning

29. Rick bought 4 sets of action heroes. Each set has 5 action heroes in it. How many action heroes did Rick buy?

30. Kara has a set of 6 nesting dolls. The tallest doll is 11 inches high. Each doll after that is 2 inches shorter than the doll before it. How tall is the shortest doll?

31. **Analyze** Miguel has 16 toy robots. He wants to put them in boxes that hold 5 robots each. How many boxes can he fill completely?

Math Is Everywhere!

SOCIAL STUDIES

Wood-carved animals like this owl are made by the Zapotec Indians of Mexico. Artists use a special kind of wood that is soft and easy to carve.

If an artist made 5 wooden owls, how many owl feet would the artist carve?

Mixed Review • Test Prep

Write each time by using numbers. *(pages 70–72)*

32. five minutes after three
33. eleven-fifteen

34. Which shows fifty-eight thousand twenty-nine? *(pages 32–33)*

A 58,290 **B** 58,209 **C** 58,029 **D** 5,829

Extra Practice See Set C on page 243.

LESSON 5 Multiply With 10

You will learn different ways to multiply when 10 is a factor.

Learn About It

Justine is helping to set up a book display for National Children's Book Week. She decides to display 10 books on each table. How many books will Justine display if there are 4 tables?

Multiply. **4 × 10 = ■** or $\begin{array}{r} \mathbf{10} \\ \mathbf{\times\ 4} \\ \hline ■ \end{array}$

Different Ways to Multiply

You can skip count.

Skip count by 10s until you say 4 numbers.

Say 10, 20, 30, 40.

$\begin{array}{r} 10 \\ \times\ 4 \\ \hline 40 \end{array}$

You can use a pattern.

Think: When a number is multiplied by 10, write a zero after the number to show the product.

1 × 10 = 10
2 × 10 = 20
3 × 10 = 30
4 × 10 = 40

Think: 4 × 1 = 4.
So 4 × 10 = 40.

You can write a multiplication sentence.

4 × 10 = ■
4 × 10 = 40

Think: 4 groups of 10 = 40.

Solution: Justine will display 40 books.

Explain Your Thinking

► When you multiply a number by 10, what digit is always in the ones place of the product? Explain how you know.

Guided Practice

Multiply.

1. 3 × 10 **2.** 10 × 6 **3.** 7 × 10 **4.** 10 × 9

Ask Yourself

- Can the Commutative Property help me?

Independent Practice

Find each product.

5. 10×2 **6.** 10×6 **7.** 10×8 **8.** 10×7 **9.** 10×3 **10.** 10×10

11. 4×10 **12.** 5×10 **13.** 10×0 **14.** 3×10 **15.** 10×1

16. 7×10 **17.** 10×10 **18.** 9×10 **19.** 2×10 **20.** 5×10

Algebra • Functions **Complete each table by following the rule.**

Rule: Multiply by 10

	Input	Output
	6	60
21.	3	■
22.	5	■
23.	■	80

Rule: Multiply by 5

	Input	Output
24.	4	■
25.	8	■
26.	■	30
27.	10	■

Rule: Multiply by 10

	Input	Output
28.	■	20
29.	7	■
30.	■	90
31.	■	100

Problem Solving • Reasoning

Use Data **Use the pictograph for Problems 32–35.**

32. Anyone who checks out a mystery book gets a bookmark. How many bookmarks have been given out?

33. Half of the checked-out nonfiction books are about animals. How many books is that?

34. Thirty poetry books were checked out. How many pictures would be needed to show that amount on the graph?

35. **Write Your Own** Use the graph to write a word problem. Give the problem to a classmate to solve.

Mixed Review • Test Prep

Solve. *(pages 104–106, 138–141)*

36. $538 + 29 = $ ■ **37.** $4{,}027 - 691 = $ ■ **38.** $5{,}208 + 4{,}316 = $ ■

39 Which is equal to 3 feet? *(pages 164–166)*

A 25 inches **B** 30 inches **C** 24 inches **D** 36 inches

Extra Practice See Set D on page 243.

Problem-Solving Skill: Too Much Information

You will learn how to find the information needed to solve a problem when too much information is given.

Sometimes a problem has too much information. So when you are solving a problem, it is important to decide which facts you need.

Problem Becca went to an art store. She bought 4 tubes of paint for $2 each, a brush for $3.25, and 3 sketchpads for $1.75 each. She paid the clerk $20. How much did Becca spend on the paint and brush?

What information do you need to know?

The problem asks how much Becca spent on the paint and brush. So you need to know

- the cost of each tube of paint ($2)
- how many tubes of paint Becca bought (4 tubes)
- the cost of the brush ($3.25)

What information is extra?

The problem asks how much Becca spent on the paint and brush only. So you do **NOT** need to know

- the cost of the sketchpads ($1.75 each)
- how much money Becca gave the clerk ($20)

Now that you know the information you need, use that information to solve the problem.

Step 1
Find the cost of the paint.

$$\begin{array}{r} \$2 \\ \times\ 4 \\ \hline \$8 \end{array}$$

$2 ← cost per tube
× 4 ← number of tubes

Step 2
Find the total cost.

$$\begin{array}{r} \$\ 8.00 \\ +\ 3.25 \\ \hline \$11.25 \end{array}$$

$ 8.00 ← cost of paint
+ 3.25 ← cost of brush

Becca spent $11.25 for the paint and the brush.

Look Back What question could you write that uses all of the information in the problem?

Each spring the *I Madonnari* Italian Street Painting Festival takes place in Santa Barbara, California. Students and professional artists work with hundreds of pieces of colored chalk to copy famous paintings or to create their own pictures.

Guided Practice

Solve.

1. Lynn bought 3 sketchpads and 2 boxes of colored chalk at the art store. The sketchpads cost $5 each. The boxes of chalk cost $6.50 each. How much did Lynn spend on chalk?

Do you need the information about the sketchpads?

2. Origami paper is sold in 10 different colors. Steve bought 8 sheets of paper in each color. The total cost for the paper was $24. How many sheets of paper did Steve buy?

What information is not needed?

Choose a Strategy

Solve. Use these or other strategies.

Problem-Solving Strategies

- **Act It Out**
- **Draw a Picture**
- **Use Logical Thinking**

3. Markers come in packages of 8. Colored pencils come in packages of 12. How many markers are there in 5 packages of markers?

4. Ribbon costs $1.50 a yard. Kate buys 12 yards of wide ribbon and 9 yards of thin ribbon. How many yards of ribbon does Kate buy?

5. Stencil shapes are on display on a shelf. Circles are to the left of triangles. Squares are to the right of triangles. Rectangles are farthest to the right. Draw a picture showing how the stencils are displayed.

6. A store had one can of paint in red, in blue, and in green. Mary, Ken, and Tom each bought a can. Mary did not buy the red can. Tom did not buy the blue can. Ken bought the blue can. Which can did each buy?

7. Naresh spent $8 on brushes. Then he spent $15 on paper and watercolor paints. He spent twice as much money on the paints as on the paper. How much money did he spend on the paints?

8. A small bottle of glue costs $0.90. A medium bottle costs $1.45 and a large bottle costs $2.05. An art teacher orders 6 small bottles of glue and 4 large bottles of glue. About how much will she spend for the glue?

Extra Practice See 1–4 on page 245.

Quick Check

Check Your Understanding of Lessons 1–6

Write two multiplication sentences for each array.

1. 

2. 

Multiply.

3. 2×7

4. 2×4

5. 8×2

6. 2×2

7. 2×9

8. 5×6

9. 5×3

10. 7×5

11. 9×5

12. 5×4

13. $10 \times 2 =$ ■ **14.** $6 \times 10 =$ ■ **15.** $8 \times 10 =$ ■ **16.** $10 \times 10 =$ ■

Solve.

17. Mary can fit 5 pictures on each page of her photo album. She can fit 10 stamps on each page of her stamp album. How many pictures can she fit on 9 pages of her photo album? What information is not needed?

How did you do?

If you had difficulty with any items in the Quick Check, you can use the following pages for review and extra practice.

Items	Review These Pages	Do These Extra Practice Items
1–2	pages 214–217	Set A, page 242
3–7	pages 218–219	Set B, page 242
8–12	pages 220–221	Set C, page 243
13–16	pages 222–223	Set D, page 243
17	pages 224–225	1–4, page 245

Test Prep • Cumulative Review

Maintaining the Standards

Write the letter of the correct answer. If a correct answer is *not here,* choose NH.

1. What number makes the number sentence true?

$$7 \times \blacksquare = 5 \times 7$$

A 4
B 5
C 6
D 7

2. There are 10 dogs at the pet store. The dog shelter has 3 times that number of dogs. How many dogs does the shelter have?

F 15 **H** 30
G 25 **J** NH

Use the table for Questions 3–4.

Input	Output
2	4
4	8
6	12
8	■

3. What is the rule?

A Input × 2 = Output
B Input + 2 = Output
C Output − 2 = Input
D Output × 2 = Input

4. If the input is 8, what is the output?

F 10
G 14
H 16
J 18

5. Tammy put her marbles into 5 groups. There were 8 marbles in each group. How many marbles did Tammy have in all?

A 30 **C** 40
B 35 **D** 45

6. Which unit of measure is used to measure the weight of an object?

F inch
G quart
H pound
J pint

7. A leopard weighs between 80 pounds and 175 pounds. What is the difference between 175 and 80?

A 90
B 100
C 255
D NH

8. Ellen read 4 pages of her library book. Dylan read 5 times this number of pages. How many pages did Dylan read?

Explain How did you find your answer?

Safe Site

Internet Test Prep
Visit **www.eduplace.com/kids/mhm** for more *Test Prep Practice.*

LESSON 7

Multiply With 1 and 0

You will learn that there are special rules when 1 or 0 is a factor.

Learn About It

Fill it up! Jack made tacos for his family. He put each taco on a different plate. If Jack used 6 plates, how many tacos did he make?

Find 6 × 1.

$6 \times 1 = \blacksquare$

$6 \times 1 = 6$

When 1 is a factor, the product is always equal to the other factor.

Solution: Jack made 6 tacos.

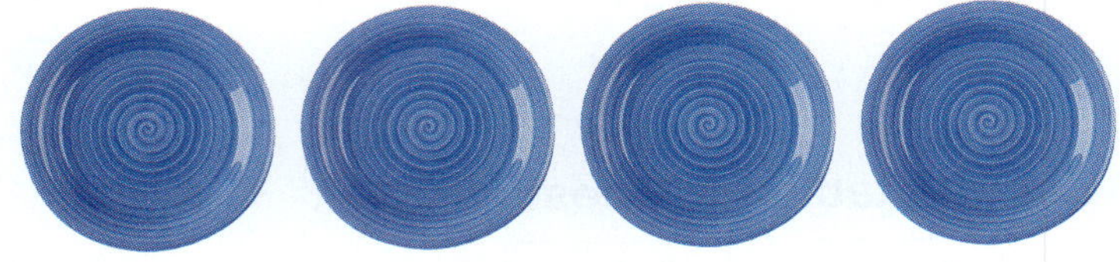

Jack has 4 more plates. There are no tacos on them. How many tacos are on these plates?

Find 4 × 0.

$4 \times 0 = \blacksquare$

$4 \times 0 = 0$

When 0 is a factor, the product is always 0.

Solution: There are 0 tacos on the four plates.

Explain Your Thinking

- ► Is it easier to multiply 438 × 1 or 438 × 2? Explain why.
- ► Is it easier to multiply 5 × 0 than 598 × 0? Explain why.

Guided Practice

Multiply.

1. $\begin{array}{r} 1 \\ \times\ 6 \\ \hline \end{array}$ **2.** $\begin{array}{r} 0 \\ \times\ 7 \\ \hline \end{array}$ **3.** $\begin{array}{r} 1 \\ \times\ 5 \\ \hline \end{array}$ **4.** $\begin{array}{r} 0 \\ \times\ 9 \\ \hline \end{array}$

5. 4 × 1 **6.** 8 × 0 **7.** 0 × 2 **8.** 1 × 3

Ask Yourself

- If 1 is a factor, what must the product be?
- If 0 is a factor, what must the product be?

Independent Practice

Find each product.

9. $\begin{array}{r} 0 \\ \times 8 \\ \hline \end{array}$ **10.** $\begin{array}{r} 1 \\ \times 7 \\ \hline \end{array}$ **11.** $\begin{array}{r} 0 \\ \times 2 \\ \hline \end{array}$ **12.** $\begin{array}{r} 1 \\ \times 9 \\ \hline \end{array}$ **13.** $\begin{array}{r} 5 \\ \times 1 \\ \hline \end{array}$ **14.** $\begin{array}{r} 0 \\ \times 4 \\ \hline \end{array}$

15. $\begin{array}{r} 7 \\ \times 0 \\ \hline \end{array}$ **16.** $\begin{array}{r} 1 \\ \times 6 \\ \hline \end{array}$ **17.** $\begin{array}{r} 8 \\ \times 1 \\ \hline \end{array}$ **18.** $\begin{array}{r} 0 \\ \times 1 \\ \hline \end{array}$ **19.** $\begin{array}{r} 5 \\ \times 0 \\ \hline \end{array}$ **20.** $\begin{array}{r} 10 \\ \times 1 \\ \hline \end{array}$

21. 6×0 **22.** 1×7 **23.** 1×1 **24.** 0×3 **25.** 10×0

26. 1×9 **27.** 4×0 **28.** 5×1 **29.** 1×0 **30.** 0×7

Algebra • Properties **Find each missing number.**

31. $4 \times 0 = \blacksquare \times 4$ **32.** $8 \times \blacksquare = 7 \times 0$ **33.** $1 \times 6 = 6 \times \blacksquare$

34. $8 \times \blacksquare = 8$ **35.** $10 \times 0 = 5 \times \blacksquare$ **36.** $2 \times 3 = \blacksquare \times 6$

Problem Solving • Reasoning

Use the number sentences at the right for Problems 37–38.

37. What number does each shape stand for?

38. Marissa has 8 empty plates. Which multiplication sentence shows how many tacos she has?

39. **Logical Thinking** Shannon is making burritos. She uses 3 more peppers than tomatoes. She uses twice as many tomatoes as onions. If she uses 1 onion, how many peppers does Shannon use?

4 × ▲ = 4

2 × ● = 0

■ × 8 = 0

◆ × 8 = 8

Mixed Review • Test Prep

Name the digit in the tens place. *(pages 18–19, 32–33)*

40. 1,486 **41.** 9,017 **42.** 18,405 **43.** 31,062 **44.** 94,305 **45.** 74,629

Choose the letter for the correct answer. *(pages 70–72)*

46 Which shows the time fifteen minutes past seven?

A 6:45 **C** 7:15
B 7:00 **D** 7:45

47 Which shows the time twenty minutes before three?

F 2:30 **H** 3:00
G 2:40 **J** 3:20

Extra Practice See Set E on page 243.

Multiply With 3

You will learn different ways to multiply when 3 is a factor.

Learn About It

Tennis balls are on sale! Suppose you buy 7 cans. If each can contains 3 balls, how many tennis balls will you get?

Multiply. $7 \times 3 = \blacksquare$ or $\begin{array}{r} 3 \\ \times\, 7 \\ \hline \blacksquare \end{array}$

Different Ways to Multiply

You can skip count.

Skip count by 3s until you say 7 numbers.

Say 3, 6, 9, 12, 15, 18, 21.

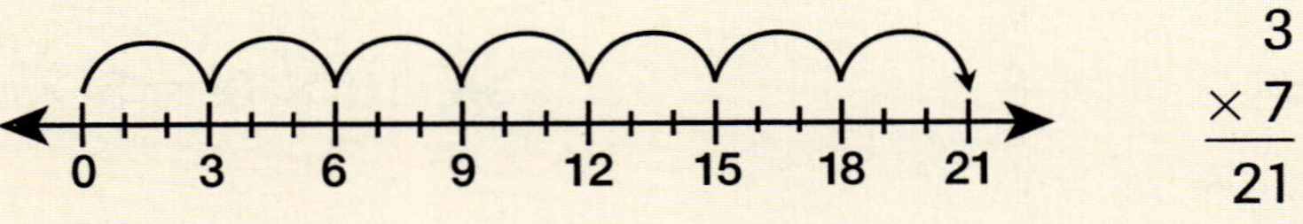

$\begin{array}{r} 3 \\ \times\, 7 \\ \hline 21 \end{array}$

You can draw a picture.

Then use repeated addition.

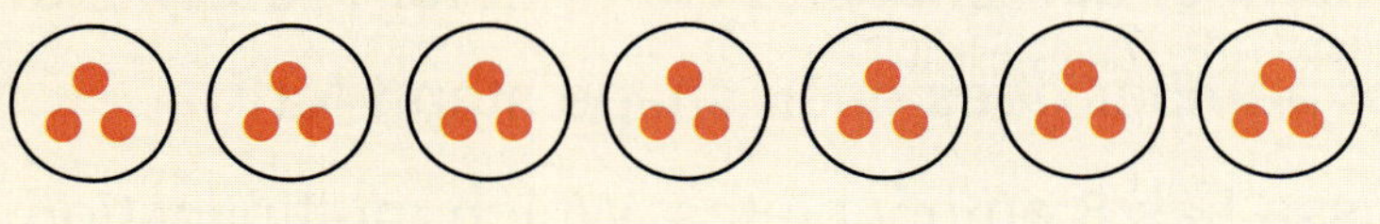

$3 + 3 + 3 + 3 + 3 + 3 + 3 = 21$

You can write a multiplication sentence.

$7 \times 3 = \blacksquare$

$7 \times 3 = 21$

Think: 7 groups of 3 = 21.

Solution: You will get 21 tennis balls.

Explain Your Thinking

▸ How can knowing $4 \times 2 = 8$ help you find 4×3?

Guided Practice

Multiply.

1. $\begin{array}{r} 3 \\ \times\, 2 \\ \hline \end{array}$ **2.** $\begin{array}{r} 1 \\ \times\, 3 \\ \hline \end{array}$ **3.** $\begin{array}{r} 3 \\ \times\, 3 \\ \hline \end{array}$ **4.** $\begin{array}{r} 5 \\ \times\, 3 \\ \hline \end{array}$

Ask Yourself

- Can the Commutative Property help me?

Independent Practice

Find each product.

5. 3×6 **6.** 3×4 **7.** 3×8 **8.** 9×3 **9.** 7×3 **10.** 3×1

11. 5×3 **12.** 3×3 **13.** 2×3 **14.** 8×3 **15.** 6×3 **16.** 3×0

17. 8×3 **18.** 2×3 **19.** 6×3 **20.** 3×5 **21.** 3×7

22. 3×4 **23.** 9×3 **24.** 3×1 **25.** 3×3 **26.** 10×3

Draw an array for each. Then copy and complete each multiplication sentence.

27. $7 \times 3 =$ ■ **28.** $4 \times 3 =$ ■ **29.** $3 \times 6 =$ ■ **30.** $3 \times 2 =$ ■

Problem Solving • Reasoning

31. Kendra's dog chews up 3 tennis balls each month. How many tennis balls does the dog chew up in 5 months?

32. **Money** Shari spent $16 on a soccer ball and a kick ball. The soccer ball cost 3 times as much as the kick ball. How much did each ball cost?

33. **Compare** Baseballs are going on sale next week for $8 each. Mario plans to buy 3 baseballs. He figures he will save a total of $6 if he waits to buy the balls on sale. What is the regular price of a baseball?

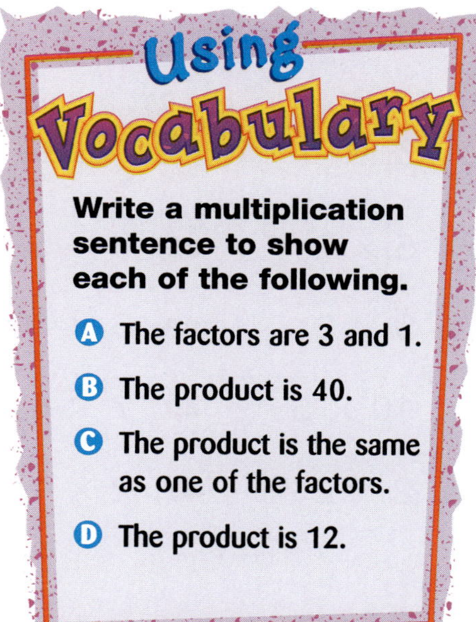

Using Vocabulary

Write a multiplication sentence to show each of the following.

- **A** The factors are 3 and 1.
- **B** The product is 40.
- **C** The product is the same as one of the factors.
- **D** The product is 12.

Mixed Review • Test Prep

Round each number to the nearest ten. *(pages 6–10)*

34. 43 **35.** 98 **36.** 429 **37.** 175 **38.** 541 **39.** 745

Choose the letter for the correct answer. *(pages 108–109, 120–121)*

40 $685 + 298 =$ ■

- **A** 387
- **B** 873
- **C** 973
- **D** 983

41 $4,205 + 1,367 =$ ■

- **F** 2,838
- **G** 5,562
- **H** 5,572
- **J** 55,712

Extra Practice See Set F on page 244.

Multiplication Facts Practice

Be sure you memorized your facts. Then find each product as quickly as you can.

1. 2×4 **2.** 3×1 **3.** 10×2 **4.** 1×7 **5.** 7×3

6. 5×7 **7.** 3×4 **8.** 2×9 **9.** 5×4 **10.** 10×5

11. 2×7 **12.** 5×9 **13.** 0×8 **14.** 3×8 **15.** 1×6

16. 10×6 **17.** 3×0 **18.** 2×5 **19.** 1×4 **20.** 8×5

21. 5×5 **22.** 0×9 **23.** 10×1 **24.** 3×3 **25.** 3×9

26. 6×0 **27.** 8×10 **28.** 5×3 **29.** 9×1 **30.** 3×2

31. 5×2 **32.** 6×5 **33.** 10×3 **34.** 4×3 **35.** 8×2

36. 9×3 **37.** 6×10 **38.** 6×2 **39.** 4×10 **40.** 2×9

41. 10×5 **42.** 7×4 **43.** 8×0 **44.** 1×5 **45.** 5×0

46. 2×2 **47.** 2×1 **48.** 7×0 **49.** 6×3 **50.** 10×10

Copy and complete each table.

51.

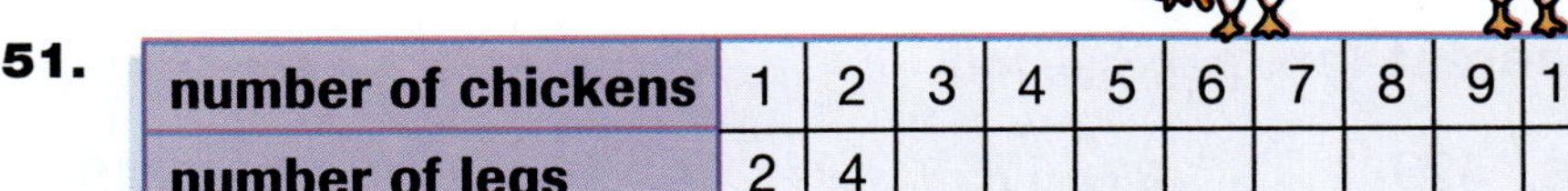

number of chickens	1	2	3	4	5	6	7	8	9	10
number of legs	2	4								

52.

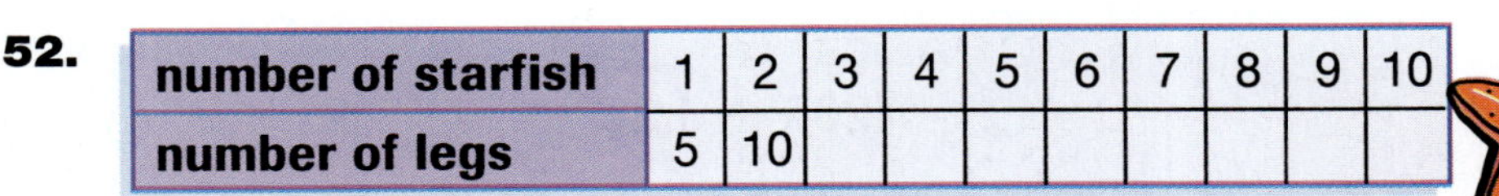

number of starfish	1	2	3	4	5	6	7	8	9	10
number of legs	5	10								

Practice Game

Multiplying Dots!

Practice multiplication by playing this game with a partner. Try to have the most dots at the end of the game!

What You'll Need

Players 2

For each pair

- *a number cube labeled 0, 1, 2, 3, 5, and 10*
- *2 sheets of paper, each divided into 4 equal spaces (Teaching Tool 2)*

Here's What to Do

1. On their sheets of paper, players draw 2 large circles in the first space, 3 in the second space, 4 in the third space, and 5 in the fourth space.
2. The first player rolls the number cube and chooses a space on his or her paper. The number rolled is the number of dots the player makes in **each** circle in that space. Then the player writes a multiplication sentence to show how many dots were drawn in that space.
3. Players take turns repeating Step 2 until all the spaces on their papers have been used. (If zero is rolled, like any other number, it counts as a turn.) The player with more dots wins!

Share Your Thinking If you roll a low number, is it better to choose a space that has many circles or few circles? Explain why.

Problem-Solving Strategy: Use Models to Act It Out

You will learn how to solve a problem by using models to act it out.

Sometimes acting out a problem can help you organize information and see the answer more clearly.

Problem This third-grade chorus has 12 singers. They want to sing in groups at the school talent show. In how many different ways can they form groups so that there is the same number of singers in each group?

Understand

What is the question?

How many different ways can the singers form equal groups?

What do you know?

There are 12 singers.

How can you find the answer?

Use counters to stand for the singers. Arrange all 12 counters in equal groups in as many ways as you can.

Here are the ways that all 12 counters can be arranged with the same number in each group.

1 group of 12

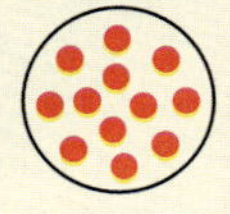

2 groups of 6

6 groups of 2

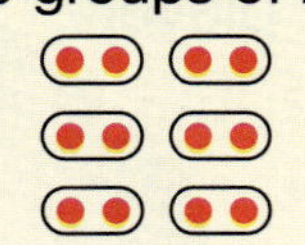

4 groups of 3

3 groups of 4

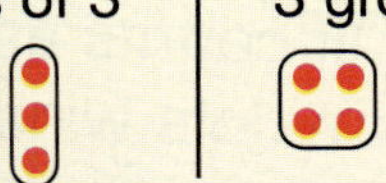

12 groups of 1

The singers can be arranged in 6 different ways.

Look Back

Look back at the problem.

How did using counters help you solve the problem?

Remember:
- Understand
- Plan
- Solve
- Look Back

Guided Practice

Solve each problem, using the Act It Out strategy.

1. There are 18 dancers in the country dance number. They need to be in equal groups of 2 or more. What are the different ways the 18 dancers can be grouped?

How could you use counters to act it out?

2. Luis, Cathy, Doug, and Julia are standing in line for the talent show. Julia is after Doug but before Luis. Cathy is before Doug. In what order are the 4 friends standing?

What could you use to act out the problem?

Choose a Strategy

Solve. Use these or other strategies.

Problem-Solving Strategies

- **Act It Out**
- **Work Backward**
- **Find a Pattern**

3. The stage crew is attaching 2 red lights and 2 blue lights to a rod. The lights need to be placed so that the red lights are not next to each other. In what ways can the lights be arranged in a row?

4. The first row of theater seats is blue. The second row is red. Then there are 2 blue rows, 2 red rows, followed by 3 blue rows, 3 red rows. If the pattern continues, what colors are the next 8 rows likely to be?

5. Four students performed a comedy act. Each actor shook hands with every other actor exactly one time. How many handshakes were there in all?

6. Billy performed for 20 minutes. Then Carlin played the piano for 10 minutes. When she finished, it was 1:15 P.M. What time did Billy begin his performance?

7. Students are arranging 30 mats for younger students to sit on in the auditorium. The mats need to be in equal rows. There is room for no more than 6 rows. In what ways can all 30 mats be arranged?

8. Four friends are doing an animal skit. In the skit the cat comes on-stage before the bird. The frog comes on before the cat. The turtle comes on last. In what order do the animals come on-stage?

Extra Practice See 5–6 on page 245.

Multiply With 4

You will learn different ways to multiply when 4 is a factor.

Learn About It

Hold on! It's time to go white-water rafting. There are 6 rafts going down a river. If each raft has 4 people in it, how many people are rafting?

Multiply. $6 \times 4 = \blacksquare$ or $\begin{array}{r} 4 \\ \times 6 \\ \hline \blacksquare \end{array}$

Different Ways to Multiply

You can skip count.

Skip count by 4s until you say 6 numbers.

Say 4, 8, 12, 16, 20, 24.

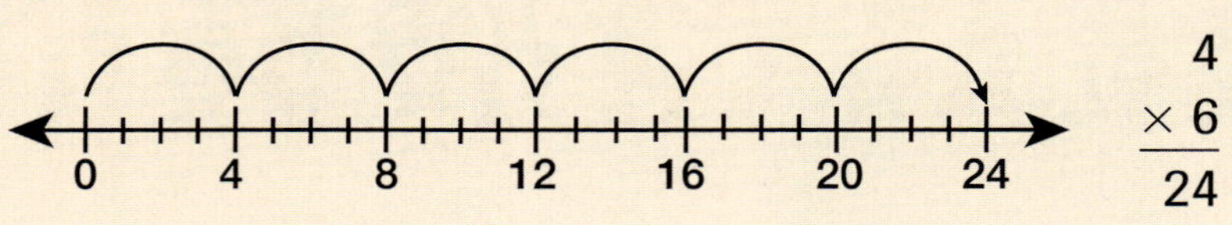

$\begin{array}{r} 4 \\ \times 6 \\ \hline 24 \end{array}$

You can draw a picture.

Then use repeated addition.

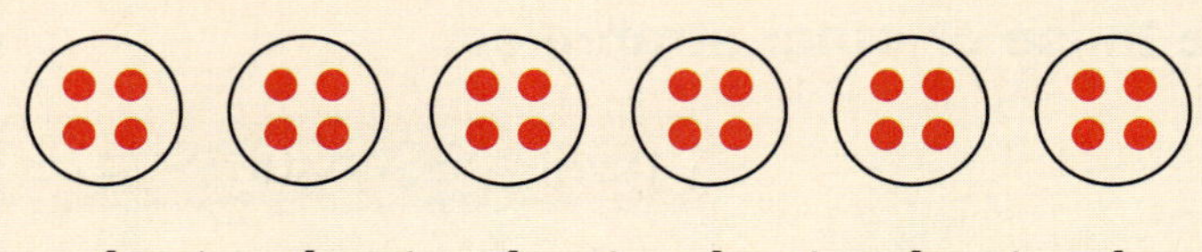

4 + 4 + 4 + 4 + 4 + 4 = 24

You can write a multiplication sentence.

$6 \times 4 = \blacksquare$

$6 \times 4 = 24$

Think: 6 groups of 4 = 24.

Solution: There are 24 people rafting.

Explain Your Thinking

- How can knowing $7 \times 2 = 14$ help you find 7×4?
- Is the product always an even number when 4 is a factor?

Guided Practice

Multiply.

1. $\begin{array}{r} 2 \\ \times 4 \\ \hline \end{array}$ **2.** $\begin{array}{r} 4 \\ \times 5 \\ \hline \end{array}$ **3.** $\begin{array}{r} 7 \\ \times 4 \\ \hline \end{array}$ **4.** $\begin{array}{r} 4 \\ \times 9 \\ \hline \end{array}$

Ask Yourself

- Can the Commutative Property help me?

Independent Practice

Find each product.

5. 1×4 **6.** 4×5 **7.** 4×3 **8.** 6×4 **9.** 4×4 **10.** 4×8

11. 9×4 **12.** 4×6 **13.** 10×4 **14.** 4×0 **15.** 3×4 **16.** 4×7

17. 4×10 **18.** 1×4 **19.** 9×4 **20.** 4×5 **21.** 6×4

22. 3×4 **23.** 4×8 **24.** 4×6 **25.** 0×4 **26.** 7×4

27. 8×2 **28.** 4×4 **29.** 3×7 **30.** 5×6 **31.** 3×8

Problem Solving • Reasoning

32. On an overnight rafting trip, campers sleep in tents that hold 4 people each. How many people can sleep in 9 tents?

33. It costs $4 to rent a child's rafting helmet. How much does it cost to rent 7 children's helmets?

34. **Analyze** John brought his camera on a 4-day rafting trip. Each day he took 6 more pictures than the day before. He took 15 pictures on the third day. How many pictures did John take during the trip?

35. **Write About It** Jesse has 5 packages of 4 flashlight batteries. Seth has 5 packages of 3 batteries. Without multiplying, how can you tell who has more batteries?

Mixed Review • Test Prep

Write the numbers from greatest to least. *(pages 22–23)*

36. 42 28 84 **37.** 735 357 375 **38.** 2,014 2,104 2,410

39 Which is 627 rounded to the nearest hundred? *(pages 8-10)*

A 500 **C** 630
B 600 **D** 700

Extra Practice See Set G on page 244.

LESSON 11

Problem-Solving Application: Use a Pictograph

You will learn how to use pictographs to solve problems.

Problem The pictograph on the right shows the number of computers that schools in Bayville have ordered. How many computers did the elementary schools order?

School Computer Orders

Alden Elementary School	4 computer symbols
Maple Elementary School	6 computer symbols
Bayville Middle School	7 computer symbols
Bayville High School	6 computer symbols

Each computer symbol stands for 5 computers.

Understand

What is the question?

How many computers did the elementary schools order?

What do you know?

The pictograph shows the number of computers each school has ordered. Each computer symbol stands for 5 computers.

Plan

How can you solve the problem?

Count the number of computer symbols next to the two elementary schools. Multiply each school's number of computer symbols by 5. Then add the products.

Solve

Find the number of computer symbols for each school.	Multiply each number by 5.	Add the products.
• Alden has 4 computer symbols.	$4 \times 5 = 20$	$20 + 30 = 50$
• Maple has 6 computer symbols.	$6 \times 5 = 30$	

The elementary schools ordered 50 computers.

Look Back

Look back at the question.

How can you use skip counting to decide whether your answer is reasonable?

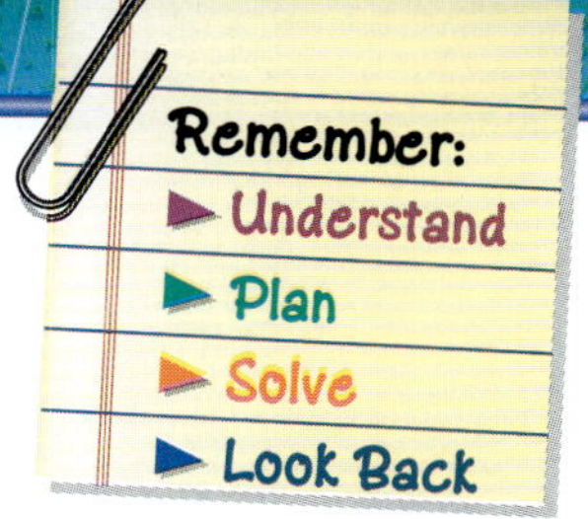

Guided Practice

Use the data in the pictograph on page 238 to solve each problem.

1. Which school ordered the most computers? How many computers did that school order?

Which row next to the name of a school has the most pictures?

2. How many more computers did the middle school order than the high school?

How many more pictures are there in the third row than in the fourth?

Choose a Strategy

The graph shows the number of CDs each grade at Maple Elementary School ordered. Choose a strategy to solve each problem.

Problem-Solving Strategies

- **Write a Number Sentence**
- **Work Backward**
- **Use Logical Thinking**

3. Write a number sentence to show the number of CDs Grade 3 ordered.

4. Janna's grade ordered the fewest CDs. How many more CDs did Grade 4 order than Janna's grade?

5. Darren's grade ordered more CDs than the grade below it but fewer CDs than the grade above it. What grade is Darren in?

Maple Elementary School
Number of CDs Ordered

Grade 1	💿💿💿
Grade 2	💿💿
Grade 3	💿💿💿💿
Grade 4	💿💿💿💿💿💿💿💿
Grade 5	💿💿💿💿💿💿💿

Each 💿 stands for 10 CDs.

6. There is a 98¢ shipping charge for every 10 CDs mailed to the school. About how much will Grade 3 spend on shipping?

7. Karyn's grade ordered twice as many CDs as one grade but only half as many CDs as another grade. What grade is Karyn in?

8. Suppose each picture in the pictograph stood for 5 CDs. How many pictures would have to be added to show the number of CDs the second grade ordered?

9. After the fifth-graders receive their order of CDs, they will need only 8 more CDs to have 100 CDs in all. How many CDs did the fifth grade have before placing the order?

Extra Practice See 7–10 on page 245.

Quick Check

Check Your Understanding of Lessons 7–11

Multiply.

1. $5 \times 0 = \blacksquare$
2. $8 \times 1 = \blacksquare$
3. $1 \times 4 = \blacksquare$
4. $0 \times 9 = \blacksquare$
5. 3×6
6. 3×8
7. 9×3
8. 3×4
9. 7×3
10. 4×8
11. 4×5
12. 4×4
13. 7×4
14. 10×4

Solve.

15. The pictograph shows how many CDs a group of friends have. Who has the most CDs? How many CDs does that friend have?
16. How many fewer CDs does Lisa have than Mario?

Number of CDs

Mario	◉ ◉ ◉ ◉ ◉
Lisa	◉ ◉ ◉
Felix	◉ ◉ ◉ ◉
Cora	◉ ◉ ◉ ◉ ◉ ◉ ◉

Each ◉ stands for 3 CDs.

How did you do?

If you had difficulty with any items in the Quick Check, you can use the following pages for review and extra practice.

Items	Review These Pages	Do These Extra Practice Items
1–4	pages 228–229	Set E, page 243
5–9	pages 230–231	Set F, page 244
10–14	pages 236–237	Set G, page 244
15–16	pages 238–239	7–10, page 245

Test Prep • Cumulative Review

Maintaining the Standards

Write the letter of the correct answer. If a correct answer is *not here,* choose NH.

1. Which number sentence could be used to find the number of pints in 2 quarts?
   - **A** ■ pints = 2 × 2
   - **B** ■ pints = 2 × 3
   - **C** ■ pints = 2 × 4
   - **D** ■ pints = 2 × 5

2. Which number sentence is modeled by this array?

   - **F** 2 × 10 + 20
   - **G** 10 + 10 = 20
   - **H** 5 + 4 = 9
   - **J** 5 × 4 = 20

3. Suppose a Beluga whale weighs 2,107 pounds. Which of the following is equal to 2,107?
   - **A** 200 + 10 + 7
   - **B** 2,000 + 100 + 70
   - **C** 2,000 + 100 + 7
   - **D** 2,000 + 100 + 10 + 7

4. Look at the table.

Input	Output
1	3
2	6
3	9
4	■

   Which number sentence would you use to find the missing number?
   - **F** 8 + 4 = 12
   - **G** 4 × 3 = 12
   - **H** 6 × 2 = 12
   - **J** 10 + 2 = 12

5. What symbol makes the number sentence true?

   3 ● 0 = 0

   - **A** +
   - **B** −
   - **C** ×
   - **D** <

6. Mrs. Holt baked 120 muffins for the bake sale. Mr. Jenkins baked 96 muffins. How many more muffins did Mrs. Holt bake?
   - **F** 24
   - **G** 76
   - **H** 176
   - **J** NH

7. Tim bought 10 packs of gum. Each pack had 5 sticks of gum. How many sticks of gum did Tim buy?

   Explain How did you find your answer?

Safe Site

Internet Test Prep
Visit **www.eduplace.com/kids/mhm** for more *Test Prep Practice.*

Extra Practice

Set A *(Lesson 2, pages 214–217)*

Write a multiplication sentence for each array.

1. 

2. 

Fill in the missing numbers.

3. $8 \times 3 = 24$
$3 \times 8 = ■$

4. $9 \times 2 = 18$
$2 \times ■ = 18$

5. $5 \times 4 = 20$
$■ \times 5 = 20$

6. $6 \times 5 = 30$
$5 \times ■ = 30$

7. $3 \times ■ = 24$
$8 \times 3 = 24$

8. $4 \times 8 = 32$
$8 \times 4 = ■$

Set B *(Lesson 3, pages 218–219)*

Write a multiplication sentence for each picture.

1.

2. 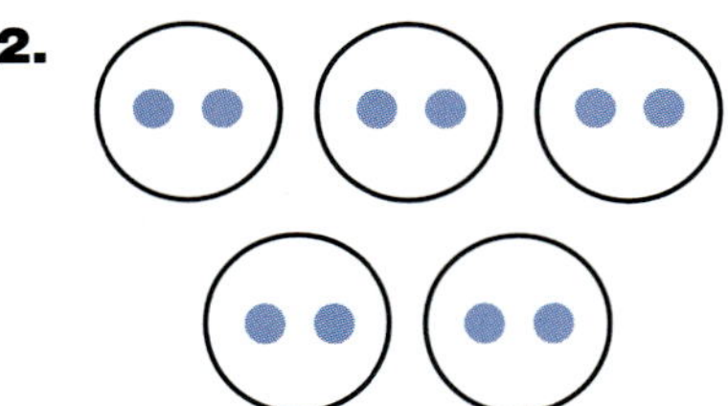

3. 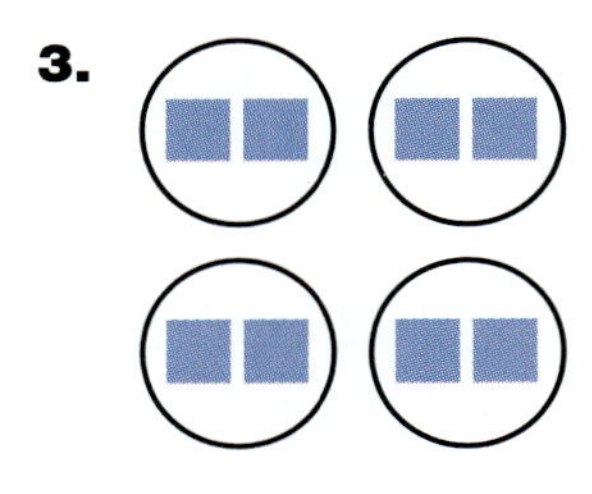

Multiply.

4. $\begin{array}{r} 2 \\ \times\ 4 \\ \hline \end{array}$

5. $\begin{array}{r} 2 \\ \times\ 5 \\ \hline \end{array}$

6. $\begin{array}{r} 8 \\ \times\ 2 \\ \hline \end{array}$

7. $\begin{array}{r} 7 \\ \times\ 2 \\ \hline \end{array}$

8. $\begin{array}{r} 6 \\ \times\ 2 \\ \hline \end{array}$

9. $\begin{array}{r} 2 \\ \times\ 9 \\ \hline \end{array}$

10. $\begin{array}{r} 2 \\ \times\ 7 \\ \hline \end{array}$

11. $\begin{array}{r} 10 \\ \times\ 2 \\ \hline \end{array}$

12. $\begin{array}{r} 2 \\ \times\ 2 \\ \hline \end{array}$

13. $\begin{array}{r} 2 \\ \times\ 3 \\ \hline \end{array}$

14. 3×2

15. 2×2

16. 9×2

17. 2×10

18. 5×2

19. 4×2

20. 2×7

21. 2×10

22. 8×2

23. 2×6

Extra Practice

Set C (Lesson 4, pages 220–221)

Multiply.

1. 2×5
2. 5×6
3. 5×7
4. 5×3
5. 5×4
6. 5×9
7. 6×5
8. 10×5
9. 5×5
10. 8×5
11. 5×8
12. 4×5
13. 6×5
14. 9×5
15. 5×5

Set D (Lesson 5, pages 222–223)

Find each product.

1. 10×6
2. 10×8
3. 7×10
4. 10×5
5. 3×10
6. 10×10
7. 2×10
8. 10×4
9. 10×9
10. 5×10
11. 2×10
12. 4×10
13. 8×10
14. 5×10
15. 10×10

Fill in the missing numbers.

16. $5 \times ■ = 10$
17. $10 \times ■ = 70$
18. $40 = 5 \times ■$
19. $10 \times 6 = ■$
20. $4 \times ■ = 20$
21. $10 = 10 \times ■$
22. $■ = 10 \times 10$
23. $5 \times ■ = 30$

Set E (Lesson 7, pages 228–229)

Find each product.

1. 0×2
2. 0×8
3. 1×7
4. 5×1
5. 9×0
6. 0×3
7. 4×1
8. 0×10
9. 6×1
10. 0×7
11. 1×8
12. 1×1
13. 5×0
14. 0×4
15. 10×1

Extra Practice

Set F (Lesson 8, pages 230–231)

Find each product.

1. $\begin{array}{r} 3 \\ \times 1 \\ \hline \end{array}$
2. $\begin{array}{r} 4 \\ \times 3 \\ \hline \end{array}$
3. $\begin{array}{r} 3 \\ \times 9 \\ \hline \end{array}$
4. $\begin{array}{r} 5 \\ \times 3 \\ \hline \end{array}$
5. $\begin{array}{r} 2 \\ \times 3 \\ \hline \end{array}$
6. $\begin{array}{r} 8 \\ \times 3 \\ \hline \end{array}$
7. $\begin{array}{r} 3 \\ \times 3 \\ \hline \end{array}$
8. $\begin{array}{r} 10 \\ \times 3 \\ \hline \end{array}$
9. $\begin{array}{r} 6 \\ \times 3 \\ \hline \end{array}$
10. $\begin{array}{r} 3 \\ \times 7 \\ \hline \end{array}$
11. 3×3
12. 0×3
13. 4×3
14. 7×3
15. 6×3

Compare. Write >, <, or = for each ⬬.

16. 3×2 ⬬ 2×3
17. 3×3 ⬬ 5×2
18. 3×6 ⬬ 3×5
19. 3×9 ⬬ 8×3
20. 3×4 ⬬ 2×6
21. 10×2 ⬬ 3×7

Set G (Lesson 10, pages 236–237)

Find each product.

1. $\begin{array}{r} 6 \\ \times 4 \\ \hline \end{array}$
2. $\begin{array}{r} 9 \\ \times 4 \\ \hline \end{array}$
3. $\begin{array}{r} 4 \\ \times 5 \\ \hline \end{array}$
4. $\begin{array}{r} 0 \\ \times 4 \\ \hline \end{array}$
5. $\begin{array}{r} 2 \\ \times 4 \\ \hline \end{array}$
6. $\begin{array}{r} 10 \\ \times 4 \\ \hline \end{array}$
7. $\begin{array}{r} 4 \\ \times 8 \\ \hline \end{array}$
8. $\begin{array}{r} 3 \\ \times 4 \\ \hline \end{array}$
9. $\begin{array}{r} 4 \\ \times 7 \\ \hline \end{array}$
10. $\begin{array}{r} 1 \\ \times 4 \\ \hline \end{array}$
11. 4×5
12. 0×4
13. 9×4
14. 4×4
15. 4×7

Follow the rule to complete each table.

Rule: Multiply by 4

	Input	Output
16.	3	■
17.	6	■
18.	■	20
19.	■	36

Rule: Multiply by 3

	Input	Output
20.	5	■
21.	■	30
22.	8	■
23.	■	21

Extra Practice • Problem Solving

Solve. *(Lesson 6, pages 224–225)*

1. Bill's dog is 5 years old. Bill buys food and a new leash for his dog. The leash costs $7. A can of food costs $2. Bill buys 10 cans. How much does he spend on dog food?

2. Jessie wants to buy 7 angelfish and 3 guppies. Angelfish cost $3 each. Guppies cost $1.50 each. How much money will Jessie spend on the angelfish?

3. There are 22 students in the art class. Ten of the students each used 3 sheets of red paper and 2 sheets of blue paper. How many sheets of paper were used?

4. Jerry has 3 different types of marbles. He puts 4 marbles in each of 5 bags to give to his friends. How many marbles does Jerry give to his friends in all?

Solve each problem using the Act It Out strategy. *(Lesson 9, pages 234–235)*

5. There are 12 dogs in a dog show. They need to be in equal groups of 2 or more. What are the different ways 12 dogs can be grouped?

6. Jenny, Al, Rita, and Len are performing in a talent show. Al will sing after Len but before Jenny. Rita will sing before Len. In what order will the 4 friends sing?

Use the data in the pictograph to solve each problem.
(Lesson 11, pages 238–239)

7. How many guppies and tetras are in Erica's aquarium?

8. Does Erica have more mollies or neons? How many more?

9. How many more neons are there than tetras?

10. If Erica buys 10 more guppies, how will the graph change?

Fish in Erica's Aquarium

Tetras	🐟🐟🐟🐟
Mollies	🐟🐟🐟🐟🐟🐟🐟
Neons	🐟🐟🐟🐟🐟🐟
Guppies	🐟🐟

Each 🐟 stands for 5 fish.

Chapter Review

Reviewing Vocabulary

Write *true* or *false* for each statement. Explain your answers.

1. An array is the answer in a multiplication problem.
2. The numbers you multiply are called factors.
3. Rows and columns make up an array.
4. Changing the order of factors in multiplication will change the product.

Reviewing Concepts and Skills

Write a multiplication sentence for each array or picture. *(pages 214–217, 220–221)*

5.

6. 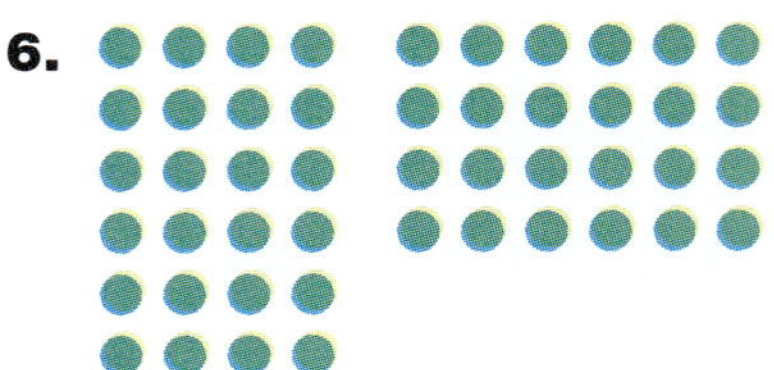

7. 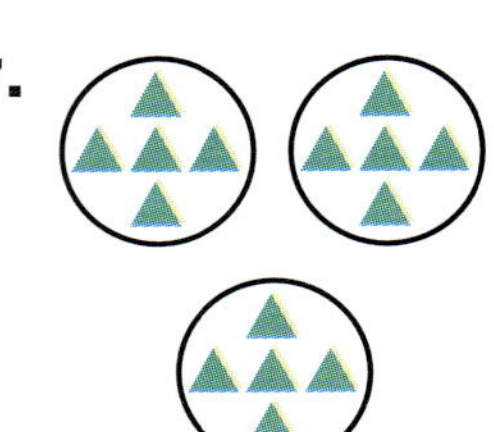

Fill in the missing numbers. *(pages 214–217)*

8. $7 \times 3 = 21$
$3 \times 7 = ■$

9. $9 \times 5 = 45$
$5 \times ■ = 45$

10. $6 \times 4 = 24$
$■ \times 6 = 24$

11. $4 \times 8 = 32$
$8 \times 4 = ■$

12. $1 \times 5 = 5$
$5 \times ■ = 5$

13. $3 \times 8 = 24$
$8 \times 3 = ■$

Multiply. *(pages 218–223, 228–231, 236–237)*

14. $\begin{array}{r} 5 \\ \times 6 \\ \hline \end{array}$ **15.** $\begin{array}{r} 4 \\ \times 2 \\ \hline \end{array}$ **16.** $\begin{array}{r} 9 \\ \times 0 \\ \hline \end{array}$ **17.** $\begin{array}{r} 6 \\ \times 4 \\ \hline \end{array}$ **18.** $\begin{array}{r} 3 \\ \times 7 \\ \hline \end{array}$

19. $\begin{array}{r} 8 \\ \times 4 \\ \hline \end{array}$ **20.** $\begin{array}{r} 2 \\ \times 3 \\ \hline \end{array}$ **21.** $\begin{array}{r} 1 \\ \times 3 \\ \hline \end{array}$ **22.** $\begin{array}{r} 7 \\ \times 5 \\ \hline \end{array}$ **23.** $\begin{array}{r} 0 \\ \times 8 \\ \hline \end{array}$

24. $\begin{array}{r} 2 \\ \times 9 \\ \hline \end{array}$ **25.** $\begin{array}{r} 8 \\ \times 3 \\ \hline \end{array}$ **26.** $\begin{array}{r} 10 \\ \times 9 \\ \hline \end{array}$ **27.** $\begin{array}{r} 4 \\ \times 7 \\ \hline \end{array}$ **28.** $\begin{array}{r} 7 \\ \times 1 \\ \hline \end{array}$

29. 8×2 **30.** 4×9 **31.** 8×1 **32.** 7×0 **33.** 3×3

34. 10×8 **35.** 9×3 **36.** 7×10 **37.** 5×9 **38.** 3×10

Find the missing factors. *(pages 220–223, 228–231, 236–237)*

39. $5 \times ■ = 0$

40. $45 = ■ \times 5$

41. $60 = ■ \times 10$

42. $■ \times 4 = 24$

43. $■ \times 5 = 15$

44. $■ \times 9 = 36$

Solve. *(pages 224–225, 234–235)*

45. Molly is buying T-shirts at a sale. Small T-shirts cost $6. Large T-shirts cost $8. She buys 4 small T-shirts. How much money does Molly spend?

46. Roberto has 18 sports trophies. He wants to arrange them into equal rows on a table. In what ways can Roberto arrange the trophies?

Use the data in the pictograph to solve Problems 47–48. *(pages 238–239)*

47. Write a number sentence to show how many books the fourth grade bought.

48. Any grade that buys 30 or more books will receive a prize. Which of the grades will receive a prize?

Books Sold at the Book Fair

Second grade	📖 📖 📖 📖 📖 📖
Third grade	📖 📖 📖 📖 📖 📖 📖
Fourth grade	📖 📖 📖 📖 📖
Fifth grade	📖 📖 📖 📖 📖 📖 📖 📖

Each 📖 stands for 5 books.

Brain Teasers Math Reasoning

Working Backward

Jane chose two different one-digit numbers. She multiplied one of them by 10. She multiplied the other by 2. Then she added the products. Her answer was 78. What numbers did Jane chose?

Nickels and Dimes

Peter has 16 coins. The coins are all nickels and dimes. The value of his coins is $1.15. How many of each coin does Peter have?

Internet Brain Teasers

Visit **www.eduplace.com/kids/mhm** for more *Brain Teasers.*

Chapter Test

Write a multiplication sentence for each array or picture.

1. 

2.

3. 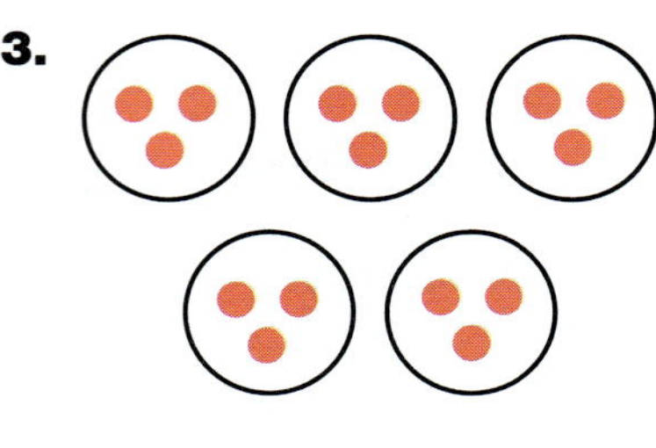

Multiply.

4. 6×4 **5.** 1×6 **6.** 10×9 **7.** 3×2 **8.** 3×7

9. 7×5 **10.** 5×0 **11.** 4×4 **12.** 9×5 **13.** 2×8

14. 7×2 **15.** 8×5 **16.** 1×10 **17.** 3×3 **18.** 4×7

19. 2×5 **20.** 5×5 **21.** 8×3 **22.** 9×2 **23.** 9×1

24. 5×6 **25.** 8×4 **26.** 3×10 **27.** 0×4

28. 3×4 **29.** 2×2 **30.** 2×0 **31.** 4×5

32. 4×9 **33.** 6×3 **34.** 7×10 **35.** 9×3

Fill in the missing numbers.

36. $5 \times ■ = 15$ **37.** $9 \times ■ = 0$ **38.** $4 \times ■ = 28$

39. $1 \times ■ = 8$ **40.** $80 = ■ \times 10$ **41.** $■ \times 2 = 8$

42. $■ = 8 \times 4$ **43.** $■ \times 5 = 5$ **44.** $■ = 6 \times 2$

45. $10 \times 10 = ■$ **46.** $7 \times ■ = 21$ **47.** $10 \times ■ = 40$

Solve.

48. Beth has $40. She buys 8 books. Each book costs $4. How much does she spend on books?

Use the data in the pictograph to solve Problems 49 and 50.

49. How many more butterfly photos than cat photos does Moira have?

50. Moira wants to put bird photos in her album. Up to 8 photos can fit on each page. She wants to put the same number of photos on each page. How many different ways can Moira arrange the photos?

Moira's Photo Collection
Number of Photos

Cat photos	□□□□□
Dog photos	□□□□□□□
Bird photos	□□□□
Butterfly photos	□□□□□□□□

Each □ stands for 4 photos.

Write About It

Solve each problem. Use correct math vocabulary to explain your thinking.

1. Alex helps his father arrange dishes in the kitchen cabinet. His father wants to make 3 stacks of dishes. He wants 8 dishes in each stack. How many dishes is that in all?

a. Draw a picture to solve the problem.

b. Write an addition sentence to solve the problem.

c. Write a multiplication sentence to solve the problem.

2. Andy wrote the multiplication sentence shown at the right.

a. How can you check his answer?

b. Write the correct multiplication sentence.

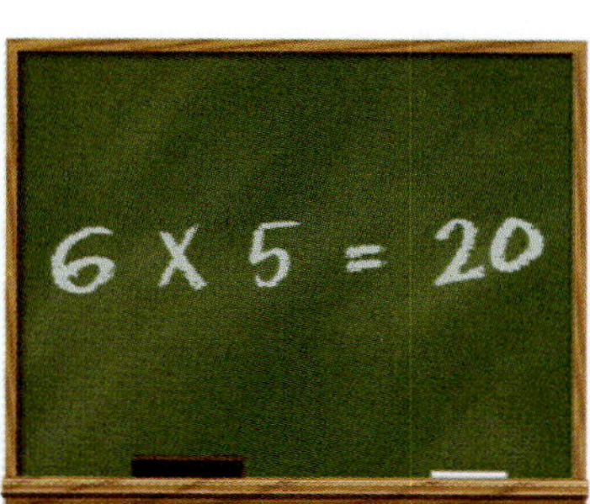

Another Look

Use the pictures below to find the answer to each question. Show your work using pictures, numbers, or words.

1. Brian is helping his aunt order toys for her toy store from the Reed Toy Company. List each toy and how much a box of each toy would cost.

2. Brian's aunt found another toy company that charges less for toys. Each toy costs $1 less than the prices listed above. How much would a box of each kind of toy from the new toy company cost?

3. **Look Back** How did you find the cost of a box of each kind of toy in Question 1? How could you use skip counting to find the cost? How could you use repeated addition?

4. **Analyze** Suppose Brian's aunt sold the toy cars she bought from the Reed Toy Company for twice what she paid for them. How much money should she collect if she sold 2 boxes of toy cars?

Enrichment

New Vocabulary
tree diagram

Making A Tree Diagram

When there are many possible ways to arrange things, you can show all the ways by making a **tree diagram**.

The tree diagram below shows all the sandwiches that can be made at Sammy's Sandwich Shop.

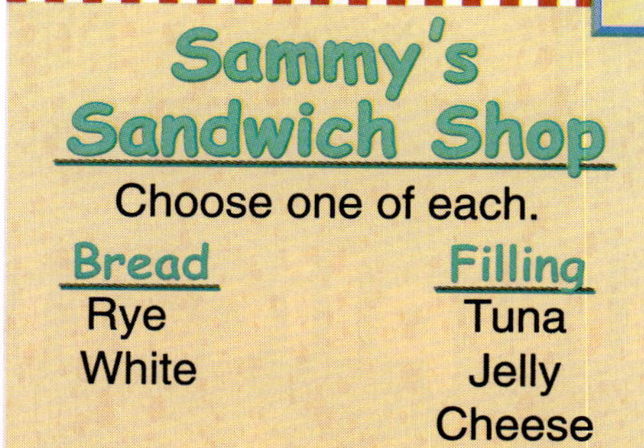

Use the tree diagram to answer these questions.

1. How many different sandwiches can you make with rye bread? How many different sandwiches can you make with white bread?
2. How many different sandwiches can you make in all?
3. Suppose whole wheat is added to the list of breads. Make a tree diagram to show all the sandwiches that can be made with whole wheat. How many different kinds of sandwiches can be made now?

Explain Your Thinking

- Suppose that Sammy's Sandwich Shop had a choice of 4 breads and 4 fillings. How many different sandwiches can be made? Explain.

Multiplication Facts

Why Learn About Multiplication Facts?

Knowing multiplication facts can help you quickly find the total number of items when you have several equal-sized groups.

You can multiply to find how many pencils you have if you buy several packages with the same number in each package.

Each of these children has a pair of skates. There are 4 wheels on each skate. You can use multiplication to find the total number of wheels on all the skates.

Reading Mathematics

Reviewing Vocabulary

Understanding math language helps you become a successful problem solver. Here are some math vocabulary words you should know.

multiplication	finding the total number of objects that are in equal groups
product	the answer in multiplication
factors	numbers that are multiplied
array	a group of objects arranged in rows and columns
Commutative Property of Multiplication	changing the order of the factors in multiplication does not change the product

Reading Words and Symbols

When you read mathematics, sometimes you read only words, sometimes you read words and symbols, and sometimes you read only symbols.

All of these describe the array of stars shown below.

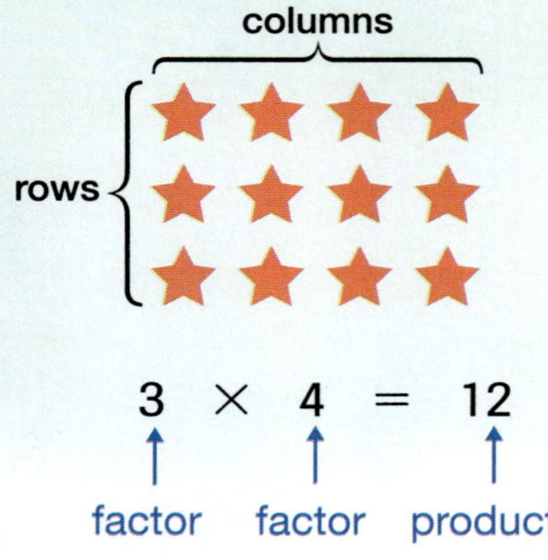

- There are 3 rows with 4 stars in each row.
- There are 4 columns with 3 stars in each column.
- There are 12 stars in the array.

$3 \times 4 = 12$ (3: factor, 4: factor, 12: product)

$4 \times 3 = 12$ (4: factor, 3: factor, 12: product)

Try These

1. Tell whether 10 is a *factor* or a *product*.

   a. $5 \times 2 = 10$ b. $10 \times 7 = 70$ c. $4 \times 10 = 40$

   d. $\begin{array}{r} 3 \\ \times\ 10 \\ \hline 30 \end{array}$ e. $\begin{array}{r} 10 \\ \times\ 2 \\ \hline 20 \end{array}$ f. $\begin{array}{r} 2 \\ \times\ 5 \\ \hline 10 \end{array}$

2. Use the vocabulary words to complete each sentence.

   a. You can draw an ____ to find a product.

   b. You can skip count on a ____ to find a product.

   c. You can use repeated ____ to find a product.

Vocabulary
addition
array
number line

3. Write a multiplication sentence for each statement.

   a. The product of five and seven is thirty-five.

   b. Four is a factor, five is a factor, and twenty is the product.

   c. The product is eight, and two is a factor.

Upcoming Vocabulary

Write About It **Here are some other vocabulary words** you will learn in this chapter. Watch for these words. Write their definitions in your journal.

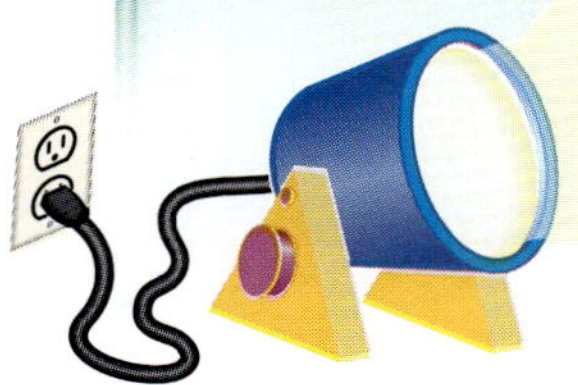

multiple

square number

Associative Property of Multiplication

Using a Multiplication Table

You will learn how to find patterns by using a multiplication table.

Review Vocabulary
multiplication
factors
product

Learn About It

Use a multiplication table to find patterns.

Materials

grid paper or Teaching Tool 3

Step 1 Use grid paper to make a **multiplication** table like the one on the right. Include the numbers shown.

Step 2 The numbers in the purple squares are **factors**. Find the row for 2. Find the column for 4. Then find the square where the row and column meet. Write the **product** of 2 × 4 in that square.

Step 3 Fill in all the other squares that have products you know.

column ↓

row →

×	0	1	2	3	4	5	6	7	8	9	10
0	0	0	0	0	0	0	0	0	0	0	0
1	0	1	2	3	4						
2	0	2	4	6	8						
3	0										
4	0										
5	0										
6	0										
7	0										
8	0										
9	0										
10	0										

2 × 4 = 8

Step 4 Look for patterns in the table.

- Which row and column have the same number in each square?
- Which row has the same numbers as Column 4?
- Which row and column have products that increase by 2 each time?
- Which rows and columns have even numbers only?

Try It Out

Use your multiplication table to answer each question.

1. When you multiply a number by 0, what is the product?
2. When you multiply a number by 1, what is the product?
3. What do all the products in Column 10 have in common?
4. Look for other patterns in the table. Describe two patterns that you find.

Below are parts of a multiplication table.
In which row or column is each part found?

5. 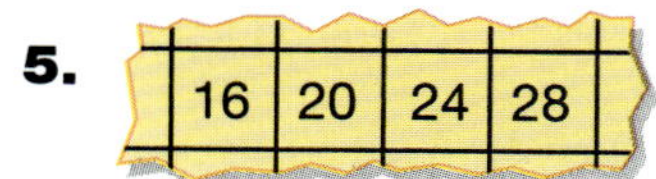

16	20	24	28

6. 

10	15	20	25

7. 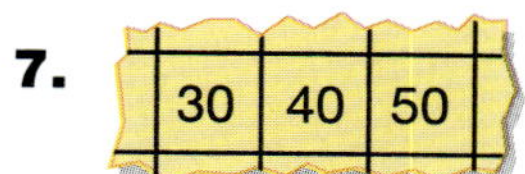

30	40	50

8. 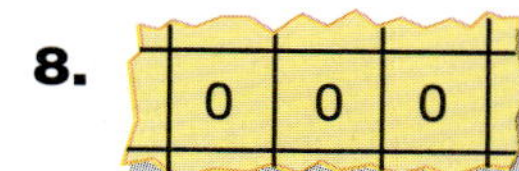

0	0	0

9. 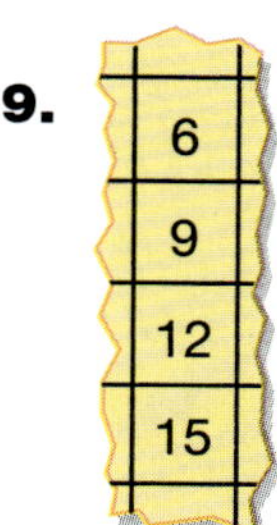

6
9
12
15

10. 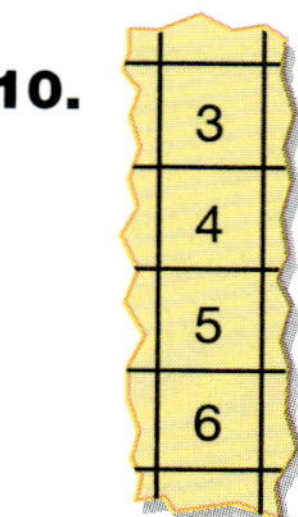

3
4
5
6

11. 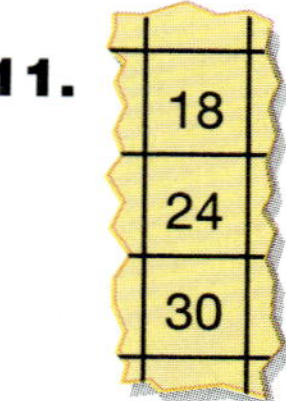

18
24
30

12.

32
36
40

Write *true* or *false* for each statement.
Give examples to support your answers.

13. The product will always be 0 when you multiply by 0.
14. The product will always be 1 when you multiply by 1.
15. Each product appears at least two times in the multiplication table.

Write about it! Talk about it!

Use what you have learned to answer these questions.

16. How could you use the products in Row 2 to help you find the products in Row 4?
17. For each row, is there a column that has the same products? Explain why or why not.

Multiply With 6

You will learn different ways to multiply when 6 is a factor.

Learn About It

During a soccer drill, each team has 6 players on the field. There are 7 teams in all. How many players are on the field?

Multiply. $7 \times 6 = \blacksquare$ or $\begin{array}{r} 6 \\ \times 7 \\ \hline \blacksquare \end{array}$

Different Ways to Multiply

You can use doubling.

7×6 is double 7×3.

$7 \times 3 = 21$
$7 \times 6 = 21 + 21$

$21 + 21 = 42$

So $7 \times 6 = 42$.

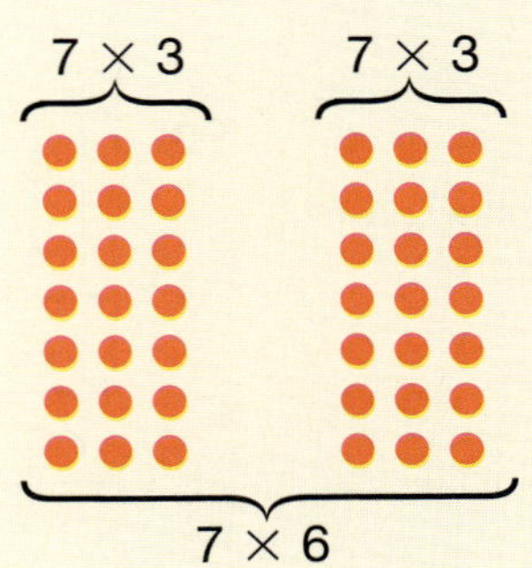

You can use repeated addition.

$6 + 6 + 6 + 6 + 6 + 6 + 6 = 42$

You can write a multiplication sentence.

$7 \times 6 = \blacksquare$
$7 \times 6 = 42$

Think: 7 groups of 6 = 42.

Solution: There are 42 players on the field.

Explain Your Thinking

► Why is 6×8 greater than 5×8?

Guided Practice

Multiply.

1. $\begin{array}{r} 6 \\ \times 2 \\ \hline \end{array}$ **2.** $\begin{array}{r} 5 \\ \times 6 \\ \hline \end{array}$ **3.** $\begin{array}{r} 6 \\ \times 4 \\ \hline \end{array}$ **4.** $\begin{array}{r} 9 \\ \times 6 \\ \hline \end{array}$

5. 3×6 **6.** 6×1 **7.** 6×8 **8.** 10×6

Ask Yourself

- What 3s fact can I use to find the product?
- Is there another fact I can use?

Independent Practice

Find each product.

9. 6×1 **10.** 6×3 **11.** 5×6 **12.** 10×6 **13.** 6×7 **14.** 6×8

15. 4×6 **16.** 6×0 **17.** 6×6 **18.** 1×6 **19.** 6×2 **20.** 9×6

21. 3×4 **22.** 2×8 **23.** 5×3 **24.** 4×9 **25.** 10×1 **26.** 3×0

27. 8×6 **28.** 6×3 **29.** 9×6 **30.** 1×6 **31.** 6×7

32. 4×6 **33.** 2×6 **34.** 6×0 **35.** 6×9 **36.** 5×6

Choose a Method

Solve. Choose a method.

Computation Methods

- **Mental Math**
- **Estimation**
- **Paper and Pencil**

37. There are 48 players signed up for a soccer clinic. Each player will get a pair of kneepads. About how many kneepads will be given out to the players?

38. **Money** There are 6 players on a volleyball team. It costs $4 for each player to play in a tournament. How much will it cost the team to play in the tournament?

39. **Compare** Mark made 8 baskets in a basketball game. In the next game he made 6 baskets. Each basket was worth 2 points. How many more points did Mark make in the first game than in the second?

40. There are 16 games on the first day of a tournament. There are 8 games on the second day and 4 on the third day. If the pattern continues, on what day will there likely be one game?

Mixed Review • Test Prep

Round each number to the nearest hundred. *(pages 8–10, 24–26)*

41. 258 **42.** 417 **43.** 850 **44.** 3,251 **45.** 1,620 **46.** 9,473

47 Which number sentence is true? *(pages 108–109)*

A $28 + 17 = 11$ **B** $106 = 54 + 62$ **C** $98 + 27 = 115$ **D** $121 = 63 + 58$

Extra Practice See Set A on page 284.

LESSON 3

Multiply With 8

You will learn different ways to multiply when 8 is a factor.

Learn About It

Did you know that a spider has 8 legs? This terrarium has 6 spiders in it. How many legs do the 6 spiders have altogether?

Multiply. $6 \times 8 = \blacksquare$ or $\begin{array}{r} 8 \\ \times\, 6 \\ \hline \blacksquare \end{array}$

Different Ways to Multiply

You can use doubling.

6×8 is double 6×4.

$6 \times 4 = 24$

$6 \times 8 = 24 + 24$

$24 + 24 = 48$

So $6 \times 8 = 48$.

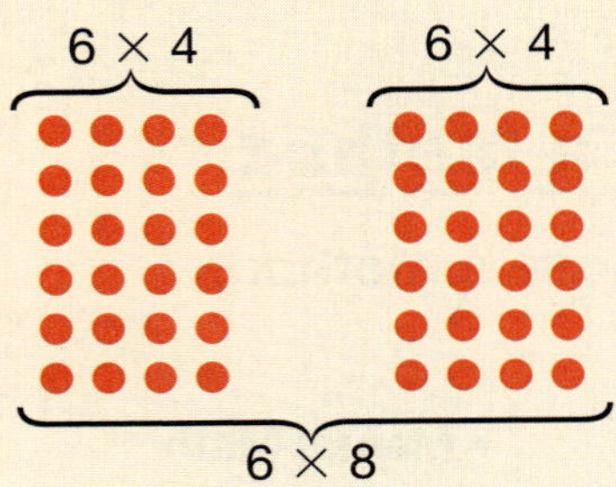

You can use repeated addition.

$8 + 8 + 8 + 8 + 8 + 8 = 48$

You can use a fact you know.

You know that $8 \times 6 = 48$, so $6 \times 8 = 48$.

Remember: Changing the order of the factors does not change the product.

Solution: The 6 spiders have 48 legs altogether.

Explain Your Thinking

► How can you use $3 \times 8 = 24$ to find 3×16?

Guided Practice

Find each product.

1. $\begin{array}{r} 8 \\ \times\, 3 \\ \hline \end{array}$ **2.** $\begin{array}{r} 7 \\ \times\, 8 \\ \hline \end{array}$ **3.** $\begin{array}{r} 8 \\ \times\, 1 \\ \hline \end{array}$ **4.** $\begin{array}{r} 5 \\ \times\, 8 \\ \hline \end{array}$

Ask Yourself

- What 4s fact can I use to find the product?
- Is there another fact I can use?

Independent Practice

Multiply.

5. 8 × 7 **6.** 8 × 2 **7.** 1 × 8 **8.** 3 × 8 **9.** 8 × 9 **10.** 10 × 8

11. 8 × 0 **12.** 6 × 8 **13.** 5 × 8 **14.** 8 × 8 **15.** 2 × 8 **16.** 4 × 8

17. 3 × 8 **18.** 7 × 8 **19.** 5 × 8 **20.** 8 × 9 **21.** 10 × 8

Algebra • Expressions **Compare. Write $>$, $<$, or $=$ for each ●.**

22. 5 × 4 ● 5 × 8 **23.** 10 × 8 ● 9 × 8 **24.** 3 × 8 ● 8 × 3

25. 6 × 4 ● 3 × 8 **26.** 7 × 5 ● 6 × 5 **27.** 2 × 5 ● 3 × 5

Problem Solving • Reasoning

28. An ant has 6 legs. Which have more legs in all, 7 spiders or 9 ants? How many more?

29. Cara, Andy, and Brett are studying ants. Cara has 9 ants. Andy has twice as many ants as Cara. Brett has 5 fewer ants than Andy. How many ants do they have in all?

30. **Analyze** Elena made up this problem: "I have some ants and spiders. There are 34 legs in all. How many ants do I have?" What is the answer to her problem?

31. **Write Your Own** Write a word problem that can be solved by multiplying by 8. Give your problem to a classmate to solve.

Math Is Everywhere!

SCIENCE Ants live together in colonies. Some colonies may have 10 ants. Other colonies have thousands of ants.

Suppose one ant colony has 38 ants and another has 21 ants. About how many ants do the two colonies have in all?

Mixed Review • Test Prep

Write the next 3 numbers that would likely continue each pattern. Explain why. *(pages xxvi–xxvii, 28–29)*

32. 3, 6, 9, 12, ■, ■, ■ **33.** 4, 8, 12, 16, ■, ■, ■ **34.** 8, 16, 24, 32, ■, ■, ■

35 What is the value of 3 quarters, 1 dime, and 6 pennies? *(pages 56–57)*

A 91¢ **B** 86¢ **C** 82¢ **D** 10¢

Extra Practice See Set B on page 284.

Multiplication Facts Practice

Be sure you memorized your facts. Then find each product as quickly as you can.

1. 6×5 **2.** 3×2 **3.** 4×7 **4.** 10×8 **5.** 4×6

6. 5×7 **7.** 1×7 **8.** 2×6 **9.** 4×5 **10.** 6×8

11. 3×7 **12.** 0×6 **13.** 3×1 **14.** 8×8 **15.** 9×4

16. 4×0 **17.** 2×7 **18.** 1×9 **19.** 6×6 **20.** 5×3

21. 9×6 **22.** 8×3 **23.** 7×8 **24.** 3×3 **25.** 6×0

26. 1×8 **27.** 4×9 **28.** 5×8 **29.** 0×1 **30.** 8×6

31. 4×2 **32.** 0×3 **33.** 8×1 **34.** 3×6 **35.** 10×9

36. 10×3 **37.** 5×5 **38.** 1×6 **39.** 6×8 **40.** 5×0

41. 4×7 **42.** 6×4 **43.** 3×9 **44.** 10×5 **45.** 1×8

46. 8×3 **47.** 7×6 **48.** 9×8 **49.** 6×9 **50.** 8×5

Copy and complete each table.

51.

number of marker boxes	1	2	3	4	5	6	7	8	9	10
number of markers	6	12								

52.

number of crayon boxes	1	2	3	4	5	6	7	8	9	10
number of crayons	8	16								

Practice Game

Coloring Counts

Practice multiplication by playing this game with a partner. Try to color in the most squares on your hundred chart.

What You'll Need

For each pair

- *2 sets of index cards labeled 2 to 9*
- *2 hundred charts (Teaching Tool 4)*
- *2 crayons of different colors*

Players 2

2 3 4 5 6 7 8 9

1	2	3	4	5	6	7	8	9	10
11	12	13	14	15	16	17	18	19	20
21	22	23	24	25	26	27	28	29	30
31	32	33	34	35	36	37	38	39	40
41	42	43	44	45	46	47	48	49	50
51	52	53	54	55	56	57	58	59	60
61	62	63	64	65	66	67	68	69	70
71	72	73	74	75	76	77	78	79	80
81	82	83	84	85	86	87	88	89	90
91	92	93	94	95	96	97	98	99	100

Here's What to Do

1. Shuffle and place the cards facedown in a pile. Each player takes a hundred chart and crayon.
2. The first player picks the top card from the pile. The player can use the number picked in **one** of these ways.
   - Color all numbers on the chart that have the number as a factor.
   - Color all numbers on the chart that have the number in the ones place.
   - Color all numbers on the chart that have the number in the tens place.
3. Players take turns repeating Step 2 until all of the cards have been used. The player with more squares colored at the end of the game wins!

Share Your Thinking Will you ever be able to color 1? 11? Explain why or why not.

Problem-Solving Skill: Multistep Problems

You will learn how to solve problems that have more than one step.

Sometimes you must do two or more steps to solve a problem. Then you need to decide what steps to do and in what order to do them.

Problem Eric has 9 pictures from a trip to Maine. He has twice as many pictures from a trip to California. How many pictures does Eric have from his 2 trips?

Decide what to do.

- First, find the number of pictures Eric has from California.
- Then find the total number of pictures from his 2 trips.

Do each step in order.

Step 1 Eric has twice as many California pictures as Maine pictures. Multiply the number of Maine pictures by 2 to find the number of California pictures.

$$\begin{array}{r} 9 \\ \times\ 2 \\ \hline 18 \end{array}$$

9 ← Maine pictures
18 ← California pictures

Eric has 18 California pictures.

Step 2 Now add the number of California pictures and the number of Maine pictures.

$$\begin{array}{r} 18 \\ +\ 9 \\ \hline 27 \end{array}$$

18 ← California pictures
9 ← Maine pictures
27 ← total number of pictures

Eric has 27 pictures from his 2 trips.

Look Back Could you have done the steps in a different order? Explain why or why not.

In Riverside, California, in 1998, over 100 children took part in a free day of picture taking. After receiving a quick photography lesson, the children walked around town taking pictures with their new cameras.

Guided Practice

Solve.

1. Amy put 47 photos in her album. The album has 10 pages. Each page holds 6 photos. How many more photos can Amy put in the album?

How many photos can fit in the album?

2. Dana has 8 state patches. Daryl has 13 more patches than Dana. How many patches do the two friends have in all?

How many patches does Daryl have?

Choose a Strategy

Solve. Use these or other strategies.

Problem-Solving Strategies

- **Act It Out**
- **Write a Number Sentence**
- **Find a Pattern**

3. Eliza is arranging 20 trip pictures in an array. The array has one more column than it has rows. How many pictures will be in each row of the array?

4. Pam brought in 8 post cards to show her class. She has three times as many post cards at home. How many post cards does Pam have altogether?

5. Nim received 3 letters with stamps on them. The letters had a total of 7 stamps. No letter had the same number of stamps. How many stamps were on each letter?

6. A map collector has 2 old maps. Each map is worth $1,500. He paid $428 for each map. How much more are the 2 maps worth now than when he bought them?

7. Leo put a roll of film in his camera. He took 13 pictures of a hike and 16 pictures of a picnic. He can take 7 more pictures before the film runs out. How many pictures can be taken with the roll of film?

8. Tory made a poster of state flags. The first row had 2 flags. Each row after that had 3 more flags than the row before it. If there were 5 rows in all, how many flags were on Tory's poster?

Extra Practice See Set 1–2 on page 287.

Quick Check

Check Your Understanding of Lessons 1–4

Multiply.

1. $\begin{array}{r} 6 \\ \times\ 3 \\ \hline \end{array}$

2. $\begin{array}{r} 6 \\ \times\ 5 \\ \hline \end{array}$

3. $\begin{array}{r} 4 \\ \times\ 6 \\ \hline \end{array}$

4. $\begin{array}{r} 9 \\ \times\ 6 \\ \hline \end{array}$

5. $8 \times 7 = ■$

6. $8 \times 6 = ■$

7. $4 \times 8 = ■$

8. $8 \times 9 = ■$

9. $8 \times 8 = ■$

10. $5 \times 8 = ■$

Solve.

11. Harry arranged his picture collection in 6 rows. He put 7 pictures in each row. Then he gave 6 pictures to his friend Tina. How many pictures does Harry have left?

12. Jessica collected 123 cans for recycling. Ashley collected 35 more cans than Jessica. How many cans did the two children collect in all?

How did you do?

If you had difficulty with any items in the Quick Check, you can use the following pages for review and extra practice.

Items	Review These Pages	Do These Extra Practice Items
1–4	pages 258–259	Set A, page 284
5-10	pages 260–261	Set B, page 284
11–12	pages 264–265	1–2, page 287

Test Prep • Cumulative Review

Maintaining the Standards

Write the letter of the correct answer. If a correct answer is not here, choose NH.

1 Which number sentence is true?

A $6 \times 7 = 5 \times 6$
B $6 \times 7 = 9 \times 6$
C $6 \times 7 = 7 \times 6$
D $6 \times 7 = 8 \times 6$

2 Samantha is 3 feet tall. Her father is twice as tall as Samantha. How tall is Samantha's father?

F 5 feet
G 7 feet
H 8 feet
J NH

3 Which number makes the number sentence true?

$$6 \times \blacksquare = 0$$

A 0
B 1
C 2
D 3

4 Which of the following is the best estimate of the mass of a third grader?

F 5 grams
G 100 grams
H 30 kilograms
J 500 kilograms

5 What symbol makes the number sentence true?

$$8 \bullet 1 = 8$$

A + **C** ×
B − **D** <

6 What is the greatest whole number you can make using the digits 7, 1, 9, and 5?

F 5,197 **H** 9,751
G 1,957 **J** 9,571

7 What time does the clock show?

A 1:25 **C** 5:00
B 9:30 **D** 12:25

8 Fred did 9 math problems in 10 minutes. His older brother did 8 times that number in the same amount of time. How many math problems did Fred's brother do in 10 minutes?

Explain How did you find your answer?

Multiply With 7

You will learn different ways to multiply when 7 is a factor.

Learn About It

Suppose your class is having a party exactly 6 weeks from today. How many days away is the party?

Multiply. $6 \times 7 = \blacksquare$ or $\begin{array}{r} 7 \\ \times\ 6 \\ \hline \blacksquare \end{array}$

Different Ways to Multiply

You can use repeated addition.

$7 + 7 + 7 + 7 + 7 + 7 = 42$

You can draw an array.

6 rows of 7 = 42

You can remember a multiplication fact.

$6 \times 7 = \blacksquare$

$6 \times 7 = 42$

Think: 6 groups of 7 = 42.

Solution: The party is 42 days away.

Explain Your Thinking

► Why is it useful to know that you can multiply factors in any order?

Guided Practice

Ask Yourself

- What fact can I use to find the product?

Multiply.

1. $\begin{array}{r} 7 \\ \times\ 6 \\ \hline \end{array}$ **2.** $\begin{array}{r} 5 \\ \times\ 7 \\ \hline \end{array}$ **3.** $\begin{array}{r} 7 \\ \times\ 2 \\ \hline \end{array}$ **4.** $\begin{array}{r} 10 \\ \times\ 7 \\ \hline \end{array}$

5. 8×7 **6.** 7×3 **7.** 4×7 **8.** 7×7

9. 1×7 **10.** 7×9 **11.** 7×0 **12.** 10×7

Independent Practice

Find each product.

13. 7×2 **14.** 7×5 **15.** 7×8 **16.** 4×7 **17.** 7×7 **18.** 3×7

19. 0×7 **20.** 7×9 **21.** 10×7 **22.** 7×1 **23.** 7×6 **24.** 5×7

25. 7×2 **26.** 9×7 **27.** 8×7 **28.** 0×7 **29.** 7×7

30. 3×7 **31.** 7×6 **32.** 7×1 **33.** 5×7 **34.** 10×7

35. 7×4 **36.** 5×8 **37.** 6×3 **38.** 9×6 **39.** 0×8

Algebra • Expressions **Compare. Write $>$, $<$, or $=$ for each ●.**

40. 4×7 ● 5×7 **41.** 7×7 ● 6×6 **42.** 0×7 ● 1×7

43. 7×2 ● 2×7 **44.** 8×7 ● 6×9 **45.** 7×3 ● 7×4

Problem Solving • Reasoning

46. Except for leap years, there are exactly 4 weeks in February. How many days is that?

47. **Estimate** Jessica's birthday is in 32 days. Julia's birthday is 41 days after that. About how many days away is Julia's birthday?

48. **Money** Terell spent $15 on 2 animal calendars. The dog calendar cost $3 more than the cat calendar. How much did the cat calendar cost?

49. **Logical Thinking** Tim is 7 years old. Lisa is four times as old as Tim. If Lisa is half as old as Uncle Ed, how old is Uncle Ed?

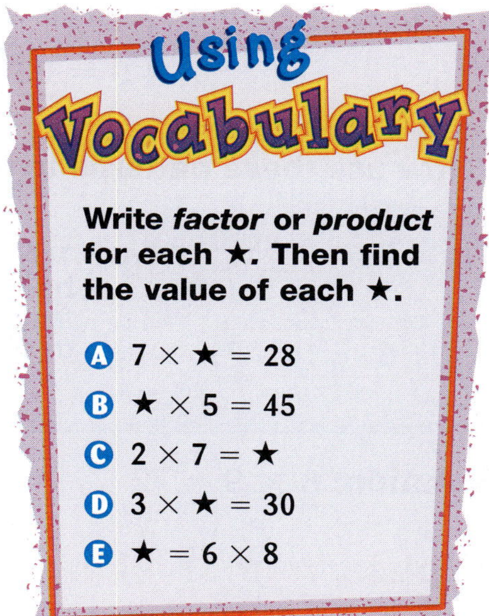

Mixed Review • Test Prep

Add or subtract. *(pages 108–109, 128–130)*

50. 715 + 268 **51.** 864 − 309 **52.** 438 − 150 **53.** 309 + 491

54 Which shows eighteen thousand, fifty-six in standard form? *(pages 32–33)*

A 1,856 **B** 18,056 **C** 18,506 **D** 18,560

LESSON 6

Multiply With 9

You will learn how to use patterns to multiply when 9 is a factor.

Learn About It

This table shows most of the 9s facts. The next fact on the table would be 8 × 9. What is 8 × 9?

Fact	Product
1 × 9	9
2 × 9	18
3 × 9	27
4 × 9	36
5 × 9	45
6 × 9	54
7 × 9	63
8 × 9	
9 × 9	
10 × 9	

Multiply. **8 × 9 = ■** or

$$\begin{array}{r} 9 \\ \times\ 8 \\ \hline ■ \end{array}$$

You can use patterns to find 9s facts.

- Look at each row in the table. Notice that the tens digit of the product is always 1 less than the underlined factor.

  7 × 9 = 63

- Look at each product in the table. Notice that the sum of the digits is always 9.

  7 × 9 = 63 → 6 + 3 = 9

Now use these patterns to find 8 × 9.

8 × 9 = 7_

8 − 1 = 7

Think: The tens digit will be 1 less than the factor you are multiplying with 9.

8 × 9 = 72

7 + 2 = 9

Think: The sum of the digits in the product will be 9.

Solution: 8 × 9 = 72

Explain Your Thinking

► How can you use patterns to help you find 9 × 9?

Guided Practice

Multiply.

1. 9 × 3 **2.** 7 × 9 **3.** 9 × 2 **4.** 5 × 9

5. 4 × 9 **6.** 1 × 9 **7.** 6 × 9 **8.** 10 × 9

Ask Yourself

- What fact can I use to find the product?
- How can I use patterns to find the product?

Independent Practice

Multiply.

9. 9 × 2 **10.** 9 × 6 **11.** 4 × 9 **12.** 9 × 0 **13.** 1 × 9 **14.** 9 × 5

15. 3 × 9 **16.** 9 × 8 **17.** 9 × 7 **18.** 10 × 9 **19.** 9 × 9 **20.** 6 × 9

21. 4 × 9 **22.** 10 × 9 **23.** 9 × 3 **24.** 9 × 7 **25.** 5 × 9

26. 6 × 9 **27.** 9 × 1 **28.** 8 × 9 **29.** 9 × 0 **30.** 2 × 9

31. 9 × 9 **32.** 3 × 9 **33.** 9 × 5 **34.** 9 × 10 **35.** 9 × 4

36. 7 × 4 **37.** 3 × 8 **38.** 5 × 6 **39.** 2 × 8 **40.** 1 × 7

Problem Solving • Reasoning

Use Data **Use the sign on the right for Problems 41–44.**

41. There are 9 planets in our solar system. What would the total cost be if you bought a small poster of each one?

42. **Estimate** About how much more does an Earth globe cost than a solar system kit?

43. **Compare** Glow-in-the-dark star sets normally cost $12. How much money do you save if you buy 4 sets on sale?

44. **Write About It** Mrs. Gomez has $37 to spend on science-fair prizes. She plans to spend all of the money on posters. How many prizes will she have? Explain how you found your answer.

Mixed Review • Test Prep

Write the value of the underlined digit. *(pages 18–19, 32–33, 34–35)*

45. 4,0$\underline{3}$9 **46.** 7$\underline{1}$,624 **47.** $\underline{5}$3,265 **48.** 3$\underline{1}$6,902 **49.** $\underline{8}$24,164

50 How many minutes are there between 10:15 A.M. and 11:30 A.M.? *(pages 78–79)*

A 135 min **B** 105 min **C** 75 min **D** 15 min

Extra Practice See Set D on page 285.

Problem-Solving Strategy: Choose a Strategy

You will learn to choose a strategy to solve a problem.

If there is more than one strategy that can be used to solve a problem, you need to decide which one to use.

Problem Erica collected shells at the beach. She gave all the shells to 3 friends. If she gave 4 shells to each friend, how many shells did Erica collect at the beach?

What is the question?
How many shells did Erica collect at the beach?

What do you know?
She gave 4 shells to each of 3 friends.

How can you find the answer?
You can use models to act it out or you can write a number sentence.

Use Models to Act It Out

- Use counters to stand for the shells. Ask 3 classmates to be the friends.
- Give 4 counters to each friend.
- Count all of the counters that your friends have.

Write a Number Sentence

Find the number of shells Erica gave her friends.

$3 \times 4 = n$

The letter n is another way to write ■. It stands for a missing number.

$3 \times 4 = 12$

3 ↑ number of friends; 4 ↑ shells given to each friend; 12 ↑ $n = 12$

Erica collected 12 shells from the beach.

Look back at the problem.
What is another number sentence you could use?

Guided Practice

Solve.

1. Ben bought 5 starfish and a display case. He spent $17 in all. If the starfish cost $2 each, how much did Ben pay for the display case?

   Think: Which step should you do first to solve the problem?

2. Min has 3 more shells than Leah. Leah has 5 more shells than Kim. Kim has 10 shells. How many shells does Min have?

   Think: For which girl do you know the number of shells?

Choose a Strategy

Solve. Use these or other strategies.

Problem-Solving Strategies

- Find a Pattern
- Act It Out
- Work Backward
- Guess and Check

3. Karyn bought some painted shells and rocks at a craft fair for 10¢ each. She bought 3 rocks. She spent 90¢ in all. How many shells did Karyn buy?

4. Roberto has 3 identical shells and 4 rocks. He wants to paint each shell yellow or green. What are all the ways Roberto could paint the shells?

5. Sue has a poster of shells. Each row shows 5 shells. Shells in the first row are numbered 1 to 5, those in the second row, 6 to 10, and so on. What number is the last shell in the sixth row likely to be?

6. Christopher had 17 sand dollars in his collection. Then he bought 2 sets of sand dollars. There are 5 sand dollars in each set. How many sand dollars does Christopher have now?

7. Todd and Matt collect beach glass. Todd has 5 more pieces than Matt. If they multiply the number of pieces each has, the product is 36. How many pieces of beach glass does Todd have?

8. Lisa put 30 shells arranged in the pattern shown below. How many small shells does Lisa have?

Extra Practice See Set 3–6 on page 287.

Patterns on a Multiplication Table

You will learn how to find patterns by using a multiplication table.

New Vocabulary
multiple
square number

Learn About It

You can use a multiplication table to see different patterns.

Materials
grid paper or Teaching Tool 5

Step 1 Copy and complete the multiplication table on the right. Use patterns to fill in the products for 11 and 12.

column ↓

row →

×	0	1	2	3	4	5	6	7	8	9	10	11	12
0	0	0	0	0	0	0	0	0	0	0	0		
1	0	1	2	3	4	5	6	7	8	9	10		
2	0	2	4	6	8	10	12	14	16	18	20		
3	0	3	6	9	12	15	18	21	24	27	30		
4	0	4	8	12	16	20	24	28	32	36	40		
5	0	5	10	15	20	25	30	35	40	45	50		
6	0	6	12	18	24	30	36	42	48	54	60		
7	0	7	14	21	28	35	42	49	56	63	70		
8	0	8	16	24	32	40	48	56	64	72	80		
9	0	9	18	27	36	45	54	63	72	81	90		
10	0	10	20	30	40	50	60	70	80	90	100		
11	0												
12	0												

Step 2 Look at the row for 2. All of the numbers in this row are multiples of 2.

A **multiple** of 2 is any product that has 2 as a factor.

0, 2, 4, 6, 8, 10, and so on are multiples of 2.

- Which column shows the same multiples of 2?

Step 3 Make a list of the multiples of 2 shown in the row for 2. Make a list of the multiples of 4 shown in the row for 4. Compare the numbers in both lists. What pattern can you find?

Step 4 Repeat Step 3 to find multiples of 3 and 6. Repeat Step 3 again to find multiples of 5 and 10.

- What patterns do you see?
- Can you find other pairs of numbers in which this same pattern happens?

Step 5 Look at the shaded products in the table shown at the right. Then look at the factors shown in the purple boxes.

- What can you say about the factors that make each of these products?

When the two factors of a product are the same, the product is called a **square number**.

0, 1, 4, 9, 16, and so on are square numbers.

×	0	1	2	3	4	5
0	0	0	0	0	0	0
1	0	1	2	3	4	5
2	0	2	4	6	8	10
3	0	3	6	9	12	15
4	0	4	8	12	16	20
5	0	5	10	15	20	25

- Shade all the square numbers you see on your multiplication table.
- How could you find some other square numbers that are not in the table?

Try It Out

Use your completed multiplication table to help you answer each question.

1. What multiples of 7 are shown in the table?
2. Are multiples of 5 always even numbers? Explain why or why not.
3. Is 8 a square number? Explain why or why not.
4. What do you notice about the multiples of 11?

Write *true* or *false* for each statement.
Give an example to support each answer.

5. Any multiple of 4 is also a multiple of 2.
6. Any multiple of 2 is also a multiple of 4.
7. All square numbers are even numbers.
8. If a number is odd, all of its multiples will be odd.
9. If a number is even, all of its multiples will be even.

Copy and complete each multiplication sentence.

10. $4 \times \blacksquare = 12$ **11.** $\blacksquare \times 8 = 56$ **12.** $5 \times 9 = \blacksquare$

13. $\blacksquare \times 1 = 10$ **14.** $12 \times \blacksquare = 36$ **15.** $\blacksquare \times \blacksquare = 1$

16. $3 \times \blacksquare = 9$ **17.** $8 \times 8 = \blacksquare$ **18.** $5 \times \blacksquare = 25$

Write whether each array shows a square number.
If not, find the least number of squares that could be added to make the array a square number.

19. 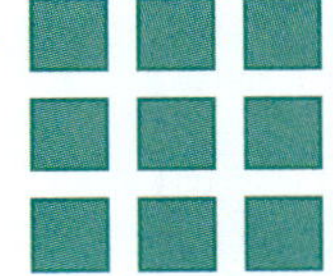

20. 

21. 

22.

23. 

24.

Use what you have learned to answer these questions.

25. How can you use a multiplication table to show that you can multiply factors in any order?
26. In the table, why is the number above a square number the same as the number to the left of that square number?

Show What You Know

Using Vocabulary

Use the clues to find each number.

1. What's the number?
- It is odd.
- Is it greater than 1.
- It is a factor of 12.
- Its multiples include 15, 18, and 21.

2. What's the number?
- It is even.
- Is it less than 19.
- 5 is one of its factors.
- Its multiples all have the same ones digit.

Looking for Signs

Write the correct operation sign to complete each number sentence. Choose +, −, or ×.

1. 3 ⬭ 2 = 5

2. 4 = 1 ⬭ 4

3. 9 ⬭ 8 = 72

4. 10 ⬭ 4 = 6

5. 0 ⬭ 8 = 8

6. 4 = 6 ⬭ 2

7. 5 ⬭ 3 = 15

8. 9 = 3 ⬭ 3

9. 16 = 4 ⬭ 4

Getting Into Shapes

Different shapes stand for different numbers. Same shapes stand for same numbers. Find the value of each shape.

1. ■ − ▲ = 1

■ × ▲ = 6

■ = ? ▲ = ?

2. ★ − ● = 8

★ × ● = 20

★ = ? ● = ?

3. ◆ + ◆ = 14

◆ × ◆ = 49

◆ = ?

LESSON 9 Multiply Three Numbers

You will learn that you can multiply factors in any order to find the product of 3 or more numbers.

New Vocabulary
Associative Property

Learn About It

When Reni's class was studying Japan, her mom came to show how sushi is made. Reni's mom put 5 pieces of sushi on each tray. She placed 2 trays on each table. There were 4 tables. How many pieces of sushi did she make?

$5 \times 2 \times 4 = \blacksquare$

- 5 ↑ pieces of sushi
- 2 ↑ number of trays
- 4 ↑ number of tables

Associative Property of Multiplication

The way factors are grouped does not change the product.

You can multiply 5 × 2 first.

$(5 \times 2) \times 4 = \blacksquare$

$10 \times 4 = 40$

You can multiply 2 × 4 first.

$5 \times (2 \times 4) = \blacksquare$

$5 \times 8 = 40$

No matter which two factors are multiplied first, the product will be the same.

Remember: The parentheses ( ) tell you which factors to multiply first.

Solution: Reni's mom made 40 pieces of sushi.

Explain Your Thinking

► In which order would you multiply $3 \times 2 \times 6$? Explain why.

Guided Practice

Find each product. Multiply factors in parentheses first.

1. $6 \times (1 \times 7) = \blacksquare$
$(6 \times 1) \times 7 = \blacksquare$

2. $3 \times (4 \times 2) = \blacksquare$
$(3 \times 4) \times 2 = \blacksquare$

Ask Yourself
- Which two numbers should I multiply first?

Independent Practice

Find each product. Multiply factors in parentheses first.

3. $(3 \times 1) \times 2 = ■$ **4.** $4 \times (9 \times 0) = ■$ **5.** $3 \times (3 \times 2) = ■$

6. $(5 \times 2) \times 3 = ■$ **7.** $(9 \times 1) \times 8 = ■$ **8.** $(0 \times 7) \times 4 = ■$

Use parentheses. Find each product in two different ways.

9. $3 \times 2 \times 4 = ■$ **10.** $2 \times 5 \times 1 = ■$ **11.** $3 \times 3 \times 1 = ■$

12. $1 \times 2 \times 6 = ■$ **13.** $4 \times 1 \times 8 = ■$ **14.** $9 \times 0 \times 9 = ■$

15. $2 \times 4 \times 2 = ■$ **16.** $7 \times 0 \times 3 = ■$ **17.** $8 \times 1 \times 9 = ■$

Problem Solving • Reasoning

Use Data **Use the graph for Problems 18–20.**

18. How many more students chose the food activity than the song activity?

19. Each student in the crafts group used 2 packages of origami paper. Each package had 7 sheets of paper. How many sheets of paper did the group use?

20. Each student signed up for only 1 activity. How many students signed up in all? Explain how you know.

21. **Write About It** When do you need to multiply more than 2 numbers? Use examples to show your thinking.

Mixed Review • Test Prep

Add or subtract. *(pages 108–109, 120–121, 132–133)*

22. $74 + 98$

23. $401 - 297$

24. $658 + 219$

25. $4{,}628 + 3{,}947$

26. $2{,}708 - 649$

27 Which shows 7,415 rounded to the nearest hundred? *(pages 24–26)*

A 7,000 **B** 7,400 **C** 7,410 **D** 7,500

Extra Practice See Set E on page 286.

Problem-Solving Application: Use Operations

You will learn how to use operations to help you solve problems.

Problem Maria is going with her family to the Summer Strawberry Festival. There will be 4 children and 3 adults going to the festival for one day. How much will the family spend on admission tickets?

What is the question?
How much will Maria's family spend on tickets to the festival?

What do you know?
- There are 4 children going to the festival.
- There are 3 adults going to the festival.

How can you solve the problem?
Find the cost of the children's tickets and the cost of the adults' tickets. Then find the cost of all the tickets.

Find the cost of the children's tickets and the adults' tickets.

Cost of the children's tickets	Cost of the adults' tickets
$4 \times \$6 = \$24$	$3 \times \$9 = \$27$

Find the cost of all the tickets.

$\$24 + \$27 = \$51$

The family will spend $51 on admission tickets.

Look Back

Look back at the question.
How could you solve the problem another way?

Remember:
- Understand
- Plan
- Solve
- Look Back

Guided Practice

Use the signs below to solve each problem.

1. Darren used nickels to buy 4 tickets. How many nickels did Darren use?

   Think: How much do 4 tickets cost?

2. Mary bought exactly enough tickets to go on 3 rides. How much did she spend on tickets?

   Think: How many tickets are needed for 1 ride?

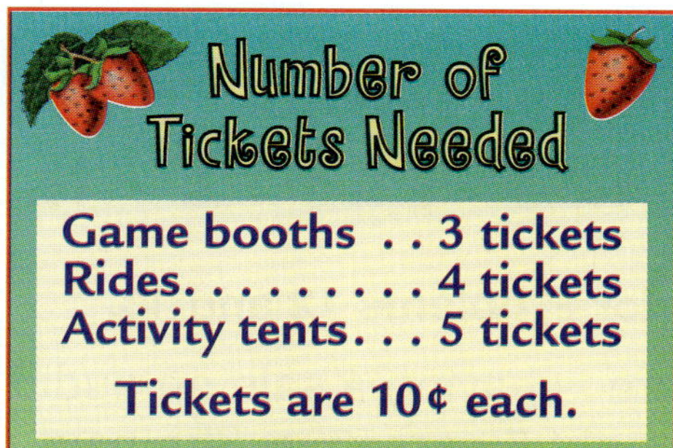

Choose a Strategy

Use the signs above to solve. Use these or other strategies.

Problem-Solving Strategies

- Write a Number Sentence
- Work Backward
- Draw a Picture

3. Don went on all the family rides and half of the kiddie rides. How many rides did he go on in all?

4. How many tickets will you need if you want to go to each game booth and activity tent once?

5. Pedro bought some tickets. First he went on 3 rides. Then he visited 2 activity tents. Now Pedro has 6 tickets left. How many tickets did he buy?

6. Matthew used twice as many tickets for rides as he used for game booths. He used 6 game-booth tickets. How many rides did Matthew go on?

7. Hannah went to a play that lasted 1 hour. After it ended, she spent an hour at the game booths and an hour going on rides. When she was done, it was 6:30 P.M. When did the play begin?

8. The 5 game booths are all in a row. Diving Darts is the booth in the middle. The Ring Toss booth is right next to it. How many more booths are there on one side of the Ring Toss booth than the other?

Extra Practice See Set 7–9 on page 287.

Quick Check

Check Your Understanding of Lessons 5–10

Multiply.

1. $\begin{array}{r} 7 \\ \times 1 \\ \hline \end{array}$
2. $\begin{array}{r} 7 \\ \times 7 \\ \hline \end{array}$
3. $\begin{array}{r} 7 \\ \times 9 \\ \hline \end{array}$
4. $\begin{array}{r} 5 \\ \times 7 \\ \hline \end{array}$
5. $\begin{array}{r} 9 \\ \times 5 \\ \hline \end{array}$
6. $\begin{array}{r} 9 \\ \times 6 \\ \hline \end{array}$
7. $\begin{array}{r} 9 \\ \times 9 \\ \hline \end{array}$
8. $\begin{array}{r} 4 \\ \times 9 \\ \hline \end{array}$

Muliply in any order to find the product.

9. $4 \times 2 \times 4 = \blacksquare$
10. $3 \times 2 \times 3 = \blacksquare$
11. $2 \times 4 \times 6 = \blacksquare$

Solve. Use the picture for Problems 12 and 13.

12. The electronics store is having a sale on audio cassettes. Irene bought 5 cassettes. She paid with a twenty dollar bill. How much change did she get back?

13. Rick bought twice as many CDs as audio cassettes. He paid $16 for cassettes. How many CDs did he buy?

How did you do?

If you had difficulty with any items in the Quick Check, you can use the following pages for review and extra practice.

Items	Review These Pages	Do These Extra Practice Items
1–4	pages 268–269	Set C, page 285
5-8	pages 270–271	Set D, page 285
9–11	pages 278–279	Set E, page 286
12	pages 272–273	3–6, page 287
13	pages 280–181	7–9, page 287

Test Prep • Cumulative Review

Maintaining the Standards

Write the letter of the correct answer. If a correct answer is not here, choose NH.

1 The population of a town is 5,654. What is the value of the underlined digit in 5,<u>6</u>54?

A 6,000
B 60
C 600
D 6

2 Which number sentence is not true?

F $4 \times 1 = 1 \times 4$
G $2 \times 3 = 3 \times 2$
H $3 \times 3 = 3 \times 5$
J $6 \times 1 = 1 \times 6$

3 Look at the number pattern below. What is the next number likely to be?

0, 6, 12, 18, ____

A 20
B 22
C 24
D 28

4 Which number sentence is true?

F $7 \times 3 = 22$
G $5 \times 0 = 5$
H $8 \times 5 = 45$
J $9 \times 0 = 0$

5 The club has three hundred sixty-two members. How is that number written in standard form?

A 3,062
B 3,620
C 362
D 636

6 Which number makes the number sentence true?

$3 \times \blacksquare = 3$

F 0
G 1
H 2
J 3

7 Mrs. Jacobs divided her class into 7 groups. Each group had 7 students. How many students were there in all?

A 35
B 49
C 56
D NH

8 Mr. Cooper needs to put shoes on all his horses. If he has 8 horses, how many shoes will he need?

Explain How did you find your answer?

Safe Site

Internet Test Prep
Visit **www.eduplace.com/kids/mhm** for more *Test Prep Practice.*

Extra Practice

Set A (*Lesson 2, pages 258–259*)

Find each product.

1. $\begin{array}{r} 6 \\ \times\ 3 \\ \hline \end{array}$ **2.** $\begin{array}{r} 7 \\ \times\ 6 \\ \hline \end{array}$ **3.** $\begin{array}{r} 6 \\ \times\ 4 \\ \hline \end{array}$ **4.** $\begin{array}{r} 0 \\ \times\ 6 \\ \hline \end{array}$ **5.** $\begin{array}{r} 6 \\ \times\ 5 \\ \hline \end{array}$

6. $\begin{array}{r} 1 \\ \times\ 6 \\ \hline \end{array}$ **7.** $\begin{array}{r} 6 \\ \times\ 6 \\ \hline \end{array}$ **8.** $\begin{array}{r} 8 \\ \times\ 6 \\ \hline \end{array}$ **9.** $\begin{array}{r} 6 \\ \times\ 2 \\ \hline \end{array}$ **10.** $\begin{array}{r} 6 \\ \times\ 9 \\ \hline \end{array}$

11. 6×1 **12.** 2×6 **13.** 9×6 **14.** 6×7 **15.** 4×6

16. 6×3 **17.** 5×6 **18.** 6×6 **19.** 0×6 **20.** 6×8

Compare. Write >, <, or = for each ⬬.

21. 4×6 ⬬ 4×5 **22.** 9×6 ⬬ 8×6 **23.** 5×6 ⬬ 6×6

24. 3×6 ⬬ 6×3 **25.** 3×6 ⬬ 2×6 **26.** 7×6 ⬬ 6×8

Set B (*Lesson 3, pages 260–261*)

Find each product.

1. $\begin{array}{r} 6 \\ \times\ 8 \\ \hline \end{array}$ **2.** $\begin{array}{r} 8 \\ \times\ 3 \\ \hline \end{array}$ **3.** $\begin{array}{r} 4 \\ \times\ 8 \\ \hline \end{array}$ **4.** $\begin{array}{r} 9 \\ \times\ 8 \\ \hline \end{array}$ **5.** $\begin{array}{r} 8 \\ \times\ 0 \\ \hline \end{array}$

6. $\begin{array}{r} 2 \\ \times\ 8 \\ \hline \end{array}$ **7.** $\begin{array}{r} 8 \\ \times\ 7 \\ \hline \end{array}$ **8.** $\begin{array}{r} 1 \\ \times\ 8 \\ \hline \end{array}$ **9.** $\begin{array}{r} 8 \\ \times\ 8 \\ \hline \end{array}$ **10.** $\begin{array}{r} 5 \\ \times\ 8 \\ \hline \end{array}$

11. 8×7 **12.** 8×8 **13.** 2×8 **14.** 10×8 **15.** 1×8

16. 8×5 **17.** 8×9 **18.** 0×8 **19.** 4×8 **20.** 3×8

Compare. Write >, <, or = for each ⬬.

21. 4×8 ⬬ 8×4 **22.** 9×8 ⬬ 8×8 **23.** 5×8 ⬬ 8×5

24. 3×8 ⬬ 4×6 **25.** 8×0 ⬬ 1×8 **26.** 8×3 ⬬ 2×8

Extra Practice

Set C (Lesson 5, pages 268–269)

Find each product.

1. 4 × 7
2. 7 × 3
3. 2 × 7
4. 9 × 7
5. 7 × 8
6. 7 × 7
7. 7 × 6
8. 10 × 7
9. 7 × 5
10. 7 × 0

Compare. Write >, <, or = for each ●.

11. 3 × 7 ● 4 × 7
12. 9 × 7 ● 7 × 6
13. 0 × 7 ● 7 × 5
14. 2 × 7 ● 7 × 2
15. 8 × 7 ● 7 × 8
16. 7 × 1 ● 3 × 3
17. 7 × 7 ● 5 × 10
18. 7 × 4 ● 3 × 9
19. 7 × 2 ● 1 × 7

Set D (Lesson 6, pages 270–271)

Multiply.

1. 9 × 3
2. 7 × 9
3. 9 × 1
4. 2 × 9
5. 9 × 8
6. 9 × 6
7. 5 × 9
8. 9 × 0
9. 9 × 4
10. 9 × 9
11. 9 × 0
12. 2 × 9
13. 9 × 9
14. 1 × 9
15. 9 × 10
16. 9 × 4
17. 6 × 9
18. 9 × 8
19. 7 × 9
20. 9 × 3

Follow the rule to complete each table.

Rule: Multiply by 9

	Input	Output
21.	7	■
22.	■	18
23.	5	■

Rule: Multiply by 7

	Input	Output
24.	4	■
25.	8	■
26.	■	49

Rule: Multiply by 8

	Input	Output
27.	■	24
28.	9	■
29.	■	40

Extra Practice

Set E *(Lesson 9, pages 278–279)*

Find each product. Multiply factors in ( ) first.

1. $(3 \times 1) \times 3$
$3 \times (1 \times 3)$

2. $2 \times (4 \times 2)$
$(2 \times 4) \times 2$

3. $3 \times (3 \times 2)$
$(3 \times 3) \times 2$

4. $(3 \times 0) \times 9$
$3 \times (0 \times 9)$

5. $(3 \times 1) \times 9$
$3 \times (1 \times 9)$

6. $5 \times (2 \times 5)$
$(5 \times 2) \times 5$

7. $2 \times (3 \times 3)$
$(2 \times 3) \times 3$

8. $(4 \times 2) \times 3$
$4 \times (2 \times 3)$

9. $8 \times (1 \times 4)$
$(8 \times 1) \times 4$

10. $5 \times (1 \times 6)$

11. $1 \times (9 \times 6)$

12. $(5 \times 3) \times 0$

13. $6 \times (5 \times 2)$

14. $5 \times (3 \times 0)$

15. $(9 \times 3) \times 1$

Use parentheses. Find each product in two different ways.

16. $4 \times 2 \times 4$

17. $7 \times 0 \times 9$

18. $7 \times 1 \times 5$

19. $1 \times 6 \times 10$

20. $5 \times 2 \times 3$

21. $1 \times 8 \times 3$

22. $3 \times 2 \times 4$

23. $3 \times 4 \times 1$

24. $3 \times 2 \times 5$

25. $1 \times 2 \times 3$

26. $3 \times 3 \times 3$

27. $1 \times 2 \times 7$

28. $4 \times 2 \times 5$

29. $8 \times 1 \times 10$

30. $9 \times 1 \times 9$

Find the missing factor.

31. $(4 \times 2) \times \blacksquare = 8$

32. $(9 \times 1) \times \blacksquare = 18$

33. $(1 \times 2) \times \blacksquare = 10$

34. $(3 \times 3) \times \blacksquare = 27$

35. $(9 \times 7) \times \blacksquare = 63$

36. $(7 \times 5) \times \blacksquare = 0$

37. $\blacksquare \times (1 \times 9) = 45$

38. $\blacksquare \times (2 \times 4) = 56$

39. $\blacksquare \times (5 \times 5) = 25$

40. $\blacksquare \times (8 \times 1) = 0$

41. $\blacksquare \times (1 \times 10) = 40$

42. $\blacksquare \times (6 \times 2) = 12$

Extra Practice • Problem Solving

Decide what operations to do and the order in which you will do them. Then solve. *(Lesson 4, pages 264–265)*

1. Leon shared 45 marbles with his brothers. He gave 15 marbles to his older brother and 23 marbles to his younger brother. How many marbles did Leon have left?

2. Lu bought 3 packs of 8 post cards. She sent one post card to each of 18 friends and put the rest in an album. How many post cards did Lu put in her album?

Solve. *(Lesson 7, pages 272–273)*

3. Kate fed 2 cups of dog food to Sparky. She fed 3 times that amount to Woofer. She has 3 cups of dog food left. How much dog food did Kate have to start with?

4. Sue and Peg knitted squares for a blanket. Sue knitted 12 squares more than Peg did. Together they knitted 32 squares. How many squares did each girl knit?

5. Each time that Tran puts $2 into his bank, his father puts $1 into it. When Tran has put $12 into his bank, how much money will his father have put into the bank?

6. Bobby gave 6 cookies to each of his 2 sisters. He ate 2 cookies and had 12 cookies left over. How many cookies did Bobby have to begin with?

Use the table to solve each problem. *(Lesson 10, pages 280–281)*

7. Helen plans to spend 4 hours watching rented movies on Saturday. Can she watch *Laddie Come Home* and *Gone in the Night*? Explain.

8. Richie's parents rented *Dusty Boots*, *Gone in the Night*, and *Laddie Come Home*. How many hours will it take to watch these 3 movies?

9. How many hours would it take to watch all of the movies listed in the table?

Movie Lengths

Movie	Running Time
Gone in the Night	2 h 30 min
Laddie Come Home	2 h 10 min
The Puppets Movie	1 h 30 min
Dusty Boots	1 h 50 min

Chapter Review

Reviewing Vocabulary

Answer each question.

1. Which numbers on the right are multiples of 4?
2. Which number on the right is a square number?
3. What is the Associative Property of Multiplication?
4. What is the answer in multiplication called?
5. What are the numbers that are multiplied called?

12		8
	15	
21		16

Reviewing Concepts and Skills

Find each product. *(pages 258 – 262, 268 – 271)*

6. 4×6
7. 6×1
8. 3×6
9. 6×6
10. 6×9
11. 8×3
12. 7×8
13. 5×8
14. 10×8
15. 8×8
16. 3×7
17. 7×6
18. 4×7
19. 7×7
20. 7×9
21. 9×5
22. 9×4
23. 3×9
24. 8×9
25. 9×9
26. 7×2
27. 9×10
28. 6×1
29. 3×6
30. 7×8
31. 8×6
32. 4×7
33. 9×8
34. 5×7
35. 9×6
36. 7×7
37. 8×9
38. 10×6
39. 3×8
40. 5×6

Compare. Write >, <, or = for each ⬬. *(pages 258 – 262, 268 – 271)*

41. 5×6 ⬬ 6×5
42. 8×1 ⬬ 1×9
43. 4×3 ⬬ 5×3
44. 2×9 ⬬ 9×1
45. 8×3 ⬬ 3×8
46. 9×7 ⬬ 6×9
47. 6×4 ⬬ 5×7
48. 3×7 ⬬ 4×6
49. 8×3 ⬬ 6×4

Find each product. Multiply factors in ( ) first. *(pages 278 – 279)*

50. $(0 \times 8) \times 7$ **51.** $2 \times (5 \times 2)$ **52.** $(1 \times 6) \times 7$

53. $6 \times (2 \times 4)$ **54.** $(8 \times 0) \times 5$ **55.** $4 \times (2 \times 2)$

Use parentheses. Find each product in two different ways.

56. $3 \times 4 \times 1$ **57.** $1 \times 9 \times 7$ **58.** $1 \times 6 \times 3$

59. $2 \times 7 \times 1$ **60.** $5 \times 2 \times 2$ **61.** $3 \times 7 \times 0$

62. $1 \times 3 \times 9$ **63.** $8 \times 2 \times 1$ **64.** $4 \times 2 \times 3$

Solve. Use the sign for Problems 65–67. *(pages 264 – 265, 272 – 273, 280 – 281)*

65. Wanda bought 3 pints of strawberries and 2 pints of blueberries. How much money did she spend?

66. Ms. Lyons is making pies for a party. She needs 4 pints of raspberries and 2 pints of huckleberries. How much will Ms. Lyons spend on the berries?

67. Carl wants to buy one pint of each of the strawberries, raspberries, blueberries, and huckleberries. He has $15. Does he have enough money? Explain.

Brain Teasers Math Reasoning

Mystery Multiple

Jim is thinking of a number less than 100 that is a multiple of 9.

The number is also 5 more than a multiple of 7.

What is the number?

Mystery Numbers

Tina is thinking of two numbers that are both less than 10.

If she multiplies the numbers, the answer is 34 more than if she adds them.

What are the numbers?

Internet Brain Teasers
Visit **www.eduplace.com/kids/mhm** for more *Brain Teasers.*

Chapter Test

Find each product.

1. $\begin{array}{r} 6 \\ \times\ 0 \\ \hline \end{array}$ **2.** $\begin{array}{r} 2 \\ \times\ 7 \\ \hline \end{array}$ **3.** $\begin{array}{r} 5 \\ \times\ 8 \\ \hline \end{array}$ **4.** $\begin{array}{r} 9 \\ \times\ 1 \\ \hline \end{array}$ **5.** $\begin{array}{r} 6 \\ \times\ 5 \\ \hline \end{array}$

6. $\begin{array}{r} 7 \\ \times\ 3 \\ \hline \end{array}$ **7.** $\begin{array}{r} 4 \\ \times\ 8 \\ \hline \end{array}$ **8.** $\begin{array}{r} 10 \\ \times\ 9 \\ \hline \end{array}$ **9.** $\begin{array}{r} 6 \\ \times\ 6 \\ \hline \end{array}$ **10.** $\begin{array}{r} 2 \\ \times\ 9 \\ \hline \end{array}$

11. $\begin{array}{r} 8 \\ \times\ 7 \\ \hline \end{array}$ **12.** $\begin{array}{r} 6 \\ \times\ 3 \\ \hline \end{array}$ **13.** $\begin{array}{r} 0 \\ \times\ 7 \\ \hline \end{array}$ **14.** $\begin{array}{r} 1 \\ \times\ 8 \\ \hline \end{array}$ **15.** $\begin{array}{r} 6 \\ \times\ 9 \\ \hline \end{array}$

16. $\begin{array}{r} 3 \\ \times\ 8 \\ \hline \end{array}$ **17.** $\begin{array}{r} 9 \\ \times\ 4 \\ \hline \end{array}$ **18.** $\begin{array}{r} 8 \\ \times\ 8 \\ \hline \end{array}$ **19.** $\begin{array}{r} 9 \\ \times\ 0 \\ \hline \end{array}$ **20.** $\begin{array}{r} 7 \\ \times\ 6 \\ \hline \end{array}$

21. $\begin{array}{r} 7 \\ \times\ 7 \\ \hline \end{array}$ **22.** $\begin{array}{r} 10 \\ \times\ 6 \\ \hline \end{array}$ **23.** $\begin{array}{r} 5 \\ \times\ 7 \\ \hline \end{array}$ **24.** $\begin{array}{r} 2 \\ \times\ 6 \\ \hline \end{array}$ **25.** $\begin{array}{r} 0 \\ \times\ 8 \\ \hline \end{array}$

26. 4×7 **27.** 5×9 **28.** 6×8 **29.** 1×7

30. 2×8 **31.** 4×6 **32.** 10×7 **33.** 8×9

34. 7×9 **35.** 9×9 **36.** 8×10 **37.** 9×3

Use parentheses. Find each product in two different ways.

38. $5 \times 1 \times 4$ **39.** $3 \times 1 \times 9$ **40.** $1 \times 4 \times 7$

41. $5 \times 2 \times 4$ **42.** $2 \times 2 \times 3$ **43.** $2 \times 4 \times 2$

44. $9 \times 3 \times 1$ **45.** $4 \times 8 \times 1$ **46.** $3 \times 3 \times 3$

Solve.

47. Small toy trucks are on sale for $4 each. Ben has saved $28. How much more money does he need to buy 9 toy trucks?

48. Laura and 6 friends went to see a movie. The tickets cost $5 each. Each person spent $3 on refreshments. How much money did Laura and her friends spend in all?

49. During their summer break, Ann read 5 more books than Jesse. Jesse read 4 more books than Paul. Paul read 8 books. How many books did Ann read?

50. Gina put stamps into her album. On one page, she put 8 rows of 8 stamps each. On the next page, she put 6 rows of 8 stamps each. How many stamps did Gina put in altogether?

Write About It

Solve each problem. Use correct math vocabulary to explain your thinking.

1. The sign shows the cost of board games in a store.

Board Games	
Who	$8.00
Up and Down	$6.00
Cookieland	$9.00

   a. Explain how you can find the total cost if you bought one of each game.

   b. Explain how you can find the total cost if you bought 2 games of *Cookieland* and 3 games of *Up and Down.*

   c. Tyrell had $25. He bought 1 game of *Who* and 2 games of *Up and Down.* Explain how you can find how much money Tyrell had left.

2. Kelly bought a package of crayons for each of her 3 cousins. There are 2 boxes of crayons in each package. There are 8 crayons in each box.

   a. Write a number sentence that shows how to find how many crayons Kelly bought in all.

   b. Find how many crayons Kelly bought. Explain how you found the answer.

Another Look

Use the sign from the Zoo Gift Shop to find the answer to each question.

1. On Monday, visitors to the Zoo Gift Shop bought 6 mammal books, 8 reptile books, 7 hats, and 9 T-shirts. Make a list to show the total sales for each kind of item.
2. Ms. Brown works in the Zoo Gift Shop. On Thursday, she sold 9 zoo spoons, 6 boxes of writing paper, 8 packs of post cards, and 7 world maps. What is the total amount of these sales?
3. **Look Back** In Question 1, you found how much 6 mammal books cost. How could you use the pattern for 9s facts to help find the answer?
4. **Analyze** Suppose you want to buy three packs of post cards and three hats. How can doubling help you find how much money you will need to buy the post cards and hats?

Enrichment

Making Multiplication Tables

You can make multiplication tables to explore even and odd products. Look at the two multiplication tables below.

Remember:
Any whole number that has 2 as a factor is an even number.
Any whole number that is not even is odd.

Multiplication Table A

×	0	2	4	6	8	10
0	0	0				
2		4				
4						
6					48	
8						
10						

$6 \times 8 = 48$

Multiplication Table B

×	1	3	5	7	9
1					
3					
5					
7					
9					

1. Copy and complete both multiplication tables. What do you notice about the factors in Table *A*? What do you notice about the factors in Table *B*?
2. When you multiply two even numbers, is the product odd or even?
3. When you multiply two odd numbers, is the product odd or even?

Explain Your Thinking

If you multiply an odd number by an even number, will the product be even or odd? Give examples to support your answer.

Geometry and Measurement

Why Learn About Geometry and Measurement?

You use geometry and measurement every day to describe the shapes and sizes of objects in your environment.

When you put a puzzle together or figure out how long a piece of wood you need for a shelf, you're using geometry and measurement.

This boy is building a model airplane. He is measuring the parts and looking at their shapes to figure out how to put the airplane together.

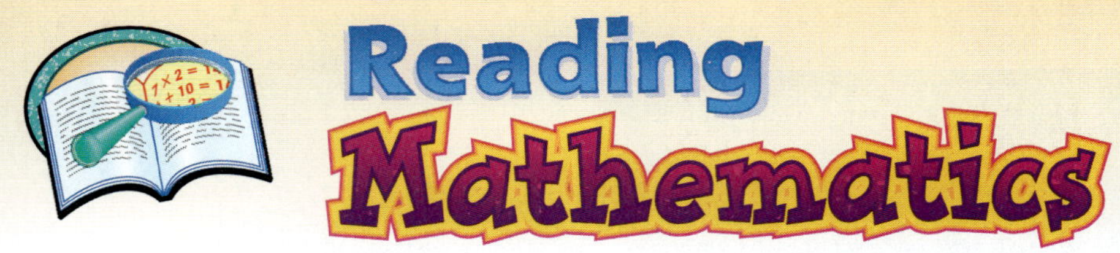

Reviewing Vocabulary

Understanding math language helps you become a successful problem solver. Here are some math vocabulary words you should know.

solid figure	a figure that has 3 dimensions
face	a flat surface of a solid figure
edge	a line segment formed where two faces of a solid figure meet
vertex	a point where three or more edges of a solid figure meet
congruent	the same shape and size
area	the number of square units needed to cover a figure
perimeter	the distance around a closed plane figure
line of symmetry	a line on which a figure can be folded so that both sides match

Reading Words and Symbols

When you read mathematics, sometimes you read words to identify figures.

Look at the different names that figures have.

Plane Figures

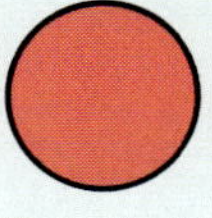
circle

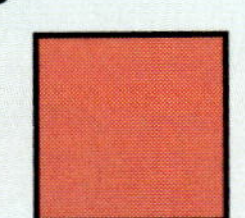
square

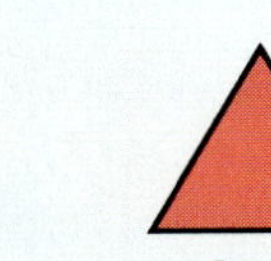
rectangle

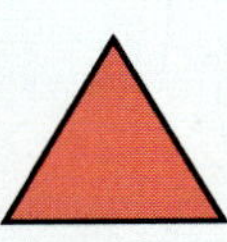
triangle

Solid Figures

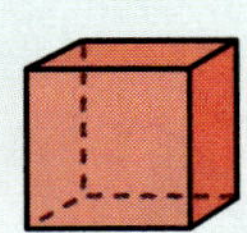
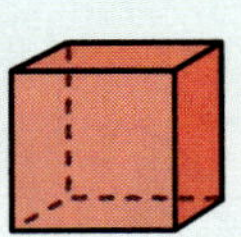
cube

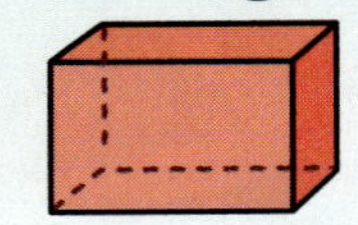
rectangular prism

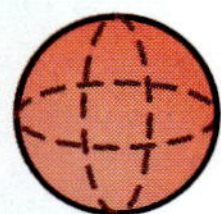
sphere

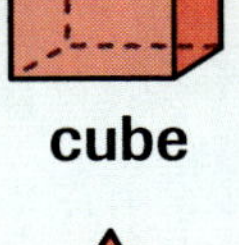
cone

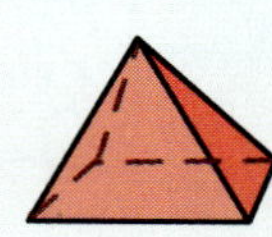
pyramid

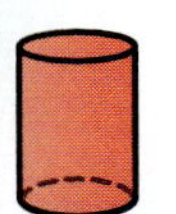
cylinder

Try These

1. Use the words on the right to complete each sentence.

   Julie sees many shapes at school.

   a. The round clock on the wall looks like a ____.

   b. Her math book is in the shape of a ____.

   c. The flag on the boat has 3 straight sides, so it must look like a ____.

   d. Each of the 4 sides of the bulletin board is four feet long, so the bulletin board could look like a ____.

Vocabulary
rectangle
triangle
square
circle

2. Write *true* or *false*.

   a. A triangle has 4 sides.

   b. All of the faces of a cube are squares.

   c. A rectangle has 4 sides of equal length.

   d. A line of symmetry divides a figure into congruent parts.

3. Name each part of the cube. Write *face, edge,* or *vertex* for each letter.

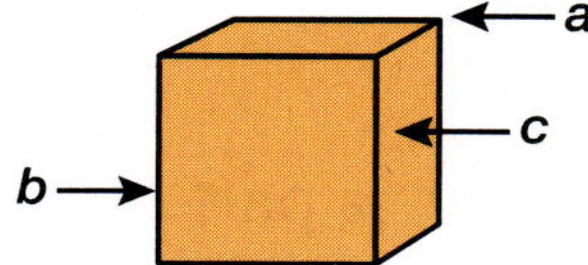

Upcoming Vocabulary

Write About It **Here are some math vocabulary words** you will learn in this chapter. Watch for these words. Write their definitions in your journal.

line	**parallel**
line segment	**quadrilateral**
ray	**equilateral triangle**
angle	**isosceles triangle**
right angle	**right triangle**
polygon	**volume**

Lines, Line Segments, Rays, and Angles

You will learn about lines, line segments, rays, and angles.

New Vocabulary
line
line segment
ray
angle
right angle

Learn About It

Have you ever seen a laser light show at an amusement park? Light from a laser travels in a narrow beam. It goes in only one direction. A laser light beam looks like a ray.

Geometric Figures

Line	A **line** is a straight path that goes on without end in two directions.	The arrows show that the line does not end.
Line segment	A **line segment** is part of a line. It has two endpoints.	
Ray	A **ray** is part of a line. It has one endpoint. A ray goes on without end in one direction.	
Angle	An **angle** is formed by two rays with the same endpoint.	

A **right angle** has a square corner.

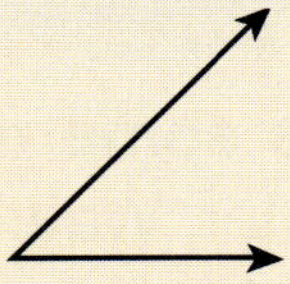

Some angles are less than right angles.

Some angles are greater than right angles.

Explain Your Thinking

► Do you think you could measure a line? a line segment? a ray? Explain your thinking.

Guided Practice

Tell whether each figure is a *line, line segment,* or *ray*.

1. 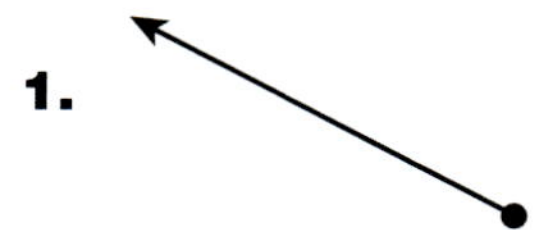
2.
3.
4.

Tell whether each angle is a *right angle, less than a right angle,* or *greater than a right angle*.

5. 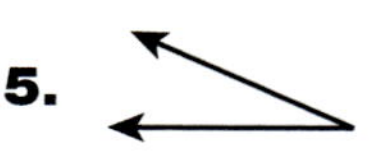
6. 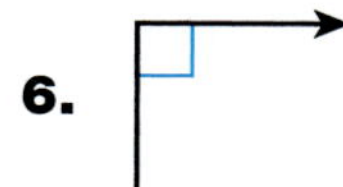
7. 

Independent Practice

Write whether each figure is a *line, line segment,* or *ray*.

8.
9.
10.
11. 
12.
13.
14.
15.

Write *right angle, less than a right angle,* or *greater than a right angle* for each angle.

16. 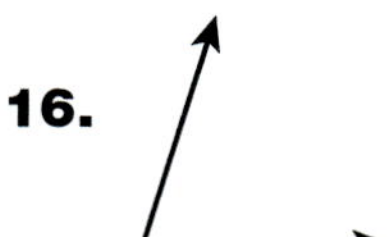
17. 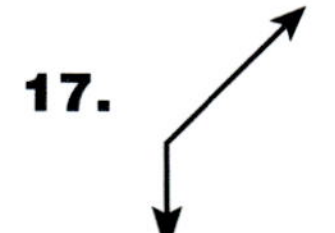
18. 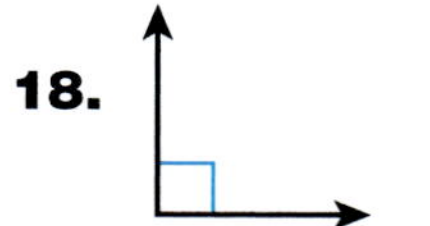
19. 
20.
21. 
22. 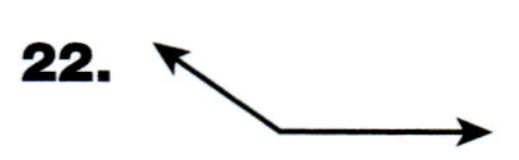
23. 

Use the figure on the right for Questions 24–28.

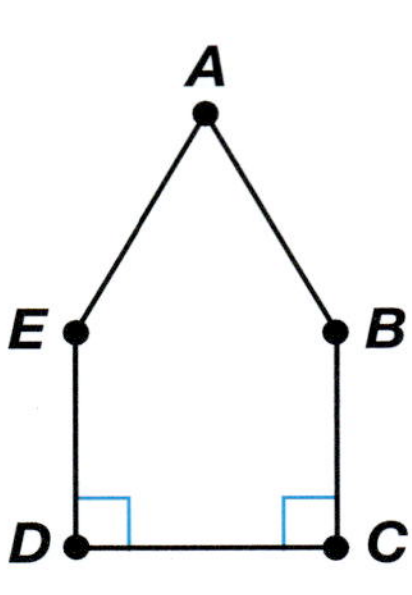

24. How many line segments are shown?

25. How many angles are shown?

26. How many angles less than a right angle are shown?

27. How many angles greater than a right angle are shown?

28. How many right angles are shown?

Write *true* or *false* for each sentence. Write a sentence or draw a picture to explain your answer.

29. An angle is part of a line segment.

30. A ray has one endpoint.

31. A line segment has two endpoints.

32. A line has an endpoint.

33. A ray goes on without end in one direction.

34. A ray is formed by two angles.

Problem Solving • Reasoning

Use the sign for Problems 35–37.

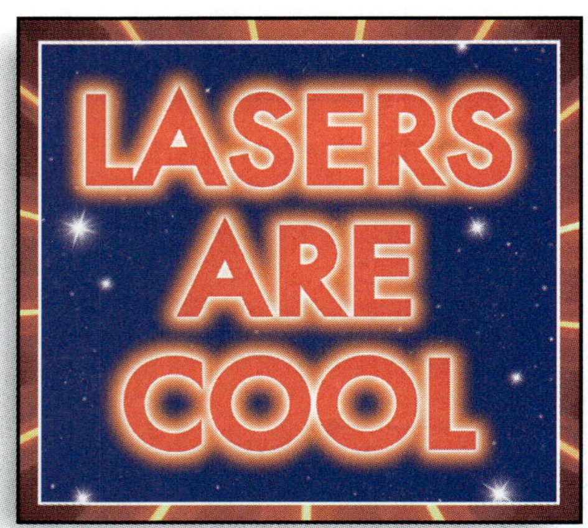

35. Which letters show right angles?

36. **Analyze** What kinds of angles are found in the letter A?

37. Which letters do not have any line segments?

38. **Write Your Own** Draw a simple picture, using line segments, rays, and angles. Write three questions about the geometric figures in your picture. Have a classmate answer your questions.

Mixed Review • Test Prep

Write the next two numbers that would likely continue each pattern. Explain how you decided. *(pages xxvi–xxvii, 28–29)*

39. 3, 6, 9, ■, ■

40. 15, 20, 25, 30, ■, ■

41. 4, 8, 12, 16, ■, ■

42. 7, 17, 27, 37, ■, ■

43. 1, 2, 4, 7, 11, ■, ■

44. 1, 2, 4, 8, ■, ■

45 How many ounces equal 2 pounds? *(pages 172–174)*

A 8 **B** 16 **C** 20 **D** 32

Extra Practice See Set A on page 340.

Visual Thinking

Moving Patterns

Look at each pattern. Draw the positions of the next two objects in the pattern.

Explain Your Thinking

► Which patterns above show objects that have turned? Explain.

Plane Figures

You will learn how to identify and describe different geometric figures.

New Vocabulary
plane figure
polygon
side
vertex/vertices

Learn About It

Look around you. You will see many different shapes.

Plane figures are flat figures. They can be closed or not closed. A circle is a closed plane figure.

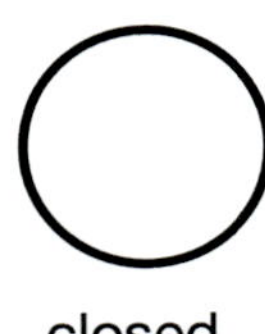
closed

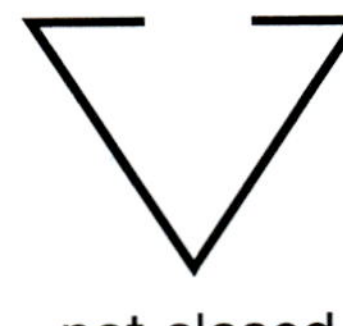
not closed

Closed plane figures that are made up of three or more line segments are called **polygons**.

This is a **side**. Each side is a line segment.

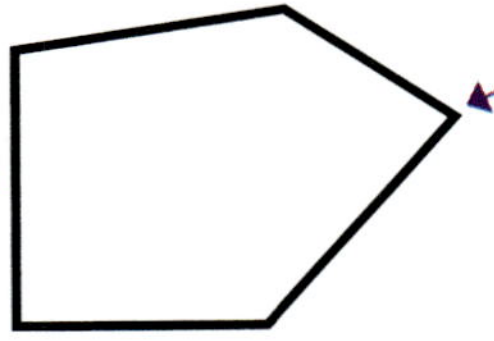

A **vertex** is a point where two sides meet.

Some polygons have special names.

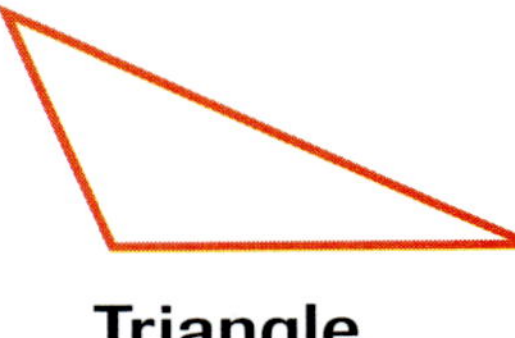
Triangle
3 sides

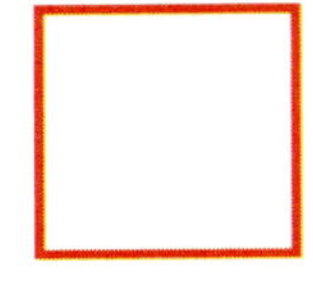
Square
4 equal sides

Rectangle
4 sides

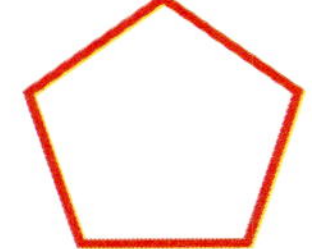
Pentagon
5 sides

Hexagon
6 sides

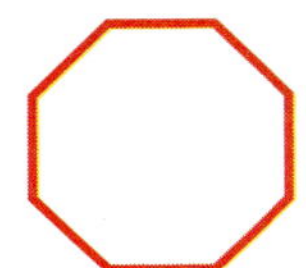
Octagon
8 sides

Explain Your Thinking

- ► Explain why a circle is not a polygon.
- ► Is an angle a polygon? Explain why or why not.

Guided Practice

Tell whether each figure is a polygon. If it is, write its name.

1. 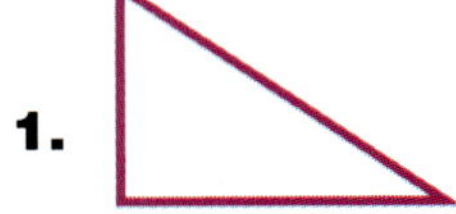

2. 

3. 

- Is the figure closed?
- How many sides does the figure have?

4. 

5. 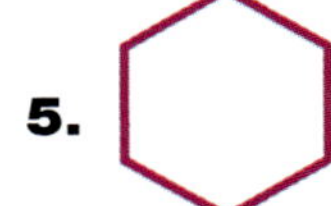

6. 

Independent Practice

Tell whether each figure is a polygon. If it is, write its name.

7. **8.** **9.** **10.**

11. **12.** **13.** **14.**

15. **16.** **17.** **18.**

Name the polygons that make up each shape.

19. 

20. 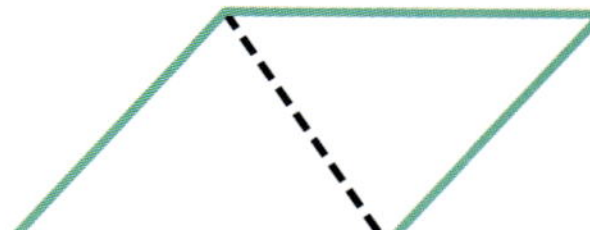

21. 

Problem Solving • Reasoning

Use the picture on the right for Problems 22–24.

22. What colors are the triangles?

23. Which kind of polygon is blue?

24. **Analyze** What color is the figure that is not a polygon? What is the name of that figure?

25. **Write Your Own** Create your own design using at least two kinds of polygons. Describe your design, naming the polygons you used.

Mixed Review • Test Prep

Solve. *(pages 108–109, 128–130, 222–223)*

26. 0×5 **27.** $68 + 77$ **28.** $25 - 19$ **29.** 5×10

30 Which is a good estimate of the answer to $985 - 654$? *(pages 134–135)*

A 1,700 **B** 1,600 **C** 400 **D** 300

Extra Practice See Set B on page 340.

Quadrilaterals

You will learn how to identify, describe, and classify different four-sided figures.

New Vocabulary
quadrilateral
parallel

Learn About It

Look around your classroom. You will see many quadrilaterals. A **quadrilateral** is a polygon with 4 sides and 4 angles.

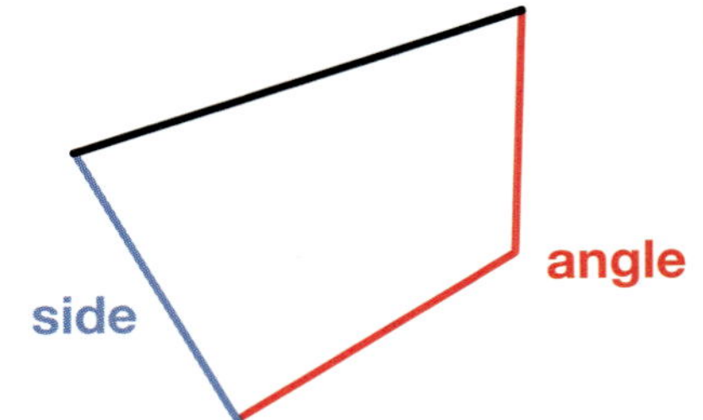

Some quadrilaterals have a pair of opposite sides that are **parallel**. These sides are always the same distance apart.

Some pairs of opposite sides are parallel.

Some quadrilaterals have no pair of sides that are parallel.

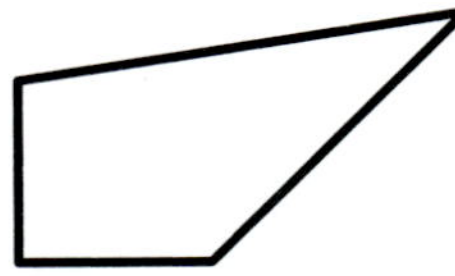
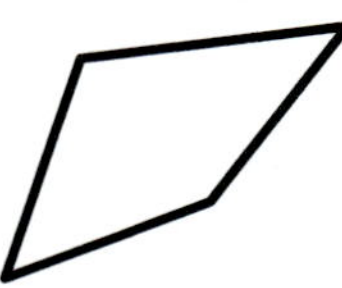

No pair of opposite sides are parallel.

Some quadrilaterals have special names.

Quadrilateral
- 4 sides
- 4 angles

Rectangle
- 4 sides
- 4 right angles
- opposite sides are parallel

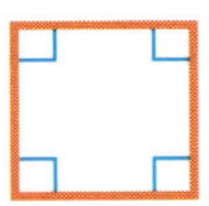

Square
- 4 equal sides
- 4 right angles
- opposite sides are parallel

Parallelogram
- 4 sides
- 4 angles
- opposite sides are parallel

Explain Your Thinking

► Explain why a square is both a rectangle and a parallelogram.

Guided Practice

Tell whether the figure is a quadrilateral. If it has a special name, write it.

1. 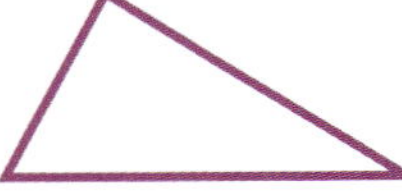 **2.**  **3.** 

Ask Yourself
- How many sides are there?
- Are the sides parallel?
- Are there four angles?

Independent Practice

Tell whether the figure is a quadrilateral. If it has a special name, write it.

4. 

5. 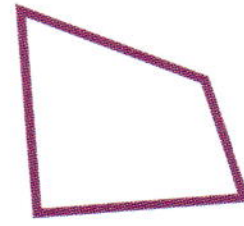

6. 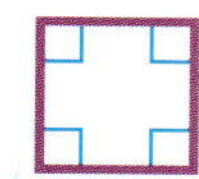

7. 

8. 

9. 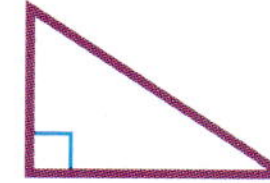

10. 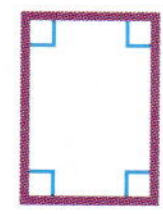

11. 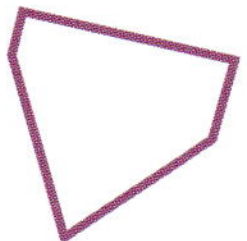

Name the figures that could be classified as

12. a quadrilateral with 4 equal sides and 4 right angles.

13. a quadrilateral with parallel opposite sides and 4 right angles.

14. a polygon with 8 sides.

15. a polygon with 6 sides.

Problem Solving • Reasoning

16. Write the names for the quadrilaterals you see in the room on the right.

17. **Analyze** Look back at Exercises 4–11. Describe two ways to sort the figures.

18. Draw a picture, using quadrilaterals. Outline squares in blue, rectangles in red, and any other quadrilaterals in green.

19. **Write About It** Are all rectangles squares? Are all squares rectangles? Explain.

Mixed Review • Test Prep

Estimate each sum or difference by rounding each number to the nearest hundred. *(pages 110–111, 134–135)*

20. 347 + 51 **21.** 923 − 695 **22.** 479 + 99 **23.** 835 − 592

24 Which number would likely go in the empty space? *(pages 28–29)*

29, 32, ___, 38, 41, 44

A 33 **B** 34 **C** 35 **D** 36

Extra Practice See Set C on page 340.

Triangles

You will learn special names for triangles.

New Vocabulary
equilateral triangle
isosceles triangle
right triangle

Learn About It

On sunny days, Jorge likes to set up his tent in the back yard and pretend that he is on a camping trip. The front and the back of Jorge's tent remind him of triangles.

Triangles are polygons that have 3 sides and 3 angles.

Some triangles have special names. These names describe the sides or the angles of the triangles.

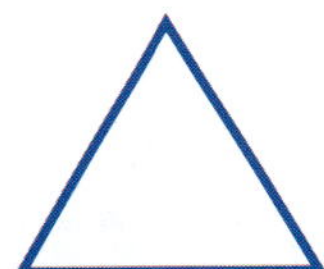

Equilateral triangle
All of the sides have equal lengths.

Isosceles triangle
Two of the sides have equal lengths.

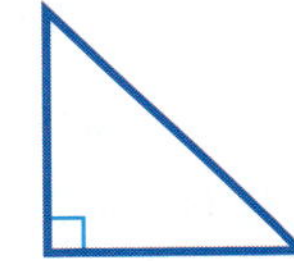

Right triangle
One angle is a right angle.

Explain Your Thinking

- ► Are all polygons triangles? Are all triangles polygons? Explain.
- ► Look at an equilateral triangle. What do you think is true about its angles?

Guided Practice

Name the kind of triangle shown. Write *equilateral, isosceles,* or *right*.

1. 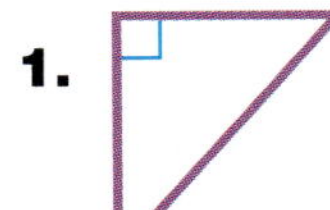

2. 

3. 

Ask Yourself
- Are any of the sides the same length?
- Are any of the angles right angles?

Independent Practice

Name the kind of triangle shown.
Write *equilateral, isosceles,* or *right*.

4. 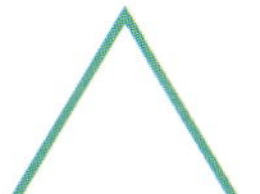

5. 

6.

7. 

8. 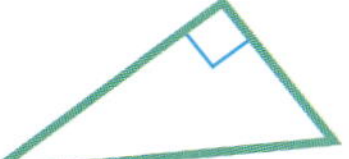

9. 

10.

11. 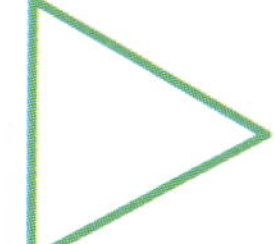

Use the triangles on the right for Questions 12 and 13.

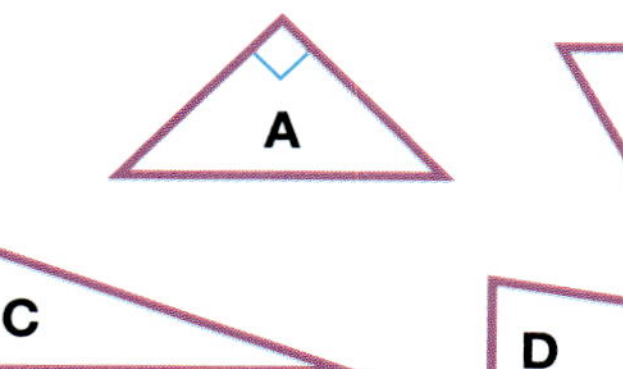

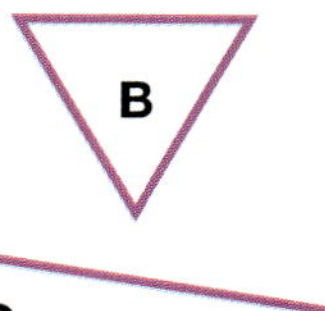

12. In which of the triangles are all the angles less than a right angle?

13. Which of the triangles has an angle that is greater than a right angle?

Problem Solving • Reasoning

14. Look back at Exercises 4–11. Describe 2 ways to sort the triangles.

15. **Logical Thinking** Can a triangle have two sides that are parallel? Explain your reasoning.

16. **Analyze** Can a triangle have a right angle and be an isosceles triangle? Explain why or why not. Use a drawing to support your answer.

17. **Write About It** An isosceles triangle has one side that is 8 inches long and another side that is 10 inches long. What do you know about the length of the third side? Explain your thinking.

Math Is Everywhere!

SOCIAL STUDIES
Some Native Americans used tepees that were easy to move. This made it easier to follow buffalo herds.

Suppose 15 wooden poles were needed to make a tepee. How many poles would be needed to make 3 tepees?

Mixed Review • Test Prep

Choose the metric unit you would use to measure each. Write *centimeters, meters,* or *kilometers*. *(pages 182–185)*

18. a classroom **19.** a road **20.** a math book **21.** a bug

22 Find the product of 9 and 8. *(pages 270–271)*

A 56 **B** 64 **C** 68 **D** 72

Problem-Solving Skill: Visual Thinking

You will learn how to solve problems that require visual thinking.

Sometimes you need to use visual thinking in order to solve problems.

Problem Jamie is making a tile design out of purple, green, and orange tiles. She wants to continue the pattern that she has started. Which of the arrangements of tiles shown below should she use to complete the pattern?

First find the pattern.

- Look at the tiles from top to bottom.
- Then look at them from left to right.
- Then look at the diagonal rows.

If you look at the diagonal rows, you will see a purple row, a green row, an orange row, then a purple row, a green row, and so on.

Then decide which of the choices below completes the pattern.

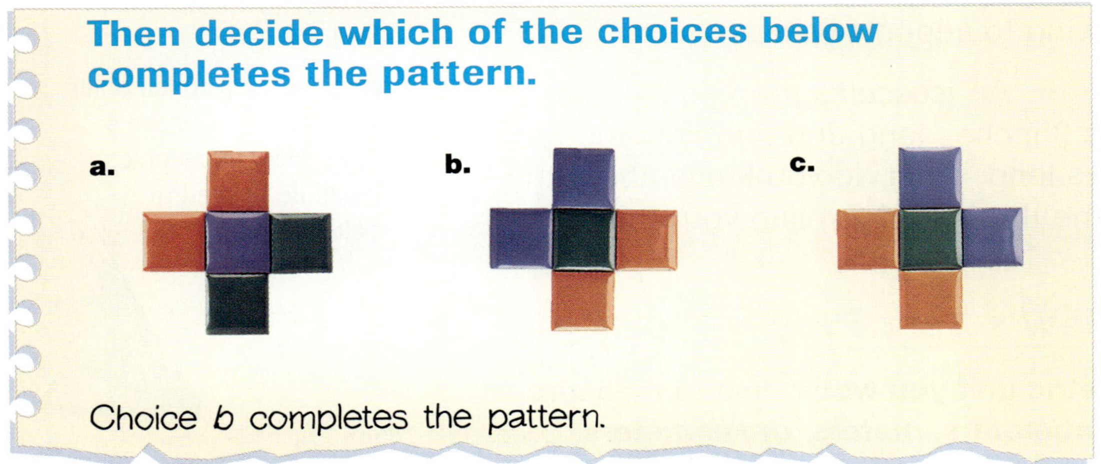

Choice *b* completes the pattern.

Look Back Why would *a* or *c* not complete the pattern?

Guided Practice

Choose the letter of the missing piece.

1 

a. c. b. d.

Think: Look at the diagonal rows to find the pattern.

2 

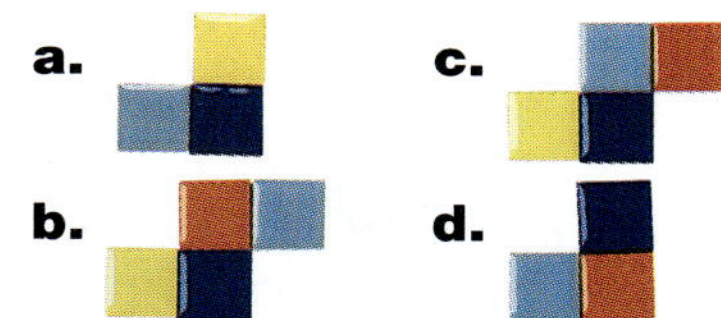

a. c. b. d.

Think: Look at the rows in different ways to find the pattern.

Choose a Strategy

Solve. Use these or other strategies.

Problem-Solving Strategies

- Use Logical Thinking
- Find a Pattern
- Act it Out
- Draw a Picture

3 A triangle is between a hexagon and a square. The square is to the left of the hexagon, but to the right of the rectangle. Which figure is first?

4 I am a polygon with fewer sides than an octagon, but more sides than a rectangle. I have an even number of sides. What is my name?

Choose the letter of the missing piece.

5 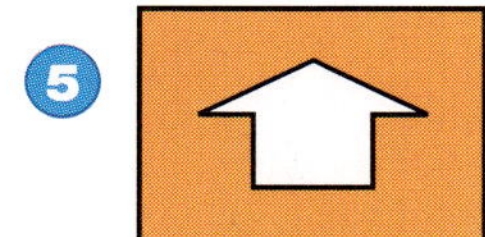

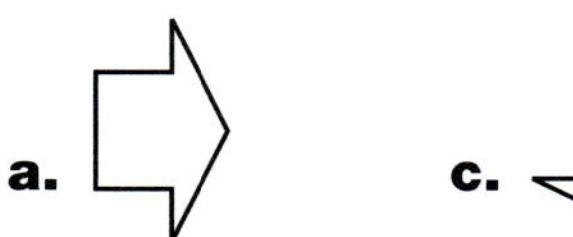

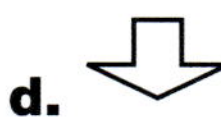

a. c. b. d.

6 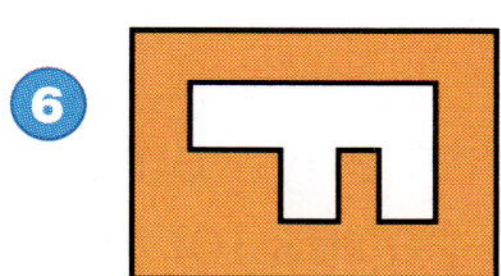

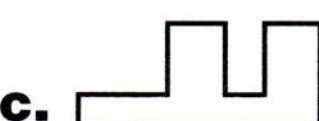

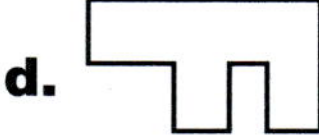

a. c. b. d.

Extra Practice See 1–2 on page 343.

Quick Check

Check Your Understanding of Lessons 1–5

Write whether each figure is a *line, line segment,* or *ray*.

1. 

2. 

3. 

Write *right angle, less than a right angle,* or *greater than a right angle* for each angle.

4. 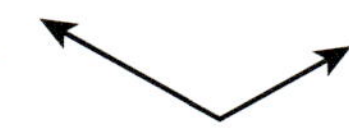

5. 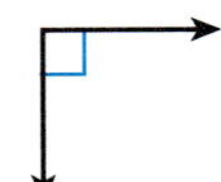

6. 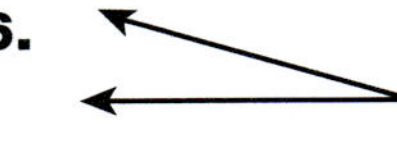

Write the special name of each polygon.

7. 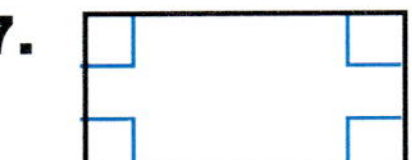

8. 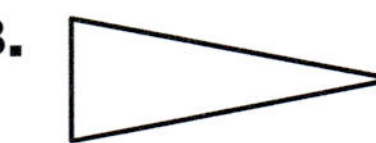

9. 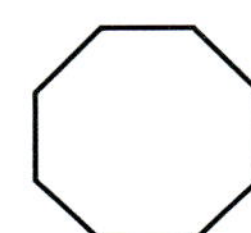

Solve.

10. Look at the figure at the right. How many rectangles are there? How many triangles are there? Explain.

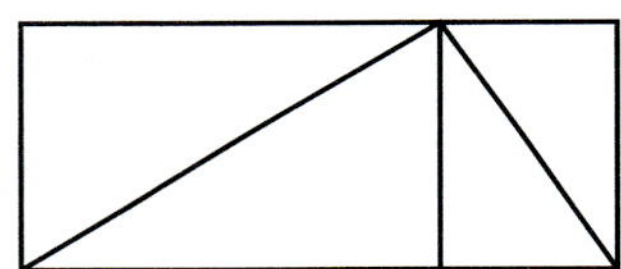

How did you do?

If you had difficulty with any items in the Quick Check, you can use the following pages for review and extra practice.

Items	Review These Pages	Do These Extra Practice Items
1–6	pages 298–300	Set A, page 340
7–9	pages 302–307	Sets B–D, page 340
10	pages 308–309	1–2, page 343

Test Prep • Cumulative Review

Maintaining the Standards

Choose the letter of the correct answer.

1 What number makes this number sentence true?

$$3 \times 4 = \blacksquare \times 3$$

A 1
B 2
C 3
D 4

2 Which figure has 4 right angles?

F triangle
G octagon
H rectangle
J parallelogram

Use the table for Questions 3–4.

Number of Rulers	Cost
2	\$4
3	\$6
4	\$8
5	\$10

3 What is the cost of 1 ruler?

A \$1
B \$1.50
C \$2
D \$3

4 How much will 10 rulers cost?

F \$12
G \$16
H \$18
J \$20

5 Which of the following is the best estimate of the length of a book?

A 2 centimeters
B 25 centimeters
C 75 centimeters
D 1 meter

6 Which triangle has an angle that is greater than a right angle?

F
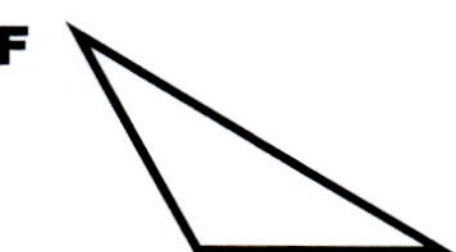

H
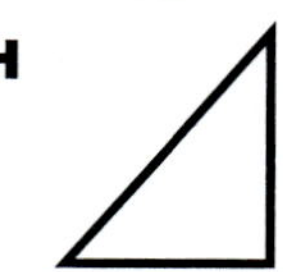

G

J

7 How many equal sides must an isosceles triangle have?

A 0
B 1
C 2
D 3

8 What is the name of this figure?

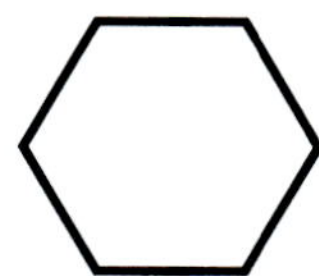

Explain How did you find your answer?

Safe Site

Internet Test Prep
Visit **www.eduplace.com/kids/mhm** for more *Test Prep Practice.*

Congruent Figures

You will learn about figures that are the same size and shape.

Review Vocabulary
congruent

Learn About It

Plane figures with the same size and shape are **congruent**.

Look at the two triangles. Are the triangles congruent?

To find out, follow these steps.

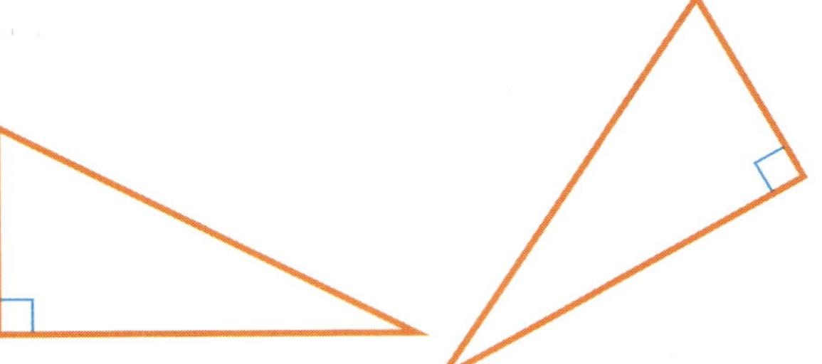

- Trace one of the triangles.
- Place the traced triangle on top of the other triangle. Turn or flip the triangle to try to match the sides and angles.

If the two triangles match exactly, they are congruent. Are the triangles congruent?

Other Examples

A. Different Sizes

The figures are not congruent.
They are not the same size.

B. Different Shapes

The figures are not congruent.
They are not the same shape.

Explain Your Thinking

► All circles are the same shape. Are all circles congruent? Explain.

► Can a rectangle and a hexagon be congruent? Explain why or why not.

Guided Practice

Trace one of the two figures. Place the traced figure on top of the other figure. Are the figures in each pair congruent?

1. 

2. 

3. 

Ask Yourself

- Are the figures the same size?
- Are the figures the same shape?

Independent Practice

Trace one of the two figures. Place the traced figure on top of the other figure. Are the figures in each pair congruent?

4. 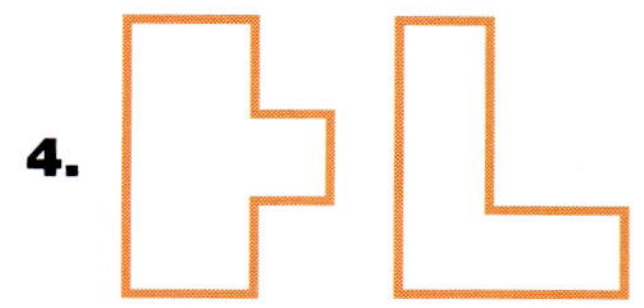

5. 

6. 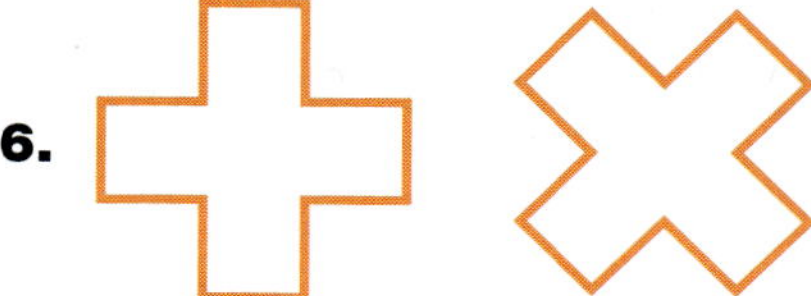

7. 

8. 

9. 

Trace the first figure. Then choose the figure that is congruent to it. Write *a*, *b*, or *c*.

10.

a. 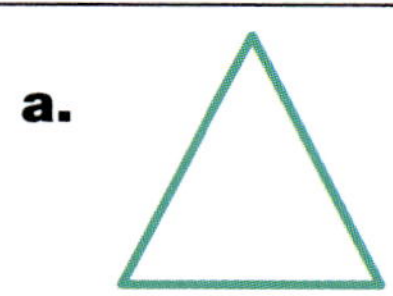

b. 

c. 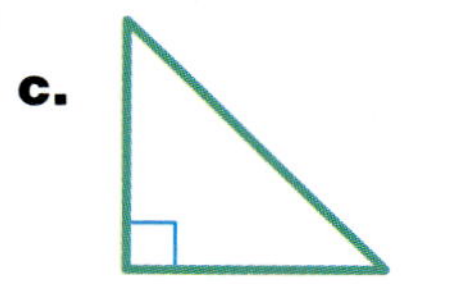

11.

a. 

b. 

c. 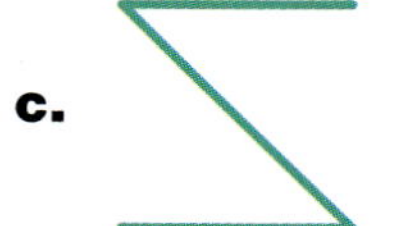

12. 

a. 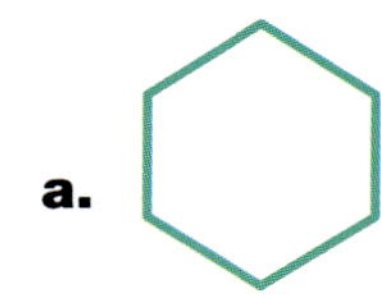

b. 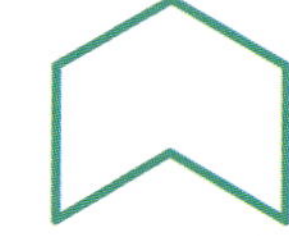

c. 

Problem Solving • Reasoning

Match each shape below with its congruent shape on the poster. For each numbered shape, write the letter of its place on the poster.

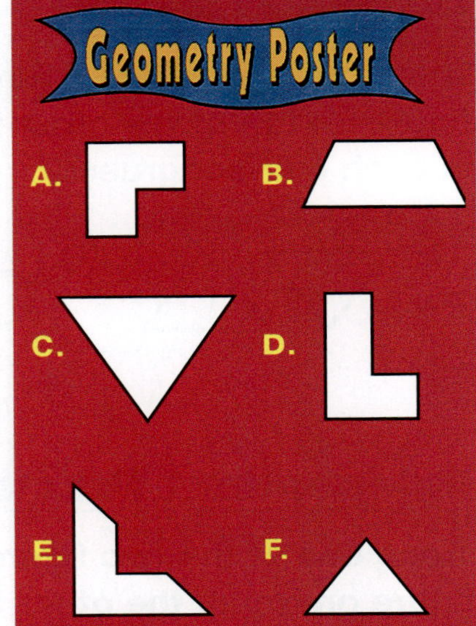

13. 

14. 

15.  

16. 

17. 

18. 

19. Do all rectangles have the same shape? Draw pictures to support your answer.

20. **Measurement** Alan drew a square with sides that were 9 cm long. Ruth drew a square congruent to Alan's square. How long were the sides of Ruth's square?

21. **Analyze** Susan drew an octagon. Steven drew a hexagon. Can Susan's figure be congruent to Steven's figure? Explain your reasoning.

Mixed Review • Test Prep

Write the value of the underlined digit. *(pages 18–19, 32–33)*

22. 4$\underline{7}$6 **23.** $\underline{8}$24 **24.** 7,43$\underline{8}$ **25.** $\underline{6}$,425 **26.** 76,52$\underline{0}$

27. 4,$\underline{5}$68 **28.** 5$\underline{2}$,367 **29.** $\underline{7}$6,520 **30.** 75,00$\underline{5}$ **31.** $\underline{8}$6,016

32 Which clock shows the time 5 hours and 30 minutes after 2:15 P.M.? *(pages 78–79)*

A 

B 

C 

D 

Extra Practice See Set E on page 341.

Visual Thinking

Similar Figures

Figures that are the same shape but not necessarily the same size are **similar** figures.

New Vocabulary
similar

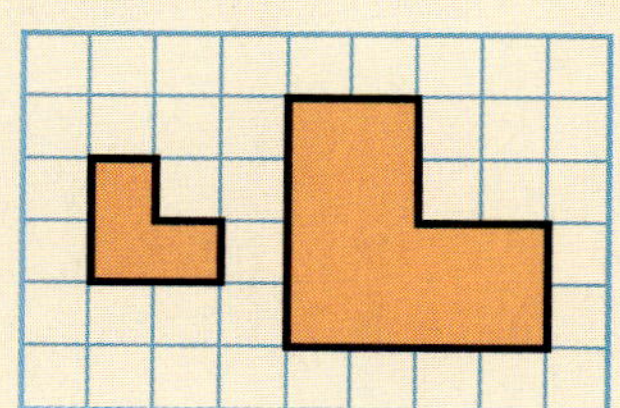

These figures are similar.
They are the same shape.
They are not the same size.

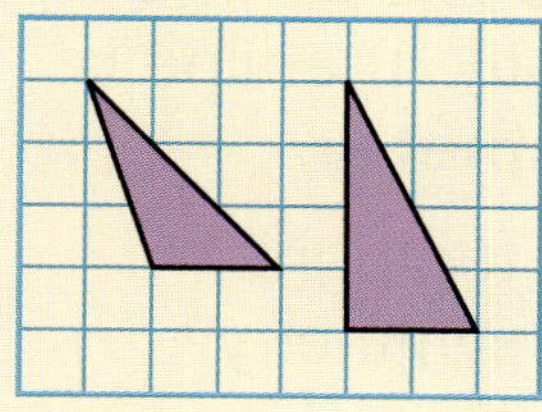

These figures are not similar.
They are not the same shape.

Tell whether the two shapes in each exercise are similar.

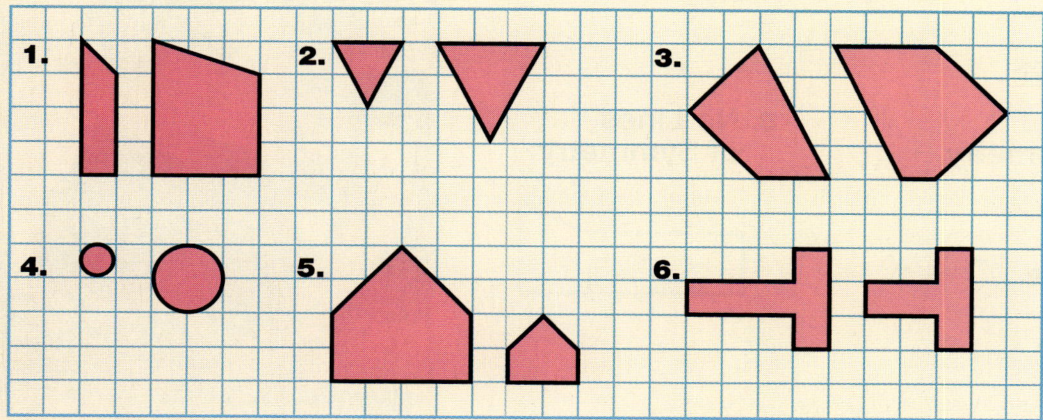

Write *true* or *false* for each sentence.
Then write a sentence or draw an example to explain your answer.

7. All circles are similar.

8. All quadrilaterals are similar.

9. All rectangles are similar.

10. All squares are similar.

11. Some triangles are similar.

12. No circles are congruent.

Explain Your Thinking

► Are all equilateral triangles similar? Explain.

Line of Symmetry

You will learn about figures that can be folded into matching parts.

Review Vocabulary
symmetry
line of symmetry

Learn About It

A plane figure that has **symmetry** can be folded along a line so that the two parts match exactly. That line is called a **line of symmetry**.

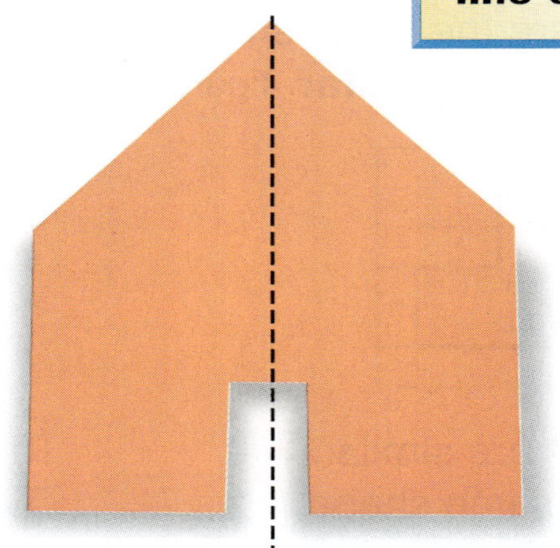

Look at the figure on the right. Does the figure have symmetry?

To find out, follow these steps.

- Trace and cut out the figure.
- Try to fold the figure so that both parts match exactly.

Other Examples

A. One or More Lines of Symmetry

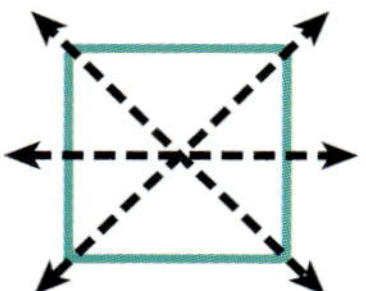

B. No Lines of Symmetry

Explain Your Thinking

► Do all squares have symmetry? Why or why not?

► How many lines of symmetry do you need to find to decide whether a figure has symmetry? Explain.

Guided Practice

Look at each figure. Tell whether each line appears to be a line of symmetry.

1. 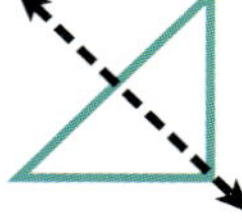

2. 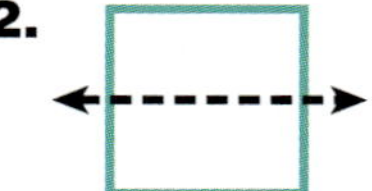

3. 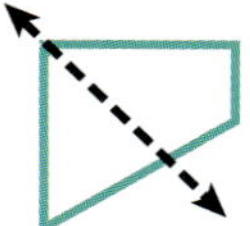

Ask Yourself

- If I fold along the line, will I have two parts that match exactly?
- If I am not sure, how can I check?

Independent Practice

Tell whether each line appears to be a line of symmetry.

4. 

5. 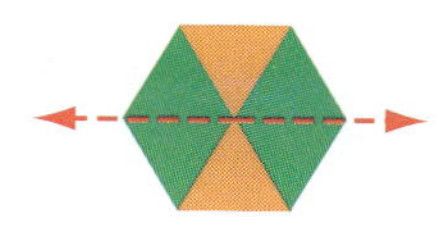

6. 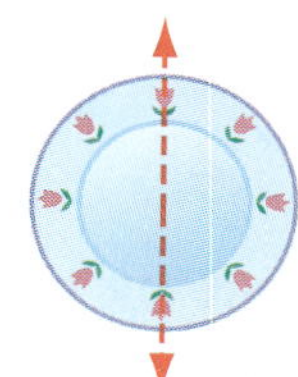

7. 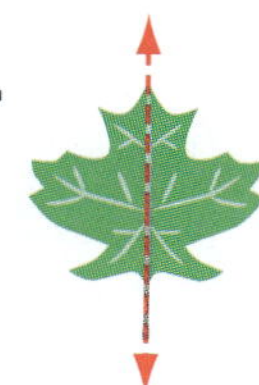

8. 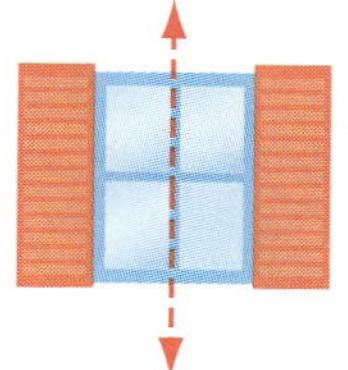

9. 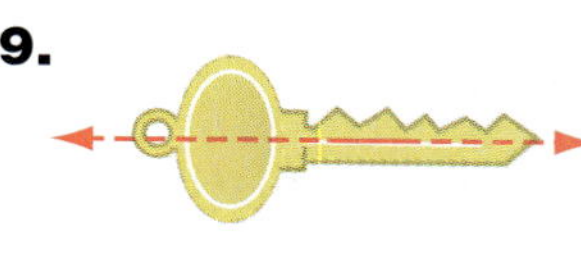

Trace each figure. Then draw a line of symmetry.

10. 

11. 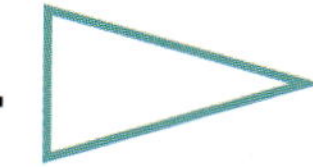

12. 

Problem Solving • Reasoning

13. Look at the letters on the right. Which letter has one line of symmetry? Which have two or more lines of symmetry? Which have no lines of symmetry?

14. Draw the numeral eight so that it has two lines of symmetry. Then draw another numeral that has symmetry.

15. **Analyze** How many lines of symmetry do you think a circle has? Draw a picture to explain your thinking.

Mixed Review • Test Prep

Choose the greater money amount. *(pages 58–60)*

16. 1 quarter or 2 dimes

17. 3 nickels or 20 pennies

18. 4 dimes or 1 half-dollar

19. 3 quarters and 3 dimes or 1 dollar

Choose the letter of the correct answer. *(pages 4–5, 18–19, 32–33)*

20 Which number is five hundred six?

A 506 **C** 5,006
B 560 **D** 5,060

21 Which number is seven thousand, fifty-four?

F 70,054 **H** 7,504
G 7,540 **J** 7,054

Extra Practice See Set F on page 341.

LESSON 8

Perimeter

You will learn how to find the distance around a figure.

Review Vocabulary
perimeter

Learn About It

Nikki drew a Wild West picture. She wants to frame her picture with rope. How many inches of rope does she need?

The distance around a figure is its **perimeter**.

To find the perimeter add the lengths of the sides.

14 + 9 + 14 + 9 = 46

The perimeter is 46 inches.
So Nikki needs 46 inches of rope.

Another Example

Find the perimeter of this pentagon.

7 + 2 + 4 + 7 + 3 = 23

The perimeter is 23 feet.

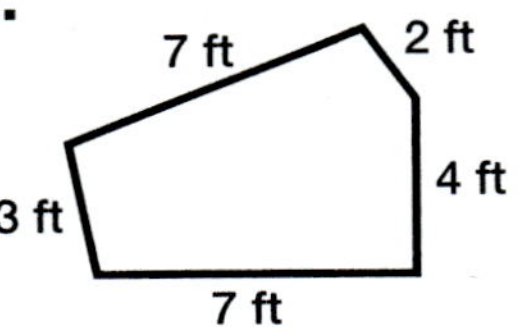

Explain Your Thinking

- ► Can you find the perimeter of a rectangle if you know the length of one side? Why or why not?
- ► Can you find the perimeter of a square if you know the length of one side? Why or why not?

Guided Practice

Find the perimeter of each figure.

1. 6 ft, 6 ft, 6 ft

2. 10 in., 12 in., 12 in., 10 in.

3.

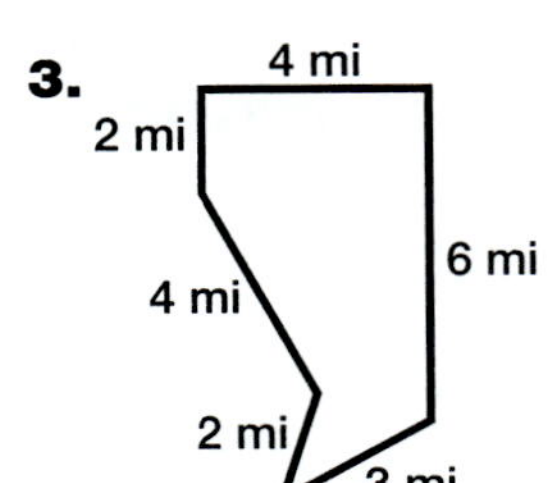

Ask Yourself

- What numbers should I add?
- How will I label my answer?

Independent Practice

Find each perimeter. Label your answer.

4.

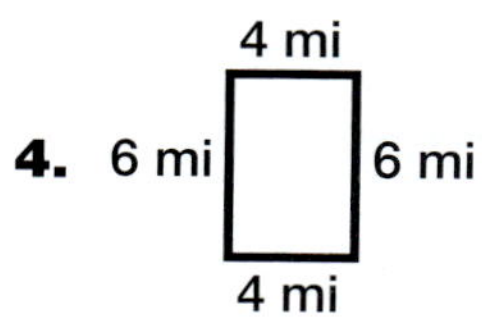

5. 3 ft, 5 ft, 4 ft

6. 7 in., 7 in., 7 in., 7 in.

7. 6 in., 4 in., 1 in., 5 in.

8. 8 ft, 8 ft, 8 ft, 8 ft, 8 ft, 8 ft

9.

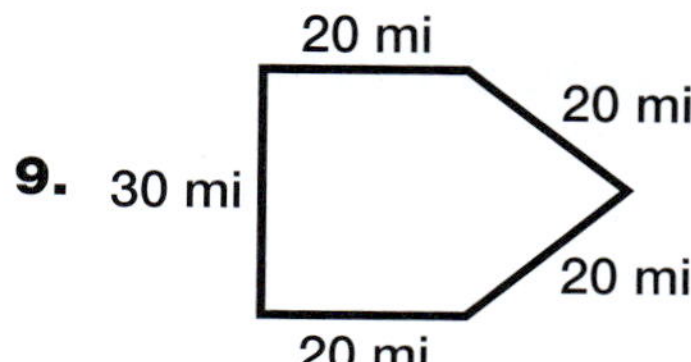

Problem Solving • Reasoning

Solve. Choose a method.

Computation Methods

- Mental Math
- Estimation
- Paper and Pencil

10. The perimeter of a triangle is 41 cm. Two of its sides are each 18 cm long. What is the length of the third side?

11. **Money** Luis needs 9 feet of edging for his garden. The edging costs $2 for each foot. How much will Luis have to pay for the edging?

12. A garden is shaped like a rectangle. The lengths of two sides of the garden are 84 feet and 65 feet. About how long is the garden's perimeter?

13. **Write Your Own** Write a problem that involves finding perimeter. Give your problem to a classmate to solve. Which computation method did you use to solve the problem?

Mixed Review • Test Prep

Write the numbers in order from greatest to least. *(pages 22–23)*

14. 475 457 4,457 4,754

15. 301 310 210 320

16. 6,805 6,508 6,580 6,850

17. 9,290 9,289 9,390 9,250

18 Find the difference between 700 and 259. *(pages 140–141)*

A 421 **B** 441 **C** 521 **D** 579

Extra Practice See Set G on page 341.

Estimating Area

You will learn how to estimate the number of square units that cover a figure.

Review Vocabulary
area

Learn About It

You can use square units to estimate the area of a figure.

One square unit

$\frac{1}{2}$ square unit

$\frac{1}{2}$ square unit

About $\frac{1}{2}$ square unit

Materials

For each pair:
1-inch grid paper

The **area** of a figure is the number of square units needed to cover the figure without overlapping.

Work with a partner to estimate the area of the bottom of your partner's shoe.

Step 1 Make an outline of the bottom of your partner's shoe on 1-inch grid paper.

Step 2 Count the number of square units inside the outline of the shoe. Two partly covered squares can be counted as one square unit.

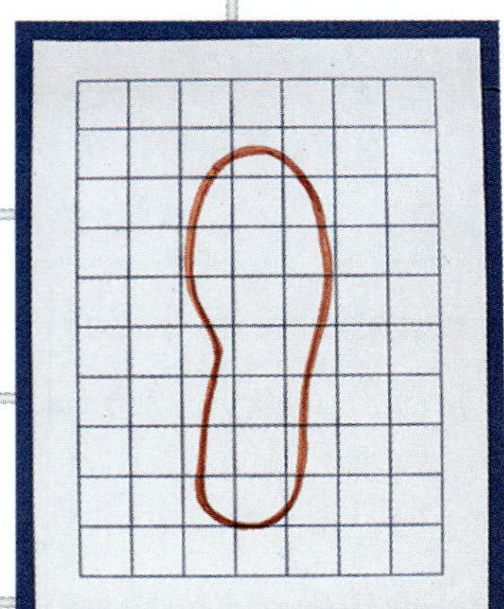

Step 3 Estimate the total area of the drawing. Write the number of square units.

Try It Out

Estimate the area of each figure. Each □ = 1 square unit.

1. 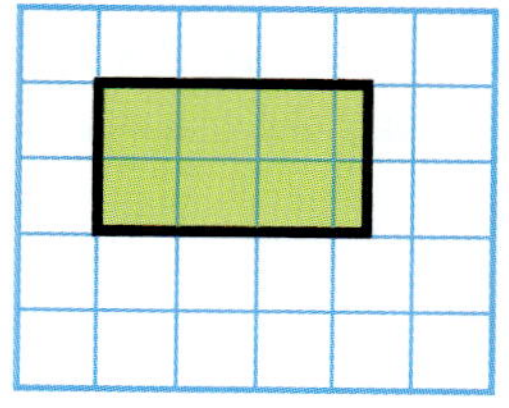

2. 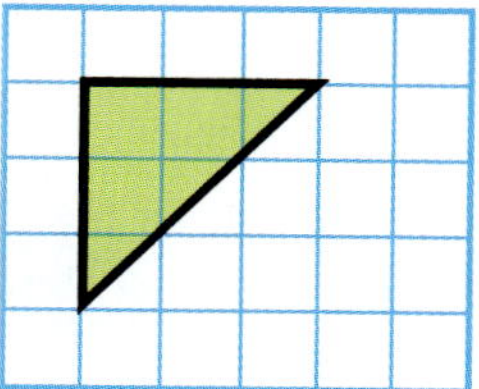

3. 

4. 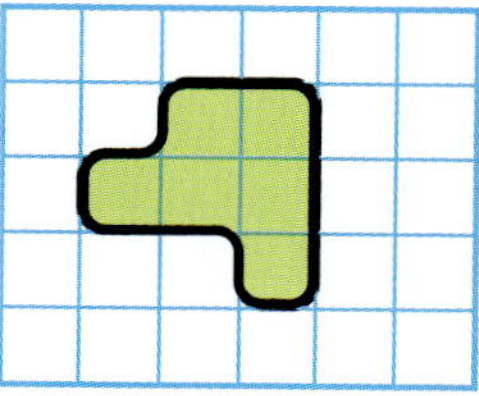

5. 

6. 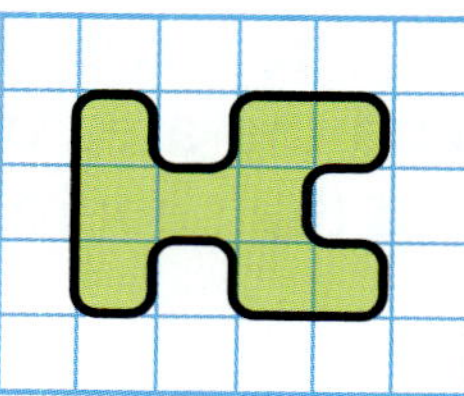

7. 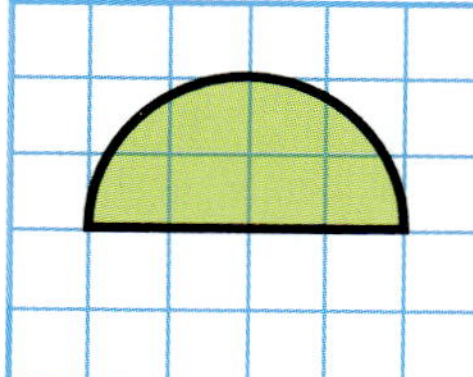

8. 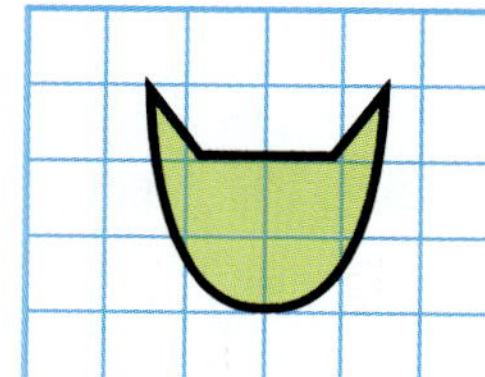

9. 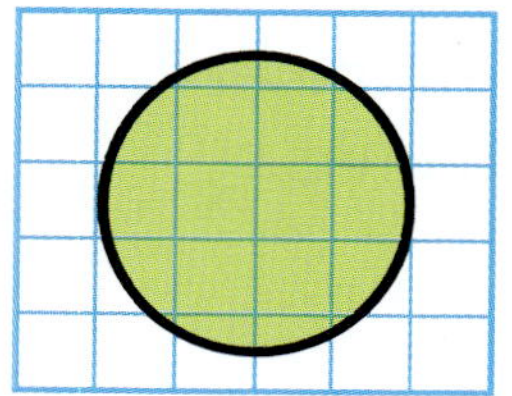

Use grid paper for Problems 10 and 11.

10. Have a friend trace around each of your hands. Estimate the area of each drawing. Are the areas the same?

11. Draw a square. Draw a line of symmetry. Count the square units to estimate the area of each part. What is true about the estimated areas? Explain why.

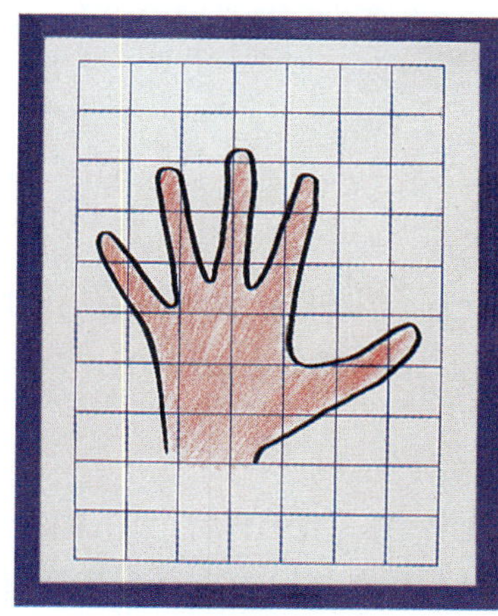

Write about it! Talk about it!

Use what you have learned to answer these questions.

12. Look at Exercises 1 and 5. Was it easier to estimate the area of the rectangle or the heart? Explain.

13. What are some differences between area and perimeter?

Find Area

You will learn how to find the number of square units that cover a figure.

Review Vocabulary
area

Learn About It

Look at the quilt on the right. What is the area of the quilt?

Area is the number of square units needed to cover a figure. You can find the area of the quilt by counting the square units.

1	2	3	4	5	6
7	8	9	10	11	12
13	14	15	16	17	18
19	20	21	22	23	24

Each □ = 1 square unit.

The area of the quilt is 24 square units.

Other Examples

A. Area of an Irregular Figure

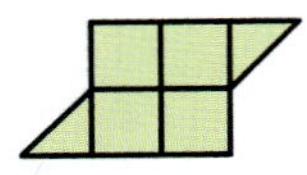

Each □ = 1 square unit.
So the area is 5 square units.

B. Area of a Right Triangle

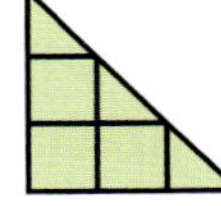

Each □ = 1 square unit.
So the area is $4\frac{1}{2}$ square units.

Explain Your Thinking

► Look at the triangle in Example *B* above. If two of these triangles were put together to form a square, what would the area of the square be? Explain.

Guided Practice

Find each area. Label your answer in square units.
Each □ = 1 square unit.

1. 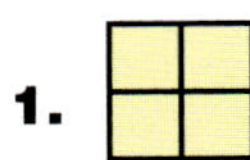

2. 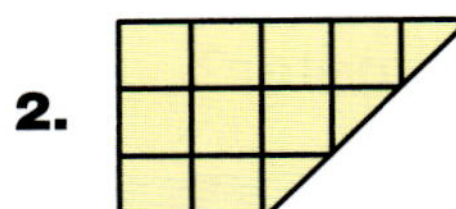

3. 

Ask Yourself

- How do I find area?
- What do I do with $\frac{1}{2}$ squares?
- Did I label my answer?

Independent Practice

Find the area of each. Label your answer in square units. Each ▢ = 1 square unit.

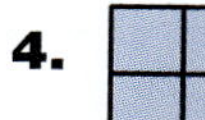

4. 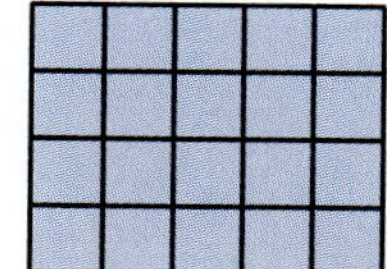

5.

6. 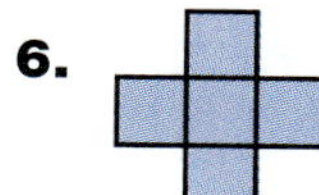

7. 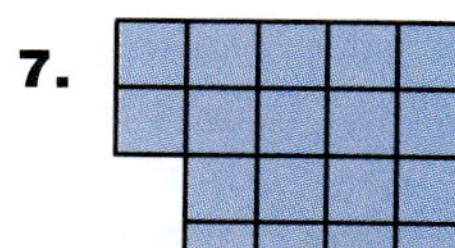

8. 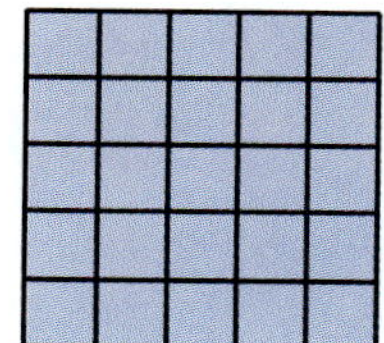

9. 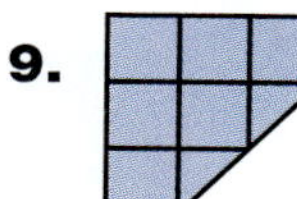

10. 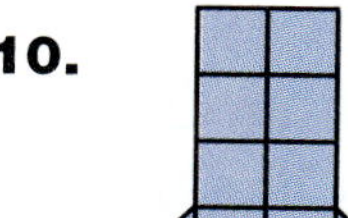

11. 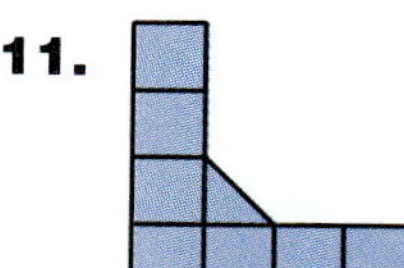

Estimate the area of each figure in square units.

12. 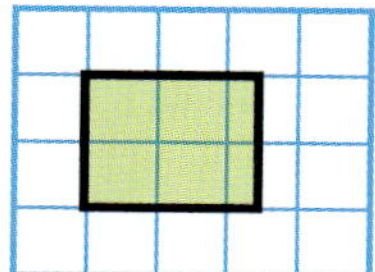

13. 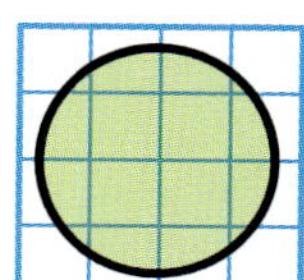

14. 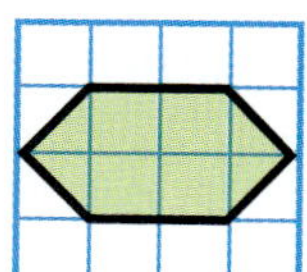

15. 

Problem Solving • Reasoning

16. Use grid paper. Draw two different polygons. Each polygon should have an area of 12 square units.

17. **Analyze** How could you find the area in Exercise 4 without counting each square?

18. **Write About It** Look at two congruent figures. Do they have the same area? Why or why not?

Using Vocabulary

Use *perimeter* or *area* to complete each sentence.

A If you add the lengths of all sides of a polygon, you are finding the ____ of that polygon.

B If you count the number of square units needed to cover a polygon, you are finding the ____ of that polygon.

Mixed Review • Test Prep

Write each time by using words. *(pages 68–72)*

19. 5:30 **20.** 7:15 **21.** 9:20 **22.** 11:55

23 What is the sum of \$29 + \$18 + \$26? *(pages 116–118)*

A \$47 **B** \$53 **C** \$73 **D** \$523

Extra Practice See Set H on page 342.

Problem-Solving Strategy: Find a Pattern

You will learn how to solve problems by finding and completing patterns.

Patterns can be found on walls, furniture, clothing, jewelry, and decorations.

Problem Toby made these cranes and placed them in a pattern. What would the colors of the next 2 cranes likely be?

What is the question?
What would the colors of the next 2 cranes likely be?

What do you know?
The colors of the cranes are blue, green, and red.

Plan

How can you find the answer?
You can find the pattern and continue it.

Solve

The pattern repeats these colors: blue, green, green, red.
Toby ended the pattern with the colors blue and green. To continue the pattern, the colors of the next 2 cranes should be green and red.

Look back at the problem.
Is there another way to describe the pattern?

Remember:
- Understand
- Plan
- Solve
- Look Back

Guided Practice

Solve these problems, using the Find a Pattern strategy.

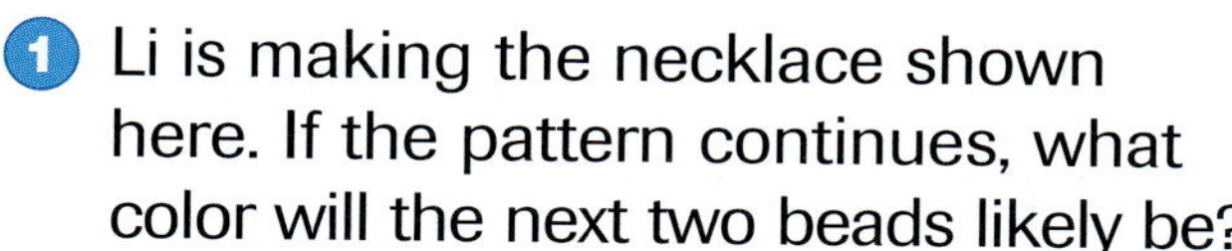

1. Li is making the necklace shown here. If the pattern continues, what color will the next two beads likely be?

Think: How do the colors repeat?

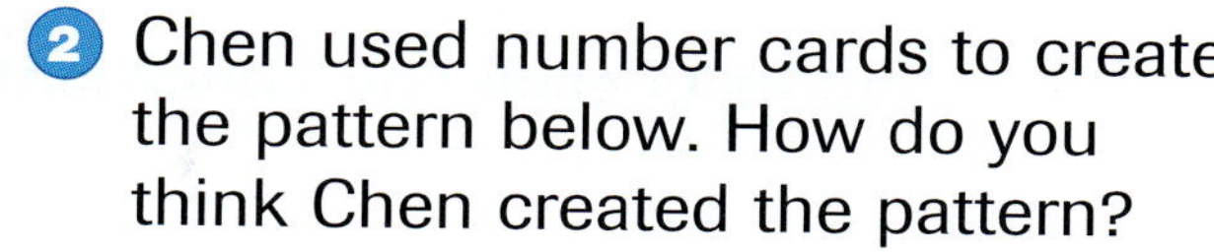

2. Chen used number cards to create the pattern below. How do you think Chen created the pattern?

Think: How do the numbers change?

Choose a Strategy

Solve. Use these or other strategies.

Problem-Solving Strategies

- **Work Backward**
- **Find a Pattern**
- **Draw a Picture**
- **Act It Out**

3. Jay plants flowers in this pattern: red, white, pink, red, white, pink. If he starts with a red flower and continues this pattern, what color will the twelfth flower likely be?

4. John has a ball. He passes it to Kim. Kim passes the ball to Alicia. Alicia passes it back to John. If they continue in this order, who will have the ball after the seventh pass?

5. Karl made 12 paper cranes. Lisa made twice as many paper cranes as Elaine. Elaine made 3 fewer cranes than Karl. How many paper cranes did Elaine, Lisa, and Karl make altogether?

6. Malik puts coins into a piggy bank. First he puts in a nickel, then a dime, then a quarter. If he continues this pattern, how much money will be in the piggy bank when he has put in 14 coins?

7. Look at the pattern of blocks shown below. If the pattern continues, what will the next two blocks likely look like?

8. If 4 more blocks are added to the pattern of blocks below, how many blocks will likely have a red square in the top row?

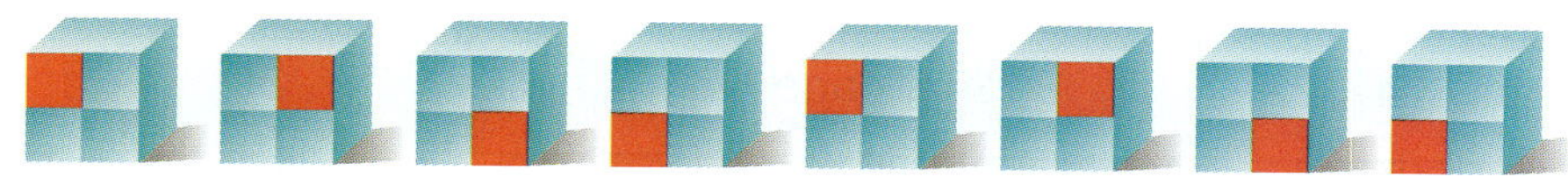

Extra Practice See 3–4 on page 343.

Quick Check

Check Your Understanding of Lessons 6–11

Are the figures in each pair congruent?

1. 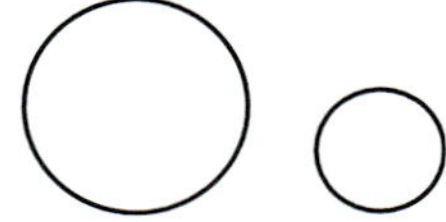

2. 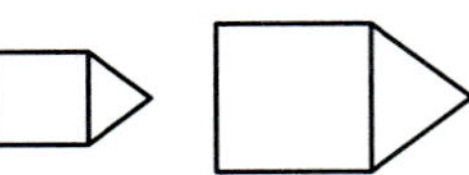

Write whether each line appears to be a line of symmetry.

3. 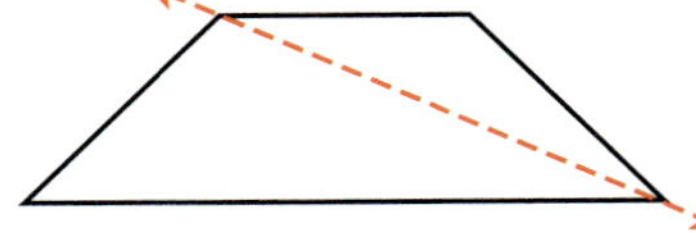

4. 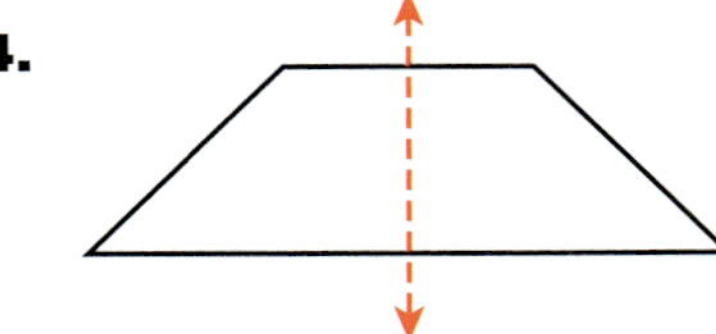

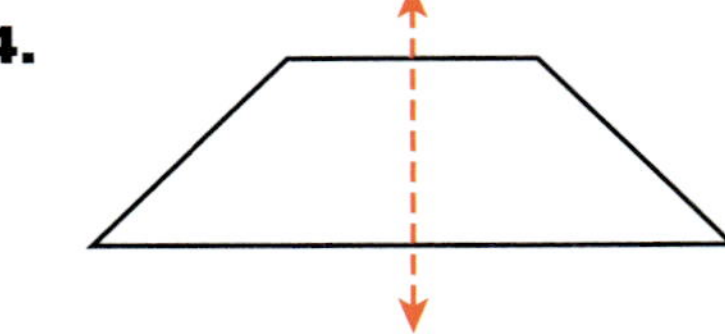

Find the perimeter.

5. 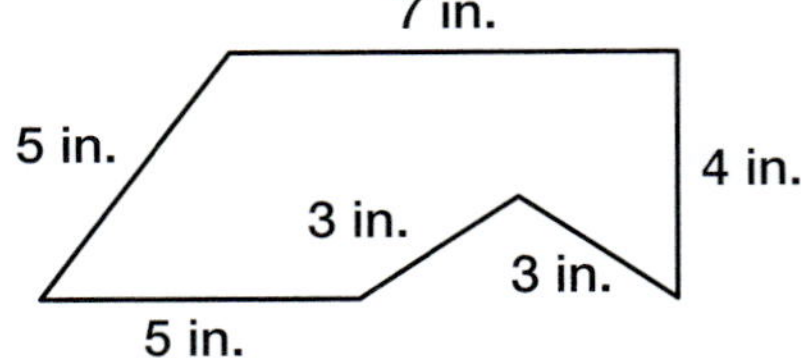

Find each area in square units.

6. 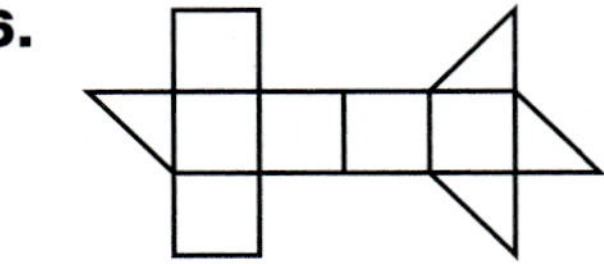

7. 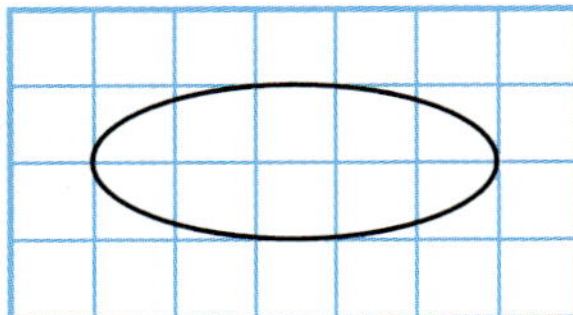

Solve.

8. Annie made a pattern with these number cards. Describe how Annie created this number pattern. What is the next number likely to be?

2 

8 11 14

How did you do?

If you had difficulty with any items in the Quick Check, you can use the following pages for review and extra practice.

Items	Review These Pages	Do These Extra Practice Items
1–2	pages 312–315	Set E, page 341
3–4	pages 316–317	Set F, page 341
5–7	pages 318–319, 322–323	Sets G–H, pages 341–342
8	pages 324–325	3–4, page 343

Test Prep • Cumulative Review

Maintaining the Standards

Choose the letter of the correct answer.

1. Which of the following is the best estimate of the area of the figure?

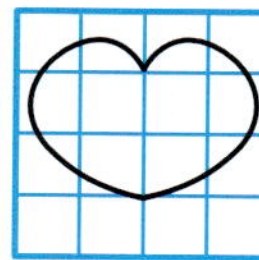

A 1 square unit
B 3 square units
C 7 square units
D 11 square units

2. What is the area of this figure?

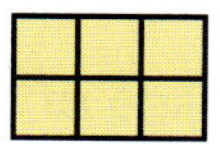

F 5 square units
G 6 square units
H 8 square units
J 10 square units

3. If each kind of figure represents a different number, and no figure is equal to zero, which statement must be true?

A △ × □ = △ × △
B △ × □ = □ × ○
C △ × ○ = ○ × △
D □ × △ = ○ × △

4. What is the perimeter of the polygon?

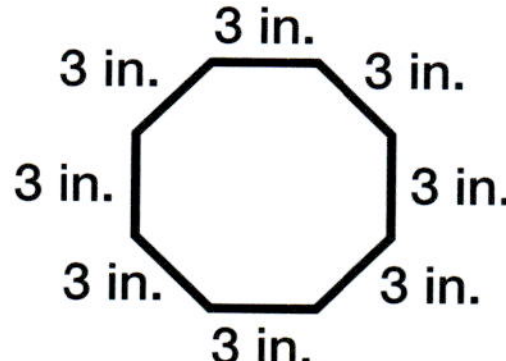

F 18 inches
G 21 inches
H 24 inches
J 27 inches

5. Which statement is not true?

A All squares have 4 sides.
B All rectangles have 4 right angles.
C All parallelograms are rectangles.
D Opposite sides of a square are parallel.

6. Which of the following is an equilateral triangle?

F
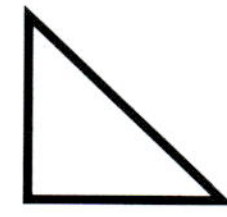

H

G

J

7. What is the perimeter of a square with sides that measure 4 meters?

Explain How did you find your answer?

Safe Site

Internet Test Prep
Visit **www.eduplace.com/kids/mhm** for more *Test Prep Practice.*

Solid Figures

You will learn to identify, describe, and classify solid figures.

New Vocabulary
rectangular prism
cube
sphere
cone
cylinder
pyramid

Learn About It

The figures below are solid figures.
They are 3-dimensional, not flat like plane figures.

Solid Figures

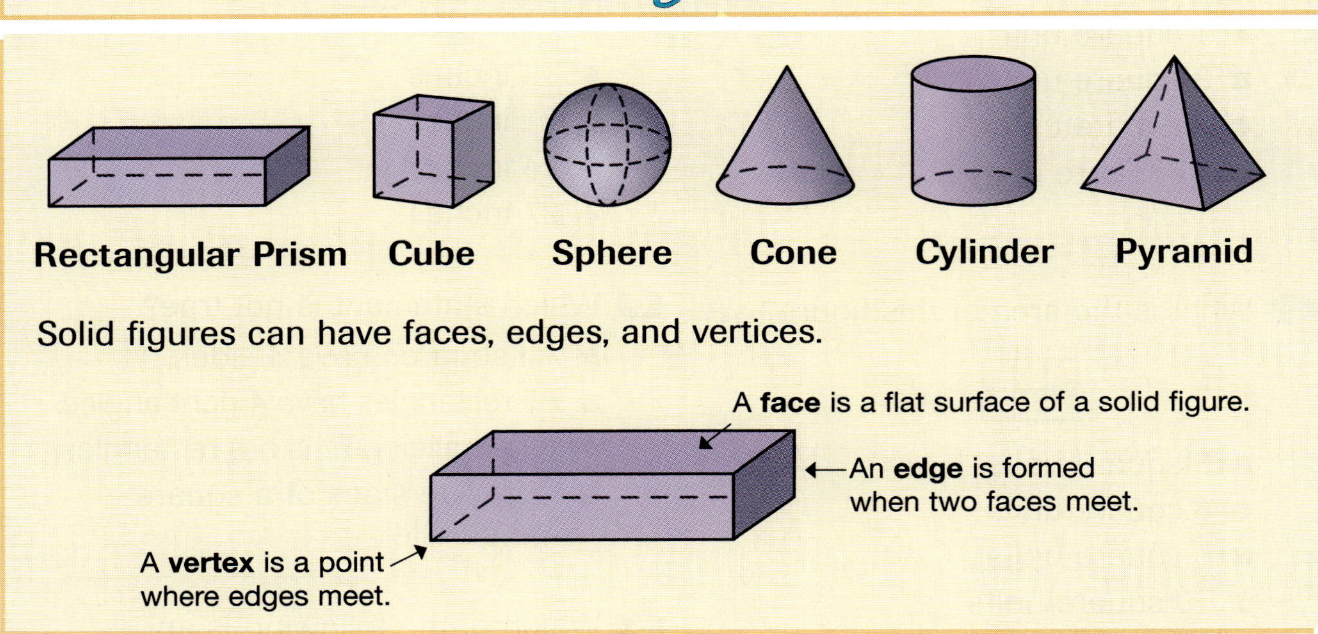

Complex Solid Figures

Complex solid figures are made up of two or more solid figures.

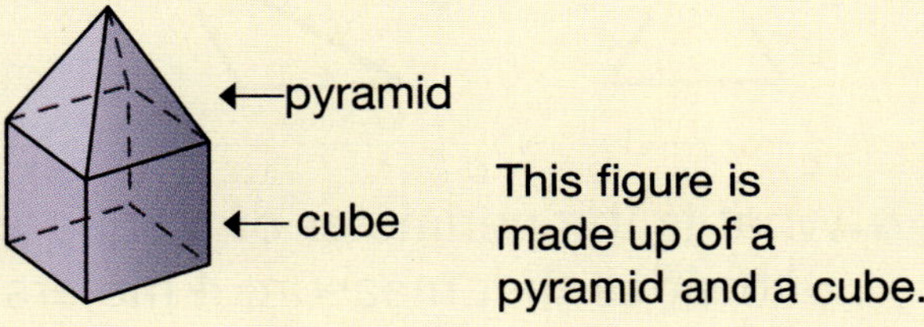

This figure is made up of a pyramid and a cube.

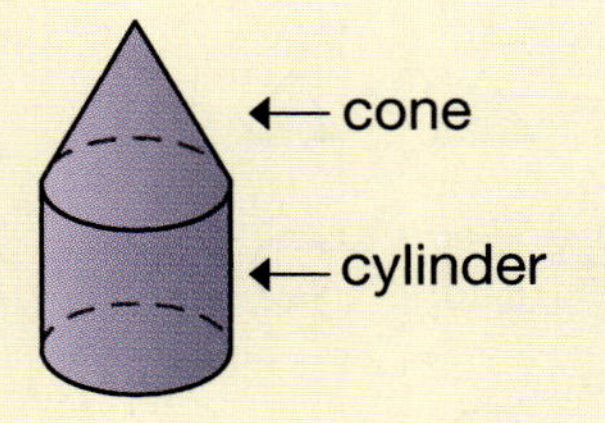

This figure is made up of a cone and a cylinder.

Explain Your Thinking

► Look at the solid figures above. Describe how you can sort the figures in two different ways.

Guided Practice

Name the solid figure or figures.

1. 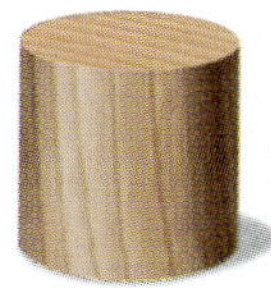

2. 

3. 

Ask Yourself

- Is the figure made up of more than one simpler solid figure?

Independent Practice

Name the solid figure that each object looks like.

4. 

5. 

6. 

7. 

8. 

9. 

10. 

11. 

Name the solid figures that make up each object.

12. 

13. 

14. 

15. 

Look at the solid figures on page 328.
Then copy and complete the table below.

	Solid Figure	Number of Faces	Number of Edges	Number of Vertices
16.	Cube			
17.	Rectangular Prism			
18.	Pyramid			

Remember:
Count the faces, vertices, and edges that are hidden.

19. Which solid figures in the table have the same number of faces, edges, and vertices?

20. Describe two ways to sort the solid figures in the table.

Problem Solving • Reasoning

Use Data **Use the graph for Problems 21–23.**

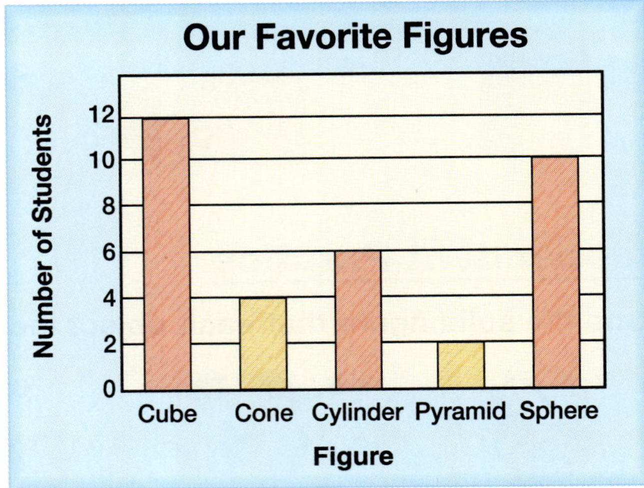

21. Lynn asked the students in her class what solid figure they liked the best. Which figure was chosen by the most students?

22. If each student voted for 1 figure, how many students are in Lynn's class?

23. How many more students chose cube than chose pyramid?

24. **Write About It** A cube is a special kind of rectangular prism. Explain what is special about a cube.

Mixed Review • Test Prep

Solve. *(pages xxiii, xxv, 236–237)*

25. $\begin{array}{r} 7 \\ \times\ 4 \\ \hline \end{array}$

26. $\begin{array}{r} 11 \\ -\ 5 \\ \hline \end{array}$

27. $\begin{array}{r} 9 \\ +\ 8 \\ \hline \end{array}$

28. $\begin{array}{r} 18 \\ -\ 9 \\ \hline \end{array}$

29. $\begin{array}{r} 9 \\ \times\ 4 \\ \hline \end{array}$

30 Anton needs 2 kg of food for his pets. How many grams of food is that? *(pages 190–191)*

A 20 **B** 200 **C** 2,000 **D** 20,000

Analogies

Look at the way the first pair of words is related. Choose the letter that shows a similar relationship for the second pair.

31. **Pyramid** is to **triangle** as **cube** is to ____.

A triangle **C** cone

B square **D** pyramid

32. **Quadrilateral** is to **4 sides** as **octagon** is to ____ **sides.**

F 3 **H** 6

G 5 **J** 8

Extra Practice See Set I on page 342.

Practice Game

Meet Your Match

Practice using what you know about plane figures and solid figures by playing this game with a partner. Try to get the most matches!

Players
2

What You'll Need

- *12 blue cards with solid figures (Teaching Tool 6)*
- *12 red cards with plane figures (Teaching Tool 7)*

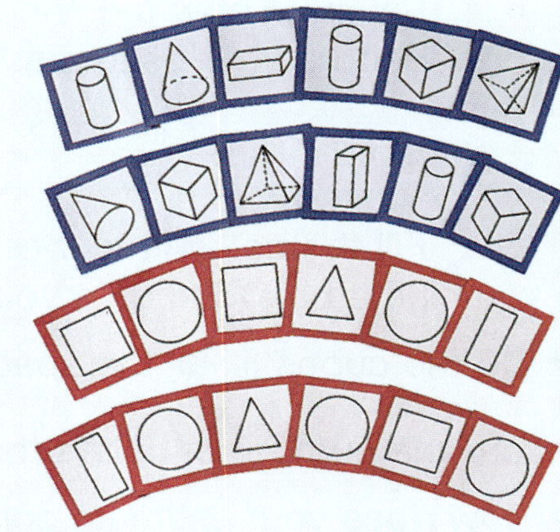

Here's What to Do

1. Shuffle the blue cards. Place them facedown in a 3 by 4 array. Shuffle the red cards. Place them facedown in a 3 by 4 array next to the first array.
2. The first player turns over one card of each color. If the plane figure can be found on the solid figure, the first player takes both cards. If the plane figure cannot be found on the solid figure, the player turns the cards over.
3. Players take turns until all the cards have been taken or no matches can be made. The player with the greatest number of matches wins.

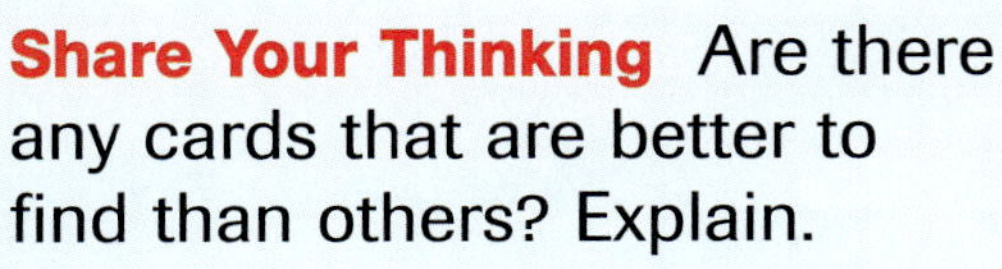

Share Your Thinking Are there any cards that are better to find than others? Explain.

Estimating Volume

You will learn how to estimate the number of cubes that fit in a container.

New Vocabulary
volume

Learn About It

The number of unit cubes that make up a solid figure is the **volume** of the figure.

Materials
For each group:
unit cubes
small box

Work with a group to estimate the number of unit cubes that will fill a small box.

Step 1 Estimate how many cubes it will take to fill the box. Record your estimate.

Step 2 Fill the box with cubes. Count the cubes as you fill the box to find its volume.

- Do the cubes fill all the space in the box?

Record the number of cubes that fit in the box.

- How does your estimate compare with the volume?

Step 3 Now empty the cubes from the box. Use all of the cubes to build another figure.

- What is the volume of the new figure?

Try to build more figures with the same cubes.

- What is the volume of each new figure?

Try It Out

1. Find 3 containers like these that are shaped like a box.

2. Find 3 containers like these that can roll.

Estimate how many cubes it will take to fill each container you have found. Record your estimate in a table like the one shown below. Then fill each container with cubes. Record the number of cubes you used.

	Container	Estimate	Number of Cubes Used
3.	Gift box		
4.	Tea box		
5.	Juice box		
6.	Coffee can		
7.	Cup		
8.	Funnel		

9. Explain how finding the area of a plane figure is different from finding the volume of a container.

Write about it! Talk about it!

Use what you have learned to answer these questions.

10. If two solid figures have about the same volume, must they have the same shape?

11. Do you think that the number of cubes used to fill the coffee can is greater than or less than the actual volume of the can? Explain.

12. Can you estimate the volume of a square? Why or why not?

Find Volume

You will learn how to find volume.

New Vocabulary
cubic unit

Learn About It

This is a unit cube. It has a volume of 1 **cubic unit.** Volume is the number of cubic units that make up a solid figure.

To find the volume of a solid figure, count the cubic units that make up the solid figure.

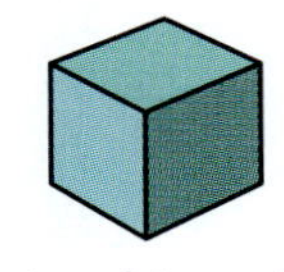

1 cubic unit
Each edge has a length of 1 unit.

Find the volume of the figure on the right.
Eight cubic units make up the figure.
The volume is 8 cubic units.

Remember:
Count the cubes that are hidden.

Find the volume of the solid figure at the right.
The volume is 8 cubic units.

Explain Your Thinking

► Why can different solid figures have a volume of 8 cubic units? Explain.

Guided Practice

Find the volume of each figure.

Each 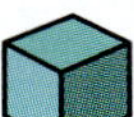 **= 1 cubic unit.**

1. 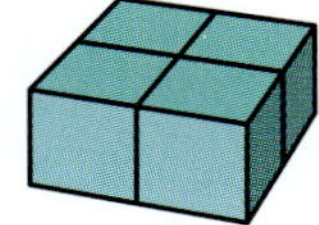

2. 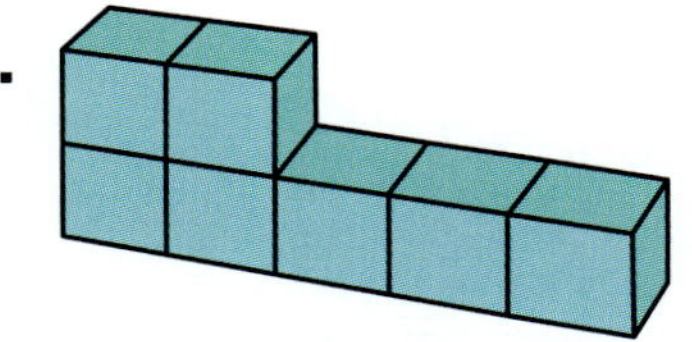

Ask Yourself

- What unit do I use to measure volume?
- How can I find the volume of a solid figure?

Independent Practice

Find the volume of each figure. Each  **= 1 cubic unit.**

3. 

4. 

5. 

6. 

7. 

8. 

Problem Solving • Reasoning

9. Look at the figures below. Write the volume of each figure in cubic units.

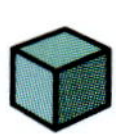  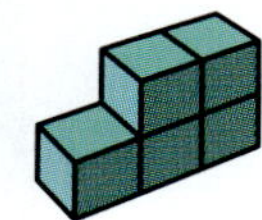 

10. Patterns In the picture above, how many cubes would likely make up the next figure? Explain why.

11. Analyze Is there a way to find the volume of the figure on the right without counting every unit cube? Explain.

Using Algebra

Solve for *n*.

A $7 + n = 6 + 6$

B $n + 8 = 9 + 1$

C $6 + 5 = n + 6$

D $n + 4 = 8 + 3$

E $5 + 8 = 8 + n$

F $9 + 6 = 8 + n$

Mixed Review • Test Prep

Write each number in expanded form. *(pages 4–5, 18–19, 32–33)*

12. 632 **13.** 814 **14.** 906 **15.** 1,930 **16.** 18,034 **17.** 49,203

18 Which number makes the number sentence true? *(pages 220–221)*

$40 = 5 \times \blacksquare$

A 4 **C** 6

B 8 **D** 9

Extra Practice See Set J on page 342.

Problem-Solving Application: Use Measurement

You will learn to use what you know about area, perimeter, and volume to solve problems.

Problem Kristen needs a tank for her pet iguana that has a floor area of at least 4 square feet. Look at the diagrams below. Which tanks have enough floor area for Kristen's iguana?

1 foot

1 foot

1 square foot

Each side has a length of 1 foot

TANK A

TANK B

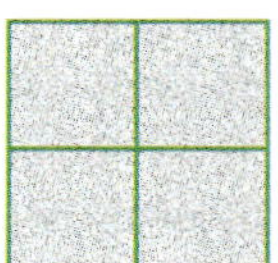

TANK C

What is the question?

Which tanks have enough floor area?

What do you know?

The tank needs to have a floor area of at least 4 square feet.

How can you find the area of the floor?

Count the number of squares on the bottom of the tank. Then compare your answer to 4 square feet.

Tank A has a floor area of 2 square feet.

Tank B has a floor area of 6 square feet.

Tank C has a floor area of 4 square feet.

So Tank B and Tank C have enough floor area.

Look back at the question.

Which tank should Kristen buy? Explain your choice.

Guided Practice

Solve each problem.

1. The pet store clerk suggested that the tank have at least 4 cubic units of space inside. Is the space inside this tank big enough? Explain.

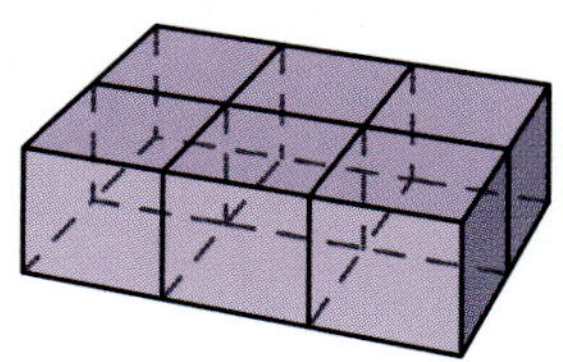

Think: Do I need to find the perimeter, area, or volume?

2. Kristen wants to put a border along the top of this iguana tank. How much border will she need to put around the tank?

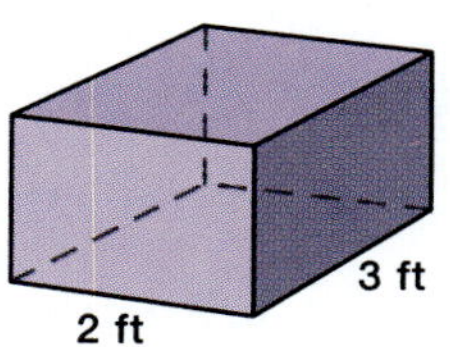

Think: Do I need to find the perimeter, area, or volume?

Choose a Strategy

Solve. Use these or other strategies.

Problem-Solving Strategies

- **Find a Pattern**
- **Draw a Picture**
- **Use Logical Thinking**
- **Write a Number Sentence**

3. Mandy wants to put outdoor carpeting on the floor of her pet's doghouse. Will $32 be enough to pay for the carpeting?

Doghouse Floor

3 ft

4 ft

Each □ of carpeting costs $4.

4. Jason wants to put a fence around a play area for his dog. How much fencing does he need if the entrance is 2 feet wide?

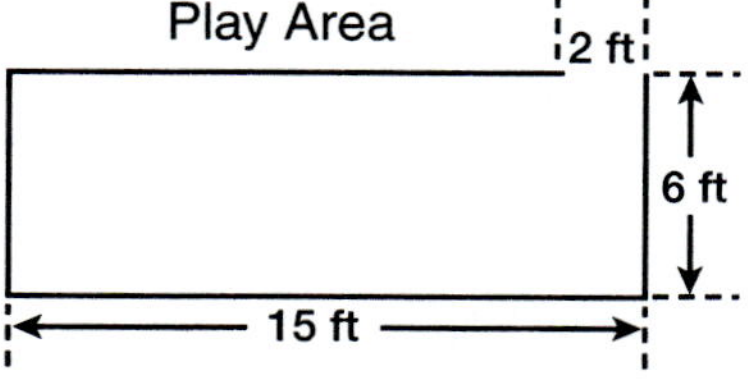

5. Tammy bought a puppy ID tag for $2 and a collar for $4. She got $4 in change. How much money did she give the clerk?

6. Elise is thinking of an odd number. The number is greater than 20 and less than 30. The sum of the digits is 9. What number is Elise thinking of?

7. The numbers 1, 2, 4, 8, and 16 form a pattern. What number would likely continue the pattern? Explain your thinking.

8. Bob is making a design that is 5 inches by 8 inches. How many 1-inch square tiles does he need to fill the area of the design?

Extra Practice See 5–7 on page 343.

Quick Check

Check Your Understanding of Lessons 12–15

Name the solid figure or figures.

1. 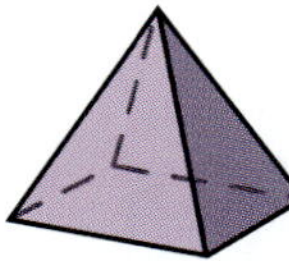

2. 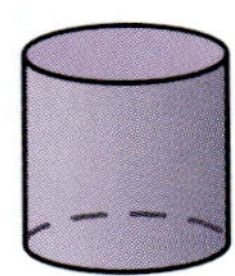

3. 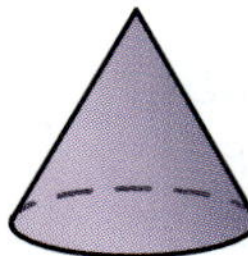

4. 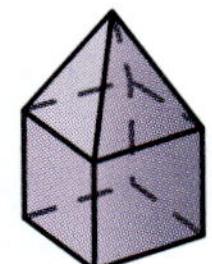

Estimate the volume of each container in unit cubes.

5. 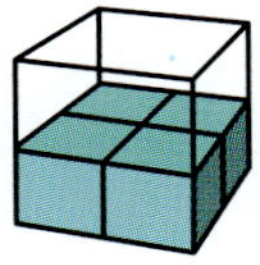

6. 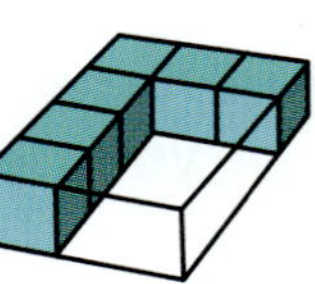

Find the volume of each figure.

7. 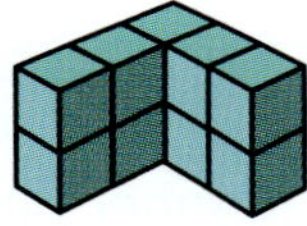

8. 

Solve.

9. Sue needs a box with at least 8 cubic units inside for her hiking gear. Is the space inside this box big enough? Explain.

How did you do?

If you had difficulty with any items in the Quick Check, you can use the following pages for review and extra practice.

Items	Review These Pages	Do These Extra Practice Items
1–4	pages 328–330	Set I, page 342
5–8	pages 332–335	Set J, page 342
9	pages 336–337	5–7, page 343

Test Prep • Cumulative Review

Maintaining the Standards

Choose the letter of the correct answer.

1. What is the name of this figure?

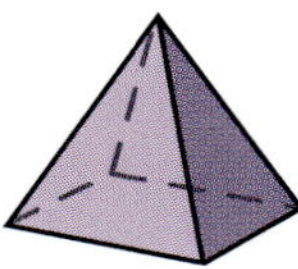

A triangle **C** sphere
B pyramid **D** cylinder

2. What two solid figures make up this complex figure?

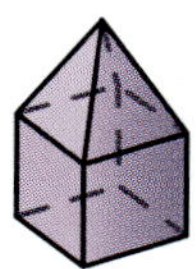

F cube, sphere
G cube, pyramid
H pyramid, sphere
J pyramid, cylinder

3. What is the area of this figure?

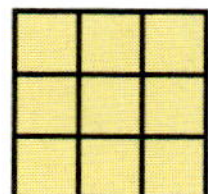

A 9 units **C** 9 square units
B 12 units **D** 9 cubic units

4. In which triangle are all the angles less than a right angle?

F

H
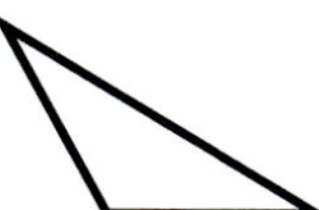

G
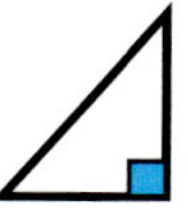

J
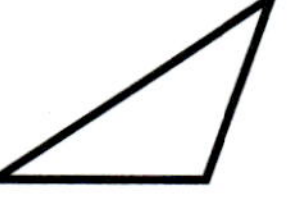

5. Which statement is true?

A A right triangle has 4 right angles.
B An isosceles triangle has 2 equal sides.
C An equilateral triangle has 1 right angle.
D All triangles have at least 1 right angle.

6. What two solid figures make up this complex figure?

F circle, cone
G cylinder, cone
H sphere, cone
J cylinder, sphere

7. What is the name of this figure?

A cylinder **C** pyramid
B cone **D** sphere

8. What is the volume of this figure in cubic units?

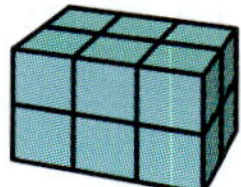

Explain How did you find your answer?

Extra Practice

Set A (Lesson 1, pages 298–300)

Write whether each figure is a *line, line segment,* or *ray*.

1. 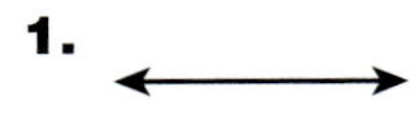
2. 
3. 
4. 

Write *right angle, less than a right angle,* or *greater than a right angle* for each angle.

5. 
6. 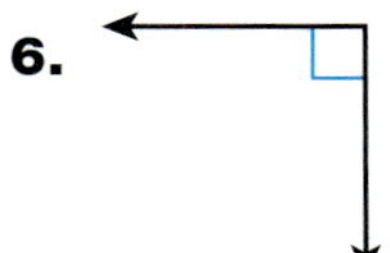
7. 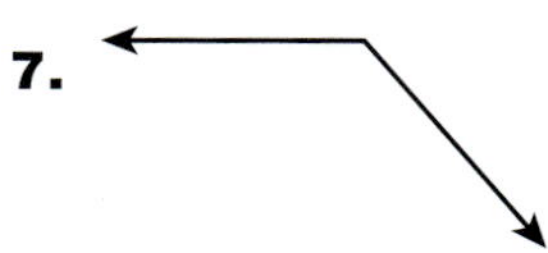
8. 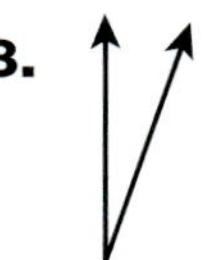

Set B (Lesson 2, pages 302–303)

Write whether the figure is a polygon. If it is, write its name.

1. 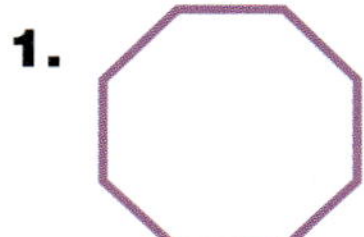
2. 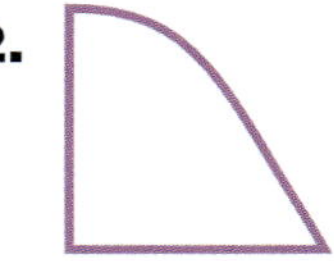
3. 
4. 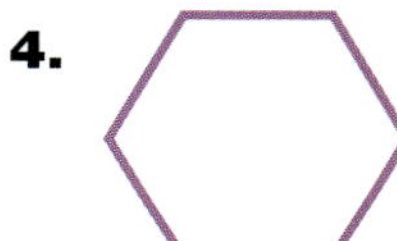

Set C (Lesson 3, pages 304–305)

Tell whether the figure is a quadrilateral. If it has a special name, write it.

1. 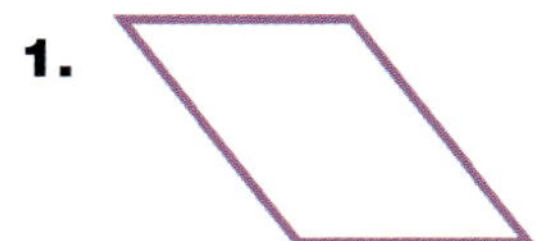
2. 
3. 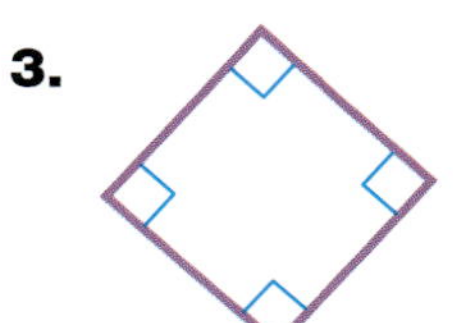
4. 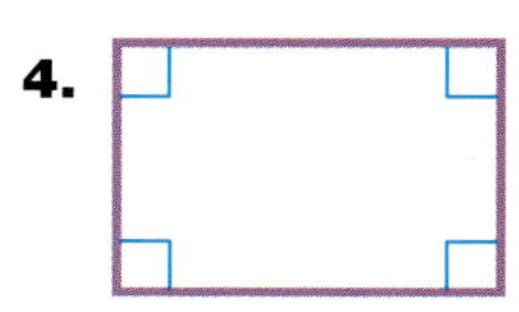

Set D (Lesson 4, pages 306–307)

Name the kind of triangle shown. Write *equilateral, isosceles,* or *right*.

1. 
2. 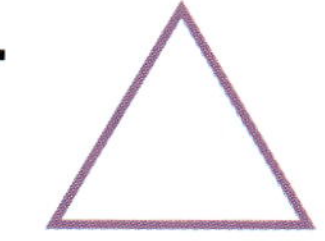
3. 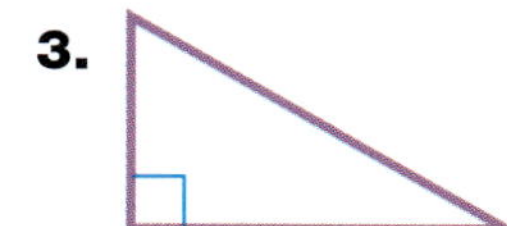
4. 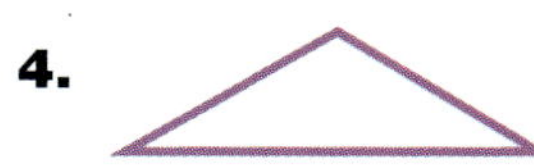

Extra Practice

Set E (Lesson 6, pages 312–314)

Trace one of the two figures. Place the traced figure on top of the other figure. Are the figures in each pair congruent?

1. 

2. 

3. 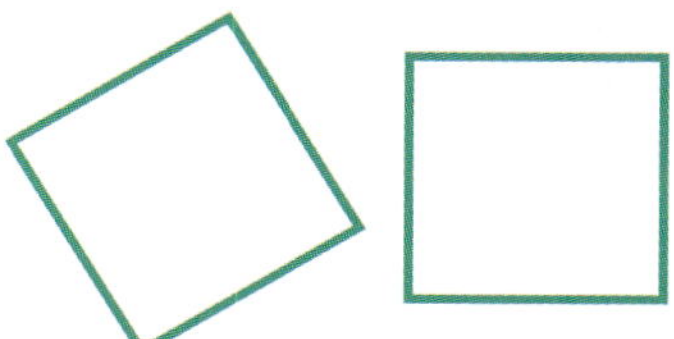

Set F (Lesson 7, pages 316–317)

Tell whether each line appears to be a line of symmetry.

1. 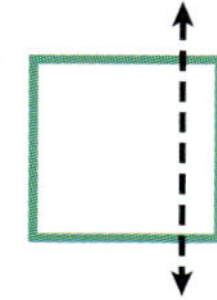

2. 

3. 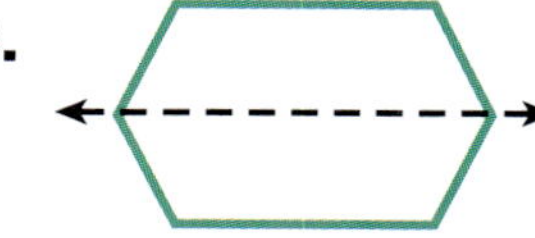

Trace each figure. Then draw a line of symmetry.

4. 

5. 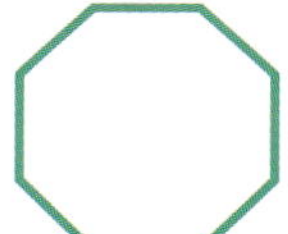

6. 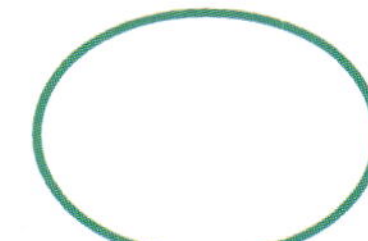

Set G (Lesson 8, pages 318–319)

Find each perimeter. Label your answer.

1. 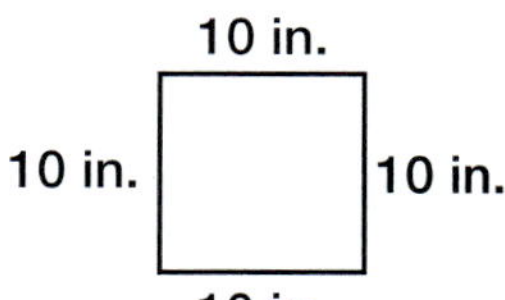

2. 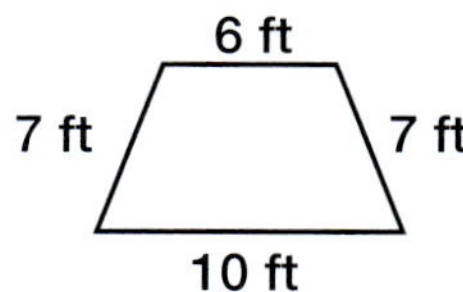

3. 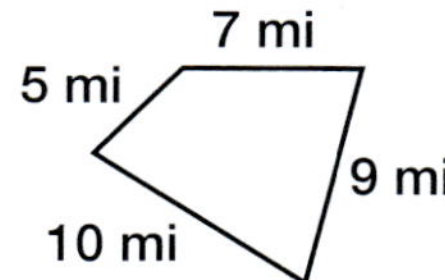

4. 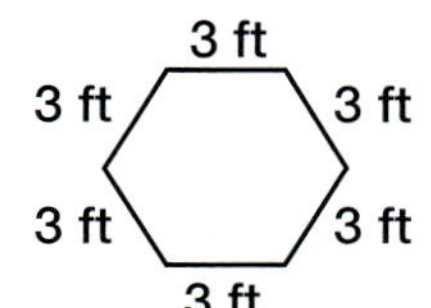

5. 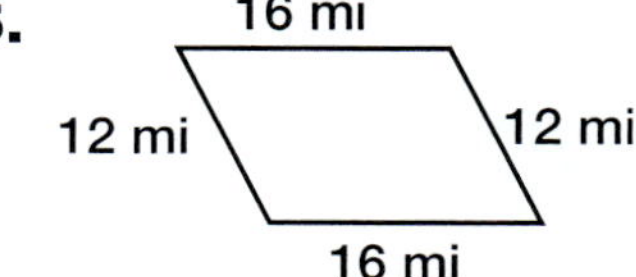

6. 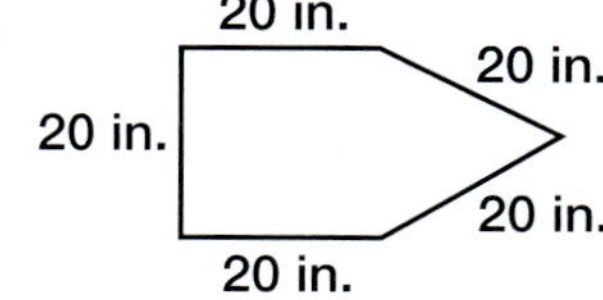

Extra Practice

Set H (Lesson 10, pages 322–323)

Find the area of each figure.
Label your answer in square units. Each ☐ = 1 square unit.

1. 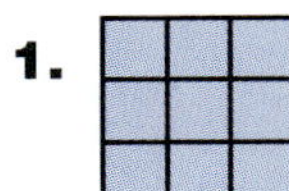

2. 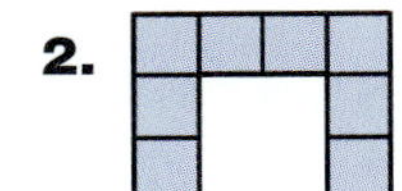

3. 

4. 

5. 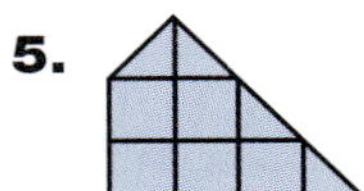

6. 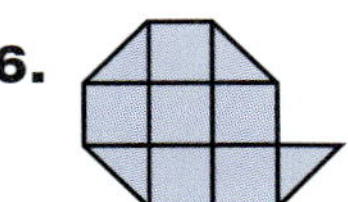

Set I (Lesson 12, pages 328–330)

Name the solid figure that each object looks like.

1. 

2. 

3. 

4. 

5. 

6. 

7. 

8.

Set J (Lesson 14, pages 334–335)

Find the volume of each figure.
Label your answer in cubic units. Each 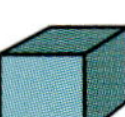 = 1 cubic unit.

1. 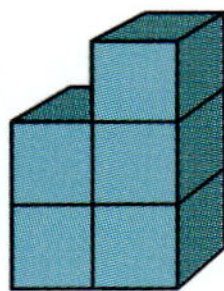

2. 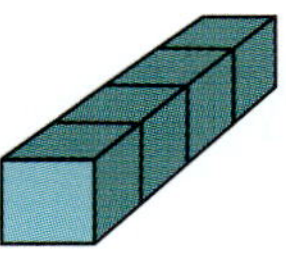

3. 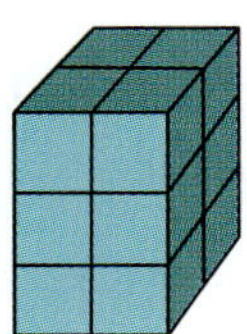

4. 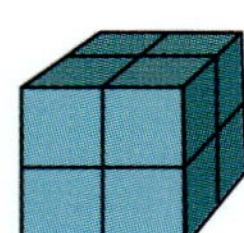

5. 

6. 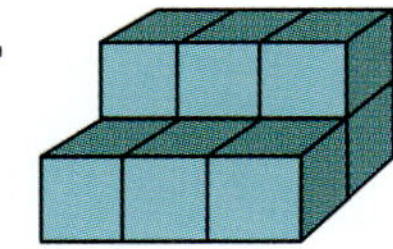

Extra Practice • Problem Solving

Choose the letter of the missing piece. *(Lesson 5, pages 308–309)*

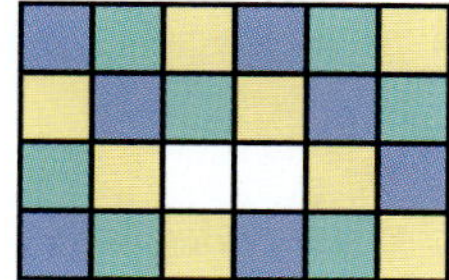

a.

b.

c.

d.

2

a. 

b. 

c.

d.

Solve these problems, using the Find a Pattern strategy. *(Lesson 11, pages 324–325)*

3. Dee is making a scarf like the one shown. She begins with a blue stripe. If she continues the pattern, what colors are the next three stripes likely to be?

4. Hank made this pattern with blocks. He asks Ted to continue the pattern. What two blocks is Ted likely to use next?

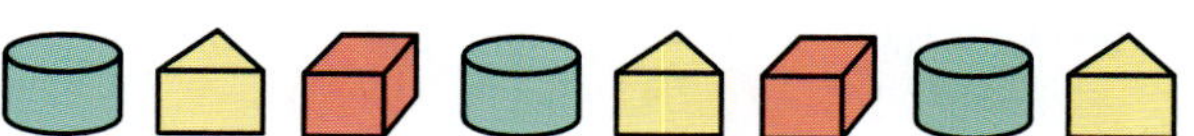

Solve. Use the picture at the right for Problems 5 and 6. *(Lesson 15, pages 336–337)*

5. Susan wants to put a wallpaper border along the top of the walls in her bedroom. How much border will she need?

6. Susan also wants to buy carpeting for her room. How much carpeting will she need?

Susan's Bedroom

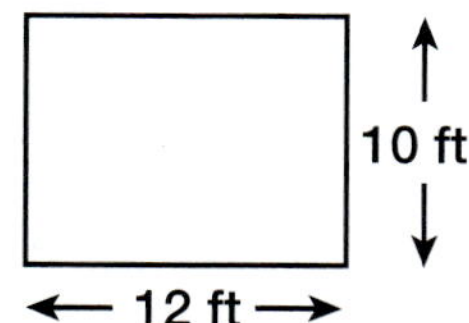

7. Look at the figure shown on the right. What is the volume of the figure in cubic units?

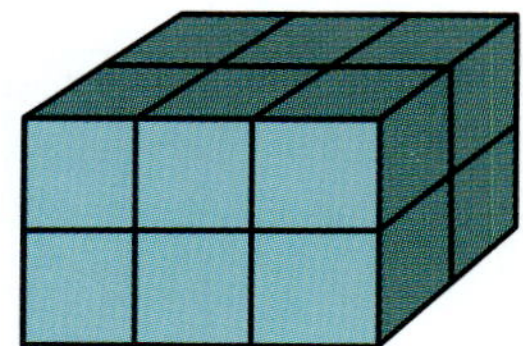

Chapter Review

Reviewing Vocabulary

Answer each question.

1. What is the name of a straight path that goes on in two directions without end?
2. What is the name of a part of a line that has one endpoint and goes on without end in one direction?
3. What is the name of a figure formed by two rays with the same endpoint?
4. What is the name of any four-sided polygon?
5. What is the name for a solid figure shaped like a ball?

Reviewing Concepts and Skills

Name each figure. *(pages 298–300)*

6.

7.

8.

9. 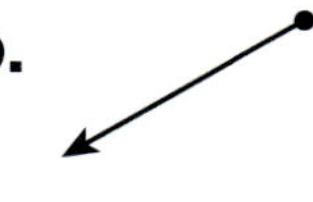

Write *right angle, less than a right angle,* or *greater than a right angle* for each angle. *(pages 298–300)*

10. 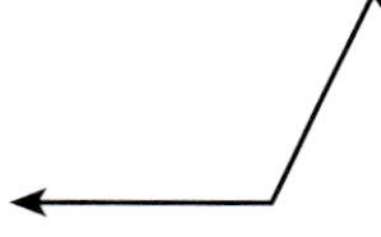

11. 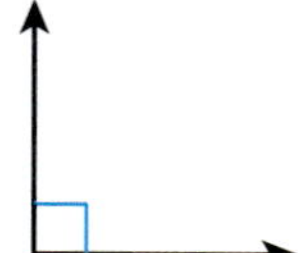

12. 

13. 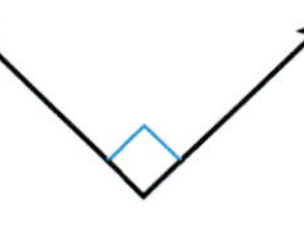

Write the special name of each figure. *(pages 302–307)*

14. 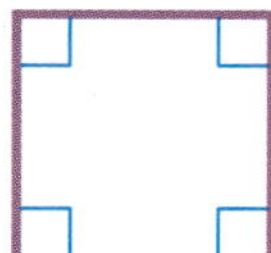

15. 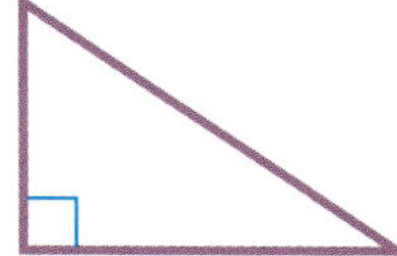

16. 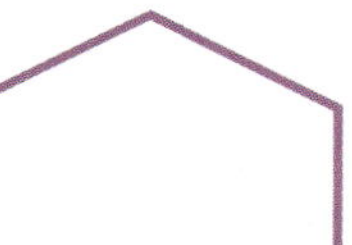

17. 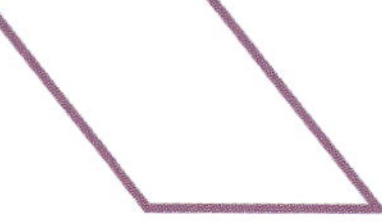

Do the figures in each pair appear congruent? *(pages 312–314)*

18. 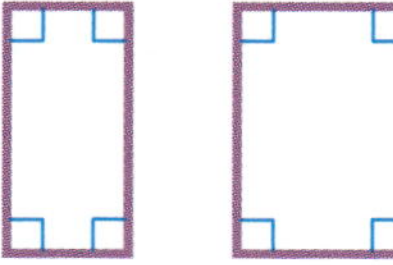

19. 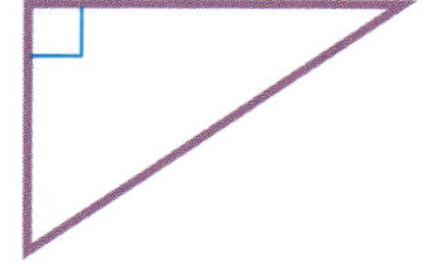

Tell whether each dashed line appears to be a line of symmetry. *(pages 316–317)*

20. 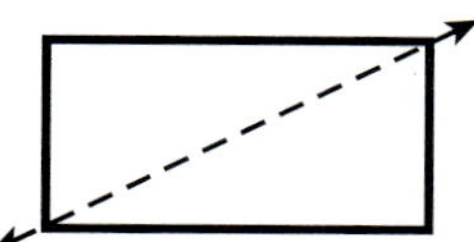

21. 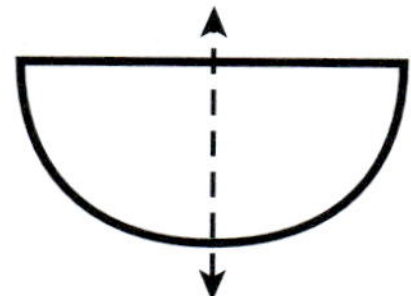

22. 

Name the solid figure or figures. *(pages 328–330)*

23. 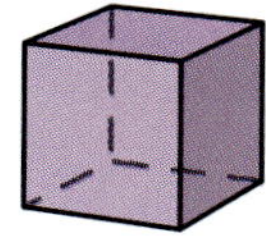

24. 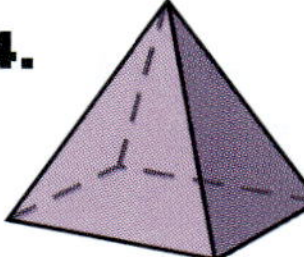

25. 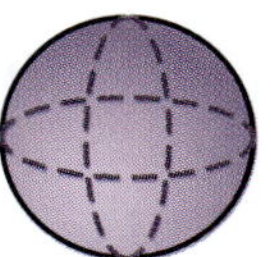

26. 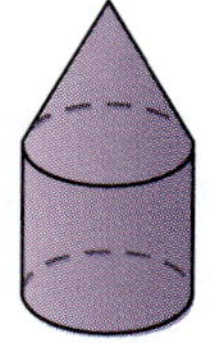

27. Find the perimeter.
(pages 318–319)

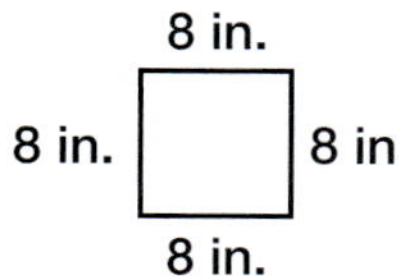

28. Find the area.
(pages 322–323)

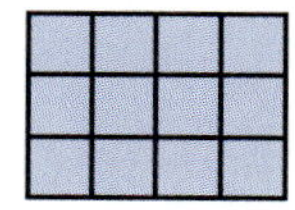

29. Find the volume.
(pages 334–335)

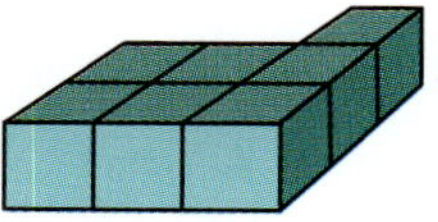

Solve. *(pages 308–309, 324–325)*

30. Choose the correct letter for the missing piece.

a. 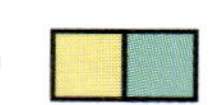

b. 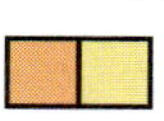

c. 

d. 

31. Al made the pattern on the right. Which card is likely to come next?

1	2	4	8	16	32

Brain Teasers Math Reasoning

Right Angles

Draw a picture to show one way to make an octagon that has 4 right angles.

Twelve Cubes

What are all the different rectangular prisms you can make using 12 unit cubes.

Internet Brain Teasers
Visit **www.eduplace.com/kids/mhm** for more *Brain Teasers.*

Chapter Test

Write whether each figure is a *line, line segment,* or *ray*.

1. 
2. 
3. 
4. 

Write *right angle, less than a right angle,* or *greater than a right angle* for each angle.

5. 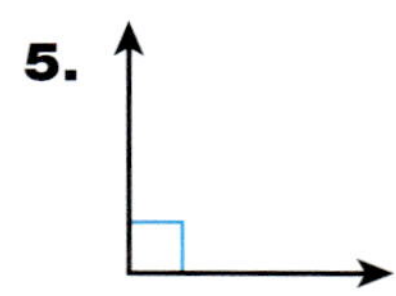
6. 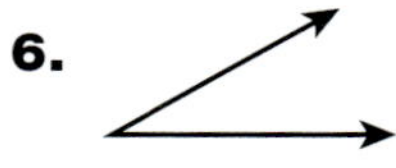
7. 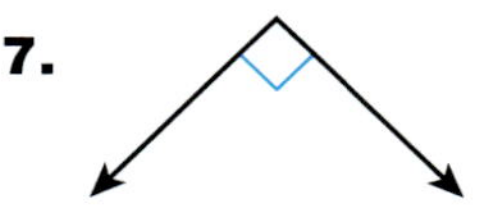
8. 

Write the special name of each figure.

9. 
10.
11. 
12. 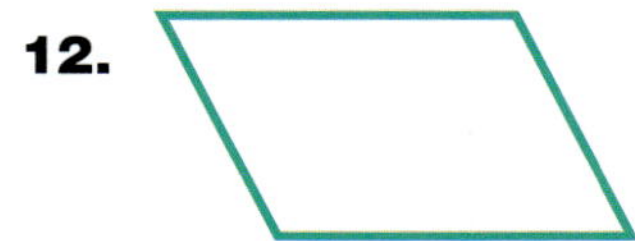

Name the kind of triangle shown. Write *equilateral, isosceles,* or *right*.

13. 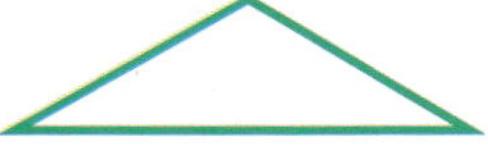
14. 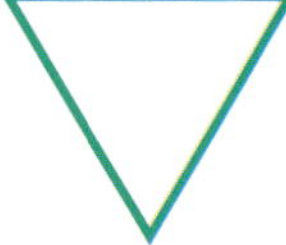
15. 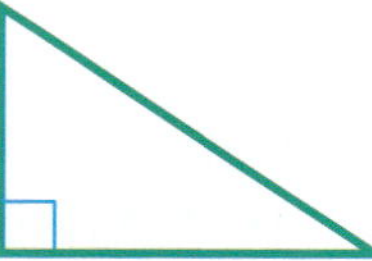

Name the solid figure or figures.

16. 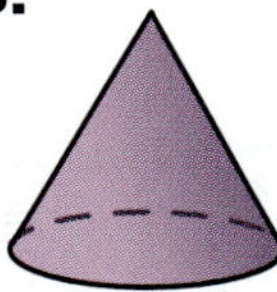
17. 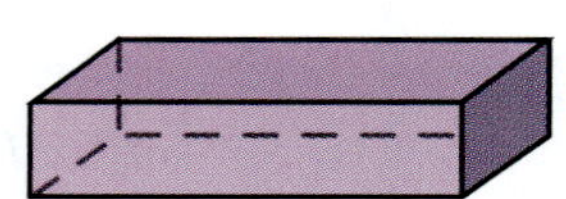
18. 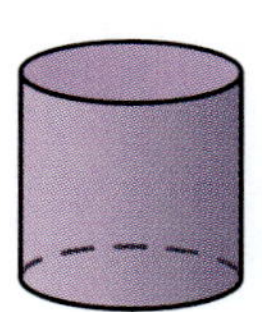
19. 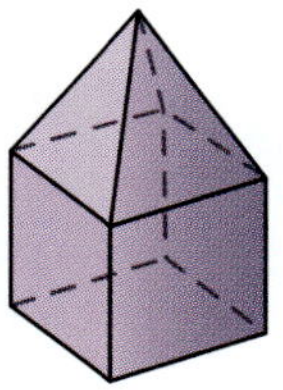

20. Find the perimeter.

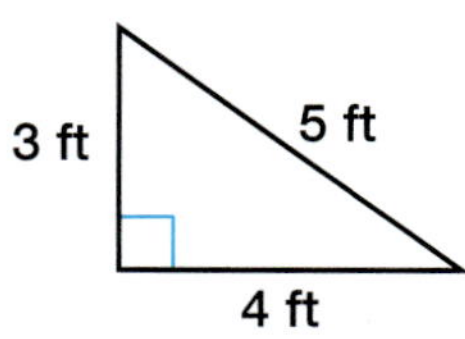

21. Find the area.

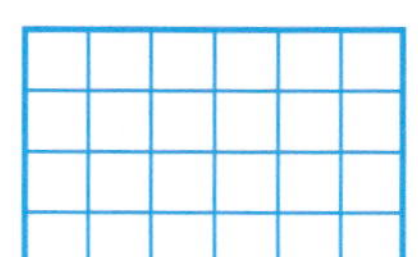

Solve.

22. Do the figures below appear to be congruent? Trace one figure to help you decide.

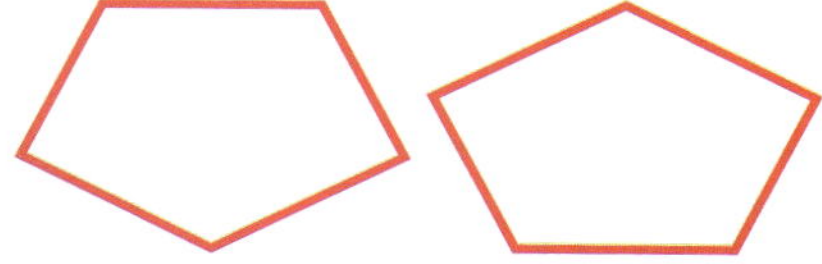

23. Does the dashed line appear to be a line of symmetry? Trace and fold to check.

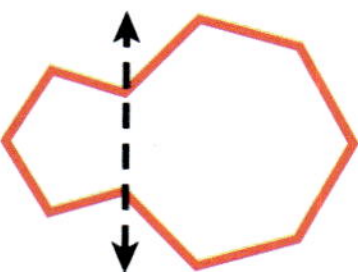

Solve.

24. Frank is making a row of colored squares. So far, he has used these colors: red, orange, yellow, red, orange, yellow, red, and orange. If he continues the pattern, what are the next two colors likely to be?

25. Look at the figure shown on the right. What is its volume in cubic units?

Write About It

Solve each problem. Use correct math vocabulary to explain your thinking.

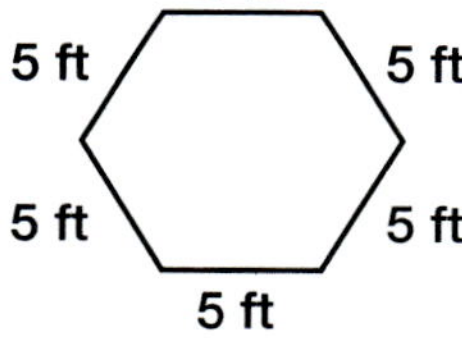

1. Look at the figure at the right.

- **a.** Is the figure a polygon? Is it a quadrilateral? Explain.
- **b.** Does the figure have at least one line of symmetry? If it does, trace the figure and show a line of symmetry.
- **c.** Explain how to find the perimeter of the figure.

2. Ann made two quilts, using congruent squares. The first quilt has 5 rows of squares with 6 squares in each row. The second quilt has 4 rows of squares with 8 squares in each row.

- **a.** Ann wants to sew a ribbon border around one of the quilts. Explain how you can tell which quilt's border will need less ribbon.
- **b.** Which quilt has the greater area? Explain how you know.

Another Look

Use the road signs to find the answer to each question.

a. 

b. 

c. 

d. 

e. 

f. 

g. 

1. Which sign is not in the shape of a polygon? How can you tell? What is the shape of this sign?
2. Write the letters of the signs that are shaped like polygons. Write the name of the polygon next to each letter. Put a check mark next to the polygons that have right angles.
3. **Look Back** What is the letter of the road sign that is an equilateral triangle? How do you know?
4. **Analyze** Suppose the width of Sign *c* is 12 inches and the sign is twice as long as it is wide. What would the perimeter of the sign be? Explain how you found your answer.

Enrichment

Nets

A **net** is a pattern that can be cut out and folded to form a solid figure. This net is for a cube.

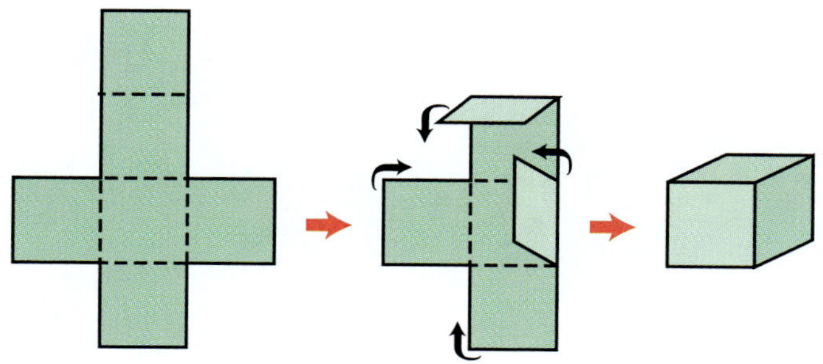

If you traced the net, cut it out, and folded it along the dotted lines, it would form a cube.

Look at the nets below. Write which of these nets will form cubes. You can check by tracing each one, cutting it out, and folding it.

1. 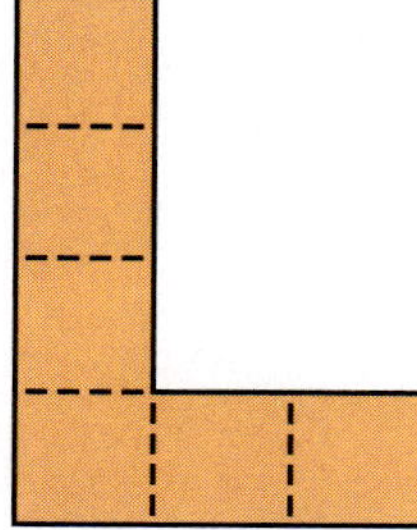

2. 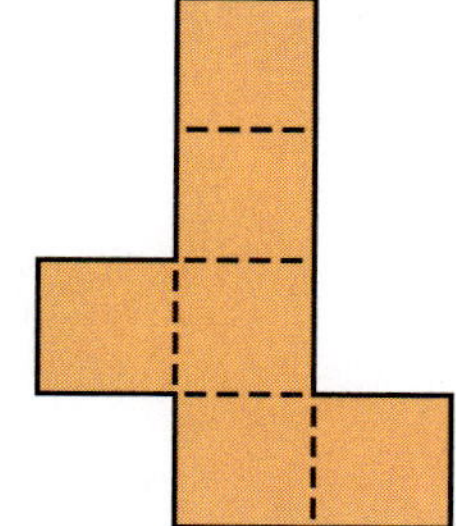

3. 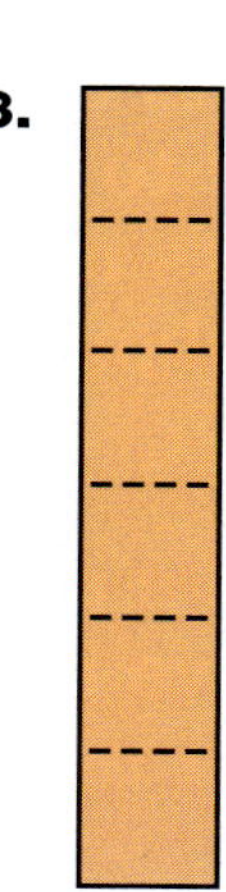

4. 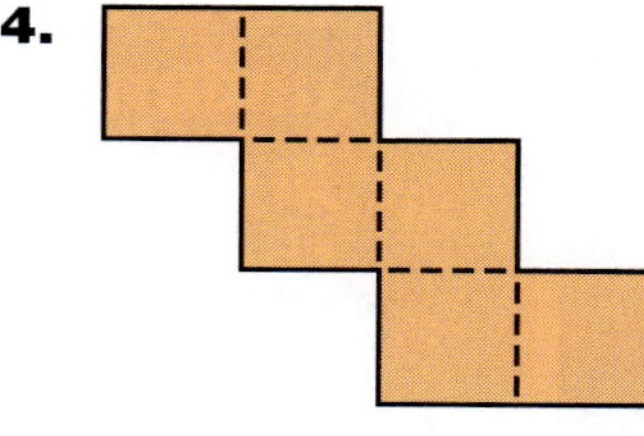

Explain Your Thinking

Draw what a net for this rectangular prism would look like.
How did you decide on the shapes of the faces?

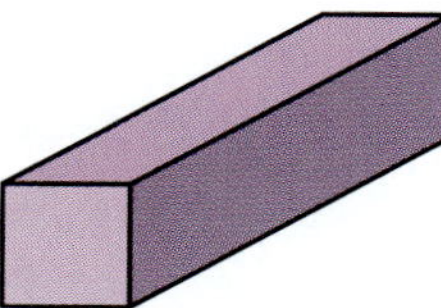

Division Concepts

Why Learn About Division Concepts?

Division concepts can help you understand how to form equal groups of objects or how to find the number of objects in each equal group.

When you share a pizza, for example, and give each person an equal number of slices, you're using division.

There are two people in each car of this roller coaster. The person in charge of the ride uses division to figure out how many cars will be needed to get everyone waiting in line on the roller coaster.

Reading Mathematics

Reviewing Vocabulary

Understanding math language helps you become a successful problem solver. Here are some math vocabulary words you should know.

equal groups	groups that have the same number of objects
divide	to separate objects into equal groups
division	an operation that divides objects into equal groups
division sentence	a sentence that shows how numbers are related in division

Reading Words and Symbols

When you read mathematics, sometimes you read only words, sometimes you read words and symbols, and sometimes you read only symbols.

Here are different ways to describe this array.

- ► Ten counters are divided into two groups of five.
- ► Ten divided by two equals five.
- ► $10 \div 2 = 5$

Try These

1. Does each sentence describe division? Write *yes* or *no*.
   a. Dan gave 15 apples to 5 friends. Each friend got 3 apples.
   b. Six students are in two cars. Four students are in one car. The other two students are in the other car.
   c. Andrea has 10 pictures in 2 picture frames. There are 5 pictures in each frame.

2. Copy and complete the table for each array.

a.

b. 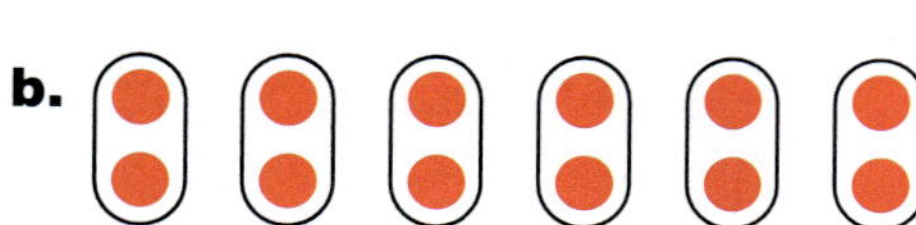

Number in All	Number in Each Group	Number of Equal Groups

3. Choose the missing factor to complete each multiplication sentence.

a. $5 \times ■ = 20$ b. $■ \times 6 = 12$

c. $3 \times ■ = 30$ d. $■ \times 2 = 14$

Missing Factors

4 10 7 2

Upcoming Vocabulary

Write About It **Here are some other vocabulary words** you will learn in this chapter. Watch for these words. Write their definitions in your journal.

dividend
divisor
quotient
unit cost

Modeling Division

You will learn two ways to think about division.

Review Vocabulary
divide
division

Learn About It

You can use counters to show two ways to think about dividing.

Materials

30 counters

You can **divide** to find how many to put into each group. Suppose you have 18 counters and you want to make 6 equal groups.

Draw 6 circles on a sheet of paper. Divide 18 counters equally among them.

- How many counters are in each group?

This **division** sentence shows how to find how many are in each equal group.

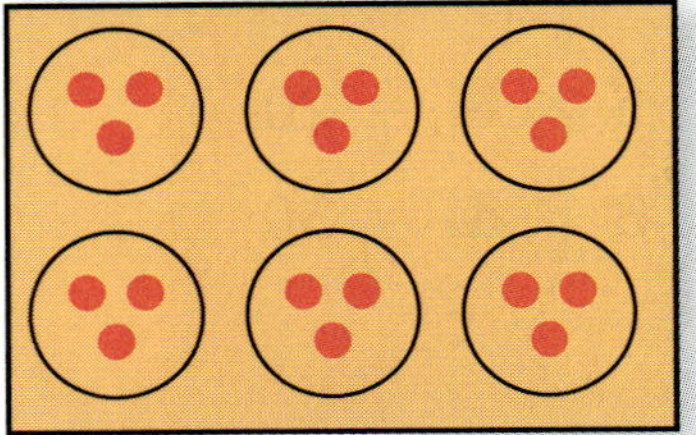

18	÷	6	=	3
↑		↑		↑
number of counters		number of groups		number in each group

You can also **divide** to find the number of equal groups. Suppose you have 18 counters and you want to put them into equal groups, with 6 counters in each group.

Put 18 counters into groups of 6.

- How many groups of 6 are there?

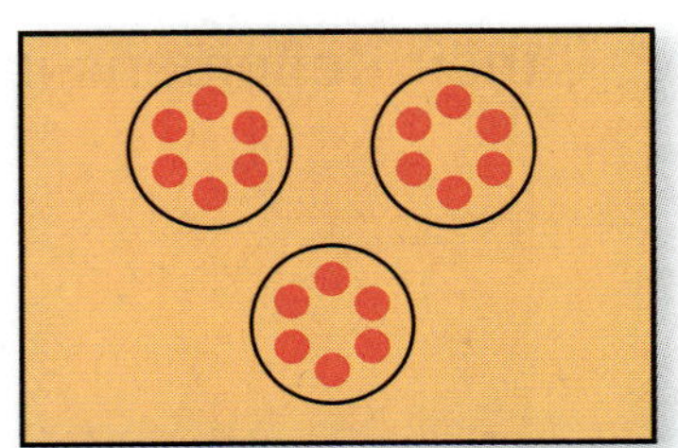

This **division** sentence shows how to find the the number of equal groups.

18	÷	6	=	3
↑		↑		↑
number of counters		number in each group		number of groups

Try It Out

Use counters to find the number in each equal group. Then complete each division sentence.

	Number of Counters	Number of Equal Groups	Number in Each Group	Division Sentence
1.	6	2		$6 \div 2 = ■$
2.	18	3		$18 \div 3 = ■$
3.	16	4		$16 \div 4 = ■$

Use counters to find the number of equal groups. Then complete each division sentence.

	Number of Counters	Number of Equal Groups	Number in Each Group	Division Sentence
4.	9		3	$9 \div 3 = ■$
5.	14		2	$14 \div 2 = ■$
6.	30		6	$30 \div 6 = ■$

Write a division sentence to describe each picture.

7. **8.**

9. **10.**

Write about it! Talk about it!

Use what you have learned to answer these questions.

11. Describe two ways to divide 8 objects into equal groups.

12. Bill is dividing 15 counters into equal groups. He puts more than one counter in each group. What is the greatest number of groups Bill can make? How many counters would be in each group?

LESSON 2

Relate Multiplication and Division

You will learn how multiplication and division are related.

New Vocabulary
dividend
divisor
quotient

Learn About It

The 12 animal pictures shown on the right form an array.

You can use arrays to help you understand how multiplication and division are related.

Multiply to find the number of pictures in all.

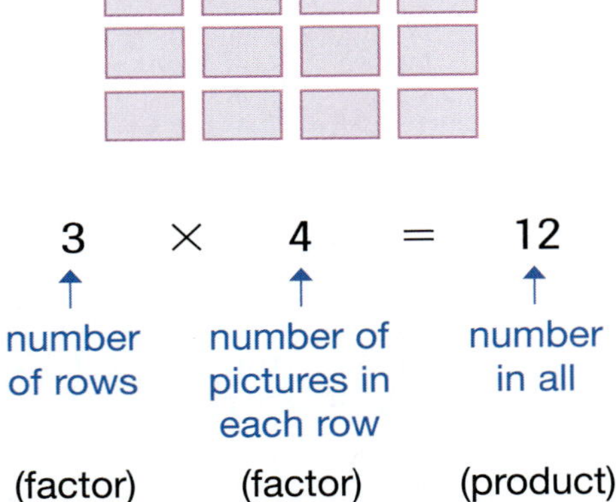

$3 \times 4 = 12$

3	×	4	=	12
↑ number of rows		↑ number of pictures in each row		↑ number in all
(factor)		(factor)		(product)

Divide to find the number of pictures in each row.

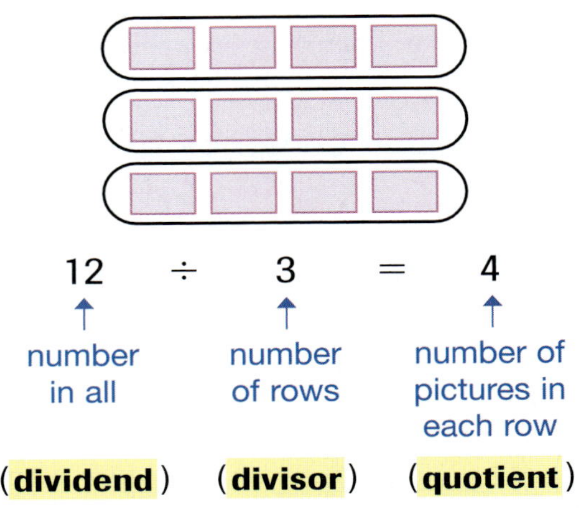

$12 \div 3 = 4$

12	÷	3	=	4
↑ number in all		↑ number of rows		↑ number of pictures in each row
(**dividend**)		(**divisor**)		(**quotient**)

Look at these arrays of 16 counters.

● ● ● ● ● ● ● ●
● ● ● ● ● ● ● ● } 2 rows, 8 in each row

$2 \times 8 = 16$

2	×	8	=	16
↑ factor		↑ factor		↑ product

● ● ● ● ● ● ● ●
● ● ● ● ● ● ● ● } 16 in all, 2 rows of 8

$16 \div 2 = 8$

16	÷	2	=	8
↑ dividend		↑ divisor		↑ quotient

Explain Your Thinking

► Look at each pair of number sentences above. Why are the product and the dividend the same in each pair?

Guided Practice

Use the array to complete each number sentence.

1\. 

$2 \times 7 = \blacksquare$

$14 \div 2 = \blacksquare$

> **Ask Yourself**
> - How many rows are there?
> - How many are in each row?
> - How many are there in all?

2\. 

$4 \times \blacksquare = 20$

$20 \div \blacksquare = 5$

3\. 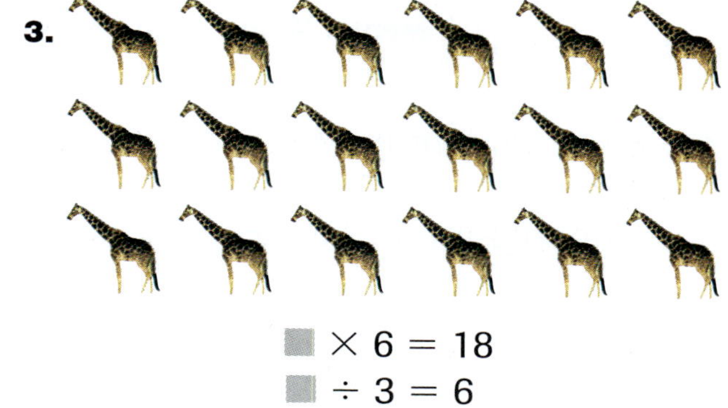

$\blacksquare \times 6 = 18$

$\blacksquare \div 3 = 6$

Independent Practice

Write a multiplication sentence and a division sentence for each array.

4\. 

5\. 

6\. 

7\. 

Draw an array for each pair of number sentences.

8\. $2 \times 6 = 12$
$12 \div 2 = 6$

9\. $3 \times 5 = 15$
$15 \div 3 = 5$

10\. $4 \times 6 = 24$
$24 \div 4 = 6$

11\. $5 \times 5 = 25$
$25 \div 5 = 5$

Draw an array for each multiplication sentence. Then write two related division sentences.

12. $3 \times 2 = 6$ **13.** $4 \times 3 = 12$ **14.** $1 \times 7 = 7$ **15.** $2 \times 7 = 14$

16. $2 \times 10 = 20$ **17.** $3 \times 9 = 27$ **18.** $3 \times 8 = 24$ **19.** $4 \times 9 = 36$

Problem Solving • Reasoning

Use the pictograph to solve Problems 20–24. Choose a method.

Computation Methods

- Mental Math
- Estimation
- Paper and Pencil

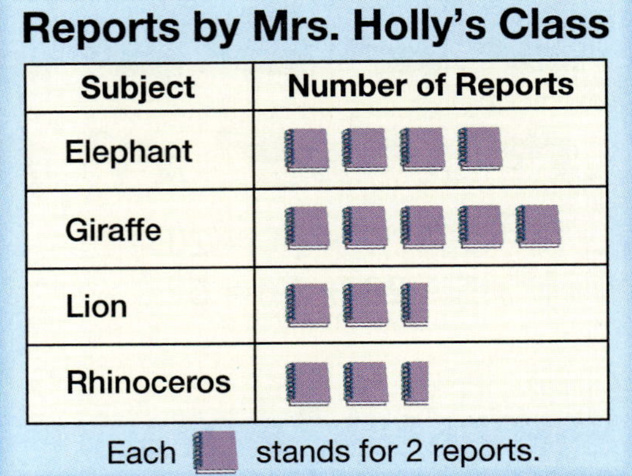

20. Each student in Mrs. Holly's class wrote one report. How many students are in Mrs. Holly's class?

21. **Analyze** Three students shared their reports. Jay talked for 18 minutes, Cara talked for 23 minutes, and Lauren talked for 21 minutes. About how many minutes in all did they talk?

22. How many more giraffe reports were written than elephant reports?

23. Rick wants to display the lion reports in 3 equal rows. Draw an array to show if it is possible for him to display the reports this way.

24. **Write Your Own** Use the information in the pictograph to write a division problem. Then give your problem to a classmate to solve.

Mixed Review • Test Prep

Look at each pair of times. How much time has elapsed? *(pages 78–79)*

25. Start: 4:23 P.M.
End: 8:43 P.M.

26. Start: 6:05 A.M.
End: 6:25 A.M.

27. Start: 10:25 A.M.
End: 11:29 A.M.

Choose the letter of the correct answer. *(pages 4–5)*

28 $900 + 70 + 6$

A 9,076 **C** 976
B 9,706 **D** 796

29 $850 - 50$

F 800 **H** 580
G 850 **J** 805

Extra Practice See Set A on page 382.

Number Sense

Dividing a Different Way

There are different ways to find the quotient when you divide. One way is to use repeated subtraction.

You can skip count backward on a number line to show repeated subtraction.

Find 30 ÷ 5.

- Start at 30.
- Count back by 5s until you reach 0.
- Count the number of times you subtracted.

The number of times you subtracted 5 is the quotient. You subtracted 5 six times.

So 30 ÷ 5 = 6.

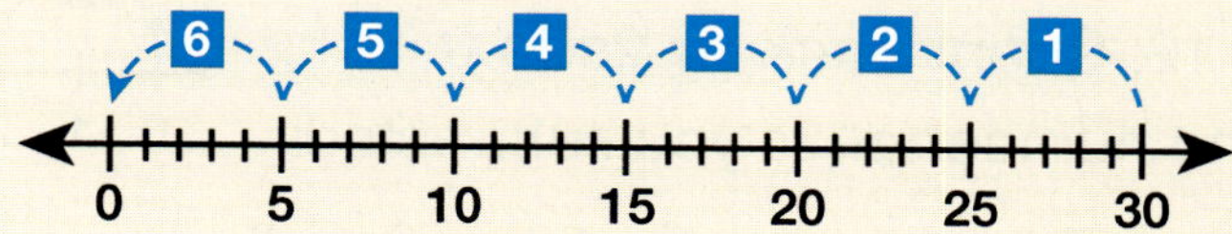

Use the number line to find each quotient.

1. 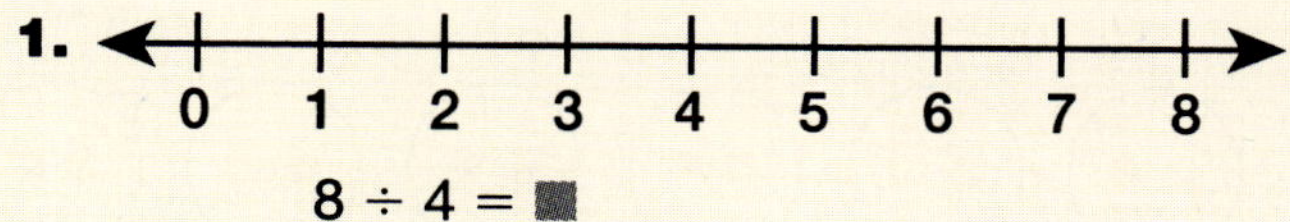

8 ÷ 4 = ■

2. 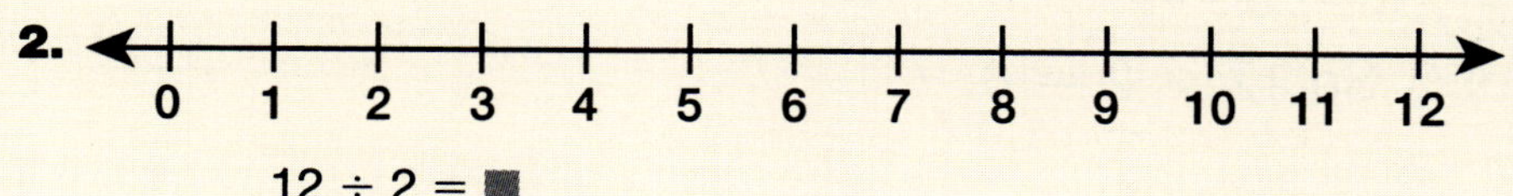

12 ÷ 2 = ■

3. 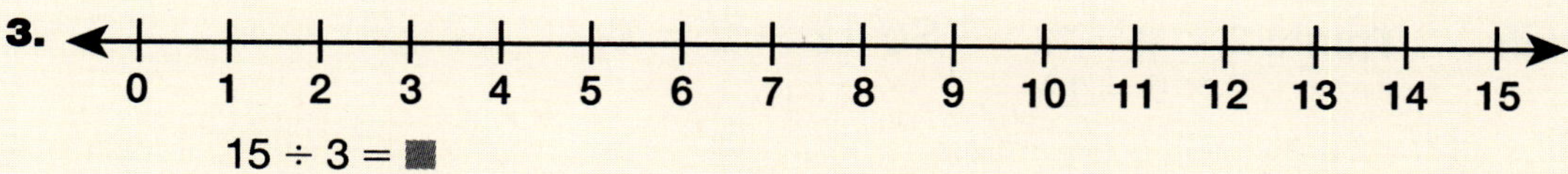

15 ÷ 3 = ■

Explain Your Thinking

► How is using a number line to divide similar to using a number line to multiply? How is it different?

Lesson 3

Divide by 2

You will learn different ways to divide by 2.

Learn About It

There are 12 students who want to ride in go-carts. If 2 students can ride in each go-cart, how many go-carts will be needed?

12	÷	2	=	6
↑ dividend		↑ divisor		↑ quotient

Different Ways to Divide

You can use a number line to model division as repeated subtraction.

- Start at 12. Count back by 2s to 0.
- Count the number of 2s you subtracted.

6 5 4 3 2 1

0 1 2 3 4 5 6 7 8 9 10 11 12

You subtracted 2 six times. So $12 \div 2 = 6$.

You can use counters to model division as repeated subtraction.

- Use 12 counters.
- Put 2 counters in each group.
- Count the number of equal groups.

There are 6 groups of 2. So $12 \div 2 = 6$.

You can use a related multiplication fact.

$12 \div 2 = ■$ **Think:** $2 \times ■ = 12$ So $12 \div 2 = 6$.
$2 \times 6 = 12$

Solution: Six go-carts will be needed.

Explain Your Thinking

► How does the number line above show that each go-cart holds 2 students?

Guided Practice

Use the picture to help you find each quotient.

1. 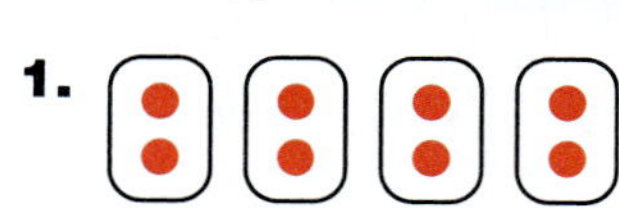

$8 \div 2$

2. 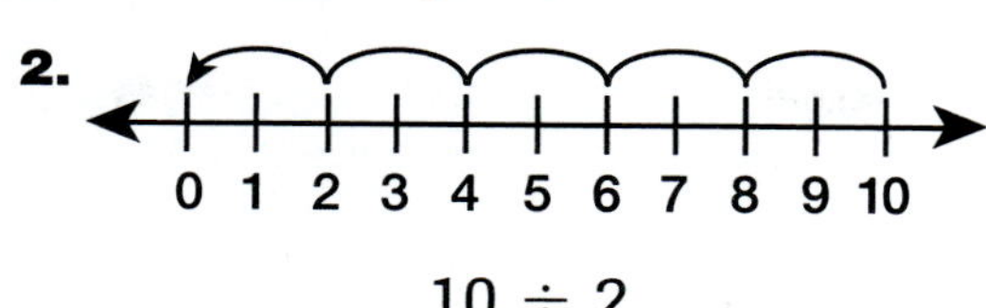

$10 \div 2$

> **Ask Yourself**
> - Are there equal groups?
> - What multiplication fact can help me?

Independent Practice

Use the multiplication fact to help you find each quotient.

3. $1 \times 2 = 2$
$2 \div 2 = ■$

4. $6 \times 2 = 12$
$12 \div 2 = ■$

5. $5 \times 2 = 10$
$10 \div 2 = ■$

6. $2 \times 2 = 4$
$4 \div 2 = ■$

7. $7 \times 2 = 14$
$14 \div 2 = ■$

8. $3 \times 2 = 6$
$6 \div 2 = ■$

9. $9 \times 2 = 18$
$18 \div 2 = ■$

10. $8 \times 2 = 16$
$16 \div 2 = ■$

Divide.

11. $8 \div 2$ **12.** $2 \div 2$ **13.** $12 \div 2$ **14.** $4 \div 2$ **15.** $10 \div 2$

16. $14 \div 2$ **17.** $10 \div 2$ **18.** $16 \div 2$ **19.** $6 \div 2$ **20.** $18 \div 2$

Problem Solving • Reasoning

Use Data **Use the sign for Problems 21 and 22.**

21. **Measurement** Matt's brother is 4 feet 4 inches tall. Can he ride the roller coaster? Explain.

22. There are 7 friends in line for the roller coaster. They have 14 tickets to share. Can all of the friends take a ride on the roller coaster?

23. **Logical Thinking** A log-flume car can fit 4 people. Beth sits in front. Ken sits behind Haley and in front of Shawn. In what order do the friends sit?

Mixed Review • Test Prep

Solve. *(pages 108–109)*

24. $142 - 19$ **25.** $648 + 46$ **26.** $381 + 16$ **27.** $1,172 - 960$

28 Which has a product of 27? *(pages 258–259, 268–271)*

A 6×6 **B** 7×4 **C** 5×9 **D** 9×3

Extra Practice See Set B on page 382.

LESSON 4

Divide by 5

You will learn different ways to divide by 5.

Learn About It

There are 20 students who want to play basketball. If 5 players are on a team, how many teams can there be?

Divide. $\mathbf{20 \div 5 = n}$

Different Ways to Divide

You can use a number line.

- Start at 20. Count back by 5s to 0.
- Count the number of 5s you subtracted.

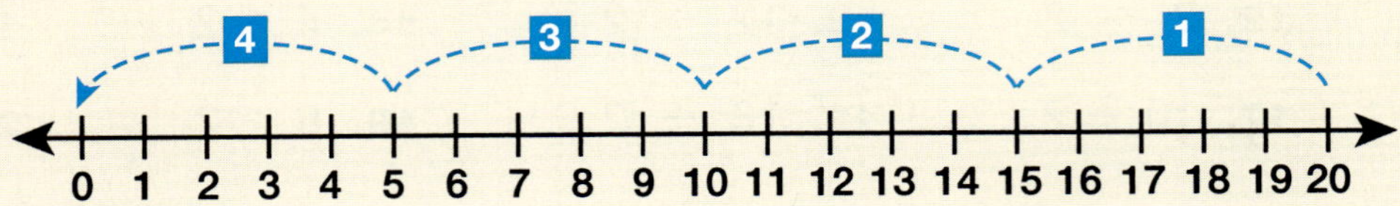

You subtracted 5 four times. So $20 \div 5 = 4$.

You can use counters.

- Use 20 counters.
- Put 5 counters in each group.
- Count the number of equal groups.

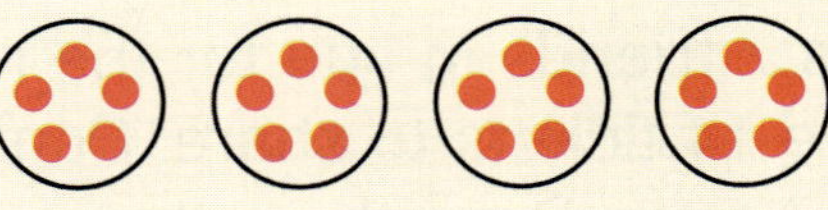

There are 4 groups of 5. So $20 \div 5 = 4$.

You can use a related multiplication fact.

$20 \div 5 = n$ **Think:** $5 \times n = 20$
$5 \times 4 = 20$
So $20 \div 5 = 4$.

Solution: There can be 4 teams.

Explain Your Thinking

- ► Can you divide 27 into equal groups of 5? Explain why or why not.
- ► How does knowing that $5 \times 4 = 20$ help you find $20 \div 5$?

Guided Practice

Use the array to help you find the quotient.

1. 

$10 \div 5 = n$

2. 

$15 \div 5 = n$

> **Ask Yourself**
> - Can I make equal groups?
> - What multiplication fact can help me?

Independent Practice

Find the missing factor. Then find the quotient.

3. $5 \times n = 5$
$5 \div 5 = n$

4. $5 \times n = 35$
$35 \div 5 = n$

5. $5 \times n = 45$
$45 \div 5 = n$

6. $5 \times n = 40$
$40 \div 5 = n$

Divide.

7. $10 \div 5$ **8.** $4 \div 2$ **9.** $5 \div 5$ **10.** $15 \div 5$ **11.** $30 \div 5$

12. $25 \div 5$ **13.** $10 \div 2$ **14.** $40 \div 5$ **15.** $20 \div 5$ **16.** $8 \div 2$

17. $14 \div 2$ **18.** $35 \div 5$ **19.** $18 \div 2$ **20.** $16 \div 2$ **21.** $45 \div 5$

Problem Solving • Reasoning

22. There are 45 students signed up to play basketball. How many teams of 5 can there be?

23. **Analyze** Students had 5 days to sign up for basketball camp. On the first day, 12 students signed up. Each day after that, 5 students signed up. How many students signed up altogether?

24. Don spent 45 minutes practicing 5 basketball drills. He spent an equal amount of time on each drill. How long did he practice the first drill?

Solve for *n*.

A $35 - 5 = n$

B $30 + n = 35$

C $n \times 7 = 35$

D $5 \times n = 30$

E $35 \div 5 = n$

Mixed Review • Test Prep

Find the missing measure. *(pages 164–166)*

25. 3 feet = ____ inches **26.** 24 inches = ____ feet **27.** 6 feet = ____ yards

28 Find the sum of \$5.64 + \$3.41. *(pages 108–109)*

A \$7.15 **B** \$8.05 **C** \$9.05 **D** \$10.05

Extra Practice See Set C on page 383.

LESSON 5

Problem-Solving Skill: Choose the Operation

You will learn how to decide which operation to use to solve a problem.

Sometimes you need to decide whether to add, subtract, multiply, or divide to solve a problem.

Sometimes you add to find the total.

For a school picnic, 185 ham sandwiches and 160 tuna sandwiches were made. How many sandwiches were made?

$$\begin{array}{r} 185 \\ +\ 160 \\ \hline 345 \end{array}$$

185 ← ham sandwiches
+ 160 ← tuna sandwiches
345 ← total number of sandwiches

Sometimes you multiply to find the total.

There were 3 tomato slices in each sandwich. How many slices were there in 10 sandwiches?

3 ← tomato slices in 1 sandwich
× 10 ← sandwiches
30 ← number of slices in 10 sandwiches

You subtract to find the difference.

Suppose 546 slices of white bread and 294 slices of wheat bread were used. How many more slices of white bread than wheat bread were used?

546 ← slices of white bread
− 294 ← slices of wheat bread
252 ← how many more slices of white bread used

You divide to find equal groups.

Suppose 30 cheese sandwiches were made. If 5 sandwiches were put in each bag, how many bags were used?

$30 \div 5 = 6$ ← number of bags

30 ↑ total number of sandwiches; 5 ↑ sandwiches in each bag

Look Back What is another operation you could use to find the number of tomato slices in 10 sandwiches?

Not in the mood for a sandwich? How about a 4-ton burrito? This 4,290-foot long burrito is the largest burrito in the world. It was made on May 8, 1999 in Kennewick, Washington.

Guided Practice

Tell which operation you would use. Then solve.

1. There are 40 people eating on blankets and 21 people eating at tables. How many more people are eating on blankets than at tables?

   Think: Do you need to compare numbers or find the total?

2. Six bags of oranges have been brought to the picnic. There are 9 oranges in each bag. How many oranges have been brought in all?

   Think: Are you combining equal groups or unequal groups?

Choose a Strategy

Solve. Use these or other strategies.

Problem-Solving Strategies

- **Write a Number Sentence**
- **Guess and Check**
- **Work Backward**
- **Draw a Picture**

3. At the picnic, there were 10 more third-graders than second-graders. There were 5 fewer fourth-graders than third-graders. There were 40 fourth-graders. How many second-graders were at the picnic?

4. The third-grade students had bananas and oranges for dessert. The students ate 3 more bananas than oranges. Altogether they ate 25 pieces of fruit. How many bananas did they eat?

5. Two students can sit on each side of a square picnic table. If 2 square picnic tables are pushed together, how many students can sit at the tables?

6. Students made teams of 4 for the sack races. There were 20 students in the first race and 16 students in the second race. How many teams in all were in the two races?

7. Students finished eating lunch at 2:00 P.M. Then a softball game began 15 minutes later. The game ended at 3:45 P.M. How long was the game?

8. There are 2 pints in a quart. If a jug of lemonade holds 18 pints of lemonade, how many quarts does the jug hold?

Extra Practice See 1–4 on page 385.

Quick Check

Check Your Understanding of Lessons 1–5

Write two related division sentences.

1. $7 \times 3 = 21$ **2.** $9 \times 7 = 63$ **3.** $8 \times 6 = 48$ **4.** $6 \times 5 = 30$

Divide.

5. $4 \div 2$ **6.** $20 \div 2$ **7.** $2 \div 2$ **8.** $6 \div 2$ **9.** $14 \div 2$

10. $12 \div 2$ **11.** $10 \div 2$ **12.** $8 \div 2$ **13.** $18 \div 2$ **14.** $16 \div 2$

15. $10 \div 5$ **16.** $40 \div 5$ **17.** $25 \div 5$ **18.** $5 \div 5$ **19.** $35 \div 5$

20. $15 \div 5$ **21.** $20 \div 5$ **22.** $30 \div 5$ **23.** $50 \div 5$ **24.** $45 \div 5$

Solve.

25. Adela made 35 sandwiches for a picnic. She put the same number of sandwiches in each of 7 bags. How many sandwiches were in each bag? Are you finding equal groups or unequal groups? Explain.

How did you do?

If you had difficulty with any items in the Quick Check, you can use the following pages for review and extra practice.

Items	Review These Pages	Do These Extra Practice Items
1–4	pages 356–358	Set A, page 382
5-14	pages 360–361	Set B, page 382
15–24	pages 362–363	Set C, page 383
25	pages 364–365	1–4, page 385

Test Prep • Cumulative Review

Maintaining the Standards

Choose the letter of the correct answer. If a correct answer is not here, choose NH.

1 What number makes the number sentence true?

$2 \times ■ = 12$

A 0
B 5
C 6
D 24

2 What is the perimeter of this figure?

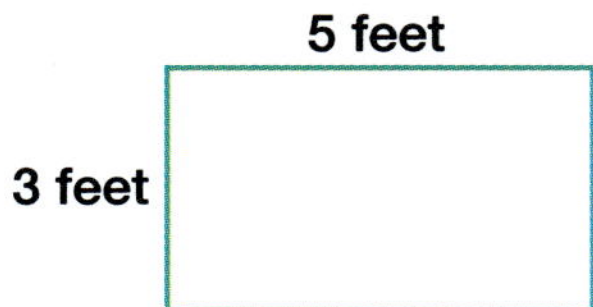

F 6 feet
G 10 feet
H 15 feet
J 16 feet

3 The chess club and the glee club are lined up in 5 equal rows for pictures. The chess club has 8 members, and the glee club has 7 members. How many students are in each row?

A 3
B 4
C 5
D NH

4 Theater tickets cost $10 each. How much will 4 tickets cost?

F $36
G $48
H $60
J NH

5 If $5 \times 9 = ■$, then which statement must be true?

A $5 \times ■ = 9$
B $9 \times ■ = 5$
C $■ \div 5 = 9$
D $■ \div 9 = 0$

6 What is the volume of this figure?

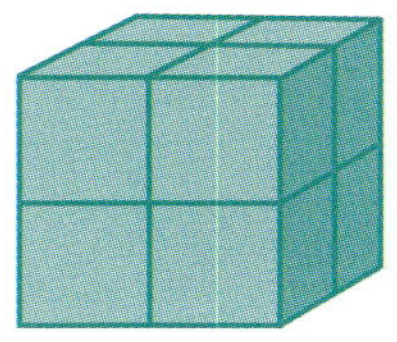

F 2 cubic units
G 4 cubic units
H 6 cubic units
J 8 cubic units

7 Bob has a total of 18 model cars. They are kept in 2 boxes. If the same number of cars are in each box, how many cars are in a box?

A 7
B 8
C 9
D 16

8 Al bought 2 packages of muffins. Each package contained 10 muffins. Al gave each of his 5 friends the same number of muffins. How many muffins did each friend receive?

Explain How did you find your answer?

Safe Site

Internet Test Prep
Visit **www.eduplace.com/kids/mhm** for more *Test Prep Practice.*

Division Rules

You will learn special rules for dividing when you use 0 and 1.

Learn About It

Counters can help you understand division involving 0 and 1.

Division Rules

When any number except 0 is divided by itself, the quotient is 1.

Put 5 counters into 5 groups.

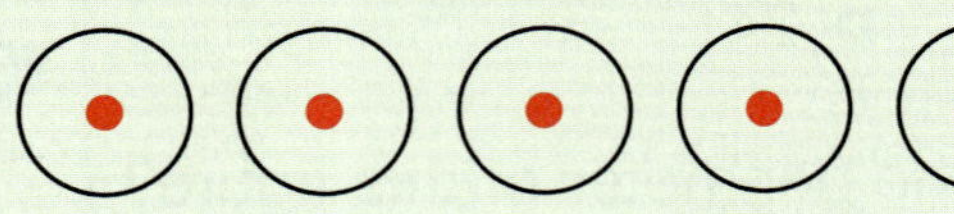

Think: 5 ÷ 5 = 1

There is 1 counter in each group.

When any number is divided by 1, the quotient is that number.

Put 5 counters into 1 group.

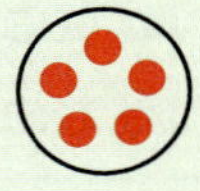

Think: 5 ÷ 1 = 5

There are 5 counters in the group.

When 0 is divided by any number except 0, the quotient is 0.

Put 0 counters into 5 groups.

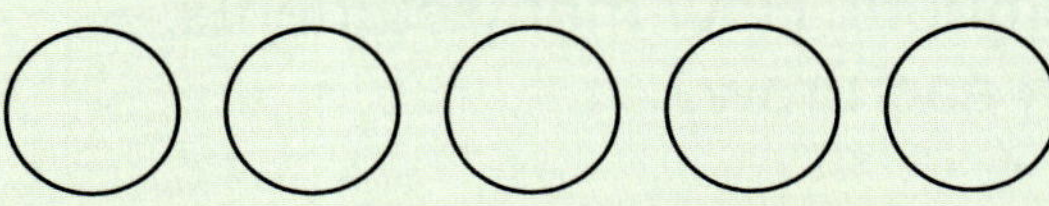

Think: 0 ÷ 5 = 0

There are 0 counters in each group.

You cannot divide a number by 0.

Try to put 5 counters into 0 groups.

It is not possible to put 5 counters into 0 groups.

Explain Your Thinking

- Which of the rules above could help you find 295 ÷ 295?
- Which of the rules above could help you find 486 ÷ 1?

Guided Practice

Find each quotient.

1. 2 ÷ 1　**2.** 1 ÷ 1　**3.** 0 ÷ 9　**4.** 4 ÷ 4

5. 6 ÷ 6　**6.** 0 ÷ 8　**7.** 5 ÷ 1　**8.** 7 ÷ 7

Ask Yourself

What is the rule for
- dividing by 1?
- dividing by 0?
- dividing a number by itself?

Independent Practice

Divide.

9. 2 ÷ 2　**10.** 0 ÷ 3　**11.** 3 ÷ 1　**12.** 5 ÷ 5　**13.** 9 ÷ 9

14. 0 ÷ 1　**15.** 6 ÷ 1　**16.** 8 ÷ 8　**17.** 7 ÷ 1　**18.** 4 ÷ 1

19. 0 ÷ 7　**20.** 3 ÷ 3　**21.** 9 ÷ 1　**22.** 0 ÷ 4　**23.** 8 ÷ 1

Algebra • Functions **Follow the rule to complete each table.**

Rule: Divide by 1

	Input	Output
24.	0	■
25.	1	■
26.	■	4
27.	7	■

Rule: Divide by 5

	Input	Output
28.	0	■
29.	■	1
30.	40	■
31.	■	7

Problem Solving • Reasoning

Write *true* or *false* for each sentence. Draw or write an example to support your answer.

32. You cannot divide 0 by 1.

33. When you divide by 1, the answer is always the same as the dividend.

34. You can never divide by 0.

Using Vocabulary

Write *always, never,* or *sometimes* for each sentence.

A An array ______ has the same number of rows and columns.

B The divisor is ______ zero.

C The quotient and the divisor ______ are the same number.

Mixed Review • Test Prep

Write each total amount. *(pages 56–57)*

35. 3 dimes, 2 nickels　**36.** 3 quarters, 1 dime　**37.** 2 quarters, 3 nickels, 4 pennies

38 Which set has only odd numbers? *(page 27)*

A 2, 3, 6, 10　**B** 3, 5, 9, 13　**C** 3, 6, 9, 11　**D** 4, 6, 11, 15

Extra Practice See Set D on page 383.

LESSON 7

Divide by 3

You will learn different ways to divide by 3.

Learn About It

A class is decorating 3 windows with paper flowers. There are 15 flowers. If the same number of flowers is put in each window, how many flowers will be in each window?

You can show 15 divided by 3 in two ways.

15 ÷ 3 = ■ or **3)15**

■ ← quotient
15 ← dividend
3 ← divisor

Different Ways to Divide

You can use counters.

- Use 15 counters.
- Put the counters in 3 groups.
- Count the number in each group.

There are 3 groups of 5.

15 ÷ 3 = 5 or 3)15 (quotient 5)

You can use a related multiplication fact.

15 ÷ 3 = ■

Think: 3 × ■ = 15
3 × 5 = 15

So 15 ÷ 3 = 5.

Solution: There will be 5 flowers in each window.

Explain Your Thinking

► Can you divide 19 into 3 equal groups? Explain why or why not.

Guided Practice

Find each quotient.

1. 3)9 **2.** 3)3 **3.** 3)27 **4.** 3)0

5. 6 ÷ 3 **6.** 12 ÷ 3 **7.** 24 ÷ 3 **8.** 3)15

Ask Yourself

- What multiplication fact can help me?

Independent Practice

Divide.

9. $3\overline{)6}$ **10.** $3\overline{)9}$ **11.** $3\overline{)0}$ **12.** $3\overline{)12}$ **13.** $3\overline{)18}$

14. $3\overline{)15}$ **15.** $3\overline{)24}$ **16.** $3\overline{)3}$ **17.** $3\overline{)21}$ **18.** $3\overline{)27}$

19. $0 \div 3$ **20.** $9 \div 3$ **21.** $15 \div 3$ **22.** $3 \div 3$ **23.** $18 \div 3$

24. $27 \div 3$ **25.** $0 \div 3$ **26.** $24 \div 3$ **27.** $21 \div 3$ **28.** $6 \div 3$

Algebra • Expressions **Compare. Write >, <, or = for each ●.**

29. $15 \div 3$ ● $15 + 3$ **30.** $5 \div 5$ ● $3 - 3$ **31.** 4×2 ● $16 \div 2$

32. $45 \div 5$ ● 7×3 **33.** $21 - 3$ ● $21 \div 3$ **34.** $18 \div 2$ ● 2×10

Problem Solving • Reasoning

35. A class made 27 paper flowers. The flowers are either yellow, red, or blue. If there are the same number of flowers of each color, how many red flowers are there?

36. **Money** Sam, Tim, and Gina bought supplies to make paper flowers. The paper cost $6, and the glue cost $3. If the children shared the cost equally, how much did each child pay for the supplies?

37. **Write About It** A class made 27 red flowers, 21 blue flowers, and 24 pink flowers. They want to put the flowers in 3 vases so that each vase has the same number of flowers of each color. How can they do it?

Math Is Everywhere!

SOCIAL STUDIES

Leis are necklaces made of flowers. Visitors to Hawaii are often given leis to welcome them.

If 12 leis are divided equally among 3 visitors, how many leis does each visitor get?

Mixed Review • Test Prep

Solve. *(pages 102–103, 278–279)*

38. $(2 \times 3) \times 4$ **39.** $5 \times (4 \times 2)$ **40.** $5 + (7 + 3)$ **41.** $(3 + 6) \times 2$

42 Which is equal to 1 pound? *(pages 172–174)*

A 8 ounces **C** 16 ounces
B 14 ounces **D** 32 ounces

Extra Practice See Set E on page 384.

Problem-Solving Strategy: Draw a Picture

You will learn how to solve a problem by drawing a picture.

Sometimes drawing a picture makes it easier to solve a problem.

Problem Linda's mom is making birdhouses. She cuts a 24-inch board into 3 equal pieces. Then she cuts each of those pieces in half. How many small pieces of wood are there? How long is each piece?

What are the questions?

How many small pieces of wood are there? How long is each piece?

What do you know?

- The board is 24 inches long.
- Linda's mom cuts the board into 3 equal pieces.
- Then she cuts each of those pieces in half.

How can you find the answer?

You can draw a picture to show the information and use the picture to find the answer.

Draw a picture of the 24-inch board. Divide it into 3 equal parts.

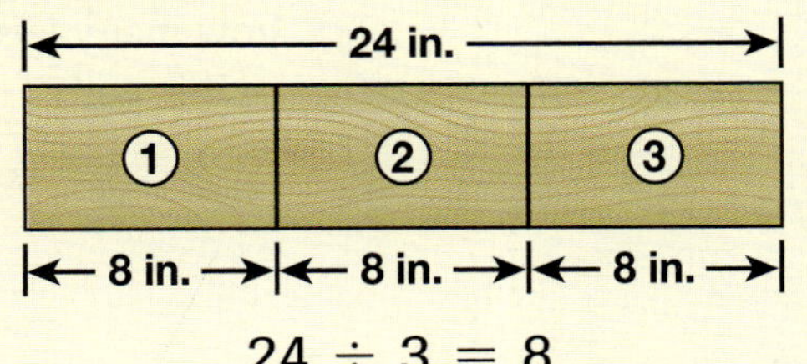

$24 \div 3 = 8$

Now divide each 8-inch piece in half.

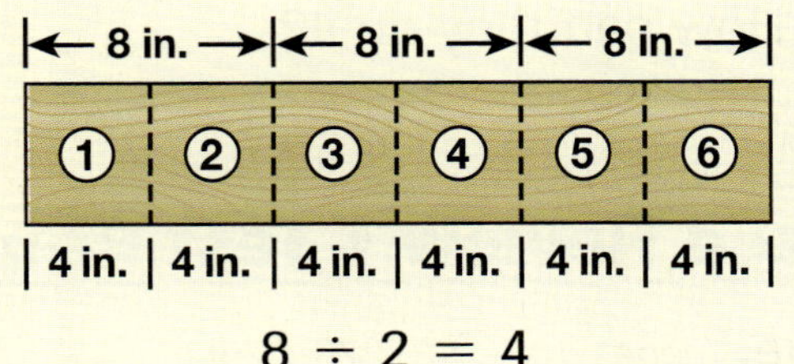

$8 \div 2 = 4$

There are 6 small pieces of wood. Each piece is 4 inches long.

Look Back

Look back at the problem.

How does drawing a picture help you answer each question?

Remember:
- Understand
- Plan
- Solve
- Look Back

Guided Practice

Solve each problem, using the Draw a Picture strategy.

1. Chris paints birdhouses red, yellow, or green. One day he painted 12 houses. He painted every third house green. How many houses did Chris paint green that day?

How can you show which houses are painted green?

2. Wendy used a 36-inch piece of yarn to make a bracelet. First she cut the yarn in half. Then she cut each half into 3 equal pieces. How many pieces did Wendy have then?

How can you show each half cut into 3 equal pieces?

Choose a Strategy

Solve. Use these or other strategies.

Problem-Solving Strategies

- **Find a Pattern**
- **Write a Number Sentence**
- **Work Backward**
- **Draw a Picture**

3. Ana spent 20 minutes making paper stars for a collage. Then she spent 15 minutes gluing the stars in place. If Ana finished the collage at 2:15 P.M., what time did she start?

4. Li has 19 red beads and 10 blue beads. She wants to make a bracelet that has no beads of the same color next to each other when worn. How many beads can Li use?

5. Ruth spent $12 on 3 jars of glitter. Each jar cost the same amount. How much would Ruth have paid if she had only bought 2 jars?

6. Chip made knots in a rope to divide it into 15 sections. He also made knots at each end of the rope. How many knots in all did Chip make?

7. Alan is making a block pattern. What are the next 3 figures likely to be?

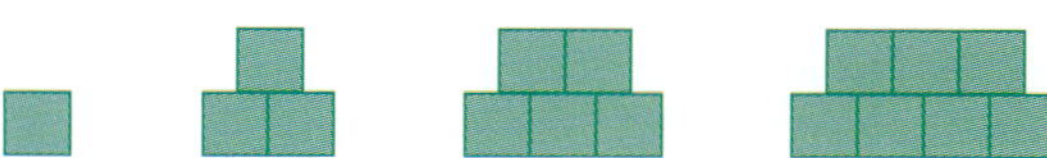

8. Erin is using a piece of ribbon to make bows. Each bow uses 6 inches of ribbon. After making 5 bows, Erin has 5 inches of ribbon left. How long was the piece of ribbon Erin started with?

Extra Practice See 5–8 on page 385.

Divide by 4

You will learn different ways to divide by 4.

Learn About It

Each member of a juggling team juggles 4 balls that glow in the dark. If the audience sees 24 balls, how many jugglers are there?

Divide. $24 \div 4 = ■$ or $4\overline{)24}$ (quotient ■)

Different Ways to Divide

You can use a number line.

- Start at 24. Count back by 4s to 0.
- Count the number of 4s you subtracted.

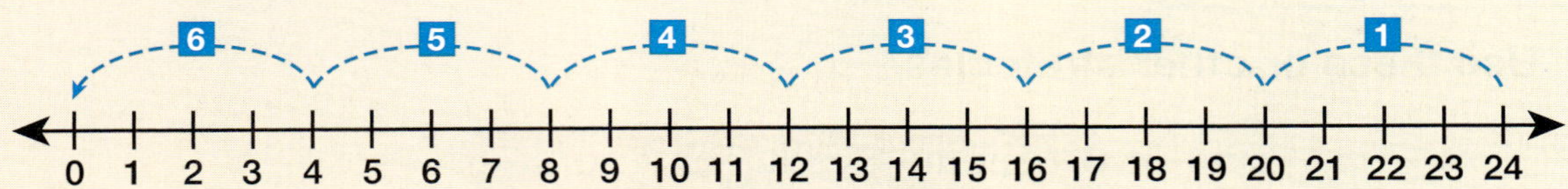

You subtracted 4 six times. So $24 \div 4 = 6$.

You can use counters.

- Use 24 counters. Put 4 in each group.
- Count the number of equal groups.

There are 6 groups of 4. So $24 \div 4 = 6$.

You can use a related multiplication fact.

$24 \div 4 = ■$ **Think:** $4 \times ■ = 24$
$4 \times 6 = 24$ So $24 \div 4 = 6$.

Solution: There are 6 jugglers.

Explain Your Thinking

► How are the dividends, divisors, and quotients related in the problems $16 \div 2 = 8$ and $32 \div 4 = 8$?

Guided Practice

Divide.

1. $4\overline{)36}$ **2.** $4\overline{)28}$ **3.** $4\overline{)16}$ **4.** $4\overline{)20}$

5. $8 \div 4$ **6.** $0 \div 4$ **7.** $12 \div 4$ **8.** $32 \div 4$

> **Ask Yourself**
> - What multiplication fact can help me?
> - Can I make equal groups?

Independent Practice

Find the quotient.

9. $4\overline{)12}$ **10.** $4\overline{)0}$ **11.** $4\overline{)20}$ **12.** $4\overline{)8}$ **13.** $4\overline{)32}$

14. $4\overline{)28}$ **15.** $4\overline{)24}$ **16.** $4\overline{)4}$ **17.** $4\overline{)16}$ **18.** $4\overline{)36}$

19. $4 \div 4$ **20.** $12 \div 4$ **21.** $24 \div 4$ **22.** $8 \div 4$ **23.** $16 \div 4$

24. $20 \div 4$ **25.** $0 \div 4$ **26.** $36 \div 4$ **27.** $28 \div 4$ **28.** $32 \div 4$

Problem Solving • Reasoning

Use Data **Use the graph for Problems 29–31.**

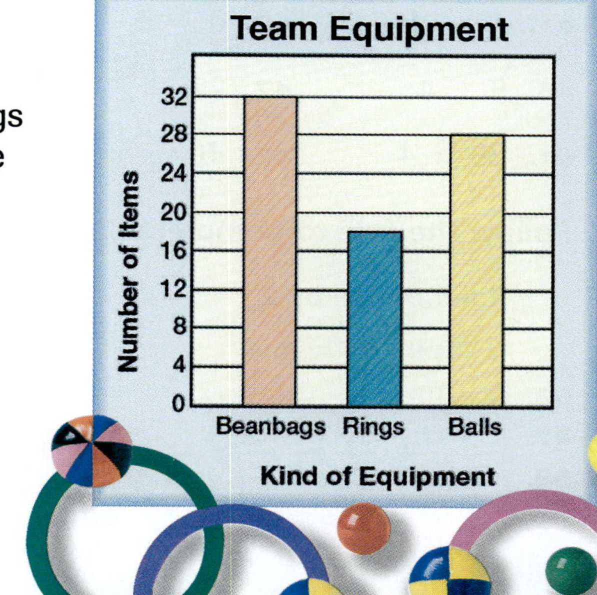

29. Each juggler on the team juggles 4 beanbags at once. How many jugglers can work at the same time?

30. **Analyze** The balls are red, yellow, pink, or green. If there are the same number of each color, how many red balls are there?

31. **Write About It** During a juggling act with 4 jugglers, one juggler used 6 rings. Were the rings shared equally among the 4 jugglers? Explain why or why not.

Mixed Review • Test Prep

Write the value of each underlined digit. *(pages 4–5, 18–19, 32–33)*

32. 4,$\underline{8}$32 **33.** 6$\underline{7}$2 **34.** $\underline{9}$,142 **35.** 1$\underline{4}$,389 **36.** 2$\underline{4}$3,740

37 Which unit would you use to measure the water in a bathtub? *(pages 168–171, 172–174)*

A ounce **C** cup
B pound **D** gallon

Extra Practice See Set F on page 384.

Division Facts Practice

Have you memorized your facts? Find each quotient as quickly as you can.

1. $3\overline{)21}$	**2.** $1\overline{)3}$	**3.** $4\overline{)8}$	**4.** $2\overline{)14}$	**5.** $5\overline{)5}$	**6.** $2\overline{)2}$
7. $5\overline{)25}$	**8.** $2\overline{)16}$	**9.** $3\overline{)6}$	**10.** $5\overline{)35}$	**11.** $3\overline{)27}$	**12.** $1\overline{)6}$
13. $4\overline{)16}$	**14.** $3\overline{)15}$	**15.** $2\overline{)6}$	**16.** $5\overline{)10}$	**17.** $4\overline{)24}$	**18.** $3\overline{)9}$
19. $8\overline{)8}$	**20.** $3\overline{)18}$	**21.** $2\overline{)4}$	**22.** $1\overline{)1}$	**23.** $5\overline{)30}$	**24.** $4\overline{)36}$
25. $4\overline{)4}$	**26.** $5\overline{)30}$	**27.** $3\overline{)12}$	**28.** $2\overline{)8}$	**29.** $4\overline{)28}$	**30.** $5\overline{)0}$

31. $12 \div 4$	**32.** $10 \div 2$	**33.** $40 \div 5$	**34.** $7 \div 1$	**35.** $3 \div 3$
36. $5 \div 1$	**37.** $32 \div 4$	**38.** $24 \div 3$	**39.** $20 \div 5$	**40.** $18 \div 2$
41. $45 \div 5$	**42.** $0 \div 3$	**43.** $9 \div 1$	**44.** $1 \div 1$	**45.** $20 \div 4$
46. $8 \div 4$	**47.** $21 \div 7$	**48.** $35 \div 5$	**49.** $18 \div 2$	**50.** $12 \div 2$
51. $28 \div 4$	**52.** $40 \div 5$	**53.** $3 \div 3$	**54.** $0 \div 5$	**55.** $2 \div 1$

Follow the rule to complete each table.

Rule: Divide by 2

	Input	Output
56.	10	■
57.	■	9
58.	0	■
59.	■	8

Rule: Divide by 4

	Input	Output
60.	16	■
61.	36	■
62.	■	7
63.	12	■

Rule: Divide by 5

	Input	Output
64.	45	■
65.	■	7
66.	20	■
67.	■	3

Find the rule. Then complete each table.

68. Rule: ________

	Input	Output
	12	4
69.	6	■
70.	18	■
71.	■	7

72. Rule: ________

	Input	Output
	7	35
73.	2	■
74.	■	30
75.	■	0

76. Rule: ________

	Input	Output
	6	24
77.	■	4
78.	8	■
79.	■	16

Practice Game

Make a Match

Practice division by playing this game with a partner. Try to be the first player to use all your cards!

What You'll Need

- *24 division fact cards like the ones shown (Teaching Tool 8)*

Players
small group

8 ÷ 2	12 ÷ 3	16 ÷ 4	20 ÷ 5
10 ÷ 2	15 ÷ 3	20 ÷ 4	25 ÷ 5
12 ÷ 2	18 ÷ 3	24 ÷ 4	30 ÷ 5
14 ÷ 2	21 ÷ 3	28 ÷ 4	35 ÷ 5
16 ÷ 2	24 ÷ 3	32 ÷ 4	40 ÷ 5
18 ÷ 2	27 ÷ 3	36 ÷ 4	45 ÷ 5

Here's What to Do

1. A player deals 5 fact cards to each player and places the remaining cards facedown in a pile. The top card is turned over and placed faceup next to the pile.
2. The first player chooses a card from his or her hand to put on the faceup pile. The card must have the same quotient, divisor, or dividend as the card that is faceup. If no match can be made, the player takes cards from the facedown pile until there's a match.
3. Players take turns repeating Step 2. If the facedown pile runs out, the cards below the top faceup card are shuffled to make a new facedown pile. The first player without cards wins!

Share Your Thinking Can you get the same quotient with different division facts? Give an example to explain your thinking.

LESSON 10

Problem-Solving Application: Find Unit Cost

You will learn how to find the cost of a single item.

New Vocabulary
unit cost

Sometimes you want to buy just one item, but the only price shown is for several items. You can divide to find the cost of a single item. The cost of a single item is called the unit cost.

CDs . . . . 3 FOR $27
MUSIC TAPES . . . . . . 4 FOR $24

Music Pins	Concert Tickets	Band Posters
5 for $10	2 for $18	3 for $15

Problem Cory is a big music fan! He went to Marty's Music and bought 3 CDs by his favorite group. How much did each CD cost?

What is the question?
How much did each CD cost?

What do you know?
• The cost of 3 CDs is $27.

What can you do to find the answer?
You can divide to find the unit cost of the CD.

Solve

Divide $27 by 3 to find the cost of 1 CD.

$$\$27 \div 3 = \$9$$

Each CD cost $9.

Look Back

Look back at the question.
How can you use multiplication to check that your answer is correct?

Guided Practice

Use the information below to solve.

1. Laura bought 2 song books and 4 blank videotapes. How much more is the unit cost of a song book than the unit cost of a videotape?

What will you divide to find the unit cost of a song book?

2. At the Music Mall, a blank videotape costs $5. How does that price compare to the unit cost of the videotapes shown below?

What is the unit cost of 1 videotape when you buy 4?

Choose a Strategy

Use the information on page 378 to solve.
Use these or other strategies.

Problem-Solving Strategies

- **Write a Number Sentence**
- **Work Backward**
- **Guess and Check**
- **Use Logical Thinking**

3. About how much would it cost Jack to buy 3 CDs and 4 music tapes at Marty's Music?

4. Music Mall sells CDs 4 for $32. At Marty's, CDs are 3 for $27. Which store offers the better buy?

5. Tyrell has exactly enough money to buy 6 band posters. If he decides to buy music pins instead, how many pins can he buy? Will he have money left over?

6. Kyle wants to record a 10-hour TV program. Each blank videotape has 4 hours of recording time on it. How many blank videotapes does Kyle need?

7. One music tape usually costs $8. The sale price for a tape is $6. How much will you save if you buy 4 tapes on sale instead of at the usual price?

8. Leah bought twice as many videos as posters. She bought 3 more CDs than videos. If she bought 7 CDs, how many posters did she buy?

9. Ellen bought a total of 10 CDs and music tapes. She bought 4 more CDs than music tapes. How many of each did she buy?

10. Devon bought a box of videos for $16.99. The clerk gave him $3.01 in change. What bill did Devon use to pay for the videos?

Extra Practice See 9–11 on page 385.

Quick Check

Check Your Understanding of Lessons 6–10

Divide.

1. $7 \div 7$
2. $4 \div 1$
3. $0 \div 9$
4. $0 \div 6$
5. $5 \div 5$

Find the quotient.

6. $3\overline{)9}$
7. $3\overline{)15}$
8. $3\overline{)27}$
9. $3\overline{)12}$
10. $3\overline{)3}$
11. $24 \div 4$
12. $36 \div 4$
13. $12 \div 4$
14. $16 \div 4$
15. $28 \div 4$

Solve.

16. Look at the information on the right. What is the unit cost of a videotape? What is the unit cost of a CD?

17. Jo makes bows. She starts with a piece of ribbon that is 12 feet long. First she cuts the piece in half. Then she cuts each half into 3 equal pieces. How many pieces of ribbon does Jo have? How long is each piece?

How did you do?

If you had difficulty with any items in the Quick Check, you can use the following pages for review and extra practice.

Items	Review These Pages	Do These Extra Practice Items
1–5	pages 368–369	Set D, page 383
6–10	pages 370–371	Set E, page 384
11–15	pages 374–375	Set F, page 384
16	pages 372–373	5–8, page 385
17	pages 378–379	9–11, page 385

Test Prep • Cumulative Review

Maintaining the Standards

Choose the letter of the correct answer. If a correct answer is not here, choose NH.

1 Which number sentence is true?

A $5 \div 5 = 0$
B $5 \div 1 = 1$
C $0 \div 5 = 0$
D $0 \div 1 = 1$

Use the table to answer Questions 2–3.

Game Sales	
Game	**Number Sold**
Topsy-Turvey	498
Circles	179
Jumps and Slides	125

2 How many more games of Topsy-Turvey were sold than Circles and Jumps and Slides combined?

F 194 **H** 373
G 250 **J** NH

3 About how many games were sold in all?

A 500
B 800
C 1,000
D 1,200

4 If $14 \div 2 = ■$, then which statement must be true?

F $14 \times 2 = ■$
G $■ \times 14 = 2$
H $2 \times ■ = 14$
J $■ \div 2 = 14$

5 Which symbol makes the number sentence true?

$4 \bullet 3 = 12$

A $+$ **C** $\times$
B $-$ **D** $\div$

6 Patty divided her 15 dolls into 3 groups. If the same number of dolls is in each group, how many dolls are in a group?

F 2
G 4
H 6
J NH

7 What symbol makes the number sentence true?

$27 \bullet 3 = 5 + 4$

A $+$ **C** $\times$
B $-$ **D** $\div$

8 Mark is a waiter. He gave each customer at the table a fork, a spoon, and a knife. If Mark gave out 18 utensils in all, how many customers were at the table?

Explain How did you find your answer?

Safe Site

Internet Test Prep
Visit **www.eduplace.com/kids/mhm** for more *Test Prep Practice.*

Extra Practice

Set A (Lesson 2, pages 356–358)

Write a multiplication sentence and a division sentence for each array.

1.

2. 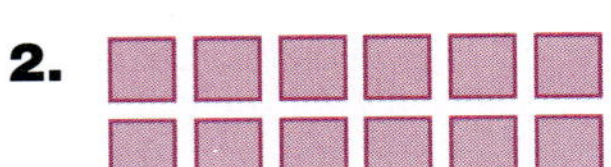

3. 

4.

5. 

6.

Draw an array for each multiplication sentence. Then write two related division sentences.

7. $4 \times 2 = 8$ **8.** $5 \times 3 = 15$ **9.** $5 \times 4 = 20$ **10.** $6 \times 3 = 18$

11. $3 \times 5 = 15$ **12.** $2 \times 7 = 14$ **13.** $3 \times 1 = 3$ **14.** $4 \times 4 = 16$

Set B (Lesson 3, pages 360–361)

Use the related multiplication fact to find each quotient.

1. $3 \times 2 = 6$
$6 \div 2 =$ ■

2. $4 \times 2 = 8$
$8 \div 2 =$ ■

3. $7 \times 2 = 14$
$14 \div 2 =$ ■

4. $8 \times 2 = 16$
$16 \div 2 =$ ■

5. $2 \times 2 = 4$
$4 \div 2 =$ ■

6. $5 \times 2 = 10$
$10 \div 2 =$ ■

7. $1 \times 2 = 2$
$2 \div 2 =$ ■

8. $9 \times 2 = 18$
$18 \div 2 =$ ■

9. $8 \times 2 = 16$
$16 \div 2 =$ ■

10. $6 \times 2 = 12$
$12 \div 2 =$ ■

11. $3 \times 2 = 6$
$6 \div 2 =$ ■

12. $7 \times 2 = 14$
$14 \div 2 =$ ■

Find each quotient.

13. $8 \div 2$ **14.** $10 \div 2$ **15.** $16 \div 2$ **16.** $18 \div 2$ **17.** $2 \div 2$

18. $6 \div 2$ **19.** $12 \div 2$ **20.** $4 \div 2$ **21.** $14 \div 2$ **22.** $10 \div 2$

Extra Practice

Set C (Lesson 4, pages 362–363)

Find the missing factor. Then write the quotient.

1. 5 × ■ = 20
20 ÷ 5 = ■

2. 5 × ■ = 30
30 ÷ 5 = ■

3. 5 × ■ = 45
45 ÷ 5 = ■

4. 5 × ■ = 10
10 ÷ 5 = ■

5. 5 × ■ = 25
25 ÷ 5 = ■

6. 5 × ■ = 15
15 ÷ 5 = ■

7. 5 × ■ = 5
5 ÷ 5 = ■

8. 5 × ■ = 35
35 ÷ 5 = ■

9. 5 × ■ = 40
40 ÷ 5 = ■

10. 5 × ■ = 30
30 ÷ 5 = ■

11. 5 × ■ = 10
10 ÷ 5 = ■

12. 5 × ■ = 20
20 ÷ 5 = ■

Divide.

13. 40 ÷ 5 **14.** 45 ÷ 5 **15.** 5 ÷ 5 **16.** 15 ÷ 5 **17.** 25 ÷ 5

18. 10 ÷ 5 **19.** 35 ÷ 5 **20.** 30 ÷ 5 **21.** 20 ÷ 5 **22.** 45 ÷ 5

Set D (Lesson 6, pages 368–369)

Divide.

1. 7 ÷ 7 **2.** 0 ÷ 4 **3.** 3 ÷ 1 **4.** 3 ÷ 3 **5.** 5 ÷ 5

6. 0 ÷ 1 **7.** 1 ÷ 1 **8.** 2 ÷ 2 **9.** 0 ÷ 5 **10.** 2 ÷ 1

Follow the rule to complete each table.

Rule: Divide by 1

	Input	Output
11.	0	■
12.	■	1
13.	4	■
14.	■	5
15.	7	■

Rule: Divide by 2

	Input	Output
16.	■	0
17.	2	■
18.	■	2
19.	8	■
20.	■	8

Rule: Divide by 5

	Input	Output
21.	0	■
22.	■	1
23.	25	■
24.	■	8
25.	45	■

Extra Practice

Set E (Lesson 7, pages 370–371)

Divide.

1. $3\overline{)9}$ 2. $3\overline{)15}$ 3. $3\overline{)21}$ 4. $3\overline{)0}$ 5. $3\overline{)3}$

6. $3\overline{)6}$ 7. $3\overline{)12}$ 8. $3\overline{)18}$ 9. $3\overline{)27}$ 10. $3\overline{)24}$

11. $9 \div 3$ 12. $0 \div 3$ 13. $18 \div 3$ 14. $3 \div 3$ 15. $27 \div 3$

16. $21 \div 3$ 17. $15 \div 3$ 18. $6 \div 3$ 19. $12 \div 3$ 20. $24 \div 3$

Compare. Write >, <, or = for each ●.

21. $12 \div 2$ ● $12 \div 3$ 22. $24 \div 4$ ● $24 \div 3$ 23. $15 \div 3$ ● $15 \div 5$

24. $40 \div 5$ ● $24 \div 3$ 25. $2 \div 2$ ● $3 \div 3$ 26. $12 \div 2$ ● $14 \div 2$

Set F (Lesson 9, pages 374–375)

Divide.

1. $4\overline{)32}$ 2. $4\overline{)16}$ 3. $4\overline{)28}$ 4. $4\overline{)24}$ 5. $4\overline{)4}$

6. $4\overline{)36}$ 7. $4\overline{)12}$ 8. $4\overline{)8}$ 9. $4\overline{)20}$ 10. $4\overline{)16}$

11. $24 \div 4$ 12. $12 \div 4$ 13. $36 \div 4$ 14. $8 \div 4$ 15. $28 \div 4$

16. $16 \div 4$ 17. $32 \div 4$ 18. $20 \div 4$ 19. $4 \div 4$ 20. $0 \div 4$

Follow the rule to complete each table.

Rule: Divide by 4

	Input	Output
21.	8	■
22.	16	■
23.	24	■
24.	28	■

Rule: Divide by 5

	Input	Output
25.	■	1
26.	10	■
27.	■	4
28.	25	■

Rule: Divide by 3

	Input	Output
29.	27	■
30.	15	■
31.	18	■
32.	■	8

Extra Practice • Problem Solving

Solve. *(Lesson 5, pages 364–365)*

1. There are 38 dancers in the ballet class and 19 dancers in the tap-dancing class. How many more dancers are in the ballet class?

2. Brittany collects stamps. She has 247 stamps from the United States and 199 stamps from other countries. How many stamps does she have?

3. There are 8 computers in the library. If 4 students are at each computer, how many students are at the computers?

4. Nadia, Keisha, and Jerry share 15 seashells equally. How many seashells does each friend have?

Solve these problems, using the Draw a Picture strategy. *(Lesson 8, pages 372–373)*

5. Lin paints model cars black, blue, and red. One week she painted 13 cars. She painted every fourth car black. How many cars did she paint black that week?

6. Will has 5 red blocks and 9 blue blocks. He wants to stack one block on top of another so that no blocks of the same color are touching. Will any blocks be left over? Explain.

7. Stephen is using a wooden rod for an art project. He has cut it into 9 pieces. How many cuts does he need to make?

8. A necklace is made of 10 black beads and 1 yellow bead. The bead in the middle is yellow. Is the fifth bead yellow? Explain your answer.

Use the table to solve each problem. *(Lesson 10, pages 378–379)*

9. Lou bought 1 hockey poster and 1 basketball poster. Did he pay more for the basketball poster or the hockey poster? How much more did he pay?

10. Jim bought 2 baseball cards, 1 hockey poster, and 1 football card. How much money did he spend?

11. Sarah has $8. How many baseball cards can she buy?

Item	Price
Baseball cards	3 for $6
Football cards	5 for $15
Hockey posters	2 for $10
Basketball posters	4 for $12

Chapter Review

Reviewing Vocabulary

Answer each question.

1. In $36 \div 4 = 9$, which number is the dividend?
2. In $15 \div 5 = 3$, which number is the divisor?
3. In $24 \div 6 = 4$, which number is the quotient?

Reviewing Concepts and Skills

Write a multiplication sentence and division sentence for each array. *(pages 356–358)*

4.

5. 

6. 

7.

Draw an array for each multiplication sentence. Then write two related division sentences. *(pages 356–358)*

8. $4 \times 2 = 8$ **9.** $5 \times 3 = 15$ **10.** $5 \times 1 = 5$ **11.** $6 \times 3 = 18$

Divide. *(pages 360–363)*

12. $12 \div 2$ **13.** $18 \div 2$ **14.** $6 \div 2$ **15.** $8 \div 2$

16. $14 \div 2$ **17.** $10 \div 2$ **18.** $4 \div 2$ **19.** $16 \div 2$

20. $10 \div 5$ **21.** $20 \div 5$ **22.** $5 \div 5$ **23.** $35 \div 5$

24. $45 \div 5$ **25.** $40 \div 5$ **26.** $30 \div 5$ **27.** $15 \div 5$

28. $18 \div 3$ **29.** $6 \div 3$ **30.** $27 \div 3$ **31.** $12 \div 3$

32. $9 \div 3$ **33.** $3 \div 3$ **34.** $21 \div 3$ **35.** $15 \div 3$

36. $12 \div 4$ **37.** $4 \div 4$ **38.** $32 \div 4$ **39.** $16 \div 4$

40. $8 \div 4$ **41.** $24 \div 4$ **42.** $20 \div 4$ **43.** $36 \div 4$

Follow the rule to complete each table. *(pages 360–363, 374–375)*

Rule: Divide by 4

	Input	Output
44.	0	■
45.	■	7
46.	32	■
47.	24	■

Rule: Divide by 2

	Input	Output
48.	■	0
49.	2	■
50.	■	7
51.	18	■

Rule: Divide by 5

	Input	Output
52.	5	■
53.	■	5
54.	45	■
55.	■	4

Solve. Use the sign for Problem 56. *(pages 364–365, 378–379)*

56. Ms. Brown bought 1 sweater, 1 skirt, and 2 shirts. How much money did she spend?

57. Judith and 4 of her friends each bought 3 flower barrettes. How many flower barrettes did they buy in all?

58. Ava cut a 16-in. ribbon into 2 equal strips. Then she cut each strip into 4 equal pieces. How many pieces of ribbon did she have?

Brain Teasers Math Reasoning

Read Jaime's Mind

Jaime thought of a mystery number. If you divide the number by 5 and then you divide the answer by 2, you get 4. What was Jaime's mystery number?

One Left Over

Sherry has some cookies. If she makes groups of 2, she has 1 left over. If she makes groups of 5, she still has 1 left over. She has fewer than 26 cookies. How many cookies could Sherry have?

Internet Brain Teasers
Visit **www.eduplace.com/kids/mhm** for more *Brain Teasers.*

Chapter Test

Write two related division sentences.

1. $4 \times 2 = 8$
2. $5 \times 3 = 15$
3. $5 \times 1 = 5$
4. $6 \times 3 = 18$
5. $3 \times 7 = 21$
6. $6 \times 4 = 24$
7. $2 \times 5 = 10$
8. $4 \times 9 = 36$
9. $2 \times 9 = 18$

Find each quotient.

10. $2\overline{)18}$
11. $5\overline{)15}$
12. $3\overline{)24}$
13. $2\overline{)8}$
14. $4\overline{)32}$
15. $3\overline{)21}$
16. $4\overline{)12}$
17. $2\overline{)16}$
18. $5\overline{)35}$
19. $3\overline{)9}$
20. $4\overline{)24}$
21. $2\overline{)14}$
22. $5\overline{)30}$
23. $3\overline{)3}$
24. $5\overline{)40}$
25. $15 \div 3$
26. $28 \div 4$
27. $25 \div 5$
28. $10 \div 2$
29. $45 \div 5$
30. $36 \div 4$
31. $18 \div 3$
32. $20 \div 4$
33. $12 \div 2$
34. $20 \div 5$
35. $27 \div 3$
36. $16 \div 4$

Use the table for Problems 37 and 38.

37. Ken went to a garage sale. He bought 4 games and 3 books. How much did he spend?

38. Theresa bought 2 games and 4 dolls. Her brother Anthony, bought 10 books and 2 games. Who spent more money? How much more was spent? Explain how you got your answer.

Garage-Sale Prices

Item	Price
Games	4 for \$16
Dolls	2 for \$6
Books	5 for \$10

Solve.

39. There are 28 birds for sale at a pet store. The owner puts 4 birds in each cage. How many cages of birds are there?

40. Lisa collects buttons. She has 15 of them lined up to make a necklace. Every fourth button is silver. How many silver buttons are there?

Write About It

Solve each problem. Use correct math vocabulary to explain your thinking.

1. Some friends earned a total of $30 for helping a neighbor with chores.

a. Explain how you would share the money equally among 5 people.

b. If each of the 5 people was given at least one five-dollar bill, how many bills would each person get? Explain.

c. Could you use only five-dollar bills to share the $30 equally among 6 people? Explain.

2. Jordan has 12 animal cards. He wants to put them in equal groups on the pages on an album.

a. Draw pictures to show how many different ways Jordan can put the cards in equal groups.

b. Write a division sentence for each way Jordan can put the cards in equal groups on pages in his album.

Another Look

**Use the picture below to answer each question.
Show your work using pictures, counters, or numbers.**

1. Which of the items in the packages pictured above can 3 friends share equally with no items left over? How many of each item would each friend receive?

2. Which of the items can 5 friends share equally with no items left over? How many of each item would each friend receive?

3. **Look Back** Which items can be shared equally by 3 and by 5 friends? Explain why by the use of division or multiplication number sentences.

4. **Analyze** Suppose 4 friends want to share soccer cards equally. How many packs of soccer cards should they buy? Explain.

Enrichment

Choosing the Operation Signs

Jenny, Lee, and Sandra practiced their math by playing two games.

In the Hit 5 game, they "made" the number 5 by picking two or more of these numbers: 1, 3, 6, and 8. Then they used one or more of the operations (addition, subtraction, multiplication, and division) to make the number 5.

Here's how Jenny made the number 5.	Here's how Lee made the number 5.	Here's how Sandra made the number 5.
She wrote: **$6 - 1 = 5$**	He wrote: **$8 - 6 + 3 = 5$**	She wrote: **$(3 \times 8) \div 6 + 1 = 5$**

Then Jenny, Lee, and Sandra played the Hit 6 game. This time, they picked from the numbers 1, 3, 5, and 9 to make the number 6.

Write +, −, ×, or ÷ in each ● to complete each child's number sentence.

1. 5 ● 1 = 6
2. 9 ● 3 = 6
3. (3 ● 5) ● 9 = 6
4. 3 ● 9 ● 5 ● 1 = 6
5. 9 ● 1 ● 5 ● 3 = 6
6. 3 ● (9 ● 1) ● 5 = 6

Explain Your Thinking

► What is the greatest number you can make by using all of the numbers 1, 3, and 4 and any operation? Explain.

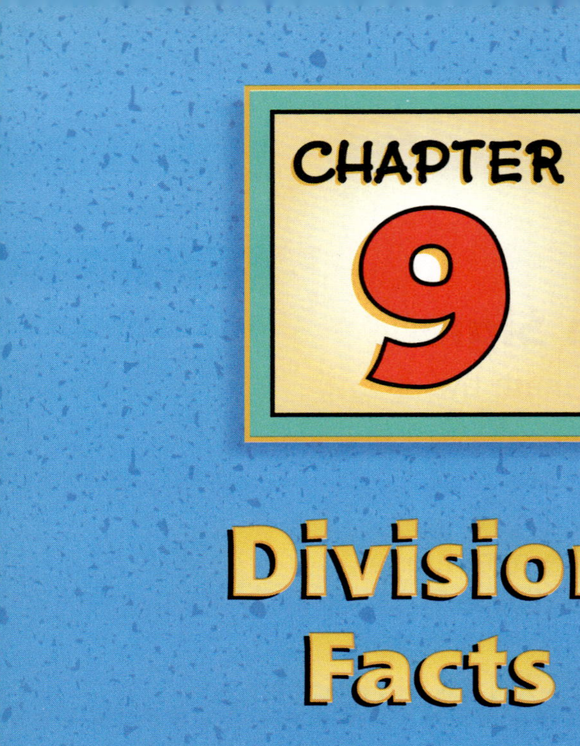

CHAPTER 9

Division Facts

Why Learn About Division Facts?

Knowing division facts can help you find the number of equal-sized groups or the number of items in each group.

When you share sports cards equally among friends or when you figure out how many equal groups of cards you can make from a collection, you are using division.

These students just finished playing a game of soccer. They used division to form two equal-sized teams.

Reading Mathematics

Reviewing Vocabulary

Understanding math language helps you become a successful problem solver. Here are some math vocabulary words you should know.

dividend	a number that is divided
divisor	a number that a dividend is divided by
quotient	the answer in a division problem
fact family	related multiplication and division facts that use the same numbers

Reading Words and Symbols

When you read mathematics, sometimes you read only words, sometimes you read words and symbols, and sometimes you read only symbols.

All of these statements describe the same division problem.

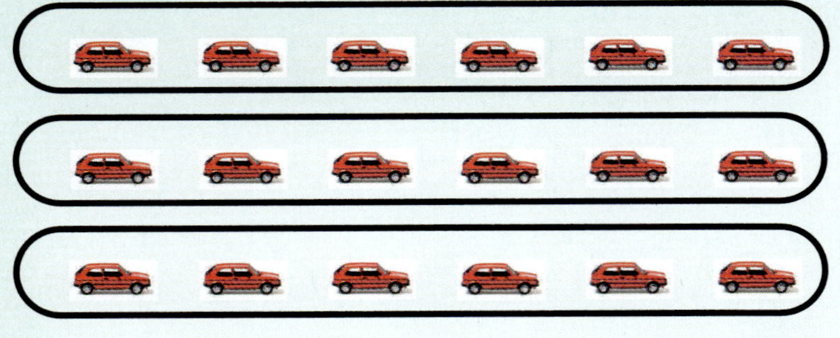

- Eighteen cars are divided into three groups of six.
- Eighteen divided by three is equal to six.
- The quotient of eighteen and three is six.

$18 \div 3 = 6$

18 ← dividend, 3 ← divisor, 6 ← quotient

$3\overline{)18}$ with 6 above

divisor → 3; 18 ← dividend; 6 ← quotient

Try These

1. Replace each ■ with *divisor, dividend,* or *quotient.*

a. ■ ÷ 3 = 9 **b.** 32 ÷ ■ = 8 **c.** 6 ÷ ■ = 1 **d.** 45 ÷ 5 = ■

e. $9\overline{)\blacksquare}$ with quotient 9 **f.** $\blacksquare\overline{)20}$ with quotient 5 **g.** $5\overline{)\blacksquare}$ with quotient 6 **h.** $4\overline{)40}$ with quotient ■

2. Write *true* or *false.*

a. When a dividend is divided by one, the quotient is the same number as the dividend.

b. The dividend and quotient can never be the same number.

c. The quotient is always less than the divisor.

d. You can use repeated subtraction to find a quotient.

e. You can use an array to show how multiplication and division are related.

3. Write each as a division sentence.

a. The divisor is five. The quotient is four. The dividend is twenty.

b. The quotient of twenty-four and three is eight.

c. Thirty-six divided by four is equal to nine.

d. The quotient is eight. The dividend is eight. The divisor is one.

e. Fifty-six divided by seven is eight.

Using a Multiplication Table to Divide

You will learn how to use a multiplication table to see how divisors, quotients, and dividends are related.

Review Vocabulary
divisor
dividend
quotient

You have used a multiplication table like the one below to multiply. You can also use the table to help you divide.

Step 1 Use the table to find 24 ÷ 4.

First, find the row marked 4.
This number is the **divisor.**

Move across this row to the column that shows 24.
This number is the **dividend.**

Look at the number 6 at the top of the column.
This number is the **quotient.**

Why can you use the table to divide?

column ↓ (6); row → (4)

×	0	1	2	3	4	5	6	7	8	9	10
0	0	0	0	0	0	0	0	0	0	0	0
1	0	1	2	3	4	5	6	7	8	9	10
2	0	2	4	6	8	10	12	14	16	18	20
3	0	3	6	9	12	15	18	21	24	27	30
4	0	4	8	12	16	20	24	28	32	36	40
5	0	5	10	15	20	25	30	35	40	45	50
6	0	6	12	18	24	30	36	42	48	54	60
7	0	7	14	21	28	35	42	49	56	63	70
8	0	8	16	24	32	40	48	56	64	72	80
9	0	9	18	27	36	45	54	63	72	81	90
10	0	10	20	30	40	50	60	70	80	90	100

Step 2 Make and complete a chart like the one below. Use the multiplication table to help you complete your chart for the examples shown.

Example	Divisor	Dividend	Quotient
24 ÷ 6			
35 ÷ 7			
56 ÷ 8			
81 ÷ 9			

Step 3 Find the number 20 in 4 different places in the multiplication table. Use 20 as the dividend. Record the divisors and quotients in your chart. Then use your chart to help you write divison sentences for each.

How are your division sentences the same? How are they different?

Step 4 Now find the number 25 in the table.

Use the table to help you write a division sentence with 25 as the dividend.

Find another number that appears only once in the table.

Write a division sentence using that number as a dividend.

Why can you write only one division sentence for each of these dividends?

Try It Out

Use the multiplication table to find each quotient.

1. 12 ÷ 2	**2.** 9 ÷ 1	**3.** 36 ÷ 4	**4.** 0 ÷ 5
5. 15 ÷ 5	**6.** 28 ÷ 4	**7.** 30 ÷ 6	**8.** 28 ÷ 7
9. 16 ÷ 8	**10.** 27 ÷ 9	**11.** 45 ÷ 9	**12.** 49 ÷ 7

Write about it! Talk about it!

Use what you have learned to answer these questions.

13. Explain how you can use a multiplication table to find 32 ÷ 4.

14. If the dividend and the divisor are both even numbers, must the quotient also be an even number? Give examples to support your answer.

Fact Families

You will learn how to use fact families to show how multiplication and division are related.

Review Vocabulary
fact family

Learn About It

Look at the picture. How many rows of toy dogs are there? How many toy dogs are in each row? How many toy dogs are in the box?

You can use the fact family for 3, 4, and 12 to tell about the toy dogs.

A **fact family** is a group of number sentences that use the same numbers. Fact families show how multiplication and division are related.

Fact Family for 3, 4, and 12

$3 \times 4 = 12$ 3 ↑ rows; 4 ↑ number in each row; 12 ↑ total	$4 \times 3 = 12$ 4 ↑ number in each row; 3 ↑ rows; 12 ↑ total
$12 \div 4 = 3$ 12 ↑ total; 4 ↑ number in each row; 3 ↑ rows	$12 \div 3 = 4$ 12 ↑ total; 3 ↑ rows; 4 ↑ number in each row

Solution: There are 12 toy dogs in the box.
There are 4 toy dogs in each row. There are 3 rows of toy dogs.

Other Examples

A. Fact Family for 3, 5, and 15

$3 \times 5 = 15$

$5 \times 3 = 15$

$15 \div 3 = 5$

$15 \div 5 = 3$

B. Fact Family for 4, 4, and 16

$4 \times 4 = 16$

$16 \div 4 = 4$

Explain Your Thinking

► How are the products and dividends related in each fact family?

Guided Practice

Copy and complete each fact family.

> **Ask Yourself**
> - Do I need to find the number of rows?
> - Do I need to find the number of columns?
> - Do I need to find the total?

1. 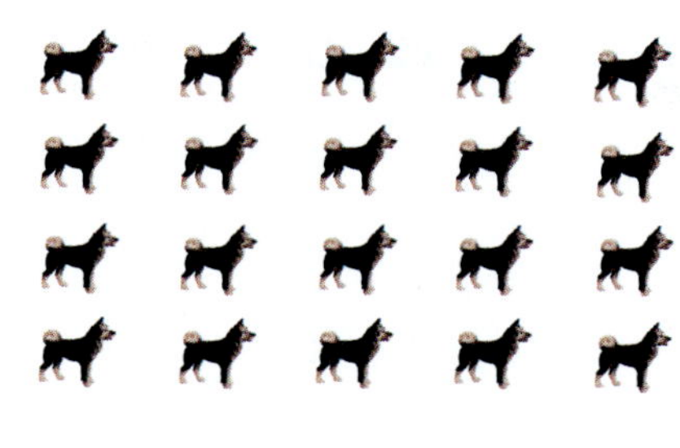

4 × 5 = 20　　20 ÷ 4 = ■
5 × 4 = ■　　20 ÷ 5 = ■

2. 

3 × 3 = 9
9 ÷ 3 = ■

3. 

2 × 4 = ■　　8 ÷ ■ = 4
4 × 2 = ■　　8 ÷ ■ = 2

4. 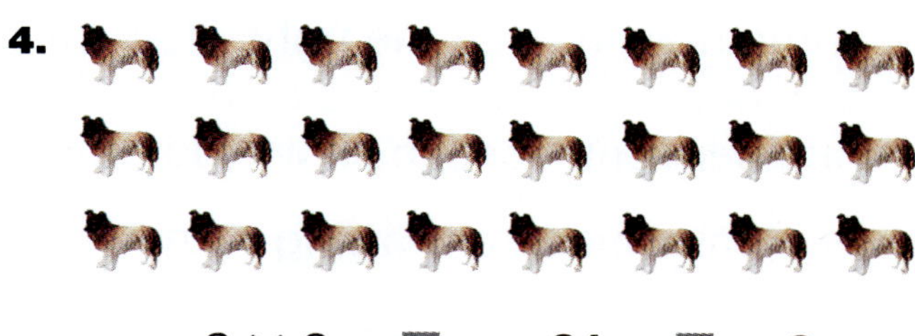

3 × 8 = ■　　24 ÷ ■ = 8
8 × 3 = ■　　24 ÷ ■ = 3

Independent Practice

Copy and complete each fact family.

5. 1 × 8 = 8
8 × ■ = 8
8 ÷ 1 = ■
8 ÷ ■ = 1

6. 2 × 7 = 14
7 × ■ = 14
14 ÷ 2 = ■
14 ÷ ■ = 2

7. 4 × 6 = 24
6 × ■ = 24
24 ÷ 4 = ■
24 ÷ ■ = 4

8. 3 × 7 = 21
7 × ■ = 21
21 ÷ 3 = ■
21 ÷ ■ = 7

9. 5 × 8 = 40
8 × ■ = 40
40 ÷ 5 = ■
40 ÷ ■ = 5

10. 3 × 10 = 30
■ × 3 = 30
30 ÷ ■ = 10
30 ÷ ■ = 3

11. 5 × 9 = 45
■ × 5 = 45
45 ÷ ■ = 9
45 ÷ 9 = ■

12. 6 × 5 = 30
■ × 6 = 30
30 ÷ ■ = 5
30 ÷ 5 = ■

Write a fact family for each array.

13. 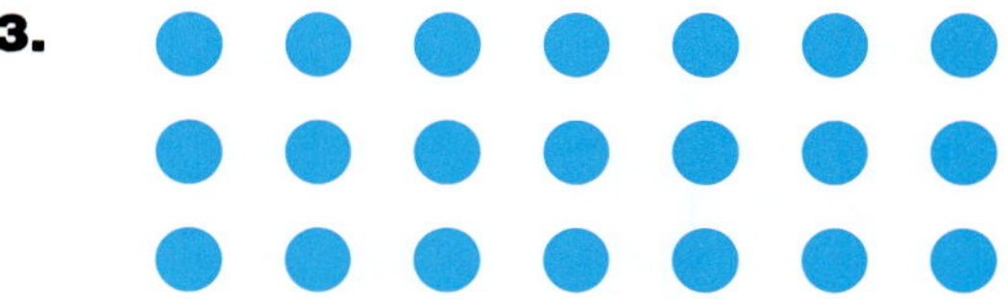

14. 

Write a fact family for each set of numbers.

15. 2, 3, 6 **16.** 10, 2, 20 **17.** 8, 3, 24 **18.** 4, 9, 36

19. 1, 5, 5 **20.** 5, 7, 35 **21.** 7, 7, 49 **22.** 6, 8, 48

Problem Solving • Reasoning

Solve. Choose a method.

Computation Methods

- Estimation
- Mental Math
- Paper and Pencil

23. Look at the drawings on the right. How many more paw prints did Paul make than Samantha? Write number sentences to show your answer.

24. **Compare** Jake made a drawing with 77 paw prints. About how many more paw prints did Jake make than Samantha?

25. Becky collects glass animals. She has 15 glass dogs, 25 glass cats, and 12 glass horses. How many more cats than dogs does Becky have?

26. **Logical Thinking** Suppose you have 21 toy dogs. You want to put as many of them as you can in a array that has the same number of rows and columns. What is the greatest number of dogs you can use? How many dogs will be left over? Explain.

▲ Samantha's Array

▲ Paul's Array

Mixed Review • Test Prep

Multiply or divide. *(pages 270–271, 362–363, 370–371)*

27. 9×7 **28.** $18 \div 3$ **29.** 5×9 **30.** $35 \div 5$ **31.** $21 \div 3$

Choose the letter that shows each number in standard form. *(pages 4–5, 18–19)*

32 200 + 40 + 3

A 2,403 **C** 270
B 2,043 **D** 243

33 5,000 + 70 + 1

F 5,710 **G** 5,071
H 5,701 **J** 571

Extra Practice See Set A on page 424.

Number Sense

Working With Parentheses

You know that parentheses show which operation to do first. Look at the examples below to see how the answers change depending on where the parentheses are placed.

Example 1		Example 2	
$(2 + 6) \div 2 = n$	$2 + (6 \div 2) = n$	$(12 - 8) \div 2 = n$	$12 - (8 \div 2) = n$
$8 \div 2 = n$	$2 + 3 = n$	$4 \div 2 = n$	$12 - 4 = n$
$4 = n$	$5 = n$	$2 = n$	$8 = n$

Try These

Find the value of *n*.

1. $(2 \times 4) - 3 = n$
$2 \times (4 - 3) = n$

2. $(8 \div 2) + 2 = n$
$8 \div (2 + 2) = n$

3. $4 + (12 \div 2) = n$
$(4 + 12) \div 2 = n$

4. $(18 \div 3) - 2 = n$
$18 \div (3 - 2) = n$

5. $6 + (9 \div 3) = n$
$(6 + 9) \div 3 = n$

6. $(3 \times 4) - 1 = n$
$3 \times (4 - 1) = n$

Copy each number sentence. Then place the parentheses to make each sentence correct.

7. $2 \times 2 + 4 = 8$

8. $2 + 8 \div 4 = 4$

9. $16 \div 4 + 4 = 8$

10. $16 \div 4 - 3 = 1$

11. $2 + 7 \div 3 = 3$

12. $15 \div 3 + 2 = 7$

Explain Your Thinking

► Is the value of *n* the same for these number sentences? Explain why or why not.

$(2 \times 8) \div 4 = n$ $\quad$ $2 \times (8 \div 4) = n$

LESSON 3

Divide by 10

You will learn different ways to divide by 10.

Learn About It

Laura decorates purses to give away as gifts. She puts 10 buttons on each purse. How many purses can Laura decorate if she has 40 buttons?

Divide. $40 \div 10 = n$ or $10\overline{)40}$ with n as the quotient

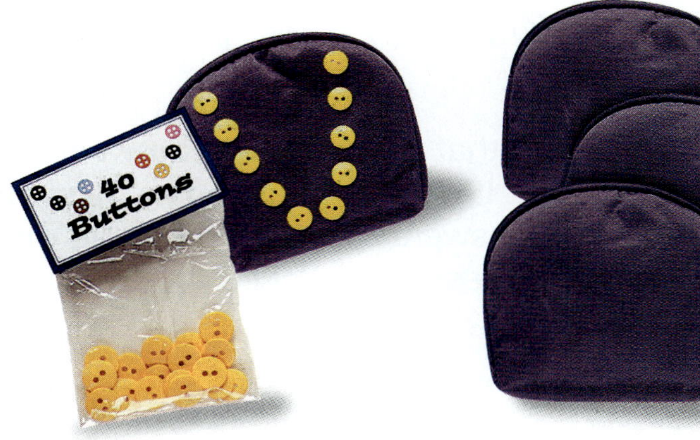

Different Ways to Divide

You can use a number line.

- Start at 40. Count back by 10s to 0.
- Count the number of times you subtracted 10.

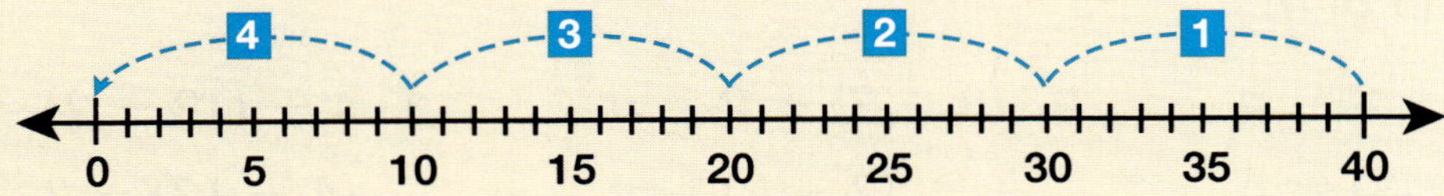

You subtracted 10 four times.

So $40 - 10 = 4$.

You can use a related multiplication fact.

$40 \div 10 = n$

Think $10 \times n = 40$

$10 \times 4 = 40$

So $40 \div 10 = 4$.

You can use a related division fact.

$40 \div 10 = n$

Think $40 \div n = 10$

$40 \div 4 = 10$

So $40 \div 10 = 4$.

Solution: Laura can decorate 4 purses.

Explain Your Thinking

► How can thinking of 60 as 6 tens help you find $60 \div 10$?

Guided Practice

Find each quotient.

1. $10\overline{)60}$ 2. $10\overline{)100}$ 3. $10\overline{)90}$
4. $10 \div 10$ 5. $30 \div 10$ 6. $20 \div 10$

Ask Yourself

- What multiplication fact can help me?
- What related division fact can help me?

Independent Practice

Divide.

7. $10\overline{)0}$ 8. $10\overline{)30}$ 9. $10\overline{)10}$ 10. $10\overline{)50}$ 11. $10\overline{)80}$
12. $10\overline{)20}$ 13. $10\overline{)40}$ 14. $10\overline{)60}$ 15. $10\overline{)90}$ 16. $10\overline{)70}$
17. $100 \div 10$ 18. $0 \div 10$ 19. $90 \div 10$ 20. $80 \div 10$ 21. $30 \div 10$

n **Algebra • Equations** **Find each missing number.**

22. $50 \div n = 5$ 23. $n \div 10 = 7$ 24. $10 \times n = 30$ 25. $n \times 4 = 40$
26. $60 = n \times 6$ 27. $10 = 100 \div n$ 28. $n \times 8 = 80$ 29. $10 = 90 \div n$

Problem Solving • Reasoning

30. Metal buttons cost 10¢ each. How many buttons can you buy with 80¢?

31. **Money** A store sells special bags of 10 glow-in-the-dark buttons for $3 a bag. Kenny bought 60 buttons. How much money did he spend?

32. Tia has 10 more white buttons than black buttons. If she has 24 buttons that are black or white, how many white buttons does she have?

Using Vocabulary

Write a number sentence for each.

A. The quotient is 6.
B. The dividend is 14.
C. The divisor is 5.
D. The product is 27.
E. The sum is 35.

Mixed Review • Test Prep

Find the missing number. *(pages 220–221; 236–237; 374–375)*

33. $4 \times n = 32$ 34. $20 \div n = 5$ 35. $n \times 9 = 45$ 36. $24 \div 4 = n$

37. **Find the product of $(2 \times 5) \times 7$.** *(pages 278–279)*

A 20 **B** 49 **C** 70 **D** 100

Extra Practice See Set B on page 425.

Problem-Solving Skill: Too Much or Too Little Information

You will learn how to decide what information you need to solve a problem.

If there is too much information in a problem, you need to decide which facts to use. If there is not enough information, you need to decide what information is missing.

At the Super Rock Shop, small rocks cost 10¢ each. Magnifying glasses cost \$3.50 each. A bag of small rocks costs \$1.00. Each large rock weighs 1 pound.

Suppose you have 90¢. How many small rocks can you buy?

Sometimes you have too much information.

What facts do you need?

- the cost of a small rock (10¢)
- how much money you have (90¢)

There is more information in the problem, but it is not needed.

How can you solve the problem?

Divide by the cost of a small rock.

90¢ ÷ 10¢ = 9

You can buy 9 small rocks.

How much do 4 large rocks and 3 small rocks weigh?

Sometimes you have too little information.

What facts do you need?

- the weight of a large rock (1 pound)
- the weight of a small rock (not given)

The weight of a small rock is not given.

How can you solve the problem?

You need to know the weight of a small rock but that information is missing.

Look Back Why is it important to read a question carefully when a problem gives too much information?

The rocks on the right are called geodes. The hollow walls inside a geode are lined with crystals. The size, color, and formation of the crystals make each geode different.

Guided Practice

Use the information on page 404 to solve.

1. Ellie buys 3 bags of small rocks. If she gives the clerk $5, what should her change be?

   Think: Do you know the cost of a bag of small rocks?

2. Rich bought 6 pounds of small rocks. How many small rocks did Rich buy?

   Think: Do you know how much a small rock weighs?

Choose a Strategy

Solve. Use these or other strategies. If not enough information is given, tell what information is needed.

Problem-Solving Strategies

- **Draw a Picture**
- **Guess and Check**
- **Write a Number Sentence**
- **Work Backward**

3. Carla is looking at a rock catalog. Each page shows 3 rows of 4 rocks. How many rocks are shown in the catalog?

4. A local nature store has 23 volcanic rocks on sale. The rocks cost $3.89 each. About how much do 4 volcanic rocks cost?

5. A 20-pound bag of sand costs $4. A 30-pound bag costs $6 and a 40-pound bag costs $8. How much would it cost to buy sand in a 20-pound bag and a 40-pound bag?

6. Fernando owns 2 rocks that weigh 43 pounds altogether. One rock weighs 5 pounds more than the other. The 2 rocks are worth $15. How much does each rock weigh?

7. **Write About It** Samuel brought 40 rocks and 20 shells to school. He made an array with all of the rocks. There were 3 more rows than columns. How many rows were in the array?

8. Rick, Chris, Molly, and Jennifer collect rocks. Jennifer has twice as many rocks as Rick. Rick has 4 more rocks than Chris. Molly has 8 rocks. Chris has 6 rocks. How many rocks does Jennifer have?

Extra Practice See 1–4 on page 427.

Quick Check

Check Your Understanding of Lessons 1–4

Write a fact family for each set of numbers.

1. 3, 5, 15 **2.** 6, 7, 42 **3.** 4, 7, 28 **4.** 3, 9, 27

Divide.

5. $10\overline{)40}$ **6.** $10\overline{)80}$ **7.** $10\overline{)50}$ **8.** $10\overline{)30}$ **9.** $10\overline{)60}$

10. $70 \div 10$ **11.** $100 \div 10$ **12.** $90 \div 10$ **13.** $10 \div 10$ **14.** $20 \div 10$

Solve. If not enough information is given, tell what information is needed.

15. Rosa wants to buy 3 red roses. If she gives the clerk $5.00, how much change will she get back?

16. Tyler needs 3 pounds of plant food. How much money will he spend?

Ally's Flower Shop	
Roses	$1.50 each
Tulips	$2.50 for 6
Vases	$5.50 each
Plant Food	$3.25 a bag

How did you do?

If you had difficulty with any items in the Quick Check, you can use the following pages for review and extra practice.

Items	Review These Pages	Do These Extra Practice Items
1–4	pages 398–400	Set A, page 424
5–14	pages 402–403	Set B, page 425
15–16	pages 404–405	1–4, page 427

Test Prep • Cumulative Review

Maintaining the Standards

Choose the letter of the correct answer. If a correct answer is not here, choose NH.

Use the table to answer Question 1.

Gallons of Gas	1	2	3	4
Price	\$2	\$4	\$6	\$8

1. How much will 10 gallons of gas cost?
   - **A** \$10
   - **B** \$15
   - **C** \$20
   - **D** \$25

2. If ■ × 9 = 27, then which number sentence must be true?
   - **F** 27 ÷ 9 = ■
   - **G** 9 ÷ ■ = 27
   - **H** 9 × 27 = ■
   - **J** 27 × ■ = 9

3. What symbol makes the number sentence true?

   30 ● 10 = 3
   - **A** +
   - **B** −
   - **C** ×
   - **D** ÷

4. If 10 schools each sent a team of 9 students to compete in a math contest, how many students were in the contest?
   - **F** 72
   - **G** 81
   - **H** 90
   - **J** NH

5. What is the name of this figure?

   - **A** square
   - **B** cube
   - **C** triangle
   - **D** rectangle

6. Parker has 18 socks. Each sock is part of a pair. How many pairs of socks does Parker have?
   - **F** 2
   - **G** 8
   - **H** 9
   - **J** NH

7. Which is the best estimate of the area of this figure?

   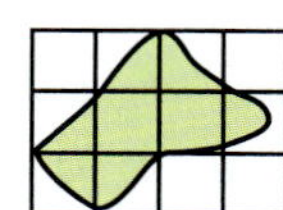

   - **A** 1 square unit
   - **B** 2 square units
   - **C** 5 square units
   - **D** 8 square units

8. Peggy invited 14 girls to her party. She bought enough pizza so that she and her friends could have 2 slices each. If each pizza was cut into 10 slices, how many pizzas did she need to buy?

   Explain How did you find your answer?

Safe Site

Internet Test Prep
Visit **www.eduplace.com/kids/mhm** for more *Test Prep Practice.*

LESSON 5

Divide by 6

You will learn different ways to divide by 6.

Learn About It

Twenty-four students have signed up for the junior ice-hockey league. Each team will have 6 players. How many teams can be formed?

Divide. **24 ÷ 6 = ■** or $6\overline{)24}$ (■ above)

Different Ways to Divide

You can use a number line.

- Start at 24. Count back by 6s to 0.
- Count the number of times you subtracted 6.

You subtracted 6 four times.

So 24 ÷ 6 = 4.

You can use a related multiplication fact.

24 ÷ 6 = ■

Think 6 × ■ = 24

6 × 4 = 24

So 24 ÷ 6 = 4.

You can use a related division fact.

24 ÷ 6 = ■

Think 24 ÷ ■ = 6

24 ÷ 4 = 6

So 24 ÷ 6 = 4.

Solution: Four teams can be formed.

Explain Your Thinking

► What related multiplication and division facts can you use to help you find 42 ÷ 6?

Guided Practice

Divide.

1. $6\overline{)36}$ **2.** $6\overline{)60}$ **3.** $6\overline{)42}$ **4.** $6\overline{)54}$

5. $6 \div 6$ **6.** $0 \div 6$ **7.** $12 \div 6$ **8.** $24 \div 6$

Ask Yourself

- What multiplication fact can help me?
- What related division fact can help me?

Independent Practice

Find each quotient.

9. $6\overline{)0}$ **10.** $6\overline{)18}$ **11.** $6\overline{)6}$ **12.** $6\overline{)24}$ **13.** $6\overline{)12}$

14. $6\overline{)42}$ **15.** $6\overline{)54}$ **16.** $6\overline{)48}$ **17.** $6\overline{)30}$ **18.** $6\overline{)60}$

19. $18 \div 6$ **20.** $36 \div 6$ **21.** $0 \div 6$ **22.** $30 \div 6$ **23.** $6 \div 6$

24. $48 \div 6$ **25.** $24 \div 6$ **26.** $54 \div 6$ **27.** $42 \div 6$ **28.** $60 \div 6$

Problem Solving • Reasoning

Use Data **Use the sign for Problems 29–31.**

29. Ben spent $18 to rent a pair of hockey skates. How many hours did he rent the skates?

30. **Compare** Mark plans to play hockey one hour a week for 10 weeks. Would it be less expensive for him to rent skates or buy a pair for $54? Explain your thinking.

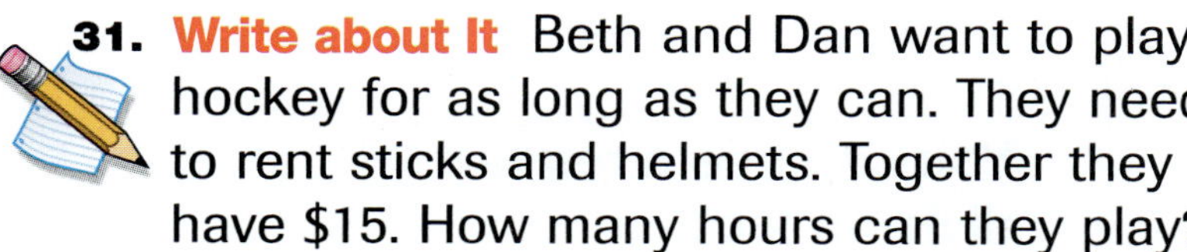

31. **Write about It** Beth and Dan want to play hockey for as long as they can. They need to rent sticks and helmets. Together they have $15. How many hours can they play?

Mixed Review • Test Prep

Solve. *(pages 102–103)*

32. $3 + 4 + 7$ **33.** $9 + 1 + 5$ **34.** $2 + 3 + 8$ **35.** $6 + 4 + 7 + 3$

Choose the letter of the correct answer. *(pages 102–103)*

36 $8 + \blacksquare + 4 = 18$

A 2 **C** 4
B 3 **D** 6

37 $5 + 3 + \blacksquare + 9 = 19$

F 1 **H** 5
G 2 **J** 10

Extra Practice See Set C on page 425.

LESSON 6 Divide by 7

You will learn different ways to divide by 7.

Learn About It

Come and get it! Every day, Shana gives the same number of biscuits to her dog, Fido. If Fido eats 21 biscuits a week, how many biscuits does he eat each day?

Divide. $21 \div 7 = n$ or $7\overline{)21}$ with quotient n

Different Ways to Divide

You can use counters.

- Use 21 counters. Divide them into 7 equal groups.
- Count the number in each group.

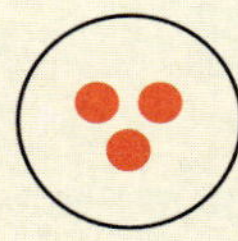 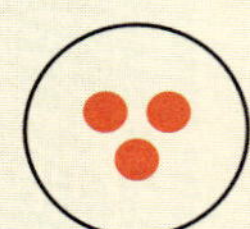 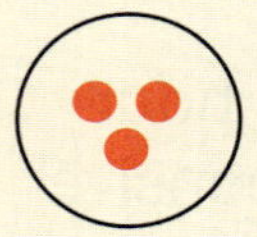 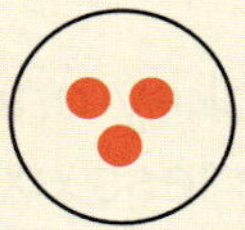 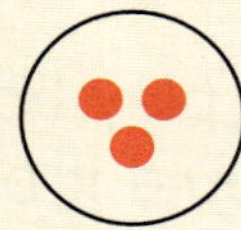 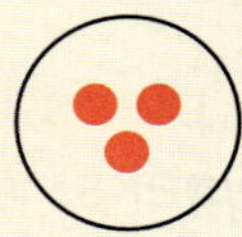 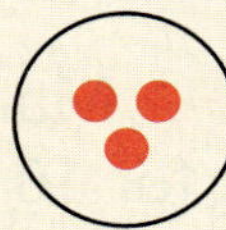

There are 3 counters in each group.

So $21 \div 7 = 3$.

You can use a related multiplication fact.

$21 \div 7 = n$

Think $7 \times n = 21$

$7 \times 3 = 21$

So $21 \div 7 = 3$.

You can use a related division fact.

$21 \div 7 = n$

Think $21 \div n = 7$

$21 \div 3 = 7$

So $21 \div 7 = 3$.

Solution: Fido eats 3 biscuits each day.

Explain Your Thinking

► What would you see if you divided the 21 counters into 3 equal groups?

Guided Practice

Find each quotient.

1. $7\overline{)14}$
2. $7\overline{)49}$
3. $7\overline{)56}$
4. $7\overline{)35}$
5. $7\overline{)63}$
6. $7\overline{)28}$
7. $21 \div 7$
8. $70 \div 7$
9. $42 \div 7$

Ask Yourself

- What multiplication fact can help me?
- What division fact can help me?

Independent Practice

Find each quotient.

10. $7\overline{)0}$
11. $3\overline{)21}$
12. $5\overline{)35}$
13. $7\overline{)28}$
14. $7\overline{)42}$
15. $7\overline{)56}$
16. $7\overline{)14}$
17. $7\overline{)63}$
18. $6\overline{)42}$
19. $7\overline{)70}$
20. $60 \div 10$
21. $28 \div 7$
22. $42 \div 7$
23. $48 \div 6$
24. $21 \div 7$
25. $56 \div 7$
26. $70 \div 7$
27. $49 \div 7$
28. $35 \div 7$
29. $63 \div 7$

Problem Solving • Reasoning

30. Fido's favorite dog biscuits come in 7 different flavors. A box has 56 dog biscuits with the same number of each of the 7 flavors. How many biscuits of each flavor are in a box?
31. Fido runs with Shana's father 4 times a week. They run 2 miles each time. How many miles does Fido run with Shana's father in 3 weeks?
32. **Analyze** Shana has 3 leashes. The red leash is 2 feet shorter than the blue leash. The blue leash is 4 feet shorter than the tan leash. If the tan leash is 14 feet long, how long is the red leash?

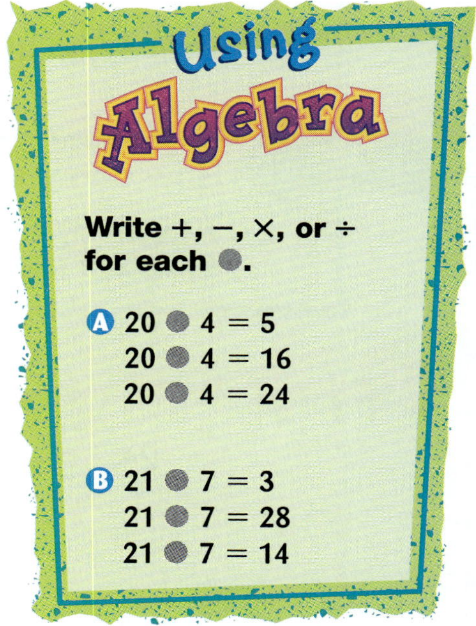

Mixed Review • Test Prep

Round each number to the nearest ten. *(pages 8–9, 24–26)*

33. 476
34. 1,035
35. 602
36. 999
37. 2,124
38. 5,365

39. **Write the letter of the best estimate.** *(pages 182–183)*

Your foot is about _____ cm long.

A 2 **B** 20 **C** 200 **D** 2,000

Extra Practice See Set D on page 426.

Problem-Solving Strategy: Write a Number Sentence

You will learn how to solve a problem by writing a number sentence.

Sometimes you can write a number sentence to help you solve a problem.

Problem Cara's class is learning an Irish folk dance for her school's International Dance Festival. If 24 students are put into 4 equal groups, how many students are in each group?

Understand

What is the question?

How many students are in each group?

What do you know?

- There are 24 students.
- There are 4 equal groups.

Plan

How can you find the answer?

You can write a division number sentence to solve the problem.

Solve

Write and solve a division number sentence.

24	÷	4	=	n
↑ number of students		↑ number of equal groups		↑ number in each group

$24 \div 4 = 6$

There are 6 students in each group.

Look Back

Look back at the problem.

Is there a multiplication sentence you could write to help you solve the problem? Explain your thinking.

Remember:
- Understand
- Plan
- Solve
- Look Back

Guided Practice

Solve these problems, using the Number Sentence strategy.

1. Students practice a Greek line dance for 10 minutes each day. If students practice for 90 minutes in all, how many days do they practice the dance?

   Think: What operation helps you find the number of equal groups?

2. Three groups of 6 students each will do a Hungarian dance called the czardas. Each of the students will need a costume. How many costumes will be needed?

   Think: How can you find the total when there are equal groups?

Choose a Strategy

Solve. Use these or other strategies.

Problem-Solving Strategies

- **Write a Number Sentence**
- **Draw a Picture**
- **Find a Pattern**
- **Guess and Check**

3. The hora is a circle dance. To learn the dance, 30 students formed 3 circles. Each circle had the same number of students. How many students were in each circle?

4. During a dance, 2 students bow. Then 4 students bow, then 8 students, then 16 students. If the pattern continues, how many students will likely bow the fifth time?

5. There are already 14 rows of chairs set up for the dance festival. There are 45 more chairs that need to be set up. How many rows will there be altogether if each new row will have 9 chairs?

6. Ms. Kim's 25 students chose to be in either the African dance or the Japanese dance. Three more students are in the African dance than are in the Japanese dance. How many students are in each dance?

7. Students practiced a Greek dance for 25 minutes. Then they took a 10-minute break. After that they practiced a Spanish dance for 30 minutes. How much time did students spend dancing?

8. In one dance, students form 4 rows of 6 dancers. Then all of the dancers who have dancers to their right, left, front, and back kneel down. How many students kneel down during the dance?

Extra Practice See 5–6 on page 427.

Divide by 8

You will learn different ways to divide by 8.

Learn About It

Forty students are taking a trip to Pennsylvania for the Groundhog Day celebration. They are riding in 8 minivans. If each minivan holds the same number of students, how many students are in each van?

Divide. $40 \div 8 = ■$ or $8\overline{)40}$

Different Ways to Divide

You can use counters.

- Use 40 counters. Divide them into 8 groups.
- Count the number in each group.

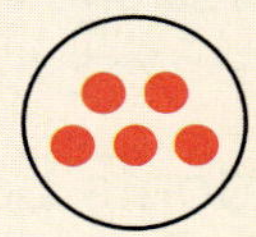 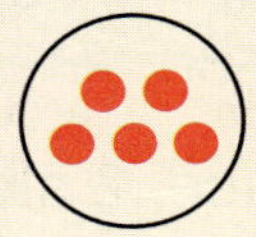 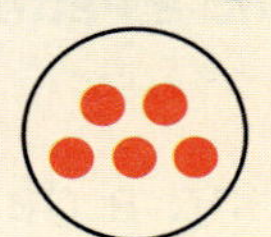 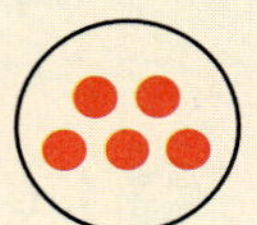 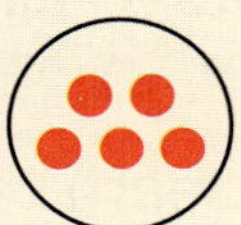 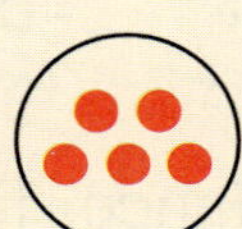 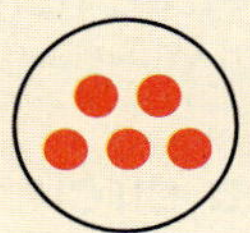 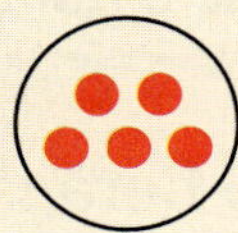

There are 5 in each group.

So $40 \div 8 = 5$.

You can use a related multiplication fact.

$40 \div 8 = ■$

Think $8 \times ■ = 40$
$8 \times 5 = 40$

So $40 \div 8 = 5$.

You can use a related division fact.

$40 \div 8 = ■$

Think $40 \div ■ = 8$
$40 \div 5 = 8$

So $40 \div 8 = 5$.

Solution: Five students are in each van.

Explain Your Thinking

► How could knowing $40 \div 8 = 5$ help you find $48 \div 8$?

Guided Practice

Find each quotient.

1. $8\overline{)8}$
2. $8\overline{)24}$
3. $8\overline{)48}$
4. $16 \div 8$
5. $0 \div 8$
6. $64 \div 8$

Ask Yourself

- What multiplication fact can help me?
- What division fact can help me?

Independent Practice

Divide.

7. $8\overline{)16}$
8. $8\overline{)32}$
9. $8\overline{)64}$
10. $8\overline{)0}$
11. $8\overline{)24}$
12. $8\overline{)40}$
13. $8\overline{)80}$
14. $8\overline{)56}$
15. $8\overline{)48}$
16. $8\overline{)72}$
17. $8 \div 8$
18. $24 \div 8$
19. $32 \div 8$
20. $72 \div 8$
21. $48 \div 8$
22. $42 \div 7$
23. $54 \div 6$
24. $0 \div 5$
25. $49 \div 7$
26. $40 \div 4$

Problem Solving • Reasoning

27. Chen shared 32 pretzels equally with the 7 other students in her minivan. How many pretzels did each student get?

28. **Analyze** Groundhog stickers cost 20¢ each, and post cards cost 40¢ each. Gary bought the same number of each. He paid with a $5 bill and received only dollar bills as change. How many stickers did Gary buy?

29. **Write About It** Look back at page 414. How many minivans would be needed if 43 students were going on the trip?

Math Is Everywhere!

SCIENCE When a groundhog hibernates in its winter den, its breathing and heart rate slow down to save energy.

If a groundhog breathes once every 6 minutes during hibernation, about how many breaths does it take in 1 hour?

Mixed Review • Test Prep

Draw each figure. *(pages 302–303)*

30. square
31. pentagon
32. circle
33. trapezoid

Choose the letter of the correct answer. *(pages 116–118)*

34. 332 + 114 + 272
   - **A** 618
   - **B** 718
   - **C** 628
   - **D** 728

35. 501 + 318 + 424
   - **F** 1,138
   - **G** 1,238
   - **H** 1,243
   - **J** 1,348

Extra Practice See Set E on page 426.

Divide by 9

You will learn different ways to divide by 9.

Learn About It

Bags of apples are sold at a farm stand. Each bag holds 9 apples. Natalie and her mother need 27 apples to make pies. How many bags of apples will they need to buy?

Divide. **27 ÷ 9 = ■** or **9)27** (quotient ■)

Different Ways to Divide

You can use a number line.

- Start at 27. Count back by 9s to 0.
- Count the number of times you subtracted 9.

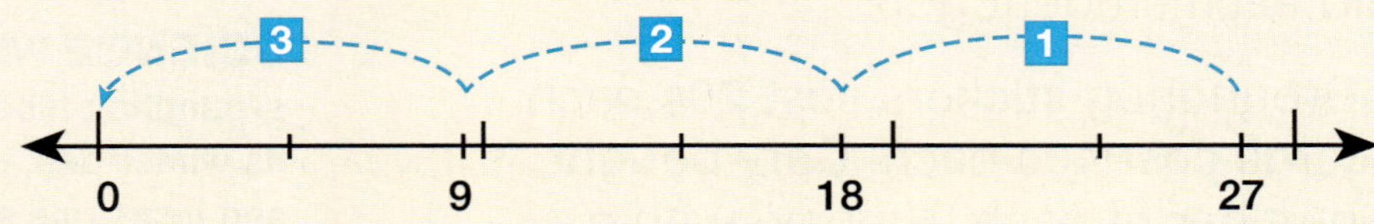

You subtracted 9 three times.

So 27 ÷ 9 = 3.

You can use a related multiplication fact.

$27 \div 9 = n$

Think $9 \times n = 27$

$9 \times 3 = 27$

So 27 ÷ 9 = 3.

You can use a related division fact.

$27 \div 9 = n$

Think $27 \div n = 9$

$27 \div 3 = 9$

So 27 ÷ 9 = 3.

Solution: They will need 3 bags of apples.

Explain Your Thinking

► Why is 36 ÷ 9 greater than 27 ÷ 9?

Guided Practice

Divide.

1. $9\overline{)72}$
2. $9\overline{)63}$
3. $9\overline{)54}$
4. $9 \div 9$
5. $27 \div 9$
6. $81 \div 9$

Ask Yourself

- What multiplication fact can help me?
- What division fact can help me?

Independent Practice

Find each quotient.

7. $9\overline{)0}$
8. $9\overline{)27}$
9. $9\overline{)90}$
10. $9\overline{)54}$
11. $9\overline{)45}$
12. $4\overline{)36}$
13. $7\overline{)56}$
14. $6\overline{)36}$
15. $8\overline{)64}$
16. $7\overline{)42}$
17. $18 \div 9$
18. $0 \div 9$
19. $27 \div 9$
20. $45 \div 9$
21. $63 \div 9$
22. $72 \div 9$
23. $63 \div 9$
24. $81 \div 9$
25. $36 \div 9$
26. $90 \div 9$

Problem Solving • Reasoning

Use Data **Use the table for Problems 27–29.**

Fruit Sold on Thursday	
Fruit	**Number Sold**
Apples	36
Pears	37
Peaches	45
Oranges	54

27. Peaches are sold in baskets at the fruit stand. Each basket holds 9 peaches. How many baskets of peaches were sold on Thursday?

28. When Lucy got to the fruit stand on Thursday, there were 18 peaches left. How many baskets of peaches had already been sold?

29. **Analyze** The fruit stand sells green apples and red apples. On Thursday, twice as many red apples as green apples were sold. How many apples of each color were sold on Thursday?

Mixed Review • Test Prep

Order the numbers from least to greatest. *(pages 22–23)*

30. 4,954 4,495 4,594 4,945

31. 6,106 6,160 6,610

32. What is the value of 1 quarter, 4 dimes, and 6 pennies? *(pages 56–57)*

A \$0.75 **B** \$0.71 **C** \$0.65 **D** \$0.61

Extra Practice See Set F on page 426.

Division Facts Practice

Be sure you memorized your facts. Then find each quotient as quickly as you can!

1. $6\overline{)42}$ **2.** $9\overline{)27}$ **3.** $8\overline{)8}$ **4.** $10\overline{)70}$ **5.** $7\overline{)56}$ **6.** $9\overline{)72}$

7. $8\overline{)32}$ **8.** $7\overline{)35}$ **9.** $10\overline{)20}$ **10.** $6\overline{)30}$ **11.** $8\overline{)56}$ **12.** $7\overline{)63}$

13. $9\overline{)45}$ **14.** $6\overline{)18}$ **15.** $7\overline{)49}$ **16.** $8\overline{)64}$ **17.** $10\overline{)90}$ **18.** $9\overline{)18}$

19. $8\overline{)48}$ **20.** $7\overline{)28}$ **21.** $6\overline{)54}$ **22.** $9\overline{)36}$ **23.** $7\overline{)42}$ **24.** $10\overline{)40}$

25. $7\overline{)21}$ **26.** $6\overline{)60}$ **27.** $8\overline{)72}$ **28.** $10\overline{)50}$ **29.** $9\overline{)54}$ **30.** $6\overline{)36}$

31. $70 \div 7$ **32.** $24 \div 8$ **33.** $60 \div 10$ **34.** $81 \div 9$ **35.** $80 \div 10$

36. $42 \div 7$ **37.** $63 \div 9$ **38.** $16 \div 8$ **39.** $36 \div 6$ **40.** $90 \div 9$

41. $24 \div 6$ **42.** $14 \div 7$ **43.** $9 \div 9$ **44.** $40 \div 8$ **45.** $12 \div 6$

46. $80 \div 8$ **47.** $7 \div 7$ **48.** $100 \div 10$ **49.** $56 \div 7$ **50.** $54 \div 9$

51. $30 \div 10$ **52.** $45 \div 9$ **53.** $48 \div 6$ **54.** $10 \div 10$ **55.** $6 \div 6$

Follow the rule to complete each table.

Rule: Divide by 7.

	Input	Output
56.	70	■
57.	■	3
58.	56	■
59.	14	■
60.	■	6

Rule: Divide by 8.

	Input	Output
61.	48	■
62.	■	9
63.	16	■
64.	■	4
65.	56	■

Rule: Divide by 9.

	Input	Output
66.	■	5
67.	81	■
68.	36	■
69.	■	7
70.	18	■

Find the rule. Then complete the table.

71. Rule: ______________.

	Input	Output
	42	7
	30	5
72.	18	■
73.	■	4
74.	48	■

75. Rule: ______________.

	Input	Output
	70	7
76.	30	■
	50	5
77.	■	8
78.	■	9

79. Rule: ______________.

	Input	Output
	24	3
80.	64	■
	8	1
81.	40	■
82.	■	10

Practice Game

Math Scramble

Practice making multiplication and division number sentences.
Try to use all your number cards!

What You'll Need

- *3 sets of number cards labeled 0 to 9 (Teaching Tool 9)*
- *15 cards for each of these symbols: ×, ÷, and = (Teaching Tools 10 and 11)*

Players
2

Here's What to Do

1. Player 1 deals all the number cards. Players take symbol cards as needed.
2. Player 1 builds a multiplication or division sentence using the number cards and any symbol cards needed.
3. Player 2 builds a number sentence onto Player 1's number sentence.
4. Players take turns building connecting number sentences until one player has used all his or her number cards or neither player is able to build another number sentence. The player who runs out of cards first wins. If both players have cards left, the player with fewer cards wins.

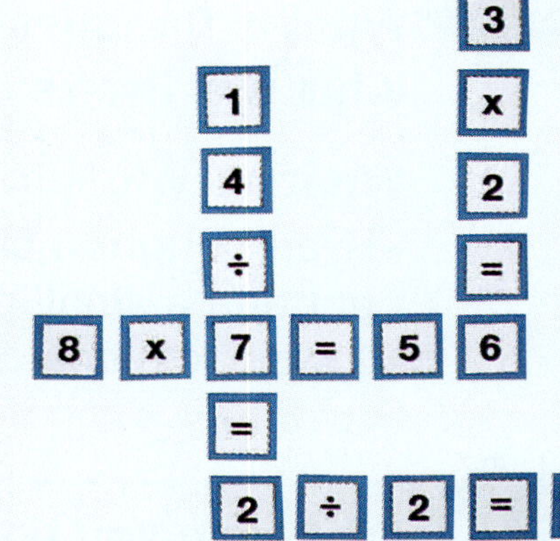

Share Your Thinking How does knowing multiplication and division facts help you play the game?

Problem-Solving Application: Use Money

You will learn how to solve problems about money.

You can use what you know about addition, subtraction, multiplication, and division to solve problems about money.

Problem Hilltop School is having a plant sale. Ryan bought a clay pot and a small plant. He paid with a $10 bill. What was Ryan's change?

School Plant Sale

Pots	clay	2 for $8.00
	plastic	$2.50 each
Plants	small	$5.00
	medium	$6.00
	large	$8.00
Flowers	tulips	4 for $1.00
	daffodils	10¢ each

Understand

What is the question?

What was Ryan's change?

What do you know?

- Ryan bought a clay pot and a small plant.
- 2 clay pots cost $8.
- 1 small plant costs $5.
- Ryan paid with a $10 bill.

Plan

What can you do to find the answer?

- First, divide to find the cost of 1 clay pot.
- Then add the cost of the plant to the cost of the clay pot.
- Then subtract the total cost from $10.

Solve

Find the cost of 1 clay pot.

$$2\overline{)\$8} = \$4 \leftarrow \text{cost of 1 clay pot}$$

Find the cost of the plant and the clay pot.

$$\$4 + 5 = \$9 \leftarrow \text{total cost}$$

Subtract to find the change.

$$\$10.00 - 9.00 = \$\ 1.00 \leftarrow \text{change}$$

Ryan's change was $1.

Look Back

Look back at the question.

What other number sentence could you use to help you find the cost of 1 clay pot?

Each spring more than a million people come to the Skagit County Tulip Festival in the state of Washington. Visitors can see thousands of colorful tulips growing on tulip farms.

Guided Practice

Use the sign on page 420 to solve each problem.

1. Erin buys 12 tulips and 6 daffodils. If she pays with a $5 bill, what should her change be?

   Think: How many flowers are in a dozen?

2. Carl wants to buy 4 pots. How much will he save if he buys plastic pots instead of clay pots?

   Think: How much will 4 clay pots cost?

Choose a Strategy

Use the sign on page 420 to solve. Choose these or other strategies.

Problem-Solving Strategies

- Write a Number Sentence
- Use Logical Thinking
- Make a Table
- Guess and Check

3. Greg bought only two items at the sale. He spent $14. What two items did Greg buy?

4. Mr. Peters has $35. He wants to buy 4 plants and 4 clay pots. Does he have enough money? Explain.

5. Laurie spent more than $2.50 but less than $3.00 on flowers. She bought the same number of tulips as daffodils. How many of each kind of flower did Laurie buy?

6. Marla bought medium and large plants. She spent the same amount of money on each size plant. What is the least amount of money Marla could have spent? Explain.

7. Carlos, Jackie, and Scott each bought 2 plants at the plant sale. Scott spent $12. Carlos spent less money than Scott but more money than Jackie. What plants did Carlos buy?

8. Some plants were put in a 5 x 4 array. The first row and column had small plants. The rest of the array had large plants. How many small plants were in the array?

Extra Practice See Set 7–8 on page 427.

Quick Check

Check Your Understanding of Lessons 5–10

Divide.

1. $6\overline{)42}$ **2.** $6\overline{)36}$ **3.** $6\overline{)18}$ **4.** $6\overline{)24}$ **5.** $6\overline{)6}$

6. $7\overline{)70}$ **7.** $7\overline{)21}$ **8.** $7\overline{)35}$ **9.** $7\overline{)14}$ **10.** $7\overline{)56}$

11. $24 \div 8$ **12.** $40 \div 8$ **13.** $64 \div 8$ **14.** $16 \div 8$ **15.** $32 \div 8$

16. $18 \div 9$ **17.** $36 \div 9$ **18.** $81 \div 9$ **19.** $27 \div 9$ **20.** $63 \div 9$

Solve.

21. In square dance, 4 pairs of dancers are needed to make a square. If 32 people are square dancing, how many squares will they make? Write number sentences to show your work.

22. Anita bought 2 roses for $2.50 each. She bought 3 carnations for $1.25 each. She gave the clerk a $10 bill. How much change did she get back?

How did you do?

If you had difficulty with any items in the Quick Check, you can use the following pages for review and extra practice.

Items	Review These Pages	Do These Extra Practice Items
1–5	pages 408–409	Set C, page 425
6–10	pages 410–411	Set D, page 426
11–15	pages 414–415	Set E, page 426
16–20	pages 416–417	Set F, page 426
21	pages 412–413	5–6, page 427
22	pages 420–421	7–8, page 427

Test Prep • Cumulative Review

Maintaining the Standards

Choose the letter of the correct answer. If a correct answer is not here, choose NH.

1. A package of 3 puzzles costs \$6. What is the unit price?

   A \$1
   B \$2
   C \$3
   D NH

2. The museum is selling a package of dinosaur books for \$30. There are 6 books in a package. What is the unit price?

   F \$2
   G \$10
   H \$36
   J NH

3. What symbol makes the number sentence true?

   6 ● 6 = 12

   A +
   B −
   C ×
   D ÷

4. Look at the table.

Input	Output
12	2
18	3
36	6
48	8

What is the output if the input is 60?

F 9 **H** 11
G 10 **J** 12

5. Which symbol makes the statement true?

   48 ÷ 8 ● 54 ÷ 9

   A > **C** =
   B < **D** +

6. What is the perimeter of this figure?

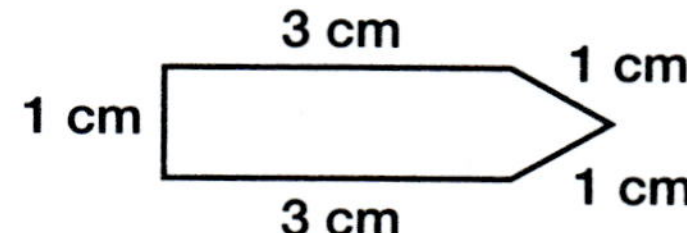

   F 3 cm
   G 6 cm
   H 8 cm
   J 9 cm

7. The elevator holds 1,000 pounds. Two boxes weighing 375 pounds each and one box weighing 125 pounds were placed in the elevator. How many more pounds can the elevator hold?

   A 125
   B 175
   C 225
   D 275

8. A theater has 8 rows of seats, with 9 seats in each row. If 64 seats are filled, how many are empty?

   Explain How did you find your answer?

Safe Site

Internet Test Prep
Visit **www.eduplace.com/kids/mhm** for more *Test Prep Practice*.

Extra Practice

Set A (Lesson 2, pages 398–400)

Copy and complete each fact family.

1. $2 \times 8 = 16$
$8 \times ■ = 16$
$16 \div 2 = ■$
$16 \div ■ = 2$

2. $1 \times 5 = 5$
$5 \times ■ = 5$
$5 \div 1 = ■$
$5 \div ■ = 1$

3. $4 \times 9 = 36$
$9 \times ■ = 36$
$36 \div 4 = ■$
$36 \div ■ = 4$

4. $5 \times 9 = 45$
$9 \times ■ = 45$
$45 \div 5 = ■$
$45 \div ■ = 5$

5. $3 \times 7 = 21$
$7 \times ■ = 21$
$21 \div 3 = ■$
$21 \div ■ = 3$

6. $4 \times 7 = 28$
$7 \times ■ = 28$
$28 \div 4 = ■$
$28 \div ■ = 4$

7. $2 \times 6 = 12$
$6 \times ■ = 12$
$12 \div 2 = ■$
$12 \div ■ = 2$

8. $5 \times 8 = 40$
$8 \times ■ = 40$
$40 \div 5 = ■$
$40 \div ■ = 5$

9. $1 \times 3 = 3$
$3 \times ■ = 3$
$3 \div 1 = ■$
$3 \div ■ = 1$

Write a fact family for each array.

10. 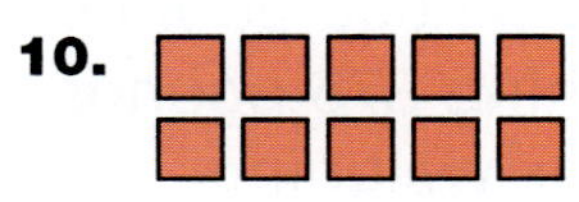

11. 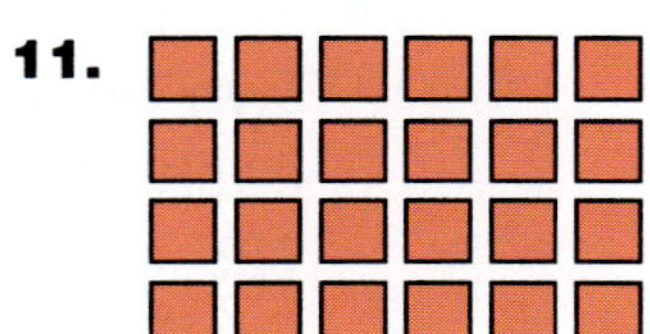

12. 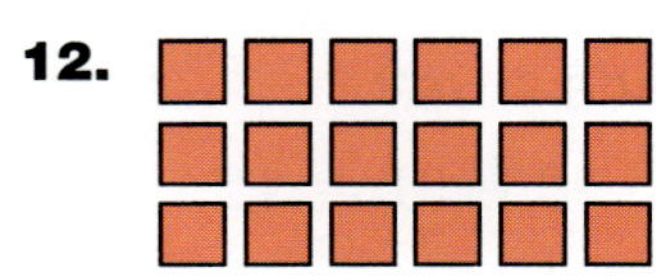

13. 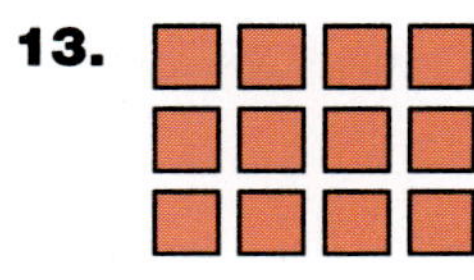

14. 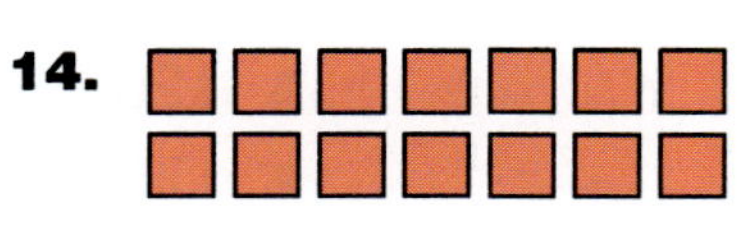

15. 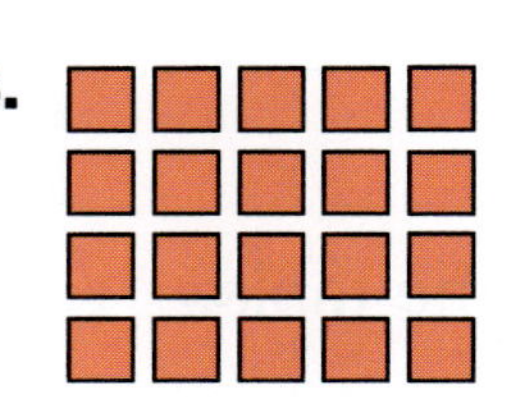

Write a fact family for each set of numbers.

16. 2, 4, 8 **17.** 4, 8, 32 **18.** 3, 4, 12 **19.** 10, 3, 30

20. 1, 7, 7 **21.** 9, 3, 27 **22.** 5, 5, 25 **23.** 7, 6, 42

Extra Practice

Set B *(Lesson 3, pages 402–403)*

Divide.

1. $10\overline{)90}$ **2.** $10\overline{)50}$ **3.** $10\overline{)20}$ **4.** $10\overline{)10}$ **5.** $10\overline{)80}$

6. $10\overline{)70}$ **7.** $10\overline{)30}$ **8.** $10\overline{)90}$ **9.** $10\overline{)60}$ **10.** $10\overline{)40}$

11. $50 \div 10$ **12.** $40 \div 10$ **13.** $80 \div 10$ **14.** $10 \div 10$

15. $90 \div 10$ **16.** $20 \div 10$ **17.** $100 \div 10$ **18.** $60 \div 10$

19. $30 \div 10$ **20.** $40 \div 10$ **21.** $90 \div 10$ **22.** $70 \div 10$

Find each missing number.

23. $70 \div ■ = 7$ **24.** $■ \div 10 = 3$ **25.** $10 \times ■ = 50$

26. $■ \times 8 = 40$ **27.** $■ \times 10 = 60$ **28.** $■ \times 9 = 90$

29. $■ \div 10 = 2$ **30.** $■ \times 7 = 70$ **31.** $80 \div ■ = 8$

Set C *(Lesson 5, pages 408–409)*

Divide.

1. $6\overline{)30}$ **2.** $6\overline{)60}$ **3.** $6\overline{)18}$ **4.** $6\overline{)24}$ **5.** $6\overline{)48}$

6. $6\overline{)42}$ **7.** $6\overline{)12}$ **8.** $6\overline{)36}$ **9.** $6\overline{)54}$ **10.** $6\overline{)60}$

11. $36 \div 6$ **12.** $12 \div 6$ **13.** $18 \div 6$ **14.** $30 \div 6$

15. $54 \div 6$ **16.** $60 \div 6$ **17.** $6 \div 6$ **18.** $42 \div 6$

19. $24 \div 6$ **20.** $48 \div 6$ **21.** $36 \div 6$ **22.** $60 \div 6$

Compare. Write $>$, $<$, or $=$ in the ●.

23. 2×4 ● $42 \div 6$ **24.** $36 \div 4$ ● $36 \div 6$

25. $40 \div 5$ ● $24 \div 3$ **26.** $2 \div 2$ ● $3 \div 3$

27. $45 \div 5$ ● $32 \div 4$ **28.** $12 \div 6$ ● $12 \div 4$

29. $30 \div 6$ ● $20 \div 4$ **30.** $70 \div 10$ ● 7×1

Extra Practice

Set D (Lesson 6, pages 410–411)

Divide.

1. $7\overline{)35}$ 2. $7\overline{)56}$ 3. $7\overline{)21}$ 4. $7\overline{)28}$ 5. $7\overline{)7}$

6. $7\overline{)42}$ 7. $7\overline{)14}$ 8. $7\overline{)49}$ 9. $7\overline{)63}$ 10. $7\overline{)70}$

11. $35 \div 7$ 12. $14 \div 7$ 13. $21 \div 7$ 14. $28 \div 7$

15. $63 \div 7$ 16. $42 \div 7$ 17. $0 \div 7$ 18. $70 \div 7$

19. $49 \div 7$ 20. $56 \div 7$ 21. $7 \div 7$ 22. $63 \div 7$

Set E (Lesson 8, pages 414–415)

Divide.

1. $8\overline{)32}$ 2. $8\overline{)56}$ 3. $8\overline{)24}$ 4. $8\overline{)80}$ 5. $8\overline{)8}$

6. $8\overline{)40}$ 7. $8\overline{)16}$ 8. $8\overline{)48}$ 9. $8\overline{)64}$ 10. $8\overline{)72}$

11. $32 \div 8$ 12. $24 \div 8$ 13. $8 \div 8$ 14. $48 \div 8$

15. $64 \div 8$ 16. $80 \div 8$ 17. $0 \div 8$ 18. $40 \div 8$

19. $16 \div 8$ 20. $56 \div 8$ 21. $48 \div 8$ 22. $72 \div 8$

Set F (Lesson 9, pages 416–419)

Divide.

1. $9\overline{)36}$ 2. $9\overline{)27}$ 3. $9\overline{)54}$ 4. $9\overline{)90}$ 5. $9\overline{)9}$

6. $9\overline{)45}$ 7. $9\overline{)18}$ 8. $9\overline{)81}$ 9. $9\overline{)63}$ 10. $9\overline{)0}$

11. $36 \div 9$ 12. $90 \div 9$ 13. $27 \div 9$ 14. $9 \div 9$

15. $81 \div 9$ 16. $18 \div 9$ 17. $0 \div 9$ 18. $72 \div 9$

19. $45 \div 9$ 20. $54 \div 9$ 21. $90 \div 9$ 22. $63 \div 9$

Find each missing number.

23. $8 \times ■ = 40$ 24. $■ \div 7 = 7$ 25. $■ \times 9 = 72$

26. $45 \div ■ = 9$ 27. $28 \div ■ = 4$ 28. $80 \div ■ = 10$

Extra Practice • Problem Solving

Use the information in the table. If not enough information is given, tell what information is needed to solve the problem. *(Lesson 4, pages 404–405)*

Marble Works	
Kind of Marble	**Price**
Small	$0.50 each
Medium	$0.75 each
Large	$1 each
Mixed bag	$4 each

1. Liz wants to buy 4 mixed bags of marbles. If she gives the clerk $20, what should her change be?

2. Jessie wants to buy 2 mixed bags of marbles and 22 medium marbles. Does Jessie have enough money to buy them?

3. Steve bought 2 bags of mixed marbles, 4 small marbles, and 2 medium marbles. He gave the clerk $15. What should his change be?

4. Mark bought 2 pounds of large marbles and 1 pound of medium marbles. How many large marbles did Mark buy?

Write a number sentence to solve each problem. *(Lesson 7, pages 412–413)*

5. A chorus practiced a song for 10 minutes each day. If they practiced 90 minutes in all, how many days did they practice the song?

6. Four groups with 5 students in each group practice a Mexican folk song. Each student needs a costume. How many costumes are needed?

Use the information in the sign to solve each problem. *(Lesson 10, pages 420–421)*

Bake Sale		
Breads	Whole Grain	2 loaves for $4
	White	50¢ per loaf
Cookies	Oatmeal Raisin	2 cookies for $1
	Chocolate Chip	3 cookies for $1
	Lemon	5 cookies for $1

7. Judith's mother bought 4 loaves of whole grain bread and 12 oatmeal raisin cookies at the bake sale. If she paid with a $10 bill and a $5 bill, what was her change?

8. Alec wants to buy 15 cookies. How much will he save if he buys lemon cookies instead of chocolate chip cookies?

Chapter Review

Reviewing Vocabulary

Copy and complete each sentence.

1. The answer in a division problem is the ____.
2. The number that is divided in a division problem is called the ____.
3. The number that you divide by in a division problem is called the ____.
4. Related facts that use the same numbers are called a ____.

Reviewing Concepts and Skills

Copy and complete each fact family. *(pages 398–399)*

5. $3 \times 8 = 24$
$8 \times \blacksquare = 24$
$24 \div 3 = \blacksquare$
$24 \div \blacksquare = 3$

6. $8 \times 5 = 40$
$5 \times \blacksquare = 40$
$40 \div 8 = \blacksquare$
$40 \div \blacksquare = 8$

7. $6 \times 9 = 54$
$9 \times \blacksquare = 54$
$54 \div 6 = \blacksquare$
$54 \div \blacksquare = 6$

8. $7 \times 10 = 70$
$10 \times \blacksquare = 70$
$70 \div 7 = \blacksquare$
$70 \div \blacksquare = 7$

9. $8 \times 3 = 24$
$3 \times \blacksquare = 24$
$24 \div 8 = \blacksquare$
$24 \div \blacksquare = 8$

10. $10 \times 4 = 40$
$4 \times \blacksquare = 40$
$40 \div 10 = \blacksquare$
$40 \div \blacksquare = 10$

Write a fact family for each set of numbers.

11. 2, 6, 12 **12.** 4, 7, 28 **13.** 5, 4, 20 **14.** 10, 6, 60

Divide. *(pages 402–403, 408–411, 414–417)*

15. $10\overline{)0}$ **16.** $10\overline{)90}$ **17.** $10\overline{)60}$ **18.** $10\overline{)10}$ **19.** $10\overline{)40}$

20. $6\overline{)36}$ **21.** $6\overline{)48}$ **22.** $6\overline{)18}$ **23.** $6\overline{)54}$ **24.** $6\overline{)60}$

25. $7\overline{)49}$ **26.** $7\overline{)7}$ **27.** $7\overline{)70}$ **28.** $7\overline{)21}$ **29.** $7\overline{)63}$

30. $8\overline{)24}$ **31.** $8\overline{)80}$ **32.** $8\overline{)72}$ **33.** $8\overline{)40}$ **34.** $8\overline{)64}$

35. $9\overline{)0}$ **36.** $9\overline{)81}$ **37.** $9\overline{)9}$ **38.** $9\overline{)90}$ **39.** $9\overline{)36}$

Write each quotient. *(pages 402–403, 408–411, 414–417)*

40. $32 \div 8$ **41.** $12 \div 6$ **42.** $42 \div 7$ **43.** $0 \div 8$ **44.** $27 \div 9$

45. $30 \div 10$ **46.** $48 \div 8$ **47.** $6 \div 6$ **48.** $100 \div 10$ **49.** $56 \div 7$

50. $63 \div 9$ **51.** $35 \div 7$ **52.** $18 \div 9$ **53.** $30 \div 6$ **54.** $80 \div 10$

Use the sign on the right for Problems 55 and 56. If not enough information is given, tell what information is needed to solve the problem. *(pages 404–405, 412–413, 420–421)*

55. Suppose Betsy buys a small pizza and pays for it with a $10 bill. About how much change will she receive?

56. Kristin bought a meal at Mario's Pizza for $2.99. The meal included 2 pieces of pizza and a small drink. How much did the pieces of pizza cost?

57. Jim bought flowers for his mother. He bought a dozen carnations at 6 for $1 and 6 daisies at 4 for $1. He paid with a $5 bill. How much change did he get?

TODAY'S SPECIALS

1 large pizza $8.99

1 small pizza $6.99

2 pieces of pizza
with a small drink $2.99

Brain Teaser Math Reasoning

Fill in the blanks with the digits from 0–9. You may not use a digit more than once.

4 × ___ = 3___

3 × ___ = ___

___0 ÷ 1___ = 6

7 × ___ = ___

___ × ___ = 20

Internet Brain Teasers
Visit **www.eduplace.com/kids/mhm** for more *Brain Teasers.*

Chapter Test

Copy and complete each fact family.

1. $6 \times 5 = 30$
$5 \times ■ = 30$
$30 \div 6 = ■$
$30 \div ■ = 6$

2. $1 \times 9 = 9$
$9 \times ■ = 9$
$9 \div 1 = ■$
$9 \div ■ = 1$

3. $4 \times 6 = 24$
$6 \times ■ = 24$
$24 \div 4 = ■$
$24 \div ■ = 4$

4. $8 \times 7 = 56$
$7 \times ■ = 56$
$56 \div 8 = ■$
$56 \div ■ = 8$

Write a fact family for each set of numbers.

5. 2, 8, 16 **6.** 7, 6, 42 **7.** 3, 7, 21 **8.** 8, 10, 80

Divide.

9. $10\overline{)20}$ **10.** $7\overline{)28}$ **11.** $8\overline{)8}$ **12.** $6\overline{)24}$ **13.** $9\overline{)54}$

14. $6\overline{)0}$ **15.** $9\overline{)45}$ **16.** $10\overline{)70}$ **17.** $7\overline{)14}$ **18.** $8\overline{)32}$

19. $9\overline{)72}$ **20.** $8\overline{)16}$ **21.** $7\overline{)0}$ **22.** $6\overline{)42}$ **23.** $10\overline{)50}$

24. $7\overline{)56}$ **25.** $10\overline{)100}$ **26.** $9\overline{)36}$ **27.** $8\overline{)40}$ **28.** $6\overline{)18}$

29. $64 \div 8$ **30.** $9 \div 9$ **31.** $21 \div 7$ **32.** $90 \div 10$

33. $54 \div 6$ **34.** $72 \div 8$ **35.** $36 \div 6$ **36.** $48 \div 8$

37. $81 \div 9$ **38.** $49 \div 7$ **39.** $35 \div 7$ **40.** $90 \div 9$

41. $40 \div 10$ **42.** $24 \div 6$ **43.** $32 \div 8$ **44.** $12 \div 6$

45. $63 \div 9$ **46.** $0 \div 10$ **47.** $56 \div 8$ **48.** $60 \div 10$

Solve.

49. Carnations are 6 for $1. Daisies are 4 for $1. Roses are $1 each. Ed bought 3 roses and 2 dozen carnations. He paid with a $10 bill. How much change did he get?

50. The 24 students in Mr. Nichol's class are separated into 8 equal groups. Write a number sentence to show how many students should be in a group.

Write About It

Solve each problem. Use correct math vocabulary to explain your thinking.

1. Ann is having a party with 10 guests. Each guest will receive the same kind of party favor. She finds favors that cost 60¢ each, 70¢ each, 80¢ each, 90¢ each, and $1 each. Ann has $7.00 to buy the favors.

   a. Explain how she can find out which favors she can buy.

   b. Explain how her choice of party favors might change if there were 7 people coming to the party instead of 10.

   c. Explain how her choice of party favors might change if she had $10 instead of $7.

2. Lisa wants to make flower decorations for the tables. There will be 10 guests at 2 tables. Each table will have a decoration. Each decoration will have 9 flowers.

   a. Explain how Lisa can tell how many flowers she will need in all.

   b. Lisa has $6.00 to buy the flowers. The flowers she wants to buy cost $4 for 12 flowers. How can she find out if she has enough money?

Another Look

Use the picture to answer the questions. Show your work using counters, drawings, or numbers.

1. You want to arrange 32 squares in equal rows to make a game board. What are all the different ways in which you can arrange the squares?
2. Use counters or pictures to arrange 55 squares into equal rows for a game board. How many different ways can you arrange the squares? Write division sentences for each way.
3. **Look Back** Explain why there are more ways to arrange a game board in equal rows with 32 squares than with 55 squares.
4. **Analyze** Make a game board that has 25 squares. Your board should have equal rows. No row or column may have only 1 square. What do you notice about the shape of the board? Why do you think this is so? Design 2 other boards with this shape but with a different number of squares. How many squares did you use for each board?

Enrichment

Using a Function Table

In a **function table**, the numbers in each row are related by the same rule.

This table shows how the number of in-line skates is related to the total number of wheels.

New Vocabulary
function table

Rule:__________

Number of Wheels	Number of Skates
4	1
8	2
12	3
16	4
20	
24	
28	
32	

1. When you know the number of wheels, how can you figure out the number of skates? What is the rule?

2. Copy and complete the table for 20, 24, 28, and 32 wheels.

3. A new set of 4 wheels costs $5. Make a function table. Label the columns *Cost* and *Number of Sets*. Show how many sets you can buy for $5, $10, $15, $20, $25, and $30. What is the rule?

Explain Your Thinking

A group of children went skating. The children counted the total number of wheels on their skates. They counted 32 wheels. How many children went skating? Explain your answer.

Data and Probability

Why Learn About Data and Probability?

Learning about data can help you organize information. Understanding probability helps you predict how likely it is that something will happen.

When you vote on a favorite class pet, you are collecting data. When you spin a spinner you can use probability to predict what color the spinner will most likely land on.

These children are rafting at summer camp—a very popular activity! Knowing how to collect and display data could help the children find out what other activities are popular with campers.

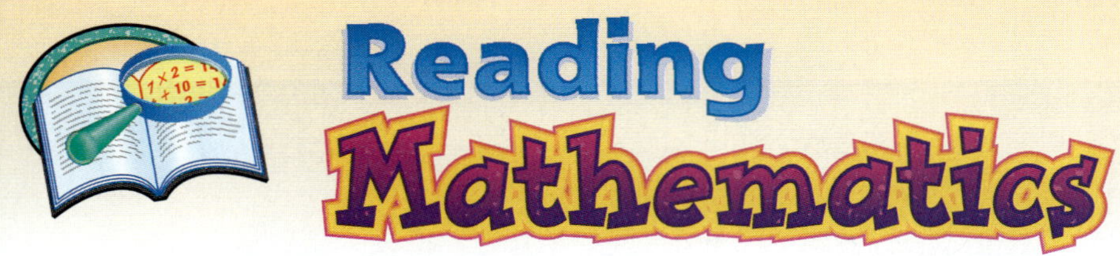

Reviewing Vocabulary

Understanding math language helps you become a successful problem solver. Here are some math vocabulary words you should know.

tally chart a chart used to record data

tally mark a vertical mark on a tally chart that stands for one

pictograph a graph that shows data with pictures

bar graph a graph that shows data with bars of different lengths

Reading Words and Symbols

When you read mathematics, sometimes you read words and sometimes you read charts and tables.

Thirteen students took turns picking marbles from the bag on the right. The marble was put back each time. The tally chart shows the number of times each color was picked.

- ► Each tally mark stands for one marble.
- ► The tally marks 𝍸 stand for 5 marbles.
- ► Thirteen marbles were picked altogether.
- ► Red was the color picked most often.

Marbles Picked

Color	Tally	Number
Red	𝍸 IIII	9
Green	II	2
Blue	II	2

Try These

1. Use the information on page 436 to answer each question.

   a. Some of the information in the tally chart is shown in the bar graph on the right. Copy and complete the bar graph.

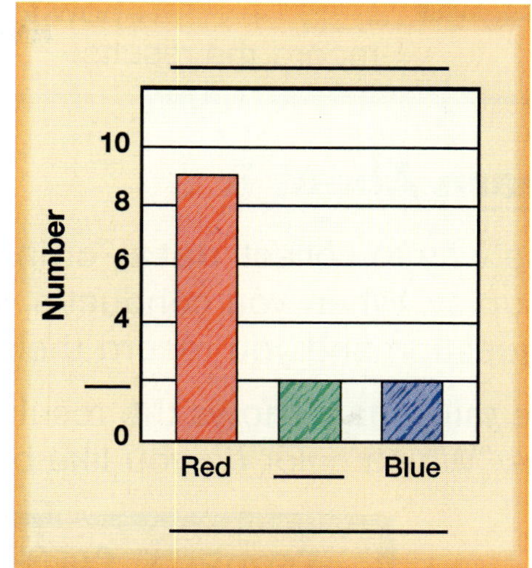

   b. Would you be *more likely* or *less likely* to pick a red marble than a blue marble on the next pick? Explain.

   c. Would you be *more likely* or *less likely* to pick a green marble than a red marble on the next pick? Explain.

2. Copy and complete each sentence. Write *always, sometimes,* or *never.*

   a. A pictograph ____ uses pictures to stand for numbers of things.

   b. A bar graph ____ has more than 3 bars.

   c. A circle is ____ used as a tally mark.

   d. The tally marks 𝍸 ____ stand for 5 on a tally chart.

Upcoming Vocabulary

Write About It **Here are some other vocabulary words** you will learn in this chapter. Watch for these words. Write their definitions in your journal.

data	**scale**
survey	**ordered pair**
line plot	**probability**
mode	**outcome**
range	**equally likely**

Collecting and Organizing Data

You will learn how to conduct a survey and record the results.

New Vocabulary
data
survey

Learn About It

One way to collect **data**, or information, is to conduct a survey. When you conduct a **survey**, you ask people a question and you record their answers.

The tally chart shows the results of a survey. The question was "Which color do you like best?"

FAVORITE COLORS

Color	Tally	Number
Red	卌	5
Blue	III	3
Green	卌 II	7
Yellow	IIII	4

Remember:
A tally mark stands for 1 vote. It looks like this: I
Five tally marks look like this: 卌

- Which color was chosen most often?
- Which color was chosen least often?

Work with a group to conduct a survey in your class.

Step 1 Think of a survey question that has at least three possible answers. Make a chart with a title, headings, and possible answers. Use the tally chart above as a model.

Step 2 Conduct a survey in your class. Record the results in a tally chart.

Step 3 Count the tally marks for each choice.

- Which choice has the greatest number of votes?

Try It Out

Use the tally chart for Questions 1–3.

1. How many children like to collect stuffed animals?
2. How many more children like collecting stuffed animals than collecting dolls?
3. How many children like collecting either rocks or stamps?

Item We Like to Collect the Most		
Item	**Tally**	**Number**
Dolls	𝍸	5
Rocks	II	2
Stamps	III	3
Stuffed animals	𝍸 II	7

Make a tally chart to record the information from the list. Then use your chart to answer Questions 4–7.

Our Favorite Pets		
Pet	**Tally**	**Number**
Bird		
Cat		
Dog		
Fish		

Our Favorite Pets	
Sue	fish
Mary	bird
Carlos	cat
Bob	dog
Kim	dog
Roger	cat
Alyssa	dog
Cynthia	bird
Rex	dog
Maggie	dog

4. How many people were surveyed?
5. Which is the favorite pet of the least number of people?
6. How many people chose either a cat or a dog?
7. Rex said, "The favorite pet is a dog." Why did Rex say this?

Write about it! Talk about it!

Use what you have learned to answer these questions.

8. Is it easier to see which pet is the favorite by looking at the list or the tally chart? Explain.
9. Write three or four sentences that summarize what your tally chart shows.

Use Line Plots

You will learn how to display data in a line plot to show how often something happens.

New Vocabulary
line plot
mode
range

Learn About It

Jim conducted a survey of 15 baseball players. He asked, "How many home runs did you hit this season?"

You can use a **line plot** like the one below to show how often something happens.

Home Runs This Season

Rick	2	John	0	Jess	1
Sally	1	Luis	2	Lynn	4
Max	3	Yoko	1	Mike	6
Amy	0	Edie	3	Ann	2
Ellen	2	Joe	2	Dave	0

```
        X
        X
X   X   X
X   X   X   X
X   X   X   X   X       X
+---+---+---+---+---+---+
0   1   2   3   4   5   6
```

Home Runs

Each X above the 3 stands for a player. Two players hit 3 home runs.

Jim used a line plot because it is a quick way to record and organize data. This line plot shows how many players hit a specific number of home runs.

The **mode** of the data is the number that occurs most often.

The number of home runs that occurred most often was 2.

The mode is 2.

The **range** of the data is the difference between the greatest number and the least number.

$$6 - 0 = 6$$

6 ↑ greatest number; 0 ↑ least number; 6 ↑ range

The range is 6.

Explain Your Thinking

► Look at the line plot above. Why are there 3 X's above both the 0 and the 1?

► Is it easier to use the data list or the line plot to find the number of home runs that was scored most often?

Guided Practice

This line plot shows the heights of five players.

1. How many players are 48 inches tall?
2. How many players are at least 52 inches tall?
3. What is the range of the data?

Ask Yourself

- What do the X's above the numbers stand for?

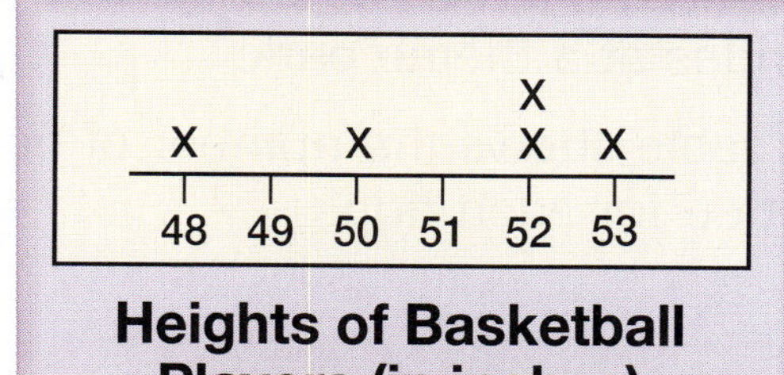

Heights of Basketball Players (in inches)

Independent Practice

This line plot represents the answers of 15 children who were asked to count the number of teams on which they play.

4. How many children play on 3 teams?
5. How many children play on at least 1 team?
6. What is the range of the data? the mode?

Number of Teams Children Play On

Problem Solving • Reasoning

Use Data **Use the line plot that shows the number of teams children play on.**

7. Suppose another child says she plays on 6 teams. How will the line plot change? Will the range or the mode of the data change? Explain.
8. **Write About It** Can you tell from the line plot which sports children play? Explain.

Mixed Review • Test Prep

Solve. *(pages 120–121, 138–141)*

9. $135.50 − 25.25
10. 5,267 + 4,327
11. 8,611 − 4,023
12. 1,016 + 2,867
13. 4,387 + 4,236

Choose the letter of the correct operation. *(pages 167, 277, 391)*

14. 7 ● 3 = 21
    - A +
    - B −
    - C ×
    - D ÷

15. 24 = 14 ● 10
    - A +
    - B −
    - C ×
    - D ÷

16. 4 = 16 ● 4
    - A +
    - B −
    - C ×
    - D ÷

Extra Practice See Set A on page 470.

Make a Pictograph

You will learn how to use pictures to show data.

Review Vocabulary
pictograph

Learn About It

One of Lucy's favorite things to do is to go on rides at a theme park.

The table shows the number of tickets needed for each ride.

Tickets Needed for Rides

Ride	Number Needed
Big Dipper	10
Carousel	4
Ferris wheel	8

You can make a pictograph to show the information from the table in a different way. A **pictograph** uses pictures to represent data.

Step 1 Draw an outline for the pictograph. Write a title and the name of each ride.

Tickets Needed for Rides

Big Dipper	
Carousel	
Ferris wheel	

Step 2 Decide what number to use for the key.

- The numbers in the table can all be divided by 2 with a quotient that is not too large. So let each 🎟 stand for 2 tickets.
- Then divide each number in the table by 2 to find the number of 🎟 to draw for each ride.

Big Dipper $10 \div 2 = 5$
Carousel $4 \div 2 = 2$
Ferris wheel $8 \div 2 = 4$

Step 3 Draw the correct number of 🎟 for each ride to complete the pictograph.

Tickets Needed for Rides

Big Dipper	🎟🎟🎟🎟🎟
Carousel	🎟🎟
Ferris wheel	🎟🎟🎟🎟
Each 🎟 stands for 2 tickets.	

Key →

Another Example

Using Parts of the Symbol

There are 21 blue balloons, 18 green balloons, and 3 red balloons.

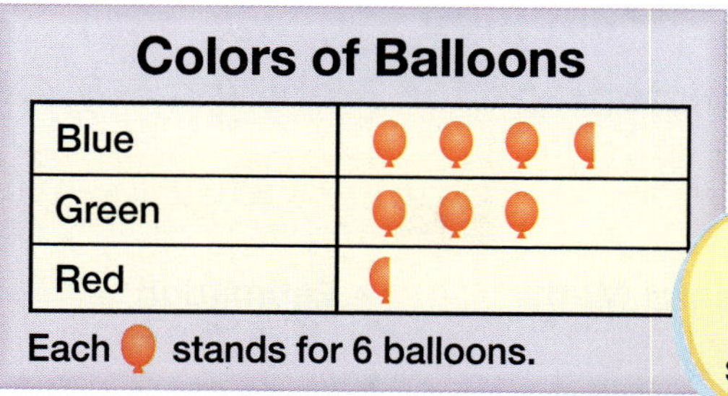

Each picture stands for 6 balloons. So one-half picture stands for 3 balloons.

Explain Your Thinking

► Why might a key where each balloon stands for 3 balloons be a good choice for the pictograph above?

Guided Practice

1. Use the table to complete the pictograph.

Books Read	
Mom	4
Dad	8
Lucy	8
Billy	16

Books Read

Mom	▪
Dad	▬

Each ▬ stands for 4 books.

Ask Yourself

- How many books does ▬ stand for?
- How many books does ▪ stand for?

Independent Practice

2. Use the table to complete the pictograph.

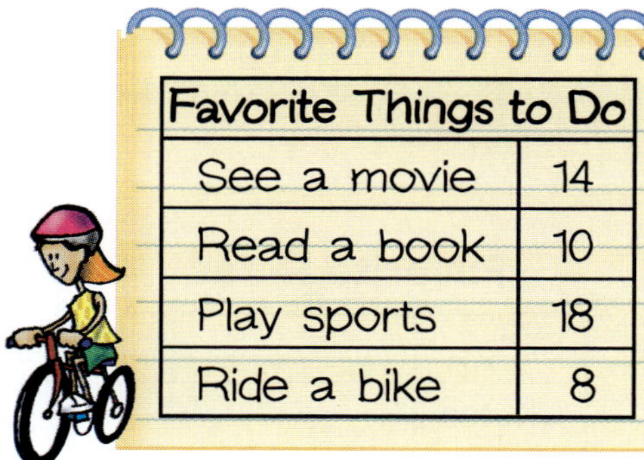

Favorite Things to Do	
See a movie	14
Read a book	10
Play sports	18
Ride a bike	8

Favorite Things to Do

See a movie	☺ ☺ ☺ ◖
Read a book	

Each ☺ stands for 4 votes.

3. Suppose the key is changed so that each ☺ stands for 2 votes. How many ☺ would you need to draw next to "Read a book"?

4. Would a key in which each ☺ stands for 10 votes be a good choice here? Why or why not?

Problem Solving • Reasoning

Use Data **Use the pictograph for Problems 5–8. Choose a method.**

Computation Methods

- Mental Math
- Estimation
- Paper and Pencil

Summer Sports Teams

Baseball	
Basketball	
Soccer	

Each stands for 10 players.

5. To the nearest 10, how many players are on summer sports teams?

6. Each person can sign up for only one team. How many people play either baseball or soccer?

7. A basketball team has 5 players. What is the greatest number of teams that can be made from the basketball players?

8. Suppose 19 new players join teams during the summer and 13 players drop out. How many players are left?

Mixed Review • Test Prep

Write the missing number. *(pages 164–166, 170–173, 182–185)*

9. 4 yd = ■ ft **10.** 64 oz = ■ lb **11.** ■ m = 300 cm **12.** ■ qt = 4 gal

13 Which number has a 3 in the ten thousands place? *(pages 32–33)*

A 43,294 **B** 23,526 **C** 37,829 **D** 73,982

14. Read the clues. Then copy and complete the pictograph.

- Six people like the Whirl.
- Eight more people like the Slide than the Whirl.
- The same number like the Chutes as the Slide.
- The number of people who like the Chutes is the same as the sum of the numbers of people who like the Whirl and the Rapids.

Favorite Rides

Slide	
Chutes	
Rapids	
Whirl	

Each stands for 2 people.

Extra Practice See Set B on page 470.

Choosing a Graph to Display Data

Mike collected data about a weekend festival in his town. Then he displayed the data in the following ways.

To show attendance, Mike made a pictograph. It is easy to show large numbers in a pictograph.

- Would Mike's data be easy to read if he used a tally mark for each person on a tally chart? Why or why not?

Festival Attendance

Friday	
Saturday	
Sunday	

Each stands for 100 people.

For the pie-eating contest, Mike made a line plot to show how many people ate a specific number of pies. A line plot makes it easy to compare small amounts of data.

- Could you show these data on a pictograph? Why or why not?

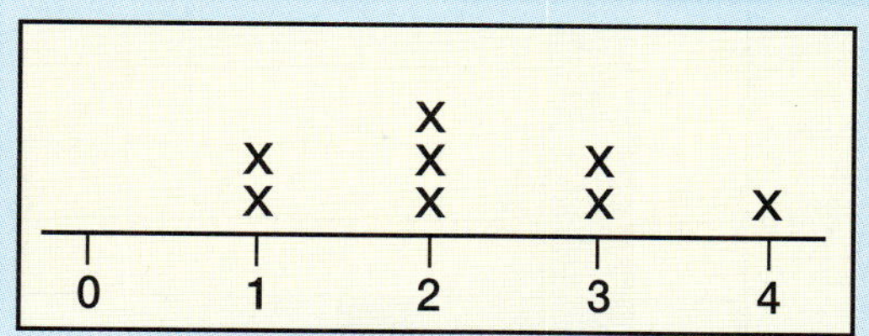

Number of Pies Eaten

Mike made a tally chart to show the number of children who had their faces painted with various designs.

- Use the data to make a pictograph or a line plot.

Face Painting

Design	Tally	Number
Rabbit	卌 卌 卌	15
Clown	卌 卌 卌 卌	20
Flower	卌 卌 卌 卌	20

Explain Your Thinking

► Which way did you choose to display the data from the tally chart? Why did you choose that way?

Problem-Solving Skill: Use a Bar Graph

You will learn how to find information in a bar graph to help you solve a problem.

Sometimes you need to get information from a bar graph in order to solve a problem.

Problem Jack volunteers at a nature center. He is helping to set up new tanks for the wood frogs. If he puts 3 wood frogs in each tank, how many tanks will he need?

Use information in the bar graph to solve the problem.

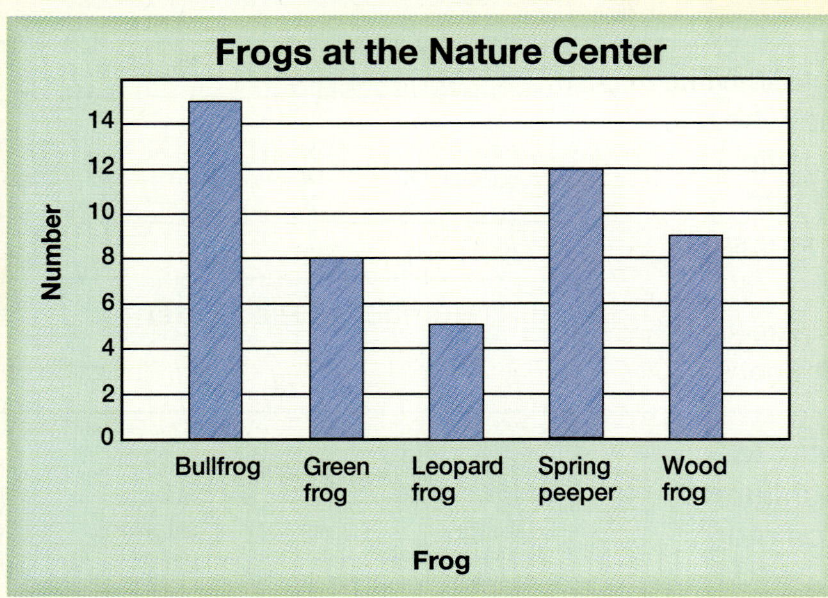

The bar for the wood frog ends halfway between 8 and 10. So the nature center has 9 wood frogs.

Divide the total number of wood frogs by 3.
$9 \div 3 = 3$

Jack will need 3 tanks.

Look Back How would you check your work?

Left: A green frog's voice sounds like a banjo string being plucked.
Right: Most leopard frogs have spots.

Guided Practice

Use the information from page 446 for Problems 1 and 2.

1. One tank holds 2 green frogs or 4 spring peepers. Which kind of frog needs more tanks? Explain.

How many green frogs and spring peepers are there?

2. There are twice as many insects as frogs at the nature center. How many insects are there?

What is the total number of frogs?

Choose a Strategy

Solve. Use these or other strategies. Use the graph for Problems 3 and 4.

Problem-Solving Strategies

- **Write a Number Sentence**
- **Draw a Picture**
- **Act It Out**
- **Use Logical Thinking**

3. How many more people visited the most popular exhibit than visited the least popular exhibit?

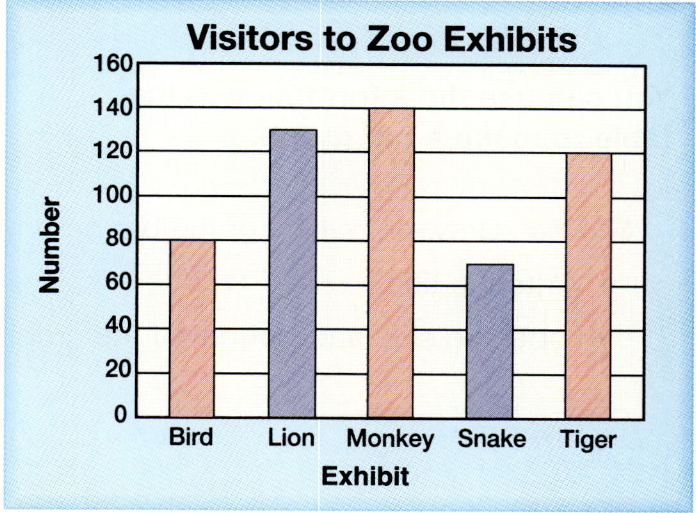

4. Twice as many people visited the gift store as visited the monkey exhibit. How many people visited the gift store?

5. Carl bought a hamburger and juice at the snack bar. The hamburger cost \$4.50. The juice cost \$0.90. Carl paid with a \$5 bill and 2 quarters. What should his change be?

6. There are four snakes in the snake house. The racer is longer than the king snake. The ringneck snake is shorter than the king snake. The coachwhip is the longest. Write the names of the snakes in order from longest to shortest.

King snake
Coachwhip

Extra Practice See 1–2 on page 473.

Make a Bar Graph

You will learn how to show data in a bar graph.

New Vocabulary
scale

Learn About It

Families often take trips on ships to watch sea animals. The table shows the number of sea animals that were seen from a ship in one day.

Animals Seen Today

Animal	Number
Dolphin	6
Seal	14
Sea otter	9
Whale	3

You can use the information in the table to make a bar graph.

Step 1 Draw an outline of the bar graph.

- Write the title.
- Label the side and bottom of the graph.

Step 2 Choose a **scale** to show the number of animals.

- You can use a scale of 1, but sometimes that makes a very large graph.
- If you use a scale of 2, some bars will end halfway between the numbers.
- Start with 0 and label the lines by 2s.

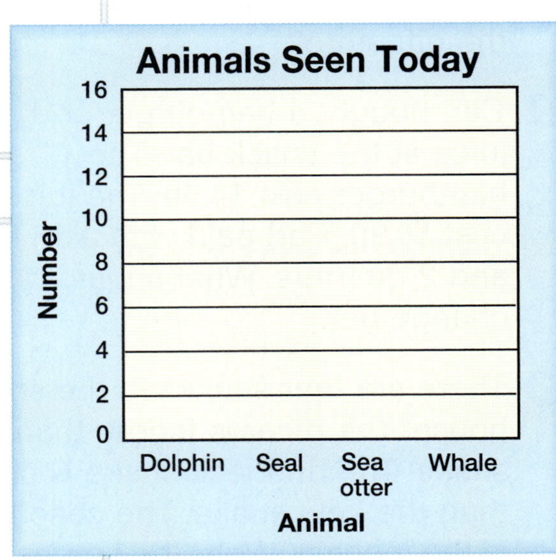

Step 3 Draw the bars.

- The bar for *sea otter* ends halfway between 8 and 10.
- The bar for *whale* ends halfway between 2 and 4.

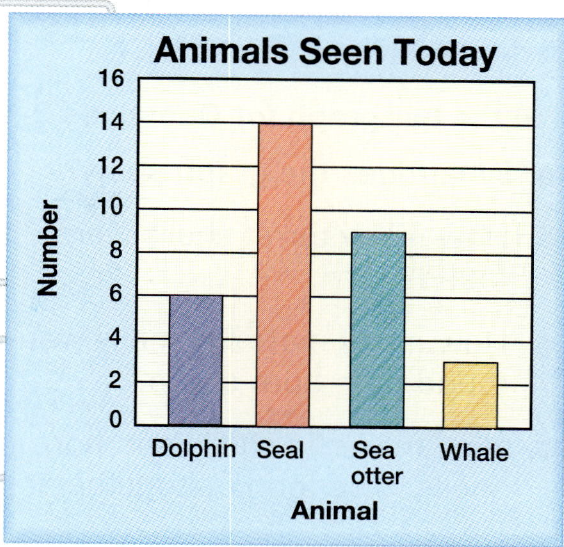

Step 4 Look back at the table to be sure that each bar is the correct height.

Another Example

Horizontal Bar Graph

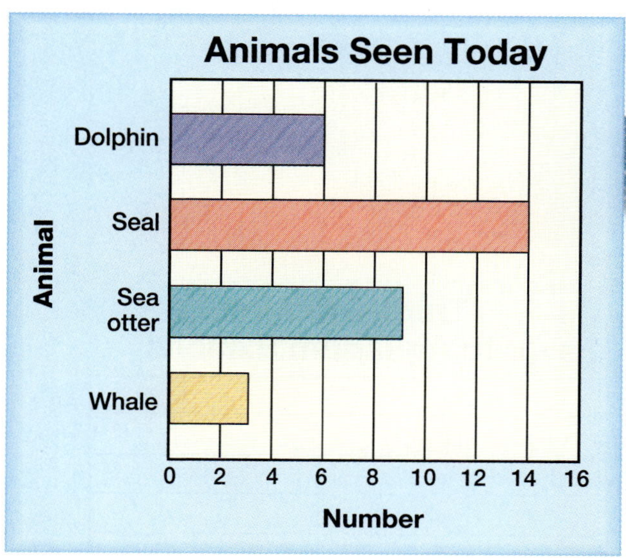

Explain Your Thinking

► Why is a scale of 10 not good for this bar graph?

Guided Practice

1. Use the data from the table to make a bar graph. Follow the steps on pages 448 and 449.

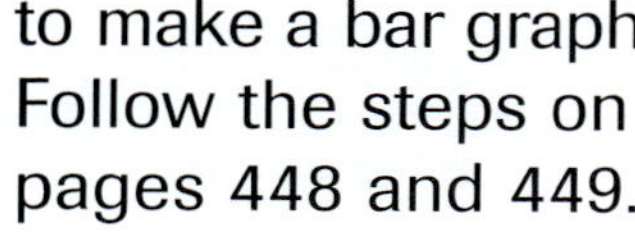

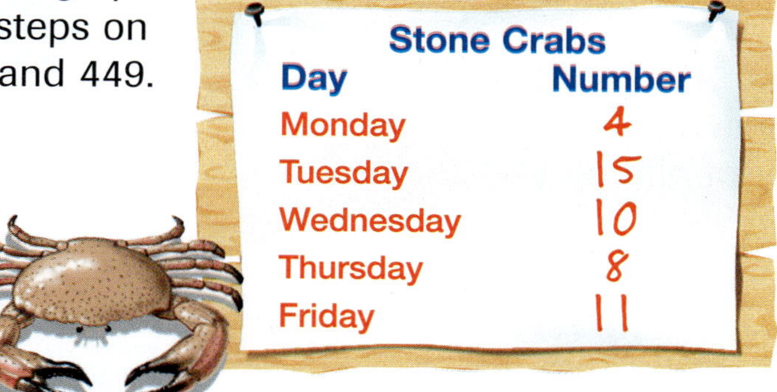

Stone Crabs

Day	Number
Monday	4
Tuesday	15
Wednesday	10
Thursday	8
Friday	11

Ask Yourself

- Do I want the bars going across or up and down?
- What are the labels for the bottom and the side?
- What scale do I want to use?

Independent Practice

Use the bar graph for Questions 2–6.

2. What does the graph show?
3. How many turret shells were found?
4. How many more fig shells were found than horn shells?
5. How many fig shells and horn shells were found altogether?
6. How many shells were found in all?

Problem Solving • Reasoning

The labels for the scale are missing from this graph. Use the graph for Problems 7–11.

7. Which exhibit was the most popular?
8. **Estimate** Which exhibit was about half as popular as Shark Cove?
9. **Compare** Which two exhibits combined were as popular as Jellyfish Junction?
10. Which exhibit was three times as popular as Coral Reef?
11. **Analyze** Suppose the scale was 0, 10, 20, 30, 40, 50, 60, 70. How many more students voted for the most popular exhibit than for the least popular one?

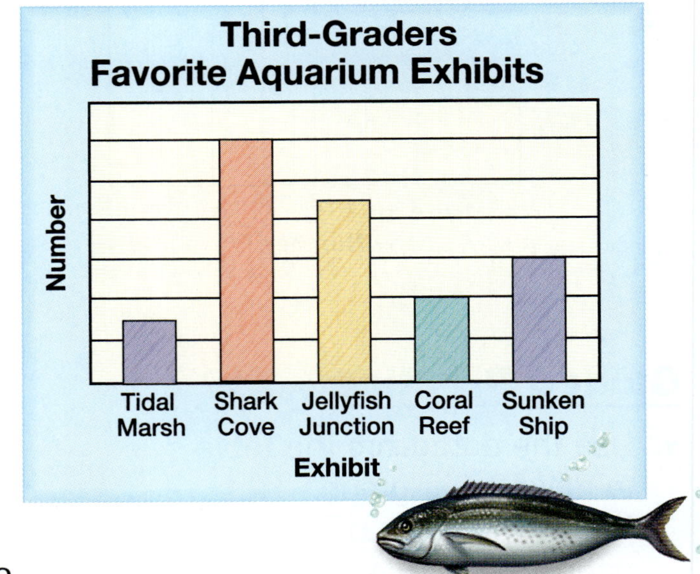

12. **Write About It** Suppose you want to make a bar graph to show the following data about the number of different types of fish at the aquarium.

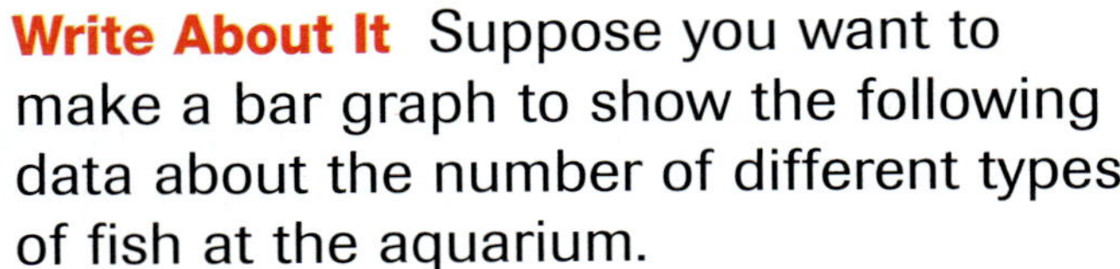

5　20　35　60　125

Tell why 10 would be a good scale.

Mixed Review • Test Prep

Compare. Write >, <, or = for each ●. *(pages 20–21)*

13. 63 + 11 ● 81 − 7 **14.** 104 + 40 ● 140 + 40 **15.** 4 × 9 ● 12 + 8

Order the numbers in each group from least to greatest. *(pages 22–23)*

16. 21 9 12 39 **17.** 56 38 44 49 **18.** 10 110 90 11

19. 83 47 28 674 **20.** 23 73 36 84 39 **21.** 273 984 237 283

Choose the letter of the correct answer. *(pages 312–317)*

22 Which dashed line is not a line of symmetry?

A 

C 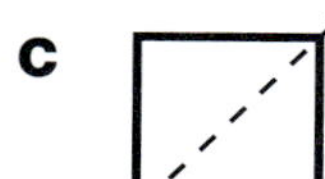

B 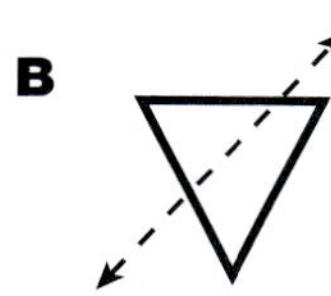

D 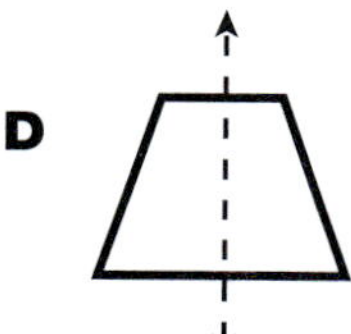

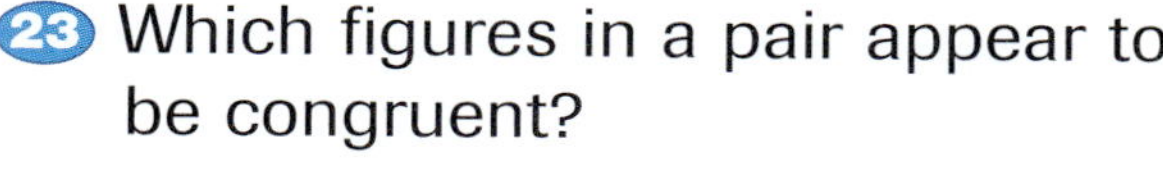

23 Which figures in a pair appear to be congruent?

F 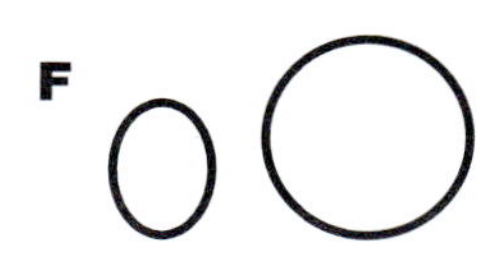

H 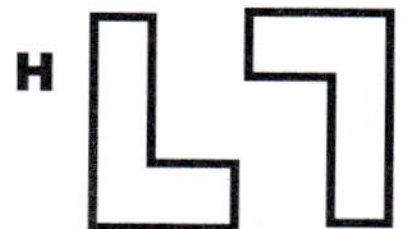

G J 

24. Use the clues to decide which post-card collection belongs to each person. Write *A, B, C,* and *D*. Then write the name of the person after the letter of his or her collection.

- Juan has twice as many post cards as Jill.
- Jill has more post cards than Beth.
- Brita has more post cards than Beth.

Extra Practice See Set C on page 471.

Graph Ordered Pairs

You will learn how to locate points on a grid.

New Vocabulary
ordered pair

Learn About It

At a zoo, visitors travel from one area to another in shuttle buses. The shuttle buses travel in a route that begins at Stop *A*. Where is Stop *A*?

Count spaces on the grid to find out.

- Start at 0.
- Move right 4 spaces.
- From there, move up 6 spaces.

The pair of numbers for the point at Stop *A* is (4, 6). The number pair (4, 6) is called an **ordered pair**.

- The first number of an ordered pair tells how far to the right to move.
- The second number tells how far up to move.

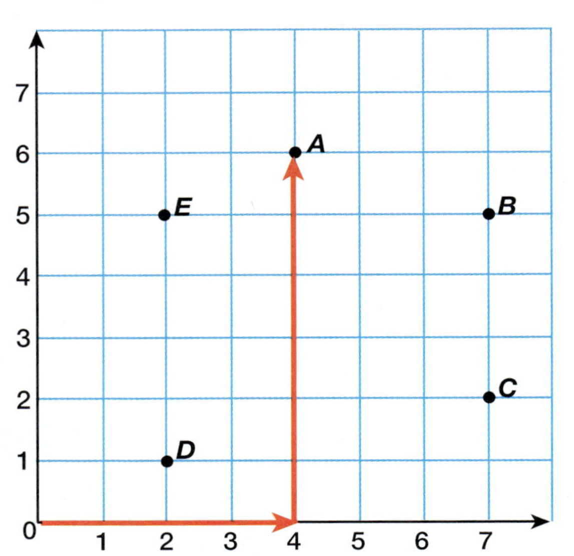

Explain Your Thinking

▶ Why are (4, 6) and (6, 4) two different ordered pairs?

▶ Why is the point (2, 5) farther up than the point (2, 3)?

Guided Practice

Use the grid above to answer Questions 1–4.

1. What ordered pair tells where Stop *C* is?
2. What ordered pair tells where Stop *E* is?
3. What stop is at (2, 1)?
4. What stop is at (7, 5)?

Ask Yourself

- Did I move to the right first?
- Did I move up next?

Independent Practice

Write each ordered pair.

5. Giraffe
6. Monkey
7. Elephant
8. Kangaroo

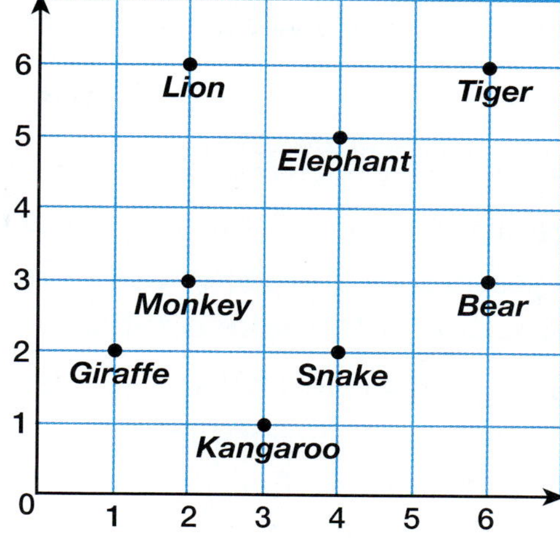

What animal is located at the point for each ordered pair?

9. (6, 6)
10. (6, 3)
11. (2, 6)
12. (4, 2)

Problem Solving • Reasoning

Make a grid like the one on the right. Then use the grid for Problems 13–16.

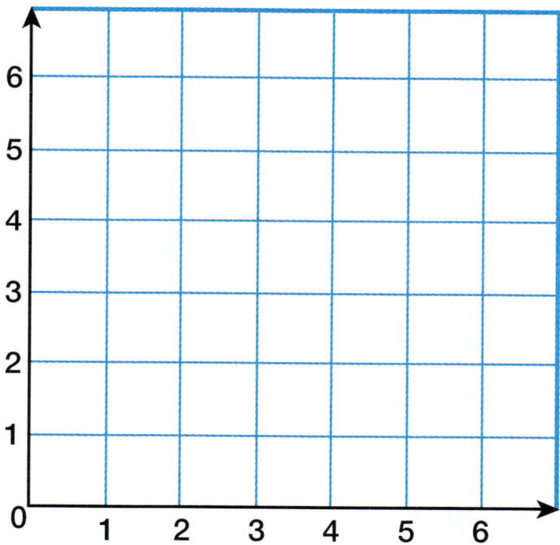

13. Draw dots on your grid to show the points for each ordered pair.

(5, 1) (5, 3) (1, 3) (1, 1)

14. Connect the points in order. Connect the last point to the first. Explain how you know that the figure is a rectangle.

15. What ordered pairs could you choose to make a square? Explain your reasoning.

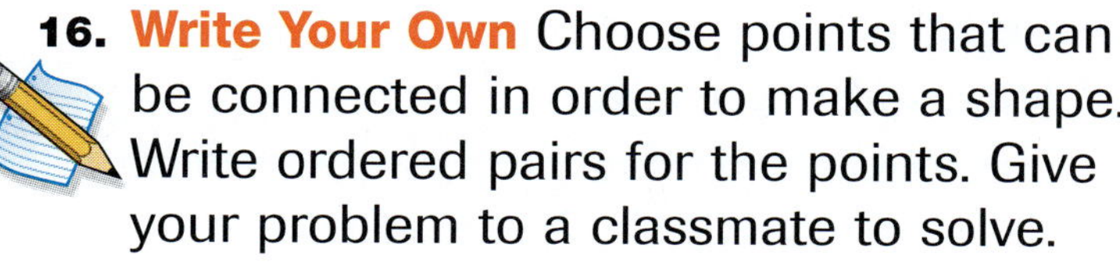

16. Write Your Own Choose points that can be connected in order to make a shape. Write ordered pairs for the points. Give your problem to a classmate to solve.

Mixed Review • Test Prep

Use the figure to answer the question. *(pages 318–319, 322–323)*

17. What are the perimeter and area of the rectangle on the right?

5 ft
3 ft

18 What is the quotient for 54 ÷ 9? *(pages 416–417)*

A 486
B 63
C 45
D 6

Problem-Solving Strategy: Make a Table

You will learn how making a table can help you solve a problem.

Sometimes you need to organize information to help you solve a problem. One way to organize information is to make a table.

Problem Meg and 3 friends will ride bikes in the Fourth of July parade. The first bike will have 2 streamers. Each of the other bikes will have 2 times as many streamers as the bike in front of it. How many streamers will the fourth bike have?

What is the question?

How many streamers will the fourth bike have?

What do you know?

- The first bike will have 2 streamers.
- Each of the other bikes will have 2 times as many streamers as the one in front of it.

How can you find the answer?

One way to solve the problem is to make a table.

Make a table.

The fourth bike will have 16 streamers.

Bike	Number of Streamers
1	2
2	4
3	8
4	16

Look back at the problem.

If there is a fifth bike that follows the same rule, how many streamers will that bike have?

Remember:
- Understand
- Plan
- Solve
- Look Back

Guided Practice

Solve these problems, using the Make a Table strategy.

1. It takes the first clown 10 minutes to put on makeup. Each clown takes 3 minutes longer than the one before. How much time does it take the fifth clown to put on makeup?

   Think: What will the parts of the table be?

2. The first car in a parade passes the reviewing stand at 10:42. Each car passes the stand 2 minutes after the one in front of it. What time is it when the tenth car passes?

   Think: By how much will the time increase?

Choose a Strategy

Solve. Use these or other strategies.

Problem-Solving Strategies

- Write a Number Sentence
- Make a Table
- Guess and Check
- Use Logical Thinking

3. For every 2 balloons you buy, the balloon seller gives you a free one. If each balloon costs $2, how much do you pay to get 6 balloons?

4. Mr. Tyson has 10 boxes of flags to sell at the parade. Each box holds 8 flags. He sells all but 4 boxes. How many flags does he have left?

5. Ms. Chan sold 150 pretzels and 325 bags of popcorn. She charged $2 for pretzels and $1 for popcorn. Did she take in more money selling popcorn or pretzels?

6. The mayor's car is behind the band and the baton twirlers. The twirlers are 3 groups ahead of the clowns. The mayor's car is not last. What is the order of these 4 groups?

7. Carlos counts a total of 18 fire trucks and ambulances in the parade. There are 8 more fire trucks than ambulances. How many ambulances are there?

8. A balloon seller sells 240 red balloons, 205 blue balloons, 125 green balloons, and 98 white balloons. How many of the balloons are red, white, or blue?

9. Nine students want to carry 3 pompoms in each hand in a parade. How many pompoms do they need?

10. Four dimes and 1 nickel pay for peanuts. What other combinations of dimes and nickels equal 45¢?

Extra Practice See 3–4 on page 473.

Quick Check

Check Your Understanding of Lessons 1-7

Use the line plot for Questions 1 and 2.

1. On how many days were more than 45 cans collected?
2. What are the range and the mode?

Cans Collected on Ten Days

25	35	45	55	65	75
X X	X	X X		X X X X	X X

Use the pictograph for Questions 3–5.

3. How many maple trees are there?
4. How many trees are there in all?
5. How many more beech trees are there than oak trees?

Number of Trees in Park

Beech	● ● ● ●
Maple	● ● ● ● ●
Oak	● ●

Each ● stands for 3 trees.

Use the bar graph for Questions 6 and 7.

6. How many chipmunks were seen?
7. How many more squirrels were seen than raccoons?

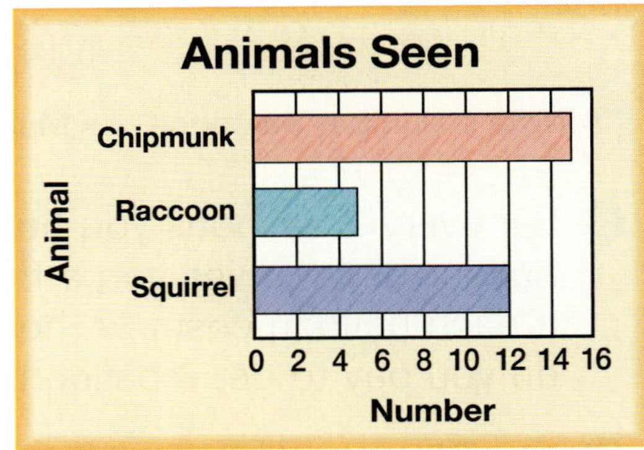

Use the grid for Questions 8 and 9.

8. What figure is located at point (4, 4)?
9. What is the ordered pair for the rectangle?

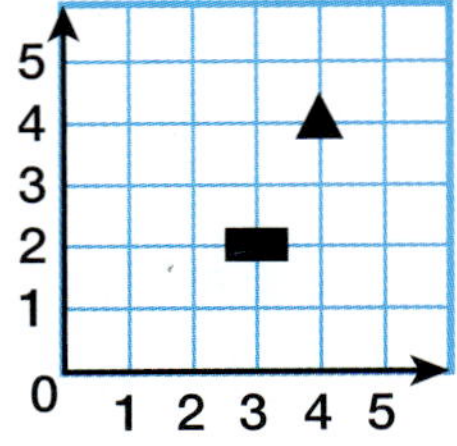

How did you do?

If you had difficulty with any items in the Quick Check, you can use the following pages for review and extra practice.

Items	Review These Pages	Do These Extra Practice Items
1–2	pages 440–441	Set A, page 470
3–5	pages 442–444	Set B, page 470
6–7	pages 446–451	Set C, page 471
8–9	pages 452–453	Set D, page 471

Test Prep • Cumulative Review

Maintaining the Standards

Choose the letter of the correct answer.
If a correct answer is not here, choose NH.

1. Which number sentence could be used to find the number of centimeters in 2 decimeters?

   A ■ cm = 2 × 10
   B ■ cm = 10 + 10 + 10
   C ■ cm = 10 × 10
   D ■ cm = 2 × 100

2. A pack of 10 pencils costs 80¢. What is the unit price?

   F 5¢
   G 8¢
   H 10¢
   J NH

3. Patrick has 68 stickers. Kenny needs 17 more stickers to equal the number Patrick has. Which number sentence could be used to find the number of stickers Kenny has?

   A 68 + 17 = ■
   B 68 − 17 = ■
   C ■ − 17 = 68
   D ■ + 68 = 17

4. Which number sentence is not true?

   F 2 × 3 × 4 = 2 × 4 × 3
   G 2 × 3 × 4 = 6 × 4
   H 2 × 3 × 4 = 8 × 3
   J 2 × 3 × 4 = 2 + 3 × 4

5. **Use the bar graph on book prices.**

   If the likely pattern continues, how much would 7 books cost?

   A $10 **C** $16
   B $14 **D** $18

6. If 42 ÷ ■ = 7, then which number sentence must be true?

   F ■ × 7 = 42
   G 42 × 7 = ■
   H ■ ÷ 7 = 42
   J ■ × 42 = 7

7. Look at the number pattern below. What is the next number likely to be?

   6, 12, 18, 24, ____

   Explain How did you find your answer?

Safe Site

Internet Test Prep
Visit **www.eduplace.com/kids/mhm** for more *Test Prep Practice.*

Probability

You will learn how to decide whether an event is impossible, unlikely, likely, or certain.

New Vocabulary
probability

Learn About It

Probability describes how likely it is that an event will happen. Using words, we can describe the probability of an event as *certain*, *likely*, *unlikely*, or *impossible*.

Pick a tile without looking.

Bag A

The probability of picking a blue tile is **certain**.

Bag B

The probability of picking a blue tile is **likely**.

Bag C

The probability of picking a blue tile is **unlikely**.

Bag D

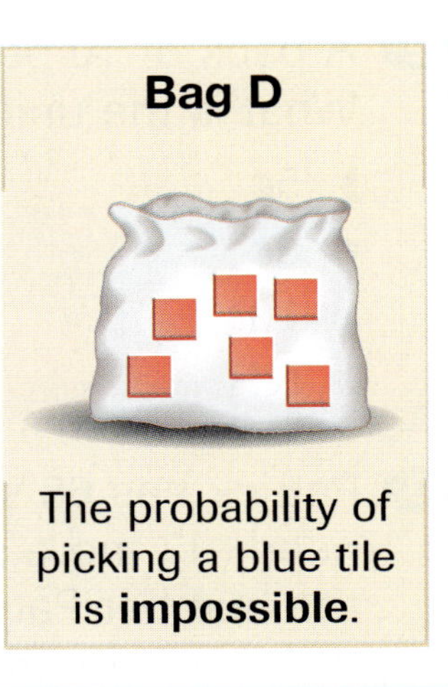

The probability of picking a blue tile is **impossible**.

Explain Your Thinking

- Why is it likely that you would pick a red tile from Bag *C*?
- Why are you certain to pick a blue tile from Bag *A*?

Guided Practice

Look at the spinner. Write whether the event is *impossible, unlikely, likely,* or *certain*.

1. Landing on yellow
2. Landing on red
3. Landing on green
4. Landing on yellow or green

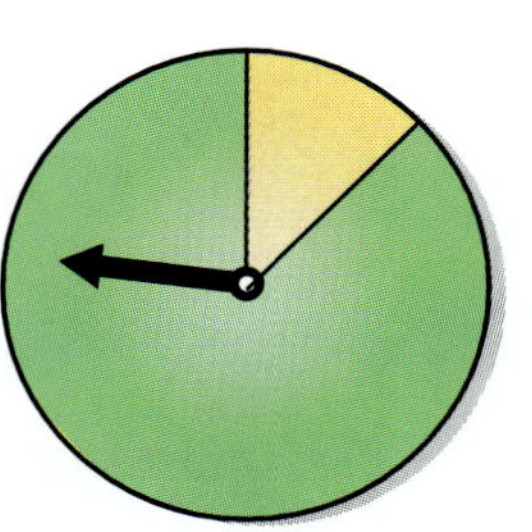

Ask Yourself

- Which color takes up the greatest area?
- Which color takes up the least area?

Independent Practice

Write the word *certain, likely, unlikely,* or *impossible* to describe the probability of picking a green tile.

5. 

6. 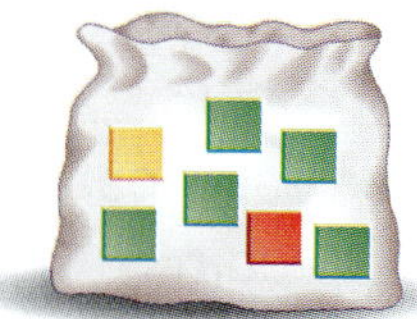

7. 

8. 

Draw a set of tiles to represent each statement.

9. Picking a blue tile is certain.

10. Picking a blue tile is impossible.

11. Picking a blue tile is possible, but unlikely.

12. Picking a blue tile is likely.

Problem Solving • Reasoning

Write whether each event is impossible, unlikely, likely, or certain. Explain your answer.

13. You were born on a day of the week that ends with the letter *y*.

14. You will win a million dollars next week.

15. The month after April is May.

16. The sum of any 2 two-digit numbers is 24.

17. It is sunny in August.

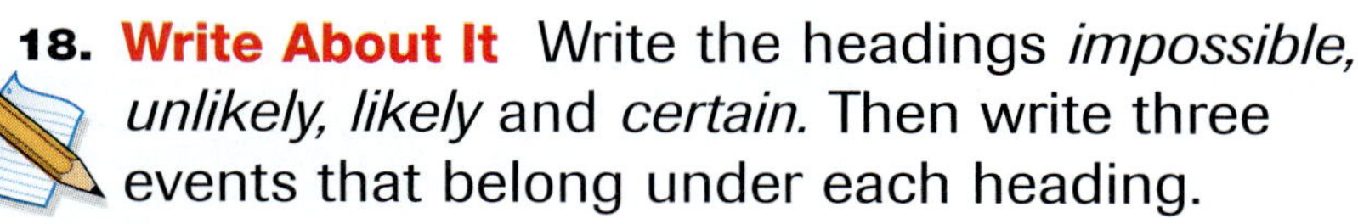

18. **Write About It** Write the headings *impossible, unlikely, likely* and *certain.* Then write three events that belong under each heading.

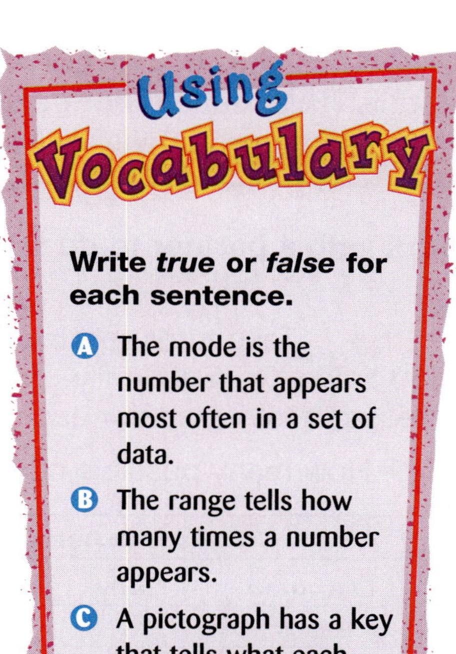

Mixed Review • Test Prep

Find the value of *n*. *(pages 258–259, 268–269, 362–363, 374–375)*

19. $7 \times n = 49$

20. $54 = n \times 6$

21. $5 = n \div 7$

22. $48 \div n = 48$

23. $n = 7 \times 3$

24. $4 = 36 \div n$

25 What time is it 3 hours before 2:30 P.M.? *(pages 78–79)*

A 11:30 A.M. **B** 12:00 noon **C** 12:30 P.M **D** 5:30 P.M.

Recording Outcomes

You will learn how to record and display the results of probability experiments.

New Vocabulary
outcome
equally likely

Learn About It

Activities such as making a spin on a spinner, rolling a number cube, and tossing a coin are examples of probability experiments.

Materials

For each pair:
coin
grid (Teaching Tool 12)
spinners (Teaching Tools 13 and 14)

If you toss a coin, there are two possible **outcomes**, or results.

- The coin can land heads up.
- The coin can land tails up.

You are **equally likely** to get heads or tails. This means that heads and tails have the same probability of occurring.

Heads

Tails

Work with a partner to do this coin-toss experiment.

Step 1 Take turns tossing a coin 50 times. On a chart like the one below, record a tally mark for each outcome.

- How many possible outcomes are there?

Coin-Toss Experiment		
Outcome	**Tally**	**Number**
Heads		
Tails		

Step 2 Find the number of times each outcome occurred. Record each total in the chart.

- How many times did the coin land heads up?
- How many times did the coin land tails up?
- Did heads come up about as often as tails?

Now look at the outcomes for a number-cube experiment.

The number cubes on the right show the possible outcomes of rolling one cube numbered 1 to 6.

Suppose Brian rolls two number cubes 100 times. Each time, he records the sum of the two numbers that are on the top faces of the cubes. The possible sums are 2, 3, 4, 5, 6, 7, 8, 9, 10, 11, and 12.

- How many possible outcomes are there?

Brian's results are shown in the table below.

Rolling Two Number Cubes											
Sum	2	3	4	5	6	7	8	9	10	11	12
Number of Occurrences	3	5	8	12	13	18	13	12	8	5	3

Work with your partner to display the results of Brian's experiment in a bar graph.

Step 1 Make a bar graph to show the outcomes.

- How many bars do you need in your graph?
- Where will the bar for the sum 2 end?

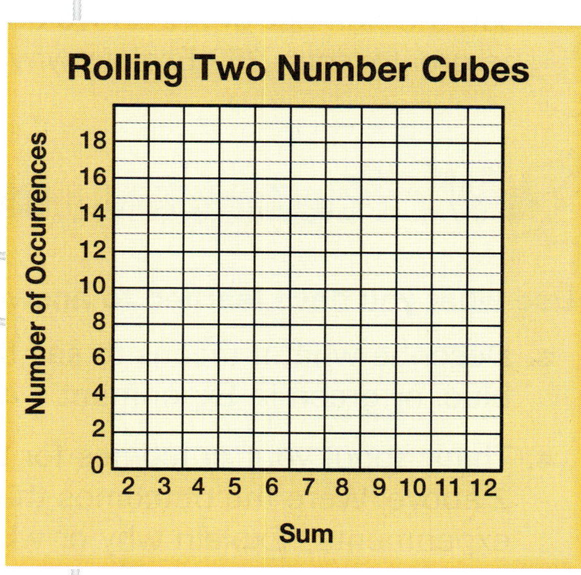

Step 2 Use the graph to tell about the results.

- Which sum occurred most often?
- What do you notice about the other sums?

Try It Out

Work with a partner to complete this spinner experiment.

1. Use a spinner like the one on the right. Make 25 spins. Record your results in a tally chart like the one below.

Spinner Experiment		
Outcome	**Tally**	**Number**
Blue		
Red		
Green		

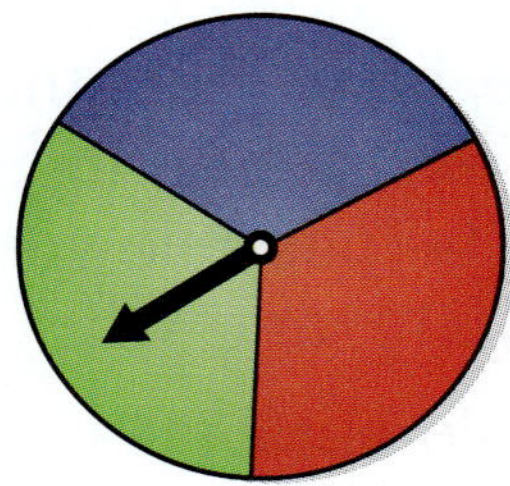

- How many possible outcomes are there?
- Did the spinner land on each color about an equal number of times?

2. Use a spinner like the one on the right. Make 25 spins. Record your results on a line plot like the one below.

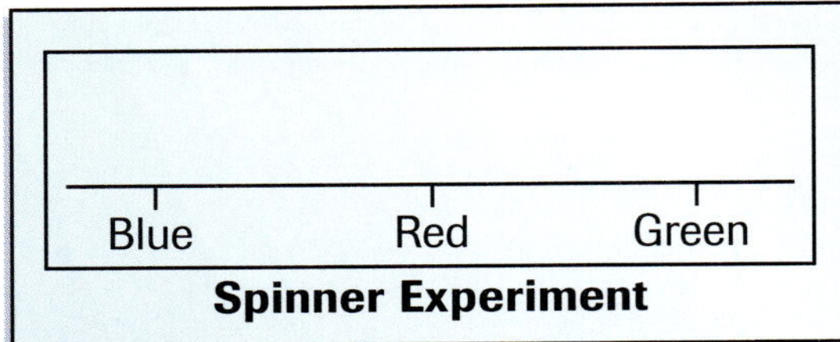

- Can the number of X's above any of the colors be greater than 25? Explain why or why not.

Write about it! Talk about it!

Use what you have learned to answer these questions.

3. Describe what it means to say that landing on red, blue, or green in Experiment 1 is "equally likely."

4. Think about your outcomes for Experiments 1 and 2 above. Were the outcomes the same for both experiments? Explain why or why not.

Practice Game

Pick and Predict

Practice predicting outcomes by playing this game with a partner. Try to predict the color of the next paper square you pick!

What You'll Need

- *a paper bag*
- *7 red and 7 blue paper squares (Teaching Tool 15)*

Players 2

Here's What to Do

1. The first player secretly puts any of the 14 paper squares in the bag and puts the remaining paper squares out of sight.
2. The second player picks a square from the bag without looking and records its color in a tally chart. Then the second player puts the square back into the bag.
3. The second player repeats Step 2 nineteen times. The second player then uses the tally chart to predict which color he or she will pick next. After predicting, the second player picks a paper square from the bag. If the prediction is correct, the player gets 1 point.
4. Players take turns repeating Steps 1 to 3. The first player to get 5 points wins.

Share Your Thinking What strategy did you use to decide which paper squares to put in the bag?

Make Predictions

You will learn how to use the results of experiments to predict outcomes.

Learn About It

You can use data from an experiment to make a prediction about what is likely to happen if the experiment is repeated.

The chart shows the results of a probability experiment in which there were 10 marbles in a bag. Without looking, a student picked a marble from the bag 25 times. The marble was put back each time.

Picking a Marble From a Bag

Outcome	Tally	Number
Red	𝍸 𝍸 𝍸 𝍸 III	23
Blue	II	2

A red marble was picked much more often than a blue marble.

These results suggest that if another marble is picked, it is more likely to be red than blue.

Explain Your Thinking

- ▶ Would you predict that there are 5 red marbles and 5 blue marbles in the bag? Why or why not?
- ▶ Would you predict that there are about 10 times as many red marbles as blue marbles in the bag? Why?

Guided Practice

The line plot shows high temperatures in a city on May 10 for the past 20 years. Suppose tomorrow is May 10.

1. What is a likely prediction of the high temperature for tomorrow?
2. What is an unlikely prediction of the high temperature for tomorrow?

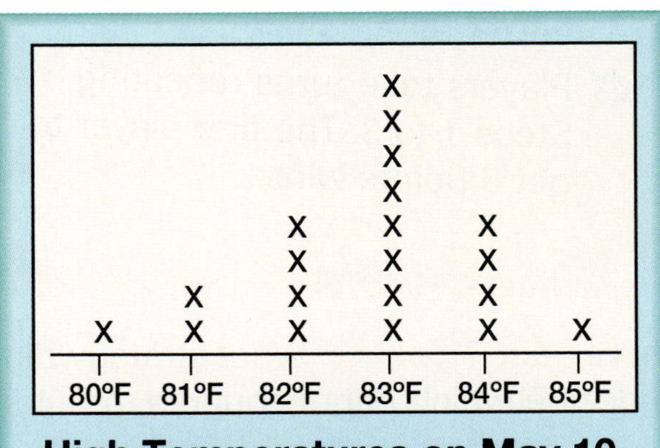

High Temperatures on May 10

Independent Practice

3. Look at the spinner. Suppose you make 50 spins. Which color do you predict the spinner is likely to land on most often?

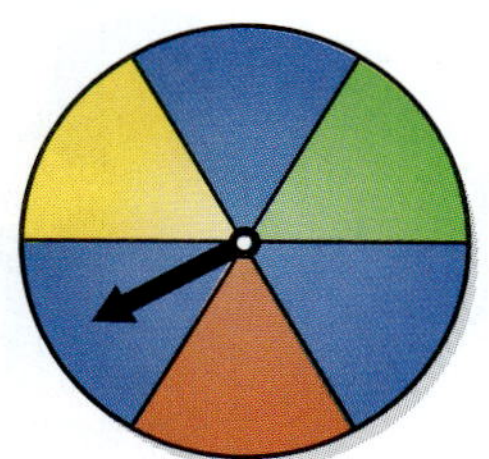

4. Make a spinner like the one on the left. Make 50 spins. Record the results in a tally chart. Then make a bar graph. Was your prediction correct?

Spinning a Spinner		
Outcome	**Tally**	**Number**
Blue		
Green		
Red		
Yellow		

Problem Solving • Reasoning

5. Two hundred children write their names on identical slips of paper and put them into a box. If 35 names are girls' names, who is more likely to be chosen on the first pick, a girl or a boy?

6. **Analyze** A bag has 10 marbles. A person picks a marble from the bag without looking, records its color, and puts it back 50 times. The results are 30 red, 10 blue, and 10 green. Make a line plot to show the results. How many of each color do you think are in the bag?

7. **Write About It** Suppose each letter of the alphabet is written on an identical slip of paper and put into a bag. If a person picks a slip without looking, is the letter more likely to be a consonant or a vowel? Explain.

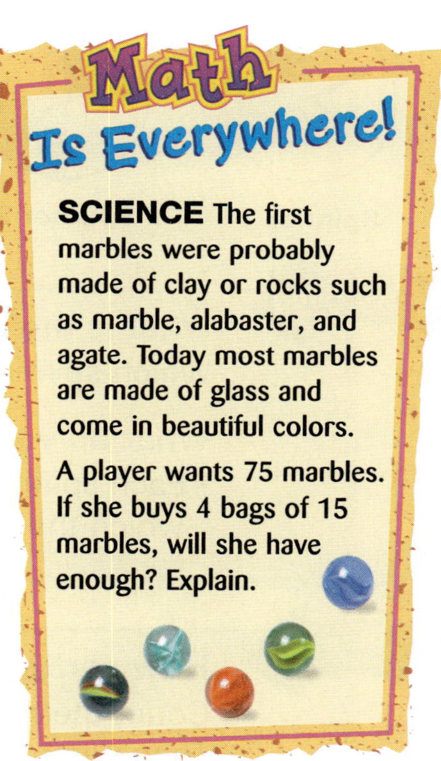

Mixed Review • Test Prep

Write the missing number. *(pages 120–121, 138–139, 140–141)*

8. 306 = 288 + ■

9. 1,042 − ■ = 981

10. ■ − 590 = 463

Write the letter of the correct quotient. *(pages 408–409, 416–417)*

11 81 ÷ 9

A 7 **B** 8 **C** 9 **D** 10

12 $6\overline{)42}$

F 6 **G** 7 **H** 8 **J** 9

Extra Practice See Set F on page 472.

Problem-Solving Application: Use Probability

You will learn how to use probability to decide if a game is fair or unfair.

A game is fair if all players have an equal chance to win.
A game is unfair if one player has a greater chance to win.

Problem Alicia and Maria are playing a game. One player moves when a spin lands on green. The other player moves when a spin lands on yellow. Which spinner makes the game fair?

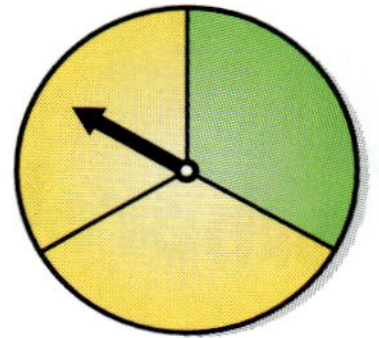

Spinner 1

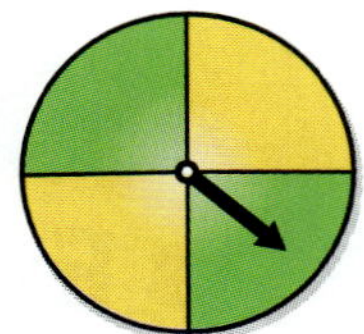

Spinner 2

Spinner 3

What is the question?

Which spinner makes the game fair?

What do you know?

- Each spinner is separated into regions in which the arrow is equally likely to land.

How can you find the answer?

Count the number of equal regions on each spinner. Then compare the number of yellow regions and the number of green regions.

There are equal numbers of green and yellow regions on Spinner 2. So Spinner 2 makes the game fair.

Look back at the problem.

Why do Spinners 1 and 3 make the game unfair?

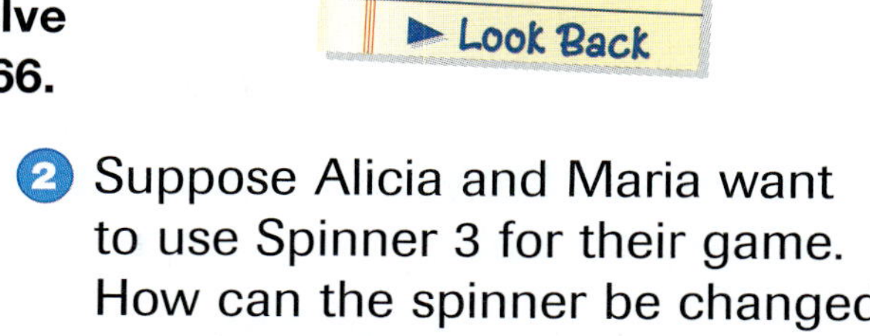

Guided Practice

Use what you know about probability to solve each problem. Use the spinners on page 466.

1. Suppose you and a friend are playing a game with Spinner 1. Which color would you choose to have a better chance of winning?

Are more of the equally likely regions green or yellow?

2. Suppose Alicia and Maria want to use Spinner 3 for their game. How can the spinner be changed to make it fair?

How many regions of each color are there? What would make the game fair?

Choose a Strategy

Solve. Use these or other strategies.

Problem-Solving Strategies

- **Use Logical Thinking**
- **Act It Out**
- **Write a Number Sentence**
- **Draw a Picture**

3. Kito is going to play a game with this spinner. One part of the spinner needs a color. Which color will make the game fair?

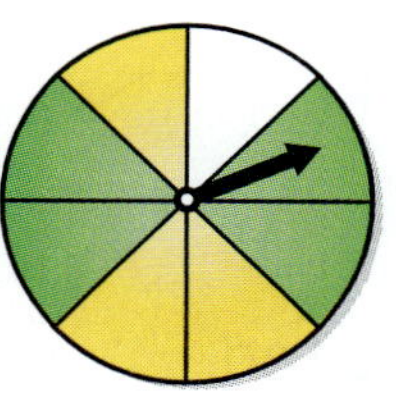

4. Jody, Ashur, and Dena are playing a game, using this spinner. Write a rule that makes the game fair.

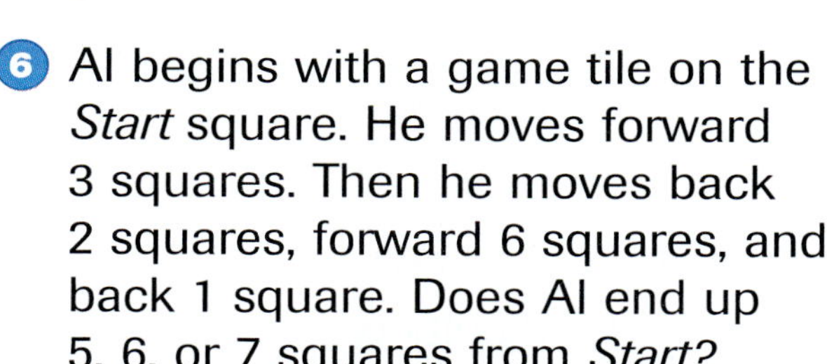

5. Sara and Vera each played a video game twice. Sara's scores were 34,189 points and 27,912 points. Vera's scores were 27,821 points and 38,233 points. Who scored more points altogether?

6. Al begins with a game tile on the *Start* square. He moves forward 3 squares. Then he moves back 2 squares, forward 6 squares, and back 1 square. Does Al end up 5, 6, or 7 squares from *Start?*

7. In Jamal's game, players toss a cube numbered 1 to 6. Player 1 gets a point if the number is 4 or greater. Player 2 gets a point if the number is less than 4. Is this game fair? Explain.

8. **Write About It** Is this spinner fair? Explain why or why not.

Extra Practice See 5–7 on page 473.

Quick Check

Check Your Understanding of Lessons 8–11

Write *certain*, *likely*, *unlikely*, or *impossible* to describe how likely the spinner is to land on green.

1. 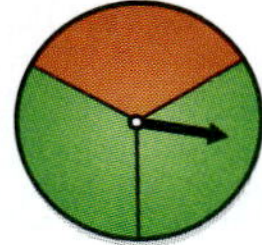

2. 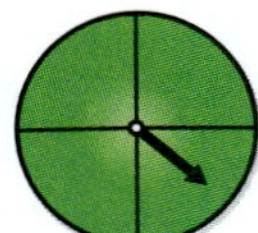

3. 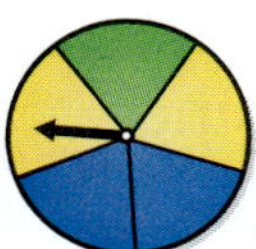

4. 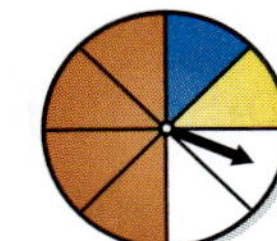

Use the spinner for Questions 5 and 6.

5. In 60 spins, which number is the spinner likely to land on most often? Explain.

6. In 60 spins, which number is the spinner likely to land on least often? Explain.

Use the line plot.

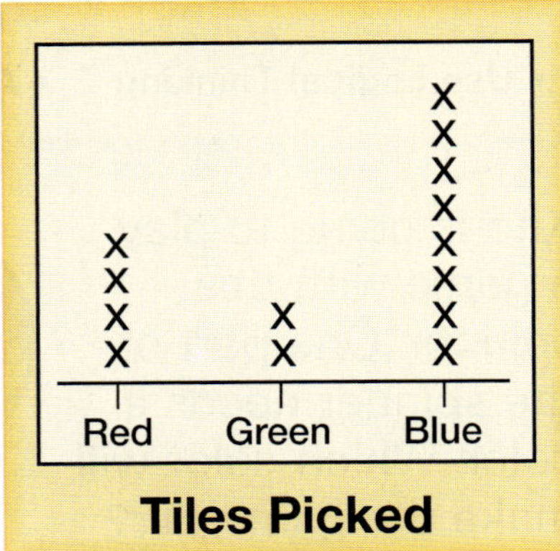

7. Without looking, a student picked a tile from a bag 14 times and put it back after each pick. When another tile is picked, which color is most likely to be picked?

Solve.

8. A spinner has four equal sections: one red, one green, and two blue. What are the possible outcomes for a spin?

How did you do?

If you had difficulty with any items in the Quick Check, you can use the following pages for review and extra practice.

Items	Review These Pages	Do These Extra Practice Items
1–4	pages 458–459	Set E, page 472
5–7	pages 464–465	Set F, page 472
8	pages 446–451	5–7, page 473

Test Prep • Cumulative Review

Maintaining the Standards

Choose the letter of the correct answer.

1 How many outcomes are possible when one coin is tossed?

A 1
B 2
C 3
D 4

2 A coin is tossed 600 times. Which bar graph shows a likely result?

F

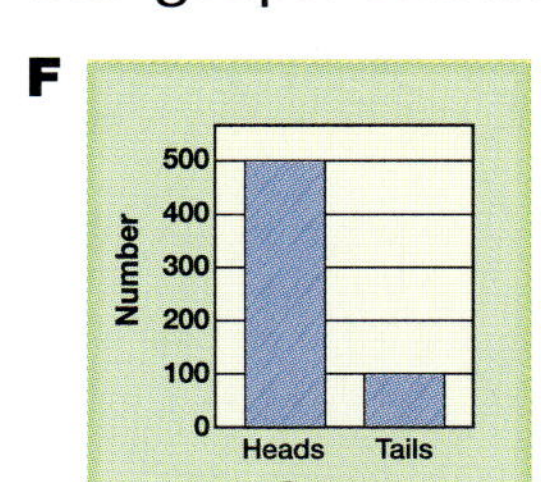

H

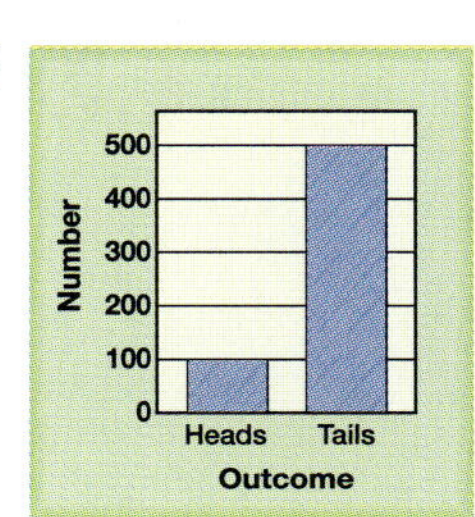

G

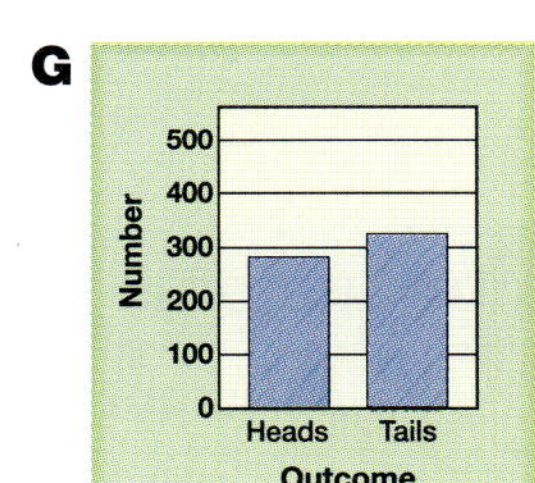

J

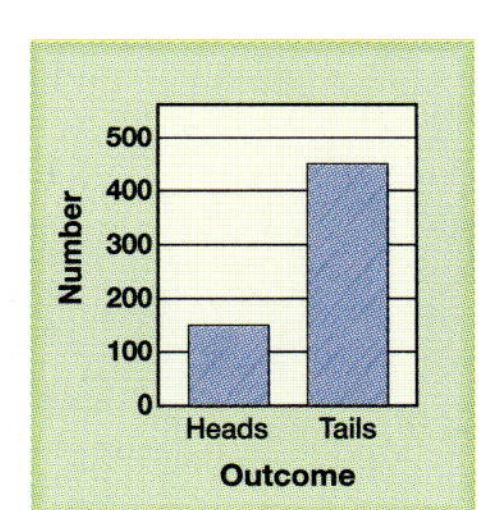

3 Which tally is likely to be the result of spinning this spinner 4 times?

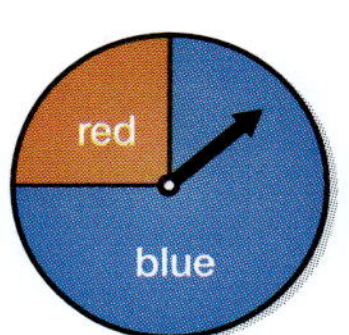

A

red	I
blue	III

B

red	IIII
blue	I

D

red	II
blue	II

E

red	IIII
blue	

4 How many sides does a hexagon have?

F 4
G 5
H 6
J 8

This line plot shows the daily high temperatures for a week. Use the line plot for Questions 5 and 6.

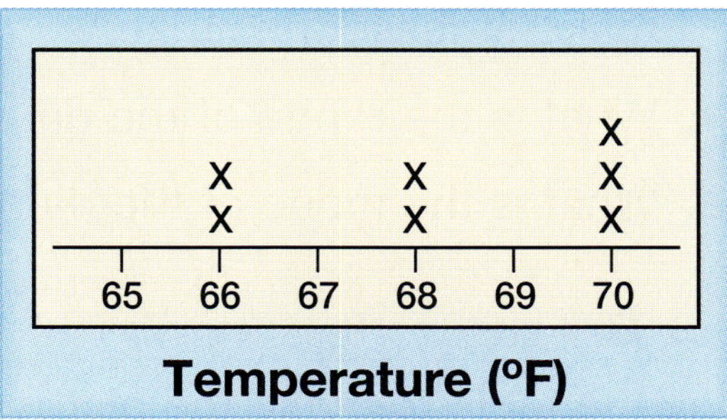

5 How many days of the week did the temperature reach 70°F?

A 0 **C** 2
B 1 **D** 3

6 Which is a likely temperature for the first day of the next week?

F 30°F **H** 90°F
G 70°F **J** 105°F

7 Kelly wants to put a lace border around a picture. If the picture is 3 inches wide and 4 inches long, how much lace does Kelly need?

Explain How did you find your answer?

Safe Site

Internet Test Prep
Visit **www.eduplace.com/kids/mhm** for more *Test Prep Practice.*

Extra Practice

Set A *(Lesson 2, pages 440–441)*

Use the line plot to answer these questions.

The line plot shows the number of strikes Ann made in each of the first 10 games she bowled this year.

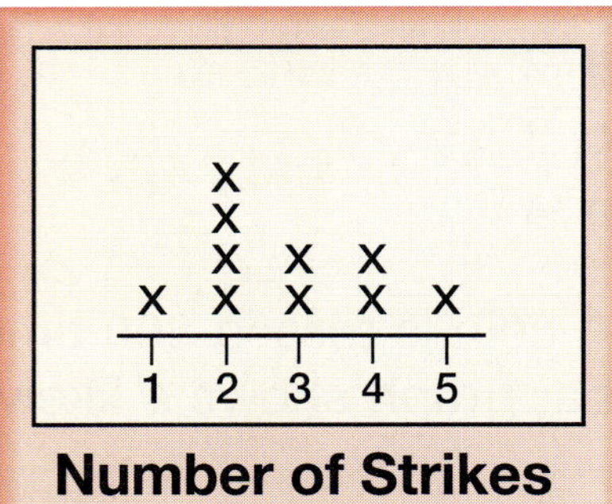

Number of Strikes

1. In how many games did Ann make 3 strikes?
2. What is the greatest number of strikes Ann made in one game?
3. In how many games did Ann make at least one strike?
4. What is the range of the data?
5. What is the mode of the data?

Set B *(Lesson 3, pages 442–444)*

Use the table to make the pictograph.

The table on the right shows how many people chose each answer when they were asked, "What is your favorite subject in school?"

Copy and complete the pictograph, using the data from the table.

Favorite Subjects

Subject	Number
Math	17
Reading	15
Science	12
Social Studies	9
Language Arts	18

Favorite Subjects

Math	☺ ☺ ☺ ☺ ☺ ☺ ☺ ☺ ◖
Reading	
Science	
Social Studies	
Language Arts	

Each ☺ stands for 2 people.

Extra Practice

Set C (Lesson 5, pages 448–451)

The table shows the number of people at a pool during 5 days. Copy and complete the bar graph, using the data in the table.

1. How many bars does your graph have?
2. What scale did you use?
3. How did you choose your scale?

People at the Pool

Day	Number
Monday	18
Tuesday	12
Wednesday	20
Thursday	15
Friday	22

Use the bar graph to answer the questions.

4. What does the graph show?
5. How many books of tickets did Juan sell?
6. How many more books of tickets did Reggie sell than Sally?
7. How many books of tickets were sold in all?

Set D (Lesson 6, pages 452–453)

Use the grid for Exercises 1–8.

Write the ordered pair for each point.

1. *X* 2. *Y* 3. *Z* 4. *W*

What letter names each point?

5. (7, 3) 6. (6, 4) 7. (7, 7) 8. (1, 5)

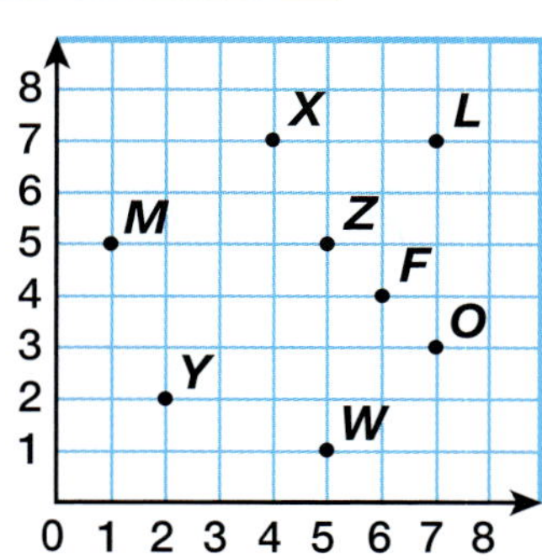

Extra Practice

Set E (Lesson 8, pages 458–459)

Look at each spinner. Write *certain, likely, unlikely,* or *impossible* to describe the probability of landing on a blue section of each spinner.

1. 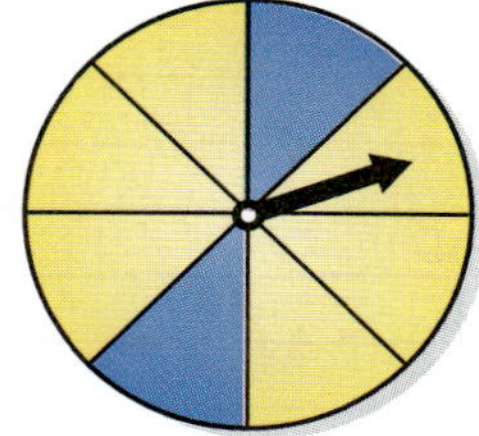

2. 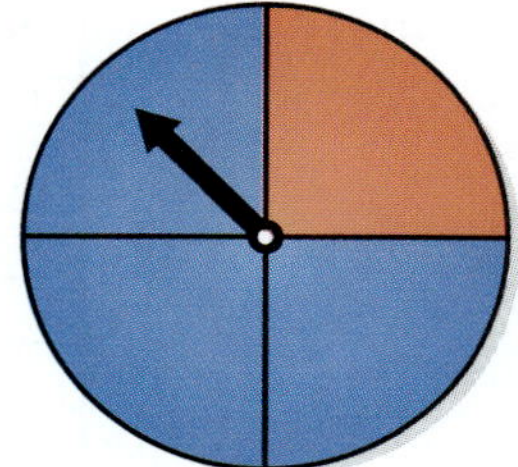

3. 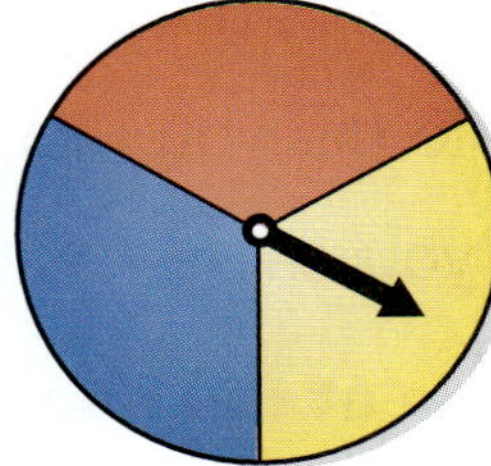

4. 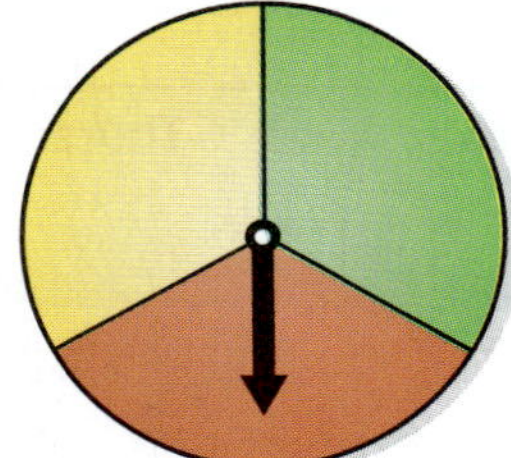

5. 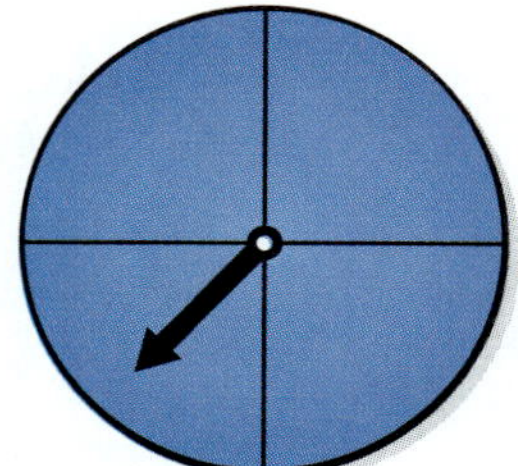

6. 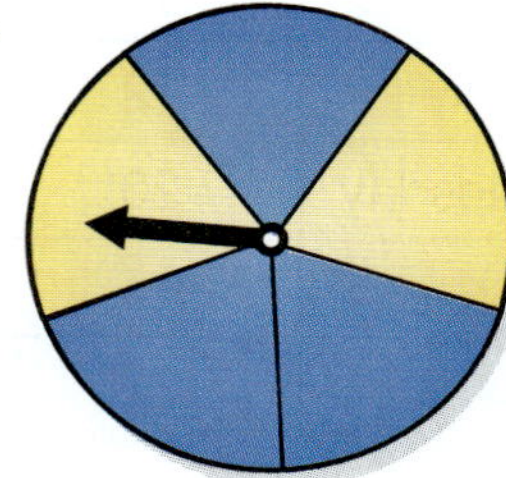

Set F (Lesson 10, pages 464–465)

Use the line plot to answer the questions.

The line plot shows the results of an experiment done using a bag of red, blue, and green marbles. Without looking, a student picked a marble from the bag 20 times and put it back after each pick.

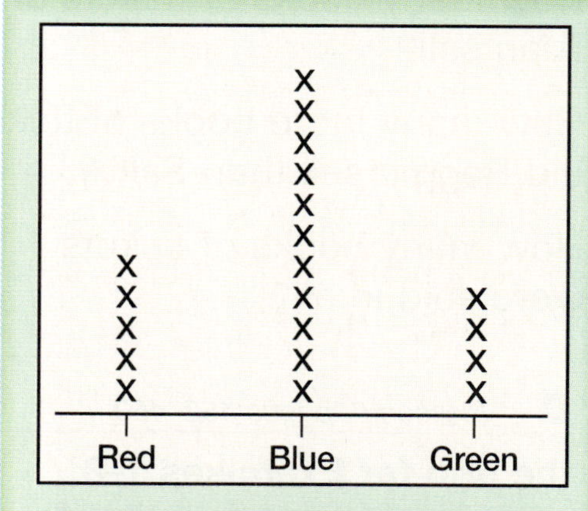

Marbles Picked From Bag

1. If there are 40 marbles in the bag, how many of each color do you predict are in the bag?
2. If another marble is picked from the bag, do you predict that it will be green? Why or why not?

Extra Practice • Problem Solving

Use the bar graph for Problems 1 and 2. *(Lesson 4, pages 446–447)*

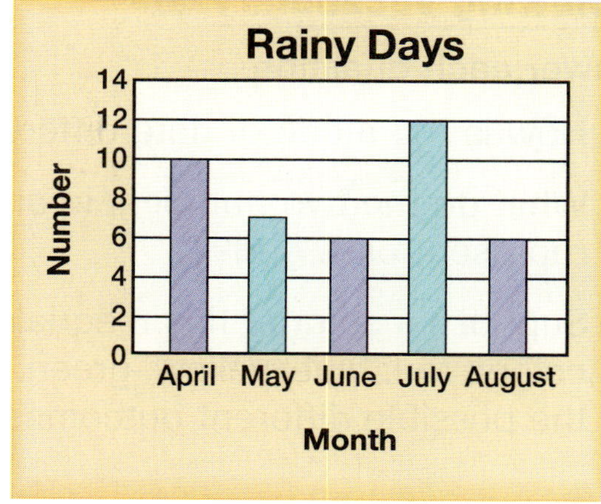

1. In July there were twice as many rainy days as in September. How many rainy days were there in September?

2. How many more rainy days were there in April than in June?

Solve these problems, using the Make a Table strategy.
(Lesson 7, pages 454–455)

3. Kate jumps rope 30 times the first week without missing a jump. Her goal is to do 6 more jumps each week than the week before. If she reaches her goal each week, how many jumps will she do by the end of the fifth week?

4. Matthew earns $5.00 a week for each yard he weeds. He weeds 3 yards the first week. If he adds 1 yard each week, how much money will he have earned altogether by the end of the sixth week?

Solve. *(Lesson 11, pages 466–467)*

5. You and a friend are playing a game with Spinner *A*. Is the spinner more likely to land on red or on blue?

6. What color should be in the blank space on Spinner *B* so that a spin has the same chance of landing on red or on blue?

7. How does Spinner *C* need to change so that a spin has the same chance of landing on red or on blue?

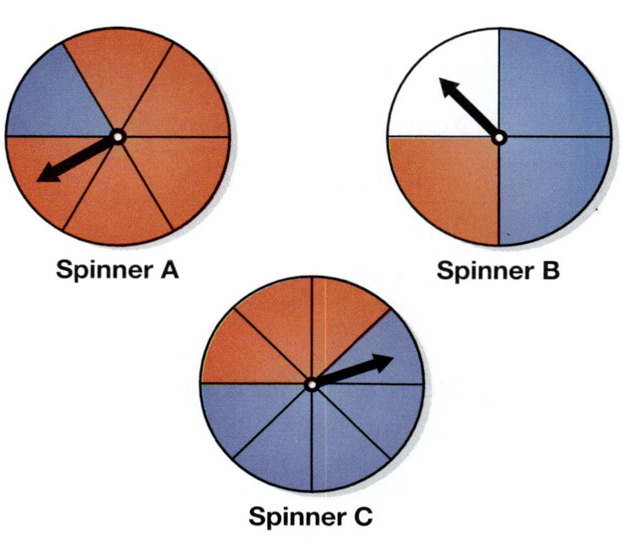

Chapter Review

Reviewing Vocabulary

Answer each question.

1. How is the mode of data different from the range?
2. What do the two numbers in an ordered pair represent on a grid?
3. Suppose a spinner has 6 equal regions with these colors: red, blue, yellow, green, red, blue. What are the possible different outcomes of a spin?

Reviewing Concepts and Skills

Use the line plot for Questions 4–6. *(pages 440–441)*

The line plot shows the number of touchdowns a football team scored in each of 8 games.

4. What do the two X's above 6 mean?
5. In how many games did the team score three or more touchdowns?
6. What are the range and the mode of the data?

Use the information in the table to make a pictograph. Then answer the questions. *(pages 442–444)*

7.

Favorite Vacation Activities	
Activity	**Number**
Swimming	32
Hiking	20
Sightseeing	40

8. Why did you choose the number you did for the key?
9. How many more people voted for swimming than for hiking?

Use the information in the table to make a bar graph. Then answer the questions. *(pages 448–451)*

10.

Birds Cindy Saw	
Bird	**Number**
Crow	4
Gull	9
Robin	11

11. Why did you choose the scale you did?
12. How many more robins than crows did Cindy see?

Write the ordered pair for each shape. *(pages 452–453)*

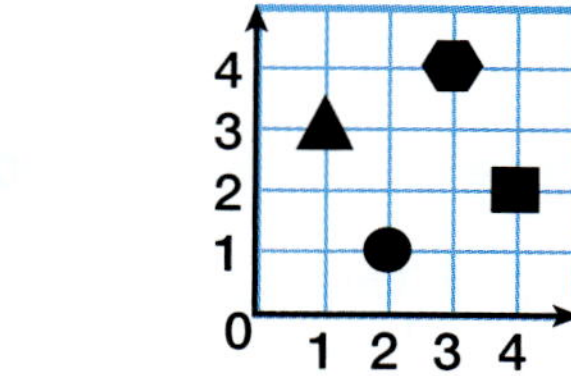

13. ▲ **14.** ● **15.** ■ **16.** ⬢

Write *certain, likely, unlikely,* or *impossible* to describe how likely each event is to occur. *(pages 458–459)*

17. A ball is square.

18. Yellow is a color.

19. You will travel in space.

Use the line plot for Questions 20–21. *(pages 464–465)*

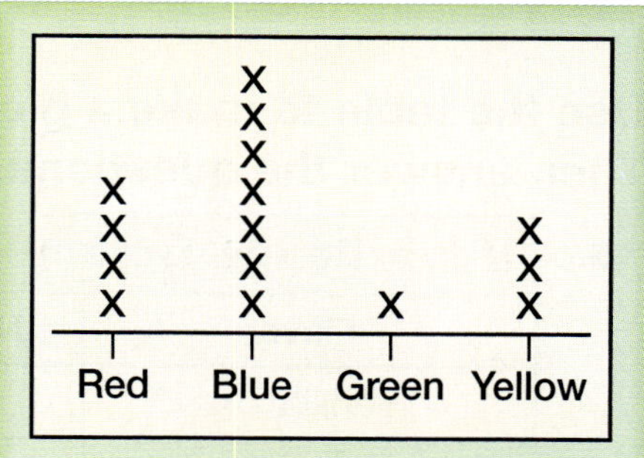

Without looking, Ira picks a button from a box 15 times, and puts it back each time.

20. If 45 buttons are in the bag, how many of each color do you predict there are?

21. If another button is picked, do you predict it is likely to be blue? Why or why not?

Solve.

22. Chen plays his flute 15 minutes the first day. If he plays 5 minutes more each day than the day before, how many minutes does he play on the seventh day?

Brain Teaser Math Reasoning

Likely Products

Suppose you multiply two numbers that are greater than 0 and less than 8. Which outcome is least likely?

A. The product is less than 8.

B. The product is odd.

C. The product is greater than or equal to 8 and less than or equal to 16.

Internet Brain Teasers
Visit **www.eduplace.com/kids/mhm** for more *Brain Teasers.*

Chapter Test

Use the line plot to answer Questions 1–4.

1. How many games were played?
2. In how many games did the team score exactly 3 runs?
3. What is the range of the data?
4. What is the mode of the data?

Use the table to make a pictograph. Then answer the questions.

5.

Favorite Ice-Cream Flavors	
Flavor	**Number**
Vanilla	9
Chocolate	18
Strawberry	6

6. What number did you use in the key? Explain why.
7. How many pictures did you draw for *Chocolate*?

Use the table to make a bar graph. Then answer the questions.

8.

Boats Rented	
Day	**Number**
Friday	9
Saturday	12
Sunday	7

9. What scale did you use? Explain why.
10. Which two bars are closest in height?

Use the grid at the right. Name the shape at each point.

11. (3, 3)
12. (1, 4)
13. (4, 2)
14. (1, 1)

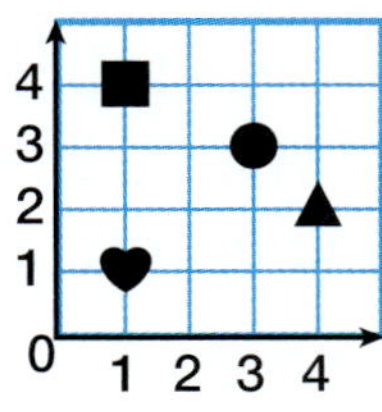

Write *certain, likely, unlikely,* or *impossible* to describe how likely each event is to occur.

15. Your fingernails will grow.
16. Wind will blow you off your feet.
17. A real pig will use its ears to fly.
18. It will rain 15 Thursdays in a row.

Solve.

19. Rosa practices violin 25 minutes this week. If she practices 5 minutes more each week than she practiced the week before, how many minutes will she practice in the sixth week?

20. Look at the spinner. What are the possible outcomes? Write *certain*, *likely*, *unlikely*, or *impossible* to describe the probability that each outcome will occur.

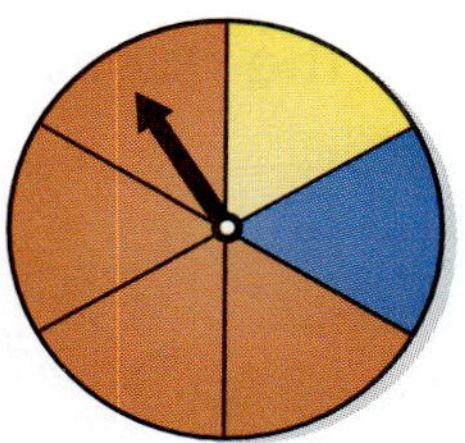

Write About It

Solve each problem. Use correct math vocabulary to explain your thinking.

1. Sandy used the data in the table to make the pictograph.

Number of Cars Washed	
Day	**Number**
Friday	32
Saturday	40
Sunday	34

Number of Cars Washed

Friday	● ● ● ● ● ● ● ●
Saturday	● ● ● ● ● ● ● ●
Sunday	● ● ● ● ● ●

Each ● stands for 4 cars.

a. Explain what Sandy did wrong.

b. Explain how to complete the pictograph correctly.

2. In a game, Player 1 scores 1 point if a spin lands on red. Player 2 scores 1 point if a spin lands on green.

a. What would the spinner look like in a fair game?

b. Would you expect the final scores for Player 1 and Player 2 to be close? Why or why not?

c. If the spinner had twice as many red spaces as green spaces, how could the rules be changed to make the game fair?

Another Look

The tally chart shows the number of soccer goals scored by five players on the Madison Whistlers during one season. Use the information in the table to answer the questions.

SOCCER GOALS

PLAYER	TALLY
LAURIE	|||
JANET	|
DEBBIE	||
MICHELE	𝍸 |||
KARLA	𝍸 |

1. Use the information on the tally chart to make a bar graph. Be sure to label your graph, choose a scale, and give your graph a title.
2. Who scored the greatest number of goals? Who scored the least number of goals? Name two players who scored 7 goals altogether.
3. **Look Back** What scale did you choose for the bar graph? Explain why you chose it.
4. **Analyze** The bar graph you made shows the number of goals scored by the five players. What else does it show?

Enrichment

Probability Experiments

When you do a probability experiment, it can be useful to display your results in an organized way. Try each of the experiments below.

Experiment 1

Make a spinner like Spinner 1. List the possible outcomes. Is one outcome any more likely to occur than another? Explain. Spin the spinner 50 times and use a tally chart to keep track of your results.

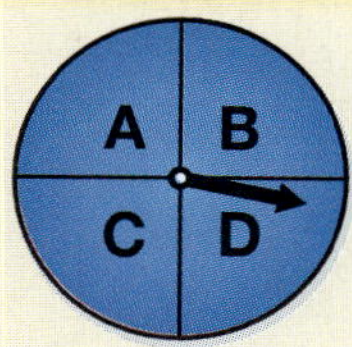

Spinner 1

Experiment 2

Make a spinner like Spinner 2. List the possible outcomes. Predict which outcome is most likely. Spin the spinner 50 times and use a line plot to keep track of your results.

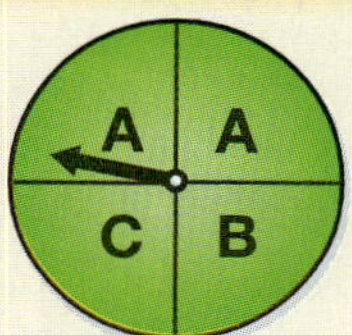

Spinner 2

Experiment 3

Make a spinner like Spinner 3. List the possible outcomes, and predict which outcome is more likely. Spin the spinner 50 times and make a bar graph to show your results.

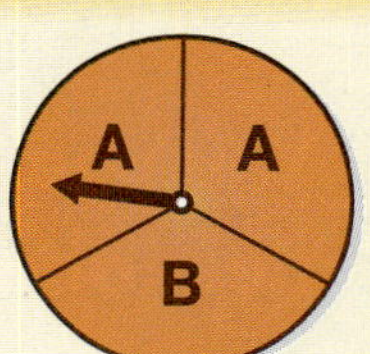

Spinner 3

1. Look at your results for each experiment. If you wanted to use the spinner that was most likely to land on A, which spinner would you use? Explain your choice.

2. How did the results of each experiment compare to your predictions? Explain why you think each prediction was correct or incorrect.

Explain Your Thinking

For Spinner 2 and Spinner 3, which outcome is more likely to happen if you spin the spinner again? Tell why.

Fractions and Decimals

Why Learn About Fractions and Decimals

You use fractions and decimals to describe and name parts of a region or group.

You use fractions when you say that $\frac{1}{2}$ of a sandwich has been eaten. When you read and write dollars and cents, you're using decimals.

Look at this group of kittens. Could you say that $\frac{2}{5}$ of the kittens are orange? How do you know?

Reviewing Vocabulary

Understanding math language helps you become a successful problem solver. Here are some math vocabulary words you should know.

fraction a number that names part of a region or part of a group

halves two equal parts that a region or group is divided into

thirds three equal parts that a region or group is divided into

fourths four equal parts that a region or group is divided into

Reading Words and Symbols

When you read mathematics, sometimes you read words, sometimes you read words and symbols, and sometimes you interpret pictures.

You can show fractions with pictures, numbers, and words.

picture: 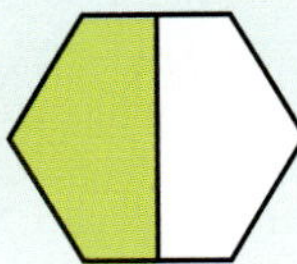

number: $\frac{1}{2}$ ← part shaded; ← equal parts

words: one half

picture: 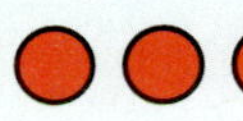

number: $\frac{3}{4}$ ← red counters; ← counters in all

words: three fourths

Try These

1. Write the number of parts. Then write whether the parts are *equal* or *not equal*.

a. 
b. 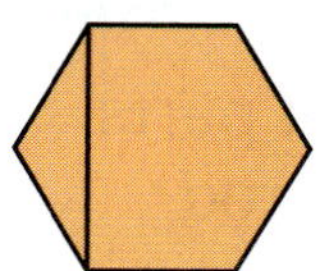
c. 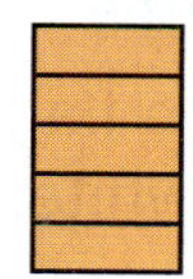
d. 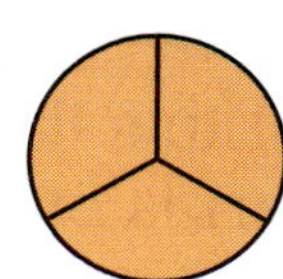

e. 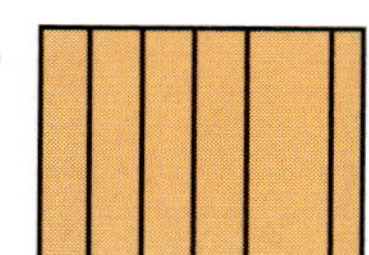
f. 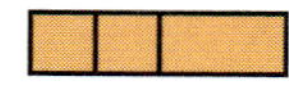
g. 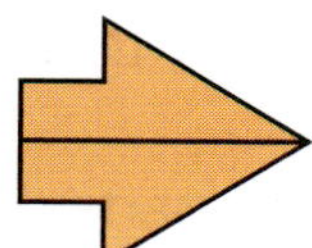
h. 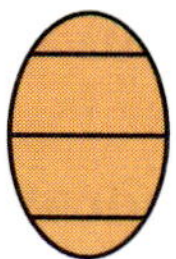

2. Write the fraction.

a. one third
b. two fourths
c. one sixth
d. three fifths
e. two halves
f. one fourth
g. one eighth
h. two thirds

3. What is each figure divided into? Write *halves, thirds,* or *fourths*.

a. 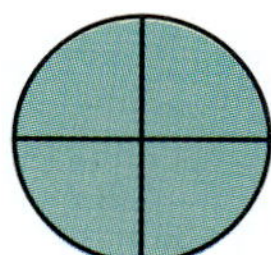
b. 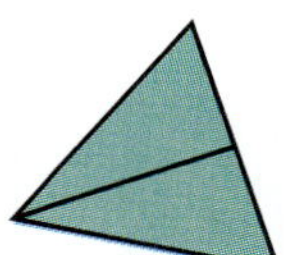
c. 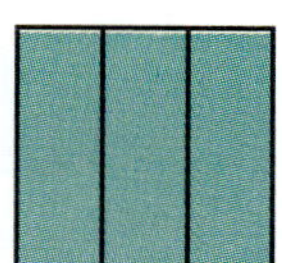
d. 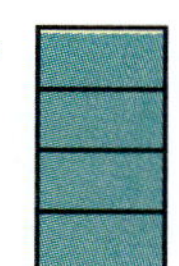

Upcoming Vocabulary

Write About It **Here are some other vocabulary words** you will learn in this chapter. Watch for these words. Write their definitions in your journal.

numerator
denominator
unit fraction
equivalent fractions
improper fraction
mixed number
decimal
decimal point
tenths
hundredths

Fractions and Regions

You will learn how to read and write fractions.

New Vocabulary
numerator
denominator

Learn About It

Look at this flag of France. The flag has 3 equal parts One part is blue. One part is white. One part is red.

A fraction shows a part of a region. You can use a fraction to tell how much of the flag is blue.

numerator → $\frac{1}{3}$ ← parts that are blue
denominator → ← total number of equal parts

We read the fraction as one third.

One third of the flag is blue.

More Examples

A. Fourths
4 equal parts

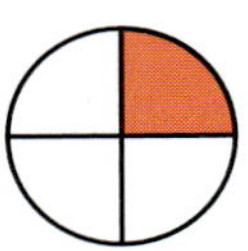

One fourth or $\frac{1}{4}$ is red.
How much is not red?

B. Eighths
8 equal parts

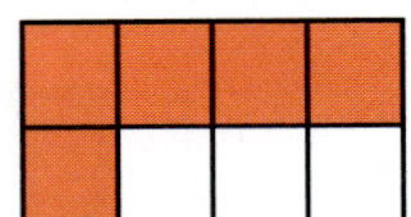

Five eighths or $\frac{5}{8}$ is red.
How much is not red?

C. Sixths
6 equal parts

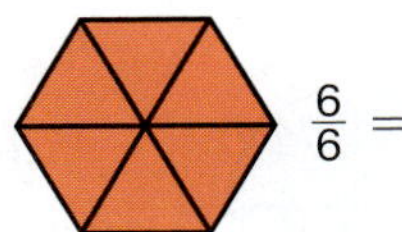

$\frac{6}{6} = 1$ whole

Six sixths or $\frac{6}{6}$ is red.
How much is not red?

Explain Your Thinking

► When a whole figure is shaded, what do you know about the numerator and the denominator of the fraction?

Guided Practice

Write a fraction for the shaded part. Then write a fraction for the part that is not shaded.

1. 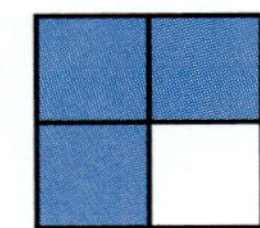

2. 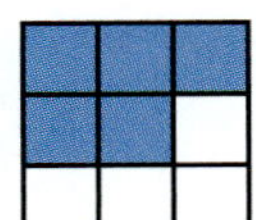

3. 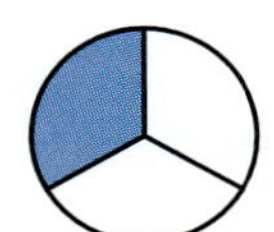

Ask Yourself

- How many parts are there in all?
- How many parts are shaded?
- How many parts are not shaded?

Independent Practice

Write a fraction for the green part. Then write a fraction for the part that is not green.

4. 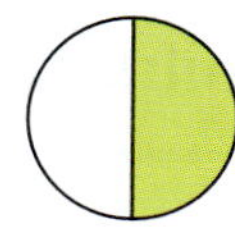

5. 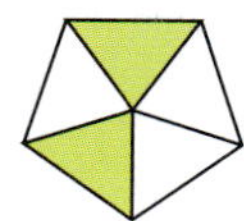

6. 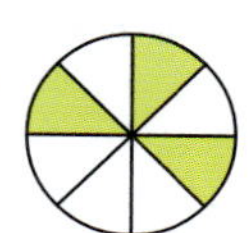

7. 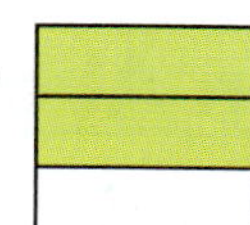

8. 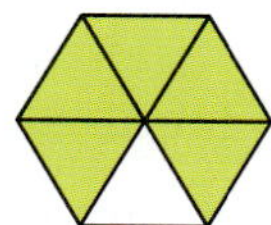

9. 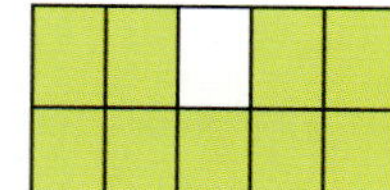

10. 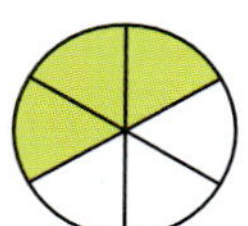

11. 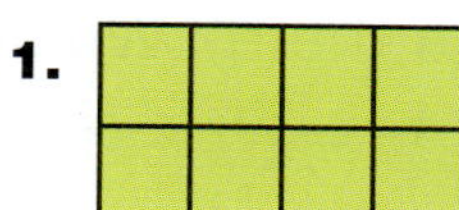

Draw a picture to show each fraction. Then name the numerator and the denominator of the fraction.

12. $\frac{2}{6}$ **13.** $\frac{4}{4}$ **14.** $\frac{1}{5}$ **15.** $\frac{10}{10}$ **16.** $\frac{5}{6}$

17. $\frac{1}{3}$ **18.** $\frac{5}{8}$ **19.** $\frac{5}{10}$ **20.** $\frac{3}{8}$ **21.** $\frac{2}{2}$

Draw a picture and write a fraction for each.

22. three fourths **23.** two thirds **24.** four fifths **25.** seven eighths

Problem Solving • Reasoning

26. Look at the flag of Nigeria on the right. Write a fraction for the part of the flag that is green.

27. **Logical Thinking** Another flag has four different color stripes that go across. The blue stripe is between the yellow stripe and the red stripe. The bottom stripe is green. The top stripe is not yellow. What color is the top stripe?

Mixed Review • Test Prep

Divide or multiply. *(pages 260–261, 410–411)*

28. 35 ÷ 7 **29.** 3 × 8 **30.** 42 ÷ 7 **31.** 6 × 8 **32.** 14 ÷ 7

Choose the letter of the correct answer. *(pages 414–415, 416–417)*

33 32 ÷ 8 = ■

A 8 **B** 6 **C** 4 **D** 3

34 63 ÷ 9 = ■

F 6 **G** 7 **H** 8 **J** 9

Extra Practice See Set A on page 530.

Fractions and Groups

You will learn that fractions can be used to name parts of a group.

Review Vocabulary
numerator
denominator

Learn About It

You can use a fraction to name part of a group.

Look at the picture on the right. How many buttons are there? What fraction of them are red?

numerator → $\frac{7}{12}$ ← number of red buttons
denominator → ← total number of buttons

Seven of the twelve buttons are red.

Seven twelfths of the buttons are red.

What fraction of the buttons are not red?

$\frac{5}{12}$ ← number of buttons that are *not* red
← total number of buttons

Five of the twelve buttons are not red.

Five twelfths of the buttons are not red.

Explain Your Thinking

► What fraction of the buttons are green? What fraction of them are yellow? Explain how you know.

Guided Practice

Ask Yourself

- How do I decide what number to write as the numerator?
- How do I decide what number to write as the denominator?

Use the picture below for Questions 1–3.

1. What fraction of the buttons have 4 holes?
2. What fraction of the buttons have 2 holes?
3. What fraction of the buttons are round?

Independent Practice

Write a fraction to name the part of each group that is round.

4. 

5. 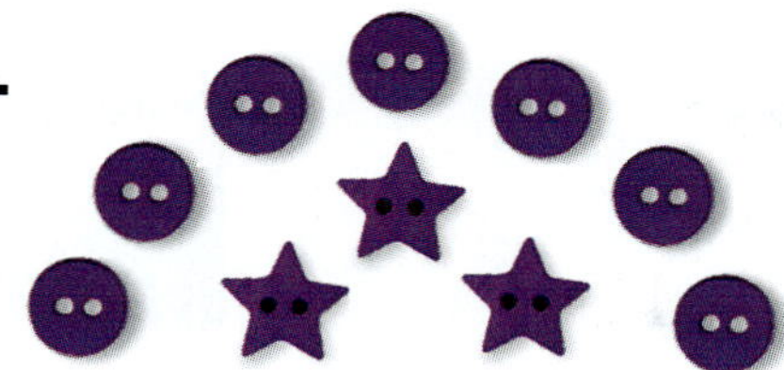

6. 

Write a fraction to name the part of each group that is red.

7. 6 of the 10 buttons are red.

8. All of the 8 buttons are red.

9. None of the 9 buttons are red.

Problem Solving • Reasoning

10. Geraldo made button art from 5 square yellow buttons and 5 square blue buttons. What fraction of the art is square buttons?

11. **Analyze** Rachel has 8 buttons. Five of the buttons are green. What fraction of the buttons are not green?

12. **Patterns** Jay followed the pattern shown below to make a button worm. If he continues the pattern to include 6 more buttons, how many orange buttons in all will he use?

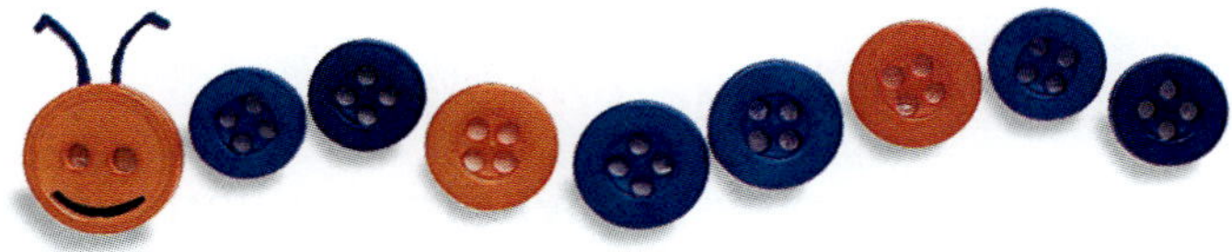

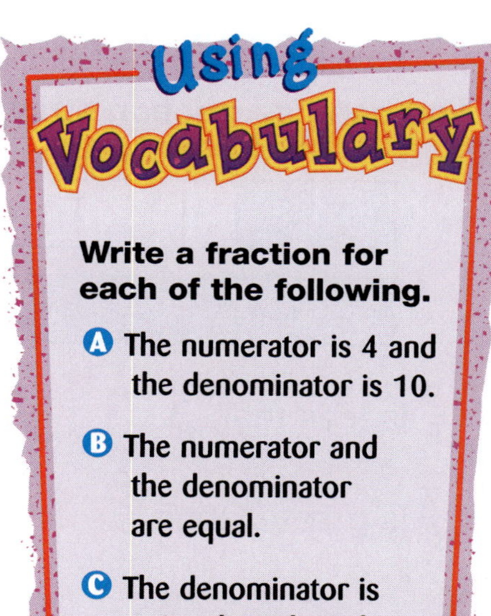

Write a fraction for each of the following.

A The numerator is 4 and the denominator is 10.

B The numerator and the denominator are equal.

C The denominator is twice the value of the numerator.

Mixed Review • Test Prep

Estimate each sum or difference. *(pages 108–109, 132–133)*

13. 647 + 293 **14.** 284 − 193 **15.** 924 − 89 **16.** 693 + 205

Choose the letter of the correct answer. *(pages 116–118, 140–141)*

17 901 − 296 = ■

A 605 **C** 705

B 615 **D** 715

18 96 + 163 + 402 = ■

F 53 **H** 714

G 661 **J** 814

Extra Practice See Set B on page 530.

LESSON 3

Compare Fractions

You will learn how to compare fractions.

New Vocabulary
unit fraction

Learn About It

Devon's class knit scarves for a service project. Look at the scarves. Which scarf has more blue?

The fractions $\frac{3}{8}$ and $\frac{7}{8}$ have the same denominator. So you can compare them in different ways.

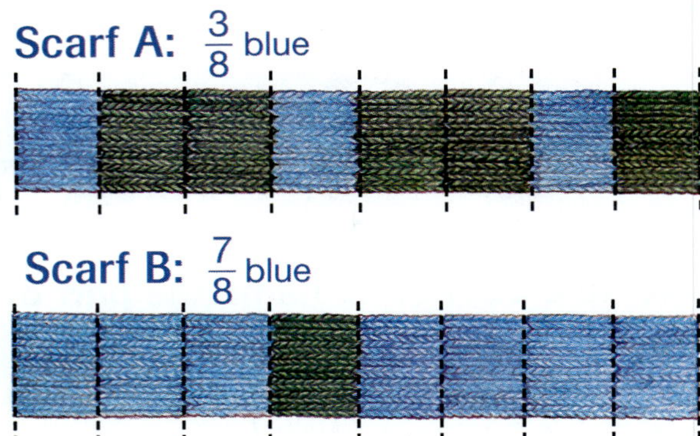

Different Ways to Compare Fractions

You can use fraction strips.

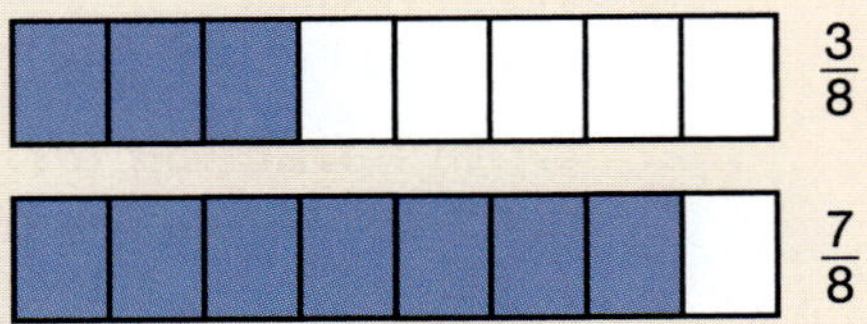

$\frac{3}{8}$ is less than $\frac{7}{8}$. $\frac{3}{8} < \frac{7}{8}$

$\frac{7}{8}$ is greater than $\frac{3}{8}$. $\frac{7}{8} > \frac{3}{8}$

You can use a number line.

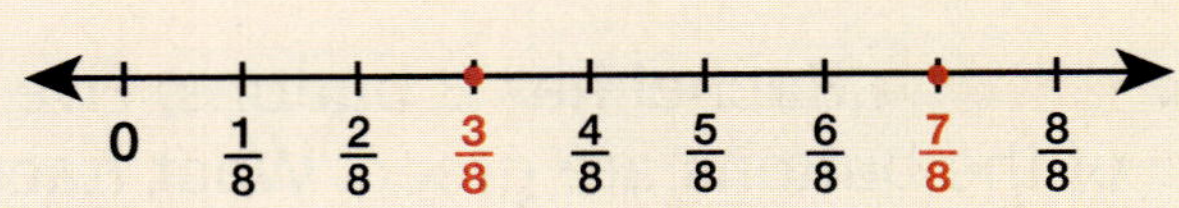

$\frac{7}{8}$ is to the right of $\frac{3}{8}$.

So $\frac{7}{8} > \frac{3}{8}$.

Solution: Scarf B has more blue.

Another Example

Compare Unit Fractions

Fractions with 1 as a numerator are **unit fractions**. You just compare the denominators of unit fractions.

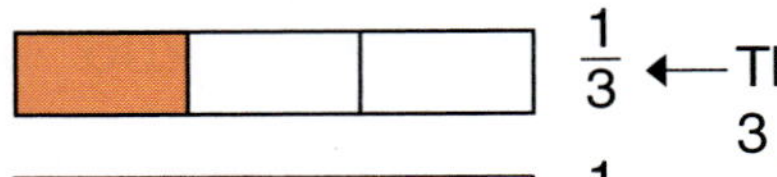

$\frac{1}{3}$ ← The whole has 3 parts.

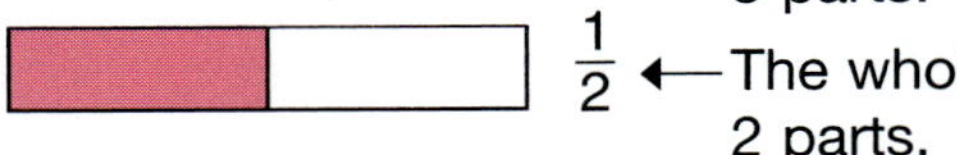

$\frac{1}{2}$ ← The whole has 2 parts.

3 parts of the whole are each less than 2 parts of the whole. So $\frac{1}{3} < \frac{1}{2}$.

Explain Your Thinking

► The circles below are the same size. One circle is divided into fourths and the other into thirds. Which is greater, $\frac{1}{3}$ or $\frac{1}{4}$? How do you know?

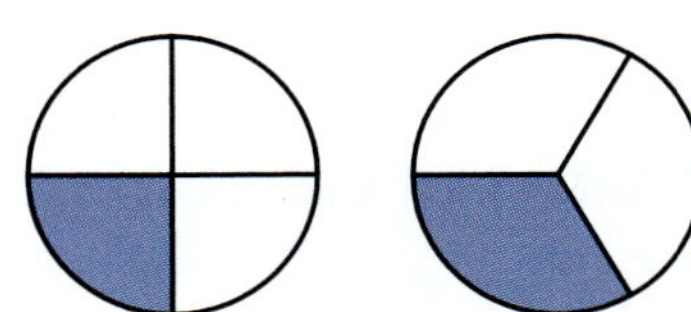

Guided Practice

Compare. Write > or < for each ⬬.

1. 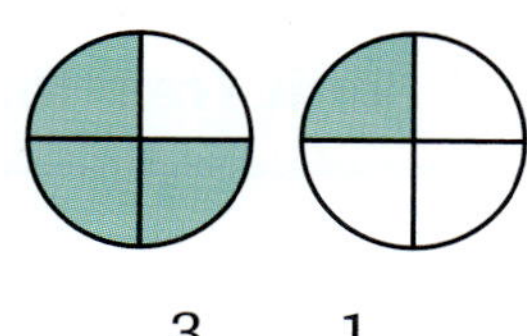

$\frac{3}{4}$ ⬬ $\frac{1}{4}$

2. 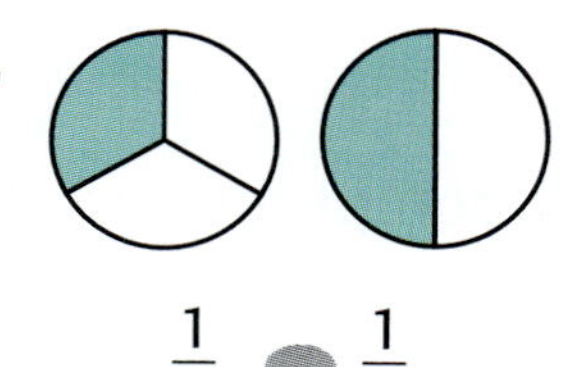

$\frac{1}{3}$ ⬬ $\frac{1}{2}$

Ask Yourself

- If the denominators are the same, which numerator is greater?
- If the fractions are unit fractions, which one represents a smaller part of a whole?

Independent Practice

Compare the fractions. Write > or < for each ⬬.

3. 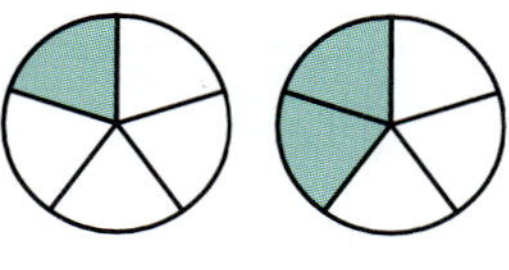

$\frac{1}{5}$ ⬬ $\frac{2}{5}$

4. 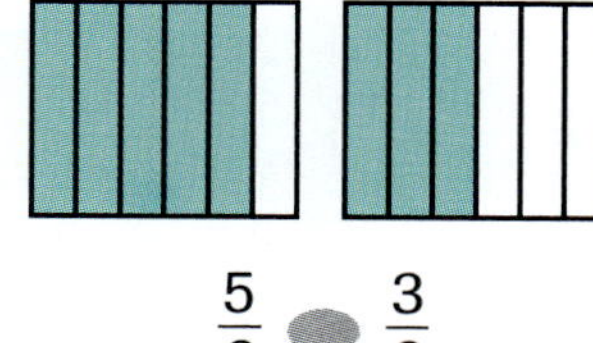

$\frac{5}{6}$ ⬬ $\frac{3}{6}$

5. 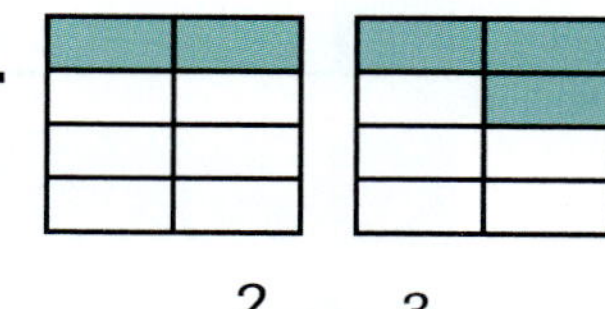

$\frac{2}{8}$ ⬬ $\frac{3}{8}$

Compare. Write > or < for each ⬬.

6. $\frac{1}{6}$ ⬬ $\frac{3}{6}$ **7.** $\frac{6}{7}$ ⬬ $\frac{3}{7}$ **8.** $\frac{5}{5}$ ⬬ $\frac{4}{5}$ **9.** $\frac{6}{9}$ ⬬ $\frac{2}{9}$ **10.** $\frac{7}{8}$ ⬬ $\frac{8}{8}$

11. $\frac{1}{5}$ ⬬ $\frac{1}{3}$ **12.** $\frac{1}{2}$ ⬬ $\frac{2}{2}$ **13.** $\frac{2}{4}$ ⬬ $\frac{3}{4}$ **14.** $\frac{7}{10}$ ⬬ $\frac{10}{10}$ **15.** $\frac{1}{9}$ ⬬ $\frac{1}{7}$

Problem Solving • Reasoning

16. Six schools each gave 4 blankets to 3 homeless shelters. If each shelter received the same number of blankets, how many blankets did each shelter receive?

17. **Compare** Paul's scarf is $\frac{2}{5}$ yellow. Emily's scarf is $\frac{4}{5}$ yellow. Susan's scarf is $\frac{1}{2}$ red and $\frac{1}{2}$ white. If each scarf is the same size, whose scarf has the most yellow?

Mixed Review • Test Prep

Write each number in standard form. *(pages 4–5, 18–19)*

18. twenty-six **19.** four hundred eight **20.** six thousand, sixty

21 Which expression has the same value as 7 × 4? *(pages 236–239)*

A 7 − 4 **B** 7 + 4 **C** 7 + 7 + 7 + 7 **D** 4 + 4 + 4 + 4

Extra Practice See Set C on page 530.

LESSON 4

Order Fractions

You will learn how to order fractions.

Review Vocabulary
unit fraction

Learn About It

You can use what you know about comparing fractions to order fractions from least to greatest or from greatest to least.

Order these fractions from least to greatest: $\frac{1}{6}$ $\frac{5}{6}$ $\frac{3}{6}$

Different Ways to Order Fractions

You can use fraction strips.

$\frac{1}{6}$ is the least. $\frac{5}{6}$ is the greatest.

So $\frac{1}{6} < \frac{3}{6} < \frac{5}{6}$.

You can use a number line.

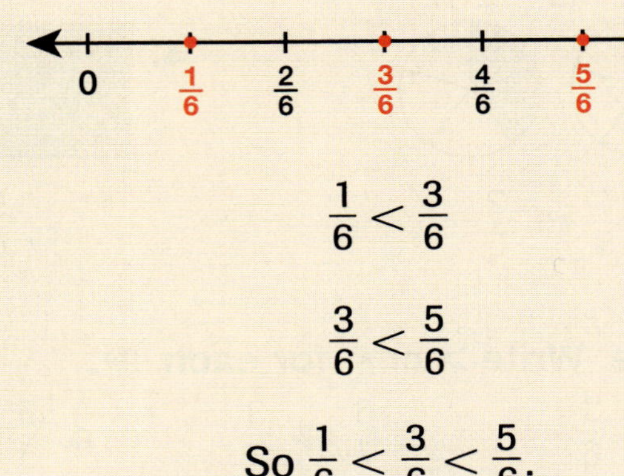

$\frac{1}{6} < \frac{3}{6}$

$\frac{3}{6} < \frac{5}{6}$

So $\frac{1}{6} < \frac{3}{6} < \frac{5}{6}$.

Solution: This is the order of the fractions from least to greatest. $\frac{1}{6}$ $\frac{3}{6}$ $\frac{5}{6}$

Another Example

Order Unit Fractions

You can order unit fractions by ordering the denominators. The greater the denominator, the smaller the fraction.

The order of fractions from greatest to least is:
$\frac{1}{2}$ $\frac{1}{3}$ $\frac{1}{6}$

Explain Your Thinking

► Look at the unit fractions above. Why does the least unit fraction have the greatest denominator?

Guided Practice

Order the fractions from least to greatest.

1. $\frac{2}{5}$, $\frac{4}{5}$, $\frac{1}{5}$

2. $\frac{1}{6}$, $\frac{1}{8}$, $\frac{1}{4}$

Ask Yourself

- If the denominators are the same, which numerator is the greatest?
- If the fractions are unit fractions, which one represents the smallest part of a whole?

Independent Practice

Order the fractions from greatest to least.

3. $\frac{1}{2}$, $\frac{1}{3}$, $\frac{1}{4}$

4. $\frac{1}{5}$, $\frac{1}{3}$, $\frac{1}{4}$

5. $\frac{3}{8}$, $\frac{7}{8}$, $\frac{1}{8}$

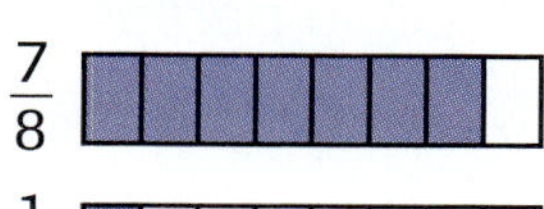

Order the fractions from least to greatest.
Use fraction strips to help you.

6. $\frac{1}{4}$ $\frac{1}{8}$ $\frac{1}{2}$

7. $\frac{4}{5}$ $\frac{2}{5}$ $\frac{3}{5}$

8. $\frac{1}{2}$ $\frac{1}{3}$ $\frac{1}{5}$

9. $\frac{6}{8}$ $\frac{5}{8}$ $\frac{2}{8}$

Problem Solving • Reasoning

10. Pam, Luke and Chen painted a mural. Pam painted the blue part. Luke painted the red part, and Chen painted the yellow part of the mural. Who painted the most?

11. **Estimate** In the school newspaper, ads cost 48¢ for $\frac{1}{8}$ page. About how much will Raul have to pay if he buys an ad that is $\frac{2}{8}$ page?

12. **Compare** At a sale, books that usually cost $8.95 now have stickers for $\frac{1}{2}$ off, $\frac{1}{4}$ off, or $\frac{1}{3}$ off. Which sticker gives the best buy?

Mixed Review • Test Prep

Write the value of each amount of money. *(pages 56–57)*

13. 3 quarters, 2 dimes

14. 6 dimes, 8 pennies

15. 2 dimes, 7 nickels

16 How many sides does a pentagon have? *(pages 302–303)*

A 6 **B** 5 **C** 4 **D** 3

Modeling Equivalent Fractions

You will learn how to use different fractions to name the same amount.

New Vocabulary
equivalent fractions

Learn About It

You can use paper circles to find out about equivalent fractions. **Equivalent fractions** are fractions that name the same amount.

Work with a partner. Each circle is the same size.

Materials
For each pair:
crayons
paper circles or Teaching Tool 17

Step 1 One person should

A. Fold a paper circle in half.

B. Open up the circle. Draw a line on the fold. Color $\frac{1}{2}$ of the circle.

A.
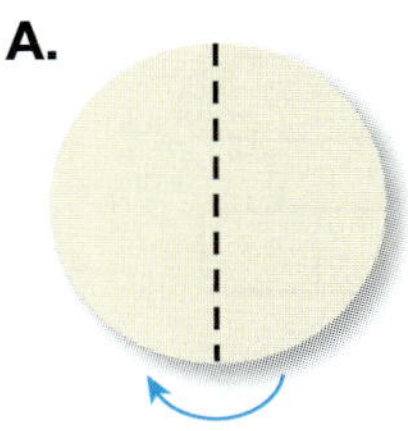

B.
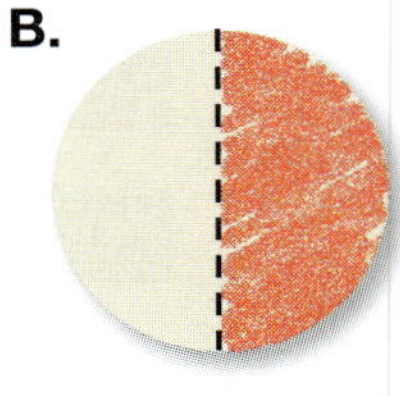

Step 2 The other person should

A. Fold a paper circle in half.

B. Fold it in half a second time.

C. Fold it in half again.

D. Open up the circle. Draw a line on each fold. Color $\frac{4}{8}$ of the circle.

A.
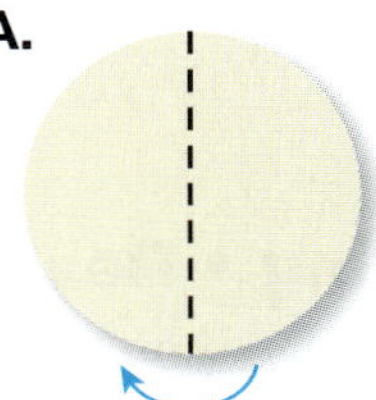

B.
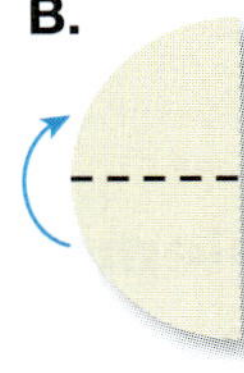

C.
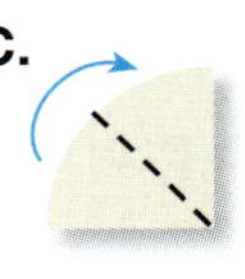

D.
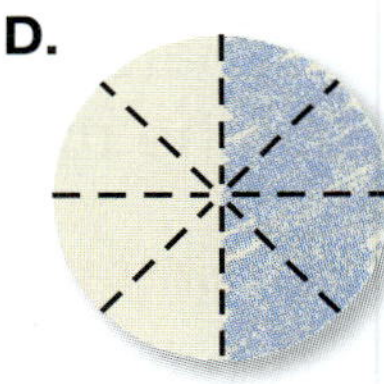

Step 3 Compare the two circles.
What fraction of each is colored?

$\frac{1}{2}$ and $\frac{4}{8}$ name the same amount.

$\frac{1}{2}$ and $\frac{4}{8}$ are equivalent fractions.

So $\frac{1}{2} = \frac{4}{8}$.

Try It Out

Write *equivalent* or *not equivalent* to describe the fractions in each pair.

1. 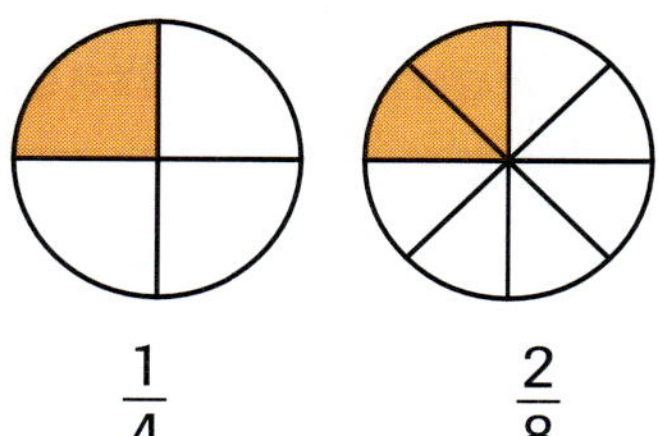

$\frac{1}{4}$ $\frac{2}{8}$

2. 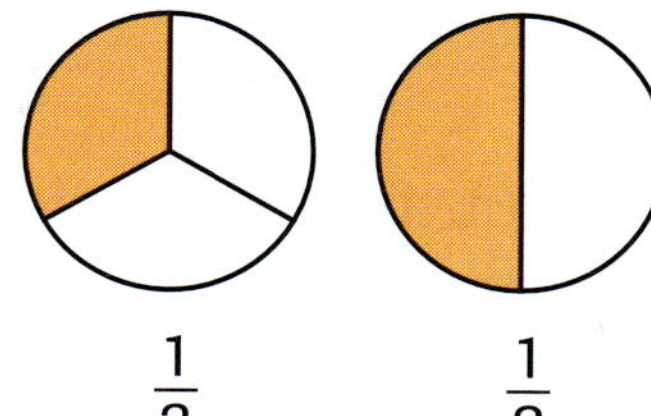

$\frac{1}{3}$ $\frac{1}{2}$

3. 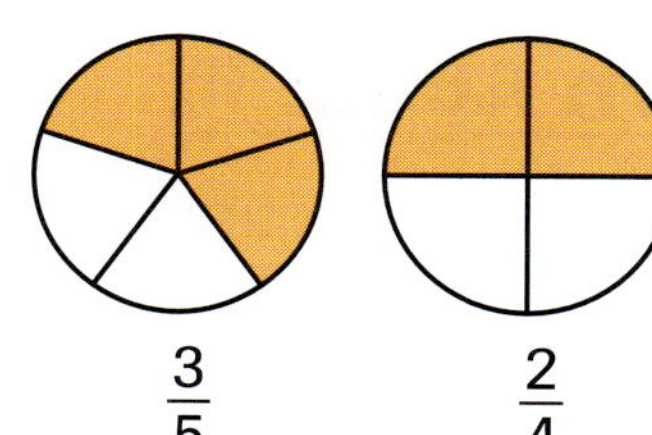

$\frac{3}{5}$ $\frac{2}{4}$

Use the drawings to complete the equivalent fractions.

4. 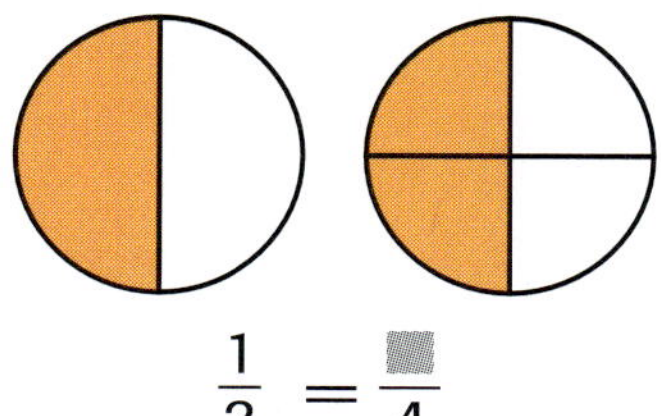

$\frac{1}{2} = \frac{\blacksquare}{4}$

5. 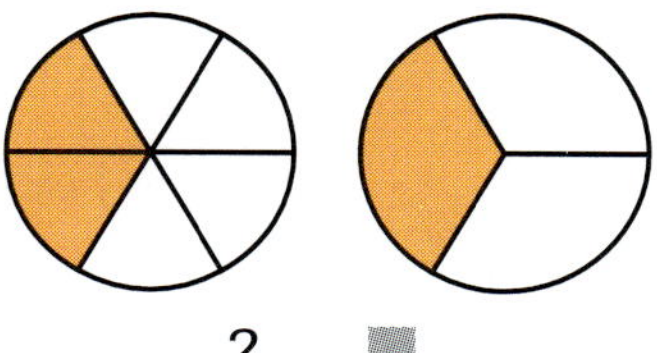

$\frac{2}{6} = \frac{\blacksquare}{3}$

6. 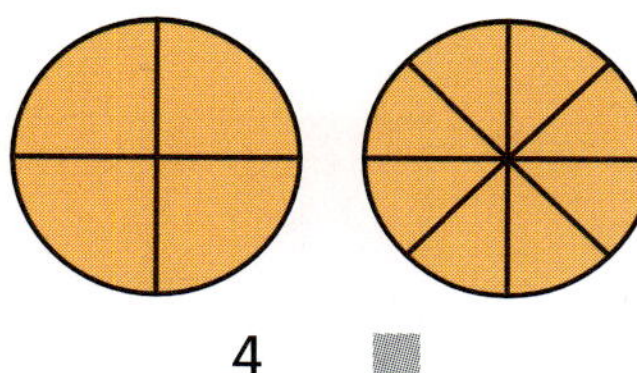

$\frac{4}{4} = \frac{\blacksquare}{8}$

7. Chad drew a square and divided it into 16 equal parts. He colored all but 2 parts. Write two equivalent fractions for the part that is not colored.

8. Dave cut a circle into 6 equal pieces. He colored $\frac{1}{2}$ of the pieces purple and $\frac{1}{2}$ yellow. How many sixths were yellow?

Write about it! Talk about it!

Use what you have learned to follow these directions.

9. Use *equivalent* or *not equivalent* to describe the fractions in each pair.

a.

b.

c.

10. Describe how you can tell whether two fractions are equivalent.

LESSON 6

Find Equivalent Fractions

You will learn more about equivalent fractions.

Review Vocabulary
equivalent fractions

Learn About It

You can use fraction strips to help you find equivalent fractions. Remember, **equivalent fractions** name the same amount.

Look at the fraction strips below.

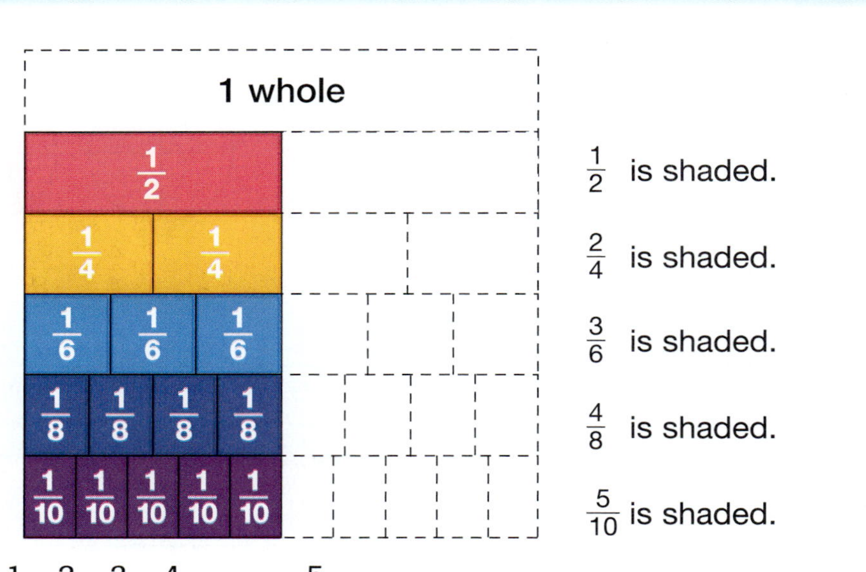

$\frac{1}{2}$ is shaded.

$\frac{2}{4}$ is shaded.

$\frac{3}{6}$ is shaded.

$\frac{4}{8}$ is shaded.

$\frac{5}{10}$ is shaded.

$\frac{1}{2}$, $\frac{2}{4}$, $\frac{3}{6}$, $\frac{4}{8}$, and $\frac{5}{10}$ all name the same amount.

$$\frac{1}{2} = \frac{2}{4} = \frac{3}{6} = \frac{4}{8} = \frac{5}{10}$$

Explain Your Thinking

- ▶ Look at the fraction strips above. Are $\frac{1}{4}$ and $\frac{2}{6}$ equivalent? Explain.
- ▶ Are $\frac{2}{2}$, $\frac{4}{4}$, and $\frac{6}{6}$ equivalent fractions? Why or why not?

Guided Practice

Name the equivalent fractions shown.

1.

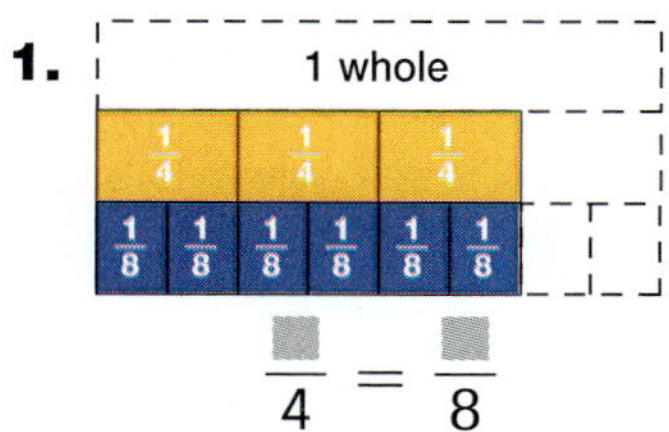

$\frac{■}{4} = \frac{■}{8}$

2.

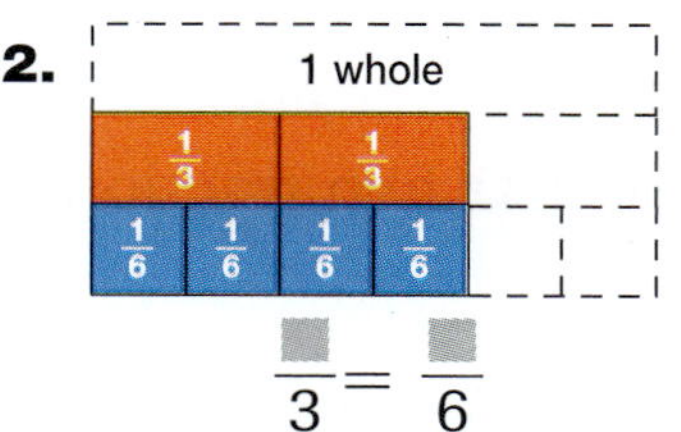

$\frac{■}{3} = \frac{■}{6}$

Ask Yourself

- How many equal parts are in each strip?
- How many parts are shaded?

Independent Practice

Name the equivalent fractions shown.

3.
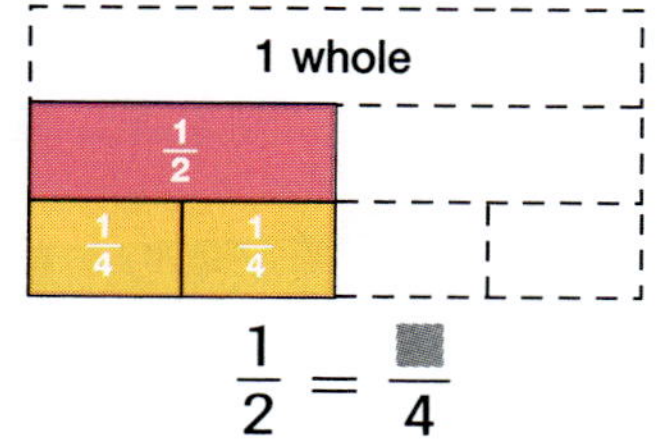

$\frac{1}{2} = \frac{■}{4}$

4.
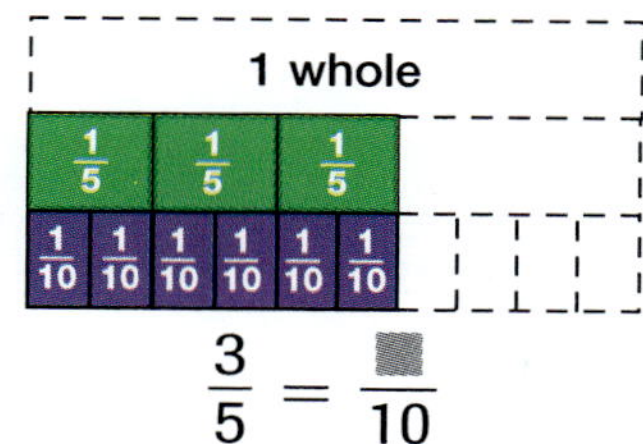

$\frac{3}{5} = \frac{■}{10}$

5.
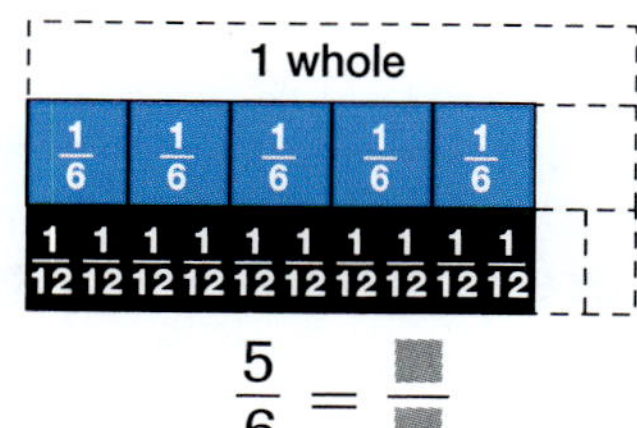

$\frac{5}{6} = \frac{■}{■}$

Write *equivalent* or *not equivalent* to describe the fractions. Draw fraction strips to support your answer.

6. $\frac{1}{4}$ and $\frac{3}{8}$ **7.** $\frac{1}{3}$ and $\frac{2}{6}$ **8.** $\frac{1}{2}$ and $\frac{3}{4}$ **9.** $\frac{2}{5}$ and $\frac{1}{4}$

Look for a pattern in the equivalent fractions. Then write 2 more equivalent fractions in each pattern.

10. $\frac{1}{2} = \frac{2}{4} = \frac{3}{6} = \frac{4}{8} = \frac{■}{10} = \frac{■}{12}$

11. $\frac{1}{3} = \frac{2}{6} = \frac{3}{9} = \frac{4}{12} = \frac{■}{15} = \frac{■}{18}$

12. $\frac{2}{3} = \frac{4}{6} = \frac{6}{9} = \frac{8}{12} = \frac{■}{15} = \frac{■}{18}$

13. $\frac{1}{10} = \frac{2}{20} = \frac{3}{30} = \frac{4}{40} = \frac{■}{50} = \frac{■}{60}$

Problem Solving • Reasoning

Use Data Use the table for Problems 14–16.

14. Which two students ran the same distance? Explain how you know.

15. **Compare** Kayla said that she ran farther than Larry. Is she right?

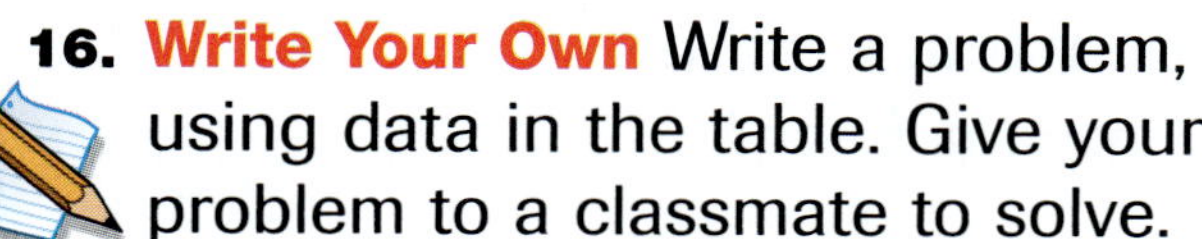

16. **Write Your Own** Write a problem, using data in the table. Give your problem to a classmate to solve.

Distances Students Ran

Student	Distance
Sven	$\frac{3}{4}$ mile
Kayla	$\frac{4}{5}$ mile
Tara	$\frac{6}{8}$ mile
Larry	$\frac{9}{10}$ mile
Joe	$\frac{10}{10}$ mile

Mixed Review • Test Prep

Add or subtract. *(pages 102–103, 104–106, 140–141)*

17. 402 − 322 **18.** 5 + 9 + 4 **19.** 306 + 207 **20.** 101 − 15

21 Which is the most likely distance from a student's home to his or her school? *(pages 164–166)*

A 2 inches **B** 2 yards **C** 2 miles **D** 200 miles

Extra Practice See Set E on page 531.

Problem-Solving Strategy: Choose a Strategy

You will learn how to choose a strategy to solve a problem.

Before starting to solve a problem, you should decide which strategy to use.

Problem Kay and Alex are building kites that are the same size. Kay colored $\frac{1}{2}$ of her kite. Alex colored $\frac{3}{4}$ of his kite. Who colored more of his or her kite, Kay or Alex?

What do you need to find?

You need to find who colored more of his or her kite.

What do you know?

- Kay colored $\frac{1}{2}$ of her kite.
- Alex colored $\frac{3}{4}$ of his kite.

How can you find the answer?

You can either Draw a Picture or Use Models to Act It Out.

Draw a Picture

Kay's Kite

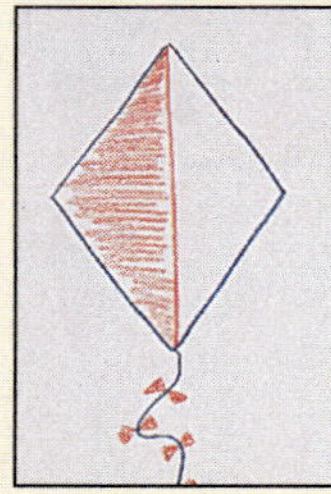

Alex's Kite

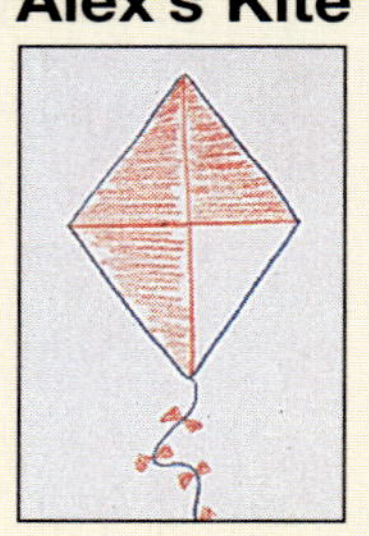

More of Alex's kite is colored.

Use Models to Act It Out

Use fraction strips.
Compare $\frac{1}{2}$ and $\frac{3}{4}$.

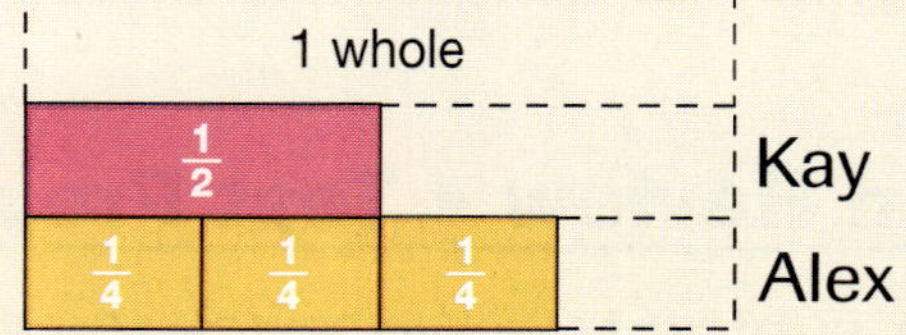

Look back at the problem.

Can you think of another way to solve the problem?

Guided Practice

Solve each problem.

1. Luisa is making a kite in the shape of a butterfly. She bought 10 feet of fabric and used 8 feet of it. What fraction of the fabric did Luisa use?

Can I draw a picture to solve the problem?

2. A kite has 12 equal panels. One half of them are green, one third are orange, and one sixth are blue. What color are most of the panels?

Think: Can I use a model to solve the problem?

Choose a Strategy

Solve. Use these or other strategies.

Problem-Solving Strategies

- **Find a Pattern**
- **Guess and Check**
- **Draw a Picture**
- **Use Logical Thinking**

3. Tom and Phyllis are making kites that are the same size. Tom colors $\frac{3}{6}$ of his kite red. Phyllis colors $\frac{3}{8}$ of her kite red. Whose kite has the least part colored red?

4. Jo spent $\frac{1}{3}$ of her time coloring a kite, $\frac{1}{4}$ of her time assembling it, $\frac{1}{3}$ of her time making a tail, and then $\frac{1}{12}$ of her time attaching it. What step took the least time?

5. Moe, Al, and Sue are flying kites. Moe's kite is twice as high as Al's kite. Al's kite is 100 feet lower than Sue's kite. If Sue's kite flies at 250 feet, how high is each kite?

6. Miguel is painting 15 stripes on a kite. The stripes are in this order: blue, green, red, blue, green, red. If the pattern continues, how many green stripes will he paint?

7. At a kite-flying contest, $\frac{1}{2}$ of the kites were diamond kites. The remaining 8 kites were box kites. How many kites were in the contest?

8. Joy bought materials for a kite. After she spent \$11 on fabric and \$4 on string, she had \$5 left. What fraction of her money did Joy spend?

Extra Practice See 1–4 on page 533.

Quick Check

Check Your Understanding of Lessons 1–7

Write a fraction to name the part that is shaded blue.

1. 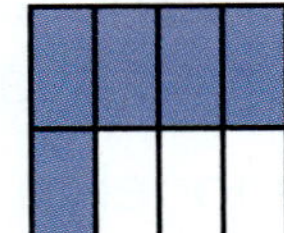

2. 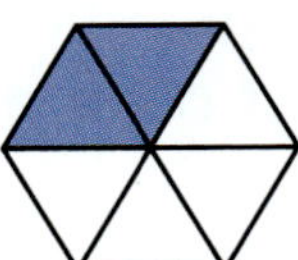

3. 

4. 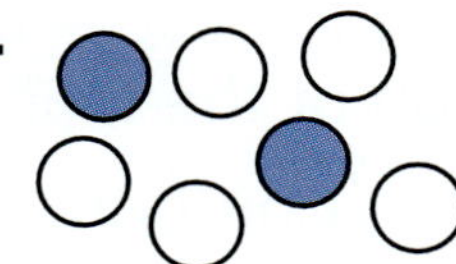

Order the fractions from greatest to least.

5. $\frac{3}{5}$ $\frac{1}{5}$ $\frac{4}{5}$

6. $\frac{1}{16}$ $\frac{1}{2}$ $\frac{1}{10}$

7. $\frac{1}{3}$ $\frac{1}{12}$ $\frac{1}{4}$

8. $\frac{8}{8}$ $\frac{6}{8}$ $\frac{7}{8}$

Write *equivalent* or *not equivalent* to describe the fractions.

9. $\frac{2}{6}$ and $\frac{1}{3}$

10. $\frac{1}{5}$ and $\frac{3}{10}$

11. $\frac{1}{4}$ and $\frac{5}{8}$

12. $\frac{3}{6}$ and $\frac{1}{2}$

Solve.

13. A pet store has 20 dog dishes. One fourth of them are red, one half are blue, one tenth are white, and the rest are green. How many dog dishes are red?

14. Ben bought a 16-ounce box of dog biscuits. Ben's dog has eaten 12 ounces of the biscuits so far. What fraction of the biscuits has the dog eaten?

How did you do?

If you had difficulty with any items in the Quick Check, you can use the following pages for review and extra practice.

Items	Review These Pages	Do These Extra Practice Items
1–4	pages 484–487	Set A, page 530 Set B, page 530
5–8	pages 488–491	Set C, page 530 Set D, page 530
9–12	pages 494–495	Set E, page 531
13–14	pages 496–497	1–4, page 533

Test Prep • Cumulative Review

Maintaining the Standards

Choose the letter of the correct answer.

1. What fraction of the square is shaded?

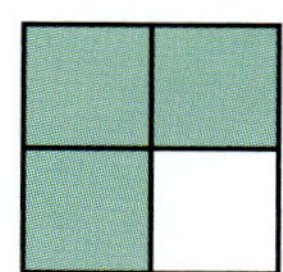

A $\frac{1}{4}$ **C** $\frac{3}{5}$

B $\frac{2}{4}$ **D** $\frac{3}{4}$

2. What plane figure has all sides equal in length and 4 right angles?

F square
G rectangle
H parallelogram
J quadrilateral

3. Which symbol makes this statement true?

$\frac{3}{8}$ ● $\frac{5}{8}$

A $>$ **C** $=$

B $<$ **D** $+$

4. A coach has 3 soccer balls and 2 basketballs. What fraction of the balls are soccer balls?

F $\frac{2}{5}$ **H** $\frac{2}{3}$

G $\frac{3}{5}$ **J** $\frac{3}{4}$

5. What is the name of this figure?

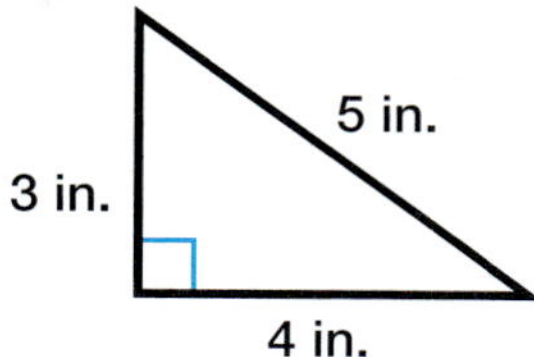

A equilateral triangle
B isosceles triangle
C right triangle
D pentagon

6. Which triangle has angles that are all less than right angles?

F
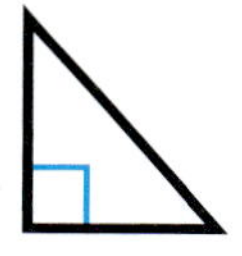

H

G
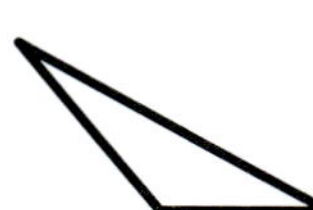

J

7. Carrie has 3 red crayons, 4 yellow crayons, and 2 blue crayons. What fraction of her crayons are blue?

Explain How did you find your answer?

Fractional Parts of a Group

You will learn how to find a fractional part of a group.

Learn About It

Look at the 12 flowers in the flower box. One third of them are red. How many of the flowers are red?

You can use counters to find the answer.

Find $\frac{1}{3}$ of 12.

- Use 12 counters to stand for the flowers.
- Put the counters into 3 equal groups.
- Count the number in one of the three groups.

$\frac{1}{3}$ of 12 is 4.

Solution: Four of the flowers are red.

Look at the picture again. Two thirds of the flowers are red or pink. How many flowers are red or pink?

Find $\frac{2}{3}$ of 12.

- Use 12 counters to stand for the flowers.
- Put the counters into 3 equal groups.
- Count the number in two of the three groups.

$\frac{2}{3}$ of 12 is 8.

Solution: Eight of the flowers are red or pink.

Another Example

With a Ruler

Use the picture of a ruler to find $\frac{1}{3}$ and $\frac{2}{3}$ foot.

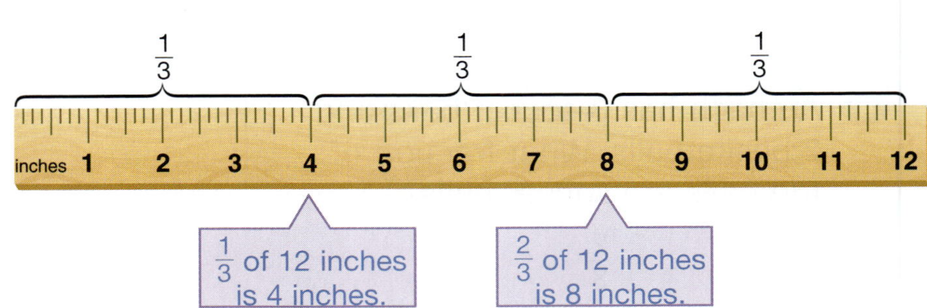

Explain Your Thinking

► How can you use the ruler to find $\frac{3}{4}$ of 12 inches?

Guided Practice

Use counters to find each answer.

1. $\frac{1}{2}$ of 10

2. $\frac{3}{5}$ of 5

Ask Yourself

- What number tells how many objects there are in all?
- What number tells how many equal groups to make?

Independent Practice

Use counters to find each answer.

3.

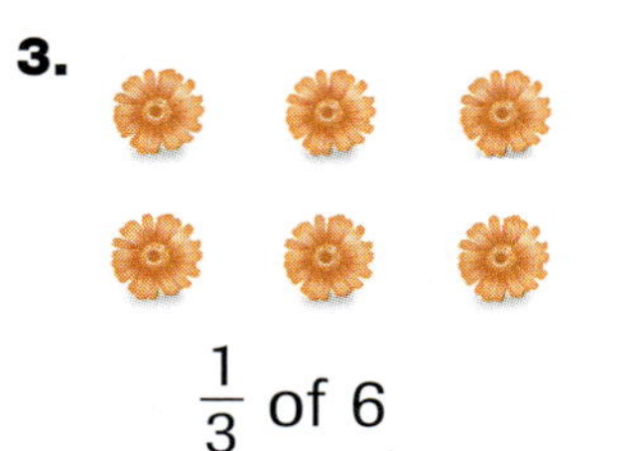

$\frac{1}{3}$ of 6

4.

$\frac{4}{9}$ of 9

5.

$\frac{1}{6}$ of 12

Draw a picture to find each answer.

6. $\frac{5}{6}$ of 12 **7.** $\frac{1}{5}$ of 15 **8.** $\frac{1}{3}$ of 15 **9.** $\frac{3}{7}$ of 14 **10.** $\frac{1}{6}$ of 6

11. $\frac{1}{4}$ of 20 **12.** $\frac{2}{3}$ of 18 **13.** $\frac{1}{8}$ of 16 **14.** $\frac{3}{10}$ of 20 **15.** $\frac{2}{9}$ of 18

Problem Solving • Reasoning

16. Liam picked 9 flowers. One third were yellow flowers. How many yellow flowers did he pick?

17. Brianna picked 16 tulips. One half were white tulips. How many white tulips did she pick?

18. **Analyze** Clark bought 12 flowers. One fourth were red flowers. The rest were white flowers. How can you find the number of white flowers Clark bought?

Math Is Everywhere!

SCIENCE The flower of the southern magnolia tree can grow to have a width of 12 inches.

A Which is wider, a flower that measures $\frac{1}{2}$ foot or 7 inches?

B Which is wider, a flower that measures $\frac{3}{4}$ foot or 10 inches?

Mixed Review • Test Prep

Complete. *(pages 164–166, 172–174)*

19. 1 ft = ___ in. **20.** 1 yd = ___ ft **21.** 1 lb = ___ oz

22 At what temperature does water freeze? *(pages 176–177)*

A 32°F **B** 50°F **C** 100°F **D** 212°F

Extra Practice See Set F on page 531.

Mixed Numbers

You will learn about fractions greater than 1.

New Vocabulary
improper fraction
mixed number

Learn About It

The peanut butter sandwiches are divided into halves.

There are 5 half-sandwiches, or $\frac{5}{2}$ sandwiches.

We can also say that there are 2 whole sandwiches and $\frac{1}{2}$ sandwich, or $2\frac{1}{2}$ sandwiches.

improper fraction → $\frac{5}{2} = 2\frac{1}{2}$ ← mixed number

An **improper fraction** has a numerator greater than or equal to its denominator.

numerator → 5
denominator → 2

A **mixed number** is made up of a whole number and a fraction.

whole number → $2\frac{1}{2}$ ← fraction

Explain Your Thinking

► Why is $1\frac{1}{3}$ equal to $\frac{4}{3}$?
Use pictures to explain your answer.

Guided Practice

Write an improper fraction and a mixed number for the shaded part.

1. 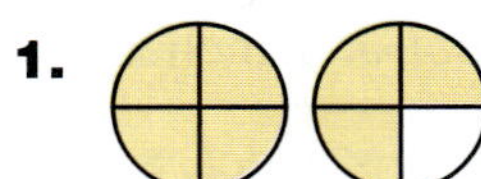

2. 

3. 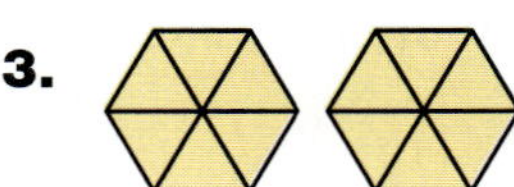

4. 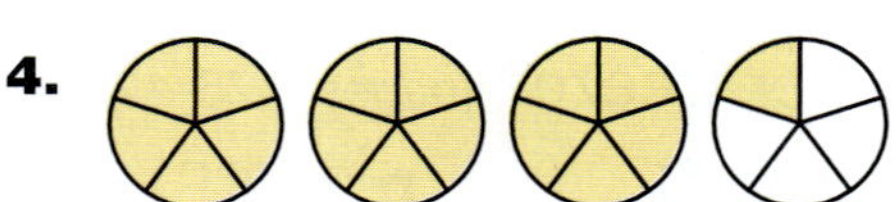

Ask Yourself

- How many whole numbers are shown?
- Are there any fractional parts left?

Independent Practice

Write an improper fraction and a mixed number for the shaded part.

5.

6. 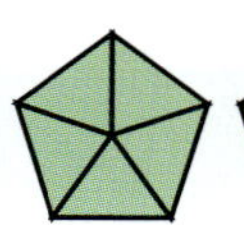

7. 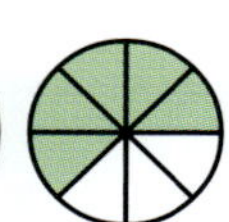

8.

9. 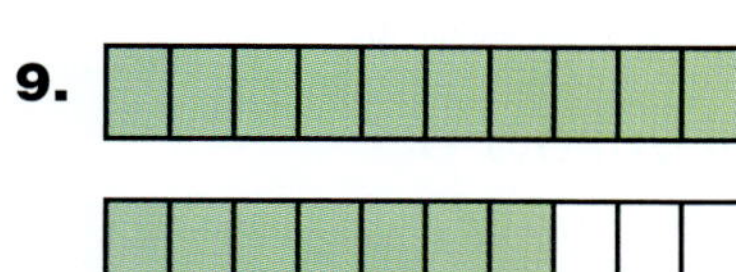

10.

Draw a picture to show each improper fraction. Then write a whole number or a mixed number for each picture.

11. $\frac{6}{3}$ **12.** $\frac{7}{6}$ **13.** $\frac{13}{5}$ **14.** $\frac{10}{3}$ **15.** $\frac{20}{5}$

16. $\frac{9}{4}$ **17.** $\frac{19}{6}$ **18.** $\frac{13}{3}$ **19.** $\frac{27}{8}$ **20.** $\frac{35}{7}$

Problem Solving • Reasoning

Use the recipe on the right for Problems 21 and 22.

21. Are $\frac{8}{4}$ teaspoons of oil enough for the recipe? Explain why or why not.

22. **Analyze** How can you use a measuring cup to measure the amount of peanuts needed for the recipe?

23. **Money** Bob and Kim bought all the ingredients for a peanut butter recipe for a total of $4.50. Bob spent $1.50 more than Kim. How much did Kim spend?

Mixed Review • Test Prep

Multiply or divide. *(pages 220–221, 408–409)*

24. 5×5 **25.** $12 \div 6$ **26.** 5×9 **27.** $54 \div 6$ **28.** 5×7

Choose the letter of the correct answer. *(pages 120–121, 138–139)*

29 7,339 − 6,309 = ■

A 1,030 **C** 1,309
B 1,039 **D** 1,390

30 3,786 + 1,224 = ■

F 2,562 **H** 5,000
G 4,910 **J** 5,010

Extra Practice See Set G on page 531.

LESSON 10

Add and Subtract Fractions

You will learn how to add and subtract fractions that have like denominators.

Learn About It

In this design, $\frac{3}{8}$ is shaded yellow, and $\frac{1}{8}$ is shaded blue. Is the amount shaded yellow or blue equal to $\frac{1}{2}$?

Add. $\mathbf{\frac{3}{8} + \frac{1}{8} = \blacksquare}$

Find $\frac{3}{8} + \frac{1}{8}$.

- Start with three $\frac{1}{8}$ fraction pieces. Add one $\frac{1}{8}$ piece.

$\frac{3}{8} + \frac{1}{8} = \frac{4}{8}$ ← When the denominators are the same, add the numerators

- Next, compare $\frac{4}{8}$ and $\frac{1}{2}$.

1/8 1/8 1/8 1/8

1/2

$\frac{4}{8} = \frac{1}{2}$

Solution: Yes, $\frac{1}{2}$ of the design is shaded yellow or blue.

How much more of the design is shaded yellow than is shaded blue? How does that answer compare to $\frac{1}{4}$?

Subtract. $\mathbf{\frac{3}{8} - \frac{1}{8} = \blacksquare}$

Find $\frac{3}{8} - \frac{1}{8}$.

- Start with three $\frac{1}{8}$ fraction pieces. Subtract one $\frac{1}{8}$ piece.

$\frac{3}{8} - \frac{1}{8} = \frac{2}{8}$

- Next, compare $\frac{2}{8}$ and $\frac{1}{4}$.

1/8 1/8

1/4

$\frac{2}{8} = \frac{1}{4}$

Solution: $\frac{2}{8}$ more of the design is shaded yellow than is shaded blue. $\frac{2}{8}$ is equal to $\frac{1}{4}$.

Explain Your Thinking

▶ How do you use what you know about adding whole numbers to add fractions with like denominators?

Guided Practice

Ask Yourself

- Should I add or subtract?
- How can I use the picture to help me?

Use the fraction strips to help you add or subtract.

1. $\frac{2}{5} + \frac{1}{5} = \blacksquare$

2. $\frac{5}{6} - \frac{3}{6} = \blacksquare$

Add or subtract. Use fraction strips or draw a picture to help you.

3. $\frac{7}{8} - \frac{2}{8}$ **4.** $\frac{2}{4} + \frac{1}{4}$ **5.** $\frac{3}{3} - \frac{1}{3}$ **6.** $\frac{7}{9} + \frac{1}{9}$

Independent Practice

Use the fraction strips to help you add or subtract.

7. $\frac{3}{6} + \frac{1}{6} = \blacksquare$

8. $\frac{3}{4} + \frac{1}{4} = \blacksquare$

9. $\frac{4}{5} - \frac{1}{5} = \blacksquare$

10. $\frac{9}{10} - \frac{6}{10} = \blacksquare$

11. $\frac{3}{8} + \frac{3}{8} = \blacksquare$

12. $\frac{7}{9} - \frac{4}{9} = \blacksquare$

Add or subtract. Use fraction strips or draw a picture to help you.

13. $\frac{1}{3} + \frac{1}{3}$ **14.** $\frac{3}{5} - \frac{2}{5}$ **15.** $\frac{2}{3} - \frac{1}{3}$ **16.** $\frac{2}{7} + \frac{5}{7}$

17. $\frac{5}{6} - \frac{2}{6}$ **18.** $\frac{3}{4} - \frac{1}{4}$ **19.** $\frac{6}{7} - \frac{4}{7}$ **20.** $\frac{2}{5} + \frac{3}{5}$

21. $\frac{5}{8} + \frac{3}{8}$ **22.** $\frac{1}{2} - \frac{1}{2}$ **23.** $\frac{6}{8} - \frac{2}{8}$ **24.** $\frac{2}{10} + \frac{3}{10}$

25. Look back at your answers in Exercises 17–24. In which exercises is the sum or difference equal to $\frac{1}{2}$? Explain.

Problem Solving • Reasoning

Solve. Choose a method. Use the picture for Problems 26 and 27.

Computation Methods

• Estimation • Mental Math • Paper and Pencil

26. Jeff made the stained glass window on the right. Write an addition sentence, using fractions to show how much of the window is red or blue.

27. Write a fraction sentence to show how much more of the window is red than green.

28. **Measurement** The window is 3 feet tall and 4 feet wide. What is the perimeter?

29. **Money** It cost Jeff about \$11 to make the window. If he sells it for \$38, will he make at least \$25? Explain your answer.

Mixed Review • Test Prep

Name each solid figure. *(pages 328–330)*

30. 

31. 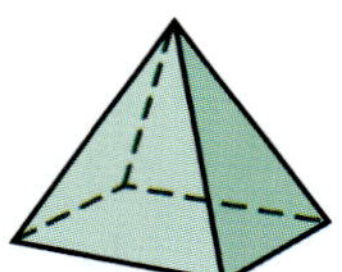

32. 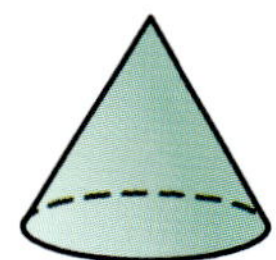

33. 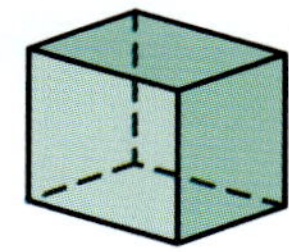

34 What is the time 30 minutes after 1:45 P.M.? *(pages 78–79)*

A 2:00 A.M. **B** 2:15 P.M. **C** 2:30 P.M. **D** 2:45 P.M.

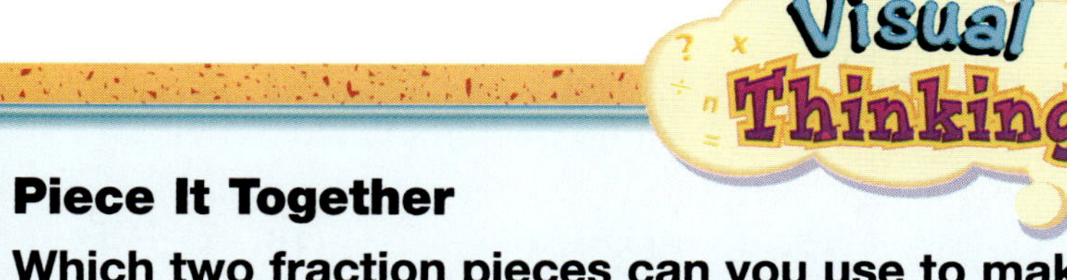

Piece It Together

Which two fraction pieces can you use to make exactly one whole?

35.  1

a. $\frac{1}{2}$ **b.** 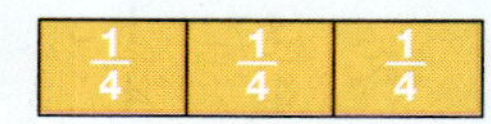 $\frac{1}{4}$ $\frac{1}{4}$ $\frac{1}{4}$ **c.**  $\frac{1}{4}$ $\frac{1}{4}$

36.  1

a.  $\frac{1}{4}$ $\frac{1}{4}$ $\frac{1}{4}$ **b.**  $\frac{1}{3}$ $\frac{1}{3}$ **c.**  $\frac{1}{8}$ $\frac{1}{8}$

Extra Practice See Set H on page 531.

Practice Game

Fraction Bingo

Practice adding and subtracting fractions by playing this game with a partner. Try to get four counters in a row!

What You'll Need

- *32 counters (16 per player)*
- *game boards (Teaching Tool 18)*
- *addition and subtraction problems (Teaching Tool 19)*
- *fraction strips (optional)*

Players
2

Here's What to Do

1. Use Teaching Tools 18 and 19. Place the addition and subtraction problems facedown in a pile.
2. Players take turns picking problems from the top of the pile. Each player solves the problem, finds the answer on his or her game board, and places a counter on top of the correct answer. Fraction strips can be used for help.
3. Repeat Step 2 until one player has four counters in a row. The row can be horizontal, vertical, or diagonal.

Share Your Thinking Explain how you would use fraction strips to find the answer to $\frac{9}{10} - \frac{4}{10}$.

Problem-Solving Skill: Multistep Problems

You will learn how to solve problems, using more than one step.

Sometimes it takes more than one step to solve a problem. You must decide both *what to do* and *in what order* to do it.

Problem Neka bought a package of paper to make greeting cards. The package had 4 sheets each of red, green, blue, yellow, orange, and pink paper. Neka used $\frac{1}{3}$ of the sheets to make cards. How many sheets of paper did Neka use?

Decide what to do.

- Find the total number of sheets in the package.
- Then find $\frac{1}{3}$ of that number.

Do each step in order.

Step 1 Multiply to find the total number of sheets Neka had in the package.

$$\begin{array}{r} 4 \\ \times\ 6 \\ \hline 24 \end{array}$$

4 ← number sheets of each color
× 6 ← number of colors
24 ← total number of sheets

Neka had 24 sheets of paper.

Step 2 Since Neka used $\frac{1}{3}$ of the sheets, find $\frac{1}{3}$ of 24.
Draw a picture to find $\frac{1}{3}$ of 24.

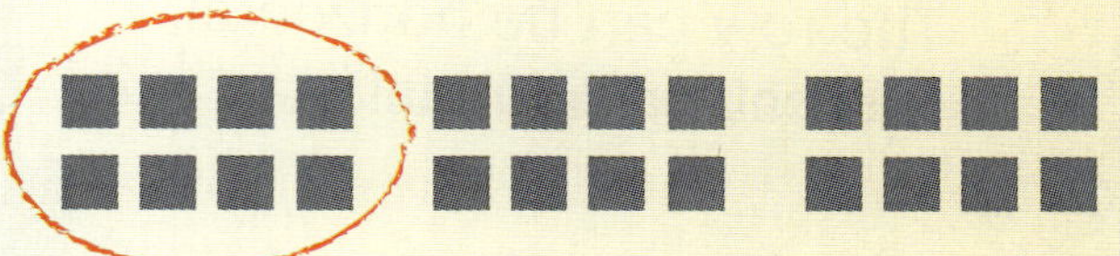

$\frac{1}{3}$ of 24 is 8

Neka used 8 sheets of paper.

Look Back Why do you divide 24 into 3 equal groups to find how many sheets of paper Neka used?

These cards were designed by students and sold on the Internet.

Guided Practice

Solve.

1. Neka had 8 markers and 16 crayons. She used $\frac{1}{2}$ of the markers and $\frac{1}{2}$ of the crayons to decorate her cards. How many crayons and markers did Neka use altogether?

What do I need to do first?

2. Neka drew 10 greeting cards. Then she made 5 more on her computer. She gave $\frac{1}{5}$ of the cards to friends. How many cards did Neka give away?

How many steps are there in this problem?

Choose a Strategy

Solve. Use these or other strategies.

Problem-Solving Strategies

- **Act It Out**
- **Find a Pattern**
- **Draw a Picture**
- **Write a Number Sentence**

3. Students made cards and arranged them in 5 rows with 4 cards in each row. Evan's class made $\frac{1}{4}$ of all the cards. How many cards did Evan's class make?

4. Anja drew a line 7 inches long. She then made the line 5 inches longer. She decided that the line was too long and erased $\frac{1}{3}$ of the line. How many inches did Anja erase?

5. Matt had a box of 8 crayons. He took $\frac{5}{8}$ of the crayons out of the box. Then he took 3 more crayons out and put 1 back. What fraction of the crayons were out of the box then?

6. Emilio made 10 paper animals for a school fair. Three tenths of the animals were blue. How many animals were blue? How many animals were not blue?

7. Shelly is making a pattern like the one below. If the pattern continues, and there are 18 triangles, how many triangles will likely be yellow?

8. Kenny bought a pack of 10 markers to decorate his cards. He lost 2 markers. He then gave $\frac{1}{2}$ of the remaining markers to John. How many markers did Kenny have left?

Extra Practice See 5–6 on page 533.

Quick Check

Check Your Understanding of Lessons 8–11

Draw a picture to find each answer.

1. $\frac{1}{3}$ of 18 **2.** $\frac{1}{4}$ of 12 **3.** $\frac{1}{5}$ of 20 **4.** $\frac{1}{6}$ of 24

Write an improper fraction and a mixed number for the shaded part.

5. 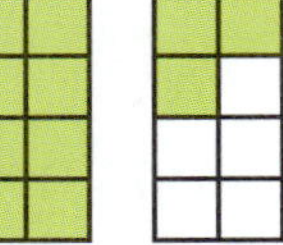

6. 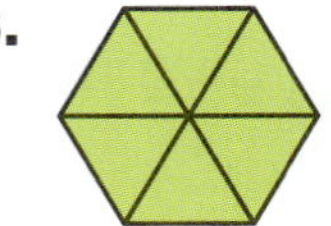 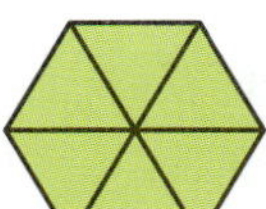 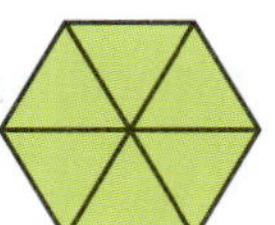 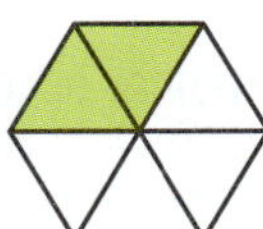

Add or subtract. Use fraction strips or draw a picture to help you.

7. $\frac{1}{5} + \frac{3}{5}$ **8.** $\frac{1}{8} + \frac{5}{8}$ **9.** $\frac{5}{7} - \frac{3}{7}$ **10.** $\frac{3}{4} - \frac{1}{4}$

Solve.

11. Andy has 5 rows of 8 stamps in his stamp album. He collected $\frac{1}{4}$ of the stamps from other countries. How many stamps are from other countries?

12. Nina made a row of 8 tiles. Then she added 7 tiles to the row. Next, she took away $\frac{1}{5}$ of the tiles. How many tiles were left in the row?

How did you do?

If you had difficulty with any items in the Quick Check, you can use the following pages for review and extra practice.

Items	Review These Pages	Do These Extra Practice Items
1–4	pages 500–501	Set F, page 531
5–6	pages 502–503	Set G, page 531
7–10	pages 504–506	Set H, page 531
11–12	pages 508–509	5–6, page 533

Test Prep • Cumulative Review

Maintaining the Standards

Choose the letter of the correct answer. If a correct answer is not here, choose NH.

1 What fraction of the circle is shaded?

A $\frac{1}{4}$ **C** $\frac{1}{2}$

B $\frac{1}{3}$ **D** $\frac{5}{8}$

2 Teddy uses $\frac{1}{3}$ of his allowance to buy a baseball. What fraction of his allowance is left?

F $\frac{1}{6}$ **H** $\frac{2}{3}$

G $\frac{1}{3}$ **J** $\frac{4}{5}$

3 What is the name of this figure?

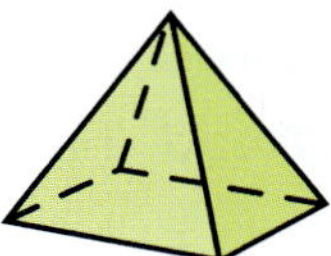

A rectangular prism
B pyramid
C cone
D triangle

4 Which figure can be formed by combining a pyramid and a cube?

F  **H** 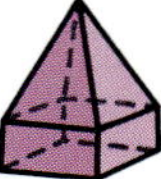

G 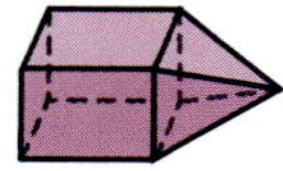 **J** 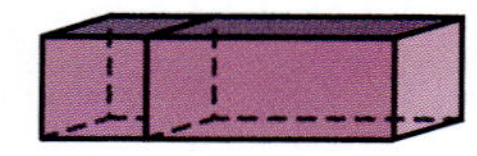

5 What is the name of this figure?

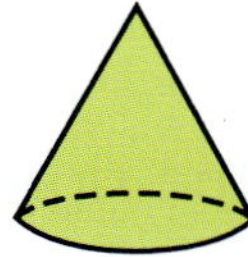

A triangle **C** pyramid
B cone **D** cylinder

6 What is the sum of $\frac{1}{4}$ and $\frac{3}{4}$?

F $\frac{1}{3}$
G $\frac{4}{8}$
H $1\frac{1}{2}$
J NH

7 What two solid figures make up this complex figure?

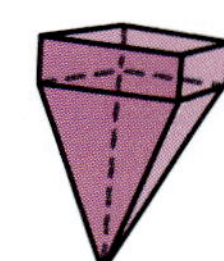

A triangle, rectangle
B pyramid, rectangular prism
C cone, rectangular prism
D cylinder, cone

8 A pizza was divided into 8 equal pieces. Megan ate $\frac{1}{8}$ of the pizza, and Tom ate $\frac{2}{8}$ of the pizza. How much of the pizza was left?

Explain How did you find your answer?

Safe Site

Internet Test Prep
Visit **www.eduplace.com/kids/mhm** for more *Test Prep Practice.*

Tenths

You will learn how to write fractions with denominators of 10 as decimals.

New Vocabulary
decimal
decimal point
tenths

Learn About It

A **decimal** is a number with one or more digits to the right of a **decimal point**.

Look at the fence on the right. It has 10 equal parts. Three of the parts are blue.

What part of the fence is blue?

Different Ways to Show Parts of a Whole

You can use a model.

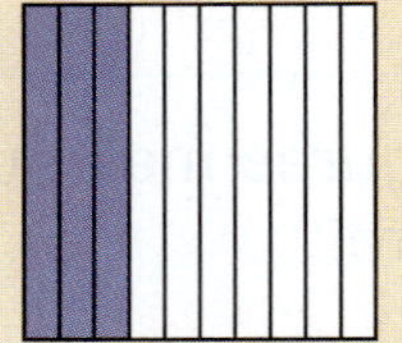

You can write a fraction.

$\frac{3}{10}$ ← blue parts / ← parts in all

You can write a decimal.

ones	.	tenths
0	.	3

↑ decimal point

Write 0.3

Read three **tenths**

$\frac{3}{10}$, or 0.3, of the fence is blue.

Explain Your Thinking

► Look at the example above. Why is there a 0 before the decimal point?

► What is the largest digit you can have in the tenths place?

Guided Practice

Write a fraction and a decimal for each shaded part.

1. 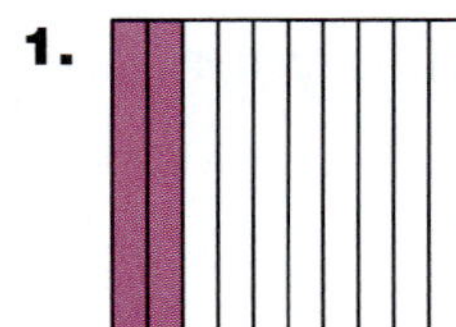

2. 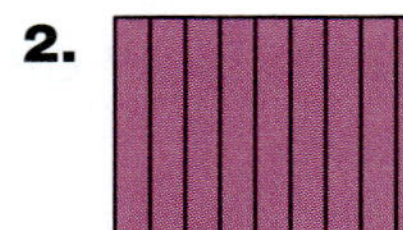

3. 

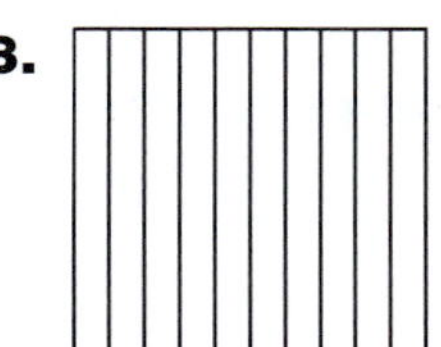

Ask Yourself

- How many equal parts are there?
- What is the number of shaded parts?

Independent Practice

Write a fraction and a decimal for each shaded part.

4. 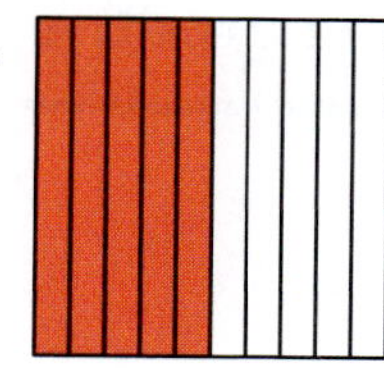

5. 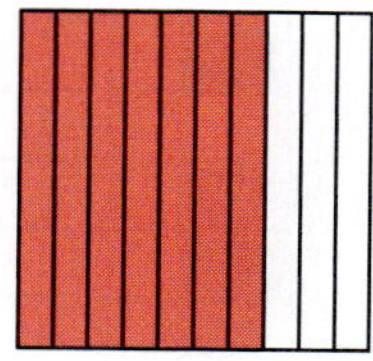

6. 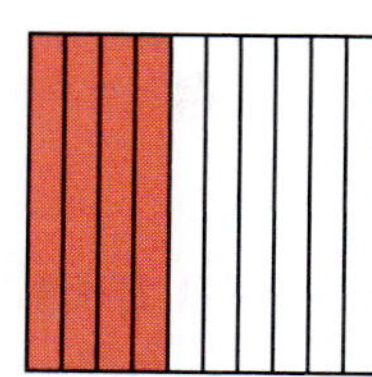

7. 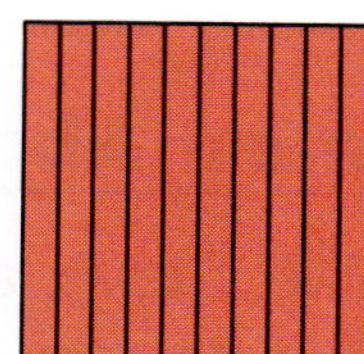

Write each as a decimal.

8. $\frac{9}{10}$ **9.** $\frac{1}{10}$ **10.** $\frac{6}{10}$ **11.** $\frac{3}{10}$ **12.** $\frac{8}{10}$ **13.** $\frac{4}{10}$

14. one tenth **15.** eight tenths **16.** five tenths **17.** two tenths

Write each as a fraction.

18. 0.3 **19.** 0.5 **20.** 0.9 **21.** 0.6 **22.** 0.1 **23.** 0.2

24. nine tenths **25.** six tenths **26.** ten tenths **27.** seven tenths

Problem Solving • Reasoning

Use the picture of a fence on page 512 for Problems 28 and 29.

28. Write a decimal for the part of the fence that is not blue.

29. Suppose it took Elaine 5 minutes to paint each board in the fence. How long would it take her to paint 0.6 of the fence?

30. **Write About It** Explain how you could write the fraction $\frac{1}{2}$ as a decimal.

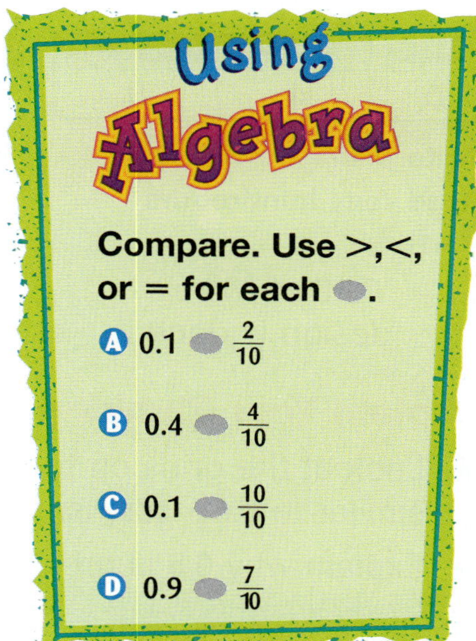

Compare. Use >, <, or = for each ●.

A 0.1 ● $\frac{2}{10}$

B 0.4 ● $\frac{4}{10}$

C 0.1 ● $\frac{10}{10}$

D 0.9 ● $\frac{7}{10}$

Mixed Review • Test Prep

Multiply or divide. *(pages 278–279, 374–375)*

31. $2 \times (2 \times 3)$ **32.** $16 \div 4$ **33.** $(2 \times 4) \times 5$ **34.** $32 \div 4$

Choose the letter of the correct answer. *(pages 278–279)*

35 $7 \times (5 + 2) = ■$

A 14 **B** 37 **C** 49 **D** 77

36 $(7 \times 5) + 2 = ■$

F 14 **G** 37 **H** 49 **J** 77

Extra Practice See Set I on page 531.

Hundredths

You will learn how to write fractions with denominators of 100 as decimals.

New Vocabulary
hundredths

Learn About It

Mike, Steve, and Jen are each making a tile design. Each design will have 100 tiles when it is done. So far Mike has used 40 tiles. Steve has used 23 tiles, and Jen has used 9 tiles.

What part of each design is done?

Mike's Design

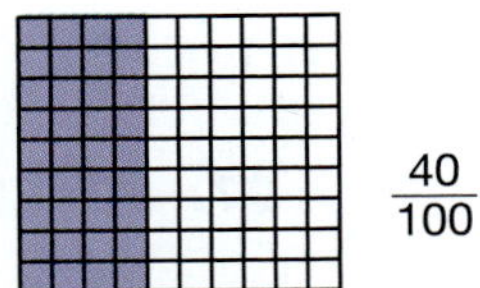

ones	.	tenths	hundredths
0	.	4	0

Write 0.40
Read forty **hundredths**

Steve's Design

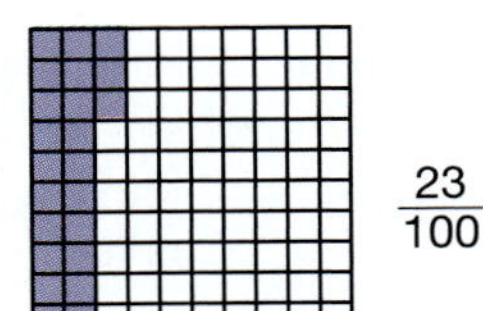

ones	.	tenths	hundredths
0	.	2	3

Write 0.23
Read twenty-three hundredths

Jen's Design

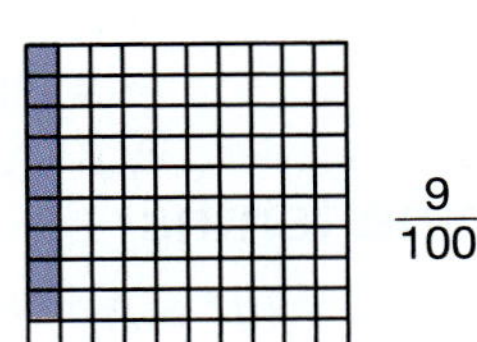

ones	.	tenths	hundredths
0	.	0	9

Write 0.09
Read nine hundredths

0.40 of Mike's design is done.

0.23 of Steve's design is done.

0.09 of Jen's design is done.

Explain Your Thinking

▶ Look at the grids on the right. How is 0.60 similar to 0.6? How is it different?

▶ Explain why 0.5 is greater than 0.05.

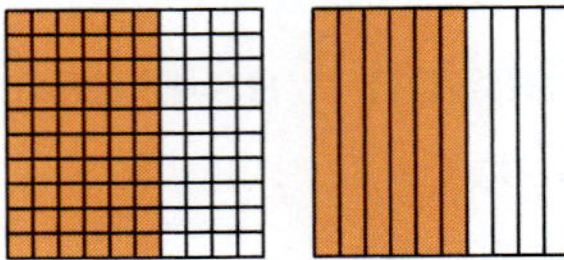

Guided Practice

Write a fraction and a decimal for each shaded part.

1. 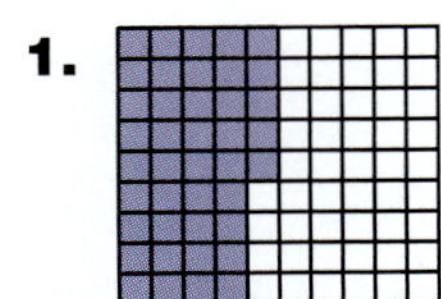

2. 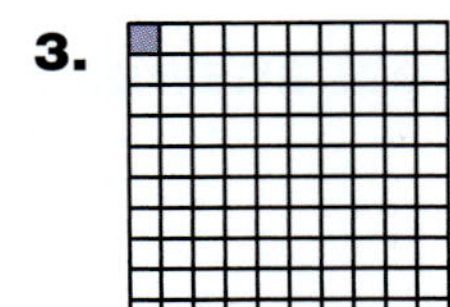

3.

Ask Yourself

- How many equal parts are there?
- How many parts are shaded?

Independent Practice

Write a fraction and a decimal for the shaded part.

4. 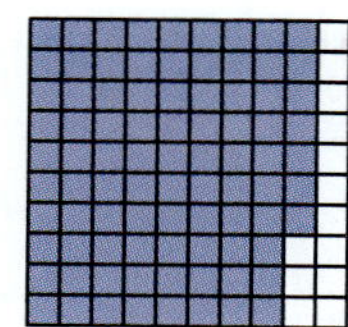

5. 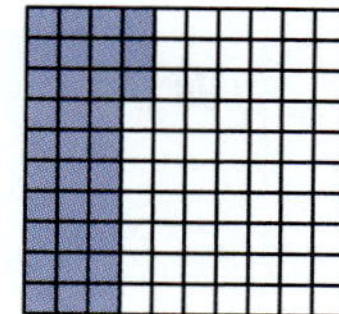

6. 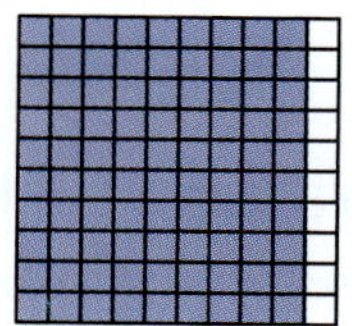

7. 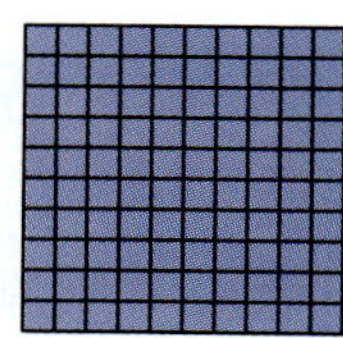

Write each as a decimal.

8. $\frac{78}{100}$ **9.** $\frac{52}{100}$ **10.** $\frac{4}{100}$ **11.** $\frac{60}{100}$ **12.** $\frac{98}{100}$ **13.** $\frac{12}{100}$

14. one hundredth **15.** thirty-seven hundredths **16.** fifty-five hundredths

Write each as a fraction.

17. 0.49 **18.** 0.23 **19.** 0.09 **20.** 0.40 **21.** 0.78 **22.** 0.10

23. four hundredths **24.** forty-four hundredths **25.** fourteen hundredths

Problem Solving • Reasoning

Use Data **Use the graph for Problems 26–29.**

26. How many tiles did Jen use?

27. What decimal shows the part of Jen's design that is blue?

28. **Compare** First, Jen puts on all of the green and red tiles. What decimal shows the part of the design that is not done?

29. **Write Your Own** Use the graph to write a problem that has a decimal as an answer. Give your problem to a classmate to solve.

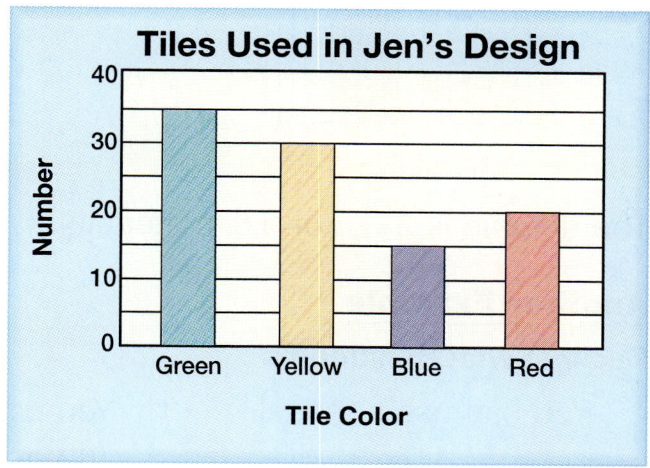

Mixed Review • Test Prep

Complete. *(pages 170–171)*

30. 1 qt = ____ pt **31.** 1 gal = ____ qt **32.** 1 gal = ____ pt **33.** 1 pt = ____ c

34 How much is $9.00 − $7.65? *(pages 140–141)*

A $0.35 **B** $1.35 **C** $1.65 **D** $2.35

Extra Practice See Set J on page 532.

Decimals Greater Than 1

You will learn how to write decimals greater than 1.

Learn About It

Bottle-nosed dolphins are mammals that live in water. However they must come to the surface often to breathe.

The bottle-nosed dolphin shown on the right measures $3\frac{5}{10}$ meters. There are different ways to show the length of the dolphin.

Different Ways to Show Decimals Greater Than 1

You can use a model.

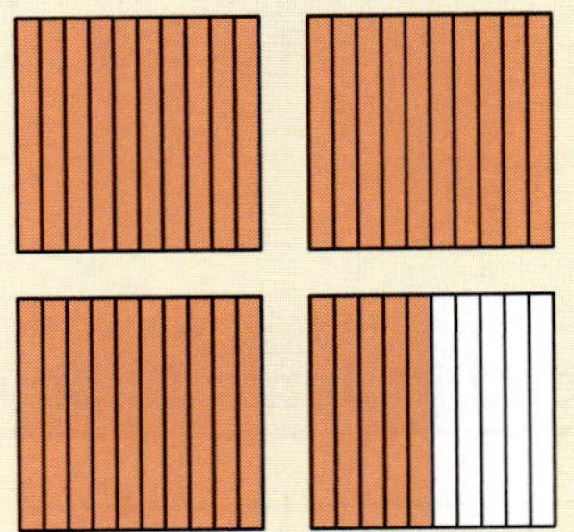

You can write a mixed number.

$3\frac{5}{10}$

You can write a decimal.

ones	.	tenths
3	.	5

Write 3.5

Read three and five tenths

Read the decimal point as "and."

The dolphin is $3\frac{5}{10}$, or 3.5, meters long.

Another Example

Decimal With Hundredths

You can use a model.

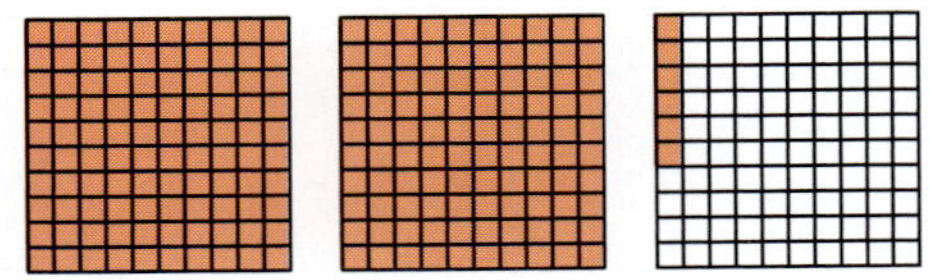

You can write a mixed number.

$2\frac{6}{100}$

You can write a decimal.

ones	.	tenths	hundredths
2	.	0	6

Write 2.06

Read two and six hundredths

Explain Your Thinking

▶ Do $\frac{23}{10}$ and 2.3 name the same amount? Explain why or why not.

▶ Why is 2.04 a different value than 2.40?

Guided Practice

Write a mixed number and a decimal for the shaded part.

1. 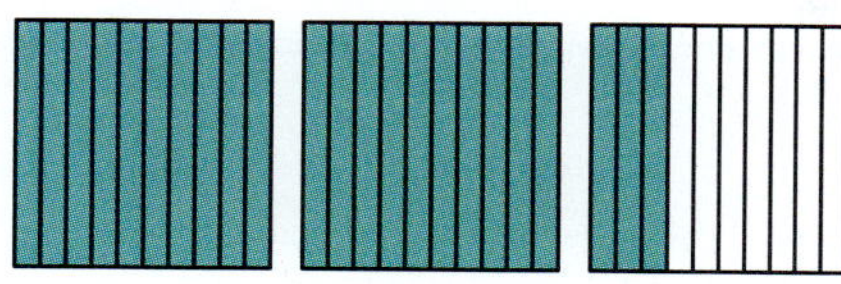

2. 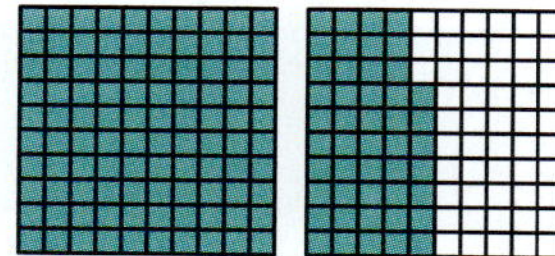

Ask Yourself

- How many wholes are there?
- How many tenths or hundredths are there?

Independent Practice

Write a mixed number and a decimal for the shaded part.

3. 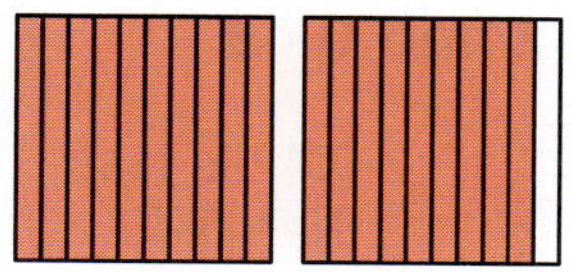

4. 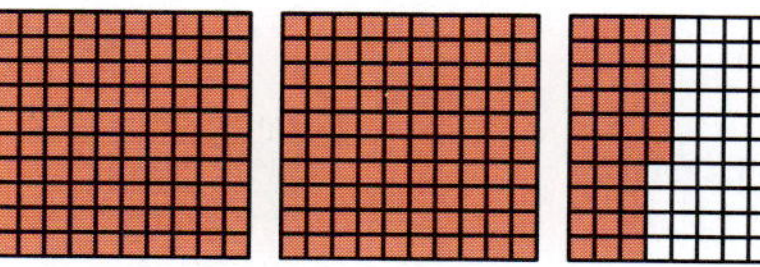

5. 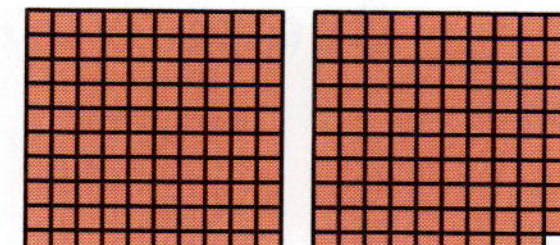

Write each as a decimal.

6. $5\frac{18}{100}$ **7.** $7\frac{8}{10}$ **8.** $9\frac{75}{100}$ **9.** $3\frac{2}{10}$ **10.** $4\frac{2}{100}$

11. six and nine tenths **12.** one and six tenths **13.** four and two hundredths

Problem Solving • Reasoning

14. A baby dolphin measures $1\frac{25}{100}$ meters. Write a decimal for the length of the baby dolphin.

15. At an aquarium, a dolphin was fed 3 whole buckets of fish and $\frac{8}{10}$ bucket of fish. Write a decimal that shows the total number of buckets of fish the dolphin was fed.

16. **Analyze** Two dolphins together weigh 450 kg. One dolphin weighs 50 kg more than the other. What is the weight of each dolphin?

SCIENCE Some bottle-nosed dolphins that live in the Pacific Ocean grow to a length of 3.7 meters. Is 3.7 meters the same as 3.70 meters? Explain.

Mixed Review • Test Prep

Compare. Write >, <, or = for each ⬬. *(pages 488–489)*

17. $\frac{7}{9}$ ⬬ $\frac{2}{9}$ **18.** $\frac{1}{2}$ ⬬ $\frac{2}{4}$ **19.** $\frac{3}{5}$ ⬬ $\frac{5}{5}$

20 Which fraction is equivalent to $\frac{1}{3}$? *(pages 494–495)*

A $\frac{1}{6}$ **B** $\frac{3}{9}$ **C** $\frac{3}{6}$ **D** $\frac{3}{1}$

Extra Practice See Set K on page 532.

LESSON 15

Compare and Order Fractions and Decimals

You will learn how to compare and order fractions and decimals.

Learn About It

You can use models or a place-value chart to help you compare and order decimals.

Compare Decimals

Compare 0.7 and 0.3.

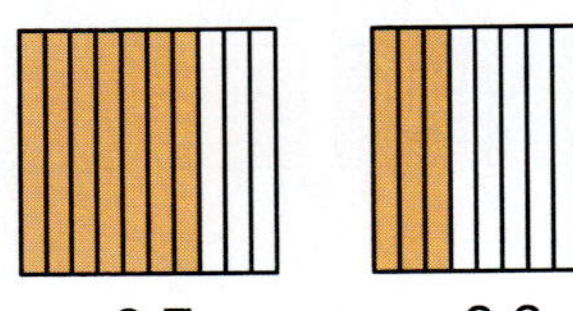

0.7 is greater than 0.3.

$0.7 > 0.3$

Compare 0.42 and 0.49.

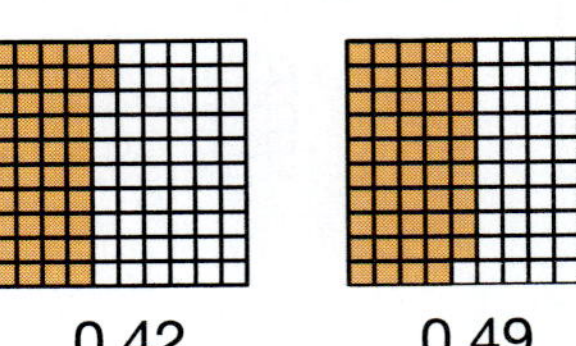

0.42 is less than 0.49.

$0.42 < 0.49$

Order Fractions and Decimals

Order these numbers from least to greatest. $\frac{24}{100}$ **0.46 0.42**

- First, write the fraction as a decimal.

$\frac{24}{100} = 0.24$

ones		tenths	hundredths
0	.	2	4
0	.	4	6
0	.	4	2

same (ones)

$2 < 4$, so 0.24 is the least number. (tenths)

$2 < 6$, so $0.42 < 0.46$ (hundredths)

- Then start at the left to compare digits in the greatest place.
- Continue comparing the other digits.

This is the order of the numbers from least to greatest. $\frac{24}{100}$ 0.42 0.46.

Explain Your Thinking

▶ Which is greater, 8.4 or 4.8? How do you know?

▶ Which is greater, 0.8 or 0.80? Explain your thinking.

Guided Practice

Compare. Write >, <, or = for each ●.

1. 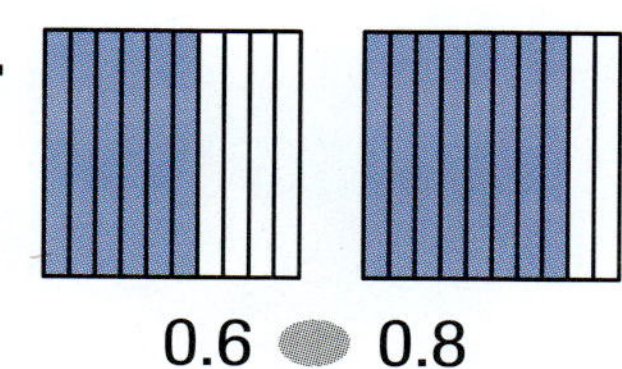
0.6 ● 0.8

2. 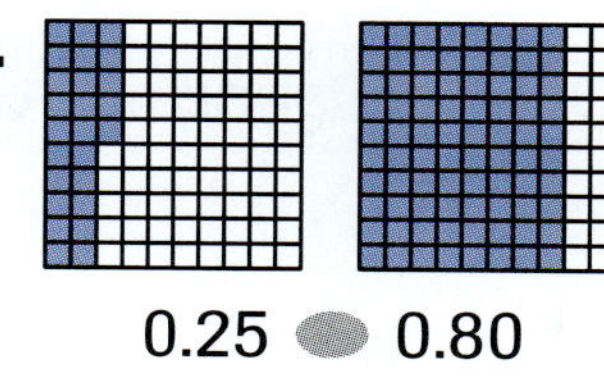
0.25 ● 0.80

Ask Yourself

- Which decimal is the greatest?
- Which decimal is the least?

Order the numbers from greatest to least.

3. 0.9 $\frac{3}{10}$ 0.4

4. 0.25 0.10 0.38

5. 2.20 2.35 2.25

Independent Practice

Compare. Write >, <, or = for each ●.

6. 1.2 ● 1.5
7. 0.39 ● 0.32
8. 0.40 ● 0.4
9. 8.06 ● 8.6
10. 3.16 ● 3.61
11. 0.64 ● 0.78
12. 4.3 ● 3.4
13. 0.99 ● 0.90

Order the numbers from least to greatest.

14. 2.1 1.3 1.9

15. 0.15 0.51 $\frac{50}{100}$

16. 1.00 1.10 1.01

Problem Solving • Reasoning

Use the bulletin board for Problems 17–19.

17. Jason tossed a water balloon 9.9 meters. Did he break the school record?

18. **Compare** Tanya tossed an egg 12.8 meters in the egg toss. Is this distance greater than or less than the record distance?

19. **Analyze** Emmy jumped 3.64 m in the long jump. Ty jumped 0.22 m farther than Emmy and 0.16 m less than Fred. Did anyone break the school record?

Mixed Review • Test Prep

Write the word name for each ordinal number. *(pages 80–82)*

20. 4th
21. 22nd
22. 31st
23. 20th
24. 16th

25. How many feet are in 6 yards? *(pages 164–166)*

A 12 **B** 18 **C** 36 **D** 72

Extra Practice See Set L on page 532.

LESSON 16 Add and Subtract Decimals

You will learn how to add and subtract decimals.

Learn About It

Jim's clubhouse has a porch and one room. The porch is 0.9 meters long. The room is 1.8 meters long. How long is Jim's clubhouse?

Add. **0.9 + 1.8 = ■**

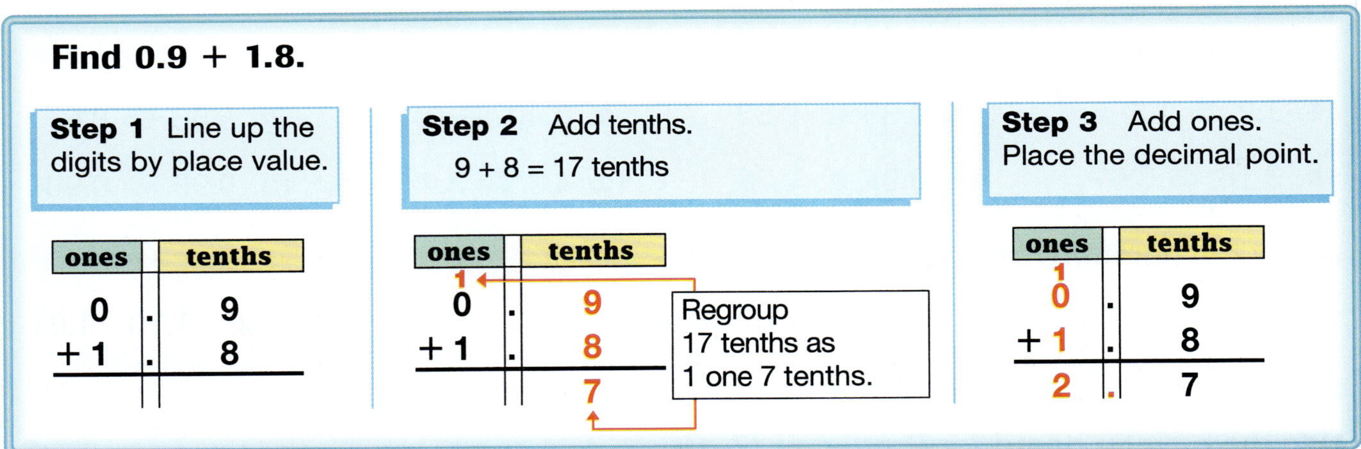

Solution: Jim's clubhouse is 2.7 meters long.

You can subtract to compare the length and width of the porch.

Subtract. **1.7 − 0.9 = ■**

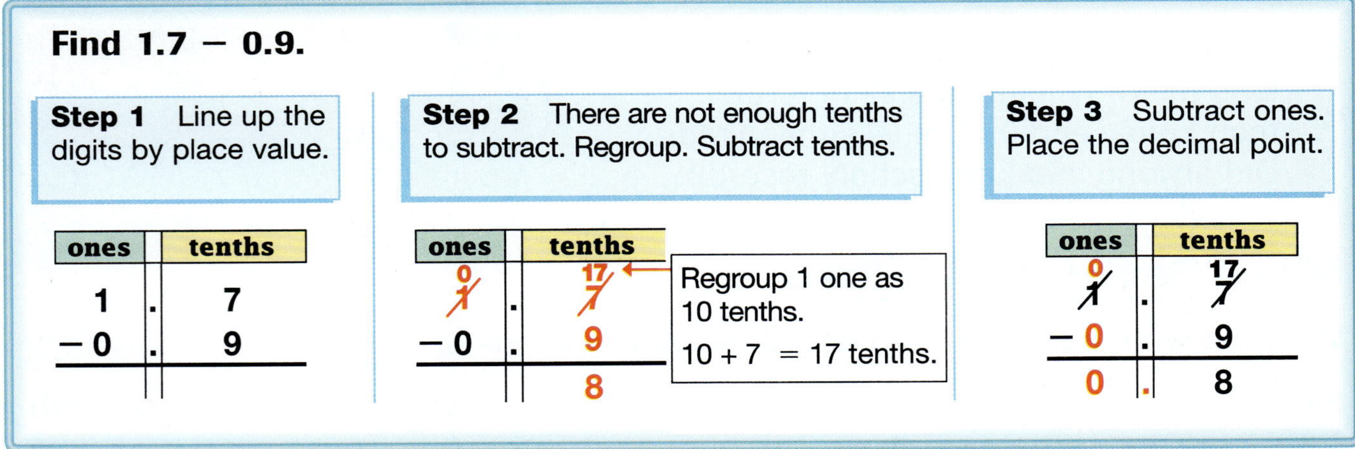

Solution: The porch is 0.8 meters longer than it is wide.

Other Examples

A. Adding Hundredths

Find 5.62 + 2.43.

$$\begin{array}{r} \scriptstyle 1 \\ 5.62 \\ +\ 2.43 \\ \hline 8.05 \end{array}$$

B. Subtracting Hundredths

Find 6.92 − 2.35.

$$\begin{array}{r} \scriptstyle 8\,12 \\ 6.\not{9}\not{2} \\ -\ 2.35 \\ \hline 4.57 \end{array}$$

Explain Your Thinking

► How is adding and subtracting decimals like adding and subtracting whole numbers?

► How do you decide where to place the decimal point in the answer?

Guided Practice

Add or subtract.

1. 1.3 + 2.5

2. 8.08 + 1.71

3. 3.52 + 0.67

4. 4.8 − 3.1

5. 3.62 − 1.23

6. 6.07 − 2.63

7. 2.2 + 0.9

8. 1.10 + 1.01

9. 9.0 − 0.9

Ask Yourself

- Which digits should I add first?
- Do I need to regroup?
- Did I write the decimal point?

Independent Practice

Add or subtract.

10. 5.4 + 2.3

11. 1.5 + 4.9

12. 6.71 + 1.56

13. 4.83 + 4.19

14. 2.67 + 5.59

15. 8.5 − 7.3

16. 7.1 − 4.8

17. 4.27 − 1.97

18. 5.49 − 4.16

19. 6.35 − 0.27

20. 3.8 + 2.8

21. 9.1 − 6.5

22. 4.56 + 2.34

23. 8.15 − 6.08

24. 7.38 − 5.23

25. 9.6 + 2.4

26. 8.4 − 6.5

27. 4.99 + 2.00

28. 11.2 − 1.1

29. 6.19 − 4.28

30. 9.09 + 0.91

31. 8.20 − 2.80

32. 17.6 − 4.8

Algebra • Functions Complete each table by following the rule. If the rule is not given, write the rule.

Rule: Add 1.5

	Input	Output
33.	1.0	■
34.	1.5	■
35.	■	3.5
36.	3.0	■

Rule: Subtract 0.5

	Input	Output
37.	5.5	■
38.	■	4.0
39.	3.5	■
40.	2.5	■

41. Rule: ____________

Input	Output
2.3	4.6
3.3	5.6
4.3	6.6
6.3	8.6

Problem Solving • Reasoning

Use the picture at the right for Problems 42 and 43.

42. How tall is Jim's clubhouse from the floor to the top of the roof?

43. Jim's clubhouse has a square window. What is the perimeter of the window?

44. **Estimate** Jim's father spent $83.75 on lumber and $12.95 on nails for the clubhouse. Was $100.00 enough to pay for the lumber and the nails?

45. **Write About It** Without adding, how can you tell whether the sum of 25.02 and 25.01 is greater than or less than 50?

Mixed Review • Test Prep

Find the area of each figure. Each □ is 1 square unit. *(pages 322–323)*

46. ⊞

47. 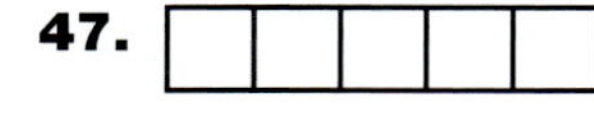

48. 

49. 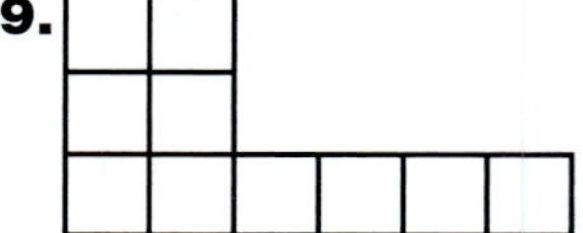

50 A 25-minute soccer practice started at 2:35 P.M. Which clock shows the time the practice ended? *(pages 70–72)*

A 

B 

C 

D 

Extra Practice See Set M on page 532.

Number Sense

Estimating Fractions and Decimals

You can use a number line to decide if a fraction or decimal is closer to 0 or 1. The fraction $\frac{1}{2}$ and the decimal 0.5 are the same distance from 0 and 1.

If a fraction is less than $\frac{1}{2}$, it is closer to 0 than to 1.

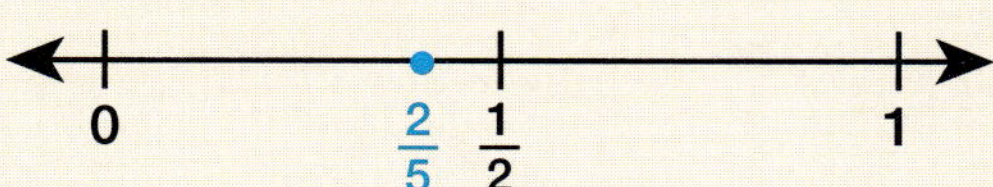

$\frac{2}{5}$ is to the left of $\frac{1}{2}$. $\frac{2}{5}$ is closer to 0 than $\frac{1}{2}$ is, so $\frac{2}{5}$ is less than $\frac{1}{2}$.

If a fraction is greater than $\frac{1}{2}$, it is closer to 1 than to 0.

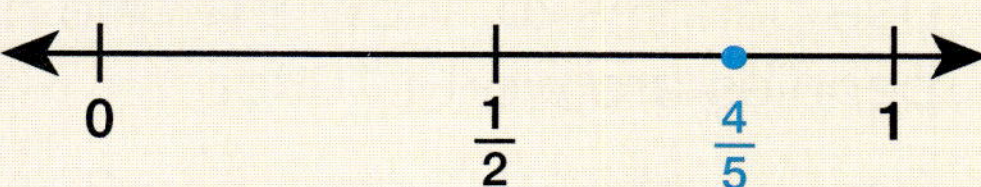

$\frac{4}{5}$ is to the right of $\frac{1}{2}$. $\frac{4}{5}$ is closer to 1 than $\frac{1}{2}$ is, so $\frac{4}{5}$ is greater than $\frac{1}{2}$.

If a decimal is less than 0.5, it is closer to 0 than to 1.

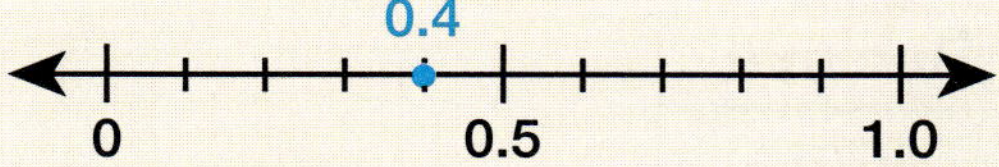

0.4 is to the left of 0.5. 0.4 is closer to 0 than 0.5 is, so 0.4 is less than 0.5.

If a decimal is greater than 0.5, it is closer to 1 than to 0.

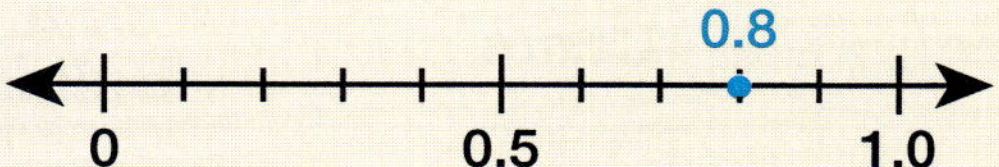

0.8 is to the right of 0.5. 0.8 is closer to 1 than 0.5 is, so 0.8 is greater than 0.5.

Tell if each fraction marked by the point is closer to 0 or to 1.

1.

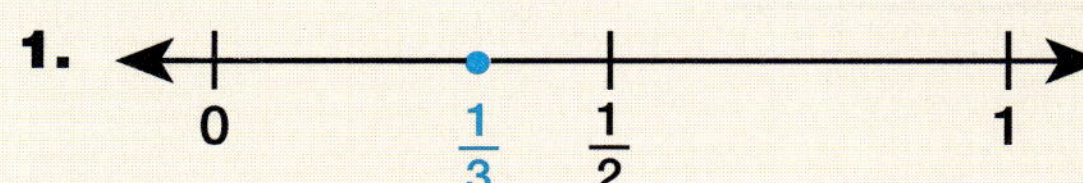

2.

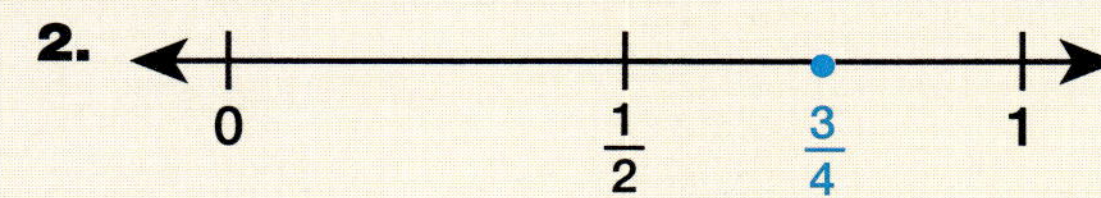

Name the decimal for each marked point.
Then tell if the decimal is closer to 0 or to 1.

3.

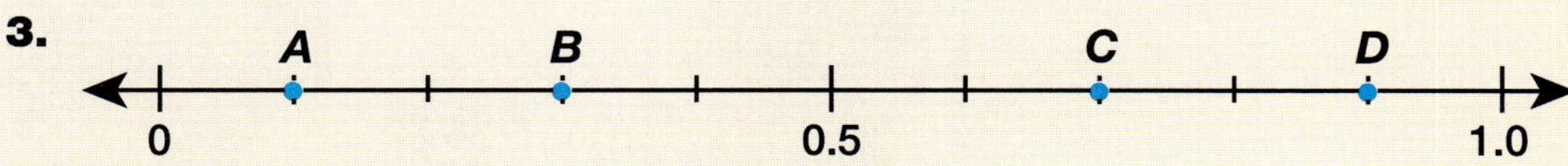

Explain Your Thinking

► How can you use a number line to show whether $3\frac{1}{4}$ is closer to 3 or 4?

Decimals, Fractions, and Money

You will learn how money can be related to fractions and decimals.

Learn About It

Materials

play money

You can use what you know about money to help you understand fractions and decimals better.

Use play money to see how different coins can be thought of as parts of a dollar.

Step 1 Use pennies to show $1. One hundred pennies are worth 100¢.

- What fraction of a dollar is 1 cent?
- How do you show 1 penny by using a dollar sign and a decimal point?

Record your work in a table like the one started below.

Name of Coin	Number of Cents	Fraction of a Dollar	Value as a Decimal
Penny	1¢	$\frac{1}{100}$ of a dollar	$0.01
Nickel			
Dime			
Quarter			
Half-Dollar			

Step 2 Repeat Step 1, using nickels, dimes, quarters, and half-dollars to show $1. Record your work in your table.

Try It Out

Match each group of coins with the correct value.

1. $\frac{5}{100}$ of a dollar
2. $\frac{1}{2}$ of a dollar
3. $\frac{3}{10}$ of a dollar
4. $\frac{3}{4}$ of a dollar

A

B

C

D

Copy and complete the table below.
Use play money to help you.

	Coins	Number of Cents	Fraction of a Dollar	Value as a Decimal
5.	10 pennies			$0.10
6.	8 dimes		$\frac{80}{100}$ of a dollar	
7.	2 quarters	50¢		
8.	25 pennies			
9.	4 nickels			
10.	2 half-dollars			

Write each amount as a fraction of a dollar.

11. $0.15 = ____ of a dollar

12. $0.25 = ____ of a dollar

13. $0.75 = ____ of a dollar

14. $0.80 = ____ of a dollar

15. $0.40 = ____ of a dollar

16. $1.00 = ____ of a dollar

Write about it! Talk about it!

Use what you have learned to answer these questions.

17. Ramona has 43 pennies. She says she has more than $\frac{4}{10}$ of a dollar. Is she correct? Explain why or why not.

18. Aaron wants to divide a dollar equally among 5 friends. Can he give each friend a quarter? Explain your thinking.

Problem-Solving Application: Use Money

You will learn how to solve problems that involve adding and subtracting money.

Problem Ryan is visiting the science museum and is eating lunch at the Comet Cafe. He orders soup and a slice of pizza. If Ryan pays with a ten-dollar bill, how much change should he get?

Item	Price
Nachos	$2.40
Slice of Pizza	$3.00
Tossed Salad	$2.80
Soup	$2.75
Chili	$3.25
Sandwiches	
Turkey	$3.95
Ham	$2.80

Understand

What do you need to find?

You need to find the amount of change Ryan should get.

What do you know?

- The soup costs $2.75.
- The slice of pizza costs $3.00.
- Ryan pays with a ten-dollar bill.

How can you find the answer?

First, add the cost of the soup to the cost of the slice of pizza to find the total cost.

Then subtract the total cost of the food from the amount of money Ryan pays.

Step 1

$2.75	← cost of soup
+ $3.00	← cost of pizza slice
$5.75	← total cost

Step 2

$10.00	← amount Ryan paid
− $5.75	← total cost
$4.25	← change

Ryan should get $4.25 in change.

Look back at the problem. How can Ryan check to be sure that his change is correct?

Guided Practice

Use the menu on page 526 to solve.

1. Eileen had chili and nachos. She gave the clerk four $1 bills, 2 quarters, 1 dime, and 1 nickel. How much more money does Eileen owe?

How much did the food cost? How much did she pay?

2. Lisa ordered soup and a tossed salad. She gave the clerk one $5 bill and three quarters. How much change should she get?

Think: What is the cost of the food? How much did she pay?

Choose a Strategy

Solve. Use these or other strategies.
Use the menu on page 526 for Problems 3–5.

Problem-Solving Strategies

- **Use Logical Thinking**
- **Act It Out**
- **Write a Number Sentence**
- **Draw a Picture**

3. Darrel has $8 to pay for his food and his sister's food at the Comet Cafe. Darrel wants chili. His sister wants a turkey sandwich. Does Darrel have enough money to also buy nachos?

4. Tony and Paula each order a sandwich and a tossed salad. Tony's sales slip shows a total of $4.60. Paula's sales slip shows a total of $5.60. Whose sales slip is incorrect? What mistake was made?

5. Lee ate lunch at the Comet Cafe. She bought nachos and paid the clerk with three $1 bills. She got five dimes and four nickels in change. Did she get the correct change? Why or why not?

6. Joan, Pam, Gina, and Carla were lining up to enter an exhibit at the science museum. Joan was first. Pam was in front of Carla but behind Gina. List the girls in order from first to last in line.

7. Mr. and Mrs. Roth and their 2 children are going to the science museum. The costs of admission are shown at the right. Mr. Roth gives the clerk three $5 bills. How much change should he receive?

Extra Practice See 7–9 on page 533.

Quick Check

Check Your Understanding of Lessons 12–18

Write a fraction and a decimal for each shaded part.

1. 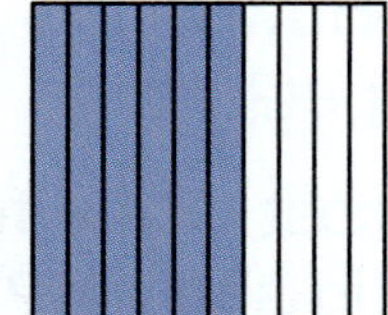

2. 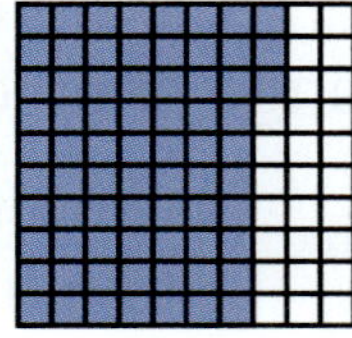

Write a mixed number and a decimal for the shaded part.

3. 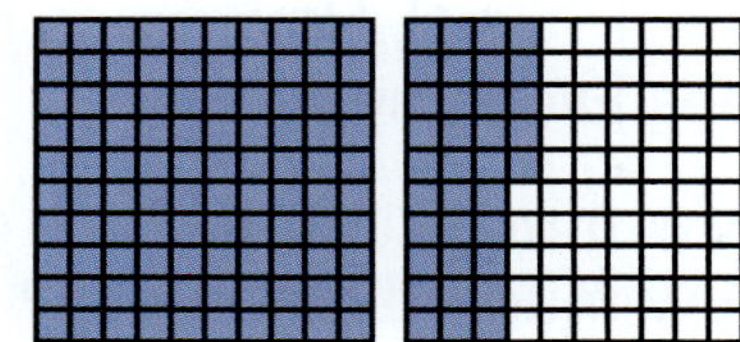

Order the decimals from greatest to least.

4. 1.2 2.1 0.25 1.65

5. 1.10 1.01 10.1 1.11

Add or subtract.

6. $7.3 + 2.4$

7. $3.28 + 2.07$

8. $7.2 - 3.4$

9. $6.58 - 3.84$

10. Kevin bought a dog toy and a bag of dog food. He gave the clerk a $10-dollar bill. How much change should he get?

Paws Pet Store	
Bag of dog food	$3.45
Box of bird seed	$1.85
Dog toy	$2.70

How did you do?

If you had difficulty with any items in the Quick Check, you can use the following pages for review and extra practice.

Items	Review These Pages	Do These Extra Practice Items
1–2	pages 512–515	Set I, page 532 Set J, page 532
3	pages 516–517	Set K, page 532
4–5	pages 518–519	Set L, page 532
6–9	pages 520–522	Set M, page 532
10	pages 526–527	7–9, page 533

Test Prep • Cumulative Review

Maintaining the Standards

Choose the letter of the correct answer. If a correct answer is not here, choose NH.

1. What is the probability of spinning a 2 on the first try?

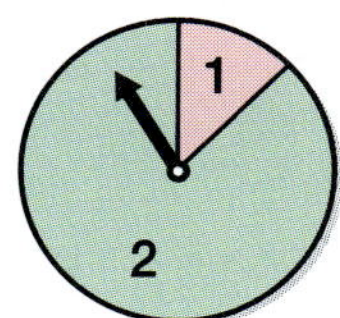

A certain
B likely
C unlikely
D impossible

2. Which of the following is $\frac{3}{4}$ of a dollar?

F \$0.25
G \$0.34
H \$0.50
J \$0.75

3. Mrs. Kennedy baked 36 cookies. She gave her neighbor $\frac{1}{4}$ of the cookies and kept the rest for herself. What fraction of the cookies did she keep?

A $\frac{1}{4}$
B $\frac{1}{2}$
C $\frac{3}{4}$
D NH

4. What decimal represents the shaded portion of this model?

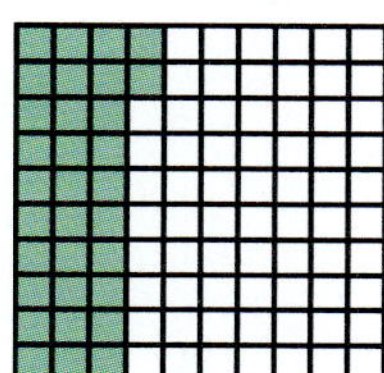

F 0.12
G 0.20
H 0.32
J 0.45

5. What is the name of this figure?

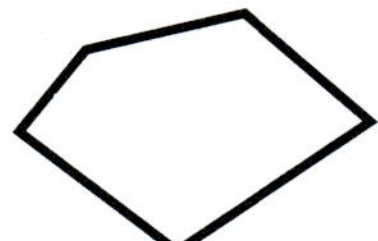

A quadrilateral
B hexagon
C pentagon
D octagon

6. How is 0.3 written as a fraction?

F $\frac{3}{100}$
G $\frac{1}{10}$
H $\frac{3}{10}$
J $\frac{10}{3}$

7. What is the sum of $\frac{1}{8}$ and $\frac{3}{8}$?

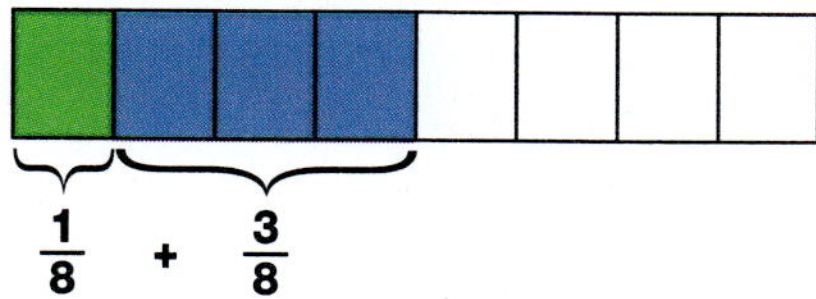

A $\frac{2}{8}$
B $\frac{4}{16}$
C $\frac{3}{8}$
D NH

8. Pauline colored 3 circles black, 5 circles blue, and the remaining 2 circles red. What fraction of the circles were not colored red?

Explain How did you find your answer?

Safe Site

Internet Test Prep
Visit **www.eduplace.com/kids/mhm** for more *Test Prep Practice.*

Extra Practice

Set A *(Lesson 1, pages 484–485)*

Write a fraction for the shaded part. Then write a fraction for the part that is not shaded.

1. 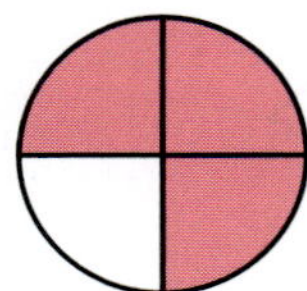

2. 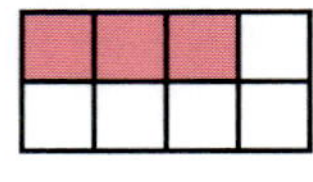

3. 

4. 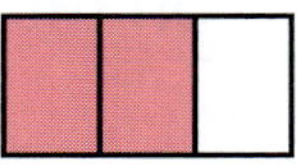

Draw a picture and write a fraction for each.

5. one fifth **6.** four eighths **7.** one third **8.** three sevenths

Set B *(Lesson 2, pages 486–487)*

Write a fraction to name the part of each group that is round.

1. 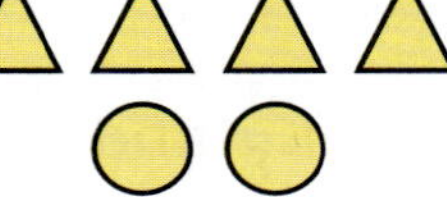

2. 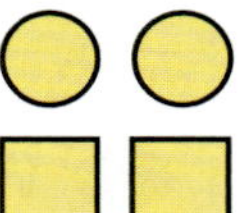

3. 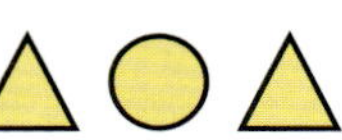

Set C *(Lesson 3, pages 488–489)*

Compare. Write > or < for each ⬬.

1. 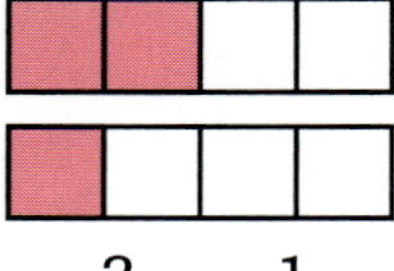

$\frac{2}{4}$ ⬬ $\frac{1}{4}$

2. 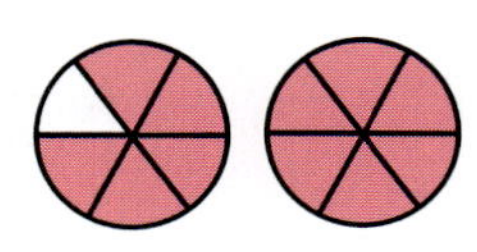

$\frac{5}{6}$ ⬬ $\frac{6}{6}$

3. 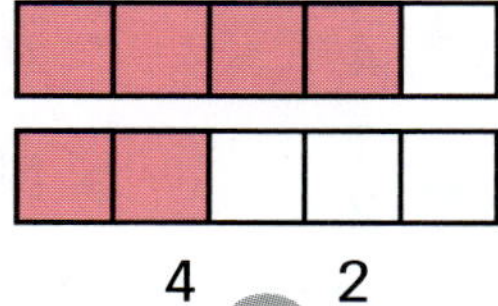

$\frac{4}{5}$ ⬬ $\frac{2}{5}$

4. $\frac{1}{5}$ ⬬ $\frac{4}{5}$ **5.** $\frac{3}{4}$ ⬬ $\frac{1}{4}$ **6.** $\frac{5}{7}$ ⬬ $\frac{2}{7}$ **7.** $\frac{1}{8}$ ⬬ $\frac{8}{8}$ **8.** $\frac{3}{3}$ ⬬ $\frac{2}{3}$

Set D *(Lesson 4, pages 490–491)*

Order the fractions from least to greatest.

1. $\frac{2}{7}$ $\frac{6}{7}$ $\frac{3}{7}$ **2.** $\frac{1}{8}$ $\frac{1}{6}$ $\frac{1}{5}$ **3.** $\frac{4}{6}$ $\frac{6}{6}$ $\frac{5}{6}$ **4.** $\frac{1}{4}$ $\frac{1}{3}$ $\frac{1}{12}$

Extra Practice

Set E (*Lesson 6, pages 494–495*)

Are the fractions *equivalent* or *not equivalent*? Make a drawing to support your answer.

1. $\frac{1}{4}$ and $\frac{2}{8}$ **2.** $\frac{1}{4}$ and $\frac{1}{3}$ **3.** $\frac{3}{6}$ and $\frac{1}{2}$ **4.** $\frac{3}{3}$ and $\frac{3}{4}$

Set F (*Lesson 8, pages 500–501*)

Draw a picture to find each answer.

1. $\frac{1}{3}$ of 6 **2.** $\frac{3}{8}$ of 32 **3.** $\frac{1}{2}$ of 8 **4.** $\frac{5}{6}$ of 24

Set G (*Lesson 9, pages 502–503*)

Write an improper fraction and a mixed number for the shaded part.

1.

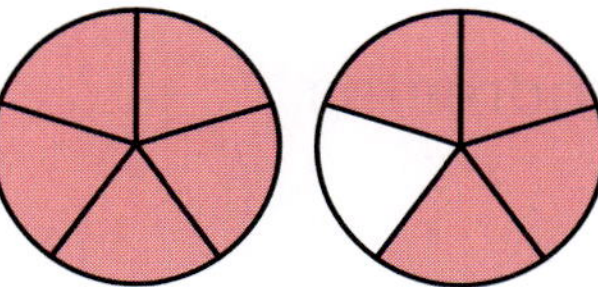

2.

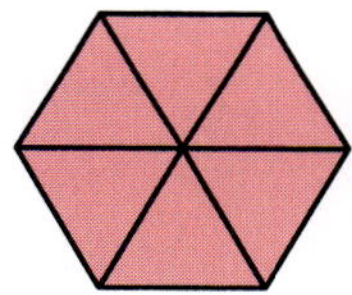

Write each as a whole number or a mixed number.

3. $\frac{9}{8}$ **4.** $\frac{5}{5}$ **5.** $\frac{7}{3}$ **6.** $\frac{4}{2}$ **7.** $\frac{13}{8}$

Set H (*Lesson 10, pages 504–506*)

Add or subtract. Use fraction strips or draw a picture if you wish.

1. $\frac{1}{3} + \frac{2}{3}$ **2.** $\frac{3}{5} + \frac{1}{5}$ **3.** $\frac{5}{6} - \frac{2}{6}$ **4.** $\frac{7}{8} - \frac{6}{8}$

5. $\frac{3}{4} + \frac{1}{4}$ **6.** $\frac{5}{7} - \frac{2}{7}$ **7.** $\frac{2}{9} + \frac{5}{9}$ **8.** $\frac{4}{6} - \frac{2}{6}$

Set I (*Lesson 12, pages 512–513*)

Write each as a decimal.

1. $\frac{6}{10}$ **2.** $\frac{9}{10}$ **3.** $\frac{7}{10}$ **4.** one tenth **5.** two tenths

Write each as a fraction.

6. 0.8 **7.** 0.9 **8.** 0.4 **9.** three tenths **10.** five tenths

Extra Practice

Set J (*Lesson 13, pages 514–515*)

Write each as a decimal.

1. $\frac{17}{100}$ **2.** $\frac{6}{100}$ **3.** $\frac{32}{100}$ **4.** $\frac{95}{100}$ **5.** $\frac{70}{100}$

Write each as a fraction.

6. 0.92 **7.** 0.19 **8.** 0.05 **9.** 0.36 **10.** 0.80

11. five hundredths **12.** sixty-eight hundredths **13.** ninety-two hundredths

Set K (*Lesson 14, pages 516–517*)

Write each as a decimal.

1. $4\frac{6}{100}$ **2.** $8\frac{34}{100}$ **3.** $2\frac{75}{100}$ **4.** $9\frac{61}{100}$ **5.** $1\frac{10}{100}$

6. three and three hundreths **7.** seventy-seven hundredths

Set L (*Lesson 15, pages 518–519*)

Compare. Write >, <, or = for each ⬬.

1. 0.7 ⬬ 0.9 **2.** 3.1 ⬬ 3.0 **3.** 0.5 ⬬ 0.05 **4.** 0.77 ⬬ 7.07

5. 3.3 ⬬ 5.4 **6.** 0.35 ⬬ 0.53 **7.** 0.09 ⬬ 0.9 **8.** 5.31 ⬬ 5.13

Order the decimals from least to greatest.

9. 0.3 3.03 3.30 **10.** 0.66 6.06 0.60 **11.** 0.20 0.22 0.02

Set M (*Lesson 16, pages 520–522*)

Add or subtract.

1. $\begin{array}{r} 4.6 \\ +\ 6.3 \\ \hline \end{array}$ **2.** $\begin{array}{r} 4.7 \\ -\ 2.8 \\ \hline \end{array}$ **3.** $\begin{array}{r} 6.6 \\ +\ 4.8 \\ \hline \end{array}$ **4.** $\begin{array}{r} 7.04 \\ -\ 1.70 \\ \hline \end{array}$ **5.** $\begin{array}{r} 9.19 \\ +\ 4.06 \\ \hline \end{array}$

6. 7.7 + 3.0 **7.** 3.9 − 0.7 **8.** 3.39 + 4.13 **9.** 8.85 − 4.43

Extra Practice • Problem Solving

Solve. *(Lesson 7, pages 496–497)*

1. Sara knitted a doll's hat. She had 10 yards of yarn. She used 4 yards for the hat. What fraction of the yarn did Sara use?

2. Trudy has 12 toy cars. Three fourths of the cars are red. One fourth of the cars are blue. Are more of the cars red or blue?

3. Luis has 12 stickers. He says that $\frac{1}{2}$ of them are bug stickers. Joe says that $\frac{3}{6}$ of them are bug stickers. Who is correct? Explain.

4. A class made 16 origami animals. Four of them are giraffes. What fraction of the origami animals are *not* giraffes?

Solve. *(Lesson 11, pages 508–509)*

5. There are 24 colors in Ellen's paint set. One half of the colors are pastels. Ellen used $\frac{1}{2}$ of the pastels to paint a picture. How many pastels did she use in her picture?

6. Barry picked 10 red delicious apples and 5 golden delicious apples. He gave $\frac{1}{3}$ of the apples he picked to his grandfather. How many apples did Barry give to his grandfather?

Use this price list to solve each problem. *(Lesson 18, pages 526–527)*

7. Ed ordered a ham and cheese sandwich and orange juice. He paid with a $10 bill. How much change should he get?

8. Betsy wants to buy a tuna fish sandwich and lemonade. She has three $1 bills, 3 quarters, and 2 dimes. How much more money does she need?

9. Penny has a $5 bill, 2 quarters, 4 dimes, and 2 nickels. If she buys a chicken salad sandwich and milk, how much money will she have left?

Sandwiches

Tuna Fish	$3.25
Chicken Salad	$4.00
Ham and Cheese	$5.25

Drinks

Milk	$1.00
Lemonade	$1.25
Orange Juice	$1.35

Chapter Review

Reviewing Vocabulary

Write *always, sometimes,* or *never* to complete each statement.

1. The denominator ____ tells the total number of equal parts.
2. The numerator of a unit fraction is ____ 1.
3. In an improper fraction, the numerator is ____ less than the denominator.
4. A decimal ____ has a digit in the hundredths place.

Reviewing Concepts and Skills

Draw a picture to show each fraction.
Then name the numerator and the denominator. *(pages 484–487)*

5. $\frac{3}{4}$
6. $\frac{2}{6}$
7. three fifths
8. four eighths

Compare. Write > or < for each ●. *(pages 488–489)*

9. $\frac{3}{10}$ ● $\frac{4}{10}$
10. $\frac{5}{8}$ ● $\frac{3}{8}$
11. $\frac{1}{3}$ ● $\frac{1}{4}$
12. $\frac{5}{6}$ ● $\frac{6}{6}$

Order the fractions from greatest to least. *(pages 490–491)*

13. $\frac{3}{5}$ $\frac{2}{5}$ $\frac{4}{5}$
14. $\frac{1}{6}$ $\frac{6}{6}$ $\frac{3}{6}$
15. $\frac{1}{4}$ $\frac{1}{3}$ $\frac{1}{6}$
16. $\frac{2}{4}$ $\frac{4}{4}$ $\frac{3}{4}$

Are the fractions *equivalent* or *not equivalent*?
Make a drawing to support your answer. *(pages 494–495)*

17. $\frac{3}{8}$ and $\frac{1}{4}$
18. $\frac{5}{10}$ and $\frac{1}{2}$
19. $\frac{3}{4}$ and $\frac{7}{8}$
20. $\frac{5}{7}$ and $\frac{3}{9}$

Find each answer. *(pages 500–501)*

21. $\frac{1}{4}$ of 8
22. $\frac{1}{3}$ of 12
23. $\frac{1}{2}$ of 6
24. $\frac{1}{8}$ of 24

Write each as a whole number or a mixed number. *(pages 502–503)*

25. $\frac{6}{2}$
26. $\frac{4}{3}$
27. $\frac{9}{6}$
28. $\frac{10}{8}$

Add or subtract. *(pages 504–505)*

29. $\frac{1}{4} + \frac{2}{4}$ **30.** $\frac{3}{5} + \frac{2}{5}$ **31.** $\frac{5}{8} - \frac{3}{8}$ **32.** $\frac{4}{6} - \frac{2}{6}$ **33.** $\frac{4}{7} - \frac{2}{7}$

Write each as a decimal or a fraction. *(pages 512–519)*

34. $\frac{8}{10}$ **35.** $\frac{3}{100}$ **36.** $\frac{39}{100}$ **37.** $4\frac{2}{10}$ **38.** $18\frac{25}{100}$

39. two tenths **40.** twenty-five hundredths **41.** two and six hundredths

Compare. Write >, <, or = for each ⬮. *(pages 518–519)*

42. 0.70 ⬮ 0.77 **43.** 0.48 ⬮ 0.43 **44.** 5.6 ⬮ 6.5 **45.** 1.02 ⬮ 1.2

Order the decimals from least to greatest.

46. 0.17 0.71 0.70 **47.** 3.03 3.30 3.00 **48.** 3.1 2.4 2.9

Add or subtract. *(pages 520–521)*

49. $\begin{array}{r} 2.4 \\ +\ 3.5 \\ \hline \end{array}$ **50.** $\begin{array}{r} 0.78 \\ -\ 0.61 \\ \hline \end{array}$ **51.** $\begin{array}{r} 9.5 \\ +\ 0.7 \\ \hline \end{array}$ **52.** $\begin{array}{r} 4.56 \\ -\ 2.73 \\ \hline \end{array}$ **53.** $\begin{array}{r} 5.08 \\ -\ 3.72 \\ \hline \end{array}$

Solve. *(pages 526–527)*

54. Ali bought a book for $3.25 and a super ball for $0.29. He paid with a $5 bill. How much change should he get?

Brain Teaser Math Reasoning

MAKE IT TRUE

How many ways can you put the numbers 1, 2, 4, and 6 into the blanks to make a true statement? The fractions must be less than 1.

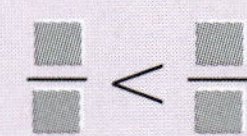

Safe Site

Internet Brain Teasers
Visit **www.eduplace.com/kids/mhm** for more *Brain Teasers.*

Chapter Test

Write a fraction for the shaded part.
Then write a fraction for the part that is not shaded.

1. 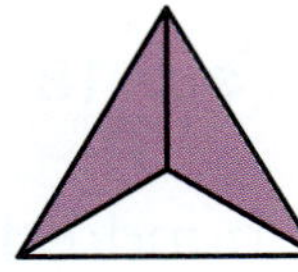

2. 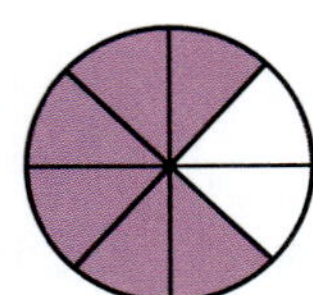

3. 

4. 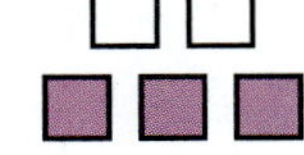

Compare. Write >, <, or = for each ●.

5. $\frac{3}{4}$ ● $\frac{6}{8}$

6. 6.08 ● 6.8

7. 0.9 ● $\frac{8}{10}$

8. 0.7 ● $\frac{7}{10}$

Order the numbers from least to greatest.

9. $\frac{5}{6}$ $\frac{4}{6}$ $\frac{3}{6}$

10. $\frac{1}{3}$ $\frac{1}{4}$ $\frac{1}{5}$

11. 3.2 4.1 3.8

12. 0.62 0.26 0.65

Are the fractions *equivalent* or *not equivalent?*
Make a drawing to support your answer.

13. $\frac{1}{2}$ and $\frac{2}{3}$

14. $\frac{3}{4}$ and $\frac{5}{8}$

15. $\frac{2}{3}$ and $\frac{2}{5}$

16. $\frac{2}{3}$ and $\frac{4}{6}$

Find each answer.

17. $\frac{1}{3}$ of 12

18. $\frac{3}{4}$ of 8

19. $\frac{1}{8}$ of 24

20. $\frac{1}{5}$ of 35

Write each as a whole number or mixed number.

21. $\frac{9}{4}$

22. $\frac{16}{8}$

23. $\frac{27}{5}$

24. $\frac{32}{6}$

Write each as a decimal.

25. $\frac{21}{100}$

26. $27\frac{4}{10}$

27. $18\frac{3}{100}$

28. $32\frac{80}{100}$

29. three and six tenths

30. seven and twelve hundredths

Add or subtract.

31. $\begin{array}{r} 4.6 \\ +\ 2.5 \\ \hline \end{array}$

32. $\begin{array}{r} 9.3 \\ -\ 3.7 \\ \hline \end{array}$

33. $\begin{array}{r} 5.26 \\ +\ 2.57 \\ \hline \end{array}$

34. $\begin{array}{r} 6.54 \\ -\ 5.49 \\ \hline \end{array}$

35. $\frac{1}{5} + \frac{3}{5}$

36. $\frac{3}{4} - \frac{1}{4}$

37. $\frac{5}{8} - \frac{2}{8}$

38. $\frac{5}{6} + \frac{1}{6}$

Solve.

39. Alexa is building a dog house. She saws a board into 8 equal parts. She uses 7 of the parts to build the dog house. What fraction of the board does Alexa use?

40. Tim has a box of 32 colored pencils. He takes $\frac{1}{4}$ of them out of the box. He uses $\frac{1}{2}$ of these pencils to color a picture. How many pencils does Tim use to color the picture?

Write About It

Solve. Use correct math vocabulary to explain your thinking.

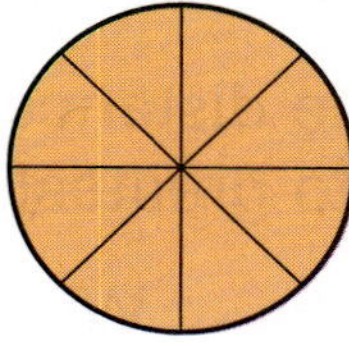

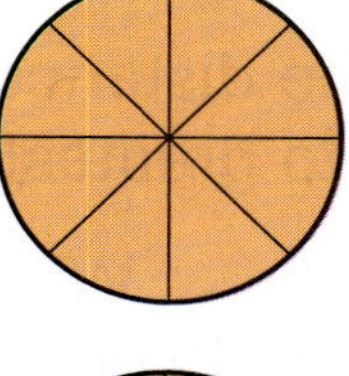

1. Jason and some friends ordered a pizza. The same pizza can be cut into either 8, 10, 12, or 16 equal slices.

   a. What fraction names 1 slice of pizza when it is cut into 8 slices? 10 slices? 12 slices? 16 slices?

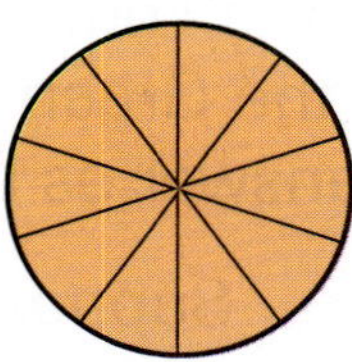

   b. How many slices should the pizza be cut into if the friends want the pizza with the large slices? How do you know?

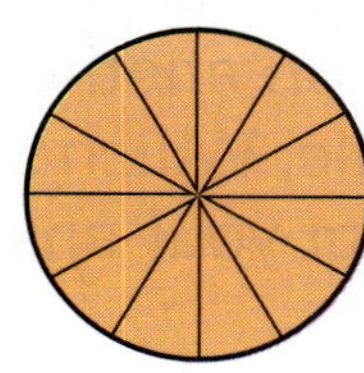

   c. There are eight people sharing the pizza. How many slices should the pizza be cut into so that each person can get an equal number of slices? Is there more than one answer? Explain.

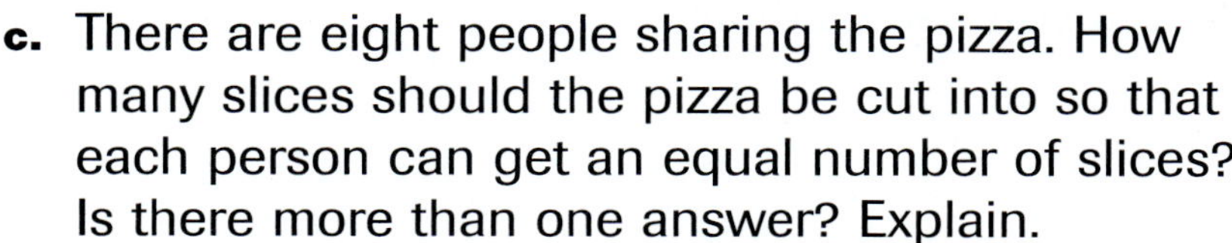

   d. If Jason and his friends each eat $\frac{1}{8}$ of a pizza with 16 slices, how many slices do they each eat?

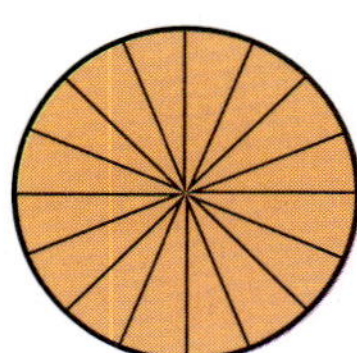

Another Look

Use the map to solve each problem. You can use fraction strips, or draw a picture to help find the answers.

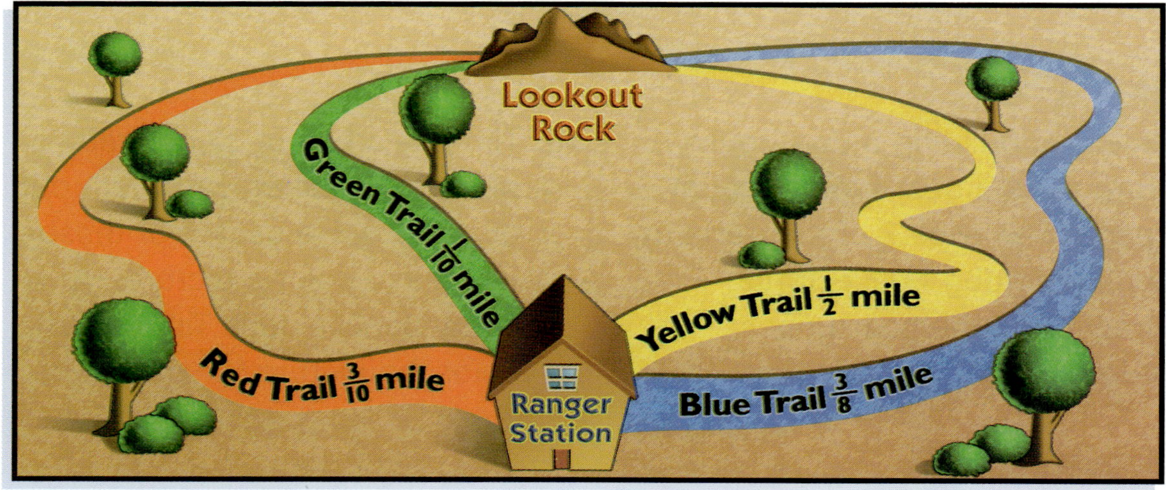

1. How long is the hike from the Ranger Station to Lookout Rock and back on each trail?
2. List the distances from Problem 1 in order from least to greatest.
3. **Look Back** Which is longer, hiking from the Ranger Station to Lookout Rock and back on the Red Trail or on the Green Trail? How much longer? Write your answer as a fraction and as a decimal.
4. **Analyze** Suppose you walked from the Ranger Station to Lookout Rock on one trail and back again on another trail. You walked a total of 0.8 mile. Which trails did you use? Explain how you got your answer.

Enrichment

Dividing Regions Into Equal Parts

Look at the figure on the right.

What fraction of the figure is shaded?

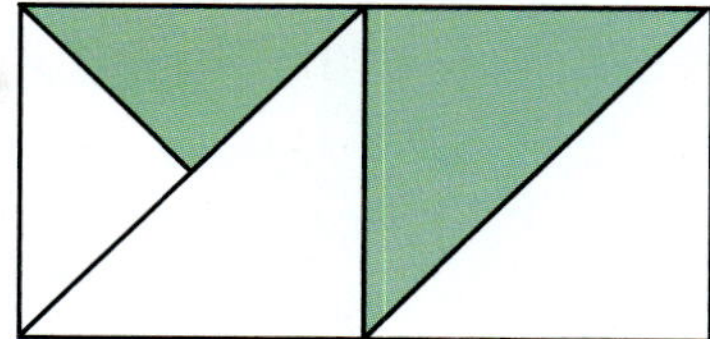

Follow these steps to find out.

- First, divide the figure into equal parts.
- Then find how many equal parts there are in all.
- Finally, find how many of the equal parts are shaded.

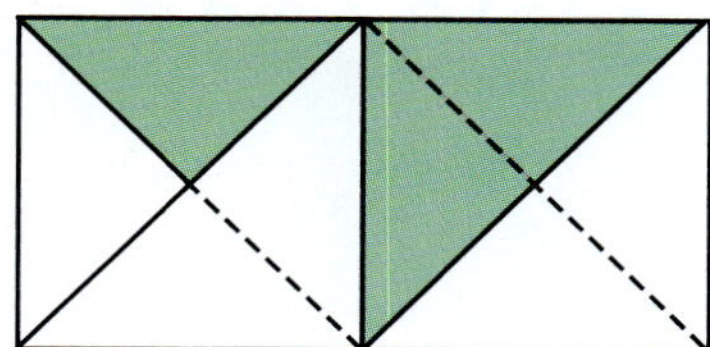

$\frac{3}{8}$ of the figure is shaded.

There are 8 equal parts.
3 of the equal parts are shaded.

Try These

Draw each figure and divide it into equal parts. Then tell what fraction of the figure is shaded.

1. 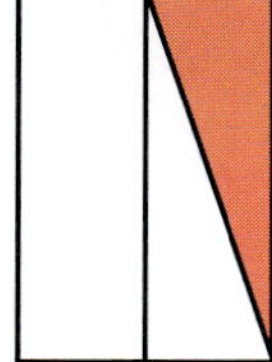

2. 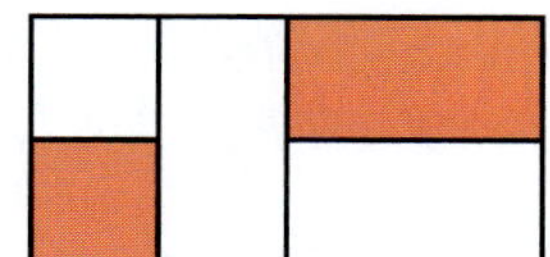

3. 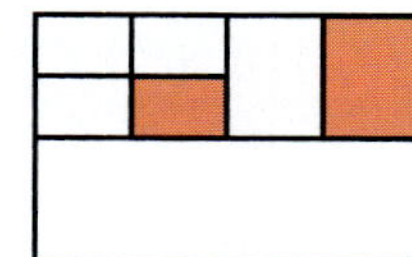

4. 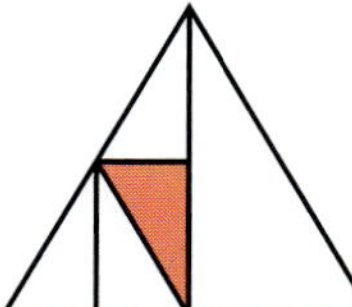

5. 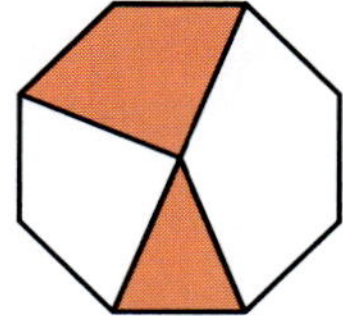

6. 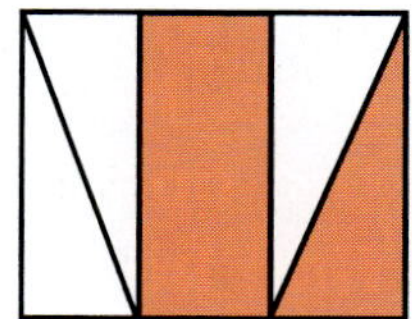

Explain Your Thinking

► Peter says that $\frac{2}{4}$ of this figure is blue. Is he right or wrong? Why or why not?

Multiplying and Dividing

Why Learn About Multiplying and Dividing Greater Numbers?

Much of the multiplication and division we do uses three- and four-digit numbers.

If you buy 3 computer games, you can multiply to find how much you owe. If you and your sister share the cost equally, you can divide to find how much each of you pay.

These bees produce enough honey to fill many jars. The beekeeper sells boxes of jars to stores. She can use multiplication to find how many jars she sells in a year.

Reviewing Vocabulary

Understanding math language helps you become a successful problem solver. Here are some math vocabulary words you should know.

multiple	the product of the number and any whole number
factors	numbers that are multiplied
product	the answer in a multiplication problem
quotient	the answer in a division problem
dividend	a number that is to be divided
divisor	a number that a dividend is to be divided by

Reading Words and Symbols

When you read mathematics, sometimes you read only words, sometimes you read words and symbols, and sometimes you read only symbols.

You can describe this array using multiplication or division.

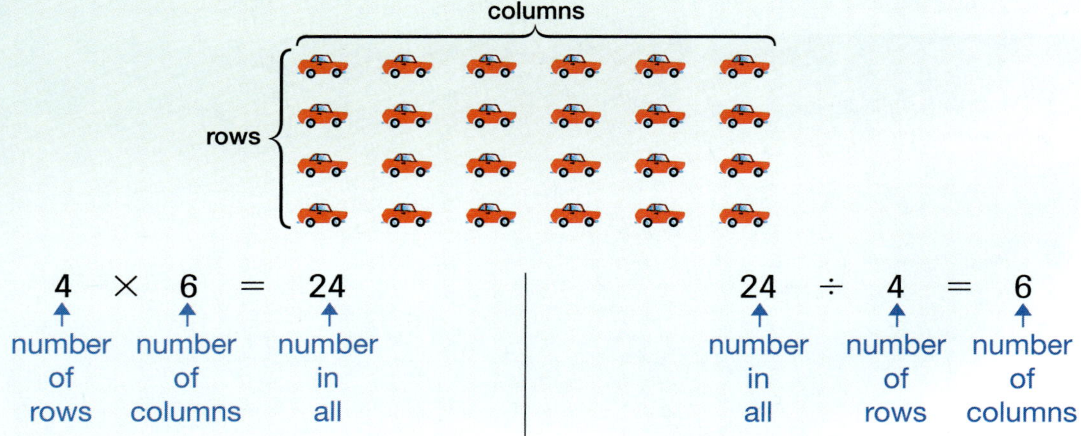

Four times six equals twenty-four.

Twenty-four divided by four equals six.

Try These

1. Use the clues to find each two-digit number.

   a. It is a multiple of 5.
   It is odd.
   The sum of its digits is 7.

   b. Both digits are the same.
   It is less than 50.
   The sum of its digits is 6.

   c. It is less than 30.
   It is a multiple of 6.
   The product of its digits is 8.

2. Write a division example that shows each of the following.

   a. The quotient is four.

   b. The divisor is less than 5.

   c. The dividend is greater than fifty.

3. Write *true* or *false*.

   a. The product of a whole number and zero is the whole number.

   b. You can use multiplication to check division.

   c. You can multiply three numbers in any order.

Upcoming Vocabulary

Write About It **Here is another vocabulary word** you will learn in this chapter. Watch for this word. Write its definition in your journal.

remainder

Mental Math: Multiply Multiples of 10, 100, and 1,000

You will learn how to use patterns and basic facts to help you multiply.

Review Vocabulary
multiples
factors

Learn About It

You can use basic facts and patterns of zeros to help you multiply **multiples** of 10, 100, and 1,000.

You need 200 beads to make a rainbow sun catcher. How many beads do you need to make 4 rainbow sun catchers?

Use the basic fact.	$4 \times 2 = 8$	**Think:** The product has the same number of zeros as the **factors**.
Then use a pattern of zeros.	$4 \times 20 = 80$ $4 \times 200 = 800$	

Solution: You need 800 beads to make 4 rainbow sun catchers.

Another Example

Zero in the Basic Fact

$5 \times 2 = 10$
$5 \times 20 = 100$
$5 \times 200 = 1{,}000$
$5 \times 2{,}000 = 10{,}000$

Think: $5 \times 2{,}000 = 5 \times (2 \times 1{,}000)$
$= (5 \times 2) \times 1{,}000$
$= 10 \times 1{,}000$
$= 10{,}000$

Since there is a zero in the basic fact, there is an additional zero in the product.

Explain Your Thinking

► How does knowing $4 \times 2 = 8$ help you find $4 \times 2{,}000$?

Guided Practice

Use a basic fact and patterns to find each product.

1. $3 \times 2 = ■$
$3 \times 20 = ■$
$3 \times 200 = ■$
$3 \times 2{,}000 = ■$

2. $4 \times 3 = ■$
$4 \times 30 = ■$
$4 \times 300 = ■$
$4 \times 3{,}000 = ■$

3. $5 \times 6 = ■$
$5 \times 60 = ■$
$5 \times 600 = ■$
$5 \times 6{,}000 = ■$

4. 6×500

5. $8 \times 3{,}000$

6. $6 \times 7{,}000$

Ask Yourself

- What basic fact can help me find the product?
- What pattern of zeros can help me?

Independent Practice

Use a basic fact and patterns to help you find each product.

7. 1 × 9 = ■
1 × 90 = ■
1 × 900 = ■
1 × 9,000 = ■

8. 3 × 7 = ■
3 × 70 = ■
3 × 700 = ■
3 × 7,000 = ■

9. 8 × 5 = ■
8 × 50 = ■
8 × 500 = ■
8 × 5,000 = ■

10. 2 × 6 = ■
2 × 60 = ■
2 × 600 = ■
2 × 6,000 = ■

11. 4 × 4 = ■
4 × 40 = ■
4 × 400 = ■
4 × 4,000 = ■

12. 7 × 5 = ■
7 × 50 = ■
7 × 500 = ■
7 × 5,000 = ■

Find each product.

13. 6 × 60 **14.** 9 × 200 **15.** 3 × 900 **16.** 6 × 9,000

17. 7 × 8,000 **18.** 2 × 50 **19.** 4 × 6,000 **20.** 5 × 300

21. 6 × 70 **22.** 8 × 60 **23.** 9 × 900 **24.** 3 × 3,000

25. 3 × 60 **26.** 5 × 400 **27.** 7 × 200 **28.** 9 × 4,000

Problem Solving • Reasoning

29. Marty wants to make 3 beaded caterpillars. It takes 90 beads to make each caterpillar. How many beads will Marty need?

30. You need 200 red beads, 200 white beads, and 100 blue beads to make 1 flag. What is the total number of beads needed to make 5 flags?

31. **Analyze** When a number is multiplied by 3, the product is 27,000. How can you use a basic fact to find the number?

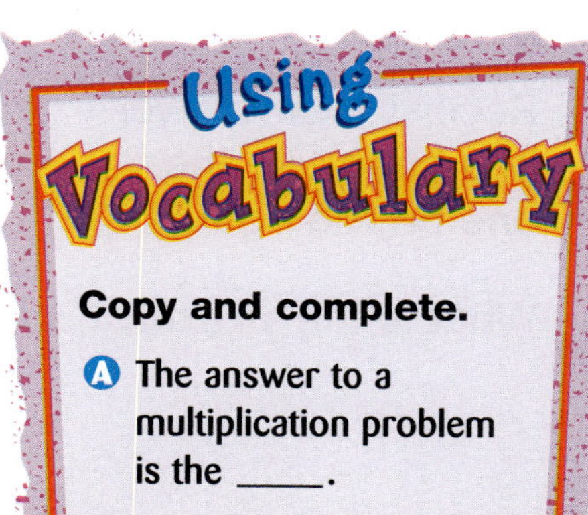

Mixed Review • Test Prep

Write the value of the underlined digit. *(pages 18–19, 32–33)*

32. 1<u>4</u>,253 **33.** <u>9</u>34 **34.** <u>2</u>,523 **35.** <u>8</u>70 **36.** <u>1</u>8,319 **37.** 9,<u>5</u>64

38 Round each number to the nearest 100 to estimate 372 + 298. *(pages 110–111)*

A 1,000 **B** 700 **C** 600 **D** 500

Extra Practice See Set A on page 586.

Modeling Multiplication

You will learn how to multiply numbers, using base-ten blocks.

Review Vocabulary
product
regroup

Learn About It

Use base-ten blocks to help you multiply a two-digit number by a one-digit number.

Materials
base-ten blocks

Problem 1 A school has three third-grade classes. Each class has 23 students. How many third-graders are in the school?

Use base-ten blocks to show 3 groups of 23.

Each row shows 2 tens 3 ones.

- How many tens blocks did you use?
- How many ones blocks did you use?

Record your answer in a chart like the one on the right.

Tens	Ones
6	9

What is the **product** of 3 and 23?

Problem 2 Now think about how you would find the number of third graders in the school if 24 students were in each class.

Use base-ten blocks to show 3 groups of 24.

- How many tens blocks did you use?
- How many ones blocks did you use?

When the number of ones blocks is 10 or greater than 10, you need to **regroup** 10 ones as 1 ten.

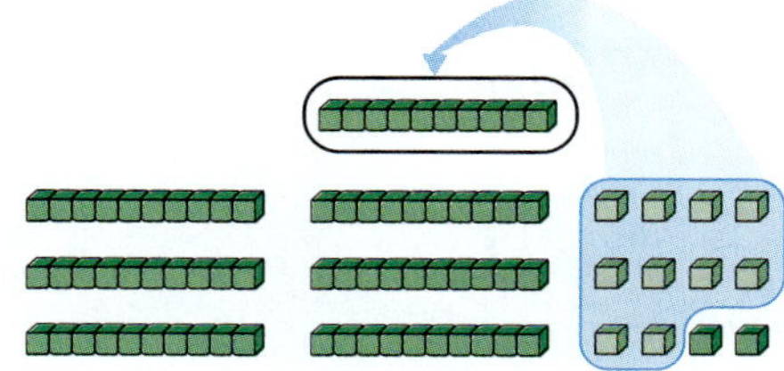

- How many tens blocks and ones blocks do you have now?

What is the product of 3 and 24?

Try It Out

Use base-ten blocks to help you find each product.

1. 2×24 **2.** 3×15 **3.** 4×22 **4.** 5×14 **5.** 2×46

6. Look back at Exercises 1–5. When did you have to regroup? Is there a way to know when you will have to regroup just by looking at the factors?

7. **Write Your Own** Write a problem that requires regrouping ones. Write another problem that requires no regrouping. Give your problems to a classmate to solve.

Algebra • Expressions **Copy and complete each number sentence.**

8. $5 \times 26 = (5 \times 20) + (5 \times \blacksquare)$

9. $4 \times 32 = (4 \times \blacksquare) + (4 \times 2)$

10. $3 \times 45 = (\blacksquare \times 40) + (3 \times 5)$

11. $6 \times 19 = (6 \times 10) + (\blacksquare \times 9)$

Write about it! Talk about it!

Use what you have learned to answer these questions.

12. How much greater will the product of 4 and 22 be than the product of 3 and 22?

13. How could you use addition to find the product of 3 and 25?

Two-Digit Numbers

You will learn how to solve multiplication problems where you have to regroup ones or tens.

Learn About It

Three groups of students are waiting for the school bus. Each group has 16 students. How many students are waiting for the school bus?

Multiply. **3 × 16 = ■**

Find 3 × 16.

Step 1 Use base-ten blocks to show 3 groups of 16.

$$\begin{array}{r} 16 \\ \times\ 3 \\ \hline \end{array}$$

Step 2 Multiply the ones.
3 × 6 ones = 18 ones
Regroup 18 ones as 1 ten 8 ones.

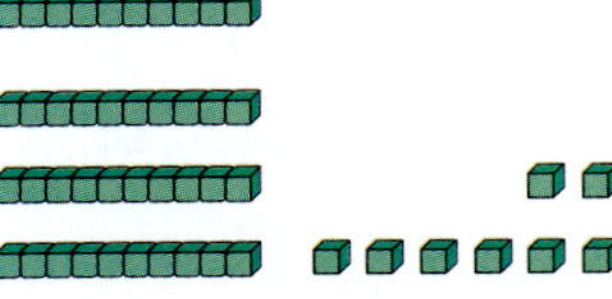

$$\begin{array}{r} \overset{1}{1}6 \\ \times\ 3 \\ \hline 8 \end{array}$$

18 ones

Step 3 Multiply the tens.
3 × 1 ten = 3 tens
Add the 1 regrouped ten.
3 tens + 1 ten = 4 tens

$$\begin{array}{r} \overset{1}{1}6 \\ \times\ 3 \\ \hline 48 \end{array}$$

4 tens

Solution: There are 48 students waiting for the school bus.

Another Example

Regroup Tens as Hundreds

$$\begin{array}{r} 83 \\ \times\ 3 \\ \hline 249 \end{array}$$

3 × 8 tens = 24 tens
24 tens = 2 hundreds 4 tens

Explain Your Thinking

- How do you know when to regroup?
- What is the most ones you can have before you need to regroup ones?
- What is the most tens you can have before you need to regroup tens?

Guided Practice

Use base-ten blocks to help you find each product.

1. 3×14

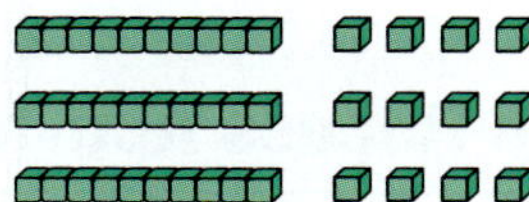

2. 5×12

Ask Yourself

- What do I multiply first?
- Do I need to regroup ones? tens?
- Do I need to add any regrouped tens? hundreds?

Multiply.

3. 21×4
4. 45×2
5. 17×5
6. 51×4
7. 32×3

Independent Practice

Find each product.

8. 2×16

9. 4×13

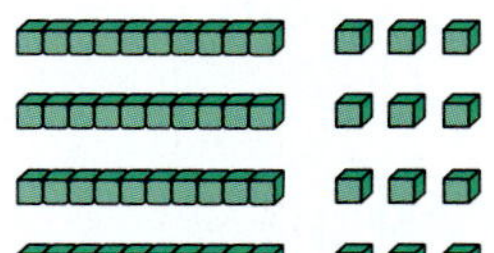

10. 3×15

11. 23×2
12. 34×2
13. 21×5
14. 33×2
15. 21×6
16. 43×3
17. 14×4
18. 38×2
19. 21×7
20. 27×3
21. 29×2
22. 14×6
23. 29×3
24. 42×4
25. 12×6
26. 2×41
27. 3×25
28. 4×32
29. 5×41
30. 3×53
31. 5×18
32. 7×31
33. 2×93

Algebra • Expressions **Write >, <, or = for each ●.**

34. 52×4 ● 4×52
35. 82×2 ● $100 + 50 + 4$
36. 0×39 ● 1×39
37. 8×31 ● $(8 \times 30) + (8 \times 1)$
38. 4×23 ● 4×32
39. $3 \times 4 \times 8$ ● $4 \times 3 \times 8$

Problem Solving • Reasoning

Use Data The graph shows the results of a survey about students' favorite recess activities. Use the graph to answer Problems 40–44.

Favorite Recess Activities

Activity	Number of Students
Tag	☺ ☺ ☺ ☺ ☺ ☺ ☺
Football	☺ ☺ ☺ ☺ ☺ ◖
Jump rope	☺ ☺ ☺ ☺
Kickball	☺ ☺ ☺ ☺ ☺

Each ☺ stands for 6 students.

40. Each student only voted for one activity. How many students voted?

41. How many students chose tag as their favorite activity? How many chose jump rope?

42. Write a number sentence to show the total number of students who chose either tag or kickball.

43. **Compare** How many more students chose tag than chose kickball? Explain how you found your answer.

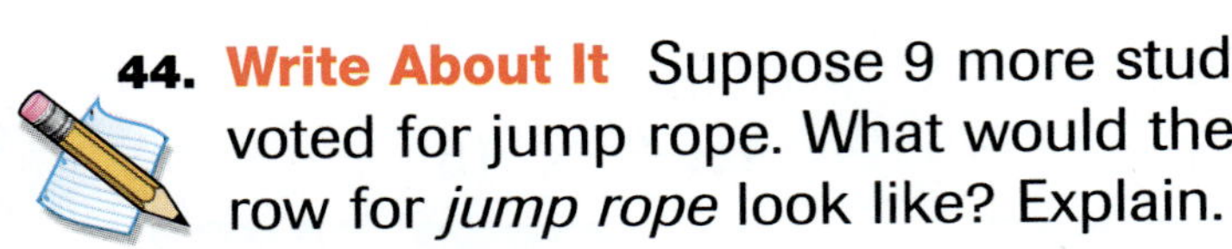

44. **Write About It** Suppose 9 more students voted for jump rope. What would the new row for *jump rope* look like? Explain.

Mixed Review • Test Prep

Compare. Write >, <, or = for each ●. *(pages 488–490)*

45. $\frac{3}{4}$ ● $\frac{1}{4}$ **46.** $\frac{3}{3}$ ● 1 **47.** $\frac{2}{5}$ ● $\frac{3}{5}$ **48.** $\frac{6}{5}$ ● $\frac{1}{5}$

49 What is the value of the 5 in 85,216? *(pages 32–33)*

A 50 **B** 500 **C** 5,000 **D** 50,000

Complete each sentence.
Write *always, never,* or *sometimes*.
Give an example to support each answer.

50. When you multiply a number that is 1 or greater than 1 by 0, the product is ____ 0.

51. When you multiply a number greater than 1 by 1, the answer is ____ 1.

Extra Practice See Set B on page 586.

Number Sense

Multiplying in Different Ways

Here are two different ways to multiply.

This is how Megan does multiplication.

$$3 \times 27 = 3 \times (20 + 7) = (3 \times 20) + (3 \times 7) = 60 + 21 = 81$$

How does writing 27 as 20 + 7 help Megan multiply the numbers?

$$4 \times 52 = 4 \times (50 + 2) = (4 \times 50) + (4 \times 2) = 200 + 8 = 208$$

How does writing 52 as 50 + 2 help Megan multiply the numbers?

This is how David does multiplication.

```
   27
 ×  3
   21 ← 3 × 7 ones
 + 60 ← 3 × 2 tens
   81 ← 21 + 60
```

How does thinking of 27 as 2 tens 7 ones help David multiply?

```
   52
 ×  4
    8 ← 4 × 2 ones
+ 200 ← 4 × 5 tens
  208 ← 8 + 200
```

How does thinking of 52 as 5 tens 2 ones help David multiply?

Try These

Find each product. Use the methods shown above and the standard method.

1. 38×2 **2.** 61×4 **3.** 43×3 **4.** 29×2 **5.** 72×4

Explain Your Thinking

► How are the methods alike? How are they different?

LESSON 4

Three-Digit Numbers

You will learn how to multiply when one factor is a three-digit number.

Learn About It

A double Ferris wheel can hold 126 people during one ride. Each half-hour, 3 rides are completed. How many people can ride the double Ferris wheel in 30 minutes?

Multiply. **3 × 126 = ■**

Find 3 × 126.

Step 1 Multiply the ones.
3 × 6 = 18
Regroup 18 ones as 1 ten 8 ones.

$$\begin{array}{r} {}^{1} \\ 126 \\ \times 3 \\ \hline 8 \end{array}$$

18 ones

Step 2 Multiply the tens.
3 × 2 = 6
Add the 1 regrouped ten.
6 + 1 = 7

$$\begin{array}{r} {}^{1} \\ 126 \\ \times 3 \\ \hline 78 \end{array}$$

7 tens

Step 3 Multiply the hundreds.
3 × 1 = 3

$$\begin{array}{r} {}^{1} \\ 126 \\ \times 3 \\ \hline 378 \end{array}$$

3 hundreds

Solution: In 30 minutes, 378 people can ride the double Ferris wheel.

Other Examples

A. No Regrouping

$$\begin{array}{r} 123 \\ \times 3 \\ \hline 369 \end{array}$$

B. Regrouping Tens

$$\begin{array}{r} {}^{2} \\ 271 \\ \times 3 \\ \hline 813 \end{array}$$

Explain Your Thinking

► How is multiplying with three-digit numbers like multiplying with two-digit numbers? How is it different?

Guided Practice

Find each product.

1. $\begin{array}{r} 234 \\ \times 2 \\ \hline \end{array}$ **2.** $\begin{array}{r} 218 \\ \times 4 \\ \hline \end{array}$ **3.** $\begin{array}{r} 273 \\ \times 3 \\ \hline \end{array}$ **4.** $\begin{array}{r} 121 \\ \times 5 \\ \hline \end{array}$

Ask Yourself

- Do I need to regroup ones? tens?
- Do I need to add any regrouped numbers?

Independent Practice

Multiply.

5. $\begin{array}{r} 124 \\ \times \quad 4 \\ \hline \end{array}$
6. $\begin{array}{r} 131 \\ \times \quad 5 \\ \hline \end{array}$
7. $\begin{array}{r} 142 \\ \times \quad 4 \\ \hline \end{array}$
8. $\begin{array}{r} 431 \\ \times \quad 2 \\ \hline \end{array}$
9. $\begin{array}{r} 136 \\ \times \quad 2 \\ \hline \end{array}$
10. $\begin{array}{r} 184 \\ \times \quad 2 \\ \hline \end{array}$
11. $\begin{array}{r} 212 \\ \times \quad 4 \\ \hline \end{array}$
12. $\begin{array}{r} 262 \\ \times \quad 3 \\ \hline \end{array}$
13. $\begin{array}{r} 394 \\ \times \quad 2 \\ \hline \end{array}$
14. $\begin{array}{r} 241 \\ \times \quad 3 \\ \hline \end{array}$
15. 2×317
16. 3×143
17. 5×115
18. 6×112
19. 7×114
20. 4×152
21. 2×493
22. 3×329

Problem Solving • Reasoning

23. If a Ferris wheel can carry 242 people each half-hour, how many people can the Ferris wheel carry in 2 hours?

24. **Money** Tickets for rides sell for 20 cents each or 6 tickets for $1.00. If you want 6 tickets, which is the better buy? Explain your answer.

25. **Analyze** Is the product of a two-digit number and a one-digit number always a three-digit number? Explain why or why not.

26. A Ferris wheel has 16 seats. Each seat holds 2 people. Suppose each seat on the Ferris wheel is filled for each ride and no person rides twice. How many people will ride in 4 rides?

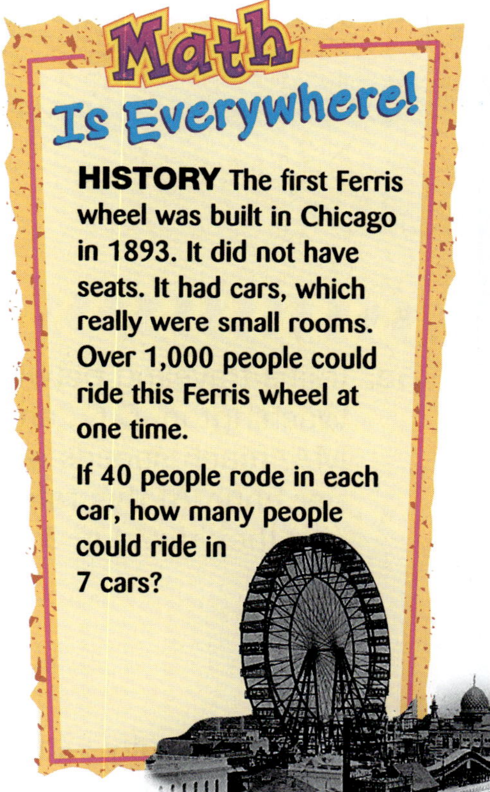

Mixed Review • Test Prep

Write a fraction to show the shaded part. *(pages 484–485)*

27. 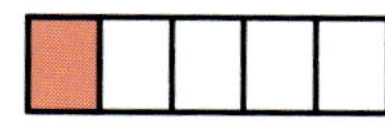

28. 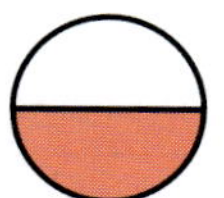

29. 

30. 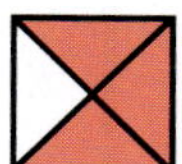

31. What is the sum of 125 and 396? *(pages 108–109)*

A 421 **C** 521
B 511 **D** 600

Extra Practice See Set C on page 587.

Quick Check

Check Your Understanding of Lessons 1–4

Find each product.

1. 7×600

2. $6 \times 4{,}000$

3. 6×800

4. $9 \times 3{,}000$

Multiply.

5. $\begin{array}{r} 27 \\ \times\ 3 \\ \hline \end{array}$

6. $\begin{array}{r} 19 \\ \times\ 5 \\ \hline \end{array}$

7. $\begin{array}{r} 52 \\ \times\ 4 \\ \hline \end{array}$

8. $\begin{array}{r} 83 \\ \times\ 3 \\ \hline \end{array}$

9. $\begin{array}{r} 126 \\ \times\ 3 \\ \hline \end{array}$

10. $\begin{array}{r} 241 \\ \times\ 4 \\ \hline \end{array}$

11. $\begin{array}{r} 136 \\ \times\ 2 \\ \hline \end{array}$

12. $\begin{array}{r} 217 \\ \times\ 3 \\ \hline \end{array}$

Solve.

13. Trains traveling between Washington, D.C., and Boston, MA, reach speeds of 125 miles per hour. At this rate, how far can they travel in 3 hours?

14. Japanese bullet trains are the fastest in the world. If a bullet train is traveling at 183 miles per hour, how many miles can it go in 3 hours?

How did you do?

If you had difficulty with any items in the Quick Check, you can use the following pages for review and extra practice.

Items	Review These Pages	Do These Extra Practice Items
1–4	pages 544–545	Set A, page 586
5–12	pages 548–550	Set B, page 586
9–14	pages 552–553	Set C, page 587

Test Prep • Cumulative Review

Maintaining the Standards

Choose the letter of the correct answer. If a correct answer is not here, choose NH.

1. Students rode in 3 buses to the Museum of Art. Each bus carried 26 students. How many students rode in the buses?

   A 72
   B 76
   C 80
   D NH

2. This pictograph shows the results of tossing a coin.

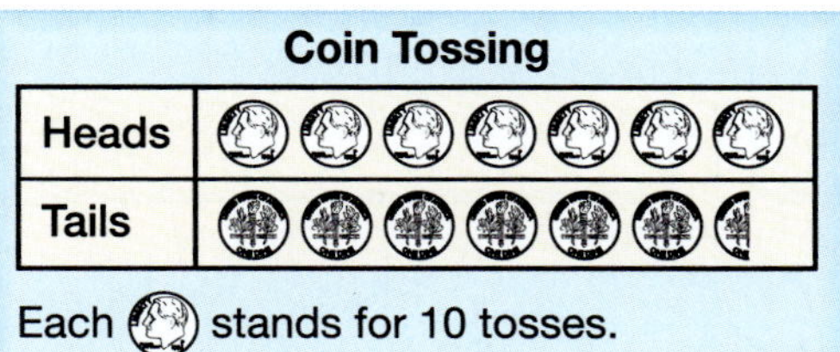

   How many times was the coin tossed?

   F 12
   G 60
   H 115
   J 135

3. What is the probability of spinning a 9 on the first try?

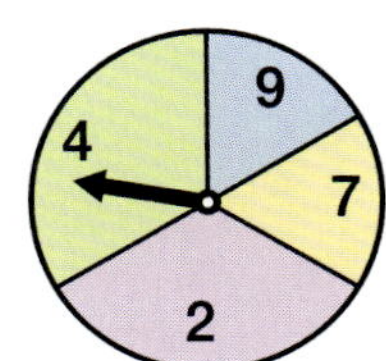

   A certain
   B likely
   C unlikely
   D impossible

4. A concert is scheduled for 4 nights. If the auditorium seats 215 people, what is the greatest number of tickets that can be sold?

   F 840
   G 860
   H 865
   J 900

5. What is the name of this figure?

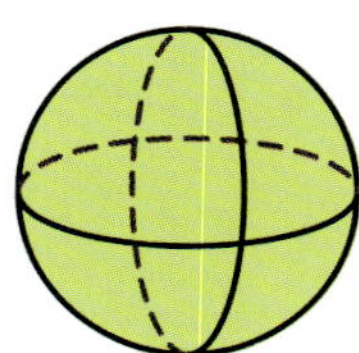

   A triangle
   B cone
   C pyramid
   D sphere

6. How many sides does an octagon have?

   F 3
   G 4
   H 6
   J 8

7. What is the perimeter of this figure?

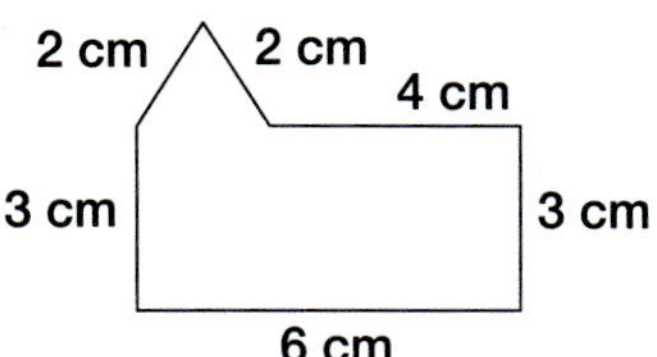

   Explain How did you find your answer?

Safe Site

Internet Test Prep
Visit **www.eduplace.com/kids/mhm** for more *Test Prep Practice.*

Regrouping Twice

You will learn how to multiply when you need to regroup more than once.

Learn About It

Don is a tour guide at a Mayan step pyramid in Mexico. He knows that he climbs 183 steps on each tour. One week he led 5 tours. How many steps did he climb that week?

Multiply. **5 × 183 = ■**

Find 5 × 183.

Step 1 Multiply the ones.
5 × 3 = 15

Regroup 15 ones as 1 ten 5 ones.

```
  1
 183
×  5
   5     15 ones
```

Step 2 Multiply the tens.
5 × 8 = 40

Add the 1 regrouped ten.
40 + 1 = 41

Regroup 41 tens as 4 hundreds 1 ten.

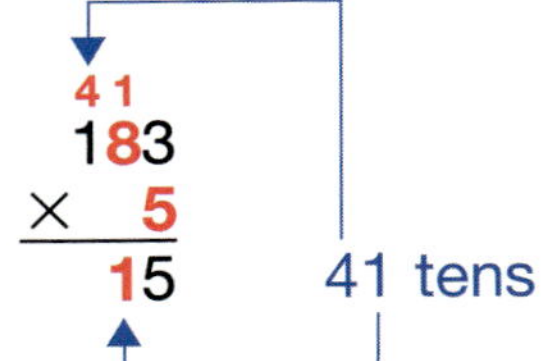

```
 41
 183
×  5
  15     41 tens
```

Step 3 Multiply the hundreds.
5 × 1 = 5

Add the 4 regrouped hundreds.
5 + 4 = 9

```
 41
 183
×  5
 915     9 hundreds
```

Solution: Don climbed 915 steps that week.

Another Example

Multiply With Four-Digit Numbers

```
  1
 8,734
×    2
17,468
```

2 × 8 thousands = 16 thousands
16 thousands + 1 thousand = 17 thousands
17 thousands = 1 ten thousand, 7 thousands

Explain Your Thinking

- What must you do with the numbers you regroup?
- When you multiply a three-digit number by a one-digit number, will you always get a three-digit product? Give examples to support your answer.

Guided Practice

Find each product.

1. 125 × 4

2. 653 × 2

3. 2,416 × 3

4. 714 × 6

5. 1,721 × 5

6. 2,621 × 4

Ask Yourself

- Do I need to regroup ones, tens, or hundreds?
- Do I need to add any regrouped numbers?

Independent Practice

Multiply.

7. 137 × 6

8. 526 × 3

9. 351 × 4

10. 418 × 3

11. 257 × 2

12. 1,126 × 3

13. 1,562 × 3

14. 3,215 × 4

15. 7,151 × 6

16. 1,171 × 7

17. 8 × 116

18. 5 × 521

19. 7 × 1,413

20. 9 × 2,811

Problem Solving • Reasoning

21. **Measurement** Rosa flew to and from Mexico twice last year. She flew 2,472 miles on each roundtrip. How many miles did she fly?

22. A store owner ordered 6 boxes of key chains. Each box had 144 key chains. How many key chains did he order?

23. **Money** Ann spent $88 on gifts. Cassie spent twice as much as Ann on gifts. How much did they spend altogether on gifts?

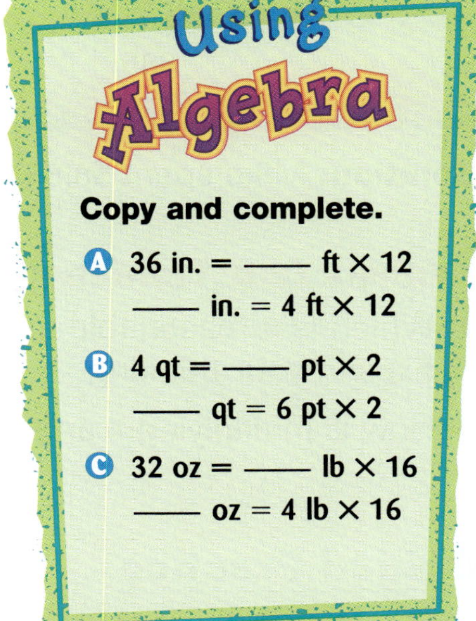

Copy and complete.

A 36 in. = ___ ft × 12
___ in. = 4 ft × 12

B 4 qt = ___ pt × 2
___ qt = 6 pt × 2

C 32 oz = ___ lb × 16
___ oz = 4 lb × 16

Mixed Review • Test Prep

Write each mixed number as a decimal. *(pages 516–517)*

24. $2\frac{3}{10}$

25. $4\frac{35}{100}$

26. $1\frac{2}{10}$

27. $3\frac{4}{100}$

28 Which unit of measurement would be best for measuring the length of a pencil? *(pages 182–183)*

A kilometer **B** meter **C** centimeter **D** millimeter

Extra Practice See Set D on page 587.

LESSON 6

Multiply Money

You will learn how multiplying money and multiplying whole numbers are alike and how they are different.

Learn About It

Mike bought 3 posters at a museum. Each poster cost \$2.95. How much did Mike spend?

Use what you know about multiplying whole numbers to multiply money.

Multiply. **3 × \$2.95 = ■**

Find 3 × \$2.95.

Step 1 Multiply as if you were multiplying whole numbers.

$$\begin{array}{r} {}^{2\,1}\\ 295 \\ \times \quad 3 \\ \hline 885 \end{array}$$

Step 2 Write the dollar sign and decimal point in the product.

$$\begin{array}{r} {}^{2\,1}\\ \$2.95 \\ \times \quad 3 \\ \hline \$8.85 \end{array}$$

Write the decimal point in the product in the same place as the decimal point in the money amount.

Solution: Mike spent \$8.85.

Explain Your Thinking

- ► Which is a reasonable answer for 2 × \$1.50, \$300 or \$3.00? Explain your thinking.
- ► How is multiplying 4 and \$1.62 like multiplying 4 and 162?

Guided Practice

Multiply.

1. \$3.24 × 2

2. \$4.53 × 3

3. \$2.25 × 4

4. \$1.15 × 3

5. \$3.18 × 4

6. \$1.13 × 5

Ask Yourself

- Do I need to regroup?
- Where will I place the dollar sign and the decimal point in the product?

Independent Practice

Multiply.

7. $1.68 × 5 **8.** $1.27 × 3 **9.** $2.78 × 2 **10.** $2.13 × 7 **11.** $1.92 × 3

12. $2.41 × 4 **13.** $1.19 × 6 **14.** $4.59 × 2 **15.** $2.81 × 4 **16.** $3.15 × 5

17. 3 × $1.35 **18.** 2 × $3.87 **19.** 3 × $2.78 **20.** 6 × $2.51

Problem Solving • Reasoning

Use Data **Use the price list for Problems 21–24.**

21. Clifford bought two telescopes at the museum gift shop. How much did he spend?

22. **Analyze** Joan wants to buy 3 different gifts. She has $16. What gifts can she buy?

23. **Money** Lana bought 3 toy dinosaurs and a package of stars. She gave the clerk $20. How much change should she get?

24. **Compare** Rex bought 2 posters, 3 toy dinosaurs, and a package of stars. Paul bought 1 telescope. Which boy spent more money?

Museum Gifts

Item	Price
Toy Dinosaur	$1.59 each
Poster	$2.95 each
Package of Stars	$1.65 each
Telescope	$12.49 each

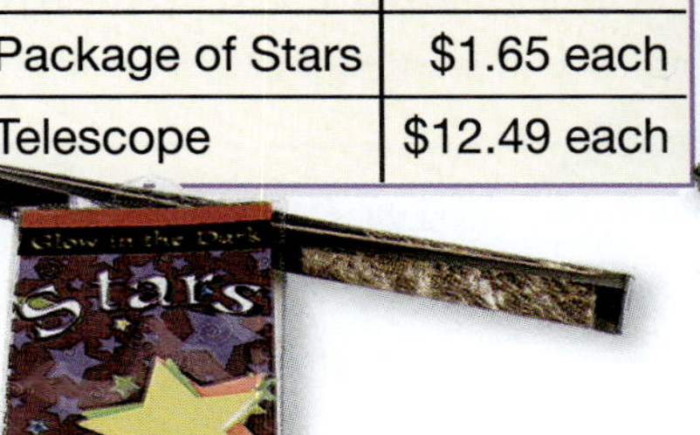

Mixed Review • Test Prep

Add or subtract. *(pages 504–506)*

25. $\frac{1}{5} + \frac{2}{5}$ **26.** $\frac{5}{8} - \frac{3}{8}$ **27.** $\frac{11}{12} - \frac{3}{12}$ **28.** $\frac{1}{4} + \frac{1}{4}$

Choose the letter of the correct answer. *(pages 298–300, 304–305)*

29 Which is a right angle?

A 
C 
B 
D 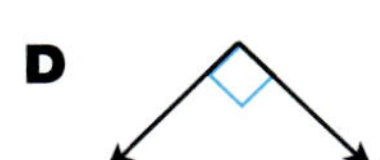

30 Which polygon is not a parallelogram?

F 
H 
G 
J

Extra Practice See Set E on page 587.

Problem-Solving Strategy: Solve a Simpler Problem

You will learn how to use a simpler problem to help you solve word problems.

Sometimes you can solve a problem by first thinking about a simpler problem.

Problem A group of 5 campers found some fossils. Then each camper made one trade with each of the other campers. How many trades were made?

Understand

What is the question?

How many trades were made?

What do you know?

- There were 5 campers.
- Each camper made one trade with every other camper.

Plan

How can you find the answer?

Solve a simpler problem. Draw a picture.

Solve

Solve the problem for fewer campers.

Show how many trades 2 or 3 campers would make.

2 campers

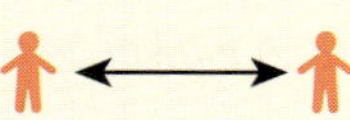

1 trade

3 campers

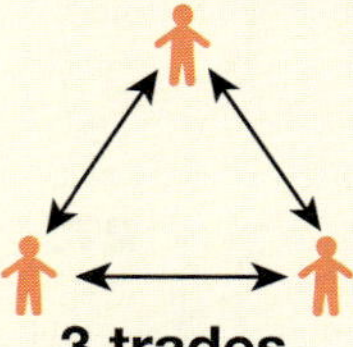

3 trades

Think: Each line stands for 1 trade.

Then use the same kind of picture for 5 campers. Draw a line to show each trade.

5 campers

10 trades were made.

Look Back

Look back at the problem.

How could you solve the problem if there were 6 campers?

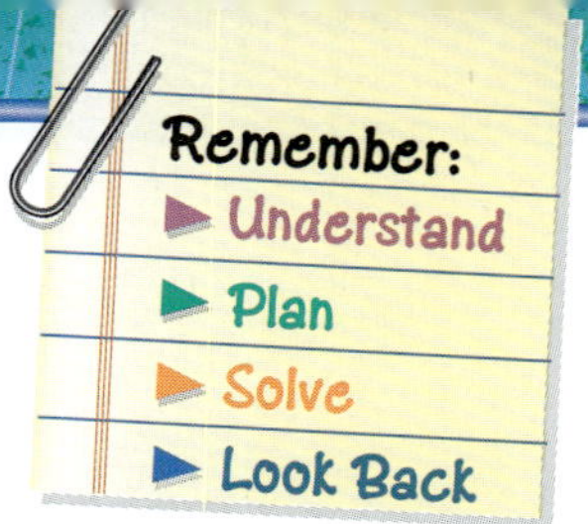

Guided Practice

Solve these problems, using the Solve a Simpler Problem strategy.

1. Four campers want to go canoeing. There is one canoe, and 2 people at a time can ride in it. How many ways could the campers pair up? How many ways could they make pairs if there were 5 campers?

   Think: How many pairs could there be if there were just 3 campers?

2. A hiking trail has signs posted every 500 yards and one posted at the start of the trail. Janey has just reached the fifth sign. How far has she hiked? How far will Janey have hiked when she reaches the ninth sign?

   How far had Janey hiked when she reached the second sign?

Choose a Strategy

Solve. Use these or other strategies.

Problem-Solving Strategies

- Write a Number Sentence
- Guess and Check
- Solve a Simpler Problem
- Draw a Picture

3. Jim and Kiera went looking for fossils. They found 50 fossils in all. Kiera found 10 more fossils than Jim. How many fossils did each person find?

4. Alicia wants to break a branch into pieces for a campfire. How many breaks must she make if she wants 10 pieces? if she wants 15 pieces?

5. A group of fossil hunters began to explore a site at 1:15 P.M. Every half-hour they took a break. How many breaks did the group take if they finished at 3:30 P.M.? if they finished at 5:30 P.M.?

6. A fossil site is shaped like a rectangle. One side is 4 feet long and another side is 3 feet long. What is the perimeter of the site? If each side were 5 feet longer, what would the perimeter of the site be then?

7. Ricky wants to divide the fossil site shown on the right into 8 equal regions. How could he do it? How could he divide the site into 16 equal regions?

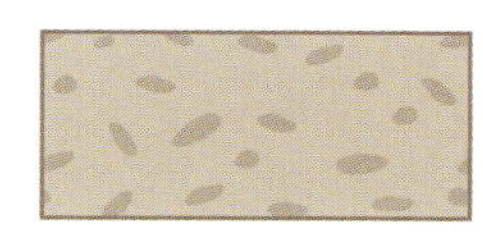

Extra Practice See 1–4 on page 589.

Quick Check

Check Your Understanding of Lessons 5–7

Multiply.

1. 246×4

2. $1{,}417 \times 5$

3. 295×3

4. $1{,}361 \times 6$

5. $\$3.15 \times 4$

6. $\$1.91 \times 8$

7. $\$4.82 \times 3$

8. $\$4.16 \times 6$

Solve. Use the table for Problems 9–10.

Camp Rentals	
Item	**Cost per day**
Dome tent	$3.95
Sleeping bag	$2.75
Camp pillow	$1.40

9. Tony's family is going camping for 4 days. How much will it cost Tony to rent a sleeping bag and a camp pillow?

10. Tessa and Colleen rented camping equipment for 3 days. Tessa rented a dome tent and Colleen rented a sleeping bag. How much more did Tessa spend than Colleen?

How did you do?

If you had difficulty with any items in the Quick Check, you can use the following pages for review and extra practice.

ITEMS	REVIEW THESE PAGES	DO THESE EXTRA PRACTICE ITEMS
1–4	pages 556–557	Set D, page 587
5–8	pages 558–559	Set E, page 587
9–10	pages 560–561	1–4, page 589

Test Prep • Cumulative Review

Maintaining the Standards

Choose the letter of the correct answer. If a correct answer is not here, choose NH.

1. Which triangle is an isosceles triangle?

A

C

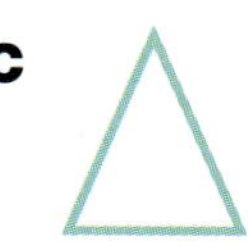

B

D

2. Which fraction represents the shaded portion of this model?

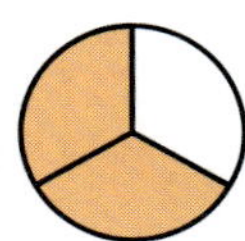

F $\frac{1}{3}$ **H** $\frac{3}{3}$

G $\frac{2}{3}$ **J** $\frac{3}{2}$

3. Mr. Wall bought 3 baskets of apples. Each basket contained 15 apples. How many apples did Mr. Wall buy?

A 35
B 40
C 55
D NH

4. Celie received 189 votes for class president. Sergio received twice that number of votes. How many votes did Sergio receive?

F 278
G 368
H 378
J NH

5. Which triangle has an angle that is greater than a right angle?

A

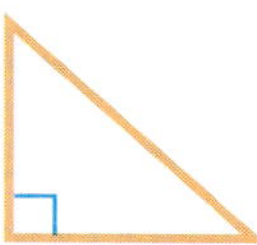

C

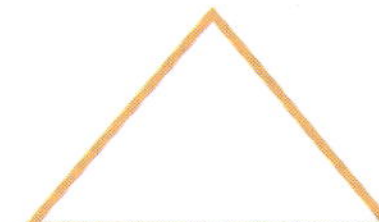

B

D

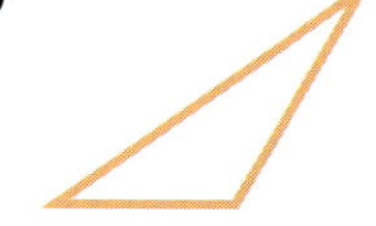

6. Which of the following is not true?

F All squares are rectangles.
G All squares have 4 equal sides.
H All parallelograms have 4 right angles.
J All rectangles have 4 right angles.

7. What is the probability that there will be a sunny day in June somewhere in the United States?

A certain
B likely
C unlikely
D impossible

8. Pedro bought 5 bottles of juice. Each bottle cost $1.99. How much did 5 bottles cost?

Explain How did you find your answer?

Internet Test Prep
Visit **www.eduplace.com/kids/mhm** for more *Test Prep Practice.*

Modeling Division With Remainders

You will learn how to find remainders in division problems.

New Vocabulary
remainder

Learn About It

Use counters to help you solve the problem.

Tricia invited 4 friends to a party. Her father bought 25 small toys to put in party-favor bags. Tricia wanted to give each friend the same number of toys. What is the greatest number of toys she could put in each bag?

Materials
counters

Step 1 Divide 25 counters into 4 equal groups. Put any leftover counters aside.

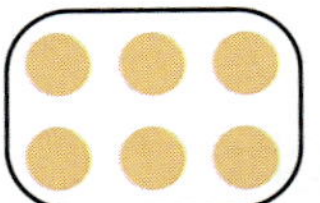
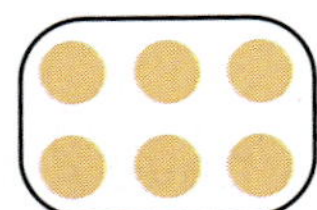
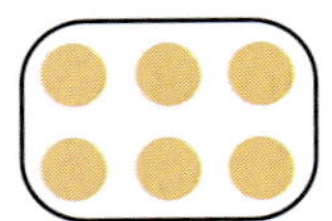
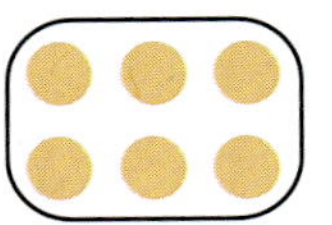

- How many counters are in each group?
- How many counters are left over?

Sometimes when you divide, you have an amount left over. This is the **remainder**. The remainder must be less than the divisor.

How many toys did Tricia put into each bag?

How many toys were left over?

Step 2 Write a division sentence that shows what you did.

25	÷	4	=	6	R1
↑ number being divided		↑ number of equal groups		↑ number in each group	↑ number left over

Remember:
R stands for *remainder.*

Step 3 Use 25 counters. Try making 5, 7, and 9 equal groups. Use the greatest number possible in each equal group. Record your work in a table like the one shown.

Total Number of Counters (Dividend)	Number of Groups (Divisor)	Number in Each Group (Quotient)	Number Left Over (Remainder)	Division Sentence
25	4	6	1	25 ÷ 4 = 6 R1
25	5			
25	7			
25	9			

- Look back at your table. Are the remainders less than, equal to, or greater than the divisors?
- Which division problem has a remainder of 0?

Try It Out

Write a division sentence for each picture.

1.

2.

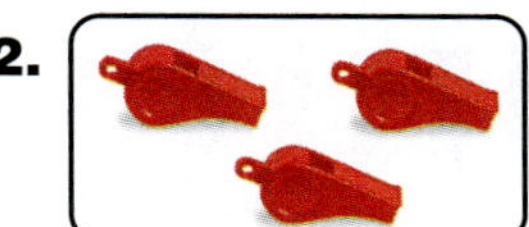

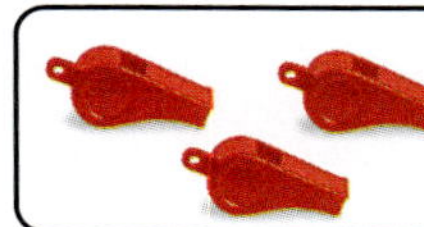

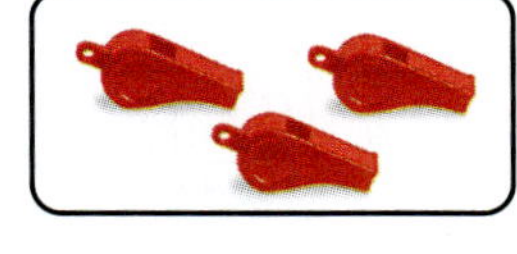

Divide. Use counters to help you.

3. 18 ÷ 3 **4.** 15 ÷ 2 **5.** 16 ÷ 4 **6.** 29 ÷ 5

7. 21 ÷ 3 **8.** 19 ÷ 4 **9.** 24 ÷ 5 **10.** 29 ÷ 3

Write about it! Talk about it!

Use what you have learned to answer these questions.

11. Diane said that 16 ÷ 5 = 3 R1. Jack said that the quotient is 2 and the remainder is 6. Who is right? Explain.

12. What is the largest remainder you can have when the divisor is 5? How do you know?

Two-Digit Quotients

You will learn how to use base-ten blocks to show division with two-digit quotients.

Review Vocabulary
quotient
dividend
divisor
remainder

Learn About It

Caryn has 47 shells. She wants to separate them equally into 2 pails. What is the greatest number of shells she can put into each pail? How many shells will be left over?

Divide. **47 ÷ 2 = ■** or **2)47**

Find 47 ÷ 2.

Step 1 Use base-ten blocks to show 47.

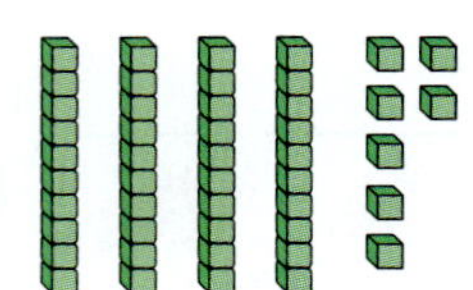

■ ← **quotient** (shells in each pail)
2)47 ← **dividend** (shells in all)
↑
divisor
(number of pails)

Step 2 Divide the 4 tens into 2 equal groups.
Put 2 tens into each group.

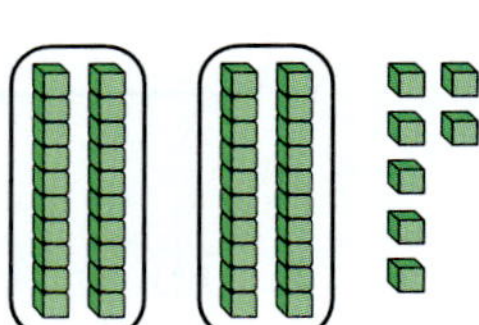

$$\begin{array}{r} 2 \\ 2\overline{)47} \\ -\ 4 \\ \hline 0 \end{array}$$

← Write 2 in the tens place.
← Multiply. 2 × 2 tens = 4 tens
← Subtract. 4 − 4
Compare. 0 < 2

Step 3 Divide the 7 ones.
Put 3 ones into each group.
There is 1 one left over.
The remainder is 1.

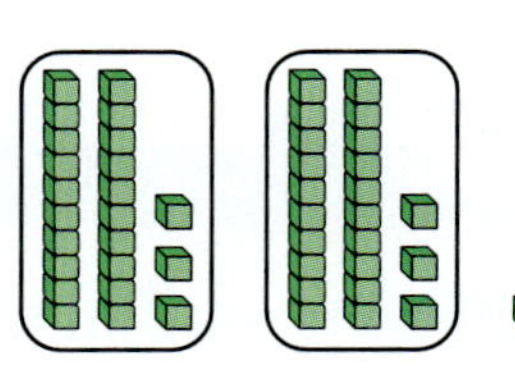

$$\begin{array}{r} 23 \\ 2\overline{)47} \\ -\ 4 \\ \hline 07 \\ -\ 6 \\ \hline 1 \end{array}$$

← Write 3 in the ones place.
← Bring down 7 ones.
← Multiply. 2 × 3 ones = 6 ones
← Subtract. 7 − 6
Compare. 1 < 2

remainder →

Remember: The remainder must be less than the divisor.

Solution: Caryn can put 23 shells in each pail. There will be 1 shell left over.

Use multiplication to check your work.

Check. $47 \div 2 = 23$ R1

Step 1 Multiply the quotient and the divisor.

$$\begin{array}{r} 23 \\ \times\ 2 \\ \hline 46 \end{array}$$

23 ← quotient
2 ← divisor

Step 2 Then add the remainder.

$$\begin{array}{r} 46 \\ +\ 1 \\ \hline 47 \end{array}$$

1 ← remainder
47 ← If the sum equals the dividend, then the quotient is correct.

$47 = (2 \times 23) + 1$

Another Example

Two-Digit Quotient With a Remainder 0

Divide.

$$\begin{array}{r} 21 \\ 4\overline{)84} \\ -8 \\ \hline 04 \\ -4 \\ \hline 0 \end{array}$$

Check.

$$\begin{array}{r} 21 \\ \times\ 4 \\ \hline 84 \end{array}$$

Explain Your Thinking

► You can use multiplication to check your answer in division. Can you use division to check your answer in multiplication? Give examples to support your thinking.

Guided Practice

Use base-ten blocks to help you divide.

1. $3\overline{)39}$ **2.** $4\overline{)85}$ **3.** $2\overline{)89}$ **4.** $5\overline{)58}$

5. $67 \div 2$ **6.** $99 \div 3$ **7.** $65 \div 3$ **8.** $88 \div 4$

Ask Yourself

- Can I divide the tens?
- Can I divide the ones?
- Are any ones left over?

Independent Practice

Divide and check. Use base-ten blocks if you wish.

9. $5\overline{)55}$ **10.** $4\overline{)48}$ **11.** $3\overline{)63}$ **12.** $2\overline{)68}$ **13.** $2\overline{)24}$

14. $3\overline{)93}$ **15.** $3\overline{)96}$ **16.** $2\overline{)43}$ **17.** $4\overline{)49}$ **18.** $3\overline{)94}$

19. $5\overline{)59}$ **20.** $4\overline{)87}$ **21.** $5\overline{)57}$ **22.** $2\overline{)85}$ **23.** $4\overline{)86}$

24. $95 \div 3$ **25.** $56 \div 5$ **26.** $49 \div 2$ **27.** $89 \div 4$ **28.** $68 \div 3$

Problem Solving • Reasoning

Use the sign for Problems 29–32.

29. Tom gave one half of his scallop shells and one half of his conch shells to his brother. How many shells did he give to his brother altogether?

30. Tom will use 6 scallop shells to decorate each picture frame. What is the greatest number of frames he can decorate? How many scallop shells will he have left over?

31. **Analyze** Tom needs 136 clam shells for an art project. Write a subtraction sentence to show how many more clam shells he needs.

32. Tom wants to store his sand dollars in more than one box. How many boxes does he need if he wants to store exactly the same number of sand dollars in each box? Explain your thinking.

Mixed Review • Test Prep

Add or subtract. *(pages 520–522)*

33. 0.4 + 1.3 **34.** 2.17 − 1.12 **35.** 3.6 − 1.1 **36.** 1.5 + 0.9

37 What time is it half an hour before 2:45 P.M.? *(pages 78–79)*

A 1:45 P.M. **B** 2:00 P.M. **C** 2:15 P.M. **D** 3:15 P.M.

Logical Thinking

Break the Code

Use the numbers on the right to find a value for each shape.

38. ■ ÷ ▲ = ● R ★

■ = ? ▲ = ? ● = ? ★ = ?

Extra Practice See Set F on page 587.

Practice Game

Remainder Race

Practice division by playing this game with a partner.
Try to be the first person to score 30 points.

What You'll Need

- *a number cube labeled 1 to 6*
- *a game board like the one shown (Teaching Tool 20)*

Players
2

5)5□	2)2□	3)3□	4)4□
3)6□	3)9□	2)6□	2)8□
2)8□	4)8□	4)4□	3)6□
3)9□	2)4□	4)8□	5)5□

Here's What to Do

1. The first player rolls the number cube. He or she then writes the number rolled in an empty ■ on the game board.
2. The first player then names the quotient and remainder for that problem. The other player checks that the quotient and remainder are correct.
3. The remainder is the number of points scored. If there is no remainder, the player scores 10 points.
4. Players take turns, repeating Steps 1–3. The first player to reach a total of 30 points wins.

Share Your Thinking

What is the best strategy for placing a number?

LESSON 10

Problem-Solving Skill: Interpret Remainders

You will learn how to use the facts in a problem to decide what a remainder means.

Sometimes you need to decide what to do with the remainder so that the answer is reasonable.

Look at the situations below.

Sometimes you increase the quotient.

There are 41 astronauts. If 6 astronauts fly together on most space shuttle flights, how many flights are needed so that each astronaut gets to fly once?

$$\begin{array}{r} 6 \text{ R}5 \\ 6\overline{)41} \\ -36 \\ \hline 5 \end{array}$$

There will be 6 flights with a crew of 6. Another flight is needed for the 5 remaining astronauts. So 7 flights are needed.

Sometimes you drop the remainder.

Suppose an astronaut in space eats 2 pounds of food each day. How many days will 19 pounds of food last one astronaut?

$$\begin{array}{r} 9 \text{ R}1 \\ 2\overline{)19} \\ -18 \\ \hline 1 \end{array}$$

The food will last 9 days.

Sometimes the remainder is the answer.

The 41 astronauts are put into groups of 8 for training. Astronauts who are not in a group work in Mission Control. How many astronauts work in Mission Control?

$$\begin{array}{r} 5 \text{ R}1 \\ 8\overline{)41} \\ -40 \\ \hline 1 \end{array}$$

There is a remainder of 1, so 1 astronaut works in Mission Control.

Look Back How do the questions help you decide what to do with the remainder?

Left: An astronaut needs a space suit to walk in space. *Right:* Without the pull of gravity, astronauts float in the space shuttle.

Guided Practice

Solve each problem.

1. Each space shuttle astronaut gets a complete set of 3 flight suits. If there are 95 flight suits, how many astronauts get a complete set of flight suits?

Can a set be made with fewer than 3 flight suits?

2. A shuttle crew wants to videotape an experiment in space. If the experiment will run 85 hours, and each tape records 4 hours, how many tapes will they need?

What does the remainder stand for?

Choose a Strategy

Solve. Use these or other strategies.

Problem-Solving Strategies

- **Use Logical Thinking**
- **Act It Out**
- **Write a Number Sentence**
- **Draw a Picture**

3. An astronaut needs 5 minutes to get into a modern space suit. It could have taken 12 times as long to get into an early space suit. How long might it have taken to get into an early space suit?

4. Vance, Shannon, Rich, and Mae are astronauts. Rich will fly a mission before Mae. Shannon will fly after Vance but before Mae. Rich will fly second. In which order will the astronauts fly?

5. Mike is an astronaut. He weighs 29 pounds on the moon. Because of differences in gravity, he weighs 6 times that amount on Earth. How much does he weigh on Earth?

6. Suppose astronauts brought back 69 pounds of rocks from the moon. If they divided this amount equally into 3 bags, how many pounds of rocks were in each bag?

7. In orbit, the space shuttle travels 467 kilometers per minute. Is it reasonable to say that the shuttle will travel more than 3,000 kilometers in 5 minutes? Explain your thinking.

8. Five friends will divide 58 space cards. Each friend will get the same number of cards. Leftover cards will be mailed to pen pals. How many post cards will go to pen pals?

Extra Practice See Set 5–8 on page 589.

Quick Check

Check Your Understanding of Lessons 8–10

Divide and check.

1. $3\overline{)98}$
2. $5\overline{)59}$
3. $2\overline{)86}$
4. $4\overline{)44}$
5. $3\overline{)69}$
6. $5\overline{)56}$
7. $2\overline{)29}$
8. $5\overline{)58}$
9. $4\overline{)87}$
10. $2\overline{)64}$
11. $4\overline{)49}$
12. $3\overline{)96}$
13. $2\overline{)47}$
14. $4\overline{)85}$
15. $3\overline{)34}$
16. $2\overline{)87}$

Solve.

17. Kayla bought a package of 25 balloons for a party. She wants to divide them equally to put into 7 party bags. The leftover balloons will be used for decorations. How many balloons will go in each bag and how many will be left for decorations?

How did you do?

If you had difficulty with any items in the Quick Check, you can use the following pages for review and extra practice.

Items	Review These Pages	Do These Extra Practice Items
1–16	pages 566–568	Set F, page 587
17	pages 570–571	5–8, page 589

Test Prep • Cumulative Review

Maintaining the Standards

Choose the letter of the correct answer.

1. What division sentence is modeled below?

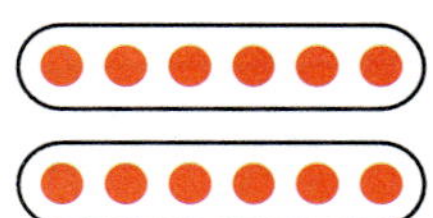

A $12 \div 2 = 6$
B $12 \div 3 = 4$
C $6 \div 2 = 3$
D $14 \div 2 = 7$

2. Which figure has a right angle?

F 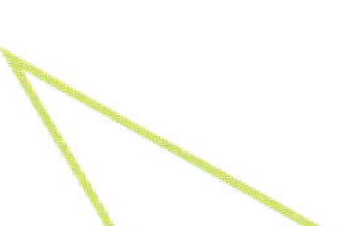
H 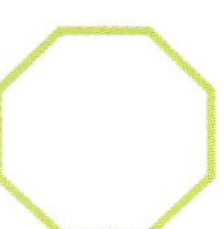
G 
J

3. What decimal represents the shaded portion of this model?

A 0.04
B 0.4
C 4.0
D 40.0

4. What is the product of 146×5?

F 500 **H** 700
G 650 **J** 730

5. Eve tossed a coin 100 times. She recorded 52 heads, and 48 tails. If she tossed the coin 200 times, which of the following is likely to be the result?

A heads—150; tails—50
B heads—100; tails—100
C heads—175; tails—25
D heads—50; tails—150

6. What solid figures make up this complex figure?

F rectangle, triangle, circle
G rectangular prism, cylinder, cone
H pyramid, cone, cylinder
J rectangular prism, cylinder, triangle

7. Dominic shuffled these cards.

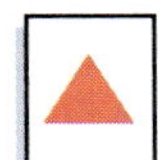    

How many outcomes are possible when 1 card is drawn?

Explain How did you find your answer?

Safe Site

Internet Test Prep
Visit **www.eduplace.com/kids/mhm** for more *Test Prep Practice.*

Regrouping in Division

You will learn how to divide with regrouping by using base-ten blocks.

Learn About It

A class is making construction-paper creatures. If 4 students share 64 sheets of paper equally, how many sheets can each student have?

Divide. **64 ÷ 4 = ■** or **4)64**

Find 64 ÷ 4.

Step 1 Show 64 with base-ten blocks.

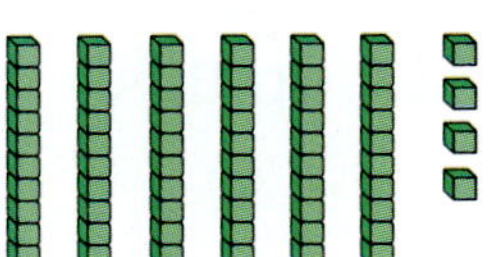

■ ← quotient
4)64 ← dividend
↑
divisor

Step 2 Divide the 6 tens into 4 groups. There is 1 ten in each group. There are 2 tens left over.

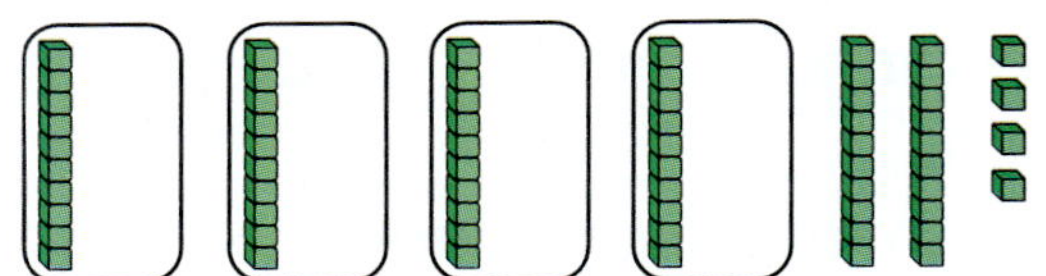

1 ← Write 1 in the tens place.
4)64
− 4 ← Multiply. 4 × 1 ten = 4 tens
2 ← Subtract. 6 − 4 = 2
Compare. 2 < 4

Step 3 Regroup the 2 tens as 20 ones.
20 ones + 4 ones = 24 ones

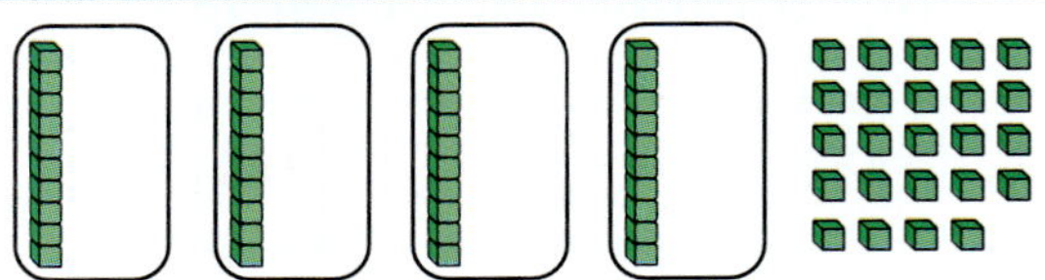

1
4)64
− 4↓
24 ← Bring down 4 ones.

Step 4 Divide the 24 ones.
Put 6 ones into each group.

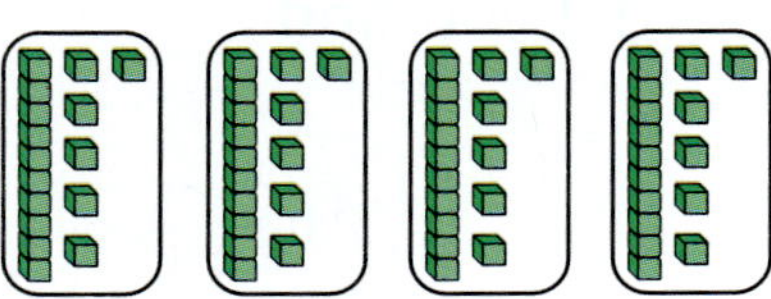

16 ← Write 6 in the ones place.
4)64
− 4
24
− 24 ← Multiply. 4 × 6 ones = 24 ones
0 ← Subtract. 24 − 24 = 0 remainder
Compare. 0 < 4

Solution: Each student can have 16 sheets of paper.

Explain Your Thinking

► If you use base-ten blocks to help you divide 32 by 2, do you have to regroup a tens block? Explain how you know.

Guided Practice

Use base-ten blocks to help you divide. Check each answer.

1. $2\overline{)52}$ **2.** $5\overline{)76}$ **3.** $4\overline{)94}$

4. 56 ÷ 4 **5.** 46 ÷ 3 **6.** 73 ÷ 3

Ask Yourself

- When I divide the tens, are any tens left over?
- When I divide the ones, are any ones left over?

Independent Practice

Divide and check.

7. $5\overline{)85}$ **8.** $2\overline{)96}$ **9.** $2\overline{)54}$ **10.** $3\overline{)76}$ **11.** $4\overline{)65}$

12. $3\overline{)81}$ **13.** $3\overline{)47}$ **14.** $4\overline{)77}$ **15.** $4\overline{)58}$ **16.** $5\overline{)99}$

17. 48 ÷ 4 **18.** 86 ÷ 5 **19.** 45 ÷ 4 **20.** 93 ÷ 2 **21.** 56 ÷ 3

Problem Solving • Reasoning

Use Data **Use the graph for Problems 22–24.**

22. Four students made all the green frogs. If each student made the same number, how many frogs did each student make?

23. **Analyze** The class started with enough supplies to make 188 creatures. How many more creatures can they make?

24. Students donated the brown bears and yellow giraffes to 5 day care centers. If each center got the same number of creatures, how many did each center get?

Mixed Review • Test Prep

Solve. *(pages 104–106, 128–130, 362–363, 556–557)*

25. 24 + 37 **26.** 156 − 85 **27.** 3 × 44 **28.** 45 ÷ 5

29 What is 1,275 rounded to the nearest hundred? *(pages 24–25)*

A 1,000 **B** 1,200 **C** 1,270 **D** 1,300

Extra Practice See Set G on page 588.

Three-Digit Quotients

You will learn to use what you know about division to find three-digit quotients.

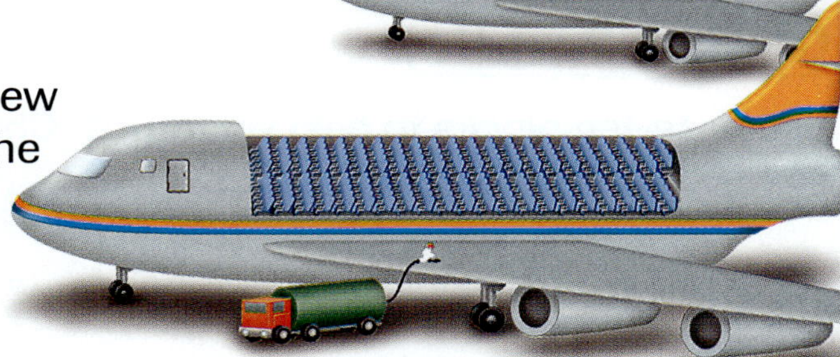

Learn About It

Three planes flew 642 passengers from New York to Los Angeles. Each plane carried the same number of passengers. How many passengers were on each plane?

Divide. **642 ÷ 3 = ■** or **3)642**

Find 642 ÷ 3.

Step 1 Divide the hundreds.

Think: $3\overline{)6 \text{ hundreds}}$? hundreds

```
  2      ← Write 2 in the hundreds place.
3)642
- 6      ← Multiply. 3 × 2 hundreds
  0      ← Subtract. 6 − 6
           Compare. 0 < 3
```

Step 2 Bring down the tens. Divide the tens.

Think: $3\overline{)4 \text{ tens}}$? tens

```
  21     ← Write 1 in the tens place.
3)642
- 6↓
  04     ← Bring down 4 tens.
 - 3     ← Multiply. 3 × 1 ten
   1     ← Subtract. 4 − 3
           Compare. 1 < 3
```

Step 3 Regroup leftover tens as ones.

Think: 1 ten 2 ones = 12 ones.

```
  21
3)642
- 6
  04
 - 3↓
  12     ← Bring down 2 ones.
           Regroup 1 ten 2 ones as 12 ones.
```

Step 4 Divide the ones.

Think: $3\overline{)12 \text{ ones}}$? ones

```
  214    ← Write 4 in the ones place.
3)642
- 6
  04
 - 3
  12     ← Multiply. 3 × 4 ones
- 12     ← Subtract. 12 − 12
   0       Compare. 0 < 3
```

Solution: There were 214 passengers on each plane.

Check your work.
Multiply the quotient by the divisor.

```
  1
 214
×  3
 642
```

Explain Your Thinking

► How do you know that the quotient is correct when you check your work?

Guided Practice

Ask Yourself

- Do I have to regroup?

Divide and check.

1. 3)951 **2.** 5)565 **3.** 2)694 **4.** 4)464

5. 684 ÷ 6 **6.** 856 ÷ 4 **7.** 972 ÷ 3 **8.** 894 ÷ 2

Independent Practice

Divide and check.

9. 3)651 **10.** 4)868 **11.** 2)652 **12.** 5)595 **13.** 2)830

14. 5)575 **15.** 3)372 **16.** 5)580 **17.** 4)468 **18.** 3)957

19. 860 ÷ 4 **20.** 452 ÷ 2 **21.** 476 ÷ 4 **22.** 642 ÷ 3

23. 696 ÷ 6 **24.** 884 ÷ 4 **25.** 981 ÷ 3 **26.** 872 ÷ 4

Problem Solving • Reasoning

27. A pilot flew the same route 4 times. She flew 852 miles altogether. How far did she fly each time?

28. **Analyze** There were 120 people on a plane when a trip ended. At one stop, 29 people got off. At another stop, 49 people got off. No one got on the plane. How many people were on the plane when the trip began?

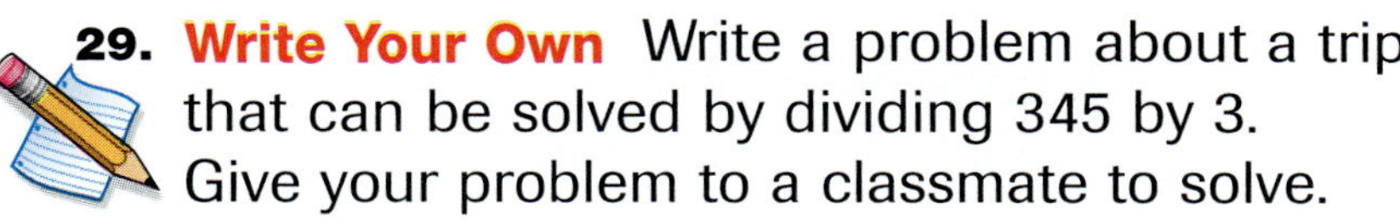

29. **Write Your Own** Write a problem about a trip that can be solved by dividing 345 by 3. Give your problem to a classmate to solve.

Math Is Everywhere!

SCIENCE The Concorde can fly faster than the speed of sound. A 747 jet does not fly as fast as the Concorde, but it holds more passengers.

One 747 jet can hold 400 passengers. That is 4 times as many passengers as the Concorde holds. How many passengers does the Concorde hold?

Mixed Review • Test Prep

Round to the greatest place to estimate each answer. *(pages 110–111, 134–135)*

30. 3,425 + 5,230 **31.** 9,342 − 1,523

32. 932 + 1,099 **33.** 4,598 − 2,865

Find the missing measure. *(pages 182–185)*

34 10 meters = ____ centimeters

A 1 **B** 100 **C** 1,000 **D** 10,000

Extra Practice See Set H on page 588.

Divide Money

You will learn that dividing money is like dividing whole numbers.

Learn About It

Sam and his brother spent a total of $8.90 to get into the railroad show. Each of their tickets cost the same amount. How much did each ticket cost?

Divide. **$8.90 ÷ 2 =** n or **2)$8.90**

Find $8.90 ÷ 2.

Step 1 Divide as if you were dividing whole numbers.

```
   445
 2)890
  - 8
   09
  - 8
    10
  - 10
     0
```

Step 2 Write the dollar sign and decimal point in the quotient.

```
  $4.45
 2)$8.90
```

Place the decimal point in the quotient directly over the decimal point in the dividend.

Solution: Each ticket cost $4.45.

Another Example

No Regrouping

```
   $3.12
 2)$6.24
  - 6
    02
   - 2
     04
    - 4
      0
```

Explain Your Thinking

- ► Look back at the example above. Why would an answer of $445 not be reasonable?
- ► How is dividing $6.24 by 2 like dividing 624 by 2?

Guided Practice

Divide.

1. 2)$8.46 **2.** 4)$4.84 **3.** 3)$3.75

4. $5.65 ÷ 5 **5.** $6.52 ÷ 2 **6.** $8.56 ÷ 4

Ask Yourself

- Do I have to regroup?
- Where should I place the dollar sign and the decimal point?

Independent Practice

Divide.

7. $3\overline{)\$6.93}$ **8.** $4\overline{)\$8.84}$ **9.** $2\overline{)\$8.28}$ **10.** $2\overline{)\$2.56}$

11. $4\overline{)\$4.60}$ **12.** $6\overline{)\$6.72}$ **13.** $5\overline{)\$5.90}$ **14.** $3\overline{)\$6.45}$

15. $3\overline{)\$9.36}$ **16.** $4\overline{)\$4.68}$ **17.** $3\overline{)\$6.96}$ **18.** $4\overline{)\$8.96}$

19. $6.50 ÷ 2 **20.** $8.64 ÷ 4 **21.** $6.81 ÷ 3 **22.** $8.74 ÷ 2

Algebra • Equations **Find each missing number.**

23. $n \div 3 = \$1.21$ **24.** $\$4.26 \div 2 = n$ **25.** $\$2.12 = n \div 4$

26. $n = \$5.55 \div 5$ **27.** $n \div 2 = \$3.24$ **28.** $n \div 3 = \$2.21$

Problem Solving • Reasoning

Use Data **Use the prices on the sign for Problems 29 and 30.**

29. What is the unit cost of a scarf?

30. Sam bought 5 train whistles. He paid the unit cost for each whistle. How much did Sam spend on whistles?

31. **Compare** A special train decal sells for $1.29. A box of 5 of the decals costs $5.50. How much do you save if you buy a box of decals instead of buying 5 individual decals?

32. **Write About It** Elise divided $4.50 by 2. She wrote $2.20 as her answer. Explain what Elise did wrong. Show how to do the division correctly.

Mixed Review • Test Prep

Solve. *(pages 504–506)*

33. $\frac{1}{5} + \frac{2}{5}$ **34.** $\frac{5}{6} - \frac{2}{6}$ **35.** $\frac{3}{7} + \frac{3}{7}$ **36.** $\frac{5}{8} - \frac{4}{8}$

37 How many sides does a quadrilateral have? *(pages 304–305)*

A 3 **B** 4 **C** 5 **D** 6

Extra Practice See Set I on page 588.

Placing the First Digit

You will learn how to decide where to place the first digit in the quotient.

Paula has 5 days to read her library book. The book has 125 pages. If Paula wants to read the same number of pages each day, how many pages must she read each day to finish the book?

Divide. **$125 \div 5 = \blacksquare$** or **$5\overline{)125}$**

Find $125 \div 5$.

Step 1 Decide where to place the first digit in the quotient.

Think: $5\overline{)1\text{ hundred}}$ — ? hundreds

$5\overline{)125}$ $1 < 5$ There are not enough hundreds to divide.

$5\overline{)125}$ (■ above the tens place) $12 > 5$ Place the first digit of the quotient in the tens place.

Step 2 Divide the tens.

Think: $5\overline{)12\text{ tens}}$ — ? tens

```
   2
5)125
 - 10   ← Multiply. 5 × 2 tens
    2   ← Subtract. 12 − 10
          Compare. 2 < 5
```

Step 3 Bring down the ones. Divide the ones.

Think: $5\overline{)25\text{ ones}}$ — ? ones

```
   25
5)125
 - 10↓
    25
  - 25  ← Multiply. 5 × 5 ones
     0  ← Subtract. 25 − 25
          Compare. 0 < 5
```

Check your work.

```
  ²
  25
×  5
 125
```

The product matches the dividend, so the quotient is correct.

Solution: Paula must read 25 pages each day.

Explain Your Thinking

- When you divide 384 by 4, will the quotient be a two-digit number or a three-digit number? Explain how you can tell without dividing.
- When you divide a three-digit number by a one-digit number, can the quotient ever be a one-digit number? Explain your answer.

Guided Practice

Divide. Check your answers.

1. $5\overline{)175}$ **2.** $2\overline{)138}$ **3.** $3\overline{)264}$ **4.** $4\overline{)328}$

5. $324 \div 6$ **6.** $465 \div 5$ **7.** $144 \div 4$ **8.** $560 \div 5$

Ask Yourself

- Can I divide the hundreds?
- Where should I write the first digit in the quotient?

Independent Practice

Divide and check.

9. $2\overline{)112}$ **10.** $3\overline{)102}$ **11.** $2\overline{)184}$ **12.** $3\overline{)285}$ **13.** $4\overline{)176}$

14. $3\overline{)141}$ **15.** $4\overline{)112}$ **16.** $5\overline{)120}$ **17.** $6\overline{)198}$ **18.** $5\overline{)320}$

19. $6\overline{)552}$ **20.** $3\overline{)282}$ **21.** $4\overline{)168}$ **22.** $3\overline{)288}$ **23.** $4\overline{)892}$

24. $480 \div 5$ **25.** $136 \div 2$ **26.** $282 \div 6$ **27.** $291 \div 3$ **28.** $388 \div 4$

Problem Solving • Reasoning

29. Lynn has 6 days to read a book that is 234 pages long. She wants to read the same number of pages each day. How many pages should she read each day?

30. **Analyze** Pete read 2 books in 4 weeks. One book had 162 pages. The other book had 154 pages. He read the same number of pages each week. How many pages did he read each week?

31. **Logical Thinking** Heather is reading a book that has twice as many pages as John's book has. John is reading a book that has 32 more pages than Ian's book has. Ian's book has 94 pages. How many pages are in Heather's book?

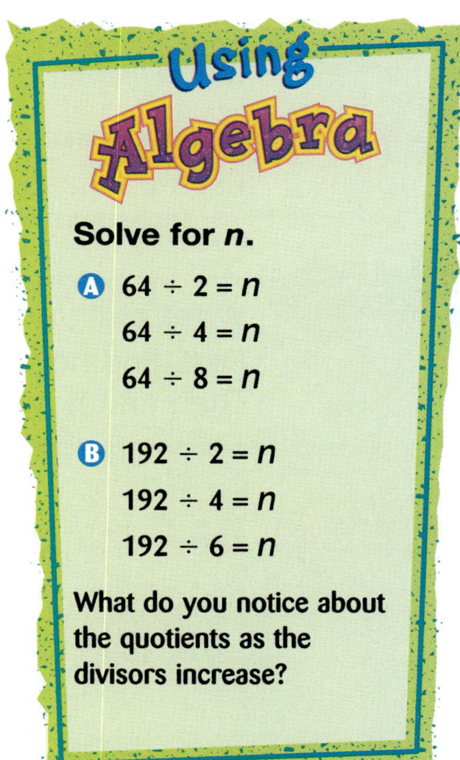

Mixed Review • Test Prep

Find each answer. *(pages 120–121, 138–139, 556–557, 574–575)*

32. $1{,}523 + 2{,}342$ **33.** $341 - 142$ **34.** 135×6 **35.** $63 \div 5$

36 Which shows the product of 3 and 158? *(pages 556–557)*

A 354 **B** 374 **C** 454 **D** 474

Extra Practice See Set J on page 588.

Problem-Solving Application: Use Operations

You will learn how to solve problems using addition, subtraction, multiplication, or division.

Sometimes when you solve a problem, you need to decide which operations to use and in what order to use them.

A zoo feeds each giant panda 150 pounds of bamboo in five days. If the pandas are fed the same amount each day, how many pounds of bamboo are 2 pandas fed in 1 day?

What is the question?
How many pounds of bamboo are 2 pandas fed in 1 day?

What do you know?
Each panda is fed 150 pounds of bamboo in five days.

Plan

What can you do to find the answer?
First, find how much one panda is fed in one day.
Then find how much two pandas are fed in one day.

$150 \div 5 = 30$ (number of pounds of bamboo 1 panda is fed in 1 day)

$2 \times 30 = 60$ (number of pounds of bamboo 2 pandas are fed in 1 day)

Two pandas are fed 60 pounds of bamboo in 1 day.

Look back at the problem.
Could you have solved the problem by multiplying first and then dividing? Explain.

Left: Giant pandas live in bamboo forests in China. *Right:* In the wild, baby giant pandas are often born in August or September.

Guided Practice

Solve.

1. There are 3 crates of bamboo and 1 crate of fruit. The 4 crates together weigh 1,500 pounds. If each of the crates of bamboo weighs 420 pounds, how much does the crate of fruit weigh?

What operations can I use to solve this problem?

2. Kay and Lou see a panda at the zoo that weighs 3 times as much as Kay. The panda weighs 213 pounds. Lou weighs 11 pounds less than Kay. How much does Lou weigh?

In what order should I do the operations?

Choose a Strategy

Solve. Use these or other strategies.

Problem-Solving Strategies

- **Work Backward**
- **Draw a Picture**
- **Write a Number Sentence**
- **Make a Table**

3. Pat works at the zoo 8 hours on Monday and 8 hours on Friday. She works 6 hours on Tuesday and 6 hours on Saturday. How many hours does she work each week?

4. Pandas eat most of the time they are awake. If a panda spends 112 hours eating each week, about how many hours does a panda spend eating each day?

5. One month at the zoo, 243 children saw the baby panda. The next month, 3 times as many children saw the baby panda. In all, how many children saw the baby panda during those two months?

6. At a petting zoo, Stacey fed some of the animals. Large food packs cost $1.25 each, and small food packs cost $0.75 each. How much did Stacy pay for 3 large food packs and 2 small food packs ?

7. A male giant panda weighs 255 pounds. A male polar bear weighs 5 times as much as the panda. How much does the polar bear weigh?

8. Some bamboo plants live to be 100 years old. If a bamboo plant sprouted in 1983 and will die when it is 100 years old, how many years from now will it die?

Extra Practice See 9–11 on page 589.

Quick Check

Check Your Understanding of Lessons 11–15

Divide and check.

1. $3\overline{)81}$ **2.** $2\overline{)92}$ **3.** $4\overline{)96}$

4. $5\overline{)675}$ **5.** $3\overline{)951}$ **6.** $4\overline{)784}$

7. $3\overline{)\$6.72}$ **8.** $5\overline{)\$5.65}$ **9.** $4\overline{)\$6.20}$

10. $8\overline{)520}$ **11.** $9\overline{)315}$ **12.** $4\overline{)292}$

Solve.

13. An American black bear that Billy saw at the zoo weighs 5 times as much as Billy does. The bear weighs 310 pounds. Billy's brother Jack weighs 22 pounds more than Billy. How much does Jack weigh? Explain how you found your answer.

14. A mallard duck can fly at speeds of 40 miles per hour. A hummingbird can fly 31 miles per hour faster. If a hummingbird could fly that fast for 4 hours, how far could it travel?

How did you do?

If you had difficulty with any items in the Quick Check, you can use the following pages for review and extra practice.

Items	Review These Pages	Do These Extra Practice Items
1–3	pages 574–575	Set G, page 588
4–6	pages 576–577	Set H, page 588
7–9	pages 578–579	Set I, page 588
10–12	pages 580–581	Set J, page 588
13–14	pages 582–583	9–11, page 589

Test Prep • Cumulative Review

Maintaining the Standards

Choose the letter of the correct answer. If a correct answer is not here, choose NH.

1 Which number makes the number sentence true?

$$4 \times \blacksquare = 52$$

A 9
B 11
C 13
D 15

2 One hundred thirty-five students were divided into 5 equal groups. How many students were in each group?

F 2 R7
G 26
H 27
J NH

3 Which symbol makes the number sentence true?

$$129 \bullet 3 = 43$$

A $+$ **C** $\times$
B $-$ **D** $\div$

4 Amy tossed a coin 50 times.

Coin Tossing Results	
Heads	~~||||~~ ~~||||~~ ~~||||~~ ~~||||~~ |||
Tails	~~||||~~ ~~||||~~ ~~||||~~ ~~||||~~ ~~||||~~ ||

How many times was tails tossed?

F 22   **H** 25
G 23   **J** 27

5 Which figure belongs in this group?

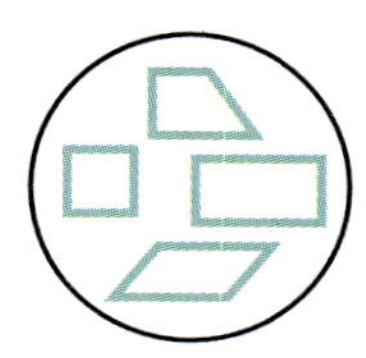

A **B** **C** **D**

6 Which color will likely be spun next?

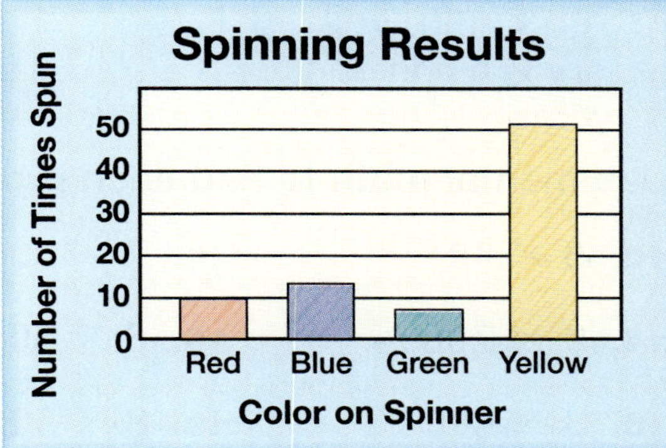

F red   **H** green
G blue   **J** yellow

7 A snack pack contains six jars of applesauce. The pack costs \$1.80. What is the unit price?

Explain How did you find your answer?

Safe Site

Internet Test Prep
Visit **www.eduplace.com/kids/mhm** for more *Test Prep Practice.*

Extra Practice

Set A (Lesson 1, pages 544–545)

Use basic facts and patterns to find each product.

1. $2 \times 4 = ■$
$2 \times 40 = ■$
$2 \times 400 = ■$
$2 \times 4{,}000 = ■$

2. $3 \times 5 = ■$
$3 \times 50 = ■$
$3 \times 500 = ■$
$3 \times 5{,}000 = ■$

3. $6 \times 7 = ■$
$6 \times 70 = ■$
$6 \times 700 = ■$
$6 \times 7{,}000 = ■$

4. $5 \times 8 = ■$
$5 \times 80 = ■$
$5 \times 800 = ■$
$5 \times 8{,}000 = ■$

5. $4 \times 6 = ■$
$4 \times 60 = ■$
$4 \times 600 = ■$
$4 \times 6{,}000 = ■$

6. $8 \times 2 = ■$
$8 \times 20 = ■$
$8 \times 200 = ■$
$8 \times 2{,}000 = ■$

7. $9 \times 9 = ■$
$9 \times 90 = ■$
$9 \times 900 = ■$
$9 \times 9{,}000 = ■$

8. $7 \times 8 = ■$
$7 \times 80 = ■$
$7 \times 800 = ■$
$7 \times 8{,}000 = ■$

9. $6 \times 5 = ■$
$6 \times 50 = ■$
$6 \times 500 = ■$
$6 \times 5{,}000 = ■$

Use mental math to find each product.

10. 5×40 **11.** 7×300 **12.** $8 \times 2{,}000$ **13.** 3×600

14. $9 \times 7{,}000$ **15.** 6×800 **16.** $4 \times 9{,}000$ **17.** 2×50

18. 3×400 **19.** 8×500 **20.** $9 \times 6{,}000$ **21.** $7 \times 4{,}000$

Set B (Lesson 3, pages 548–550)

Multiply.

1. 13×2 **2.** 41×6 **3.** 32×4 **4.** 51×4 **5.** 16×3

6. 19×5 **7.** 43×3 **8.** 21×9 **9.** 29×3 **10.** 31×7

11. 3×52 **12.** 2×27 **13.** 4×13 **14.** 5×15 **15.** 2×34

16. 6×16 **17.** 4×15 **18.** 9×21 **19.** 4×82 **20.** 7×31

Extra Practice

Set C (Lesson 4, pages 552–553)

Multiply.

1. 125×3
2. 114×4
3. 215×3
4. 427×2
5. 223×4
6. 153×2
7. 326×3
8. 131×5
9. 143×3
10. 242×4
11. 3×72
12. 2×126
13. 3×225
14. 2×114
15. 5×117

Set D (Lesson 5, pages 556–557)

Multiply.

1. 125×5
2. 314×3
3. 652×4
4. 231×5
5. 473×2
6. $1,839 \times 2$
7. $2,153 \times 4$
8. $1,316 \times 5$
9. $2,424 \times 3$
10. $2,157 \times 3$

Set E (Lesson 6, pages 558–559)

Multiply.

1. $\$3.14 \times 2$
2. $\$2.43 \times 4$
3. $\$1.47 \times 5$
4. $\$2.71 \times 3$
5. $\$4.16 \times 6$
6. $\$1.36 \times 3$
7. $\$3.61 \times 5$
8. $\$4.25 \times 2$
9. $\$2.47 \times 4$
10. $\$3.51 \times 7$

Set F (Lesson 9, pages 566–568)

Divide and check.

1. $2\overline{)48}$
2. $4\overline{)84}$
3. $3\overline{)36}$
4. $5\overline{)55}$
5. $2\overline{)85}$
6. $3\overline{)63}$
7. $5\overline{)58}$
8. $2\overline{)42}$
9. $4\overline{)87}$
10. $3\overline{)39}$
11. $64 \div 2$
12. $69 \div 2$
13. $96 \div 3$
14. $89 \div 4$
15. $84 \div 4$

Extra Practice

Set G (Lesson 11, pages 574–575)

Divide and check.

1. $5\overline{)75}$	**2.** $2\overline{)74}$	**3.** $2\overline{)70}$	**4.** $3\overline{)54}$	**5.** $4\overline{)96}$
6. $3\overline{)72}$	**7.** $3\overline{)57}$	**8.** $5\overline{)85}$	**9.** $4\overline{)68}$	**10.** $4\overline{)72}$
11. $75 \div 3$	**12.** $60 \div 5$	**13.** $78 \div 3$	**14.** $74 \div 2$	**15.** $48 \div 3$
16. $34 \div 2$	**17.** $87 \div 3$	**18.** $56 \div 4$	**19.** $95 \div 5$	**20.** $38 \div 2$

Set H (Lesson 12, pages 576–577)

Divide and check.

1. $3\overline{)942}$	**2.** $2\overline{)854}$	**3.** $5\overline{)565}$	**4.** $2\overline{)450}$	**5.** $5\overline{)575}$
6. $2\overline{)874}$	**7.** $3\overline{)651}$	**8.** $5\overline{)560}$	**9.** $3\overline{)948}$	**10.** $4\overline{)892}$
11. $864 \div 4$	**12.** $674 \div 2$	**13.** $496 \div 4$	**14.** $945 \div 3$	**15.** $872 \div 2$

Set I (Lesson 13, pages 578–579)

Write each quotient.

1. $3\overline{)\$6.39}$	**2.** $4\overline{)\$8.48}$	**3.** $2\overline{)\$4.28}$	**4.** $2\overline{)\$4.52}$
5. $4\overline{)\$8.60}$	**6.** $2\overline{)\$4.74}$	**7.** $5\overline{)\$5.70}$	**8.** $3\overline{)\$6.75}$
9. $\$9.48 \div 3$	**10.** $\$4.56 \div 4$	**11.** $\$6.84 \div 2$	**12.** $\$8.96 \div 4$
13. $\$6.78 \div 3$	**14.** $\$5.90 \div 5$	**15.** $\$4.96 \div 4$	**16.** $\$6.84 \div 3$

Set J (Lesson 14, pages 580–581)

Divide and check.

1. $4\overline{)316}$	**2.** $3\overline{)252}$	**3.** $5\overline{)475}$	**4.** $4\overline{)256}$	**5.** $2\overline{)172}$
6. $2\overline{)174}$	**7.** $3\overline{)192}$	**8.** $3\overline{)282}$	**9.** $5\overline{)315}$	**10.** $4\overline{)344}$
11. $3\overline{)285}$	**12.** $4\overline{)376}$	**13.** $2\overline{)150}$	**14.** $5\overline{)420}$	**15.** $4\overline{)272}$

Extra Practice • Problem Solving

Solve these problems, using the Solve a Simpler Problem strategy. *(Lesson 7, pages 560–561)*

1. Suppose a crate of sugar weighs 351 pounds. How many pounds do 8 crates of sugar weigh?

2. A baker's dozen is 13 items. How many items are there in 9 baker's dozens?

3. At the Doughnut Hole Bakery, Mr. Lawson uses 175 pounds of flour every week. How much flour does Mr. Lawson need for 5 weeks?

4. A baker baked 352 loaves of wheat bread and 952 loaves of white bread last week. How many loaves of bread were baked last week?

Solve. *(Lesson 10, pages 570–571)*

5. Margaret and 8 friends are going to ride bumper cars at the amusement park. Three people can fit in one bumper car. How many bumper cars will Margaret and her friends need?

6. Bob sold bags of cookies at a bake sale. He baked 85 cookies and put 4 cookies in each bag. After Bob filled all the bags he could, he ate the leftover cookies. How many cookies did he eat?

7. At a used-book sale, mystery books cost $3 each. Donald has $35. How many mystery books can he buy?

8. Bill will put his model cars in rows. He wants to put 4 cars in each row. He has 86 model cars. How many rows can he make?

Use the sign to solve each problem. *(Lesson 15, pages 582–583)*

9. Ben buys 6 shirts and 2 pairs of shoes. How much does he spend?

10. Brooke buys 3 shirts and 2 pairs of shoes. She gives the clerk four $20 bills. What should her change be?

11. Alicia's father wants to buy 4 pairs of shoes and 3 shirts. He has $75. How much more money does he need?

Chapter Review

Reviewing Vocabulary

Find a word or number that makes each sentence below false. Then change the word or number to make the sentence true.

1. Multiples of 8 are 20, 30, 40, and 50.
2. You can multiply to find the quotient.
3. A dividend is the number left over after dividing.

Reviewing Concepts and Skills

Use a basic fact and patterns to find each product. *(pages 544–545)*

4. $2 \times 7 = \blacksquare$
$2 \times 70 = \blacksquare$
$2 \times 700 = \blacksquare$
$2 \times 7{,}000 = \blacksquare$

5. $6 \times 5 = \blacksquare$
$6 \times 50 = \blacksquare$
$6 \times 500 = \blacksquare$
$6 \times 5{,}000 = \blacksquare$

6. $3 \times 9 = \blacksquare$
$3 \times 90 = \blacksquare$
$3 \times 900 = \blacksquare$
$3 \times 9{,}000 = \blacksquare$

7. $3 \times 3 = \blacksquare$
$3 \times 30 = \blacksquare$
$3 \times 300 = \blacksquare$
$3 \times 3{,}000 = \blacksquare$

8. $7 \times 7 = \blacksquare$
$7 \times 70 = \blacksquare$
$7 \times 700 = \blacksquare$
$7 \times 7{,}000 = \blacksquare$

9. $5 \times 1 = \blacksquare$
$5 \times 10 = \blacksquare$
$5 \times 100 = \blacksquare$
$5 \times 1{,}000 = \blacksquare$

Multiply. *(pages 548–559)*

10. 14×2 **11.** 16×4 **12.** 17×7 **13.** 46×2 **14.** 24×3

15. 243×2 **16.** $\$3.27 \times 3$ **17.** 193×5 **18.** 284×3 **19.** $\$1.36 \times 4$

20. $2{,}299 \times 2$ **21.** $2{,}647 \times 2$ **22.** $3{,}691 \times 2$ **23.** $2{,}127 \times 3$ **24.** $1{,}823 \times 4$

25. 5×16 **26.** 3×416 **27.** 2×39 **28.** 4×17 **29.** 5×25

30. $3 \times \$2.85$ **31.** 4×246 **32.** $6 \times \$4.31$ **33.** 5×413 **34.** 7×134

Divide and check. *(pages 566–569, 574–581)*

35. $3\overline{)39}$ **36.** $4\overline{)87}$ **37.** $2\overline{)69}$ **38.** $3\overline{)351}$ **39.** $4\overline{)896}$

40. $5\overline{)495}$ **41.** $2\overline{)692}$ **42.** $2\overline{)\$2.74}$ **43.** $5\overline{)475}$ **44.** $4\overline{)272}$

45. $3\overline{)141}$ **46.** $5\overline{)365}$ **47.** $5\overline{)435}$ **48.** $49 \div 4$ **49.** $292 \div 2$

50. $\$6.55 \div 5$ **51.** $\$2.36 \div 2$ **52.** $\$6.96 \div 3$ **53.** $\$8.52 \div 4$

Solve. *(pages 560–561, 570–571, 582–583)*

54. Deb is going on a four-week bike trip. She will bike 172 miles each week. How far will Deb bike during the entire trip?

55. The 46 students in Bill's class will go on a tour at Safari Park. They will be driven through the park in minivans. Each van can hold 5 students. How many vans will Bill's class need?

56. Bernie has $12.00 to spend at the amusement park. Tickets for 3 rides on the roller coaster are $6.00. The Ferris wheel costs $1.50 a ride. Can Bernie ride the roller coaster 3 times, ride the Ferris wheel once, and still have enough money left to buy a soda for $1.25? Explain.

Brain Teaser Math Reasoning

Changing Shapes

A string is shaped into an octagon with sides of equal length. Each side of the octagon is 85 cm long. If the string is reshaped into a pentagon with sides of equal length, how long will each side be?

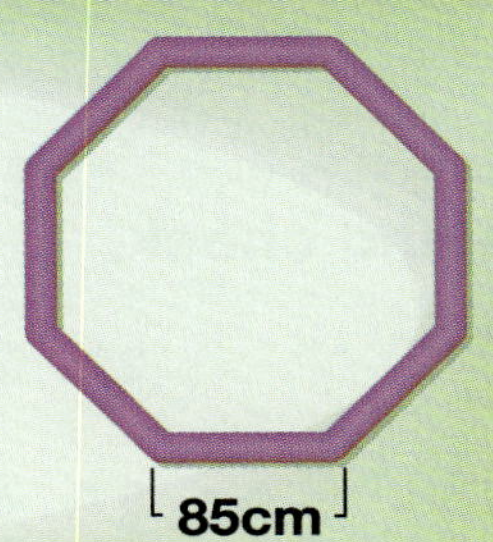

Safe Site

Internet Brain Teasers
Visit **www.eduplace.com/kids/mhm** for more *Brain Teasers.*

Chapter Test

Use a basic fact and patterns to find each product.

1. 1 × 7 = ■
1 × 70 = ■
1 × 700 = ■
1 × 7,000 = ■

2. 4 × 9 = ■
4 × 90 = ■
4 × 900 = ■
4 × 9,000 = ■

3. 5 × 6 = ■
5 × 60 = ■
5 × 600 = ■
5 × 6,000 = ■

Use mental math to find each product.

4. 7 × 60 **5.** 4 × 800 **6.** 5 × 300

7. 9 × 400 **8.** 5 × 4,000 **9.** 8 × 5,000

10. 8 × 3,000 **11.** 7 × 3,000 **12.** 6 × 9,000

Multiply.

13. 43 × 3 **14.** 29 × 2 **15.** 51 × 4 **16.** 27 × 2 **17.** 14 × 3

18. \$4.17 × 3 **19.** 274 × 3 **20.** 146 × 4 **21.** \$7.63 × 2 **22.** \$3.85 × 2

23. 1,234 × 4 **24.** 5,328 × 3 **25.** 1,132 × 5 **26.** 2,127 × 4 **27.** 7,121 × 7

28. 2 × 384 **29.** 3 × \$4.16 **30.** 2 × \$3.77

Divide and check.

31. $4\overline{)47}$ **32.** $2\overline{)67}$ **33.** $3\overline{)65}$ **34.** $2\overline{)59}$ **35.** $3\overline{)98}$

36. $5\overline{)385}$ **37.** $4\overline{)472}$ **38.** $4\overline{)324}$ **39.** $3\overline{)216}$ **40.** $5\overline{)245}$

41. 64 ÷ 3 **42.** 674 ÷ 2 **43.** \$4.84 ÷ 2

44. \$5.70 ÷ 5 **45.** 856 ÷ 4 **46.** $6\overline{)372}$

Solve.

47. Brook School spends $452 on football equipment for the 4 new members of the team. They spend the same amount on each player. How much do they spend on each new player?

48. Each student who plays football receives 2 jerseys. If there are 125 jerseys, what is the greatest number of players who can have 2 jerseys?

49. There are 5 players on a basketball team, and 49 students will come to play in a tournament. Players who are not on a team will be substitutes. How many substitutes will there be?

50. A marching band will earn money to pay for uniforms. If they earn $85 a week, how much will they earn in 9 weeks? Will that pay for uniforms that cost $725? If not, how much more will they need?

Write About It

Solve each problem. Use correct math vocabulary to explain your thinking.

1. Johanna made a mistake on this problem.
   a. Show Johanna what she did wrong.
   b. Explain how she could correct her mistake.

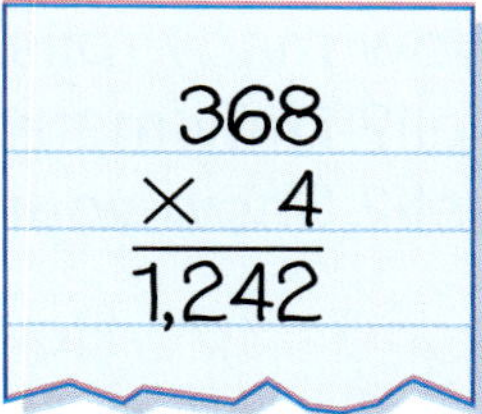

2. Tiffany and her friend are sharing a large pizza. Can they share the cost of the pizza equally?
   a. How did you decide on your answer?
   b. Suppose the girls decide to add 2 extra toppings. What will they each need to pay for the pizza now?
   c. Can 3 friends share equally the cost of a large pizza with 2 extra toppings? Why or why not?

Another Look

The students at Simpson Elementary are raising money for their band. They are selling rolls of gift-wrap and boxes of ribbon. The rolls of gift-wrap sell for $7 each. The boxes of ribbon sell for $5 each.

Use the picture to help you answer each question.

1. How many rolls of gift-wrap did the fourth grade sell? How many boxes of ribbon did the fourth grade sell? Show your work.

2. **Look Back** How can you check that your answers for Question 1 are correct?

3. **Analyze** Suppose the fifth grade sold 47 rolls of gift-wrap. They made a total of $1,089. How could you find how many boxes of ribbon they sold?

4. Suppose the 6th grade sold a different kind of ribbon. If one 6th grader sold 6 boxes for $24, what was the unit cost of each box? How many boxes did the entire 6th grade sell, if they raised a total of $208 selling boxes of ribbon?

Enrichment

Finding Perimeter

Review Vocabulary
Perimeter

You can use different operations to find the **perimeter**. Look at the examples below.

If the sides of a figure are different lengths, you can add to find the perimeter.

Add the lengths of each side.

$$\frac{5}{9} + \frac{7}{9} + \frac{6}{9} + \frac{8}{9} = \frac{26}{9} \text{ or } 2\frac{8}{9} \text{ in.}$$

Perimeter $= 2\frac{8}{9}$ in.

If the sides of a figure are the same length, you can multiply to find the perimeter.

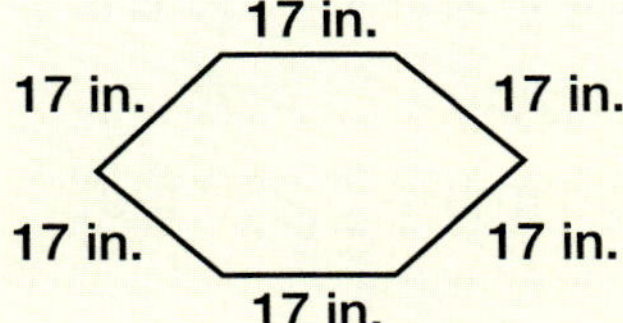

Multiply the length of one side by the total number of sides.

$6 \times 17 = 102$ in.

Perimeter $= 102$ in.

Find the perimeter of each figure. For each, tell whether you can find the perimeter by multiplying.

1. Sides: $\frac{4}{8}$ in., $\frac{3}{8}$ in., $\frac{5}{8}$ in.

2. Sides: 19 ft, 19 ft, 19 ft, 19 ft

3. Sides: $\frac{8}{10}$ yd, $\frac{6}{10}$ yd, $\frac{3}{10}$ yd, $\frac{9}{10}$ yd

4. Sides: $\frac{3}{6}$ ft, $\frac{5}{6}$ ft, $\frac{4}{6}$ ft, $\frac{2}{6}$ ft

5. Sides: 6 in., 5 in., 7 in., 10 in., 11 in.

6. Sides: 24 ft, 24 ft, 24 ft, 24 ft, 24 ft, 24 ft, 24 ft, 24 ft

Explain Your Thinking

Give an example to show that different shapes can have the same perimeter.

Table of Measures

Customary Units of Measure

Length

1 foot (ft) = 12 inches (in.)

1 yard (yd) = 36 inches

1 yard = 3 feet

1 mile (mi) = 5,280 feet

Capacity

1 pint (pt) = 2 cups

1 quart (qt) = 2 pints

1 gallon (gal) = 4 quarts

Weight

1 pound (lb) = 16 ounces (oz)

Metric Units of Measure

Length

1 meter (m) = 100 centimeters (cm)

1 decimeter (dm) = 10 centimeters

1 kilometer (km) = 1,000 meters

Capacity

1 liter (L) = 1,000 milliliters (mL)

Mass

1 kilogram (kg) = 1,000 grams (g)

Units of Time

1 minute (min) = 60 seconds (s)

1 hour (h) = 60 minutes

1 day (d) = 24 hours

1 week (wk) = 7 days

1 year = 12 months (mo)

1 year = 52 weeks

1 year = 365 days

1 leap year = 366 days

1 decade = 10 years

1 century = 100 years

1 millennium = 1,000 years

Glossary

addend A number to be added in an addition expression.

Example: In 2 + 5 + 3 = 10, the addends are 2, 5, and 3.

addition An operation on two or more numbers that gives a sum.

angle A figure formed by two rays with the same endpoint.

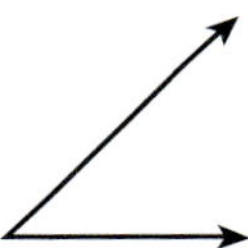

area The number of square units in a region.

array An arrangement of objects, pictures, or numbers in columns and rows.

Associative Property of Addition The property which states that the way in which addends are grouped does not change the sum. It is also called the *Grouping Property of Addition.*

Associative Property of Multiplication The property which states that the way in which factors are grouped does not change the product. It is also called the *Grouping Property of Multiplication.*

capacity The amount a container can hold.

centimeter (cm) A metric unit used to measure length.

100 centimeters = 1 meter

century A unit of time equal to 100 years.

Commutative Property of Addition The property which states that the order of addends does not change the sum. It is also called the *Order Property of Addition.*

Commutative Property of Multiplication The property which states that the order of factors does not change the product. It is also called the *Order Property of Multiplication.*

cone A solid figure that looks like this:

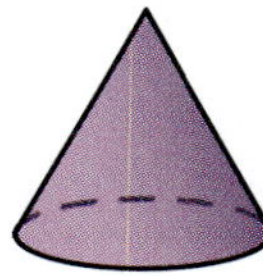

congruent figures Figures that have the same size and shape.

cube A solid figure that has six square faces of equal size.

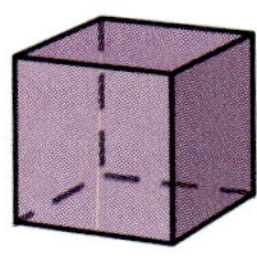

Glossary

cup (c) A customary unit used to measure capacity. There are 8 ounces in one cup.

cylinder A solid figure that looks like this:

decade A unit of time equal to 10 years.

decimal A number with one or more digits to the right of a decimal point.

Examples: 0.5, 0.06, and 12.679 are decimals.

decimeter (dm) A metric unit used to measure length.

1 decimeter = 10 centimeters

degree Celsius (°C) The metric unit used to measure temperature.

degree Fahrenheit (°F) The customary unit used to measure temperature.

denominator The number below the bar in a fraction.

Example: In $\frac{3}{5}$, 5 is the denominator.

difference The result of subtraction.

Example: In 9 − 5 = 4, the difference is 4.

digit Any of the symbols 0, 1, 2, 3, 4, 5, 6, 7, 8, 9 in the base-ten numeration system.

dividend The number that is divided in division.

division An operation that separates an amount equally into smaller groups and gives the number in each group.

divisor The number by which a number is being divided.

dollar sign A symbol ($) written to show dollars in money amounts.

equilateral triangle A triangle that has three congruent sides.

equivalent amounts Amounts that are equal or worth the same.

equivalent fractions Fractions that show the same amount.

Example: $\frac{2}{3}$ and $\frac{10}{15}$ are equivalent fractions.

estimate To find an answer that is close to the exact amount.

event In probability, a result of an experiment that can be classified as certain, likely, unlikely, or impossible to occur.

expanded form A way to write a number that shows the value of each digit.

factor of a number A number that divides evenly into a given number.

foot (ft) A customary unit used to measure length.

1 foot = 12 inches

fraction A number that names a part of a set or a part of a region.

Examples: $\frac{1}{2}$, $\frac{3}{4}$, *and* $\frac{2}{3}$ *are fractions.*

gallon (gal) A customary unit used to measure capacity.

1 gallon = 4 quarts

gram (g) A metric unit used to measure mass.

1,000 grams = 1 kilogram

hour A unit of time equal to 60 minutes.

improper fraction A fraction that is greater than or equal to 1. The numerator in an improper fraction is greater than or equal to the denominator.

Examples: $\frac{5}{5}$ *and* $\frac{8}{7}$ *are improper fractions.*

inch (in.) A customary unit used to measure length.

12 inches = 1 foot

is greater than (>) The symbol used to compare two numbers. $5 > 4$ means five is greater than 4.

is less than (<) The symbol used to compare two numbers. $4 < 5$ means four is less than five.

isosceles triangle A triangle that has two congruent sides.

kilogram (kg) A metric unit used to measure mass.

1 kilogram = 1,000 grams

kilometer A metric unit used to measure length.

1 kilometer = 1,000 meters

line A straight path that goes on forever in opposite directions.

Glossary

line of symmetry The line on which a figure can be folded so that the two halves match exactly.

line plot A diagram that organizes data using a number line.

line segment Part of a line. A line segment has two endpoints.

liter (L) A metric unit used to measure capacity.

1 liter = 1,000 milliliters

M

mass The amount of matter in an object. It is often measured using grams or kilograms.

meter A metric unit used to measure length.

1 meter = 100 centimeters

mile (mi) A customary unit used to measure length.

1 mile = 5,280 feet

milliliter (mL) A metric unit used to measure capacity.

1,000 milliliters = 1 liter

minute A unit of time equal to 60 seconds.

mixed number A number containing a whole number part and a fraction part.

Examples: $2\frac{1}{2}$ *and* $5\frac{3}{7}$ *are mixed numbers.*

mode The number or numbers that occur most often in a set of data.

multiple of a number A number that is the product of the given number and a number.

multiplication An operation on two numbers that gives a product.

numerator The number above the bar in a fraction.

Example: In $\frac{3}{4}$, *3 is the numerator.*

ordered pair A pair of numbers in which one number is named as the first and the other number as the second.

ordinal numbers Numbers used to show order or position, such as *first, second, third, fourth, fifth.*

ounce (oz) A customary unit used to measure weight.

16 ounces = 1 pound

outcome A result in a probability experiment. In tossing a coin, there are two possible outcomes, heads or tails.

parallel lines Lines that do not intersect. They are everywhere the same distance apart.

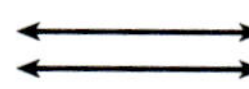

perimeter The distance around a figure.

Example: The perimeter of this rectangle is 20 inches.

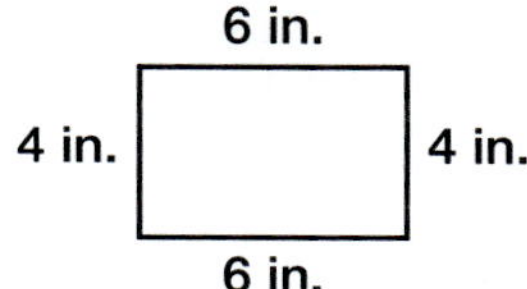

pictograph A graph that shows data by using pictures.

pint (pt) A customary unit used to measure capacity.

2 pints = 1 quart

place value The number assigned to each place that a digit occupies. In 346, the digit 3 is in the hundreds place.

plane figure A geometric figure that lies in one plane.

polygon A simple closed plane figure made up of three or more line segments.

pound (lb) A customary unit used to measure weight.

1 pound = 16 ounces

probability The chance of an event occurring.

product The result of multiplication.

Example: In $3 \times 4 = 12$, the product is 12.

pyramid A solid figure whose base can be any polygon and whose faces are triangles with a common vertex.

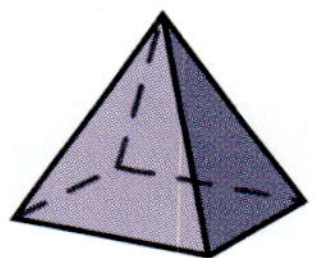

quadrilateral A polygon with four sides.

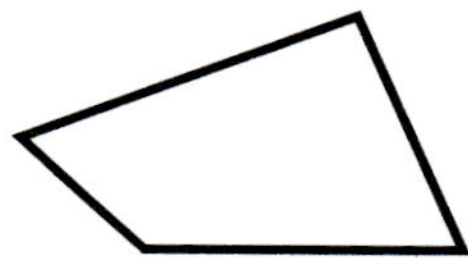

quart (qt) A customary unit used to measure capacity.

4 quarts = 1 gallon

quarter Another name for a fourth; also a coin that is worth 25 cents.

quotient The answer in division.

Glossary

range The difference between the greatest number and the least in a set of data.

ray A part of a line that has one endpoint and goes on forever in one direction.

rectangular prism A solid figure all of whose faces are rectangles.

remainder The number left over after one number is divided by another.

Example: In 14 ÷ 3 = 4 R2, 2 is the remainder.

right angle An angle that measures 90°.

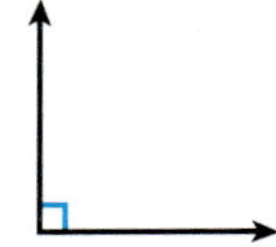

right triangle A triangle with one right angle.

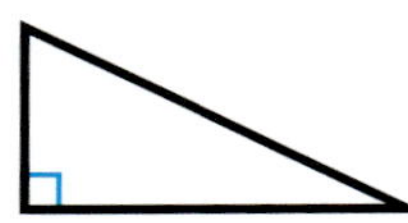

side of a polygon A line segment that is part of a polygon.

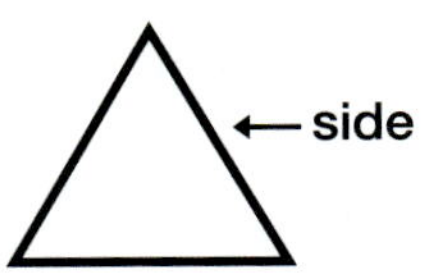

similar figures Figures that have the same shape, but not necessarily the same size.

sphere A solid figure that is shaped like a round ball.

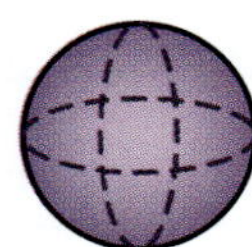

square A rectangle with four equal sides and four right angles.

square number A whole number multiplied by itself.

standard form A way to write a number by using only digits.

subtraction An operation on two numbers to find the difference.

sum The answer in addition.

Example: In 3 + 6 = 9, the sum is 9.

symmetry (line symmetry) A figure has line symmetry if it can be folded along a line so that two parts match exactly.

unit cost The price of one item.

unit fraction A fraction whose numerator is 1.
Example: $\frac{1}{3}$ *is a unit fraction.*

vertex of an angle A point common to the two sides of an angle.

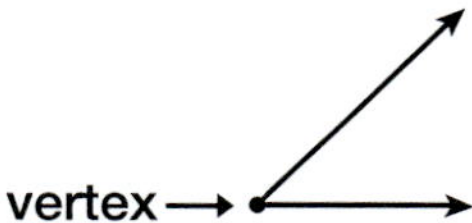

vertex of a polygon A point common to two sides of a polygon.

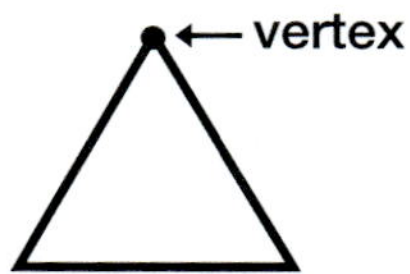

vertex of a prism A point common to the edges of a prism.

volume The number of cubic units that fit inside a solid figure.

weight The measure of how heavy something is.

yard (yd) A customary unit of length.
1 yard = 3 feet

Zero Property of Addition The property which states that the sum of any number and 0 is that number.

Zero Property of Multiplication The property which states that the product of any number and 0 is 0.

Index

Index

E

I

Index

Index

Index

Index

Credits

PHOTOGRAPHY

All photographs by Houghton Mifflin Company (HMCo.) unless otherwise noted.

Cover: *t.* James L. Amos/Peter Arnold, Inc.; *b.* Brian Kenney Wildlife Photography.

Coin photography by Mike Tesi for HMCo. xii: *l.* PhotoDisc, Inc.; *r.* Anup Shah/Dembinsky Photo Associates. xviii: C Squared Studios/PhotoDisc, Inc. xix: *b.r.* Michael Gaffney for HMCo. xx: *r.* Bob Daemmrich Photography. xxi: Don Riepe/Peter Arnold, Inc. 1: Richard Hutchings Photography. 4: Javier Galeano/AP/Wide World Photos. 6: Mark Gibson/Dembinsky Photo Associates. 8–9: Michael Gaffney for HMCo. 12: *t.* © Clem Haagner/Photo Researchers, Inc. 13: *l.* Stan Osolinski/Dembinsky Photo Associates; *r.* © Tom & Pat Leeson/Photo Researchers, Inc. 22: *l.* © Dennis Flaherty/Photo Researchers, Inc.; *m.* © Gregg Mancuso/Stock Boston; *r.* © George Ranalli/Photo Researchers, Inc. 24–25: Richard Hutchings for HMCo. 28: Tony Arruza/Bruce Coleman Inc. 32: Nubar Alexanian/Stock Boston. 35: David Toase/PhotoDisc, Inc. 50–51: Bob Daemmrich/Stock Boston. 54: *t.* Richard Hutchings for HMCo. 56: *t.l.* Courtesy, United States Mint © 1999; *b.l.* Courtesy, United States Mint © 1999. 57: *t.l* Courtesy, United States Mint © 1999; *b.l.* Courtesy, United States Mint © 1999; *b.r.* Courtesy, United States Mint © 1999. 63: *t.r.* Michael Gaffney for HMCo. 65: Courtesy, Santa Ana Public Library. 68: *r.* Michael Ventura/Bruce Coleman Inc. 70: *r.* Joe Marquette/AP/Wide World Photos. 71: PhotoDisc, Inc. 72: *l. inset* Architect of the Capitol; *r. inset* Architect of the Capitol; *bkgd.* Matthew McVay/Stock Boston. 75: Mike Tesi for HMCo. 76: *t.* Bob Daemmrich Photography. 78: Bob Daemmrich Photography. 79: Courtesy, National Square Dance Convention. 84: David Young-Wolff/PhotoEdit. 98–99: Index Stock Imagery. 103: Parker/Boon Productions for HMCo. 113: L.D. Gordon/The Image Bank. 120: *l.* "Stone Soup" by XXX Architects. Photographer Laura Fieber. CANSTRUCTION is a national charity competition sponsored by the Society of Design Administration in association with local chapters of the American Institute of Architects; *r.* "Taxi" by XXX Architects. Photographer Kevin Wick. CANSTRUCTION is a national charity competition sponsored by the Society of Design Administration in association with local chapters of the American Institute of Architects. 123: *t.* © Robert & Linda Mitchell. 132: *l.* Mike Barlow/Dembinsky Photo Associates; *r.* Anup Shah/Dembinsky Photo Associates. 133: Lynda Richardson/Peter Arnold, Inc. 134: Skjold/PhotoEdit. 139: © American Museum of Natural History. 156–157: Norris Blake/Visuals Unlimited. 158: Allan Landau for HMCo. 159: *l.* Corbis. 162: *t.* Rod Planck/Dembinsky Photo Associates; *m.* Sharon Cummings/Dembinsky Photo Associates; *b.* Christoper Thomas/Tony Stone Images. 163: *t.l.* E.R. Degginger/Color-Pic, Inc.; *t.r.* J & L Waldman/Paradux Enterprises; *m.l.* J & L Waldman/Paradux Enterprises; *m.r.* Charles Fitch/FPG International; *b.l.* J & L Waldman/Paradux Enterprises; *b.r.* J & L Waldman/Paradux Enterprises. 164: *l.* E.R. Degginger/Animals Animals/Earth Scenes; *r.* Brown Brothers. 166: © Rafael Macia/Photo Researchers, Inc. 176: *l.* Bob Daemmrich/Stock Boston; *r.* Lawrence Migdale/Pix. 178: *t.* Lawrence Migdale/Stock Boston. 184: *b.l.* Index Stock Imagery; *b.r.* Parker/Boon Productions for HMCo. 188: *t.* Jeff Foott/Bruce Coleman Inc.; *b.* Stan Osolinski/Dembinsky Photo Associates. 189: Werner Bertsch/Bruce Coleman Inc. 192: *l.* Joe McDonald/Bruce Coleman Inc.; *r.* © Galen Rowell/Corbis. 194: Tad Motoyama/Los Angeles Zoo. 195: © Tom Brakefield/Corbis. 201: PhotoDisc, Inc. 206: *b.m.* Corbis; *b.r.* PhotoDisc, Inc. 208–209: Bob & Clara Calhoun/Bruce Coleman Inc. 211: *t.l.* PhotoDisc, Inc.; *b.l.* Corbis. 221: Courtesy, Folk Art & Craft Exchange. 225: *l.* © The Photo Works/Photo Researchers, Inc.; *r.* Jesse Alexander. 252–253: Paul Barton/The Stock Market. 258: *bkgd.* David Madison/Bruce Coleman Inc.; *inset* Ken Karp for HMCo. 260: *bkgd.* © Carolyn A. McKeone/Photo Researchers, Inc.; *inset* John Markham/Bruce Coleman Inc. 261: Hans Pfletschinger/Peter Arnold, Inc. 264: *b.* Sophie Roquefort/Bruce Coleman Inc. 265: Courtesy, Expedition Riverside. 272: Richard Hutchings/PhotoEdit. 273: *t.* Larry Lipsky/Index Stock Imagery. 279: Stuart M. Williams/Dembinsky Photo Associates. 294–295: Superstock. 298: © Roger Ressmeyer/Corbis. 300: *bkgd.* © Laser Images, Inc./LASERIUM ®. 307: Index Stock Imagery. 324: *l.* David Young-Wolff/PhotoEdit/Picture Quest Network International/PNI. 329: *t.m.l.* Ken Karp for HMCo.; *b.l.* Gail Mooney/Corbis. 336: © Lawrence Migdale/Photo Researchers, Inc. 342: PhotoDisc, Inc. 350–351: Joe Schwartz. 356–357: PhotoDisc, Inc. 360: Al Hamdan/The Image Bank. 365: AP/Wide World Photos. 371: © Jeff Greenberg/PhotoEdit. 372: Richard Hutchings for HMCo. 392–393: Bob Daemmrich/The Image Works Inc. 409: C Squared Studios/PhotoDisc, Inc. 412: Tim Boyle/Liaison Agency Inc. 413: Tony Freeman/PhotoEdit. 415: Skip Moody/Dembinsky Photo Associates. 416–417: Michael Gaffney for HMCo. 421: Janice L. Reed/JL Ecklund Photography. 433: Mike Tesi for HMCo. 434–435: Mark E. Gibson/Mark and Audra Gibson Photography. 440: Don Spiro/Tony Stone Images. 442: *t.* Siegfield Layda/Tony Stone Images. 446: Michael Gaffney for HMCo. 447: *t.l.* © Skip Moody/Dembinsky Photo Associates; *t.r.* Index Stock Imagery; *b.l.* Rod Williams/Bruce Coleman Inc.; *b.r.* John H. Hoffman/Bruce Coleman Inc. 458: Michael Gaffney for HMCo. 477: Lori Adamski Peek/Tony Stone Images. 480–481: Ron Kimball. 495: Bob Daemmrich Photography. 496: *t.* Gary Buss/FPG International. 501: Kenneth W. Fink/Bruce Coleman Inc. 508: *t.* Richard Hutchings for HMCo. 509: *l.* "Yellow Flowers" © Christina Miller, Age 9, Courtesy, Kids-Did-It! Designs ® kidsdidit.com; *m.* "Yellow Cat" © Nick Abrams, Age 8 Courtesy, Kids-Did-It! Designs ® kidsdidit.com; *r.* "Three Peaches" © Lauren Van Way, Age 9, Courtesy, Kids-Did-It! Designs ® kidsdidit.com. 512: Richard Hutchings for HMCo. 516: © Francois Gohier/Photo Researchers, Inc. 517: E.R. Degginger/Dembinsky Photo Associates. 519: *l. inset* Bob Daemmrich/Stock Boston; *r. inset* Bob Daemmrich/The Image Works. 526: Charles Gupton/The Stock Market. 527: Michael Gaffney for HMCo. 540–541: David Barnes/Tony Stone Images. 552: Gary A. Conner/Index Stock Imagery. 553: Stock Montage, Inc. 556: Francis Lepine/Animals Animals/Earth Scenes. 560: Bob Daemmrich/Stock Boston/Picture Quest Network International/PNI. 570: *t.* Terry Renna/AP/Wide World Photos; *b.* NASA. 571: NASA/The Image Works Inc. 577: Don Riepe/Peter Arnold, Inc. 582: Sharon Cummings/Dembinsky Photo Associates. 583: *l.* Keren Su/Stock Boston; *r.* Keren Su/FPG International.

ILLUSTRATIONS

vi-ix: Chuck Primeau. xii: *l.* Art Thompson; *r.* Pamela Becker. xv: Doug Horne. 5: Robert Schuster. 6: David Preiss. 10: Tim Harkins. 18: Chi Chung. 20: Lori Anzalone. 26: Margo De Paulis. 29: Gary Hallgren. 33: Karen Minot. 34: Ken Batelman. 36-37: Walter Stuart. 68: Bruce MacPherson. 73: Adam Gordon. 77: Manuel King. 80, 82: Chris Lensch. 83: Bruce MacPherson. 84-85: Shelton Leong. 97: Chris Lensch. 104: Saul Rosenbaum. 110-111: Randy Hamblin. 112: Saul Rosenbaum. 122: Lori Anzalone. 128: Garry Colby. 130: Garry Colby. 132: Art Thompson. 135: Tim McGarvey. 138: Pamela Becker. 139: Dale Rutter. 141: Robert Schuster. 142: Carlyn Iverson. 145: Doug Horne. 160-162: Ken Batelman. 164: Karen Strelecki. 171: Doug Horne. 173: Saul Rosenbaum. 177: Bruce MacPherson. 182: Ken Batelman. 186-187: Saul Rosenbaum. 188: Joe Taylor. 190: Saul Rosenbaum. 191: Doug Horne. 193: Bruce MacPerson. 194: David Preiss. 199: *t.* Shelton Leong; *b.* Saul Rosenbaum. 203: Shelton Leong. 205: Shelton Leong. 207: Lori Anzalone. 217: Linda Davick. 223: Manuel King. 232: Stephen Schudlich. 235: Andrew Shiff. 236: Shelton Leong. 238-240: Doug Horne. 245: Doug Horne. 247: Ken Batelman. 249: Patrick Gnan. 250: Dan Clyne. 251: Deborah Drummond. 258: Doug Horne. 270-271: Doug Horne. 273: Carlyn Iverson. 280-282: Doug Horne. 289: Doug Horne. 292: Dan Clyne. 300-301: Art Thompson. 303: Doug Horne. 317: Deborah Drummond. 318: Nikki Rogers. 325: Ken Batelman. 328: Saul Rosenbaum. 329: Wayne Watford. 330: Patrick Gnan. 334-335, 337-339, 342: Saul Rosenbaum. 343: *t.* Leah Palmer; *b.* Saul Rosenbaum. 345-347: Saul Rosenbaum. 358: Doug Horne. 361: Doug Horne. 362: Shelton Leong. 370: Jeannie Winston. 374: John Ceballos. 378-379: Tom Powers. 380; 387: Doug Horne. 408: Shelton Leong. 409: Doug Horne. 414: Tommy Stubbs. 416: Christian Musselman. 436, 442: Ken Batelman. 443: *l.* John Kovaleski; *r.* Ken Batelman. 444-445: Ken Batelman. 448: *t.* David Preiss; *b.* Walter Stuart. 449: *t.* Walter Stuart; *bl.* Walter Stuart; *br.* David Preiss. 450: Walter Stuart. 451: Jenny Campbell. 452: Wayne Watford. 455: Chris Reed. 458-459: Ken Batelman. 470: Ken Batelman. 478: *l.* Doug Horne; *r.* Greg Scheetz. 479: Art Thompson. 485: Robert Schuster. 488: Leah Palmer. 497: Robert Schuster. 501: Gary Torrisi. 503: Pamela Becker. 506: Leah Palmer. 520, 522: Gary Torrisi. 526-527: Art Thompson. 533, 538, 542: Doug Horne. 548: Chris Reed. 561: Shelton Leong. 576: Art Thompson. 578-579: Sally Vitsky. 580: Tate Nation. 582: Sean Dwyer. 589: Doug Horne. 593-594: Patrick Gnan. 597-598, 601-602: Saul Rosenbaum.